Comparative Politics
of the Third World

Comparative Politics of the Third World

LINKING CONCEPTS AND CASES

December Green
and Laura Luehrmann

LYNNE
RIENNER
PUBLISHERS

BOULDER
LONDON

Published in the United States of America in 2003 by
Lynne Rienner Publishers, Inc.
1800 30th Street, Boulder, Colorado 80301
www.rienner.com

and in the United Kingdom by
Lynne Rienner Publishers, Inc.
3 Henrietta Street, Covent Garden, London WC2E 8LU

Library of Congress Cataloging-in-Publication Data
Green, December.
    Comparative politics of the third world : linking concepts and cases / December Green
and Laura Luehrmann.
    Includes bibliographical references and index.
    ISBN 1-58826-190-5 (alk. paper)
    ISBN 1-58826-166-2 (pbk. : alk. paper)
    1. Developing countries—Politics and government—Case studies.   2. Developing
countries—Economic policy—Case studies.   I. Luehrmann, Laura, 1969–   II. Title.
JF60.G74   2003
320.3'09172'4—dc21

                                                                    2002036823

British Cataloguing in Publication Data
A Cataloguing in Publication record for this book
is available from the British Library.

Printed and bound in the United States of America

The paper used in this publication meets the requirements
of the American National Standard for Permanence of
Paper for Printed Library Materials Z39.48-1992

    5   4   3   2   1

Contents

Illustrations

Preface

In recent years, it has become commonplace to discuss globalization, examining both its benefits and its drawbacks. Yet, such dialogue often takes place within a very limited perspective. What do globalization and its related developments mean to the majority of the world's population, most of whom are still waiting to receive the promised benefits of a more "global" world?

University students today frame their views in a world dizzied by events of great magnitude. To truly understand both the sources and the consequences of such matters, students need to look beyond the Western world. Consider an incomplete list of events that have permeated life in recent years: battles over AIDS drugs and other patents; movements based in religious fundamentalisms; the decline of national sovereignty; increased recognition of crimes against humanity; youth activism in everything from financial markets to human rights campaigns to warfare; student demonstrations against corruption, corporate greed, and authoritarian governments; "wars" on everything from drugs to poverty to terrorism; violence perpetuated by the seemingly innocuous purchase of items such as diamonds; as well as gender violence, new forms of imperialism, and more.

We prepared this book in order to provide a context in which students can begin to analyze such events, taking away with them a greater appreciation not only of the substantive issues under study, but of the larger issues behind the headlines. We approach the issues with a perspective explicitly designed to foster critical-thinking and decisionmaking skills. Our overarching goal is to increase students' exposure to dynamics in the third world. We explore issues and controversies in these countries, employing an interdisciplinary perspective. We believe that in order to be informed members of modern society, students need a solid basis in the history, society, politics, and economics of a manageable number of countries, while being reminded that no single case study is representative of such enormous and diverse regions. The complexities of our world demand it.

Throughout the book, we make a conscious attempt to show students why they should care about what happens in the third world, and how they are affected by it. We also attempt to provoke and engage students by offering them a view of the world they don't often hear, including one that is often critical of the

West. We strongly believe that, all too often, the voices of leaders and citizens in non-Western countries are sorely neglected even in case studies devoted to such countries. In addition, we work to avoid the marginalization of groups such as women, youth, and indigenous peoples. By integrating these groups into discussions of general theory, we hope that students will begin to appreciate the competing perspectives and their bases—and will walk away with a more accurate view of the world around them.

*   *   *

We received much assistance throughout the duration of this project, and we owe gratitude to many. Special thanks to Dean Mary Ellen Mazey, of the College of Liberal Arts at Wright State University, for her enthusiastic support of this project. We feel fortunate to be part of an institution that truly supports the integration of scholarship and teaching, as this project demonstrates. Our colleagues in the Department of Political Science have been particularly helpful in the formulation and completion of this book. We give special thanks to our chairperson, Donna Schlagheck, and to Charlie Funderburk for their advice and encouragement during its preparation. Joanne Ballmann, who prepared the bibliography, and Renée Harber provided excellent editorial assistance and moral support. Additionally, we thank colleagues in other departments and universities who read the text at various stages of development, and whose prescient comments led to a clearer presentation, especially Elizabeth Brads, Dick Olufs, Carol Engelhardt, and Laura Leming.

We are grateful to have been able to work with Bruce Stiver, of Wright State's Center for Teaching and Learning, who helped prepare the graphics that enhance the pages of this text.

We both want to convey our profound debt to our students, whose questions have motivated much of the shape of this book. Their insights, curiosities, and frustrations helped clarify what we believed we needed to include in an introductory text.

We are also grateful to all the wonderful people at Lynne Rienner Publishers, but particularly to Lynne Rienner, for understanding the need for this project and for going above and beyond, using her experience and expertise to refine it. Special thanks to Sally Glover for her always prompt and friendly guidance, to Steve Barr, director of production, and to Jason Cook, our excellent copyeditor, whose diligence has helped us present a clearer, more accurate product. What a joy it has been to work with such a professional and courteous staff.

Finally, our families have endured much during the preparation of this book—from truncated holidays, to late-night writing sessions, to the ups and downs of the publishing process. To our husbands, David and Joe, for their encouragement and partnership, we lovingly dedicate this book.

December Green
Laura Luehrmann

Comparative Politics
of the Third World

1

Introducing
Comparative Studies

At the end of the twentieth century, the world was riding out one of the longest economic booms in generations. DEMOCRACY* was breaking out everywhere, the United States and what was left of the Soviet Union were new friends, and technology was indeed making the world a smaller place. GLOBALIZATION was a buzzword of the era, and one of the dominant images of the times involved a lone man stopping a line of Chinese tanks by simply standing in front of it. Yet this was also a time when the majority of the world's population lost ground economically, when record numbers of people were attempting to subsist on less than one dollar a day. In addition, many of the political changes we were seeing at century's end were more virtual than real. The toppling of dictators the likes of Duvalier, Mobutu, Suharto, and Barre had the effect of taking the lid off a pot now free to boil over.[1]

Nationalism reared its ugly head in ways that post–World War II generations had never seen. The results defy the imagination. To describe some of it, we coined a new term for a very old practice—"ethnic cleansing." Rape was finally recognized as a systematic weapon of war, not simply "boys being boys" in its aftermath. In another major turnabout, Russia went from being a contributor to being a competitor for foreign aid, something that was rapidly becoming scarce as Western donors decided that the countries that needed it the most had suddenly become much less interesting. We had new concerns to keep us up at night; AIDS and the GREENHOUSE EFFECT had largely replaced mutual assured destruction as global threats. Sure, weapons of mass destruction were hardly a thing of the past, but instead of attack from a superpower now it was rogue states and nongovernmental actors that threatened to deliver their chemical and biological nasties through the most mundane of delivery systems. We all got a crash course in "dirty bombs," and learned that they were far more likely to be conveyed by suitcase or transport container than intercontinental ballistic missile. New and horrific diseases such as Ebola began to pop up from place to place. And just as we thought we had finally vanquished them, old killers that

---

* Terms appearing in small capital letters are defined in the glossary, which begins on p. 459.

1

we thought we had beaten, such as tuberculosis and smallpox, were again among us.

Until very recently most of us thought that these were the concerns of far-away countries we would never visit. Yet as much as Americans were jolted from their relative complacency into a new awareness of the world around them that crisp blue September morning in 2001, for much of the rest of the world it was just more of the same. On an individual level at least, the events of that day brought Americans closer to understanding the sense of horror, loss, fear, and even anger that so many others experience on a daily basis. While much of the world mourned with the United States, many people felt like it was time that the citizens of one of the most powerful countries on the planet begin to take more of an interest in the world around them. Such a string of tragedies is hardly something one can prepare for, but perhaps some of us would not have been taken so off-guard had we not been so insular in our concerns. Americans had just months earlier elected a president who clearly had little interest in foreign affairs and campaigned promising an isolationist approach that focused on domestic issues. His foreign policy advisers made it be known that we would not answer all the world's "911" calls, not be "the world's social worker."

However, since the September 11 attacks this president has become much more internationalist in his concerns and is leading a worldwide war on terrorism. Even if it is motivated primarily by self-interest, it is crucial that Americans attempt to understand the world that we are a part of and with which we are inextricably bound—now more than ever. And if we are to avoid some of the mistakes of the past, it is just as crucial to recognize the importance of perspective—that there are at least two sides to every story. If we are to be adequately prepared to respond to the challenges of the future, our understanding of the world must change to include attention to the ostensibly "powerless." These are the people living in the countries that compose much of what we variously term the "third world," or the "non-Western world"—the majority of the world's inhabitants whom we had, until recently, conveniently forgotten.

What's to Compare?

In this introduction to the comparative studies of Asia, Africa, Latin America, and the Middle East, we take a different spin on the traditional approach to discuss much more than politics as it is often narrowly defined. As one of the social sciences, political science has traditionally focused on the study of formal political institutions and behavior. In this book, we choose not to put the spotlight on governments and voting patterns, party politics, and so on. Rather, we turn our attention to all manner of political behavior, which we consider to include just about any aspect of life. Of interest to us is not only how people are governed, but also how they live, how they govern themselves, and what they see as their most urgent concerns.

The framework we employ is called a political interaction approach. It is an eclectic method that presents ideas from a variety of contemporary thinkers and theories. We characterize this as a comparative studies rather than a comparative

Figure 1.1   Global Village of 1,000 People

Imagine that the world is a village of 1,000 people. Who are its residents?

584 Asians
124 Africans
95 East and West Europeans
84 Latin Americans
55 Russians and citizens of the former Soviet republics
52 North Americans
6 people of the Pacific

The people of the village have considerable difficulty in communicating:

165 speak Mandarin
86 speak English
83 speak Hindu/Urdu
64 speak Spanish
58 speak Russian
37 speak Arabic

This list accounts for the native tongues of only half the villagers. The other half speak, in descending order of frequency, Bengali, Portuguese, Indonesian, Japanese, German, French, and over 5,000 other languages.

In this village of 1,000 there are

329 Christians (among them 187 Catholics, 84 Protestants, 31 Orthodox)
178 Muslims
167 people who identify themselves as non-religious
132 Hindus
60 Buddhists
45 atheists
3 Jews
86 people belonging to other religions

One-third of these 1,000 people in the world village are children, and only 60 are over the age of sixty-five. Half the children are immunized against preventable infectious diseases such as measles and polio. Just under half of the married women in the village have access to and use modern contraceptives.

This year twenty-eight babies will be born. Ten people will die, three of them from lack of food, one from cancer, two of them babies. One person will be infected with the HIV virus. With twenty-eight births and ten deaths, the population of the village next year will be 1,018.

In this 1,000-person community, 200 people receive 80 percent of the income; another 200 receive only 2 percent of the income. Only 70 people own an automobile (although some of them own more than one car). About one-third have access to clean, safe drinking water. Of the 670 adults in the village, half are illiterate.

The village has six acres of land per person:

700 acres are cropland
1,400 acres are pasture
1,900 acres are woodland
2,000 acres are desert, tundra, pavement, and wasteland

Of this land, the woodland is declining rapidly; the wasteland is increasing. The other land categories are roughly stable. The village allocates 83 percent of its fertilizer to 40 percent of its cropland—that owned by the richest and best-fed 270 people. Excess fertilizer running off this land causes pollution in lakes and wells. The remaining 60 percent of the land, with its 17 percent of the fertilizer, produces 28 percent of the food grains and feeds 73 percent of the people. The average grain yield of that land is one-third the harvest achieved by the richer villages.

In this village of 1,000 people there are

5 soldiers
7 teachers
1 doctor
3 refugees driven from their homes by war or drought

The village has a total yearly budget, public and private, of over $3 million—

Figure 1.1 *continues*

Figure 1.1   continued

$3,000 per person, if it were distributed evenly. Of this total:

$181,000 goes to weapons and warfare
$159,000 goes to education
$132,000 goes to healthcare

The village has buried beneath it enough explosive power in nuclear weapons to blow itself up many times over. These weapons are under the control of just 100 of the people. The other 900 people are watching them with deep anxiety, wondering whether they can learn to get along together; and if they do, whether they might set off the weapons anyway through inattention or technical bungling; and if they ever decide to dismantle the weapons, where in the world village they would dispose of the radioactive materials of which the weapons are made.

Sources: Adapted from Donella H. Meadows, "If the World Were a Village of One Thousand People," in *Futures by Design: The Practice of Ecological Planning,* ed. Doug Aberley (Gabriola Island, British Columbia: New Society, 1994); and North-South Centre of the Council of Europe, "If the World Were a Village of One Thousand People," www.nscentre.org.

politics textbook because our approach is multidisciplinary. We divide our attention between history, politics, society, and economics in order to convey more fully the complexity of human experience.[2] Instead of artificially confining ourselves to one narrow discipline, we recognize that each discipline offers another layer or dimension, which adds immeasurably to our understanding of the "essence" of politics.[3]

Comparative studies then is much more than simply a subject of study—it is also a means of study. It employs what is known as the comparative method. Through the use of the comparative method we seek to describe, identify, and explain trends—in some cases, even predict human behavior. Those who adopt this approach, known as comparativists, are interested in identifying relationships and patterns of behavior and interactions between individuals and groups. Focusing on one or more countries, comparativists examine case studies alongside one another. They search for similarities and differences between and among the selected elements for comparison. For example, one might compare patterns of female employment and fertility rates in one country in relation to others. Using the comparative method, analysts make explicit or implicit comparisons, searching for common and contrasting features. Some do a "most similar systems" analysis, looking for differences between cases that appear to have a great deal in common (e.g., Canada and the United States). Others prefer a "most different" approach, looking for commonalities between cases that appear diametrically opposed in experience (e.g., Bolivia and India).[4] What is particularly exciting about this type of analysis is stumbling upon unexpected parallels between ostensibly different cases. Just as satisfying is beginning to understand the significance and consequences of the differences that exist between two cases we just assumed had so much in common.

Most textbooks for courses such as the one you're just beginning take one of two roads. Either they offer CASE STUDIES, which provide loads of intricate detail on a handful of states (often the classics: Mexico, Nigeria, China, and

Figure 1.2   What's in a Name?

In this book we take a comparative approach to the study of Asia, Africa, Latin America, and the Middle East. Today it is more common to hear the states of these regions variously referred to as "developing countries," "less developed countries," or "underdeveloped countries." These are just a few of the labels used to refer to a huge expanse of territories and peoples, and none of the names we use are entirely satisfactory. First, our subject—four major world regions—is so vast and so heterogeneous that it is difficult to speak of it as a single entity. Second, each name has its own political implications and each insinuates a political message. For example, although some of them are better off than others, only an extreme optimist could include all the countries contained within these regions as "developing countries." Many of the countries we'll be looking at are simply *not* developing. They are *underdeveloping*— losing ground, becoming worse off.[5]

Those who prefer the term "developing countries" tend to support the idea that the capitalist path of free markets will eventually lead to peace and prosperity for all. Capitalism is associated with rising prosperity in some countries such as South Korea and Mexico, but even in these countries the majority has yet to share in many of its benefits. However, the relative term "less developed countries" (or LDCs) begs the question: Less developed than whom—or what? The answer, inevitably, is what we arbitrarily label "developed countries": the rich, industrialized states of Western Europe, Canada, and the United States, also known as the West (a term that, interestingly enough, includes Japan but excludes most of the countries of the Western Hemisphere).

Although the people who talk about such things often throw about the terms "developed" or "less developed" as a shorthand measure of economic advancement, often such names are resented because they imply that somehow "less developed" countries are lacking in other, broader measures of political, social, or cultural development. Use of the term "developing," or any of these terms for that matter, suggests that countries can be ranked along a continuum. Such terms can be used to imply that the West is best, that the rest of the world is comparatively "backward," and that the most its citizens can hope for is to "develop" using the West as model.

At the other end of the spectrum are those who argue that the West developed only at the expense of the rest of the world. For these analysts, underdevelopment is no natural event or coincidence. Rather, it is the outcome of hundreds of years of active underdevelopment by today's developed countries. The majority's resistance to such treatment, its efforts to change its situation, is sometimes referred to as the North-South conflict, or the war between the haves and the have-nots of the world. The names "North" and "South" are useful because they are stripped of the value judgments contained within most of the terms already described. However, they are as imprecise as the term "West," since "North" refers to developed countries, which mostly fall north of the equator, and "South" is another name for less developed countries, which mostly fall south of the equator.

Another name signifying location, the all-inclusive "non-Western world," invites still more controversy. As others have demonstrated, it is probably more honest to speak of "the West and the rest" if we are to use this kind of term, since there are many non-Wests, rather than a single "non-Western world."[6] At least "the West and the rest" is straightforward in identifying its center of reference. Blatant in its Eurocentrism, it is dismissive of 75 percent of the world's population, treating "the rest" as "other." In the same manner that the term "nonwhite" is demeaning, "non-Western" implies that something is missing. Our subject becomes defined only through its relationship to a more central "West."

During the COLD WAR, the period of U.S.-Soviet rivalry running approximately from 1947 to 1989, another set of names reflected this ideological conflict that dominated international relations. For decades fol-

Figure 1.2   *continues*

Figure 1.2 *continued*

lowing World War II the rich, economically advanced, industrialized countries, also known as the "first world," were pitted against the Soviet-led communist "second world." In this rivalry, each side described what it was doing as self-defense, and both the first and second worlds claimed to be fighting to "save" the planet from the treachery of the other. Much of this battle was over who would control the "third world," which served as the theater for many Cold War conflicts and whose countries were treated as pawns in this chess game. Defined simply as what was left, the concept of a "third world" has always been an unwieldy one. Neither first nor second, the "third world" tends to bring to most people's minds countries that are poor, agricultural, and overpopulated. Yet consider the stunning diversity that exists among the countries of every region and you can see how arbitrary it is to lump them into this category. Not all of what we once called the third world can be characterized as such today. For example, how do we categorize China? It's clearly communist (and therefore second world), but during the Cold War it viewed itself as the leader of the third world. What about Israel or South Africa? Because of the dramatic disparities occurring within these countries, they could be categorized as third world or first, depending on where you look. The same can be said for the United States. Visit parts of its inner cities, the rural South, or Appalachia and you will find the third world. And now, with the Cold War over, why aren't the former republics of the Soviet Union included in most studies of the third world? Certainly the poorest of them are more third than first world.

The fact is, many countries fall between the cracks when we use the first world/third world typology. Some of the countries labeled "third world" are oil rich, while others have been industrializing for so many years that even the term "newly industrializing country" (NIC) is dated (it is still widely used, but is gradually being replaced by names such as "new industrial economy" or "emergent economy"). Therefore, in appreciation of the diversity contained within the third world, perhaps it is useful to subdivide it, to allow for specificity by adding more categories.

Under this schema, the NICs and a few others that are most appropriately termed "developing countries" are labeled "third world" (e.g., Taiwan, South Korea, Brazil, Mexico). "Fourth world" countries become those that are not industrializing, but have some resources to sell on the world market (e.g., Ghana, Bolivia, Egypt), or some strategic value that wins them a bit of foreign assistance. The label "LDC" is the best fit in most of these cases, since it simply describes their situation and implies little in terms of their prospects for development. And finally, we have the "fifth world," which Henry Kissinger once callously characterized as "the basket cases of the world." These are the world's poorest countries. Sometimes known as "least less developed countries" (LLDCs), they are very clearly underdeveloping. With little to sell on the world market, they are eclipsed by it. The poorest in the world, with the worst ratings for virtually every marker of human development, these countries are marginalized and utterly dependent on what little foreign assistance they receive.

Clearly none of the names we use to describe the countries of Asia, Africa, Latin America, and the Middle East are satisfactory. Even the terms "Latin America" and "Middle East" are problematic. Not all of "Latin America" is "Latin," in the sense of being Spanish- or Portuguese-speaking. Yet we will use this term as shorthand for the entire region south of the U.S. border, including the Caribbean. And the idea of a region being "Middle East" only makes sense if one's perspective is distinctly European—otherwise, what is it "middle" to? The point is that most of our labels reflect some bias, and none of them are fully satisfactory. These names are all ideologically loaded in one way or another. Because there is no simple, clearly most appropriate identifier available, you will find that at some point or another we use each of them, as markers of the varying worldviews you will see presented in this text. Ultimately, we leave it to the reader to sift through the material presented here, consider the debates, and decide which arguments—and therefore which terminology—are most representative of the world and therefore most useful.

India; curiously, the Middle East is frequently left out), or they provide a CROSS-NATIONAL ANALYSIS that purports to generalize about much larger expanses of territory. Those who take the cross-national approach are interested in getting at the big picture. Texts that employ it focus on theory and concepts to broaden our scope of understanding beyond a handful of cases. They often wind up making fairly sweeping generalizations. Sure, the authors of these books make reference to any number of countries as illustration, but at the loss of detail and context that comes only through the use of case studies.

We provide both cross-national analysis and case studies, because we don't want to lose the strengths of either approach. We present broad themes and concepts, while including attention to the variations that exist in reality. In adopting this hybrid approach we have set for ourselves a more ambitious task. However, as teachers, we recognize the need for both approaches to be presented. We have worked hard to show how cross-national analysis and case study can work in tandem, how one complements the other. By looking at similar phenomena in several contexts (i.e., histories, politics, societies, economics, and international relations of the third world, more generally), we can apply our cases and compare them, illustrating the similarities and differences experienced in different settings.

Therefore, in addition to the cross-national analysis that composes the bulk of each chapter, we offer eight case studies, two from each of the major regions of the third world. For each region we include the "classics" offered in virtually every text applying the case method to the non-Western experience: Mexico, Nigeria, China, and Iran. We offer these cases for the same reasons that so many others see fit to include them. However, we go further. To temper the tendency to view these cases as somehow representative of their regions, and to enhance the basis for comparison, we submit alongside the classic other, less predictable case studies from each region. These additional cases are equally interesting and important in their own regard; they are countries that are rarely (if ever) included as case studies in introductory textbooks: Peru, Zimbabwe, Turkey, and Indonesia. (See the maps and country profiles in Figures 1.3 to 1.10 on pages 18 through 25.)

Through detailed case studies, we learn what is distinctive about the many peoples of the world, and get a chance to begin to see the world from a perspective other than our own. We can begin doing comparative analysis by thinking about what makes the people of the world alike and what makes us different. We should ask ourselves how and why such differences exist, and consider the various constraints under which we all operate. We study comparative politics not only to understand the way other people view the world, but also to make better sense of our own understanding of it. We have much to learn from how similar problems are approached by different groups of people. To do this we must consider the variety of factors that serve as context, to get a better idea of why things happen and why events unfold as they do.[7] The better we get at this, the better idea we will have of what to expect in the future. And we will get a better sense of what works and doesn't work so well—in the cases under examination, but also in other countries. You may be tempted to compare the cases under review with the situation in your own country. And that's to be encouraged, since the study of how others approach problems may offer us ideas on how to improve our lives at home. Comparativists argue that drawing from the experience of others is really the only way to understand our own systems. Seeing beyond the experience of developed countries and what is immediately familiar to us expands our minds, allows us to see the wider range of alternatives, and offers new insights into the challenges we face at the local, national, and international levels.

The greatest insight, however, comes with the inclusion of a larger circle of voices—beyond those of the leaders and policymakers. Although you will certainly hear their arguments in the chapters that follow, you will also hear the voices of those who are not often represented in texts such as this. You will hear stories of domination and the struggle against it. You will hear not only how people have been oppressed, but also how they have liberated themselves.[8] Throughout the following chapters we have worked to include the standpoint and perspectives of the ostensibly "powerless": the poor, youth, and women. Although they are often ignored by their governments, including the U.S. government, hearing their voices is a necessity if we are to fully comprehend the complexity of the challenges all of us face. Until these populations are included and encouraged to participate to their fullest potential, development will be distorted and delayed. Throughout this book, in a variety of different ways, you will find that attention to these groups and their interests interconnects our discussions of history, economics, society, politics, and international relations.

Cross-National Comparison: Recurrent Themes

As mentioned earlier, we believe that any introductory study of the third world should include both the specificity of case study as well as the breadth of the cross-national approach. Throughout the chapters that follow you will find several recurring themes (globalization, human rights, the environment, and AIDS), which will be approached from a number of angles and will serve as a basis for cross-national comparison. For example, not only is it interesting and important to understand the difference in the experience of AIDS in Zimbabwe as opposed to Iran, it is just as important to understand how religion, poverty, and war may contribute to the spread of the disease. In addition, if you're trying to understand AIDS, you should be aware of its impact on development, how ordinary people are attempting to cope with it, and what they (with or without world leaders) are prepared to do to fight it.

In a variety of ways and to varying degrees, globalization, human rights abuse, environmental degradation, the emergence of new and deadly diseases, international migration, and the drug trade are all indicative of a growing world INTERDEPENDENCE. By interdependence we are referring to a relationship of mutual (although not equal) vulnerability and sensitivity that exists between the world's peoples. This shared dependence has grown out of a rapidly expanding web of interactions that tie us closer together. Most Americans are pretty familiar with the idea that what we do as a nation often affects others—for better or worse. On the other hand, it is more of a stretch to get the average American to understand why we should care and why we need to understand what is happening in the world around us—even in far-off "powerless" countries. However, whether we choose to recognize it or not, it is becoming more and more difficult to escape the fact that our relationship with the world is a reciprocal one. What happens on the other side of the planet, even in small, seemingly "powerless" countries, does affect us—whether we like it or not.

Globalization

The end of the Cold War opened a window of opportunity that has resulted not only in some dramatic political changes, but also in a closer integration of the world's economies than ever before. As a result, the world is becoming increasingly interconnected by a single, global economy. This transformative process is commonly described as globalization, and it is supported and driven by the full force of capitalism, unimpeded now because of the absence of virtually any competing economic ideology. The world has experienced periods of corporate globalization before (the last was associated with European imperialism). What is unique about this cycle is the unprecedented speed with which globalization is tearing down barriers to trade. It is also increasing mobility, or cross-border flows of not only trade, but also capital, technology, information—and people. As it has before, technology is driving this wave. The World Wide Web is as symbolic of this era as the Berlin Wall was of the Cold War. Because of their mobility and global reach, MULTINATIONAL CORPORATIONS (MNCs) are key actors (but hardly the only actors) in this globalization. This is a process that is rapidly unfolding and under no one's control. In fact, even some of its advocates allow that globalization may be a process out of control.[9]

For those who embrace it, globalization's dynamism and power are part of its appeal. They consider globalization to be a largely benevolent process. They see it as the surest route to development and prosperity—it is even credited with sowing the seeds of democracy worldwide. Because of globalization, no corner of the world remains isolated; new values are being spread that challenge traditional belief systems such as fatalism, elitism, and authoritarianism. Poverty is alleviated as trade is increased and jobs are created; as the lines of communication are opened up we learn from and begin to accept one another. Ideally, globalization will help to make us more aware of our common interests, our mutual dependence. Among other things, it has brought people together to form the basis of the international environmental movement; it has enhanced scientific cooperation and raised human rights as a universal concern (which some refer to as "moral globalization" or "the globalization of dissent").[10]

According to its admirers, globalization is spilling over into a variety of areas, creating a "world village" based in cultural and political globalization. As it works to overcome the barriers between us, globalization enhances interdependence. It tightens the web of interrelationships that link the world's peoples. Thanks to globalization, this deepening interdependence is fostering a sense of community and sharing over the identity politics that once divided us by religion, ethnicity, language, and so on. (Although interestingly, some analysts who are generally proglobalization argue that being wired for a free flow of information can actually produce hostility and anger. Much of this "shared" information promotes stereotyping and reinforces divisions.)[11]

Some analysts go even as far as to suggest that we are moving to a "postcultural" world in which the boundaries marking where one culture ends and another begins are increasingly blurred. They contend that globalization is not promoting homogenization and that it is not the same thing as Westernization; rather, globalization is promoting eclecticism and advancing our recognition of the world's diversity. So-called traditional cultures aren't so traditional. None of the world's cultures have developed in a vacuum, unaffected by outside forces. Even those concerned about globalization's impact admit that cultures aren't static. They are always changing—globalization is just hurrying the process along.

In this sense, perhaps it can be said that globalization is producing a more homogeneous world.[12] Then again, antiglobalists maintain that a more homogeneous world means cultural devastation for the majority. Globalization is a cultural bulldozer. Already the dollar has become the de facto global currency, and English has become the de facto global language. One of the most visible signs of this is the spread of Western consumer culture. While this is something proglobalizers generally celebrate, critics despise it as "coca-colonization."[13]

Critics argue that globalization isn't so much about interdependence as it is about furthering dependence. Dependence is a form of international interdependence—except that dependence is marked by an extreme power imbalance. Antiglobalists point out that economic globalization is capitalist globalization, which means that corporations and the rich are being privileged over other social actors. The result isn't anything new. Poverty, the exploitation of the underdog, the erosion of labor and environmental standards, and the abuse of human rights all predated globalization. The difference is that globalization has accelerated and intensified these trends.

Even the proponents of corporate globalization admit that it does create winners and losers; globalization brings profits but also problems. They also recognize that globalization is not a uniform process, and that its effects are more evident in some places than in others. Certainly, aspects of globalization such as deregulation or disappearing trade barriers are more obvious in some places than in others (e.g., the creation of trading blocs within Europe and in North America). Thus far, globalization is uneven: it appears to have hardly touched the most economically underdeveloped countries in the world, such as those in the Sahel.[14] Yet this is increasingly the exception, and the rapid economic, sociocultural, and political change associated with globalization is the rule worldwide.

Its boosters argue that for better or worse, globalization is inexorable and inevitable; the integration of the world's peoples has gone so far that we can never go back. However, history shows us that even this massive force could be reversed by international events. Nationalism and economic downturns have in the past contributed to the end of previous cycles of globalization.[15] The U.S. recession (which most analysts argue began before September 11) is very definitely affecting the rest of the world. If it continues for long, it may also mean a return to economic nationalism and protectionist policies that could very quickly shred this interdependent web.

Human Rights

The idea that humans share certain natural, universal, and inherent rights—simply because they are human—dates at least as far back as John Locke's *Two*

Treatises of Civil Government (1690). The view that abusers should be held accountable for their wrongs, or that others should interfere with how a government treats its own citizens, is more recent in origins. It was not until the systematic murder of millions under Hitler's Third Reich that the world was willing to challenge two dominant principles of international relations: nonintervention, or the legal obligation to refrain from involvement in the internal affairs of other states, and SOVEREIGNTY, the widely shared belief that STATES are the principal actors in international relations and as such they are subject to no higher political authority.[16]

However, the Holocaust served as a catalyst to the development of what is now recognized as an international human rights movement. The Holocaust ostensibly taught us that in some cases the world must intervene against abusers and that state sovereignty must not always be held as sacrosanct. How a government treats its own people does affect the rest of us. If nothing else, respect for human rights is widely recognized as essential to international peace and stability. At least in theory, the international community accepts that it has a moral mandate to prevent the kinds of abuses associated with the genocide in Europe.

Over the fifty years following that genocide the world community set out to develop a variety of international norms to promote human rights and to institutionalize safeguards against the recurrence of atrocities. Prominent in this effort was the creation of the UNIVERSAL DECLARATION OF HUMAN RIGHTS (UDHR) in 1948, which is widely recognized as the most authoritative and comprehensive of all international statements on human rights. Composed of thirty articles addressing a broad range of issues, the UDHR is accepted as setting the standards to which all states should aspire. The UDHR includes attention to what are sometimes known as "first-generation" or "blue" rights: civil and political rights, such as freedom of speech, freedom of religion, freedom from torture or cruel and unusual punishment, the right to due process, the right to self-determination, and so on. These rights are based on the assumption that the individual should be protected against state actions that are unusual, arbitrary, or excessive. As long as the right to challenge the government's misuse of authority is permitted, other rights (such as freedom from torture) will be safeguarded. First-generation rights are considered by many people to be key to the enjoyment of all other rights. Yet the UDHR also recognizes the importance of "second-generation" or "red" rights: economic, social, and cultural rights, such as access to decent food, shelter, work, education, and healthcare. This conception of human rights, sometimes known as the "human-needs" approach, considers the aspects of existence necessary to secure the basic development of the person primary. Proponents of second-generation rights maintain that a government's denial of basic needs is as much a violation of human rights as the torture of dissidents.[17]

Although the governments of virtually every country in the world use the language of human rights and claim to believe in the inherent dignity of human beings, for many years the world has been divided over how most appropriately to define human rights. The governments of most developed countries, especially the United States, have traditionally argued that political and civil rights should be prioritized. They contend that these rights, which place an emphasis on liberty, should come first, because the enjoyment of such freedoms will

These Afghan refugees are exercising their right to an education in Iran (UN Photo)

enable the individual to ensure for him- or herself the provision of subsistence or red rights. Yet who cares about freedom of expression and the other blue rights when one's children are dying of hunger? As the former president of Senegal, Leopold Senghor, put it, "Human rights begin with breakfast." He and others argue that those who seek to exclude red rights have it all wrong, since until people's basic rights, or certain minimal physical needs, are met, there can be no development—let alone enjoyment of more ambitious rights, such as liberties. (Others point out that for poor countries, government guarantees of food and housing are actually much more ambitious than the relatively "cost-free" guarantees of freedoms, such as expression and assembly. Nobel laureate Amartya Sen maintains that the right to freedom of speech is a precondition for all other rights, since famine, torture, and other abuses rarely occur in countries with democratic governments and a relatively free press.)[18]

The UDHR, whose drafters included Westerners and non-Westerners, attempts to get around this debate by proclaiming that human rights are indivisible, interdependent, and interrelated, and that all are necessary for the full realization of human potential. Not everyone agrees. According to the proponents of CULTURAL RELATIVISM, including those who support the "Asian values" argument, human rights (or moral claims) should be defined as the product of a particular society's culture and historical experience. Therefore, to talk about a universality of human rights is to impose one's values on others. For them, political and civil rights are based in Western Enlightenment values, which have little appeal or relevance in Confucian cultures, wherein higher value is placed on order and discipline. Blue rights also uphold the rights of the individual over those of the community. This idea is unacceptable in many non-Western cultures, which hold that the rights of the individual should be subordinated to those of the group, since the individual has no meaning apart from the community to whom he or she belongs.[19]

Critics of the "Asian values" argument point to the complexity not only of Confucianism, which is not as conservative as many think, but also of Asian cultures themselves, of which there are a great variety and diversity. Asian cultures draw from many different influences, including Buddhism, which emphasizes individual freedoms and tolerance. Millions of non-Westerners, led by people such as Aung San Suu Kyi and Rigoberta Menchú, reject arguments that political and civil rights or freedoms (such as freedom from torture) are uniquely Western. Many non-Western traditions view the individual and community as inseparable, and the relationship between the rights of the individual and the rights of the community as one of mutual obligation. While group rights can be used to restrict individuals, they can also exist to protect individual rights.[20]

As you might imagine, this and other debates over how best to define human rights have hamstrung international efforts to promote such rights. However, there is new momentum behind the human rights movement. Just as the Holocaust once spurred a concern with human rights, perhaps it was the specter of ethnic cleansing, its mass killing and systematic rapes, and the "too little too late" responses in Bosnia and Rwanda that have propelled this renewed interest. Once again, the human rights movement is developing—and not only toward finding other ways of holding accountable those responsible for such atrocities. The challenges associated with globalization have led to calls for expanding and refining the scope of human rights and including a third generation of "new" human rights. Debate has begun over whether other values of signal importance, such as the rights to peace, development, and a safe and healthy environment (or "green" rights) qualify as human rights. Are the rights to clean drinking water and to live in safety legally enforceable claims, or merely "wishes"? The third generation of rights remains the subject of heated debate. Yet even for the older generations of rights, there remain enormous differences between the governments of the world over how to define human rights, how and when human rights law should apply, and what priority should be given to different categories of rights. While this highly politicized debate continues, it is increasingly common for analysts to return to the argument that is at the core of the Universal Declaration of Human Rights: that the distinction between human rights and human needs is an artificial one. Rather, civil, political, economic, social, and cultural rights are best understood as part of "a seamless web"— indivisible and interdependent.[21] In other words, all the rights discussed here are important because it is difficult to fully enjoy one category of rights without the security offered by the others.

The Environment

Along with globalization and human rights, the health of the planet is another issue of interdependence (and also one that is arguably everyone's business). Environmental issues will turn up in nearly all of the following chapters because the growing body of scientific evidence is becoming more difficult to refute. Development as it is currently being pursued, in both developed and in less developed countries, is contributing to a morass of environmental problems that transcend national borders and whose management will require global cooperation. Global warming, deforestation, desertification, loss of biodiversity, the depletion of fisheries and destruction of coral reefs, toxic dumping, water shortages—these are just a few of the problems whose solutions will require international cooperation.[22]

Take, for example, the issue of deforestation. Currently, the world's remaining rainforests are being destroyed at a rate of 14 million hectares (an area almost three times the size of Costa Rica) per year. And despite more attention since the 1980s to the many problems associated with the loss of rainforests, deforestation has actually increased by 34 percent since 1991. These forests are hot spots for biodiversity (they contain hundreds of species within a single hectare, whereas the average hectare of forest typically contains a handful of species). However, 70 percent of the natural cover protecting these species has been lost in the last several decades. At the current rate, in ten to twenty years these hot spots will become theaters of mass extinction—comparable in scale to the demise of the dinosaurs 65 million years ago.[23]

Of similar cataclysmic value is the threat posed by the greenhouse effect or global warming to another common resource, the atmosphere. The greenhouse effect is produced by the emission of what have come to be known as greenhouse gases: carbon dioxide released by the burning of fossil fuels, as well as naturally occurring methane and nitrogen. Industrialization and economic growth based on the use of coal, oil, and natural gas have contributed to the release of these gases, which has reached record highs. Greenhouse gases are collecting in the upper atmosphere, covering the planet in a blanket of sorts. Incoming heat from the sun penetrates this blanket but is then trapped by it. The effect is likened to a greenhouse, which traps heat indoors. In this sense, the growth of economies based on the consumption of fossil fuels has contributed substantially to warming over the last fifty years

While some scientists and politicians argue that global warming is not a manmade event, but naturally occurring and inevitable—part of a long cycle of alternating ice ages and periods of extreme heat—this is the minority view. The majority of the world's scientists agree that we are experiencing a global warming; the main issue for debate is over how bad it will be—and how soon it will come. A 2000 study conducted by the highly respected Intergovernmental Panel on Climate Change (IPCC) found that human activity is the principal cause of recent climate change and that the rate of warming is greater than estimated in earlier studies. If fossil fuel combustion continues at twentieth-century levels, virtually every natural system and human economy will be at risk. Higher temperatures will mean rising seas from melting ice caps, more frequent and severe storms, and more intense droughts. It will alter every ecosystem on the planet.

Already we are seeing its effects. This climate change is exacerbating the misery of already poor areas, and creates a vicious cycle in which poverty and environmental degradation coexist and are accelerated by globalization.[24]

In a variety of ways, globalization is just hastening processes already well under way. However, because of its speed, globalization is putting unprecedented pressures on the planet's capacities. Displaced rural populations are flooding the cities in search of their livelihood or pressing into the forests seeking new resources. This only contributes to the greenhouse effect, not only because the burning of forests releases more carbon dioxide into the atmosphere, but also because the loss of these forests means the loss of "pollution sponges," since forests absorb carbon and slow global warming. As LDCs embrace the developed country model, pursuing growth at any cost, they will increasingly become part of the problem. However, as it currently stands, the 25 percent of the world's population living in developed countries consumes 80 percent of the world's resources. The United States alone produces 25 percent of the emissions associated with global warming, yet the LDCs are likely to feel the most severe impact of environmental devastation. Not only are they more vulnerable to many of its effects, but LDCs also lack access to the technologies that might ameliorate its impact. Over the last few years, a number of creative solutions based on cooperative efforts have been proposed for dealing with the environmental problems that we share. Unfortunately, finger pointing and recriminations between developed and less developed countries, and efforts by even the richest developed countries to shift the burden of responsibility to others, suggest that the international leadership (and funding) so desperately needed to address these problems will continue to be sorely lacking.

Disease

Just as environmental degradation is taking an increasing toll on all of us, but especially the poor, so is disease. Not only is there an income gap between developed and less developed countries, but there is also a health gap. A variety of threats come together to explain why infant mortality rates remain higher in LDCs and why life expectancy has actually shortened in many LDCs: undernutrition, infectious diseases, and chronic debilitating diseases—all associated with poverty. These problems are related to much of the misery and hardship in all the regions we will study. Although malnutrition, malaria, and the dehydration associated with diarrhea are bigger killers today, HIV/AIDS stands alone as the coming plague. Although it is widely and mistakenly perceived in developing countries as a disease that has been brought under control, one that can be managed with the proper medical care, there is no cure for AIDS. In many LDCs its effects will be near apocalyptic. By conservative estimates, at the end of 2002 already 27 million people were dead, approximately 14 million children were orphaned, and 42 million men, women, and children were living with HIV or AIDS.[25] According to UN Secretary-General Kofi Annan, the disease has already set back development in some African countries by a decade or more. It now threatens to have the same effect on Eastern Europe, Asia, and the Caribbean.

HIV/AIDS is by no means a problem unique to the third world. However,

85 percent of all people with HIV/AIDS live in LDCs and the vast majority of them live in Africa. It is important to note that some areas of Africa, such as West Africa, are not as seriously affected as others. Although it is still unclear whether AIDS will explode in Asia as it has particularly in southern Africa, the infection rate is far greater than any expert or computer model predicted ten years ago.[26] This acute form of a viral infection is spread through sexual contact and other activities involving the exchange of body fluids. Around the world people become infected with HIV in a variety of ways, including blood transfusions, intravenous drug use, and both heterosexual and homosexual sex. Each country and region has its own particular mix of circumstances reflected by patterns of transmission. As you will read in Chapter 7, poverty is a major factor contributing to the spread of the disease.

In many places social norms not usually addressed also play a role in the spread of HIV.[27] Many governments refuse to recognize that especially vulnerable groups, such as drug addicts, gay men, and sex workers, exist. In addition, because of social taboos, many governments have refused to discuss the transmission of HIV through unprotected sex. The result worldwide is a striking lack of awareness concerning its dangers. In many places, multiple sexual relationships for men may be socially tolerated or even encouraged. Other practices considered traditional, such as female genital cutting and wife inheritance, contribute to the spread of the disease. Similarly, imbalances of power often put females at risk of HIV infection. Females of all ages, especially young women, often have a difficult time rejecting a man's sexual advances or insisting he wear a condom, since many cultures—Western and non-Western—teach females to be subordinate to male authority. In the long term, changing how males and females relate to each other and how men treat women and girls will be a fundamental advance not only against this disease, but also against many other barriers to development. In the near term, however, smaller, more mundane efforts must be made. In Uganda and Thailand, the governments have taken proactive measures to promote health education and safer sex. In many cultures, though, condoms are not regularly available and are stigmatized for a number of reasons. Women who use them are often treated with suspicion. Where fertility is celebrated and child mortality rates are high, condoms are rejected because they are a form of birth control.

However, condoms, vaginal microbicides, and other tools are a crucial means of helping women to take their lives (and the lives of their children) into their own hands. Without access to information and services to protect themselves, an estimated 6,300 women are infected with HIV every day.[28] These estimates are conservative, since it is likely that many people who are HIV positive have no idea that they are dying. They can't afford the tests, and given the stigma that people with AIDS face worldwide, many ask why they should bother. There is little recourse for the majority of those who would test positive, since they lack access to the medicines that could prolong their lives. Put yourself in their shoes: Why worry about something that might kill you ten years down the line when you're struggling with a host of other life-threatening problems on a day-to-day basis? Such questions provoke a variety of reactions. In the meantime, the world is facing a pandemic that has been likened to the Black Death of the fourteenth century. If it continues to go uncontained, its long-term impact may be unlike any the world has ever known.

Conclusions: It Depends on Who You Ask

Let's put it flatly: there are no simple answers to any of the questions we have raised here or will raise throughout the chapters that follow. The best any of us can do is to present you with a wide range of thinking, or alternative perspectives on many of the challenges faced to some degree by all of us—but most directly by people living in less developed countries. In this book we will be looking at a series of issues of interdependence, such as the drug trade, migration, and arms transfers, from a number of angles. We ask that before you make up your own mind about any of these contending theories, you consider each of them on its own merits. We firmly believe that it is the only way to begin to understand the complex social phenomena we now set out to discuss.

Linking Concepts and Cases

The information in this section is provided as a primer for the case studies we will be discussing throughout the rest of the book. Figures 1.3 through 1.10 on pages 18 through 25 should serve as a point of reference for you as you go on to read about the histories, economies, and politics of the eight case studies introduced here. Throughout the book, we will return to the same countries, applying the ideas introduced in the conceptual chapters to the reality of their experiences.

Now It's Your Turn

From a simple examination of this statistical information, what would you expect to be the key issue, or the most pressing problem each country faces? What can a sketch such as this tell you about life in each of these eight countries? Which ones appear most similar, and in what ways? What are some of the most striking differences between these countries? What other information not included here do you consider deserving of attention? Why?

Figure 1.3 Mexico: Profile and Map

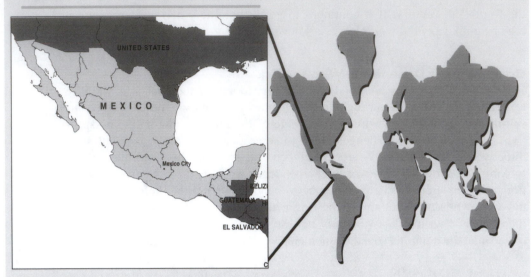

Formal Name:	United Mexican States
Area, km²:	1.97 million
Comparative Area:	Slightly less than three times the size of Texas
Capital:	Mexico City
Establishment of Present State:	September 18, 1810
Population:	101 million
Age Under 15 Years:	33%
Population Growth Rate:	1.5%
Fertility Rate (children per woman):	2.62
Infant Mortality (per 1000 births):	25
Life Expectancy:	72
HIV Incidence Adult:	0.29%
Ethnic Groups:	Mestizo 60%, Amerindian 30%, white 9%, other 1%
Literacy:	90%
Religions:	Roman Catholic 89%, Protestant 6%, other 5%
GDP per Capita (PPP):	$ 9,100
GDP Growth Rate:	7.1% (2000)
Labor by Sector:	Services 56%, Industrial 24%, Agriculture 20%
Population in Poverty:	27%
Unemployment Rate:	2.2% (urban, with considerable underemployment)
Export Commodities:	Manufactured goods, petroleum and petroleum products, silver, fruits, vegetables, coffee, cotton
External Debt:	$ 162 billion

Source: CIA, *World Factbook,* 2001

Figure 1.4 Peru: Profile and Map

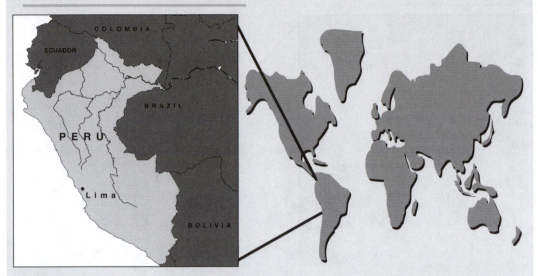

Formal Name:	Republic of Peru
Area, km²:	1.28 million
Comparative Area:	Slightly smaller than the size of Alaska
Capital:	Lima
Establishment of Present State:	July 28, 1821
Population:	27 million
Age Under 15 Years:	34%
Population Growth Rate:	1.7%
Fertility Rate (children per woman):	2.96
Infant Mortality (per 1000 births):	39
Life Expectancy:	70
HIV Incidence Adult:	0.35%
Ethnic Groups:	Mestizo 60%, Amerindian 30%, white 15%, other 3%
Literacy:	89%
Religions:	Roman Catholic 90%
GDP per Capita (PPP):	$ 4,550
GDP Growth Rate:	3.6% (2000)
Labor, Major Sectors:	Agriculture, mining, manufacturing, construction
Population in Poverty:	49%
Unemployment Rate:	7.7% (with extensive underemployment)
Export Commodities:	Fish and fish byproducts, copper, zinc, gold, crude petroleum and petroleum byproducts
External Debt:	$ 31 billion

Source: CIA, *World Factbook*, 2001

Figure 1.5   Nigeria: Profile and Map

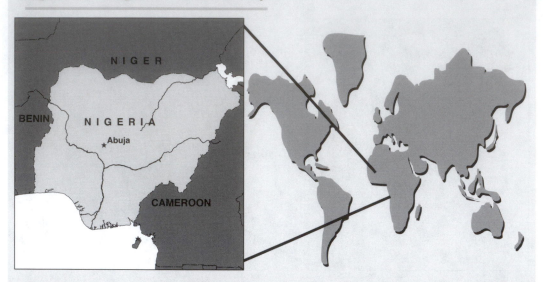

Formal Name:	Federal Republic of Nigeria
Area, km2:	923,768
Comparative Area:	Slightly more than twice the size of California
Capital:	Abuja
Establishment of Present State:	October 1, 1960
Population:	126 million
Age Under 15 Years:	44%
Population Growth Rate:	2.6%
Fertility Rate (children per woman):	5.57
Infant Mortality (per 1000 births):	73
Life Expectancy:	51
HIV Incidence Adult:	5%
Ethnic Groups:	(More than 250 groups) Hausa and Fulani 29%, Yoruba 21%, Ibo 18%, Ijaw 10%, Kaniuri 4%, Ibibio 3.5%, Tiv 2.5%
Literacy:	57%
Religions:	Muslim 50%, Christian 40%, indigenous beliefs 10%
GDP per Capita (PPP):	$ 950
GDP Growth Rate:	3.5% (2000)
Labor by Sector:	Agriculture 70%, Services 20%, Industrial 10%
Population in Poverty:	45%
Unemployment Rate:	28%
Export Commodities:	Petroleum and petroleum products, cocoa, rubber
External Debt:	$ 32 billion

Source: CIA, *World Factbook,* 2001

Figure 1.6   Zimbabwe: Profile and Map

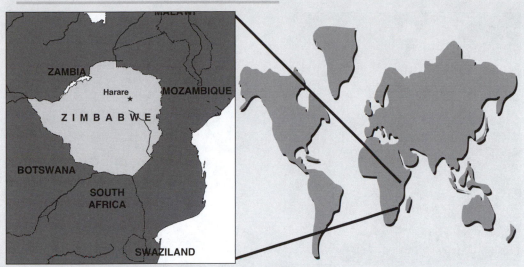

Formal Name:	Republic of Zimbabwe
Area, km2:	390,580
Comparative Area:	Slightly larger than the size of Montana
Capital:	Harare
Establishment of Present State:	April 18, 1980
Population:	11 million
Age Under 15 Years:	39%
Population Growth Rate:	0.15%
Fertility Rate (children per woman):	3.28
Infant Mortality (per 1000 births):	62
Life Expectancy:	37
HIV Incidence Adult:	25%
Ethnic Groups:	African 98% (Shona 71%; Ndebele 16%; other 11%), mixed and Asian 1%, white <1%
Literacy:	85%
Religions:	Syncretic 50%, Christian 25%, indigenous beliefs 24%, Muslim and other 1%
GDP per Capita (PPP):	$ 2,500
GDP Growth Rate:	–6.1% (2000)
Labor by Sector:	Agriculture 20%, Services 24%, Industrial 10%
Population in Poverty:	60%
Unemployment Rate:	50%
Export Commodities:	tobacco, gold, ferroalloys, cotton
External Debt:	$ 4.1 billion

Source: CIA, *World Factbook,* 2001

Figure 1.7   Iran: Profile and Map

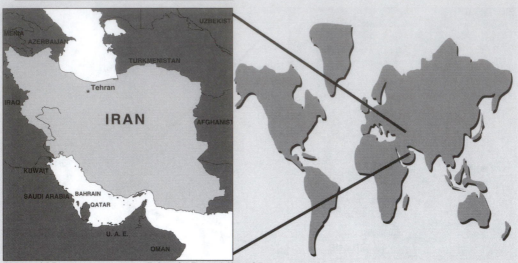

Formal Name:	Islamic Republic of Iran
Area, km²:	1.65 million
Comparative Area:	Slightly larger than the size of Alaska
Capital:	Tehran
Establishment of Present State:	April 1, 1979
Population:	66 million
Age Under 15 Years:	33%
Population Growth Rate:	0.72%
Fertility Rate (children per woman):	2.02
Infant Mortality (per 1000 births):	29
Life Expectancy:	70
HIV Incidence Adult:	0.01%
Ethnic Groups:	Persian 51%, Azeri 24%, Gilaki and Mazandarani 8%, Kurd 7%, Lur 2%, Baloch 2%, Turkmen 2%, other 1%
Literacy:	72%
Religions:	Shia Muslim 89%; Sunni Muslim 10%; Zoroastrian, Jewish, Christian, and Bahai' 1%
GDP per Capita (PPP):	$ 6,300
GDP Growth Rate:	3% (2000)
Labor by Sector:	Agriculture 33%, Services 42%, Industrial 25%
Population in Poverty:	53%
Unemployment Rate:	14%
Export Commodities:	Petroleum, carpets, fruits, nuts, iron, steel, chemicals
External Debt:	$ 7.5 billion

Source: CIA, *World Factbook,* 2001

Figure 1.8 Turkey: Profile and Map

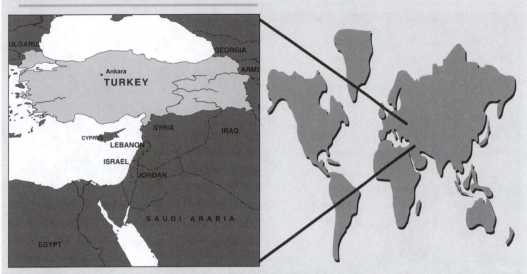

Formal Name:	Republic of Turkey
Area, km²:	780,580
Comparative Area:	Slightly larger than the size of Texas
Capital:	Ankara
Establishment of Present State:	October 29, 1923
Population:	66 million
Age Under 15 Years:	28%
Population Growth Rate:	1.24%
Fertility Rate (children per woman):	2.12
Infant Mortality (per 1000 births):	47
Life Expectancy:	71
HIV Incidence Adult:	0.01%
Ethnic Groups:	Turkish 80%, Kurdish 20%
Literacy:	85%
Religions:	Muslim (mostly Sunni) 98%, Christian and Jewish 2%
GDP per Capita (PPP):	$ 6,800
GDP Growth Rate:	6% (2000)
Labor by Sector:	Agriculture 38%, Services 38%, Industrial 24%
Population in Poverty:	not available
Unemployment Rate:	5.6%
Export Commodities:	Apparel, foodstuffs, textiles, metal manufactured products, transportation equipment
External Debt:	$ 109 billion

Source: CIA, *World Factbook,* 2001

Figure 1.9   China: Profile and Map

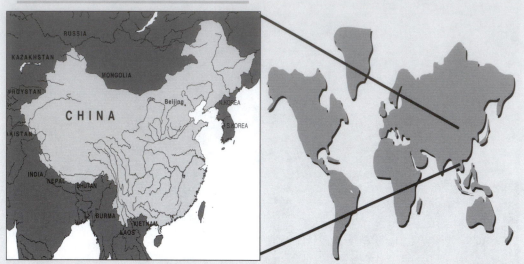

Formal Name: People's Republic of China

Area, km²: 9.60 million

Comparative Area: Slightly smaller than the size of the United States

Capital: Beijing

Establishment of
    Present State: October 1, 1949

Population: 1.27 billion

Age Under 15 Years: 25%

Population Growth Rate: 0.88%

Fertility Rate
    (children per woman): 1.82

Infant Mortality
    (per 1000 births):   28

Life Expectancy: 72

HIV Incidence Adult: 0.07%

Ethnic Groups: Han Chinese 91.9%; Zhuang, Uighur, Hui, Yi, Tebetan, Miao,
                         Manchu, Mongol, Buyi, Korean, and others 8.1%

Literacy: 82%

Religions: (Officially atheist), Taoist, Buddhist, Muslim, Christian

GDP per Capita (PPP): $ 3,600

GDP Growth Rate: 8% (2000)

Labor by Sector: Agriculture 50%, Services 26%, Industrial 24%

Population in Poverty: 10%

Unemployment Rate: 10% (urban)

Export Commodities: Machinery and equipment, textiles and clothing, footwear, toys
and   sporting goods, mineral fuels

External Debt: $ 162 billion

Source: CIA, *World Factbook,* 2001

Figure 1.10   Indonesia: Profile and Map

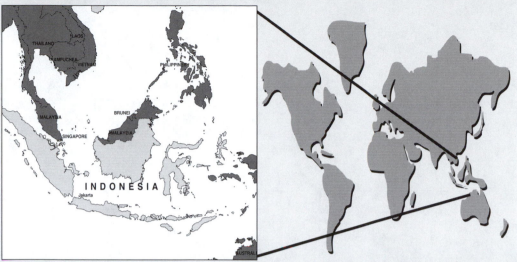

Formal Name:	Republic of Indonesia
Area, km²:	1.92 million
Comparative Area:	Slightly less than three times the size of Texas
Capital:	Jakarta
Establishment of Present State:	August 17, 1945
Population:	228 million
Age Under 15 Years:	30%
Population Growth Rate:	1.6%
Fertility Rate (children per woman):	2.58
Infant Mortality (per 1000 births):	41
Life Expectancy:	68
HIV Incidence Adult:	0.05%
Ethnic Groups:	Javanese 45%, Sundanese 14%, Madurese 7.5%, coastal Malays 7.5%, other 26%
Literacy:	84%
Religions:	Muslim 88%, Protestant 5%, Roman Catholic 3%, Hindu 2%, Buddhist 1%, other 1%
GDP per Capita (PPP):	$ 2,900
GDP Growth Rate:	4.8% (2000)
Labor by Sector:	Agriculture 45%, Services 39%, Industrial 16%
Population in Poverty:	20%
Unemployment Rate:	15–20%
Export Commodities:	Oil and gas, plywood, textiles, rubber
External Debt:	$ 144 billion

Source: CIA, *World Factbook,* 2001

PART I

HISTORICAL LEGACIES

How does one possibly condense thousands of years of the histories of four vast and diverse regions into a few chapters? It is not a simple proposition, but a necessary one. For all their differences, there are some experiences generally shared among these regions, and we will draw your attention to some common patterns. In order to make this broad sweep of time more comprehensible, we'll be speaking in generalities. We will illustrate with some specific examples throughout the chapters. However, as much as possible, we have attempted to avoid a long list of names and dates. At the risk of leaving out some exceptions to the rule, we believe that it is important at this point to come away with a general sense of the non-Western world's history. It is only with a sense of the full range of experience that one can go on to understand the complex issues that characterize life in the non-Western world today.

The most renowned historians of our time tell us that there is much still unknown about early human history. Dating back over the last 2 million years or so, much of world history is still incomplete, and (with a few exceptions) this is very much the case for the non-Western world. Unfortunately, this lack of information has provided fertile ground for the development of myths, stereotypes, and distortions—many of which continue to be popular today. As you will see, many of these beliefs—that the peoples of the non-Western world made no contributions, had no achievements, had no history—were used by Westerners to justify enslavement, conquest, and domination. Westerners' denials of the contributions of non-Westerners and portrayals of them as pagan, barbaric, warlike, or even childlike in some cases, are widely denounced today. For years, historians have worked diligently to repair the damage done by colonial apologists. A more balanced representation of the past is important work for its own sake. But it is also crucial that these histories be reconstructed because so often Western colonizers did everything they could to destroy all records of them. A greater understanding of the tremendous variety of human experience may not only help to restore the sense of identity that was taken from colonized peoples—it may also serve as a source of inspiration for indigenous solutions to some of the problems we must face today.

In their zeal to correct for the wrongs of the past, some historians have overcompensated and wound up providing an equally distorted version of history.

27

Some adopted Western value systems and focused only on the "great civiliza-tions" or empires of Asia, Africa, Latin America, and the Middle East. They ignored the vast array of smaller (but not lesser) forms of social organization. Yet the regions we are studying were inhabited for thousands of years by many different groups of people, with different ways of life. Some lived in relative isolation and some had long histories of contact with other peoples across great distances—well before these territories were "discovered" by white men. In fact, much of the non-Western world was integrated on some level into larger regional and even transcontinental networks of trade.

However, in their efforts to correct negative distortions, some historians provided overly romantic views of these empires, extolling only their virtues and portraying the world as it was before the arrival of Europeans as some sort of golden age of peace and plenty. Most analysts today agree that neither por-trayal is accurate. There is fairly wide agreement that each extreme oversimpli-fies. Because humans populated these societies, it is fair to assume that they were neither all good nor all bad. Most historians currently embrace a more bal-anced approach that seeks to understand these societies in all their complexity. And that complexity includes attention to the vast diversity of societies that existed in the long stretch of history we refer to as "precolonial"—not just empires or small bands of hunter-gatherers, but also everything in between.

2

Precolonial History
(Or, What Your "World Civ" Class Might Have Left Out)

> The past reappears because it is a hidden present.
> —Octavio Paz, writer[1]

One way of conceptualizing the many different ways in which humans organize themselves into groups is to picture a continuum. Large, hierarchical, centralized societies (or EMPIRES) lie at one end of this continuum, and much smaller, more egalitarian, decentralized societies are located at the other end, with most societies falling somewhere in between, containing elements of the two more extreme types. Without valuing one form of organization over another, anthropologists often make distinctions between STATE SOCIETIES and STATELESS SOCIETIES. Whereas the great empires have drawn most of the attention of archaeologists and historians, increasingly we are learning about somewhat smaller states. Anthropologists tell us that our earliest human ancestors lived in stateless societies. This system of organization has largely disappeared, as its members have been pushed into the most inhospitable environments or absorbed by larger groups. Yet both state and stateless societies could be found in Asia, Africa, Latin America, and the Middle East at the time of European conquest. Consequently, all these systems deserve attention, as no single type can be considered representative of these vast regions.

Stateless Societies

It is the democratic character of stateless societies that Westerners frequently find most striking. Relatively speaking, in stateless societies power is shared among the members of the group (often but not always both male and female). Also known as ACEPHALOUS SOCIETIES, they have no full-time political leaders, chiefs, presidents, or monarchs. It is not uncommon for elders to guide the affairs of the group. Or a member of the community known for his or her prowess in war or some other talent might serve on a temporary basis to lead communities in a certain function (military, religious, or economic). However, for these groups there is no tradition of a supreme ruler who governs continuously and beyond their immediate area of settlement. Unlike state systems with their courts, retinues, full-time militaries, and so on, in stateless societies people's day-to-day lives are conducted without interference from "government" as we know it.

Yet no society is truly stateless. Even in these noncentralized societies, there are widely accepted rules that provide a basis for the orderly functioning of the community. Government might appear to be more informal, in that there are no palaces, courthouses, or government buildings of any kind. However, this system is actually highly organized and there are often harsh penalties for violations of the public good. Within stateless societies, a variety of associations (such as all-male or all-female secret societies or age grades) are based on kinship, or family relationships. They exist to settle disputes among members, forge unity, and maintain order. These often-complicated arrangements promote cooperation, and time-honored rules allow families to draw on the labor they need in times of hardship. A web of kinship ties forms the basis for this kind of organization. All members of the extended families who make up the community know that the survival of all is based on this system of mutual aid and obligation.[2]

A strong sense of community pervades stateless societies, which exists among small bands or tribal groups of 20–200 people. Stateless societies are renowned for their egalitarianism. Relatively speaking, there are no divides based on class, no rich and poor. Often working as hunter-gatherers who migrate in seasonal cycles, they rarely establish themselves in one place for long, nor do members produce or accumulate wealth above the bare necessities. Whether primarily composed of hunter-gatherers or small farmers, stateless societies are often associated with subsistence economies. However, the extreme hardship such groups live under today is not traditional—they have been pushed to the most inhospitable environmental margins. Life in such societies was not always tenuous. Many hunter-gatherers preferred what they saw as the good life compared to the hard work and risk involved in food production.

Based on their intimate knowledge of the resources available, the members of stateless societies employed a wide range of techniques to support themselves.[3] Going back at least 3,000 years, statelessness is known to have existed among pastoral populations as well as more settled populations practicing slash-and-burn techniques and shifting cultivation. Some groups, such as the Guarani of Brazil, lived off of some combination of these activities. This sense of communalism and egalitarian sharing of resources based on kinship was central to the early success of wet-rice cultivation in Southeast Asia.[4] Stateless societies were identified in the sierras of northern Mexico and in the pampas of South America, as well as in the Amazon Basin.

Small, highly mobile hunter-gatherer populations often lived alongside pastoralists and larger groups of sedentary farmers in symbiotic relationships. There is a great deal of evidence of the interpenetration and complementarity of hunter-gatherer groups by food producers (and vice versa). At times, relations could be described as cooperative, as hunter-gatherer groups like the San, or the !Kung of southern Africa traded game and other goods such as wild honey for farm products and implements such as nets or other technologies. Trade was also important for forest farmers, such as the Ibo of Nigeria. Through village markets, trading has long been a tradition for women of state and stateless societies in much of West Africa.

However, at other times relations between these neighbors turned hostile. Conflicts could arise over any number of matters, most notably access to resources. Especially during times of environmental stress, it was not uncommon for settled farmers to come into conflict with pastoralists over land, as herds might destroy a field or farmers might encroach on prime pastureland. Like hunter-gatherers, pastoralists did not generally form states, but they did sometimes take them over by conquest. Pastoralists, organized and unified under a strong central regime, were known to raid settled populations. For example, Turkic nomads and other warriors on horses repeatedly swept into India to plunder sedentary societies. Herding populations such as the Masai of East Africa had a number of advantages, which enabled them, as well as larger, more centrally organized societies such as the Zulu (South Africa), to overwhelm their stateless or less centrally organized neighbors. Similarly, the Aztecs started out as a small group of tough nomads who made alliances to conquer sedentary groups. Often sedentary societies found it necessary to form larger political groupings, to make alliances and take common action in self-defense. They might erect a walled town at the center of their farmlands to serve as a refuge against raids from their neighbors. The need for defense was one of the most common factors behind the development of states.

State Societies

Historians continue to disagree about the causal relationship between population booms and increased food production. It is still a chicken or egg question: Does growth in the production of cereals such as rice, millet, and maize contribute to a population boom? Or do population booms necessitate an intensification of agricultural production? Either way, the two factors are clearly associated with the development of state societies. Once production is increased to the point of surplus, time is freed up for some people to work in capacities other than food production, including as full-time political leaders. When this happens, we begin to see more social stratification. There are divisions based on wealth, and clear differences between the rulers and ruled. A merchant class of traders emerges, markets grow, and trade becomes more regularized. In state societies in all regions the craftwork produced by an artisan class of weavers, potters, and metal- and woodworkers was highly prized. For example, the Chibcha of Colombia were known for their magnificent gold work, recognized as perhaps the finest in the ancient Americas.

At this intermediate level of social organization, clearly a state society but not an empire, government is described as comprising relatively simple small states or chiefdoms. As states grow larger we see a more centralized political organization and more complex forms of government supported by bureaucracies with increasingly specialized functions such as ambassadors, harbor masters, special judges, treasurers, tax collectors, and so on. Commercial city-states dominated the trade in the Southeast Asian archipelago. Often state societies were absorbed into larger empires in their efforts to monopolize trade. The Swahili city-states of the East African coast, such as Pemba, Mombasa, and Zanzibar, were autonomous and loosely linked through commercial ties (until they were all brought under the Omani Empire). Similarly, the city-states of Mesopotamia were eventually integrated into a single, powerful entity to ensure the security of trade routes.

States of this size existed long before the conquest of Latin America, especially in the circum-Caribbean area (Panama, Costa Rica, northern Colombia, Venezuela, Puerto Rico, Jamaica, and Cuba). A paramount chief or king arose (in some cases chosen by election, in other cases because of some exceptional talent or charisma, magical powers, skills as a protector, etc.) and was assisted by councils drawn from the heads of the lineages composing the village. At this level of organization, the chief's rule was not absolute. He was limited by his advisers and required to consult the council, although the power of the council varied by state. Often in state societies in Africa and in Southeast Asia, decisions were reached by consensus between a king and council. After lengthy deliberations, the king would pronounce a final decision representing a compromise of views.

In some cases kings had veto powers and could disregard the consensus of deliberations. Elsewhere, if the council disagreed with a chief's decisions, it could give counterorders and seek to unseat him. In the Oyo kingdoms of West Africa, a leading minister could command an extremely unpopular king to commit suicide on the basis that the people, the earth, and the gods rejected his rule. There are examples of tyrants in such societies, but generally speaking, rulers still depended on the support of the population. Kings were respected as long as they fulfilled their responsibilities as protectors and providers. There were usually no standing armies to help kings impose their will, and abuses risked reprisals. Therefore, in some states at least, there were traditional checks on the rulers' powers.

Empires

Historians tell us that the differences between chiefdoms and larger, more complex kingdoms or empires are difficult to draw. Certainly empires are distinguished by size of the territories and populations they control. Beyond this, the difference is mostly a matter of degree, as empires are in the simplest sense an expansion and deepening of tendencies found in chiefdoms.[5] The former empires of what is now called the "third world" greatly resembled those in today's "first world" in terms of size of population or expanse of territory, use of official religions, or conquest of smaller states. Larger kingdoms often developed from these smaller states. Some were very large: historians estimate that the Aztecs controlled a population of nearly 25 million people in the early sixteenth century. Europeans were often surprised at how much the empires they encountered were like the ones at home. In fact, the Aztecs dominated a total area not much smaller than that of Spain. Hernan Cortés wrote that the Aztecs lived much like people in Spain, inasmuch as harmony and order, and that it was remarkable to see what they had achieved. The Spanish conquerors of Cuzco,

Figure 2.1 Early Non-Western Empires

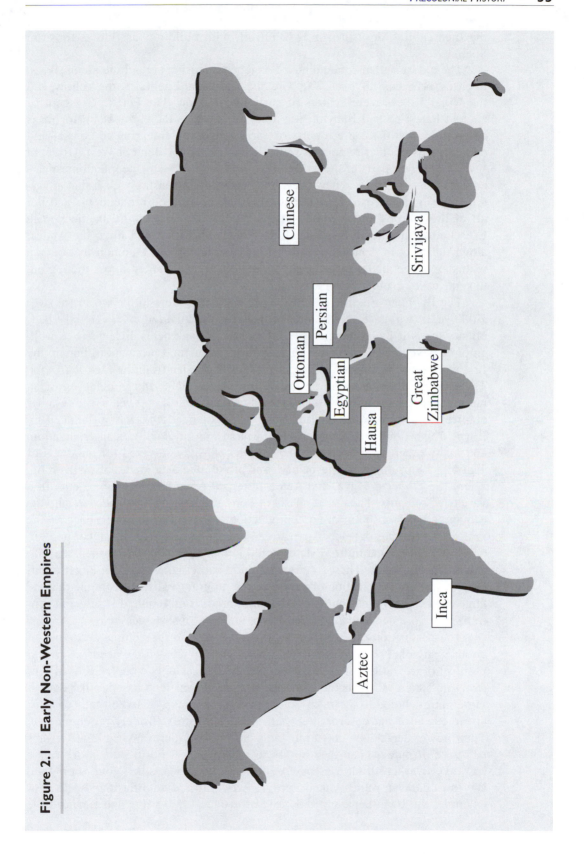

the Inca capital, described it as beautiful, with buildings as fine as those in Spain.[6]

The oldest settled communities developed intensive agriculture along rivers, in oases, or in coastal areas. The Nile, the Tigris and Euphrates, the Yellow, and the Niger Rivers were centers of early civilization. The Fertile Crescent of ancient Palestine and Babylon was long accepted as the earliest site for mass cultivation. Yet there are reports of early kingdoms emerging in coastal and delta regions in other regions as well, such as the Niger Bend of West Africa. In several different parts of the world, over thousands of years, people domesticated wild plants or adopted new ones. It is becoming increasingly clear that at various times and places there were also revolutions in food production—and not all of these crops and methods have a Middle Eastern origin. In the Fertile Crescent as in other food-producing "homelands" such as China, the Andes, along the Nile, in Amazonia, and in Mesoamerica, it was common that once a mainstay of the diet was perfected, agriculture spread swiftly across the region, in some cases to other continents.

The Egyptian Empire, one of the preeminent powers in the world for over 2,000 years, was based on the soils of the Nile floodplain. It maximized the benefits of the Nile by building canals, dikes, and embankments. Elsewhere as well, empires developed in the most successful areas of food production. Funan, the first empire in Southeast Asia, became rich off the rice from the Mekong Delta. The Chinese Empire began on the Yellow River plain, and is made up of an uninterrupted succession of two dozen dynasties over 4,000 years. Many other empires were also long-lived; although it influenced and was influenced by Egypt, Kush flourished for over 1,000 years as an original African civilization, and many other empires in the four regions of study survived for hundreds of years. In Latin America, Mesoamerica is often cited as a cradle of civilization. There the Olmecs, Maya, and Aztecs attained remarkable achievements in a variety of pursuits. The desert coasts of Peru and later its highlands became the economic base for the Inca. Food production increased there in part because the indigenous peoples developed irrigation systems that allowed for higher productivity. Moreover, centralized states could compel the cooperation necessary to extending farmlands. These large states could harness the energy of larger populations through the creation of public works programs. Historians argue that the huge projects that contributed to a boom in production required strong and centralized governments and the extension of authority over larger areas.

The production of surpluses meant an increase in the volume and types of goods available for trade. Increased trade not only created the need for greater political organization, but it also financed the increasingly complex activities of evolving states. Whereas the trade of some states was land-based, other emerging empires turned to the seas. Commercial kingdoms situated on the coasts or at the edges of the desert were often based almost exclusively on commerce. Their power depended upon a reliable means of transport (navigable waterways or beasts of burden) and their ability to secure routes. For hundreds of years a lucrative overland trade was based on cloth and beads, silks, gold, ivory, and slaves as caravan routes linked Europe, Africa, the Middle East, and Asia. For example, the trans-Saharan trade lasted for over 1,000 years and financed the great empires of Ghana, Mali, and Songhay in West Africa, whose wealth was based on monopoly control and taxation of the gold passing through their domains.

Seafaring states also amassed great riches. For example, Srivijaya, considered to be the only maritime state among the Southeast Asian classical states, was a commercial power taking revenues from passing trade. Its strategic location allowed Srivijaya to dominate maritime activity and patrol the archipelago around the Malacca Strait, one of the most significant links in the world trading system. As the dominant power in the area, Sriviijaya controlled piracy, provided harbor facilities for shipbuilding and repair, and offered reprovisioning and warehousing services—all in addition to its business in camphor, bird nests, perfumes, pearls, and peppers and spices, among other goods.[7]

Determined to maintain control over this strategically important network of sea-lanes, China and Southeast Asia were pioneers in the development of early naval capacities. Their accomplishments in this area were so substantial that China is considered to have been far ahead of any country in the world in the development of the sailing ship and navigational technology until at least the fifteenth century. Shipbuilding and naval activity were especially common in the Southeast Asian archipelago. Some ships were up to 400 feet long and large enough to carry 500–1,000 people. In the fifteenth century China sent treasure fleets with hundreds of ships across the Indian Ocean—decades before Columbus's three ships made their way to the Americas.[8] There is evidence that Indonesians and possibly the Chinese traveled as far east as Madagascar. Some historians believe Asian sailors may have traveled to the Cape of Good Hope, or even around it, long before Europeans did.

However, as early as the second century B.C.E., Arab middlemen conducted much of the trade between East Africa and Asia. From the seventh through the twelfth century the Muslim trade network was vast, and various Muslim empires functioned as free trade areas. Their central position between east and west gave them a decisive advantage in the various long-distance trades at the center of the world economy for hundreds of years. Through their commercial activities Muslim traders disseminated technological innovations and greatly advanced the areas of navigation, shipbuilding, astronomy, and geography. These coastal

Figure 2.2   Why Wasn't It China that Conquered the World?

With all of its advantages, why wasn't it China that conquered the world? Historians cite internal divisions within China in the fourteenth and fifteenth centuries. A power struggle between two factions in the Chinese court ended with the ascendance of a group who sought to turn inward. This marked a turning point in China's history, as the empire stopped sending out fleets and dismantled its shipyards. It also abandoned other technologies, in effect stepping back from the verge of its own industrial revolution—about 400 years ahead of Europe. Because it was so centralized politically, under this system China effectively retreated from technological innovation and halted it, just as Europe was rising.

merchants visited the Swahili city-states on a sea trade governed by the monsoon winds. Many stayed on and intermarried with African women, forming an elite class of merchants on East Africa's coasts.

While a corps of diplomats or ambassadors was key to maintaining stable relations along this trade, an interest in protecting or expanding trade and the accumulation of wealth also contributed to the development of another institution common to the world's empires: full-time militaries. Some kingdoms did not have standing armies. Most soldiers were actually farmers or herders who provided their own weapons and provisions. Other states, such as China by the fourth century B.C.E., had professional armies. In West Africa, Mali was renowned for its disciplined cavalry. It had horses and coats of chain mail long before its neighbors. Some Indian kingdoms, such as the Mauryan, had a cavalry of elephants and chariots. Ghana was said to have had an army of 200,000 men, including 40,000 archers. And the Ottoman militaries became regarded as a state within a state, so powerful that they could make and unmake rulers. Similar corps, such as the Mameluks, ruled Egypt for over 200 years.

Where warfare was endemic, its frequency changed the relative importance of the military, which became the core of some states, such as those of the Zulu and the Assyrians. With superior weapons and horses, some groups gained the military power to conquer neighboring groups and expand in order to collect tribute from subjugated populations or vassal states. As these states grew, they attained larger surpluses by preying on neighboring populations and requiring tribute payments. Warfare between chiefdoms became common, and captives were taken in warfare and enslaved.[9] Stronger groups imposed their wills on weaker groups. The Mongol invasions rearranged politics in India and mainland Southeast Asia. Arab invasions had a similar effect in North Africa. Tribute could come in the form of material resources or labor. For example, the Akan of West Africa wanted captive labor to mine gold, the basis of the Asante Empire in the eighteenth century. Slaves composed a large class in most empires; only slightly better off were subjugated peoples paying tribute.

Therefore, one important part of understanding empires is to see them as a collection of different communities over which there is a centralized government. These kingdoms routinely ruled over vast, sprawling, and varied areas. The Inca Empire ran north to south for over 2,000 miles. Such large states required effective political and military institutions to integrate conquered people into the system, and exercised executive, judicial, and legislative authority. They set about enforcing laws, organizing armies, and collecting taxes. Some were better administrators than others. Centralized states such as Persia (Iran) were broken into provinces and run by elaborate bureaucracies. The Inca divided their empire into four quarters, each with a lord (usually a close relative of the emperor). Besides tribute collection and organization of public works, the Inca sought to assimilate conquered peoples by encouraging their use of Quechua, the language of the empire. The imperial government required all those living under its rule to accept the official state religion, but they allowed people also to continue worshipping their own gods. Similarly, the Persian Empire imposed uniform laws and used a single language for administration, but was tolerant of local cultures.

Still, the relative egalitarianism found among stateless societies appears to have been unknown at the state level. Rather little is known about women in most early societies, and what we do know is mostly about elite women. Men dominated most state systems. This was not always the case, however, as women sometimes played key political, economic, and religious roles in their communities. Aztec women worked as doctors, artisans, merchants, and in temple service. Even in studies of the most famously patriarchal empires (such as those of the Aztecs, Inca, and Zulu—which also tended to be the most militarized), the genders are not described as equal, but as serving complementary functions. Inca noblewomen had access to land, herds, water, and other resources through their mothers, and some historians argue that their activities were viewed as of equal importance to those of men. For the Aztecs, death in childbirth for women was considered the equivalent of death in battle for men—and revered with great honor.[10]

Many of the empires of West Africa also reserved an honored place for women. In fact, women's social position and personal liberty often astonished travelers. Women are known to have served as political leaders of Swahili (Zanzibar was once governed by a Muslim Swahili queen) and Mayan city-states. More often, however, women served at lower levels, as the heads of towns and subregions within empires. Among the Yoruba in Nigeria, the *iyalode* was a female official with jurisdiction over all women, who spoke on women's issues in the king's council. Similarly, among the Aztecs there were female officials charged with overseeing the affairs of women. Women also served in some imperial armies, and there are examples of all-female regiments led by women (such as the Amazons of Dahomey and the Sotho of South Africa).

Although less commonly found in Latin America, there are examples of empresses and warrior queens in the histories of Asia and Africa. In the Hausa state of Zaria, Queen Amina outfitted her armies with iron helmets and chain mail to successfully wage a series of military campaigns. However, in most cases when women held this kind of power, it was treated as a temporary arrangement. Women served as regents, ruling when the successor to the throne was too young to assume (his) full duties. In matrilineal societies, such as the Asante in Ghana, maternal relations were crucial in determining succession, inheritance, and other matters. Here and elsewhere queen mothers and queen sisters were major power brokers, and often had considerable leverage and influence. An Asante queen mother, Ya Asantewaa, is considered a heroine for leading her kingdom in resistance against British rule in 1900.

The Asante had a relatively large empire. One of the most notable differences between empires and smaller states is that the kinship ties that unite chiefs with commoners in states do not exist in empires. Rather, in empires the ruling group claims separate origins from the masses and lives apart from them. A variety of sources tell of the spectacle and luxury of life enjoyed by elites in the empires of the non-Western world. Large retinues of ministers, scholars, and courtiers surrounded emperors. Often imperial courts included harems, as royal polygamy was not uncommon. Kings of large states such as Mwene Mutapa (Zimbabwe) distinguished themselves by having 2,000–3,000 royal wives.

Always at the pinnacle of power in this hierarchy was the emperor, who ruled as an absolute monarch. There was little left of the kind of constitutional monarchy described for smaller states, in which a king confers with a council. At the level of empire, the emperor's authority took on a divine status and usually was unquestioned. This far greater centralization of power was supported by a religious ideology that had enormous influence over the population. Every empire was linked with a state religion, and based on some mix of THEOCRACY and royal despotism. As "the son of heaven," the Chinese emperor was considered godlike. Egyptian monarchs were regarded as gods on earth. Rulers often claimed special powers of intercession with God or the gods.[11] As chief religions and philosophies of state, Hinduism and Buddhism helped provide the unity necessary for the first kingdoms of India to become larger political entities. Similarly, Islam created a unity among rival Arab clans. It was this unity based in religion that contributed to the rapid growth of the Arab Empire, known as the Caliphate. This empire rivaled Rome at its peak, and controlled an area that stretched from the Mediterranean into Central Asia from the seventh to the eleventh century.

Religious ideologies served the state in other ways as well. In all four regions, emperors were believed necessary for performing important rites. The Sapu Inca was responsible for defending the order and existence of the universe. For the Aztecs, the emperor was a renowned warrior, and conquest was necessary to the proper worship of the god Huitzilopochtli—the only assurance that the sun would continue to pass through the sky. Across empires in the non-Western world it was also common to find that kings and emperors lived lives of ritual seclusion apart from the population. They were often separated from the public behind a screen and communicated only through intermediaries—all based on the belief that the emperor was too holy for common gaze. For example, the Alafin of Oyo, considered to be the incarnation of a chief god, could only be seen through a veil and could never be seen eating. It was not unusual for emperors to be thought to possess supernatural powers. They were often the only ones allowed to transgress the ordinary rules of social life, such as incest.

In deference to emperors' unquestioned power, life at imperial courts around the world was immersed in elaborate ritual and ceremony. We know from various sources that the capitals of these empires were often lavish. These were true cities, serving not only as economic but also as cultural centers and populated by tens of thousands, even millions of people. For example, the Aztec capital Tenochtitlan was home to 150,000–300,000 people in the early sixteenth century. Described by Spaniards as an "Indian Venice," the city sat on an oval island connected to the mainland by three causeways and interlaced with numerous canals. Chang'an, the capital of the Tang Dynasty of China, was described as very grand, and was once probably the largest city in the world, with an estimated population of 2 million. Timbuktu and the other capitals of West African empires were described as awash in gold, dripping in opulence, and capable of serving thousands at banquets. The generosity and hospitality of these courts was commented on by visitors of the time. In the tenth century, the emperor of Ghana was known as the richest monarch in the world. The annual revenue of the Mongol emperor in the seventeenth century was said to be ten times that of his contemporary, Louis XIV. When the Mansa of Mali made his pilgrimage to Mecca in 1324–1325, he impressed the world with his wealth and munificence.

Besides feats of monumental architecture, many empires were renowned for their buildings of remarkable beauty and distinctiveness. Many empires also invested in enormous public works projects. The most famous of these is the Great Wall, a continuous fortification built along China's northern frontier. On a similar scale is the Grand Canal, which linked northern and southern China, running over 1,000 miles long. The massive engineering of water systems, such as the use of dams and irrigation, helped the Chinese, the Funan, the Inca, and others increase food production on limited arable land. The Inca produced a surplus in the highlands through agricultural terracing and irrigation. They maintained control over the empire through an impressive system of roads and built suspension bridges to render immense gorges passable. For many lowland Asian empires, wet-rice cultivation required sophisticated water management and regulation in order to create a higher volume of production necessary to feed larger populations.

As mentioned earlier, the surplus created by such innovations allowed for state patronage of the arts and religion, which contributed to the development of rich material cultures. Empires were known for their production and vast exchange of goods and services, including luxury items. Various empires had specialists in jewelry making and goldsmithing, feather working, silk weaving, and other adornments. Empires from all regions are known for their wall paintings and sculpture, such as the Ajanta caves in India, and the cast bronze portraits of the kings of Ife and Benin in West Africa. The Gupta kingdom not only provided for peace and prosperity by reuniting much of northern India; its two centuries of rule are described as a period of cultural brilliance, a creative age for the arts and sciences. In the Middle Ages, Muslim society was the scientific center of the world, and Arabic was synonymous with learning and science for over 500 years.[12]

Arab and other non-Western peoples contributed to the development of technologies in several different fields, such as metallurgy. For example, China used coal as metallurgical fuel and for heating houses 700 years before the West.[13] But such feats were by no means confined to Asia. Although little of the non-Western world is considered industrialized today, a variety of industries once flourished throughout these regions. Weaving, which goes back in Egypt and Nubia for a millennium, was once a primary industry in parts of Africa, Asia, the Middle East, and Latin America. The Chinese are credited with technological achievements such as the invention of water-powered mills, drought-resistant rice strains, gunpowder, and optical lenses. Some historians argue that China was near its own industrial revolution in the thirteenth century, and world history would be much different today if not for the Mongol invasion and later emperors' failures to resume the Song Dynasty's initiatives.[14]

What we today call the "third world" was the site of a series of accomplishments in the field of mathematics as well. Arab scholars introduced algebra and the use of zero to the West. Egyptians were the first to use the decimal system. The Chinese are known for their use of geometric equations and trigonometry. Several empires prioritized the study of the sciences, particularly astronomy, in which the Maya are said to have made observations and calculations of astounding complexity. This includes the development of a calendar that is more accurate than our own in making adjustments in the exact length of a solar year.

The Maya are also known for their complex glyphic writing, which has still not been decoded but is widely considered to be the most advanced in the ancient Americas. Although Sumer is believed to be the first civilization to create cuneiform writing (about 5,000 years ago), the Egyptians developed writing (about 3200 B.C.E.) and the Chinese have preserved script that dates back as far as the second millennium B.C.E. Instead of lettering, the Inca used mnemonic devices, knotted quipu strings, which were used in record keeping and accounting. Yet there were also highly artistic and prosperous urban civilizations, such as the Ife of Nigeria, who did not have writing. Oral cultures there and around the world have produced a large body of myths, legends, and poetry, as well as theater, prose, and philosophy. Griots and other professional historians have transmitted the genealogies and histories of these peoples by memory.

The Assyrians collected their literature in libraries, filled with thousands of stone tablets. The Gupta in India, the Maya, and the Persian empires are known for their patronage of scholarly activity, including the recording of official histories. In addition to being the center of trade in the Southeast Asian archipelago, Srivijaya was a center of Hindu and Buddhist learning. Correspondingly, Baghdad was such a gathering place for Muslim scholars during the Umayyad Dynasty. At the time that it was the major hub for the trans-Saharan trade and one of the most celebrated of savanna cities, Timbuktu was also famous for being a city of universities, attracting scholars of international repute. In the third millennium B.C.E. Egypt achieved high intellectual, social, and material standards that compared favorably with most other parts of the world.[15] The Greeks borrowed heavily from the Egyptians in philosophy and the sciences, transmitting to the West many of their accomplishments. Therefore, it is not only the West that has a rich intellectual history. In fact, the West became what it did because of an infusion of knowledge from the non-Western world.

For all of their strengths, however, we find a common pattern among Western and non-Western empires—authority was inversely related to distance. The larger the area conquered, the more difficult it was to maintain hegemony, or absolute control over the empire. The Songhay Empire in West Africa was almost perpetually engaged against dissidents across its vast frontier, as was the Chinese Empire, which frequently broke down into fiefdoms. Empires tended to overextend themselves and were constantly plagued by problems of administration and succession (one reason Ghana lasted so long is that it stayed relatively small). Whereas smaller groups often unified into larger states under a common cause (such as defense against an external threat), after the shared problem was eliminated these larger units tended to break back down into smaller and more local organizations. This was a cycle that repeated itself in all four regions many times before European conquest.

Yet it is for a variety of reasons (not all of them well understood) that many of the empires described here had long passed from the scene; their capitals were no longer as dazzling and prosperous by the 1500s, when Europeans began arriving in larger numbers. By the time European powers became intent on expansion, many of these empires were showing signs of distress. They were at risk of disintegration from infighting and fragmentation.[16] For example, the Mongol Empire was fragmenting when the Europeans arrived. Indian and foreign rivals defeated the Mongols, so that by the time the West began its invasion the empire was vulnerable and divided into many small successor states that were easily played off each other by the French and British. We see this pattern among empires in all four regions. There were the internecine dynastic struggles of China, the civil wars over succession crises of the Inca and Oyo (Nigeria) states, and slave raiding in Africa, which spread firearms throughout the region and contributed to endless wars between various groups. In all of these places, the once-central leadership was weakened, administrative controls broke down, and outlying tributaries attempted to break free of the empire's grasp.

The potential for revolt in these kingdoms was aggravated by heavy taxation and other stresses. These often became more burdensome as empires struggled to survive. For example, just before Spanish conquest, the Aztecs greatly stepped up the pressure on conquered groups. They demanded mass human sacrifices to assuage the gods and prevent a predicted cataclysm. Consequently, tributary and/or minority groups, long resentful of imperial domination, were eager to ally with the invaders. Europeans benefited enormously from this circumstance and employed a strategy of DIVIDE AND CONQUER.[17]

While it is important to remember that Europeans were not invited guests, there are cases in which people didn't immediately recognize the Europeans as invaders and ended up compromising themselves. There are countless stories of how non-Westerners received the European visitors peacefully—even warmly. Many societies active in the Indian Ocean network of trade accepted the Portuguese enclaves as they had other outsiders for as long as anyone could remember. They gave the Europeans a cautious welcome and sought to profit from their presence. The Aztec emperor Moctezuma at first offered generous gifts to encourage his unearthly-looking visitors to leave. When that didn't work Moctezuma warily welcomed Cortés and his men to Tenochtitlan and treated them as guests.

Once the emperor recognized his error it was too late. The Aztecs, like most of the other military empires of Africa, Asia, Latin America, and the Middle East, were unprepared to counter European penetration. In some cases, people

Figure 2.3   The Transatlantic Slave Trade

Unique in terms of the enormity of human devastation it caused, the transatlantic slave trade lasted for nearly 500 years. Although it began on a small scale in the 1400s, by the seventeenth century, labor shortages in the Americas greatly increased the demand for slaves. At its height, thousands of men and women in their most productive years were stripped from their communities on an annual basis and taken across the Atlantic on the harrowing trip known as "the Middle Passage." Because so many died along the way, the total number of people enslaved is still unknown, although most historians estimate that at least 12 million people served as human cargo in this trade.

Figure 2.4　The Opium Wars

Those states that were not so open or that didn't receive Europe so warmly were also forced into the new order—on Europe's terms. As the Middle Empire, China believed itself to be at the center of the universe. Largest in size and population, longest in history, untouchable in cultural achievement, the Chinese Empire was in many ways the premier entity when Europeans started arriving in more significant numbers in the sixteenth century. Yet Europe's appetite for Chinese porcelains, silks, and teas was not reciprocated by Chinese interest in European goods.

As a result, the Europeans (and particularly the British) struggled with their trade deficits until they did find one commodity the Chinese found habit-forming: opium. This narcotic proved to be a boon to the British economy. Although the Chinese government had recognized the devastation caused by opium addiction and outlawed its sale, the British sold the drug through a smuggling network along the coast. When China attempted to destroy the contraband trade, the British fought what were known as the Opium Wars to force open the country to foreign trade. In decline at the time, the Chinese Empire was easily overwhelmed by the British military. The resulting Treaty of Nanjing in 1842 was the first of several "unequal treaties" that established European dominance in China. The Chinese coast was carved up into five ports open to Westerners. In effect, the emperor was forced to grant concessions at gunpoint—truly a low point in the empire's history. At the mercy of foreigners, China faced 100 years of humiliation.[18]

quickly adapted to the new reality and worked hard to reclaim the advantage. However, many groups fought pitched battles against the invaders and some succeeded (at least temporarily). The emperor Menelik drove the Italians out of Ethiopia in the late nineteenth century and as a result it was one of the few territories never formally colonized. Equipped with European arms his forces had built for themselves through reverse engineering, Samory Touré was able to keep the French out of large parts of West Africa for nearly twenty years. The Inca were able to hold off the Spanish for decades, as resistance was not finally put down until 1572. These are just a few of the examples of indigenous peoples' fierce resistance to European conquest. But in most cases it was too late.

3

Colonialism: Gold, God, and Glory

Whatever happens we have got / The maxim gun and they have not.
—Hilaire Belloc, writer[1]

In most cases European conquest of what would become the "third world" did not come overnight. Rather, colonization was the culmination of processes that had begun hundreds of years earlier. The fifteenth and sixteenth centuries represented a turning point for Europe—and for the non-Western world. Most historians agree that until this time, Europe had little on Asia, Africa, the Middle East, or the Americas. It was just another of the world's regions, with its share of accomplishments and failures. In the fifteenth century few could have dreamed that Europe would dominate the world. How did it all change? How did Europe manage to conquer virtually the entire world? One currently popular view is that Europe simply took advantage of a set of fortuitous circumstances. It was willing to build on the achievements of others (such as gunpowder, the compass, and improvements in shipbuilding) and use its military power to take control of the seas and world trade.[2]

What other kinds of generalizations can we make about colonialism? Several, since the main differences between the colonizers were in degree, but not in kind. There are some interesting comparisons to be made in terms of style, but not in terms of substance.[3] Who were the colonizers, who assumed the role of "MOTHER COUNTRY"? The major colonizers in Latin America were the Spanish and the Portuguese, although the British, French, and Dutch took the Guianas and parts of the Caribbean. Spain dominated the Philippines, Puerto Rico, and Cuba until the United States replaced it after the Spanish-American War. The British took much of Asia, including India, Pakistan, Sri Lanka, Burma, and Malaysia. The French claimed Indochina (including Vietnam, Cambodia, and Laos). In Asia the Portuguese had only a few small holdings, and the Dutch controlled the vast archipelago today known as Indonesia.

The British and French were the dominant colonial powers in Africa, with the French taking much of the northern and western regions of the continent, and the British controlling much of the eastern and southern regions. Other colonial powers took pieces of the African cake as well, including the Belgians, Germans, Italians, Portuguese, Spanish, and Dutch.

Figure 3.1 How Did Europe Conquer the World?

How did a relative handful of Europeans succeed in conquering these empires? A variety of advantages served the European cause, but the shortest answer is weaponry. Europeans had enormous advantages in military technology throughout the period of conquest. By the seventeenth century, guns were the main weapons favoring Europeans (an early machine gun, the maxim gun, revolutionized violence). Yet weaponry had made all the difference even hundreds of years earlier.

In Latin America in the early sixteenth century, the Spaniards used steel swords, lances, small firearms and artillery, as well as steel body armor and helmets against far greater numbers of indigenous soldiers with much less effective weaponry and protection. The Inca and Aztecs were equipped only with clubs and axes of wood or stone, slings, bows and arrows, and quilted armor. Brought in on ships from Europe, horses provided the Spaniards with another tremendous advantage in battle. Horses gave the invaders height in combat (which protected riders by giving them a raised fighting platform) and speed in attack. Foot soldiers could never succeed against a cavalry in the open. In addition, the Spaniards unleashed massive dogs in combat. As vicious killers they terrorized the population. The invaders benefited from other psychological advantages as well. Aztec priests had been predicting the return of the god Quetzalcoatl, as well as the end of the world. The Aztecs had never before seen men with light-colored eyes and hair, let alone horses (which when mounted by Spaniards appeared to be two-headed animals). Combine these advantages with differences in battle tactics (by Aztec standards, the Spanish didn't fight fair; the Spanish fought to kill, the Aztecs to take prisoners). Add to that the death toll from the diseases Europeans brought with them. And the effect was the literal decimation of populations—not only in Latin America, but in Africa and Asia as well.[4]

Although several European powers were interested in the area, the British dominated the waters of the Persian Gulf and influenced surrounding territories from the late nineteenth until the middle of the twentieth century. After the fall of the Ottoman Empire at the end of World War I, much of the Middle East was divided as mandates between the French and British. The Russians continued to dominate Central Asia, and they vied with the British for control of Persia until the two agreed to divide it between themselves into spheres of influence.

Not all of the non-Western world was formally claimed and occupied by Europeans, but even territories that were never formally colonized fell under heavy European influence. Because China's coast was carved up between five different alien powers and its emperor rendered a puppet, it is said to have been "semicolonized" after the Opium Wars of the mid–nineteenth century. Similarly, because they were not insulated from trends ongoing elsewhere, Turkey, Thailand, Ethiopia, Liberia, and the handful of states that were never officially colonized share many of the legacies of colonialism.

Just as the players involved vary by country, so do the length and periodization of colonialism. The Spanish and Portuguese were the earliest colonizers, and Latin America was the first region to be colonized. Its era of colonial rule was relatively long, beginning in the early sixteenth century and lasting 300 years or more. Yet independence came relatively early to Latin America; with a few notable exceptions in the Caribbean and Brazil, most of the region became independent in the 1810s and 1820s.

Compared to Latin America's experience, colonialism in most of Africa, the Middle East, and Asia was relatively short-lived. After years of encroaching influence, nearly all of Asia was formally colonized after the 1850s but independent less than 100 years later, in the 1940s and 1950s. Most of Africa was parceled out to the Europeans at the Conference of Berlin in the 1880s and was (formally) self-governing by the end of the 1960s.

The Middle East's experience is somewhat different. Though the Russians had been encroaching on Central Asia since the sixteenth century, most European powers were more cautious about taking on the Ottoman Empire. During the nineteenth century, when Europe was most active in acquiring colonies, most of the Middle East (with the notable exceptions of Persia, Saudi Arabia, and Yemen) was under Ottoman control. Perhaps because of a long history of mutual antagonism between Christians and Muslims, perhaps because Europeans knew relatively little of the land and overestimated the Muslim power's military strength, or perhaps because at the time they had little economic interest in the region—European penetration of the Middle East was delayed. As a result it was the last major area to fall to the West.

However, by the end of World War I, the Ottoman Empire had bottomed out after a long decline. Despite promises of independence to the Arabs, who had risen up against the Ottomans, Ottoman territories (including former German colonies in Africa and the Pacific) were set aside by the League of Nations as mandates, or wards of the international community. The Western-dominated League granted supervision of the mandates to Britain and France. The French acquired Syria and Lebanon. Control over Iraq, Transjordan, and Palestine passed to Britain. Under this system, the Europeans' primary responsibility was to prepare their wards for eventual self-government. However, many analysts characterize the MANDATORY SYSTEM as a fig leaf for colonialism, as the mandates were treated no differently than colonial possessions elsewhere. Still, the period of mandates was relatively brief. Most of these territories declared their independence in the post–World War II period.

Whether it lasted for one generation or for many generations, most students of the non-Western world agree that colonialism was a formative experience. Although they may disagree about how long-lasting its legacy was, the fact remains that, in one form or another, colonialism is the one experience that virtually every non-Western country has shared. Why did the Europeans conquer the world? What were they after? And what impact did their policies have on the colonized? Analysts disagree in terms of the relative weight they assign the different interests that motivated the Europeans, but most agree that it was based in a mix of what Ali Mazrui characterized as "the three Gs"—gold, God, and glory.[5]

Gold

In many ways, colonialism was the culmination of a process that wrecked indigenous economies, ruined local industries, and replaced traditional networks of trade with a world system in which Europeans dominated and the rest of the world served. Gold, or the economic motive, was a major if not *the* major drive behind colonialism. By the beginning of the age of imperialism in the fifteenth century, an overland long-distance trade had linked Europe and the non-Western world for over 1,000 years. However, it was a technological revolution that would dramatically shift the balance of power—the Europeans' ability to dominate world trade by sea.

From the time of Henry the Navigator, Portugal had led Europe in decades of exploration. Early in the fifteenth century, as the Portuguese began making stops along the coast of Africa, they established plantations in Cape Verde and the Canary Islands. In Africa, the Portuguese were literally seeking gold, but later it was slaving that set in motion a process that would dramatically alter Africa's relationship with Europe. By 1487 the Portuguese had rounded the Cape of Good Hope and entered the bustling Indian Ocean trading network. The newcomers originally sought access to the highly lucrative trade in pepper and spices. They did this by setting up trading posts at strategic bases along the coasts of Africa, the Middle East, and Asia. Over the next 100 years, Portugal practiced a policy of expansionism. Seeking to eliminate the middleman and gain direct access and control of this trade, Portugal defeated fleets of Egyptians, Arabs, and Persians. Portuguese traders eventually reached as far as China by the early sixteenth century, although the European presence went largely unnoticed by the Chinese emperors until much later.[6]

Meanwhile, seeking another route to the Indies, the Portuguese were joined by the Spanish, who together claimed the Caribbean and much of the Americas as their own. In a papal bull in 1493, Pope Alexander VI randomly determined the line dividing what would become Latin America between the two Iberian powers. This pronouncement formed the basis of the Treaty of Tordesillas in 1494, which formalized their claims. All was decided even before the Portuguese landed in Brazil, but the exclusivity of this relationship would be more or less maintained for another 300 years, until the independence of these territories in the nineteenth century.

The Portuguese weren't as successful at maintaining their interests in Asia. They benefited from a near monopoly in the region for over 100 years but were later displaced by the Dutch, French, British, and others, who entered the Indian Ocean trade as competitors in the seventeenth century. The employees of chartered companies (such as the Dutch East India Company) were often the first to make contact in these distant territories. Serving as agents of the crown, these companies paved the way for imperialism. Under a royal charter granting him access to much of southern Africa, Cecil Rhodes's British South African Company had the power to conduct warfare and diplomacy and to annex territory on behalf of the British monarch. With enormous resources at their disposal, these companies established empires in Asia and Africa with a variety of economic interests in mind. They later pushed for concessions and enjoyed monopolies in the Middle Eastern mandates—these profits were also repatriated to Europe. With the exception of the early colonies established by the Spanish and Portuguese, Europeans maintained long relationships in these territories prior to outright colonization.

This was the age of MERCANTILISM, the precapitalist stage marked by the accumulation of capital through trade and plunder on a worldwide scale. Under mercantilism, each power sought commercial expansion in order to achieve a surplus in its balance of trade. Colonies were developed to suit the mother country's interest, as sources of raw materials and guaranteed markets for its manufactured goods. Colonialism was never about free trade. Rather, in the earliest days it was mercantilist, and through to the end it was protectionist. Whether it was the Spanish in the fifteenth century or the French after World War II, this exclusive arrangement served as the umbilical cord linking the mother country to her colonies.

From the earliest days of colonization this arrangement simply meant expropriation without compensation. In Spanish America, mining was the principal source of royal revenue. The crown acquired enormous wealth by hauling treasure off in its galleons, creating monopolies, and taxing all wealth produced in the colonies. Under the *quinto,* one-fifth of all gold, silver, and other precious metals belonged to the crown. Innumerable taxes weighed on the indigenous people, who paid the costs of colonial administration and defense and were expected to produce a surplus for the crown. Such wealth promoted the growth of European industry and subsidized the consolidation of European commercial and military power in Asia and Africa.[7]

With industrialization fully under way in the eighteenth and nineteenth centuries, European economic interests in the non-Western world grew. In order to assure the quantity and quality of the raw materials they desired, Europeans yearned to eliminate local middlemen and establish their own monopoly control of production and trade. Eager to sell their newly manufactured wares, the colonizers sought guaranteed markets and set about destroying their indigenous competitors. They interfered with preexisting regional and long-distance trades. For example, the Spanish colonies were prohibited from producing any goods produced by Spain. In Africa, Asia, the Middle East, and Latin America, self-sufficient economies were destroyed or transformed and subordinated. India, which once produced the world's finest cotton yarn and textiles, was flooded by cheap factory-made British fabrics and effectively eliminated as a competitor. Millions of artisans were put out of work, with little choice but to turn to farming. Similarly, the Ottoman Empire's handicrafts manufacturing couldn't compete with industrialized production techniques of the West. Colonized peoples were driven out of the most important sectors of their economies, as industrialists, craftsmen, and merchants.

Europe's industrial revolution also demanded reliable access to cheap raw materials. The colonies were established to serve as feeders to the industrial economies of the colonizer, and the result was the development of economies centered on the export of raw materials. Justified by the principle of comparative advantage, which holds that efficiency is enhanced by specialization in production, the mother countries decided what their new colonies would produce, based on the colonizer's needs and the particular resources of each territory. Monocultures were created: sugar from Cuba, hides from Argentina, coffee from Kenya, cotton from Egypt. Nigeria and India were unusual in that they exported a handful of different cash crops. The colonies were never to be self-sufficient; instead they were undiversified, vulnerable, and dependent.

To ensure the desired quality and quantity of goods, the mother countries often imposed a system of compulsory crop cultivation. Small farmers were given quotas and obliged by law to produce the assigned cash crops. Those who did not fulfill their quotas could be fined or arrested. In Latin America, Indians were forced to sell their goods at fixed prices usually well below world market value. In addition, they were compelled to buy goods at artificially high prices. Because of the relatively low value of unprocessed goods versus the high cost of imports, colonialism established a fundamental inequality of exchange. The people of the colonies ended up producing what they didn't consume and consuming what they didn't produce.[8] They were in effect marketing raw goods to the West, to repurchase them in finished form.

For all intents and purposes, the resources of one territory were drained to enrich another. The Europeans opened up mines and plantations. Germans and South Africans stripped Namibia of its once-vast diamond wealth. After the Dutch East India Company took Indonesia, all of Java was set aside as large plantations to grow export crops such as coffee and pepper. Europeans busied themselves obtaining concessions, such as a sixty-year British monopoly to find and develop petroleum and natural gas in most of Persia. Soon foreigners owned the right to control every aspect of this asset, and Persia was the richest known source of petroleum at the time.[9]

Someone had to produce these commodities, and one of the first concerns of every colonial power was how to meet its labor demands in terms of mining, portage, construction, and cultivation. Slavery, tenancy, and debt peonage existed throughout the colonial period. Although King Leopold of Belgium was unrivaled in the barbarism he used to compel labor in the Congo, other colonizers used forced labor as well. Under the Spanish system of *repartimiento* (or the *mita*), all adult male Indians had to spend part of their year laboring in Spanish mines, farms, and public works. Barely disguised slavery, the *mita* was an important source of labor for the Spanish until the end of the colonial period.[10] Similar practices, such as land curtailment, or the large-scale appropriation of territory by Europeans, denied the indigenous people an alternative source of cash income. Once-independent farmers and herders were converted to wage labor. In addition, taxes were imposed at such a rate (and to be paid in the colonizer's currency) that people were left little choice but to seek employment in the colonial economy. Perhaps the most oppressive labor regulations were found in southern Africa, where pass laws and labor contracts created a system of migrant labor that gave employers enormous advantages. To some degree it continues to this day.

Wherever colonialism existed, no matter who was doing the colonizing, the effect on the colonized was much the same. The demands of the colonial economy often resulted not only in an intensification of the exploitation of labor, but also in a great disruption of community and family. Often men and women were forced to leave their families behind to work as migrant laborers. Overall health and nutrition deteriorated as demands for labor grew. Although most people continued to work as farmers, colonial agriculture was much more extensive than anything known before, demanding more energy and resources to produce commodities for sale in markets. Most Africans, for example, were so busy in their cash-crop farming that there was little time for the production of staples or to supplement their diets with hunting or fishing as before. Often the result was vulnerability to overwork and disease, which spread rapidly with the dislocations associated with an intensification of production and trade volumes. A variety of colonial policies rendered indigenous populations landless. Under French rule in Vietnam it is estimated that two-thirds of the population were tenant farmers.[11]

In the worst cases, traditional welfare systems were destroyed. The stress and dislocation of colonialism combined with economic hardship to contribute to a rise in social violence and self-destructive behavior, such as opium addiction in southern China and alcoholism in India and South Africa. In some places populations actually declined, as death rates rose while fertility rates fell. Forced to produce government crops, Indonesians were left dependent on purchasing rice. But the low contract price for the spices they produced meant that entire regions became impoverished. The commercialization of agriculture left peasants vulnerable, and famine occurred with regularity. It is estimated that 15 million people in India died of famine between 1875 and 1900. During the first forty years of colonial rule, overwork and abuse reduced the population of the Belgian Congo by half. Perhaps the most devastating results occurred in the valley of Mexico, where the population is believed to have dropped by 90 percent during the first 100 years of colonial rule.[12]

God

Often alongside the conquistadors in Latin America and the traders in Asia and Africa were the missionaries. "God" would be invoked to justify colonialism, and to varying degrees proselytizing was a large part of the colonial effort. Priests came to Latin America on Columbus's second sailing in 1493. The Catholic Church was joined by Protestant missionaries who served as aggressive agents of cultural imperialism as well, to compete for souls in Asia, Africa, and to a lesser extent in the Middle East. Catholic or Protestant, some missionaries saw themselves as protectors of the colonized and were "pronative" in conflicts with the mother country over their treatment. However, these people of God were colonizers as well, collaborators crucial to the administrative success by helping to bring indigenous peoples under control. In a massive effort work was fused with conversion. The "heathens" were gathered together so that they could be not only more easily evangelized, but also taught "Christian virtues" of hard work and unquestioning obedience.

More than any other actor, the missionaries were responsible for compelling colonized peoples to recognize their domination by the invading culture. Missionaries assertively challenged all preexisting belief systems. Their churches were often built on holy grounds, over razed temples to drive home their message. The earliest days of conquest and pacification were often times of violence, dramatic social change, and transformation. For many people colonialism meant the destruction of their world, since indigenous religions were assaulted

Figure 3.2   Did Colonialism Benefit Women?

Colonialism is sometimes argued to have improved the status of women, since the missionaries sought to destroy indigenous customs and social practices they saw as barbaric, such as female genital cutting, polygamy, and suttee (the practice of burning widows on the funeral pyres of their husbands). However, throughout the precolonial societies of the non-Western world, women's experience varied by race, class, region, age, and other factors. In some communities non-Western women were much more "liberated" than their Western sisters. Where women had shared political authority or enjoyed economic or sexual autonomy before colonialism, European sexism and colonial policy destroyed such systems and marginalized women. Where patriarchy long predated the arrival of Europeans, colonialism laminated it. Western and non-Western patriarchies joined in an attempt to control female labor and sexuality, deny them access to education and employment, and deprive them of political power. The colonizers sought to win the allegiance of men by granting them increased authority over women. However, women were not passive victims in this process. In Zimbabwe and elsewhere, some women agitated for a return to the relatively favorable status they had held in their societies before colonialism. In a variety of ways, including the use of so-called weapons of the weak, they asserted their interests. Often colonial women (both colonizer and colonized) enjoyed more independence than is usually assumed—despite rigorous efforts to keep them "in their place."[13]

by the persistent imposition of European values. Time and again evangelization was conducted with such zeal, and was so heavy-handed, that it amounted to forced conversion. Christianity was imposed with an intolerance that was new in most regions.

Although there were some significant differences in approach (the Portuguese and Spanish were much more interested in religious conversion than the Dutch, for example), wherever colonialism existed it was based in racism and cultural imperialism. Propounding Social Darwinist theories on evolution and survival of the fittest, the Europeans saw themselves as more civilized, cleaner, smarter, and better educated than the people they colonized, who were variously described as devious, lazy, or immoral. The expression of this chauvinism or racism took different forms, depending on the colonizer. For example, whereas the policy of assimilation was based in the French belief in their own cultural superiority, the British were better known for the use of a color bar, based in their sense of racial superiority. However, institutionalized segregation and discrimination was the rule in every colony. Whereas the French were determined that their civilization should be accepted by all living under French rule, the British stressed the differences between themselves and the colonized, and were contemptuous of indigenous peoples' attempts to adopt the English language and culture.

Yet in British colonies and all the others, "white man's burden" was about more than just saving souls. It provided a rationale for domination: the fruits of Western civilization should be shared with the heathen. Again it was missionaries who took it upon themselves to bear this burden. They were given a virtual monopoly over colonial education. Building schools and clinics was an effective way of evangelizing and advancing the colonial effort. Apologists for colonialism often laud these efforts, which did provide formal education and improved healthcare for some. However, these services were grossly inadequate and unevenly distributed. It is estimated that fewer than 10 percent of Zambian children ever saw the inside of a schoolhouse. Secondary schools were rare in colonial Africa until after World War II. Few universities and technical schools were established; not a single university was built in Brazil during the entire colonial period. There was not one university in Indonesia until 1941. Where schools did exist, often it was only whites or the children of "notable natives" who received these benefits.[14]

In other ways as well, the colonial educational systems existed primarily for the benefit of European settlers and administrators. The schools served as instruments of subjugation. They perpetuated racial inequality by indoctrinating the colonized into permanent subservience and sought to convince indigenous people of their inferiority. A few professionals were trained, but mostly the colonized were prepared to work as soldiers, clerks, and low-level administrators. The curriculum was not only irrelevant to their needs, but it also taught colonized people to disown their birthrights, to give up their traditions, dress, customs, religion, language—in some cases even their own names. For example, French language, literature, and history were compulsory in colonial Syrian schools, while Arabic language, literature, and history were ignored. The achievements of non-Westerners were disregarded or denied. European institutions were assumed to be innately superior to anything that might have existed before colonialism. In effect, the children who went through these schools were taught to embrace all that was European. These students, who grew up to be the elites of their countries, ended up alienated from their own cultures. They were taught to assimilate and adore European culture and to look down on their own as decadent and worthless. The result was an identity crisis not easily resolved.[15]

Glory

A third factor commonly observed as motivating European efforts to conquer the world was the search for the glory and prestige that comes with recognition as a great power. Nationalistic rivalries for world dominion, in particular the rivalry between the French and the British, compelled the various European powers to claim a share of the cake. Strategic and economic interests combined to raise the stakes in this rivalry. No one wanted to be left out; the colonizers competed fiercely for markets. They also sought control of sea-lanes, access routes, and strategic locations such as the Suez Canal, Cape Town, Aden, Ceylon, and Hong Kong in order to protect their military, logistical, and economic interests. For example, the Suez Canal was considered by the British to be "the lifeline to India," since cutting through it from the Mediterranean to the Red Sea greatly reduced the long journey from Europe around Africa. Not only did this short cut mean an enormous increase in the volume of trade, but control of India also greatly facilitated the exploitation of China. Therefore, location made Egypt strategically pivotal and the British insisted on maintaining a strong presence there.[16]

Yet other European powers were just as determined to establish their empires. Out of concern that such intense competition might lead to war, the British, French, Germans, Belgians, and others made agreements for the orderly extension of European influence. Through various meetings, they set out rules for the "legal" appropriation of territories. At the Conference of Berlin in the 1880s, the Europeans divided Africa between themselves. The arbitrary lines they assigned as borders are largely the ones that exist today.

Similarly, the Europeans carved twenty-four nations out of the Ottoman Empire with little knowledge or care as to what they were creating. Often the partitions took place on maps that didn't reflect the interior of the territories. Some of the resulting entities were left landlocked; some were left with little base for economic development. Just as devastating in terms of long-term feasibility, the colonizers ignored local factors and drew boundaries between states that cut across religious and ethnic groups.[17] Some groups such as the Kurds became STATELESS NATIONS, spread through Iran, Iraq, and Turkey, with no government to call their own. In addition, groups with very different cultures, traditions, and beliefs about government were thrown together to live in MULTINATIONAL STATES. Where divisions are deep, such as in the Sudan, this has meant real problems for the development of national identities. Fearing dominance by larger groups, minorities often maintain their subnational loyalties. Many religious and ethnic groups in Indonesia, Lebanon, and Nigeria, for example, have little sense of national identity. As a result, state SOVEREIGNTY is weak. The existence of multinational states and stateless nations has contributed to innumerable territorial challenges over the years. The result has been attempts at secession (Nigeria, East Timor) as well as IRREDENTIST WARS to redraw boundaries (such as those between Israel, Somalia, Iraq, and their neighbors).

In hindsight it is clear that the borders established by the colonizers would pose long-term problems for the non-Western world. However, in the late nineteenth and early twentieth century Europe argued that colonialism was for the indigenous peoples' own good.[18] Perhaps to satisfy public concerns back home, the colonizers took the paternalistic position that those with a "higher civilization" should be entrusted with the responsibility of tutoring their "little brown brothers" in Western political and social institutions. Westernization was assumed to be synonymous with modernization, and modernization was identified with progress. Colonized peoples were described as childlike or nonadult. The League of Nations determined that this period of guardianship should continue until the peoples of Africa, Asia, and the Middle East were deemed by its largely European members "to be ready" for self-rule.

The role of benevolent father figure was another aspect of the glory Europe was seeking. This self-aggrandizement was clearest in the mandatory system, when the League of Nations authorized France and Britain to govern the territories of the Ottoman Empire. As stewards responsible for the area's welfare, the period of mandate was to be a "sacred trust." While the mandatory system was supposed to prepare the area for independence as soon as possible and be a benefit to its wards, in fact it was foreign occupation.

Figure 3.3   Israel

After the fall of the Ottoman Empire, a variety of interests motivated the West's desire to create a home for the Jewish people. Yet at about the same time that the British had promised to create a Jewish state, they had also committed themselves to the establishment of a Hashemite kingdom—in much the same area, then known as Palestine. Unclear as to its precise borders and without attention to the rights of the majority Arab Muslims living there, the West helped to found the state of Israel in 1948. Though many people celebrated this accomplishment, for others the creation of Israel was symbolic of the triumph of Western imperialism over the entire Arab world. Only hours after its founding, the inhabitants of the area (Muslim, Jewish, and Christian) began fighting for control over this land. The fighting has been particularly fierce over specific sites sacred to all of them, such as Jerusalem. Jews claim the land back to the time of King David as their gift from God. Christians refer to the region as the Holy Land, and for Muslims it is sacred as well. While some Arab leaders accept the existence of Israel as a reality, many Muslims regard the very existence of this state as deeply offensive. Consequently, many Israelis consider their incursions into neighboring areas as necessary for their defense, whereas others in the region regard such moves as expansionist.[19]

How much did the guardians do for their wards? How much tutelage in self-rule occurred during colonialism? What kind of lesson in government was colonialism, exactly? Although some historians get caught up in debates over the significance of style and approach, overall colonial government was rigidly hierarchical, lacking democratic forms of accountability, autonomy, or decentralization. Although colonialism's reach was concentrated in the cities and dissipated through the hinterland, its rule was authoritarian, and the primary objective of government was the imposition of order.

To this end the mother countries were abusive. They relied on repression to maintain control. Colonialism created a legacy of military privileges by rewarding soldiers as a special caste with its own set of interests, not subject to civil power.[20] They created full-time standing armies to crack down on dissent, dissolve parties, and force nationalist leaders such as Nelson Mandela underground. Others, such as Sukarno, were sent into exile. Justice was arbitrary; the colonizers imprisoned leaders such as Gandhi and Kenyatta and sometimes used appalling force to put down resistance. It was not uncommon for them to collectively punish entire populations. In one of the worst cases, the Germans fought a war of annihilation against the Herero in South West Africa, reducing the population by 85 percent. In many places the colonizers became quasimilitary authorities, reduced to imposing martial law to maintain control.

Not only was Europe determined to hold on to power, but administration was to be on the cheap, with little or no costs to the mother country. To do this, the colonizers relied on the cooperation of indigenous peoples, and distorted preexisting political systems whenever possible to administer colonial controls. Although there were differences in how much they relied on them, to some degree the British, French, and the others depended on the assistance of "native elites." Known as caciques in Mexico and the Philippines, curacas in the Andes, and mandarins in Indochina, these were indigenous peoples who either were large landholders or had held traditional power prior to colonization. If no local elites were sufficiently accommodating to colonial interests, the Europeans simply appointed what were called in some areas "warrant chiefs," ambitious men with no traditional claim to power but who had proven themselves loyal to the colonizer.[21] Rewarded with privileges such as exemption from taxes or labor service, they served as brokers for the colonial state, charged with overseeing the enforcement of colonial regulations, collecting taxes, and conscripting labor. Under colonialism, corrupt officials often became quite wealthy, administrators embezzled, and offices were bought and sold. In fact, in all four regions it is said that colonialism created a mentality of corruption. One of its longest-lasting legacies is the notion that government can be manipulated by money, and that political power is the surest route to wealth. Not only was corruption pervasive, but some colonial systems were particularly notorious for their inefficiency and immense bureaucracies.[22]

In effect, then, colonialism destroyed precolonial political systems and delegitimized traditional leaders without providing a viable alternative to authoritarianism. Individual rights and freedoms were subordinated to the mother country's desire to hold on to power. Western ideals such as egalitarianism and SELF-DETERMINATION were seldom applied to non-Westerners. The colonial model of government was a small elite maintained in power through reliance on coercion. Despite all its grandiose claims, the colonial state was no DEMOCRACY. Rather, it was government based on intolerance.

Government based on intolerance, alienation from one's own culture, and the creation of economic dependency—this was what colonialism meant to the colonized. Gold, God, and glory all had a role to play in the push for empire. Rather than attributing colonialism to any single factor, it is perhaps best to understand European motivation as based in a mix of these three motives. Certainly the impact from political, economic, and cultural imperialism is still felt throughout the former colonies. Although it would go too far to blame all of it on colonialism, much of the instability found in so many former colonies should be understood as the logical consequence of this relationship.

4

Independence or In Dependence?

> You have tampered with the women. You have struck a rock. You have dislodged a boulder. You will be crushed. The weight is heavy. We need our mothers. We won't give up, even if we're jailed. We are ready for our freedom.
> —Women's freedom song from the 1950s, South Africa[1]

Colonialism was not only a time of dislocation; it was also a time of unrest. There was always resistance to European domination. However, it grew in intensity and complexity over the years. Especially in the cities, ostensibly nonpolitical associations such as study groups, savings societies, prayer groups, and even dance clubs provided people the opportunity to congregate and discuss grievances. Such associations became nascent political parties advocating various forms of resistance. These groups became nationalist movements as they came together for larger demands such as SELF-DETERMINATION.

Groups that usually saw themselves as sharing few interests joined together against the MOTHER COUNTRY (whether Sunnis and Shiites in Iraq or members of different ethnic groups in Ghana and so on) and were relatively successful in setting aside their differences for their common goals. Yet multiethnic, multireligious revolts contained the seeds of possible fragmentation, even self-destruction. Nationalist movements in some countries such as Nigeria were always divided by bitter, regional rivalries. Ideological, ethnic, religious, and other divides simmered just under the surface of many of these movements, yet for a while at least the colonized managed to transcend their differences to unite against the colonizer.[2]

A number of factors combined to promote unity against the colonial powers. In most of Asia, Africa, and the Middle East, the rise and intensification of NATIONALISM corresponded with the period between World War I and World War II. Not only were the colonies expected to sacrifice for the war effort, but the Great Depression hit most of the non-Western world especially hard. An already difficult situation had become intolerable. Asian and African soldiers returning home from the world wars (many of them conscripted) had seen colonial doctrines of white supremacy dramatically challenged. Nationalist movements were emboldened by the Japanese defeat of Russia in 1905, and the near defeat of the Allies in the Pacific in World War II. Supported by international organizations

Figure 4.1   The Spanish American Experience

Latin America was the first of the four regions under study to be colonized, and the first to win its independence. Nationalism manifested itself there as a sense of "Americanness," which grew rapidly after the 1750s in response a power vacuum in Spain. Heavily in debt from years of wasteful expenditures, Spain was an absolutist empire decaying from within. When it undertook an assertive program of reforms that had the overall effect of increasing taxes, the colonizer's relationship with its colonies was further strained—and the colonized were already pressed to their limits.[3]

By the end of the eighteenth century, dissatisfaction with the status quo was widespread. Rebellions became more common, and in Mexico at least, it looked for a while as if self-rule would be won by the masses through social revolution. However, throughout most of Spanish America, Creoles (American-born, of Spanish descent) usurped the more radical nationalist efforts of Indians, mestizos, and people of African descent. An aristocracy with limited access to the highest levels of state and church, they had long resented the favored treatment given to Peninsulars (Spaniards born in Spain), but the Creoles also feared more fundamental social change that might threaten their interests. In the end the American-born elite exploited the crown's weakness and declared their independence. However, Spain didn't give up without a fight. It was only after years of devastating military campaigns that most of the territories colonized by Spain became independent in the period 1810–1826.[4]

such as the Pan-African Congress, these servicemen were joined by students, workers, professionals, and others who stridently expressed their revulsion toward occupation. If World War II was a struggle against racism and tyranny, then why should colonized peoples everywhere not be granted self-determination?

Beyond these common questions, nationalist movements varied greatly in terms of ideology, membership, goals, and strategy. They disagreed over whether peaceful change was possible, or if violence was necessary. And there were serious divides over how much change was necessary, if reform would suffice or if revolution was a must, and over what kind of government and economic system was preferred.

Although sometimes the split within and between nationalist movements was a matter of rival personalities and ideologies, frequently it was generational—the old versus the new elites. The older generation was composed of a relatively privileged class of teachers, religious leaders, and low-level civil servants who resented the restrictions they faced as "nonwhites." Generally social conservatives, they were very class conscious and tended to distance themselves from the masses. The self-titled "civilized natives" in Africa, for example, were calling for more rights primarily for themselves. These were not radical demands; most old-style elites were not asking for independence. Rather, they were seeking better treatment within the system.

Not only were their requests of the colonial government relatively modest, but their tactics were moderate as well. More trusting of the system, the older generation of nationalists played by the rules. During World War I, for example,

Figure 4.2 Subversion and Other "Weapons of the Weak"

Although not usually described as "nationalist" per se, people resisted colonial rule for a variety of reasons and in a variety of ways. Tax evasion, desertion, feigning illness, breaking machinery, and other means of subterfuge are known as WEAPONS OF THE WEAK. They are far more common than the revolts and wars but have not usually been covered in history books. In part, this is because some means of resistance were never recognized as such. For example, mass waves of people took flight, moving across regions during the period of conquest and "pacification" to escape colonial rule. People sought escape (another weapon of the weak) through a variety of means, including alcohol abuse and suicide. Although we generally hear that populations grew under colonialism, in some places birthrates fell because women refused to bring children into this new world of oppression. Abortions and infanticide are believed to have been common in Peru, the Congo, and elsewhere during the period of colonialism. It is important to recognize that what may appear to be individual, private actions may be linked to larger issues as a response to an insufferable situation.[5]

the Indian National Congress hoped to win favor for its cause by cooperating with the British. These activists undertook letter-writing campaigns and submitted petitions to the colonial powers asking that they end abuses and do more to provide for the welfare of the colonized. Seeking to spur the mother country to take corrective action, they wrote editorials. Some, such as the South African National Native Conference (later known as the African National Congress), used diplomatic means. Egyptians sent a delegation to London to present their case for self-rule. Elite and commoner alike even went to the colonial courts for redress of their grievances.

On the other hand, the new elite was primarily composed of a later generation of the educated class. Having mostly attended university abroad, the new elites were mobilized by Liberal notions of freedom and self-determination. These new elites formed groups such as the Nigerian Youth Movement, which were often more militant and more radical in their aims than the older generation of leaders, whom they frequently disdained as accomplices of colonialism. Many once-cautious and genteel groups who had been known for their moderation, such as the Indian National Congress and the African National Congress, were radicalized by colonial refusals to budge. As a newer generation assumed leadership of these movements it adopted a harder line.[6]

Well organized under charismatic leaders such as Castro, Nkrumah, Gandhi, Sukarno, Nasser, Ho Chi Minh, and Mandela, the nationalist movements gained in membership and strength. Instead of simply ameliorating colonialism, these new nationalists sought to completely uproot it. Their strategy was much more grassroots-based, including previously excluded groups such as women, workers, and youth. Like earlier generations the new elites used the press and international congresses to make their causes known. But whereas the resistance offered by earlier generations was marked by its politeness and civility, this generation of nationalists organized mass campaigns and were much more confrontational toward those they viewed as their oppressors. Demonstrations, strikes, boycotts, and other forms of mass resistance proliferated in Africa, Asia, and the Middle East after World War I, but boomed after World War II. Starting in the 1920s and 1930s Latin Americans joined broadly based mass parties seeking more radical change as well. At times this nationalism took the form of radical mass mobilization. Demonstrations and strikes turned into countless riots and rebellions—and sometimes even revolutions. In the Aba Women's War, one of the most famous events of this period in Nigeria, market women stripped and marched to Governor's Palace to protest taxes and unfair treatment. In response to the threat to their communities, women also led riots in Mexico and Peru, armed with spears, kitchen knives, and rocks. Men and women turned out into the streets under such circumstances, to let the authorities know that they should listen to their complaints.[7] Often these mass strikes and riots were put down with severe reprisals. In the protests at Amritsar, for example, the British responded savagely, leaving 1,000 Indians dead and many more wounded.

Often these movements did attempt to influence the terms of colonialism (or in the case of Latin America, neocolonialism). For example, West African farmers sought to alter wage rates and the prices for their crops through cocoa "holdups" of the sale of their produce, refusing to sell until they got a better price. Throughout this period there were many demonstrations of rural and urban discontent. Colonized people everywhere wanted improvement of health and educational facilities, and equality of economic opportunity. Yet the movements led by the new elite generally had larger goals in mind. More willing to use violence if necessary, and more revolutionary in their goals than the old-style elites, these nationalists were seeking some form of national self-determination—autonomy, if not independence.

In terms of their vision for the future, many of these groups stressed the positive aspects of indigenous cultures and the need for a cultural renaissance, to revive the traditional order in the face of the foreign assault. Some favored Western constitutional models for change; some advocated peaceful change, practicing techniques of noncooperation such as civil disobedience and passive resistance. Others adopted and adapted Marxist Leninism, in the belief that capitalism would never lead to development and that violent, revolutionary change was the only way independence could be achieved (Algeria, Vietnam, Angola). Others (such as the African National Congress in South Africa) used a mix of methods. Again, they disagreed not only about how independence should be achieved, but also about the best blueprint for the future.

For many years the colonizers were able to use the divide between the old and new elites to their advantage. Infighting within and between nationalist movements over goals and strategy no doubt delayed independence. Still, despite the Europeans' best efforts, eventually it became clear that the nationalist movements could not be ignored or written off by the colonizers. The anticolonial struggle was greatly assisted by the fact that after the world wars the imperial powers were weakened, impoverished, and exhausted. Public opinion in Europe had turned against unnecessary expenditures, and most of the remaining colonial powers had lost the will to hold on. The colonies were reeling as well; the wars had intensified pressures on them not only for troops, but also for forced labor and supplies. After sacrificing for the war effort, living with short-

Figure 4.3 Spiritualism and Nationalist Resistance

Just as religion was used to colonize, spirituality was used in resistance. Because of colonial attempts to co-opt or destroy traditional sources of authority, spiritual leaders were frequently the only ones left with legitimacy. Often denigrated by the colonizers as "witch doctors," priests and mullahs, prophets, spirit mediums, and healers inspired nationalist movements around the world. Some of these movements were moderate and advocated reconciliation and peaceful change. Others predicted the end of the world and the coming cataclysm for whites. In Southeast Asia, Islamic and Buddhist religious revivals mobilized populations. Pan-Islamism fused religion with nationalism, creating a JIHAD tradition that spurred resistance to imperial penetration. Separatist and millenarian churches in Latin America and Africa were often based in ancestral traditions. The common theme across the four regions is that these movements sought to recover the identity and defend the cultural dignity of colonized peoples.[8]

ages, price hikes, and wage freezes for years, the Arabs, Indians, Africans, and others expected rewards for their contribution. They wanted concessions from the mother countries and they expected to be granted more participation in running their own affairs. For example, during World War I in return for their cooperation against the Ottomans, the Allies had made promises to the Arabs for immediate self-government. They were infuriated when it became clear this was not to be. Why freedom for Czechoslovakia and Yugoslavia and not the peoples of Asia, Africa, and the Middle East?

With some notable exceptions, the United States and the Soviet Union generally supported the nationalists' demands. Whether for altruistic or not-so-altruistic reasons, both new superpowers generally adopted an anticolonial stance and pressured Europe to dismantle its EMPIRES. Moreover, in much of the diplomatic language of the times—from the Atlantic Charter, which upheld the right to self-determination, to the Charter of the newly established UNITED NATIONS—colonial powers were finding it much more difficult to maintain their LEGITIMACY.

Figure 4.4 Wars of Liberation

For many countries, the road to independence was one of intense conflict and violence, marked by insurgencies and revolts. Where peaceful means didn't work, where all efforts were met with ruthless suppression, men and women turned to armed struggle. Particularly where there were large numbers of white settlers (e.g., Zimbabwe, Algeria) these conflicts often developed into revolutions and wars of liberation. Contrary to popular perception, both men and women participated in these wars. Women risked their lives to feed and house GUERRILLAS. They performed crucial services, such as moving weapons and information to fighters. In some cases, women carried the rifle, serving as rebel soldiers in El Salvador, Zimbabwe, Algeria, and elsewhere. These women became important symbols and rallying points for their nations. For example, Hawa Ismen Ali, who became known as Somalia's "Joan of Arc," was killed standing up to Italian colonialism in 1948.[9]

Increasingly, in the international arena, they were being held accountable for their actions. The UN received complaints from the colonies, and required regular progress reports on how well it was preparing its wards for independence. In effect, a constellation of events, both domestic and international, came together to make the hold of empire less and less tenable. Buoyed by the vacuums created by international events, nationalism throughout the non-Western world was the driving force behind this change. This was as true in the early nineteenth century for Latin America (with the decline of the Iberian powers) as it was by the mid–twentieth century for Asia, Africa, and the Middle East.

The end of colonialism came about at different times and in different ways, but it is fair to say that it mostly came about over the objections of the mother countries. In most colonies, there was little power sharing until the very end. The vast majority of colonized peoples were excluded from the rights of citizenship. In much of the non-Western world, all attempts by indigenous peoples to participate in politics were squelched until after World War II. Although the British and French were more likely than the Belgians, the Dutch, or the Portuguese to allow for an independent press and the right to an associational life, overall the "best" of the colonizers hurt democratization more than they nurtured it. Even those most willing to allow some political opening made often inadequate and superficial reforms. For every concession granted there were restrictions that continued to limit political participation.

Yet these were the lucky ones. Where the colonizers recognized independence as inevitable, and the forcible retention of empire as impracticable and unprofitable, they acted pragmatically. With foresight, they initiated a gradual devolution of power so as to maintain the close ties established under colonialism after independence. While this might mean problems for the former colonies in terms of continued dependency, a graceful exit by the mother country meant a far greater likelihood that independence would at least begin with some form of DEMOCRACY.

Others were not so fortunate. For the vast majority of colonized peoples living under Belgian, Dutch, Spanish, or Portuguese rule, there was little preparation for independence or democracy.[10] Even when they left peacefully, as the Belgians and French did from most of their African colonies, they delayed the handover of power until the very end and then left virtually overnight. To punish the colonies for seeking self-determination, the former mother countries cut off aid. There are stories that the French even took the light bulbs with them when they left, and that the Portuguese destroyed water systems. Worse, where strategic interests loomed large or where white settler populations lobbied against independence, the colonizers fought long and bloody wars in a desperate attempt to hold on to power. In countries where class and race conflicts were deepest, independence was achieved with more difficulty and democracy quickly failed. Similarly, where it took a revolution to win liberation, the new government was likely anti-Western, anticapitalist, and based on one-party rule.[11]

Is It "Independence" Only in Name?

However fiercely the colonizers struggled against it, inevitably the period of empire had passed. Although most of Latin America had won its independence more than 100 years earlier, formal independence in Asia and Middle East was granted or won in the 1930s, 1940s, and 1950s. The 1960s is the decade most associated with independence in Africa, although several countries were liberated only since then—the last colony to win its freedom was South Africa in 1994.

For the majority of people living in South Africa and the other former colonies, independence was a time of great optimism and celebration. With the exception of a few elites, most citizens of the non-Western world looked forward to the freedoms associated with self-determination. Freedom was variously defined as everything from the end of forced labor, to political autonomy, self-determination, and individual liberty, to the end of colonial monopolies. Finally, it was time for the non-Westerners to control their resources for their own benefit. People anticipated a restoration of the dignity taken from them by colonialism, and in these heady days people looked forward to a smooth road ahead. However, too soon it became clear that each newly independent state would have its own problems to face. Above all, the nationalists who had brought their countries to independence faced formidable challenges of organizing new governments that would provide the political stability necessary for economic growth.

Political Development

The architects of these new systems had very different ideas about the best way of organizing government. Consequently, the first experiments in self-rule resulted in a diversity of government forms. While some independence governments were established as monarchies (e.g., Iraq, Morocco, Saudi Arabia), most became republics. In part, the mode of decolonization explains the range of experience after independence. Although those that won their independence through wars of liberation usually turned to more radical experiments, those that achieved their independence in relative peace often adopted in some form the mother country model. For example, many of the formerly British colonies experimented with a parliamentary system. Most of Latin America has spent some time under presidential systems, like that of the United States, its highly influential neighbor to the north.

Experience with constitutional government in the newly independent states varied widely. In democracies power often swung back and forth between conservatives and liberals. Over the years we have seen other shifts as well; some constitutions granted a degree of state autonomy through federalism, others provided for greater centralization in decisionmaking. In Latin America and Africa, most constitutions were short-lived; they were written and rewritten several times. In Mexico, Nigeria, Iran, and many other countries, democratic or not, there has been a constant struggle over how religious or secular government should be. Consequently, for many countries the only thing constant has been change.

For many of the people living in these new states it was their first experimentation with democracy. Others attempted to build on democratic traditions that predated colonialism. The experiment worked better in some places than others; some countries created democracies shortly after independence that continue to exist today (e.g., India and Botswana). However, such successes were relatively rare. Instead, democracies floundered in most countries just a few years after independence. In many Arab countries, for example, where the idea of popular participation was said to be an alien concept, democratic traditions grew slowly if at all. There and elsewhere power devolved from civilian to military rule and many other countries as well soon became mired in a variety of despotisms. In part this was due to a revolution of rising expectations. Governments might be following constitutional and legal procedures but they were failing to address the needs of their people. Those who had been waiting so long for a decent life soon became disillusioned with the pace of change and frustrated by the inability of their new governments to produce the desired results. As we will see in the following chapters, economic and political instability are closely linked. Across the non-Western world, governments at the helm of countries experiencing economic hardship tend to lose public support. They become weak and vulnerable to upheaval and military takeover. Then as now, people who come to view democracy as only serving the interests of elites frequently end up calling on the military to overthrow constitutional governments to establish stability and carry out speedy reforms.[12]

Whereas the demise of so many of these democratic experiments was disappointing to some, it was widely applauded by large margins in Iraq, Syria, and Egypt. There and elsewhere, dictatorship often had broad appeal because in many ways "independence" was just a change of masters. These countries' so-called independence has not necessarily meant self-government and it did not usually result in radical changes in the lives of the majority. This is most clearly the case in Latin America in the nineteenth century, but it was also largely true of Asia, the Middle East, and Africa over 100 years later. Hierarchies were reproduced, just deracialized (although in Latin America it was mostly a matter of American-born whites replacing the Iberian-born). Democratic constitutions were façades. Political and economic power was concentrated in the hands of a few linked by class, ethnicity, or religion. When elections were held, they were often blatantly manipulated and even under civilian rule authoritarianism became entrenched.

Nonetheless, more radical models resulting from revolutions were often no more successful in meeting people's expectations. Interestingly, radicals often justified their rule in the same ways conservatives did. Both left- and right-wing authoritarians maintained that their countries were in crisis, and that they could not afford democracy because it was too disruptive. In some cases it was argued that democracy should be rejected because it was not traditional to indigenous cultures. Elsewhere the justification was that the masses only dimly perceived their own interests. Until they knew what was good for them, they needed to be led by the vanguard, a revolutionary elite that could show them the way.

Dictators used any or all of these arguments to rationalize the emergence of single-party states. Many of the nationalists who led their countries to independence refused to share power through democratic means. On paper or in practice, governments were created in which executives were strong, legislatures and judiciaries weak. Government existed to serve as a rubber stamp for the party and the leader (e.g., Mexico under the Institutional Revolutionary Party [PRI],

Malawi under Banda, China under the Communist Party). Through the creation of cults of personality, leaders monopolized political and economic power.

In Latin America these strongmen were known as CAUDILLOS, and nearly every country in the region had at least one in the early years after independence—and has had since (as we will see in Chapter 14). In Africa, Asia, and the Middle East, in monarchies, and in civilian- and military-ruled republics, these leaders established themselves as "supreme protectors" or "presidents for life." Based on personal, not constitutional authority, Sukarno ruled Indonesia for two and a half decades. Ferdinand Marcos clung to power in the Philippines and Mobutu Sese Seko in Zaire for more than twenty years. Despite the fact that they were famously corrupt, these leaders portrayed themselves as all-seeing, all-knowing father figures responsible for the welfare of the nation. Much like the monarchs of long ago, their power was based on their charisma, their ability to co-opt populations by doling out favors—and their willingness to use violence to quell dissent.

With few exceptions, under civilian and military rule, in both left-wing and right-wing governments, there has been an expansion in the size and influence of militaries. Dictators dependent on the use of repression to maintain power tended to overindulge the military in order to maintain its loyalty. As a result, spending on the military ballooned in most countries, further aggravating economic difficulties. Mexico was one of the countries most generous with its military. Military spending under a series of caudillos consumed approximately 60 percent of the national budget in the 1820s and under Antonio López de Santa Anna in 1854–1855 the military share of the budget was 93.9 percent.[13] Yet Mexico was unique only in the extent of such excess. Governments around the world (including those of developed countries) have routinely put guns before butter, favoring military spending above healthcare, education, and the like. Although there are some revolutionary military governments that sought to overturn the status quo, most often militaries have tended to intervene to protect the interests of conservative landowners and urban elites. However, this relationship has on occasion become strained. Growing military contempt for civilians often resulted in coups against democratic and less-than-democratic governments. In many countries, the military's political importance grew as that of civilian authority declined.

Why has authoritarianism been such a persistent feature of politics in all four regions? At times coups have been applauded and authoritarians have enjoyed widespread popularity, simply because they provided the order that is so widely viewed as necessary to economic growth and progress.[14] Another factor motivating populations to put security issues above other needs is that very soon after independence many countries had begun falling apart. With their common enemy gone, nationalists turned on each other. Divisions that had run just under the surface during the nationalist period resurfaced to plague many of the newly independent states. With the end of colonialism, the competition for power was naked and constant. Politics quickly became regarded as a ZERO-SUM GAME, in which whatever power one group won came only at the loss of another. Although we hear a lot about "tribal" conflicts in the non-Western world, clashes were frequently based on power politics portrayed as based not only in ethnic but also in regional, linguistic, or religious differences. Across countries in all four regions, these cleavages contributed to a process of fragmentation. The result has been civil war, often involving efforts at secession, and international wars, to redraw boundaries and claim resources. In Nigeria, Guatemala, Indonesia, and elsewhere, when politicians have manipulated religious, ethnic, or other communal divides to win power, it has meant chaos.[15]

Old resentments that may have preceded colonialism but were aggravated by policies of divide and rule were rendered even more deadly by the COLD WAR. During the period running from the end of World War II until the demise of the Soviet Union in the early 1990s, non-Western countries often found themselves the targets of superpower influence. In the major ideological battle of the twentieth century, the world was divided between the United States and the Soviet Union into spheres of influence. In this struggle the United States favored conservative governments and rebel movements friendly to capitalism and routinely embraced military dictatorships because they were anticommunist. As President Harry S. Truman famously put it about his counterpart Anastacio Somoza of Nicaragua, "He's a bastard, but he's our bastard." No more idealistic in its choices, the USSR supported radical, anti-imperialist forces that had come to power (or were seeking to come to power) through revolution. In its own rivalry with China, the communist powers vied with each other to be recognized as the champion of the "third world."

In their effort to divide up the third world, the superpowers made a series of bilateral treaties and regional alliances, often based on the superpowers' promise of military and economic assistance. The people of Asia, Africa, Latin America, and the Middle East were given an ultimatum by the United States and told that they were with it or against it. They could not sit on the fence (although India and others objected to such treatment by forming the NON-ALIGNED MOVEMENT).

Once the United States and the Soviets had achieved nuclear parity, the fear that direct conflict would result in mutual assured destruction led the superpowers to seek other theaters of war. PROXY WARS were fought in Asia, Africa, Latin America, and the Middle East, with the United States supporting one side and the Soviets the other in various civil and international wars. With both the United States and the Soviets focused on their own battles, the superpowers intervened in domestic politics with little understanding of or interest in local conditions, let alone the issues at stake for their proxies. In Cuba, Afghanistan, and Vietnam, in wars between Somalia and Ethiopia, Israel and its neighbors, and in many other conflicts throughout the non-Western world, the superpowers again and again intervened, hoping to shore up their allies and overthrow governments supported by their adversary. Conflicts in these faraway countries were just a small part of a larger battle that each superpower portrayed as monumental—a war between the forces of good and evil. However, there is an African saying that goes, "When elephants fight, only the grass gets trampled." This was certainly the case for countless civilians caught between the two sides in what were often bloody wars of attrition.

Economic Development

To put it mildly, the political instability exacerbated by the Cold War was hardly conducive to the political or economic development of the non-Western world. Meanwhile, superpower efforts to prop up allies who were doing little or nothing to promote development meant prolonged economic hardship and volatile politics in many non-Western countries. Upon independence these countries had enormous needs but simply not enough resources. New leaders came to power promising to improve standards of living, increase incomes, provide essential services, and build infrastructure. Hopes were very high. However, even after formal independence, the economies of most countries were weak and under the direction of foreigners. Because of discriminatory colonial policies there was a shortage of trained and experienced indigenous professionals, since nationalist leaders had frequently been relegated to a role in the opposition or as revolutionary fighters.

Just as the way in which independence was achieved had an effect on government forms, it also had an effect on the structure of postindependence economies. Countries that were liberated through revolution were much more likely to argue that the main lesson of colonialism was that capitalism didn't work. From their view, private enterprise had contributed to a distorted development, in which wealth was shared among a few. Thus postrevolutionary governments called for a socialist or communist system that would offer protections to the masses by granting a larger role to the state in production and distribution. Yet for a variety of reasons these experiments largely failed to produce the intended results. Isolated from the capitalist world, communist- or socialist-led countries often became just as dependent on the Soviet Union as they had been on their former mother countries.

On the other hand, the majority of countries had won their independence with relatively little bloodshed. They were more likely to be capitalist and to maintain close economic ties with their former mother countries and the West. Often new leaders didn't attempt to transform the status quo. Rather, they sought to open their countries up to foreign trade, incorporate them more fully into the international economy, and replace the colonizers as the primary beneficiaries of the system. Most countries became plutocracies, in which rich families joined together to run regions and nations. With a few exceptions, landownership patterns remained largely unchanged. Indigenous elites sometimes replaced foreigners, but existing economic and social structures were largely kept intact.[16]

To the frustration of many, the colonial economic system essentially went on as if there had been no political change at all. With a few important exceptions, most countries continued as producers of raw materials—often exporting the very same commodities assigned to them under colonialism. The performance of these sectors varied; there were occasionally times of prosperity (e.g., Peru's guano boom in the nineteenth century), but for the most part their exports were more vulnerable than finished goods, subject to periodic and dramatic price changes. Cycles of international boom and bust had devastating consequences, even for those countries that had managed to industrialize.

Meanwhile, unless there was strong state intervention guiding these

Figure 4.5 Attempts at Industrialization

Why not just break out of the raw materials rut? Countries in all four regions have attempted to industrialize, to diversify their economic bases, and to lessen their dependence on foreign trade—in most cases through IMPORT SUBSTITUTION INDUSTRIALIZATION (ISI), that is, by replacing expensive foreign imports with domestically produced consumer items. Some countries (particularly in Asia) have managed to successfully industrialize, mostly due to strong state intervention and protectionism. However, more often these early attempts at industrialization have failed. STATE-OWNED ENTERPRISES (SOEs) frequently proved to be inefficient, and the infant industries they were trying to launch simply could not compete against more established enterprises in developed countries.

economies, foreign corporations continued to dominate them. This was especially the case in petroleum-producing countries, but to some degree true of all raw materials producers, since most non-Western countries had little control over production levels, pricing, processing, marketing, or the transportation of their goods. Still largely undiversified monocultures, they were dependent not only on foreign investment, but on foreign imports as well. Since these countries were earning too little from their exports to pay for imports of oil, food, medicine, and other consumer items, they soon fell into a pattern of deficit spending. Asian, African, Latin American, and Middle Eastern states became caught up in a cycle of borrowing to pay their debts and spending revenues on debt service rather than the internal improvements that might promote development. Within a few years of independence, many countries were in default on their debts and vulnerable to the whims of their creditors. Foreign influence, whether through MULTINATIONAL CORPORATIONS (MNCs) or INTERNATIONAL FINANCIAL INSTITUTIONS (IFIs) and other organizations, eventually became so pervasive that the term NEOCOLONIALISM was coined to describe the condition of many non-Western states, which were now independent only in name.[17]

Conclusions: From Interdependence to Dependence?

Although we tend to think of the INTERNATIONAL ECONOMIC SYSTEM as a contemporary phenomenon, it existed long before Europeans colonized the world. Empires in Asia, the Middle East, and Africa had prospered in the world marketplace for over 2,000 years. The Americas were linked in a busy regional trade. Although some areas remained isolated, others played an integral part in the evolving international trade. African, Middle Eastern, and Asian craftsmen and merchants once traded on an equal par with Europeans, as equal partners in the world economy.[18] It is important to understand that before the age of European empire, Europe was just one part of the international economy. A world economy and system of interdependence predates colonialism.

However, that interdependence was fundamentally changed by European imperial expansion. One major effect of this expansionism was that the economic relationship between the West and much of the world shifted substantially over time—to Europe's favor. Whether it lasted for three decades or three centuries, the mercantilist policies associated with colonialism played a decisive role in Europe's rise to power. Noneconomic interests did play a part in motivating this expansionism. But the accumulation of capital created by the transatlantic slave trade, the pillage of foreign lands, and the creation of European monopolies provided the base for Western industrialization and the development of capitalism.

Whereas this early form of GLOBALIZATION meant unprecedented wealth for Europe, for the people to be conquered the European presence was much like an apocalypse. Yes, the history of the world can be described as a series of conquests. The rise and fall of empires is a recurrent phenomenon in the histories of all regions. This wasn't the first time outsiders had swept through these territories, but this usually involved a relatively marginal disturbance to the underlying continuity of life. The European colonization of Asia, Africa, Latin America, and to a lesser extent the Middle East marked a fundamental, long-term change in institutional structures as a whole and a modification of the network of social norms and beliefs that constituted entire cultural systems. It radically altered people's lives. The effect was often devastating as indigenous political systems were undermined or destroyed. Social structures were warped, economies distorted, and cultures disintegrated.[19]

There are analysts who refute such arguments and characterize the effect of European colonialism on the colonized as essentially benign, or even a positive good. They contend that the colonial experience contributed to the overall well-being of indigenous peoples. Many non-Westerners would remind the defenders of European imperialism that by and large, colonial rule was established through conquest—it was not something that the colonized ever asked for. It is undeniable that colonial policies resulted in an opening of more international trade routes and an expansion of the volume of trade—but on what basis? The mother countries did introduce new crops and animals, and transfer new tools and techniques to the colonies, but this in no way compensated for the demographic losses and suffering associated with the slave trade and colonialism. The colonizers did bring new ideas and worldviews with them. There was a valuable interchange of ideas, but at what cost—in return for exploitation, pauperization, and humiliation?[20]

Despite all the fanfare, the formal independence of these territories did not fundamentally change the lives of the majority of people living there. Nor did it create the space for the new states' rapid economic development. Rather, colonialism left behind a number of legacies—political, economic, social, and cultural. The former colonizers had put these countries on an unhealthy course from which it has been very difficult to deviate. Much of the non-Western world continues to suffer from neocolonialism in the sense that since independence other developed countries have joined the former colonizers to reap the benefits of colonialism without its costs. During the Cold War the non-Western world was clearly allowed only as much "independence" as the superpowers deemed compatible with their interests.[21]

Then as now, during the various incarnations of globalization, the non-Western world has struggled against its dependent status. The West has regularly intervened to overthrow non-Western governments seeking radical structural changes in class relationships and income distribution. Mohammed Mossadegh in Iran, Jacobo Arbenz Guzman in Guatemala, Patrice Lumumba in the Congo—these are just a few of a string of leaders who were eliminated because they dared to challenge the status quo. But it is not just radicals who remember and have hard feelings about these foreign interventions. Ordinary people throughout Asia, Africa, Latin America, and the Middle East resent the fact that they are still not treated as equals. Far less than their counterparts in the West do they control their own destinies, plan their own development, manage their own economies, determine their own strategies and priorities, and generally manage their own affairs. Ironically, non-Westerners are uniquely deprived of a fundamental and inalienable right so lauded by the West—the right to liberty.[22]

Whether it lasted for 60 or 300 years, colonialism was not just a blip in the string of history for many people living in the third world. Rather, it was an extremely important part of their experience, a watershed event they must struggle to overcome. Yet in recent years it has become the fashion (even among some third worlders) to argue that blaming colonialism is an old and tired argument. Those who dwell on its excesses are increasingly accused of beating a dead horse. Is it high time to get over it and move on? Or is it really that simple?

5

Linking Concepts and Cases

The last three chapters have outlined in broad strokes some of the history of what would later become known as the "third world." To consider some of the legacies of this past, we invite you to explore the patterns described here in greater detail by taking a look at our case studies. Too many people believe that the third world was always "third world," that life in the non-Western world began only during the period of colonization—or that the only "civilization" is Western civilization. As you read about the specific histories of these eight case studies, consider the following questions.

How similar were these countries' precolonial experiences? How do they differ? Compare these countries in terms of their experiences under colonialism. What countries colonized them and in what manner were they colonized? How was each of these countries integrated into the world system before and after colonialism?

What if any factors can you identify as aiding the European conquest of these territories? How did each country attempt to free itself from Western domination, and why were some struggles less peaceful than others? Did the countries that became independent through the use of violence appear to have had an experience dramatically different than those that became independent through peaceful means? Since independence, what kinds of problems do all or most of these countries share? How different are they in their approach to these problems? Among the cases, what kinds of experiences have been widely shared since independence?

Case Study: Mexico

Well before it was "discovered" by Europeans, the area once called New Spain had developed a variety of civilizations based on maize surpluses and extensive trade networks. Although archaeologists are still piecing together the region's history, it appears that the Olmecs, dating back to 1200 B.C.E., may be the mother civilization to the empires of Mesoamerica. With their distinctive cities, monumental buildings, art, and sculpture, the Olmecs, and later the Maya (A.D. 250–900) played an important part in shaping the early history of this region.[1]

Relative latecomers to the fertile valley of Mexico in the thirteenth century, the Mexica were a minor group who eventually built the Aztec Empire around its city-state, Tenochtitlan. At its height, it is estimated that this powerful, complex civilization ruled a population of 25 million. Much of its wealth was based in conquest, as it subjugated its neighbors and took tribute from them. Built on the belief systems of earlier cultures, the Aztec worldview mixed war and religion. The Aztecs believed that conquest was essential to the proper worship of the Sun God. Perhaps the world's leading practitioners of human sacrifice in terms of volume, the Aztecs saw themselves as staving off the end of the world. To ensure the passage of the sun through the sky, they believed it was necessary to feed the Sun God with life—human blood from ritual killing. To satisfy the Sun God's appetites (in one year just before the Spanish invasion, it is estimated that 20,000 people were sacrificed), they warred on their neighbors, taking captives for sacrifice. As you might imagine, the Aztecs had many enemies.

But the existence of local people willing to ally with the Spanish against the Aztecs was only one factor in favor of their relatively small expedition. When these adventurers arrived in 1519, led by the conquistador Hernan Cortés, the stage was already set for a strategy of DIVIDE AND CONQUER. However, just as crucially, the Aztec response to the Spanish invasion was slow and indecisive. In part this was because for ten years prior to the arrival of the Europeans, there had been a series of foreboding omens. The emperor and absolute ruler of the Aztecs, Moctezuma II, had expected a coming cataclysm upon the return of the god-king Quetzalcoatl (the feathered serpent). Quetzalcoatl had been known as a white-skinned deity who took the shape of a man. Understandably then, the emperor was taken aback by Cortés, with his pale complexion, blue eyes, and red hair. Although still suspicious that the newcomers were men and not gods, Moctezuma initially tried to bribe the mysterious visitors to leave by offering them generous gifts of gold. Yet this only confirmed the Spaniards' resolve to march on Tenochtitlan and confiscate all its wealth. With the help of superior weaponry, the invaders were able to overcome their numerical disadvantage and quickly decapitated the empire by taking Moctezuma hostage. Although the Aztecs did rebound and made a last attempt to fight off their attackers, by 1521 they were devastated by smallpox and literally starving to death. The empire was destroyed and the rest of central Mexico fell soon thereafter.[2]

Built atop of the ruined Aztec capital, Mexico City became the center of the Viceroyalty of New Spain. The territory it covered was immense; it would eventually run from Panama to California, and include a few Caribbean islands as well as the Philippines. For 300 years, New Spain was the most productive and most populous of the Spanish colonies. Although it was eventually silver that produced the most fabulous wealth for Spain, the Spanish crown also encouraged the establishment of haciendas with the *encomienda* system. The *encomienda* rewarded the conquistadors with land grants and the guarantee of plentiful labor. For the Indians this meant their virtual enslavement, as they were now compelled to provide their colonizers with tribute and free labor, in return for the right to live on their own land. Under their agreement with the crown, the *encomenderos* were supposed to Christianize and assimilate the Indians into a faithful, Spanish-speaking work force. To help them do this, the Franciscans and other Catholic missionaries arrived early in the sixteenth century and succeeded in making widespread and rapid conversions. However, more than protecting the new converts, the *encomienda* and later colonial policies allowed for their exploitation and abuse.

Eventually it became clear that there simply was not enough labor for the colonial economy to produce the wealth Spain demanded. Indigenous peoples, decimated by the conquest, were continuing to be depopulated by their treatment under colonialism. To augment the labor force, African slaves were brought in, to share with Indians the lowest rungs of the racist social order. These groups joined mestizos in sporadic rebellions against their mistreatment. However, it was another, relatively privileged class who proved pivotal in Mexico's break from Spain. The Creoles were second-class citizens within the elite, stigmatized simply because they were born in the colonies. These "Americanos" greatly resented the privileges granted to the immigrant Peninsulars. Moreover, they chafed at the fact that the colonial economy was managed for the benefit of Spain. Instead, the Mexican Creoles wanted commercial freedom, to trade with countries other than Spain, and to become rich without the crown's interference.[3]

For these reasons many Creoles initially supported Father Miguel Hidalgo's social revolution in 1810. However, once it was clear that the changes sought by this movement were so far-reaching as to threaten their interests, Creoles joined the Peninsulars to squash this and later rebellions seeking radical change. The movement for independence was stalled for nearly a decade until in 1821, in reaction to liberal reforms in Spain, one elite, led by Agustín de Iturbide, displaced the other. Rallying broader support with talk about popular SOVEREIGNTY, Creoles claimed power for themselves. Spain was too weak to do much about it, and Mexico became independent with relatively little bloodshed.

In its first fifty years of independence, Mexico continued to suffer from chronic instability. Between 1821 and 1860 the country went through at least fifty different presidencies, each averaging less than one year—and thirty-five of Mexico's presidents during this period were army officers. Government was changed at gunpoint; it was the age of CAUDILLOS, warlords seeking wealth, promising order, and surviving on patronage. Antonio López de Santa Anna was the most notorious of them all—he held the presidency on nine separate occasions. It was also during this period that Mexico suffered its most humiliating experience, as it endured several foreign interventions. After a disastrous war with the United States in 1848, Mexico was forced to cede the huge swath of land between Texas and the Pacific (approximately half of Mexico's territory).[4]

For much of the rest of its first 100 years of independence, Mexico was polarized politically, torn apart by the rivalry between Liberals and Conservatives. In this often bitter battle, Conservatives sought to promote order and defend the Church, which was by now institutionalized as a wealthy and influential interest group in a firm alliance with elites. On the other hand, Liberals were anticlerical and argued that the Church was entirely too powerful—politically and economically—and that reforms were badly needed. The leader of the Liberal movement during much of the nineteenth century was Benito Juárez, who as president sought to strip power from both the army and the Church. Conservatives counterattacked and even supported the French, who invaded to collect on Mexico's debt and overthrew the Juárez government in 1864.

The period of French rule under Emperor Maximillian was relatively brief and Juárez was eventually reinstated, but the Liberal-Conservative divide continued to dominate politics until the rise of the last caudillo, Porfirio Díaz. Taking the post of president through a coup d'état and remaining there for over thirty years (1876–1911), it can be said that Díaz finally provided Mexico with some stability, if nothing else. Associated with the "modernization" of Mexico, Díaz made generous concessions to foreign investors, sold Indian landholdings to private entrepreneurs, and argued that the repression associated with his rule was for a good cause—to modernize Mexico. Considered a loyal friend of the United States, Díaz ensured that any "progress" for Mexicans made on his watch accrued to himself and his cronies.[5]

One lesson of history is that policies that create such widespread misery tend to invite disorder. Francisco Madero, a Liberal seeking democratic change in Mexico, ran for president against Díaz in 1910. However, after his suspicions were confirmed that Díaz would not allow himself to be voted out of power, Madero and his followers resorted to more violent means. From all over the country the people answered his call for the overthrow of Díaz, including Emiliano Zapata from the south and Pancho Villa from the north. This was the beginning of the Mexican Revolution; the movement grew rapidly and Díaz, surprisingly weak, stepped down in 1911.

But it was only the beginning of the first major social revolution of the twentieth century. Madero was now president, but he was more of a parliamentarian than a revolutionary. Because the changes he initiated were deemed too little too late, he was soon confronted by his former compadres. During the most violent phase of the revolution, the country broke down into a brutal civil war that raged until 1917. It was only after disposing of Zapata and Villa that Venustiano Carranza became president, declaring the revolution a success.

The constitution resulting from this revolution was startlingly radical for the times. It set out a framework for significant changes in Mexico's power relationships. Among other things, the constitution (which remains the foundation of Mexico's government today) places significant restrictions on the Church. Far more progressive than labor laws in the United States at the time, the 1917 Constitution established rights for labor, including the right to strike, the right to a minimum wage, and the right to a safe workplace. As one might expect after years of foreign domination, the document is intensely nationalistic, and places restrictions on foreign ownership. Most significantly, perhaps, the constitution gives the government the right to control Mexico's resources and to redistribute land.

The first years of implementation of the revolution's goals were very slow. In part this was because the government was sidetracked by a civil war in the 1920s when conservative Catholics sought to regain power for the Church. It was also partly due to the fact that the leaders who survived the revolution were not nearly as progressive as its architects. However, by the 1930s, Mexicans had in Lázaro Cárdenas a president determined to reaffirm the revolution's goals. His administration was responsible for distributing 44 million acres of land, almost twice that distributed by all his predecessors combined. Moreover, the Cárdenas government recognized the necessity of providing support services to assist land recipients, whether they lived in the communal system of ejido, or on individual family plots.

Although he attempted to steer a middle course, neither too socialist nor too capitalist, Cárdenas was most of all a nationalist, and his attempts to make real the promises of the revolution were perceived by foreign interests—including the United States—as threatening. As late as the 1930s, foreign firms had effectively controlled Mexico's oil reserves. However, invoking the constitutional right of Mexico to control its subsoil resources, Cárdenas expropriated these properties, compensated the companies, and established PEMEX as a state oil monopoly.[6]

Petroleum was only one vital industry in which the state would play a large role. However, the bulk of the Mexican economy continued to be held privately. From the 1940s to the 1960s, Mexico experienced a "miracle" in terms of economic growth, which was nearly unsurpassed, averaging 6 percent per year. Elites were the primary beneficiaries of the so-called miracle. The Mexican middle class grew, but poverty persisted and the gap between the rich and poor actually loomed wider. To address this problem and win the support of the poor, the government created a broad system of social assistance. Although it has never amounted to a significant redistribution of income, since the 1940s Mexico has had one of the most socially progressive programs in Latin America.[7]

As is indicated by its economic policy, Mexican politics since 1917 has been more pragmatic than revolutionary. Soon after the revolution, power was centralized under a single party, which took power in 1928 and controlled the government for seventy years. Known since 1945 as the Institutional Revolutionary Party (PRI), its longevity can be attributed to several, less-than-democratic, factors, including its organization. It gradually took control of the military and organized labor, and then welcomed its rivals into the fold. It operated an immense system of patronage, in effect mobilizing the support of the peasantry and buying the loyalty of those who might threaten it.

Under the PRI Mexico became known as "the perfect dictatorship" because, unlike many of its neighbors to the south, where coups were the norm, Mexico has enjoyed remarkable stability. However, it is important to remember that the PRI government was authoritarian; as we will see in later chapters, it was not above relying on electoral fraud or even physical coercion to retain power.

Still, compared to many others such as Chile and Argentina, such behavior was uncharacteristic of Mexico. As the primary force guiding Mexican politics since the revolution, the PRI was pragmatic ideologically. Although there have always been differences within this large and heterogeneous party, a "pendulum effect" ensuring a tendency toward the center worked for decades to hold all the different elements of the PRI together. For many years this was the secret of the PRI's success. Until the 1980s Mexico was effectively a single-party state; the opposition was small and seldom won elections. However, by the early 1980s that had begun to change, as elements within the PRI recognized that the party's survival was incumbent upon its ability to adapt to a variety of changed realities. The PRI split became more apparent as Mexico set out on a long road to political liberalization. The modest political opening continued gradually and the PRI appeared to reverse course on several occasions, such as when it claimed victory in the highly disputed presidential elections of 1988. However, prodded by civil society, the PRI managed its internal divisions to allow in 2000 for the freest and fairest elections in Mexico's history.

Case Study: Peru

Although the first Peruvians are believed to have been seminomadic shellfish collectors and fishermen, the earliest known permanent settlements developed with the introduction of maize and the adoption of impressive irrigation systems. The transformation of marginal lands into abundant fields formed the basis of several pre-Inca civilizations, such as the Moche and the Nazca, known for their sophisticated crafts and ceremonial buildings.

However, it is the civilization of the Inca for which Peru is best known. Its empire was immense, running 4,000 kilometers along the spine of the Andes. Heralded for their material well-being and cultural sophistication, the Inca rivaled or even surpassed other great empires in world history. Although there are still debates as to the origins of the Inca, in a relatively short period of 100 years they were able to subdue and incorporate nearly 12 million people.

At the helm of power was the emperor, who was considered both man and god. Divinely ordained, he enjoyed absolute power and controlled vast material resources. Systems of mutual assistance and expectations of reciprocity were core values of the Inca. Kin groups were allocated shares of land by the state. In return individuals were expected to work the land, keeping a third of their produce for themselves and turning over a third to support state functions and a third to serve ecclesiastical needs. Subjects were also expected to perform *mita* or draft labor, which helped construct and maintain public works, including a remarkable system of roads and bridges.

Yet this highly sophisticated, militarized state, defended by tens of thousands of warriors, was unable to stand against 168 Spanish adventurers seeking their fortunes. Clearly, the Spanish had an overwhelming military advantage. Just as crucially, the empire was already factionalized and vulnerable when the foreigners arrived, having just been through a civil war, the result of a succession crisis. The Spanish were able to capitalize on this, using a policy of divide and rule. Led by the seasoned conquistador Francisco Pizarro, the Spanish ambushed the overconfident Inca and took their ruler, Atahualpa, hostage in 1532—the empire fell soon thereafter.[8]

In the early colonial economy of plunder, Peru became Spain's great treasure house. Lima was constructed as the capital of this seat of Spanish colonial administration, known as the Viceroyalty of Peru (1543). Mining overwhelmingly dominated the colonial economy. Little else mattered; as one viceroy famously put it, "If there are no mines, there is no Peru."[9] Silver became the engine for colonial development in Peru, as the demands of the boomtowns created by mining stimulated agricultural production. In addition, Lima became a vibrant center for merchants active in the Atlantic and Pacific trades.

However, because the prosperity of Spain and its settlers was dependent on a reliable source of cheap labor, the indigenous peoples of Peru were pressed into service. Harassed and humiliated by the Spanish, in the early years of colonial rule many Indians were rendered landless and virtually enslaved under the feudal *encomienda* system. Under a form of extortion known as the *reparto,* Spanish administrators forced Indians to buy European goods at high prices. Distorting the Inca system of *mita,* the Spanish compelled all adult male Indians to spend part of their year laboring in Spanish mines, farms, and public works (without the state providing anything in reciprocity). Because the silver and mercury mines were such notorious death traps and paid little, the *mita* served as a crucial source of labor for the colonial economy.[10]

Such policies had a devastating impact on the indigenous population.[11] The *mita* drained off able-bodied workers, contributing to the social disintegration of indigenous communities. Famine became commonplace, and populations already weakened fell easily to disease. People were demoralized. Abortion, infanticide, and suicide became common forms of escape. Because of the depopulation of Indian communities, significant numbers of Africans were brought to Peru as slaves to meet the colonial economy's demand for labor.

Although they were treated as less than human by the colonial system, Africans, Indians, and mestizos were by no means passive in their acceptance of this situation. The eighteenth century was an especially tumultuous time in Peru, as over 100 popular uprisings occurred, some of them seriously threatening the established order. The most significant of these insurgencies was the "Great Rebellion" of 1780–1781. Led by a curaca who adopted the name of the last Inca king, Túpac Amaru, this revolt was based in Inca NATIONALISM and spread rapidly throughout the southern Andes. Determined to contain the well-organized mass movement, the Spanish set out to reconquer the area, terrorizing villages. Six months later this short but vicious civil war was over, with more than 100,000 dead (nearly 10 percent of the entire population).[12]

The Great Rebellion had the effect of unifying Creoles and Peninsulars against the threat to their privileges. By the early nineteenth century, compared to the rest of Spanish America, the Viceroyalty of Peru was a royalist stronghold. And because the colonial ruling class didn't fracture in Peru as it did elsewhere in Spanish America, it took an intervention of foreign armies to bring independence to the country. With General José de San Martín pressing into Peru from the south, and General Simón Bolívar coming in from the north, Peruvian Creoles reluctantly declared independence in 1821. However, it was not until Bolívar undertook his final campaign against Spain in 1824 that his troops, assisted by Indian GUERRILLA forces, finally defeated the royalists. The republic was established and Bolívar set about the difficult task of establishing the first political institutions of independent Peru.[13]

However, Peruvians were divided over what type of government to pursue, and no constitution lasted for long. Although its constitutions contained Liberal guarantees of DEMOCRACY, equality, and respect for human rights, Peru remained a highly stratified society where race and class determined privilege. Power remained dispersed to the countryside as a semifeudal network of Creole landowners controlled vast areas, free from restraint. The 1890–1930 boom in agro-exports accelerated the problem of landlessness for the majority, while the largest haciendas were owned by a group known in Peru as "the forty families." As a result, landholding in Peru is grossly unequal, and one of the most skewed in all of Latin America. During much of the twentieth century, 0.1 percent of farm families controlled 30 percent of the country's land, and more than half of its best soils.[14] This oligarchy, composed of businessmen and landowners, continued for years to dominate Peru. A COMPRADOR class, these elites manipulated politics to serve their own economic interests. For many years this oligarchy was backed by two of the most powerful institutions in the country, the military and the Church.

In the early years of independence, civilian and military strongmen fought for political power. The country fell into a long period of caudillism. Coups and countercoups were common, particularly in the first thirty years of independence, when there were twenty-four changes of regimes. This initial experience established a pattern for Peruvian politics that has persisted over the years: the use of force has been widely accepted as a means of resolving political conflict.

Just as Peru's politics have swung back and forth between civilian and military rule, its economic fortunes have alternated between boom and bust. After the wars for independence, Peru was in an economic crisis. Silver production had dropped, military spending was high, and the country suffered from chronic deficits. However, by the mid–nineteenth century, guano, or bird droppings, were to have the same effect on the economy that silver once did. Accumulating over thousands of years on the islands off Peru's coast, guano was rich in nitrogen. Once used by Indians as a fertilizer, guano was rediscovered and exported to Europe in the 1840s. For fifty years the guano boom created great prosperity for the Peruvian oligarchy and the British (who took about half the profits). However, by the 1880s the guano deposits were largely depleted, and Peru was soon unable to pay its bills. Peruvian governments began a tradition of selling off state interests to foreigners, and ended up putting the country's development in the hands of outsiders.

Eventually Peru managed to move away from its dependence on a single export, and began selling a variety of raw materials to Europe such as copper, tin, and rubber.[15] However, because the economy remained focused on production for the international market, not domestic demand, it was more vulnerable to price swings created by forces beyond its control. Adopting a program of export-led growth, Peru continued to experience boom and bust cycles. The gap between rich and poor continued to grow. Whenever a government suggested reforms that threatened the interests of traditional elites, the military stepped in.

However, when the military intervened in 1968, "politics as usual" in Peru were dramatically altered. Cuba's Fidel Castro described it "as if a fire had started in the firehouse."[16] The military, which had traditionally repressed all demands for drastic change, initiated a social revolution. At the head of this revolution was General Juan Velasco Alvarado, who as president proclaimed a new economic order that would be based on neither capitalism nor communism. At the heart of this program was a sweeping agrarian reform, to rectify the entrenched imbalance in landownership and severe inequalities, intensified by an economic decline and accompanied by a marked growth in population.

Military reformers also sought to promote a more autonomous development by nationalizing the assets of the foreign corporations that dominated the Peruvian economy, such as the International Petroleum Corporation.

However ambitious the revolution's goals, very little worked as planned, and by 1975 it was over. The reforms were halted and a new government set out once again to calm the oligarchy's fears, embrace a free market approach, and assure foreign capitalists that they were welcome in Peru. However, the economy did not recover. Rather, world prices continued to decline for the country's exports and its foreign debt ballooned. When Alan García Perez was elected president in 1985, he attempted to turn the country around by rejecting the liberal economic strategies of his predecessors. An economic nationalist, García shocked the international community by announcing he would limit Peru's interest payments on its foreign debt to 10 percent of its export earnings. The INTERNATIONAL MONETARY FUND (IMF) responded by declaring Peru ineligible for new credits. The punishment took its toll; Peru was bankrupt and suddenly the world's basketcase.[17]

Meanwhile, Peruvians had become caught up in a brutal civil war based in the glaring gap between the affluent coast and the desperately poor sierra. The highly secretive Maoist guerrilla group Shining Path (Sendero Luminoso) called for the creation of an egalitarian utopia. During the 1980s, both Shining Path and the Peruvian military became known worldwide for their use of terror. As the war grew more intense, the rebels seemed unstoppable, taking large portions of the countryside. Civilian governments declared states of emergency, giving the military a free hand in much of the country, and suspended most civil rights. Secret military trials of those suspected of ties to Shining Path landed thousands of innocents in prison. García and his successor, Alberto Fujimori, were both caught in the unenviable position of having to rely on the army against Shining Path. In 1990, after twelve years of uninterrupted civilian rule, Peru's constitution granted excessive powers to the executive, while its democratic institutions were still alarmingly weak.[18] Elected that year, Fujimori immediately took aggressive steps to deal with the economic and political instability rocking Peru. To jump-start the failing economy, he adopted an extreme policy of NEOLIBERALISM and imposed austerity measures advocated by the IMF. On the war against terror, Fujimori preferred a similarly draconian approach. In return for cooperation in the U.S. war on drugs, the president amassed enough military power to turn loose his security forces on the countryside. When questioned about the iron grip he claimed was a necessity, the democratically elected president of Peru carried out an *autogolpe* (self-coup) in 1992, taking for himself the power to rule by decree. With the help of the military, he closed the Congress and the judiciary, suspended the constitution, and proclaimed a state of emergency. Initially the public overwhelmingly supported the *autogolpe,* primarily because they were desperate for a solution.

Peruvians later reelected Fujimori president, since he was able to provide some semblance of order. Although Fujimori was eventually credited with destroying the terrorists and stabilizing the economy, over time his support dwindled, as the population began to question the necessity of his continued authoritarianism. When Fujimori once again attempted to extend his hold on power, ensuring his reelection through whatever means necessary, Peruvians risked clashing with the military and went out into the streets to demand his resignation. After scandals involving videotapes and a manhunt that now seems almost farcical, Fujimori, one of the few dictators left in the region, did finally step down in 2000, paving the way for Peru to make yet another attempt at democratic government and economic development.[19]

Case Study: Nigeria

The country today known as Nigeria contains hundreds of different ethnic groups, each with its own history. Because of the heterogeneity of these peoples it is impossible to begin to describe all of them here. However, a sketch of the Hausa, Yoruba, and Ibo gives one a sense of the diversity existing in Nigeria. They are the three largest ethnic groups, composing two-thirds of the country's population.

Situated at the edge of the Sahara, the Hausa states of northern Nigeria were kingdoms that rose to prominence based on their location as a major terminus of the trans-Saharan trade. Not only fine craftsmen and rich merchants, their kings taxed goods that traveled through their territory on caravans. A strong cavalry-based military ensured the orderly conduct of business, and offered travelers protection from raiders. From the fourteenth century on, Islamic culture and religion gradually spread through northern Nigeria, primarily through commercial networks. Kano was long a famous center of Islamic learning, although Islam did not become a mass religion among the Hausa until an Islamic revolution in the early nineteenth century. A Fulani preacher, Usman dan Fodio, led devout Muslims displeased with corrupt Hausa kings, excessive taxes, and laxity in the practice of Islam in a JIHAD against their rulers. He brought together the discontented into a powerful revival movement that incorporated the Hausa states into a vast theocracy, the Sokoto Caliphate. Conversion was brought with war, as the jihad spread Islam into central and southwestern Nigeria.[20]

One of the groups affected by this expansionist policy in the south were the Yoruba. This powerful empire was based on a confederation of ancient Yoruba kingdoms and known for its remarkable bronzes and terracottas. The most influential of these kingdoms, Oyo, was at its height between the sixteenth and eighteenth centuries. A large and prosperous megastate, it controlled the trade routes to Hausaland and had a formidable military, with overwhelming numbers of bowmen and cavalry.[21] The power of Yoruba kings was limited by a constitutional monarchy that required that kings confer with a council. However, by the late eighteenth century the Oyo king had become increasingly despotic, violating the traditional rights of the population to participate in decisionmaking. This contributed to a series of devastating civil wars that lasted for the next 100 years.

As opposed to the more centralized Hausa and Yoruba governments with their kings and hierarchies, the Ibo lived in relatively egalitarian ministates in which political power was decentralized. There was no empire, no expansionist military; in fact, there were no kings, presidents, or full-time political leaders of any kind. Rather, the Ibo lived in STATELESS SOCIETIES. If democracy is largely about the right of political participation, then traditional Ibo politics was extremely democratic. Nearly all Ibo were part of the great assemblies that came together to make important decisions for the group. A council of elders and other age- or gender-based associations enforced these decisions. Although the Ibo traditionally lived in the forests of southeastern Nigeria, they were hardly isolated. Forest farmers, the Ibo produced valuable commodities such as kola nuts (important for ceremonial reasons and one of the few stimulants allowed Muslims) to sell in the long-distance trade that crossed the Sahara.

European demand gradually redirected the caravan-based desert trade toward the coast. Nigeria was located in the heart of what became known as the Slave Coast. At the peak of the transatlantic slave trade, 20,000 people each year were taken from this area to be sold as slaves. Throughout much of Nigeria, larger military states such as those of the Hausa and Yoruba raided their neighbors for war captives, who were then passed on to African middlemen and sold to Europeans waiting at trading stations on the coast. Although some Africans became wealthy from this trade, it proved devastating for many others. As the slave trade became less profitable it was replaced by the LEGITIMATE TRADE. A number of European countries were by this time rising industrial powers intent on trading their manufactured goods for cheap raw materials. In Nigeria, British trading houses promoted the production of cash crops such as palm kernel, which could be used as an industrial lubricant and processed into a variety of products, including soap and candles.

French and German merchants were also interested in this territory, which by the late nineteenth century Britain considered to fall within its sphere of influence. In an effort to eliminate foreign competition of all kinds, African leaders were compelled to sign treaties of protection and free trade (in effect bypassing indigenous middlemen and maximizing British profits). The British sent military expeditions to "pacify" those who resisted this encroachment. With conquest still not complete, the British claimed control of the Colony of Lagos and the Protectorate of Southern Nigeria (1900) and the Protectorate of Northern Nigeria (1903). The British conquered these territories separately and they administered them separately, as two very different systems. This policy continued even after the so-called amalgamation of the northern and southern protectorates in 1914.

The architect of this policy was Sir Frederick Lugard, who believed that the north was different from the south and that each should develop autonomously. To overcome shortages of funds and personnel, the British attempted to use a policy known as "indirect rule." As opposed to the "direct rule" associated with the French and which required large numbers of French administrators, indirect rule was much less expensive because it allowed the British to govern through indigenous rulers. It depended on the cooperation of traditional elites, or "native authorities," who served as intermediaries between the British and the indigenous masses and enforced colonial policy.

Perhaps not surprisingly, in many parts of Nigeria the native authorities were hated by their own people and viewed as corrupt collaborators of colonialism. Although people from all classes found ways to indicate their displeasure with foreign rule, ironically it was the Western, Christian missionaries who educated a new elite of African nationalists. Urban and predominantly southern Nigerian teachers, clerks, doctors, and other professionals asserted themselves as agents of social change. They urged other Nigerians to join across ethnic and regional divides to form trade unions, independent churches, newspapers, and various movements that would become the country's first political parties in the 1920s. Leaders of these early political movements, such as Herbert Macaulay (considered by many the father of Nigerian nationalism), often sought reform, not independence. They criticized the colonial government and looked forward to self-rule, but expected the transfer of power to be gradual. On the other hand, radical nationalism experienced an upsurge after the 1930s, as the movement for independence spread beyond Lagos. For example, students organizing the Nigerian Youth Movement (NYM) were more militant in their demands, calling for mass education, equal economic opportunities, and a transfer of power to Nigerians.

The British reacted in a variety of ways to the nationalist demands. In some cases they resorted to repressive measures, firing on or jailing nationalists. Eventually the British offered some concessions, including a series of constitutional proposals for self-government. After years of negotiations, the transfer of power began in 1948. Suddenly Nigerians were to be prepared for the administration and development of their country. The participants agreed that upon independence they would establish a parliamentary democracy and continue with a capitalist economic system. The British left peacefully, assured that their vital economic interests would be protected.

As the date of independence neared, the nationalists abandoned the unified, pan-Nigerian approach they had adopted against colonial rule. The major ethnic groups formed regionally based political parties caught up in a three-way struggle: the Action Group (largely Yoruba), the Northern People's Congress (representing the Hausa), and the National Congress of Nigeria and the Cameroons (which drew mostly Ibo support). With the British effectively out of the way, now the enemy was other Nigerians. Perceiving politics to be a ZERO-SUM GAME, there was a polarization of the political process as each group vied for control of the country's resources.

Yet in 1960, when Nigeria finally became independent, most people were still hopeful about the ability of Nigerians to steer the country toward development. The new government was modeled on British parliamentary democracy. The country was to be administered through a federal system, and was initially divided into three regions: north, west, and east. In the first general elections, in 1964, the Northern People's Congress easily established its dominance, controlling enough seats in parliament to name Tafawa Balewa prime minister of Nigeria's First Republic, its first attempt at civilian rule. When Nigeria became a republic, a Nigerian from the east (Nnamdi Azikiwe) replaced the British queen in the ceremonial role of head of state. Obafemi Awolowo of the Action Group was to lead the loyal opposition.

However, almost immediately, all went wrong. Although technically Nigeria had a multiparty system, in each region one large ethnic group dominated all the smaller ones. Even more problematic, the northern region was given twice the area and population of the other two. Given their long history of distrust there was little prospect of the eastern and western regions ever joining together effectively against the northern region. Tensions mounted. The 1964 parliamentary elections were widely suspected of fraud, and ethnic minorities complained about their lack of representation. Violence broke out in various parts of the country and the government was too weak to contain it. Politics had become a winner-take-all game in which compromise was extremely difficult. Because the country was in constant crisis during its first six years of independence, no one was surprised by (and many Nigerians welcomed) the country's first coup d'état, led by Ibo officers in 1966.

Yet like the rest of Nigeria the military too has suffered from ethnic, regional, and other divisions. Fear of Ibo dominance contributed to a second coup in 1966, and again northerners controlled the government. The purges and pogrom that followed convinced the Ibo to secede and declare the independent Republic of Biafra. Just seven years after independence, Nigeria was fracturing, consumed by a civil war, the Biafran War, from 1967 to 1970. Determined to maintain the territorial integrity of Nigeria (as well as control over its oil wealth, much of which would have been lost to Biafra), the federal government put up a fierce resistance. The fighting was prolonged, as the federal government could not prevail against the forest fighters. In the end, the government resorted to quarantining eastern Nigeria and cutting off food supplies to the Ibo. By the time the Ibo submitted to such tactics and surrendered, an estimated 1 million people had been starved to death.

Remarkably, the country remained intact, largely because of a government program of reconciliation and reconstruction. Such a policy was greatly facilitated by the sudden windfall produced by the jump in the price of oil in the 1970s. As a member of the Organization of Petroleum-Exporting Countries (OPEC), Nigeria enjoyed great prosperity in this period. Overnight it had become one of the wealthiest countries in the world. Unfortunately, since then most of Nigeria's fortune has been stolen or squandered. This was particularly the case during the Second Republic of 1979–1983, when President Shehu Shagari turned politics into a business. The democratic process was subverted as abuse of power occurred on an unprecedented scale. Corruption was so massive and Shagari's government so audacious that fires were set in public buildings to destroy evidence. After a sham vote in which Shagari had himself reelected, the country broke out into open conflict that was only brought to a halt with another coup.

Thus Nigeria settled into a long period of military rule. During most of the 1980s and 1990s, the generals who ruled Nigeria were more authoritarian and kleptocratic than ever, even as the country slipped into a deep economic decline. After years of overspending and misusing funds it was now a major debtor. The structural adjustment prescribed by the IMF prioritized debt repayment over basic needs. Nigeria's relations with its creditors improved, but the reforms failed to correct the economy's structural ills.[22]

Meanwhile the dictatorship was under foreign and domestic pressure to make political as well as economic reforms. After putting off the transfer of power as long as possible, General Ibrahim Babangida offered up his personal design for a Third Republic. When relatively free and fair elections were finally held in 1993, one of Babangida's handpicked candidates, Moshood Abiola, was elected president. As a Muslim Yoruba, he would be the first civilian president from the predominantly Christian south. However, almost immediately Babangida annulled the result, for reasons that are still unclear. Such actions confirmed Yoruba suspicions that the north would never share power or control over the country's oil revenues. Protests shook the country and Babangida stepped down. Within just a few months, one of Babangida's advisers, General Sani Abacha, had overturned the weak interim government.

Abacha presided over the most predatory dictatorship Nigeria had ever known. Living standards fell to their lowest point in twenty years. Brazenly corrupt and notoriously cruel, Abacha set about crushing all dissent. For asserting himself to be the legitimate president, Abiola was arrested for treason (a capital offense) and imprisoned until his death, of apparently natural causes, in 1998. The government became an international pariah for its use of state terrorism against its own people. It is sometimes said that Nigeria became as quiet as a graveyard—until, in what is widely considered a "coup by God," Sani Abacha was found dead in his own bed in somewhat scandalous circumstances.[23]

Abacha's death was celebrated with dancing in the streets. His sudden departure paved the way for another attempt at a transition to civilian rule. The Fourth Republic began with elections in 1999 with all the same problems of its predecessors. This time, it was up to a former military dictator, Olusegun Obasanjo, to lead the country in correcting these problems before the cycle began yet again.

Case Study: Zimbabwe

There was great cultural, political, and economic diversity among the early people of Zimbabwe. Hunter-gatherers long preceded the Shona, Zimbabwe's largest ethnic group, who arrived in the area around A.D. 300. Among the Shona there are several subgroups, some of whom lived in empires, and others who preferred stateless societies. Although they are known to have mined and worked with a variety of minerals, most notably iron ore and gold, cattle-keeping was a more important activity for most Shona, who also worked as farmers. Perhaps the wealthiest empire of southern Africa, Great Zimbabwe was an ancient city famous for its stone buildings and vast walls. For reasons that are still unclear, Great Zimbabwe declined and was abandoned in the fifteenth century. On its heels a larger Shona empire was founded in the north, known as Mwene Mutapa ("Great Plunderer"). Like Great Zimbabwe, it too had an expansionist policy and took tribute from subjugated populations. Though without the cultural and technological achievements of Great Zimbabwe, Mwene Mutapa was also rich in resources and favored by its river access to the main trading centers on the coast. Long before the Portuguese established trading posts nearby, the Shona had been involved in a regional network of trade that connected southern central Africa to coastal trading cities and the Indian Ocean trade.

Most of Zimbabwe continued to be dominated by various Shona kingdoms until the early nineteenth century, when events in South Africa changed the balance of power dramatically. Various South African ethnic groups, including the

Ndebele, fled seeking shelter from the Zulu military onslaught known as the Mfecane, or "Great Crushing." By the 1840s the Ndebele had settled in southwestern Zimbabwe, which became known as Matabeleland. Though unable to defend themselves against the overwhelming might of the Zulu, the highly centralized Ndebele kingdom had a professional army and absorbed the resident Shona-speaking inhabitants. The Ndebele also dominated many Shona groups in eastern Zimbabwe, raiding Mashonaland periodically for cattle, grain, and women.

Another raider of sorts, Cecil John Rhodes was one of the biggest empire builders of the nineteenth century. Having come to South Africa from Britain at age seventeen, Rhodes soon became a self-made millionaire as a founder of DeBeers Diamonds. Interested in money for the power it could buy, Rhodes was a British supremacist and advocate of British imperialism. His interest in Zimbabwe was based on rumors of more gold fields to the north of South Africa's enormous Witwatersrand gold reef. Rhodes sent emissaries to Matabeleland to push for concessions. The Ndebele king, Lobengula, was deceived into signing an 1888 agreement, known as the Rudd Concession, which basically gave the British mineral rights to the entire territory, placing it in the British sphere of influence.[24]

Soon after winning the concession Rhodes formed the British South Africa Company, and obtained a royal charter to colonize and administer the area north of the Limpopo River on behalf of Britain. Rhodes recruited a "pioneer column" of settlers to invade and occupy Zimbabwe. Upon arrival in Zimbabwe in 1890, the whites first established themselves in the predominantly Shona east.

Conditions were ripe for conflict. Disappointed with its luck at striking gold, the British South African Company began looking beyond Mashonaland for new areas to mine. Yet not only were the Europeans antagonizing the Shona, but the Ndebele considered the east to be their raiding ground and resented the whites' presence. When the British attempted to establish a boundary requiring the Ndebele to confine their raids to the western side of the "border," a clash between the settlers and the Ndebele was inevitable. After a series of provocative incidents, the two parties were at war. Although the company's forces were greatly outnumbered, with their modern firearms against the Ndebele's spears the British swept into the west. Lobengula died during his escape, and with the Ndebele demoralized, Matabeleland was opened to white settlers. The British forced the Ndebele onto dry and infertile reserves and gave Lobengula's cattle to whites. The entire territory was placed under colonial rule in 1895 and became known as Rhodesia. By all appearances, the once powerful Ndebele were now prostrate, utterly defeated.

So when a series of uprisings broke out in 1895–1896 and spread over Zimbabwe, the British were taken by surprise. Yet for the Ndebele and the Shona, colonialism not only meant political oppression and economic exploitation, but it was an assault on their way of life. Aggravating their problems were a series of natural disasters. Many Ndebele and Shona believed that these misfortunes were attributable to the presence of whites in their land. Traditional religious authorities blamed the whites for angering God, and warned that Africans must fight to drive out the whites or they would continue to suffer.

Consequently, so many of the indigenous people responded to the war cry "Chimurenga!" that even with their military advantages, the whites found the uprisings difficult to put down.[25]

However, with the help of imperial troops, by 1897 the leaders of what is called the First Chimurenga War had been killed or captured. The British colonial office took over from the company responsibility for Rhodesia, although the white settlers largely ran it in their interests. Africans became second-class citizens in their own land, as racist laws enforced a color bar.[26] Blacks were systematically humiliated and exploited. The country was divided into white areas and black areas. White settlers poured in, taking the best land and establishing large farms. Most blacks were left poor and landless, forced to live in the 31 percent of the territory assigned to them—the wastelands known as reserves. Africans were compelled to work in semislave conditions. To earn money to pay taxes to the colonial state, young men had little choice but to sign contracts requiring them to leave their families behind on the reserves for a year at a time while they worked in white-owned mines or farms. There discrimination was systematic; the disparity in wages between white and black workers was enormous. As late as the 1960s, white mine workers earned twelve times as much as Africans—and white farm workers earned twenty times as much as blacks.[27]

Moreover, the colonial system did everything it could to ensure that African political participation was kept at a minimum. Theoretically, Africans could vote in elections for a legislative council, but because the property and educational qualifications for the franchise were set so high, blacks were legally denied a political voice in this "democracy." This does not mean, however, that blacks had no political voice. Against the overwhelming force of the colonial military, many Africans turned to WEAPONS OF THE WEAK, adopting postures of noncooperation or "refusal to understand." When possible, workers simply deserted the most abusive bosses and shared "market intelligence," leaving wayside messages such as signs carved on trees that alerted others to avoid those employers.[28]

Some Africans submitted to colonial rule, but this does not mean that they accepted it. Rather, in order to survive, they chose to cooperate and seek some amelioration in their treatment. Still, self-government was a long-term objective for many. By the 1920s larger numbers of Ndebele had adopted modern forms of political protest. Led by a new elite known for its moderation, they sought change through constitutional means. Black immigrants to Zimbabwe were frequently the initiators of mass-based protest. South Africans founded the Rhodesian Bantu Voters' Association, which brought together Zimbabweans from different regions and ethnic backgrounds, and appealed to ordinary people by focusing on the land issue. Churches such as the millenarian Watch Tower movement mobilized grassroots protest.[29] The first African trade union in the colony, the Industrial and Commercial Workers' Union (ICWU), was formed by a Malawian. In response to desperate conditions, Africans led a number of strikes in the first half of the twentieth century. More often than not such actions were systematically smashed by the state.[30]

In their determination not to give in to African demands, the settlers attempted to tighten their control over Africans. One way of doing this was through repression. Under a state of emergency, government was given power to put people in prison without trial. Parties were banned; activists were rounded up, detained, and imprisoned. Another strategy was to ally with traditional elites. Many of these elites, who had long worked for the colonial government as Native Authorities, were valued for their loyalty and the influence they held in their communities. By co-opting these elites and giving them more power than they traditionally held, including more power over women, whites could in effect buy their allegiance and promote a policy of divide and rule, by encouraging tribal consciousness.[31]

A third way of dealing with African nationalism was promoted by white liberals frightened by the Mau Mau killings of British settlers in Kenya. In the 1950s whites voted in an administration intent upon making Rhodesia appear to be doing something to placate Africans. This government promised land and other reforms (but not one man one vote, and franchise qualifications were actually raised). For these reasons, most blacks rejected these "multiracial" reforms as paternalistic delaying tactics.[32]

Nor did the liberal policy sit too well with whites for long. The 1962 elections were the end of the liberal experiment, as for the next two decades white voters put into office right-wing extremists led by the Rhodesian Front. In 1965, without consulting Britain (which still had ultimate responsibility for the colony), Prime Minister Ian Smith cut ties with the mother country. Through the Unilateral Declaration of Independence (UDI), the settlers displayed their disregard of international opinion and declared Rhodesia an independent, white-run state.

Despite African hopes that the British would use force against the UDI government, they were unwilling to intervene. After diplomatic efforts failed, Britain did join the UNITED NATIONS in imposing economic sanctions on Rhodesia. Sanctions were not a complete failure, but they had little effect, primarily because the United States and other Western countries broke them. While some characterize this policy as racist, in part it was because the West viewed the struggle in Rhodesia through a COLD WAR lens. For Africans the Second Chimurenga War, which began in 1966, was a war for liberation. Yet the white government was able to portray the African opposition as communist, and the conflict in Rhodesia as part of the larger East-West struggle. The two parties that dominated the anticolonial effort, the Zimbabwe African People's Union (ZAPU), led by Joshua Nkomo, and the Zimbabwe African National Union (ZANU), led by Robert Mugabe, eventually joined forces toward the end of the war in what was called the Patriotic Front. Both called for a socialist transformation of society. Even more damning, from a Western perspective, they each received military assistance from the USSR and China, as well as neighboring African countries.[33]

Pressure was building on the white government, and despite Smith's claims that majority rule would come "not in a thousand years," by the early 1970s it was becoming increasingly clear that the white government was losing the war. Desperate to hold on to power, Smith tried to preempt the guerrilla victory by promoting a political coalition. The Rhodesian Front was eager to end the war with the Internal Settlement of 1978, based on a sharing of power with noncombatant African "moderates." After years of negotiations, Smith was eventually able to win over Bishop Abel Muzorewa, a conservative who had long been associated with the anticolonial cause. Although elections were held in 1979, ZANU and ZAPU, the two parties with the largest African following, boycotted the polls. Yet Africans had achieved some semblance of political power, as Muzorewa became the titular head of government. However, whites continued to control power. The armed forces, police, civil service, and the economy remained in white hands. Because Muzorewa could not control the guerrillas and because the Patriotic Front was joined by most of the world in denouncing the new government, the internal settlement was not durable. The guerrillas refused to surrender, international sanctions remained in place, and the war intensified and was virtually won by the guerrillas in 1979.

That year the three parties met in London to negotiate a peace settlement brokered by Britain. The resulting Lancaster House Agreement served as the basis for a new constitution based on majority rule, but with protections for minority rights. It established a parliamentary system with a president acting on the advice of the prime minister and set a date for elections. The parliamentary elections held in 1980 were an extraordinary exercise in democracy, as the three bitterly hostile armies put down their weapons to campaign against each other. Voting did largely break down along ethnic lines, and though there were some irregularities, international observers found the process to be free and fair. An estimated 94 percent of the electorate voted and Robert Mugabe, because his party, ZANU (now known as the Zimbabwe African National Union–Patriotic Front [ZANU-PF]), had won an overall majority in parliament, became the first prime minister of independent Zimbabwe.

As prime minister, Mugabe recognized that Zimbabwe needed stability if it were to develop, and that there could be no stability without a policy of reconciliation. Although there were some hard feelings on all sides, Mugabe did create a coalition government, inviting Nkomo and even a few whites to serve as ministers in his cabinet. However, strains resurfaced by the end of the first year, and the country soon fell into a civil war. After years of peacemaking efforts, the two Patriotic Front rivals sat down at the bargaining table. The Unity Accord was reached in 1987 and ZAPU was absorbed into ZANU-PF.

As mentioned earlier, the government's policy of national reconciliation also applied to whites, many of whom had panicked after the Lancaster House Accords and planned to leave Zimbabwe. Some did go, but Mugabe worked hard to assure whites that their property rights would be respected. Although an avowed socialist, Mugabe abided by the Lancaster House restrictions on the redistribution of wealth and adopted an economic pragmatism that surprised many. In fact, the mixed economy continued on much as it had before, with the tiny white minority controlling a disproportionate share of the country's resources. For more than twenty years the most crucial issue of all, the land issue, has gone unresolved. So far, at least, many Zimbabweans have found freedom to offer few material rewards.[34]

Case Study: Iran

Iran, which was known as Persia until 1935, experienced a dramatic transformation from a vast Persian empire to an Islamic republic. Grandeur, triumph, invasion, and discord color the historical legacy of this land and people. As a major world empire, Persian culture and civilization endured nearly twenty-five centuries of dynastic rule. It was named for the ancient province Parsa, where the first Iranians settled, and at its height ruled over much of the area we now call the Middle East. The continued survival of Persian cultural and linguistic traditions provides Iranians a nearly continuous cultural tradition since.

Modern Iranians go out of their way to emphasize their non-Arab, Aryan heritage, including distinguishing themselves from Arabs by speaking the Persian language. By the middle of the tenth century, a new Persian language developed that grammatically is not that distinct from Pahlavi, the language of pre-Islamic Iran, with Arab script. Acceptance of Shiism (discussed in Chapter 10) also distinguished Iranians from Turks and Arabs. As evidence of the continuity of some aspects of pre-Islamic culture, the Zoroastrian tradition of celebrating the Nurooz is still celebrated today as the first day of the Iranian calendar as well as the first day of spring (March 21).

Inhabitants occupied the region now known as Iran as early as the middle paleolithic times, approximately 100,000 years ago, with sedentary cultures as far back as 18,000 to 14,000 years ago. The Elamites were the original inhabitants of southern portions of the Iranian plateau. Their language is believed to be unique, with no discernible connection to any other linguistic group.[35] The Elamites created a regional civilization, which was highlighted in both Akkadian and Babylonian texts. Iran's abundance of mineral resources was known as early as 9000 B.C.E. and copper metallurgy became common in 5000 B.C.E.

The first dynasty of Iran's pre-Islamic phase was the Achaemenid Dynasty (546–334 B.C.E.), founded by Cyrus the Great, who was known for freeing the Jews from Babylonian captivity. The Achaemenians spoke an Indo-European language and believed in Zoroastrianism, a monotheistic religion that rose in Persia before Christianity. In fact, it is believed that the biblical Three Wise Men who visited the Baby Jesus in Nazareth were likely Zoroastrian. A ruler who described his empire as Iranshahr, meaning "land of Aryans," or people who are of pure, noble, and good birth, used the name Iran as early as the third century B.C.E.[36] Achaemenid leaders created a hereditary monarchy and empire, which spread throughout the Middle East.

Contemporaneous with the Roman Empire, the Sassanid kings led one of the Persian Empire's grandest dynasties in Mesopotamia and the region now known as Iran. Leadership continued to be hereditary, with a fusion of spiritual and religious power. Sassanid kings imposed Zoroastrianism as the state religion, granting immense powers to members of the clergy. The gradual embrace of Islam began after Persia's wars with the Roman and Byzantine Empires drained the country, increasing discontent within the population. The "golden age" of Islam followed, under rulers called the Abbassids. This 400-year period was marked by tremendous amounts of trade both within the large empire and beyond its borders, widespread public education, scientific developments (especially in medicine and healthcare), and mathematical advances. Although this golden age began to collapse from within—torn apart by internal division and schism—its end was hastened by the European Crusades.

The Mongol invasions of 1258 ended Abbassid rule and divided the Islamic world. A succession of dynasties ruled until 1501, when the Safavid Dynasty—later known for its militarism and conquest—was seated. Safavid rulers battled with the Ottomans, eventually settling on frontier lines roughly equivalent to the modern Iranian-Turkish border.[37] This was also the dynasty that imposed Shia Islam as the state religion, in a succession dispute that is discussed in Chapter 10.

A new dynasty of Turkish origin, the Qajars, ruled from 1796 to 1925. Similar to what would follow later in Iran, this dynasty struggled to integrate religious authority with modern rule, all the while attempting to return to the glories of the earlier Persian Empire. It was under the Qajars that Tehran became the capital of Persia. Early-nineteenth-century educational reforms began to create elites who challenged Iran's relations with the West, fomenting local protests and rebellion and ultimately leading to the first limits on royal power. In 1902, Qajar Shah Muzaffar al-Din,[38] facing the demands of reformers, designed a constitution (based on the Belgian Constitution of 1831) that combined a national assembly (Majles) with a constitutional monarchy. The significance of this change was only eclipsed by the discovery of oil in 1908.

The religious-secular debate that colors much of Iran's modern postrevolutionary history is nothing new. In the Constitution of 1906, the government officially enshrined religious influence and recognized some rights of religious minorities (especially Zoroastrians, Christians, and Jews) by granting them the right to elect one representative to the Majles. Yet both legal protections and legal limits on power were ignored, often at the urging and intervention of imperial powers. The Majles was ended at foreign powers' intervention when England and Russia pressured it to dismiss Morgan Shuster, a U.S. adviser.

The Qajar Dynasty gave way to the Pahlavis, who became the last Iranian royal family. In 1921 a former peasant and military soldier of the Persian Cossack Brigade, Reza Khan, staged a coup, dethroned the Qajars, and founded the Pahlavi Dynasty in 1925. In keeping with tradition and alluding to Iran's historical notions of authority, he took the name Reza Shah Pahlavi (Pahlavi was the language of pre-Islamic Iran). He took the Turkish leader Mustafa Kemal Atatürk as his model, promoting secularization and limited clerical powers. In 1936 he forced women to unveil, making Iran the first Islamic country to declare veiling illegal (an ironic point to which we will return in Chapter 10). He alienated many groups in Iranian society, but especially the religious clerics. In his modernization plan, Reza Shah attempted to combine retrospective elements of Iran's pre-Islamic civilization with Western technological achievements. He nominally tried to reduce foreign power, but his desire to modernize meant he was dependent on Western technology, especially since Britain controlled the Anglo-Persian Oil Company, which financed many development projects and had fueled the British fleet in wartime.

Outside interference in Iranian affairs became one of the leading grievances of the population under Pahlavi rule, and ultimately led to the dynasty's downfall. England viewed Iran as a buffer zone to protect its interests in India and competed with Russia to gain prominent spheres of influence. British and Russian troops partitioned the country at the end of World War I. After the Bolshevik Revolution led to the withdrawal of Russian forces, the British attempted to dictate Iran's transformation into a protectorate. The controversial Anglo-Persian Agreement of 1919 provided British "advisers" to Iran—on Iran's bill—as a way to ensure Iran's stability and ultimately its ability to serve as a buffer state protecting India. The agreement was shady at best: Majles deputies never had any opportunity to comment on it, nor was it presented for discussion at the League of Nations.

Iran was again occupied during World War II, even though its leaders had proclaimed neutrality in the conflict. During the war, the Allied powers accused Reza Shah of being pro-German, forcing him to abdicate, board a British ship, and head toward exile in South Africa, where he died in 1944. Even if the Shah himself did not explicitly support the Germans, there was much public sentiment encouraging him to follow the lead of the Ottoman Empire by entering the war on the side of Germany.[39]

The British and the Russians had considered restoring the Qajar monarchy, but decided instead to continue the Pahlavi Dynasty by transferring power to Reza Shah's son, Mohammed Reza Pahlavi, who ruled from 1941 to 1979. He continued the absolute power he inherited from his father, while increasing Iran's controversial ties to the West. During his rule he was significantly challenged by two leaders—both of whom challenged Iran's ties to Western powers. The first was Dr. Mohammad Mossadeq, who was considered to be a liberal nationalist. Mossadeq, a Majles deputy educated in Switzerland, became a leading voice in the calls for the nationalization of the oil industry, which England had controlled exclusively. As Mossadeq's popularity increased, the Shah appointed him prime minister in 1953. Yet the West vilified the prime minister for nationalizing the oil industry, even though he was one of the country's leading voices for liberalism. London threatened military force, imposed economic sanctions, and even took Iran to the International Court of Justice in The Hague over oil, to no solution. The final nail in the coffin came when a joint mission between the U.S. Central Intelligence Agency (CIA) and Britain's MI6, in collaboration with the Iranian army, overthrew Mossadeq. As a result of these actions, supported if not encouraged by Pahlavi, the leader lost his domestic LEGITIMACY—already on shaky ground—and was labeled "America's Shah." There was much truth to the charge, as the weakened Shah increasingly relied on Western power games to maintain his own authority as he was vilified at home. Despite objections, the alliance between the Shah and the United States lasted for almost thirty years, as the oil industry was denationalized and the U.S. and British companies raked in the profits.

The second man to challenge the Shah, and ultimately inspire the forces that led to the end of the Pahlavis, was Ayatollah Ruhollah Khomeini, a prominent Shia fundamentalist cleric. Khomeini's first book, *Secrets Revealed,* published in 1941, defended the Persian Constitution. But after police killed theology students in the holy city of Qum, Khomeini declared war on the Shah, which led to Khomeini's arrest and exile. Khomeini was able to capitalize on the festering resentment within Iran as people grew increasingly discontent in the face of prolonged economic crises, humiliating international domination, and attempts to secularize the state. The regime's attempts to marginalize Khomeini—including articles in the official press accusing him of being an anti-Iranian British spy or a homosexual—blew up in its face.[40] Khomeini voiced his criticism of the Shah ever louder, increasing his support. The Shah's response was to increase the power of his repressive secret service, SAVAK, which went to great extremes in arresting perceived enemies of the regime. Increasingly, the Shah lost control over his own government, and in the face of widespread protests and chaos, he and his family left the country for good in January 1979. Khomeini followed on his heels, declaring the establishment of the Islamic Republic of Iran in April of that year. Rejecting secularism, Khomeini established a Council of Guardians, which institutionalized the role of clerics in interpreting Iranian laws, and ratified himself as the "Supreme Leader" of the state, answering only to God.

Khomeini ruled during an extremely turbulent decade in Iranian life: the country became increasingly isolated from the international community, was devastated by the ten-year war with Iraq, and fractured along multiple internal divisions that had disappeared during the time of opposition to the corrupt Shah. But people had united around Khomeini, and after his death in June 1989, mourning masses attempting to touch his body caused it to fall from its platform during the funeral march. Defying the Western prediction of the chaos that would follow Khomeini's death, outgoing president Ali Khamenei succeeded Khomeini as Supreme Leader in a relatively seamless transition of power. Ali Akbar Hashemi Rafsanjani, the popular speaker of Iran's Majles, was overwhelmingly elected president, and he served in this capacity for two four-year terms, from 1989 to 1997. Rafsanjani was succeeded by the surprise victory of long-shot Ayatollah Mohammad Khatami, the former minister of culture known for his advocacy of the relaxation of controls over the press and media. Khatami surprisingly defeated the clear favorite of the religious establishment, Nateq Nouri, to become president. He was reelected in the summer of 2001 and, as we discuss in upcoming chapters, has had the difficult job of attempting to balance reform and conservative elements in the country.

Case Study: Turkey

The Ottoman Empire of Turkey prevailed as one of the world's great civilizations for over 500 years. Because of its overwhelming power, the "Turk" was characterized by some as the "scourge of civilization."[41] This image was memorialized in Shakespeare's play *Othello,* in which a main character warns against the "general enemy Ottoman." Once you understand more about Turkey's historical journey, it may be clearer throughout the rest of the book why some of its leaders proclaimed the importance of secularism for its future, for religious struggle played a tremendous role in the history of this land and its people. Turkey's history is surrounded by religious domination, conquest, and development, including much of the early years of the Christian Church as well as early conflict between those desiring conversion to either Islam or Christianity.

Turkish history is rich with a sense of strength, conquest, and creativity that we now understand through archaeological discoveries, including tens of thousands of written tablets that link the ancient residents of the Hattian lands to the biblical people known as the Hittites. It is believed that people began to populate the Anatolian plateau (also known as Asia Minor) during the neolithic period, in approximately 10,000 B.C.E. Some of the earliest evidence of settlements suggests that before 7000 B.C.E., structures made of sun-dried mud, grain agriculture, and items of luxury, including mirrors, daggers, and jewelry, were prominent.[42]

The Hittite civilization (1600–1200 B.C.E.) has been important for a Turkish sense of national consciousness, even if most awareness of this civilization was scarce prior to the 1920s. The Hittite period conforms approximately to the Late Bronze Age and is known for its creation of the two-wheeled chariot. The regime collapsed around 1200 B.C.E., in spite of its defeats of the Egyptian pharaohs, largely due to its inability to maintain its reach as well as the dramatic income disparity within its rule. The breakdown of this kingdom was followed by other monarchies, marked by uncertainty, warfare, and invasion. Numerous kingdoms were born in its wake, including the Phyrygian state, the Urartian kingdom, and the Lydian state, which is known for its creation of coins for monetary exchange.

The Anatolian interior remained under Persian rule for 150 years, until conquered by Alexander the Great, who ushered in a period of Hellenistic (Greek) influence. The Anatolian lands then became a battleground between Rome and the Parthian kingdom of Iran. It was under Roman imperial rule that some of the most important early Christian church councils, including Nicaea, Ephesus, and Chalcedon, took place. The Greeks were followed by the Romans, and later, the Arabs, each bringing their own interpretations of religious tradition, opening Anatolia as a battleground of religious conflict.

Arabs began their conquest in the seventh century, although the Taurus Mountains served as a physical barrier between the developing Christian and Muslim bases. Europeans only began to refer to the lands of Anatolia as "Turchia" at the end of the twelfth century; their rise was a gradual one, taking nearly two centuries. Turks were seminomadic tribal peoples who began conversions to Islam in the tenth century. They began to rise to prominence in the region known as the Byzantine Empire (also known as the East Roman Empire) and became consumed in struggle, lessening their presence in Anatolia. This absence allowed the Turks to conquer Armenian regions and push them to the south. The Christian Crusades, which began in 1095 at the calling of Pope Urban II and ended nearly two centuries later, failed to convert the Turks to Christianity, instead reinforcing their image as the people who wanted to destroy Christianity. Martin Luther blasted, "The Turks are the people of the wrath of God."[43]

The Turkish "golden age" took place under the Ottomans, the most successful Turkish clan, which was founded by Sultan Osman. The Ottomans were early converts to Islam, as the simplicity of this faith tradition appealed to them over the complexity of Christian rituals. They conquered the Christian city of Constantinople, renaming it Istanbul. This was followed by rule over Athens, Tabriz, Damascus, Cairo, Belgrade, Baghdad, Tripoli, and Cyprus—the

Ottoman Empire included much of the Middle East and North Africa as well as most of present-day Hungary and southeastern Europe. Eclipsing the Protestant-Catholic divide in Europe, there was concern that the Ottomans would be able to go as far as Paris, for they almost conquered Vienna.[44] Despite its Islamic focus, the Ottomans organized members of the non-Muslim minority into relatively self-governing units known as millets, Turkish for "nations," which were protected by the sultan. The three primary millets were the Christian Armenians, Greek Orthodox Christians, and Jews. Although it was recognized as a period of ethnic harmony, cultural diversity, and legal codification, it was also a time of little peace and almost continual warfare.

During the Ottoman era, the Islamic Empire ruled the seas. Ottomans held powerful posts on the Mediterranean Sea and the Indian Ocean, and were viewed as the leaders of the Islamic world. Ottoman leaders were very successful in their pursuit of land and followers, and they adopted the title of sultan (a leader whose authority is granted by the caliph, the ultimate leader of the Islamic world) as a way to establish authority, both spiritual and temporal, over conquered peoples.

Yet in the eighteenth and nineteenth centuries, the Ottoman Empire declined, especially in the face of the Christian powers of Europe. Despite defeating Napoleon Bonaparte in a triple alliance between Britain, Russia, and the Ottomans, the empire became increasingly drained of resources and became widely known as the "sick man of Europe." The proud people experienced great humiliation as Ottoman sultans were forced to sign treaties with European Christians over whom they had always viewed themselves as superior. The beginning of the end was the empire's alliance with Germany in World War I, pursued in the attempt to avoid isolation and, in the view of some, as a possible way to recolonize the empire's lost areas. The Turkish people suffered immensely throughout the war, and in 1920 the empire was divided into British and French protectorates, with the Greeks occupying western Anatolia. The greatest human tragedy was the Armenian genocide of 1915–1916 by the Ottomans, in retaliation for Armenian loyalties with the Russians (the Christian Armenians had vainly hoped that the Russians would support their independence after the war). While the number of casualties is a matter of great dispute today, most estimate that, at a minimum, 800,000 Armenians were murdered, starved, or died of disease as a result. The government of Turkey, to this day, denies complicity in the affair.

Following the war, the Ottoman territories were partitioned and the remnants of the empire were centered in Anatolia. Anatolia was among the last regions discussed by the Entente statesmen after the war, and increasingly citizens resented their domination and occupation. Out of the ashes of this semicolonization, the empire eventually gave way to the Turkish Republic, largely through a one-man revolution. Mustafa Kemal Pasha, later known as Atatürk (literally "Father of the Turks") rose to prominence as the Ottoman monarchy started to rot from within. He founded a subversive group called the Committee of Union and Progress, which outsiders referred to as the "Young Turks." But it was a revolution whose gains were costly, as nationalists fought control over former Ottoman territories occupied by Greece, Italy, Britain, and France.

Atatürk had become the rallying force for a defeated nation after the German monarchy was overthrown and the Allies decreed that the empire be divided between British and French protectorates, with a small region left to the sultan, and most offensively to the Turks, the granting of power in western Anatolia to the Greeks. Istanbul was placed under international control: all Turks had left was the mountainous regions of central Anatolia. Some have called this settlement more severe than the Treaty of Versailles was to Germany.[45] Capitalizing on Turk anger over the Greek occupation of Anatolia, Atatürk and his supporters launched the independence movement from the Turkish interior, with Ankara as the new capital. Atatürk's motto, similar to those of other nationalist independence leaders, was "Turkey for the Turks." In the end, though, the Young Turks were able to reverse the most egregious terms of the peace settlement, and gain sovereignty over the Turkish people (Turkey was the only losing power of World War I to avoid reparations). Like many other revolutionary leaders, Atatürk's image went beyond hero status as the single true patriarch of the people against whom nothing negative could be said.[46] The new Turkish Republic dramatically restructured social life, especially in its promotion of a secular state unbound to Islam. Women were given the right to vote in 1930 and encouraged to work.

Following Atatürk's death in 1938, the leadership succession was complicated by the absence of competing parties. For much of Turkey's early years as a republic, it operated as a single-party state, ruled by the Republican People's Party (RPP). This legacy of weak political parties continues to mar Turkish politics today. The young republic also struggled with a military that often intervened in the name of protecting the legacy of Atatürk, referred to as Kemalism. Yet unlike other states in the third world, even though the military intervened and took power three times between 1960 and 1980, it returned rule to civilians after each power grab.

As we discuss throughout the book, the Turkish military views itself as the protector of "New Turkey's" founding virtues. Leaders who followed the "Father of the Turks" struggled with his legacy, especially his insistence on the importance of secularism for Turkey's modernization. President Ismet İnönü, who immediately followed Atatürk, attempted to liberalize life in Turkey, increasing his pressure especially after World War II. Other leaders rose to power demanding that the military be removed from the business of settling scores. The leader of the Motherland Party, Prime Minister Turgut Özal (who later became president), challenged the power of the military generals. Following Özal's death in 1993, Tansu Çiller, an economist trained in the United States, became Turkey's first female prime minister—and her years in office were plagued with economic and separatist problems. Perhaps the most controversial leader in recent Turkish history was Prime Minister Necmettin Erbakan, of the Islamist Refah Party, who came to power in 1995. The military demanded his resignation two years later, attempting to bar him from politics for challenging the secular tenets of Kemalism.

As you can see, the combination of many different thorny issues has produced great drama within the Turkish Republic, as leaders and citizens alike face a daunting number of challenges and questions—some that have been around for centuries and others that are products of the modern era. As you will discover throughout the course of this book, the modern Turkish Republic is a crossroads state, standing at the intersection of cultures (Europe and the Middle East), religious traditions (Islam, Christianity, and secularism), and identity. It is also a state that occupies a less certain role in the power plays of the twenty-first century than it did during the Cold War, when its geographic positioning attracted much superpower attention, especially from the United States. Turkey continues to be a state of great import, albeit one facing many struggles along the way.

Case Study: China

It is often said that China is at once over five millennia old and five decades young. This contrast, between one of the world's oldest civilizations and its endurance for more than fifty years as a "People's Republic," captures much of the intrigue that is China today. Ancient China had great influence over its Asian neighbors, especially in the secular rituals derived from Confucian traditions. Today, Chinese civilization is viewed as the world's oldest, charting the relatively continuous existence of human communities for approximately 20,000 years. (Isolated human skeletons have been discovered from much earlier times, contemporaneous with Indonesia's "Java Man.") China's literary tradition is over 3,500 years old, and its written words (known as "characters") can be traced to linguistic precedents dating to approximately 1500 B.C.E.

Similar to many others, Chinese civilization was centered on river systems, especially the Yellow River in the north, where China's earliest recorded history is found, and the Yangtze River in the central and southern regions. It was a region ruled by over a dozen imperial dynasties, marked by fluctuating periods of stability, chaos, conquest, and cultural progress. The leader of each dynasty exercised authority based on the belief that she or he possessed the "Mandate of Heaven," which can best be understood as receiving the favor of one's spiritual ancestors.

China's first documented dynasty, the Shang, began in approximately 1700 B.C.E. Although Chinese records indicate at least one earlier dynasty, the existence of this community through archaeological records is yet to be proven.[47] Evidence of the Shang Dynasty is found in the so-called oracle bones, discovered only in the late 1800s, which were used to receive guidance from the heavens.

China's first unified dynasty, and indeed the source of the Western name "China," was achieved during the Qin Dynasty, which began in 220 B.C.E. Lasting only fifteen years, this was a remarkable dynasty that completed two wonders of the world. The Qin emperor ordered earlier walls used for fortification and defense to be linked literally into one "Long Wall" (known in the West as the "Great Wall"), providing modern Chinese an incredibly important symbol of the endurance of their culture.[48] The second famed creation of this dynasty was the emperor's elaborate tomb, composed of over 8,000 terracotta soldiers and horses buried to protect their identity. This major capital project of the dynasty required extensive resources, including labor power and coercion, and many of the 750,000 workers who planned and constructed the tomb, located in the ancient capital of Xi'an, were killed so they could not reveal its location. China's greatest dynasty, the Han, lasted for four centuries (206 B.C.E.–A.D. 220), and introduced the world's first wheelbarrow, as well as the widespread use of paper and porcelain. It was during this dynasty, contemporaneous with the Roman Empire, that the famed Silk Road, a 7,000-mile trade route from Xi'an to Rome, increased China's interaction with the rest of the world. China's interaction with the West grew steadily after this dynasty, and by the Ming Dynasty (1368–1644), contacts with the Spaniards, Russians, and Dutch were extensive. It was during this time that the Jesuit Mission of Matthew Ricci was begun, launching China's extensive yet troubled relationship with Western religions.[49]

It is important to note that in the midst of this exploration and grandeur, ordinary Chinese citizens lived a difficult life filled with totalitarian leaders, extensive tax payments to finance imperial projects, and little freedom in either their work or their personal lives, which were mired in poverty. Advancement in Chinese society throughout most of its past was based on academic credentials achieved through a complex examination system that was based primarily on Confucian texts, affording luxury to an extremely small minority of the population (from which women were expressly excluded).

China's relative isolation and size encouraged a "Middle Kingdom" philosophy in which rulers and ordinary citizens alike viewed themselves at the center of world civilization. This attitude manifested itself in China's tributary system of trade, in which foreign powers were required to give gifts to the emperor to show respect or gain favor (and sometimes protection). Additionally, the Chinese viewed anyone outside of their cultural civilization to be "barbarians," little deserving of equal contact or negotiation. Part of the measure, in Chinese eyes, of whether one was civilized or barbarian was one's allegiance to the teachings of a man who lived approximately 2,500 years ago, Kung Fuzi, known in the West as Confucius. His teachings, which may be viewed more as a way of life than a religious tradition, produced a great degree of cultural continuity in Chinese civilization, and even though modern leaders have gone to great pains to eradicate his influence, it continues today. Confucian thought influenced almost all of Asia, well beyond the borders of the Middle Kingdom. Confucius was a traditionalist who reflected, in extremely chaotic times, on solutions to his society's problems. One of his core beliefs centered on the importance of tradition and ritual. He proposed that paternalistic kings who set good examples could govern society best. To him, the virtues of respect and reverence were most important, especially in relation to the elderly and the educated in society. Confucius taught of an inegalitarian, hierarchical system of relationships that required the more powerful person to provide care and guidance while the less powerful in the relationship was mandated to respect and obey. Confucian thought eventually became required understanding for those who wanted to consider themselves "educated Chinese," and it was officially adopted as the state ideology in the second century B.C.E. The Confucian school certainly was not the only worldview during China's past (the Taoists found these teachings restrictive and authoritarian and the legalists found them too retrospective and lacking in rules), but it certainly was the most important. As a measure of its dominance, the Qing or Manchu Dynasty, China's last, was actually introduced to China by foreigners from the north. The Chinese welcomed them, though, because of their internalization of the Confucian code of conduct and rule.

The Chinese Empire traded extensively with Arabs and Persians for hundreds of years before European contact, under the tributary system discussed above. The Chinese never regarded their trading partners as equals, and indeed, for much of its history China's power was unrivaled, especially on the seas and in its protectorates and colonies throughout Asia, including Vietnam, Burma, and Korea. China's imperial power began to decline, though, in the 1500s, as its leaders turned increasingly inward and encouraged more isolation from the rest of the world. It was the outcome of this turn of events that led, in many ways, to the eventual European conquest of much of China, beginning in the late 1700s. In their desire to increase access to Asia through a Chinese trading point, the British and others established permission for foreign citizens to live in China without being subject to Chinese authority, a system known as EXTRATERRITORI-ALITY. This was the beginning of the erosion of China's sovereignty, as foreigners began living in the country not bound by Chinese laws, but rather by the laws of their home countries. As its trade deficit with China spiraled higher, England goaded China into a series of battles referred to as the Opium Wars (see Chapter 3). China's loss of Hong Kong (and other regions, including Taiwan, Macau, and Shandong) symbolized the imposition of foreign rule over a grand imperial land, rule that was not relinquished until the end of the twentieth century. (Taiwan, which was ceded to the Japanese in 1895, remains an example of contested sovereignty—discussed in Chapter 12.) On a larger scale, to most Chinese these events symbolized the loss of the famed "Mandate of Heaven" and gave birth to a flurry of potential solutions to the crisis. It was a time when many feared that Chinese civilization would fracture endlessly, exacerbated by localized warlord politics or regional military powers.

Shortly after the collapse of the last dynasty in 1911, Beijing University students staged the first mass demonstration in China's history, on May 4, 1919, to protest the status of Shandong, administered as a German colony since 1898. The warlord-dominated government in Beijing had entered into a secret agreement with the Japanese during World War I. At the Versailles Peace Conference at the end of the war, many Chinese placed great hope in Woodrow Wilson's rhetoric about SELF-DETERMINATION, but their hopes were crushed when they learned that Shandong was granted to Japan as part of the Versailles settlement. Protests erupted throughout China and within Chinese communities abroad, and China never did sign the Versailles agreement. Out of this environment of distrust and disappointment, two dominant groups led the way to China's future: the Nationalist Party (KMT), lead by Sun Yat-sen, and the Chinese Communist Party (CCP), eventually led by Mao Zedong (even though he was a minor leader for the first years of the party). Both parties focused on rallying different Chinese groups to their cause, and engaged in bitter battles with each other despite two formal attempts to unite for China's future. The final straw was the Japanese invasion of northern China in 1931, after which the CCP was perceived as the aggressive fighter for Chinese interests and for the needs of ordinary people. Following Japan's defeat in World War II and its expulsion from China, all-out civil war ensued between the KMT and the CCP, with the defeated Nationalists eventually exiling themselves to Taiwan. The People's Republic of China was declared on October 1, 1949, although its hold on Chinese territory, and on world opinion, was less than complete, which set the stage for a rough ride especially during its first thirty years.

Mao Zedong, affectionately known as "The Chairman," led China for over two and a half decades, from the beginning of the PRC in 1949 until his death in 1976. His legacy remains a mixed one: he united the country and made the Chinese people proud of their heritage and achievements, while inflicting incredible civil disarray during his attempt to "continue the revolution" from 1966 to 1976, in the period known as the CULTURAL REVOLUTION (discussed in Chapter 13). Mao was followed by another longtime member of the CCP, Deng Xiaoping, who had been a member of the party during its rise to power in the 1930s and 1940s. As you will read, Deng dramatically changed the face of China, by opening it to the outside world, promoting the development of political and economic institutions, and attempting to move away from the charismatic rule of his predecessor. Deng, who died in 1997, has also left a mixed legacy: while the lives of ordinary Chinese citizens improved dramatically under his watch, the blood of the Tiananmen Square demonstrations of 1989 is also on his hands. Leaders who followed in his footsteps, including Jiang Zemin and Hu Jintao, faced the difficult task of trying to preserve the Communist Party's monopoly on power while attempting to integrate China more closely into the world economy. It is a balancing act that continues to challenge China's leaders today.

Case Study: Indonesia

Modern Indonesia is an identity born of trade routes and colonial experience. Despite regional prominence and rich cultural traditions, there was little sense of commonality among the peoples who lived on the thousands of islands in the South Pacific prior to the early nineteenth century. Throughout this book, you should not be surprised to read about the division and tense unity that exist in modern Indonesia at the beginning of the twenty-first century, as unity was a concept rarely evidenced in the islands of the archipelago.

The region known today as Indonesia was long populated by human beings. You may be familiar with "Java Man," the fossilized bones of a hominid that were discovered in 1891. It is believed that this human, known as *Pithecanthropus erectus,* lived over 750,000 years ago and had the capacity for fire-building and language. Subsequent archaeological discoveries confirmed populations extending 35,000–40,000 years ago, including Solo Man, named after a river in central Java, and the later Wajak Man, who lived 12,000–13,000 years ago.

Despite the presence of human communities almost 1 million years ago, the majority of today's Indonesians descended from two ethnic groups who immigrated to the islands from the north. These groups include the Melanesian peoples, who are believed to have inhabited the islands approximately 6,000 years ago, and the Austronesians, who migrated to the Indonesian archipelago from Taiwan at approximately the same time.

The Indonesian archipelago was an active player in the early Malay world, with a handful of states and kingdoms that thrived in trading. Early settlements prospered on the main islands, including Ho-Ling in central Java. Chinese records of this civilization report extensive war exploits, labor surpluses, and entertainment based on shadow plays and drums. By the sixth century, major kingdoms developed on Java and Sumatra, highlighted by the Srivijaya kingdom in southern Sumatra. Considered one of the most powerful kingdoms in Southeast Asia, Srivijaya emerged as the chief state and the only maritime state among the classical states in the region. As a commercial state, it began and ended earlier than others. Srivijaya's rulers controlled the critical Straits of Malacca, the preferred travel route between China and India, and its influence reached to southern Vietnam.[50] The exchange of commercial goods was not the only type of trade in this kingdom: it was also viewed as the center both of Hindu and Buddhist studies.[51]

Not surprisingly, due to its location Srivijaya was famous for its navy, financed largely by taxes collected on foreign ships traversing its path. It eventually controlled a vast territory, including most of Sumatra, present-day Malaysia, and Singapore, yet the authority of the king expanded farther, to Borneo and Sri Lanka. The wealth of this kingdom was memorialized in the story that each day the king would toss a gold bar into the sea to acknowledge it as the source of Srivijaya's prosperity. At the end of his reign, the number of gold bars retrieved from the waters quantified the king's power.[52] Yet because of its export focus, it was a vulnerable state, dependent on the economic situation in India and China.

Even after Srivijaya's decline, Indonesia's prominence in Asian trade continued, and the city port of Malacca rose to prominence in its absence. Asian states (especially China and India) as well as Arab states provided ideal export markets for products abundant on the archipelago, especially spices. The region's abundance of spices, especially cloves, nutmeg, and pepper, were sought by traders around the world. Early Indonesians had established colonies in Madagascar for the transport of spices abroad, especially to the Romans (today, Austronesian languages can still be found there as remnants of this influence).

Increased trade led to heightened cultural interaction between islanders and their mainland Asian neighbors. By the third century A.D., both Hindu and Buddhist traditions had filtered into the western islands from India. Neither system was adopted writ large; they were both regionally adapted and made to fit earlier customs, especially animism, a tradition based on the reverence for all living things. Islam did not become a major influence until the thirteenth century, and even then it was often combined with native religious traditions, as well as Hinduism and Buddhism. The Portuguese and the Dutch introduced Christianity much later, in the sixteenth and seventeenth centuries. Another cultural artifact of Indonesia's status as the trading center of Southeast Asia was the adoption of the Malay language by dissimilar people: it became the unifying factor facilitating trade between diverse groups. As Islam spread through the archipelago, the use of Malay became even more predominant.

Islamic traditions existed in parts of Indonesia as early as the thirteenth century, primarily through the rise of Malacca as a prominent trade port, and the spice-trading route between Malacca, northern Java, and Maluku was a major avenue for the spread of Islam. Even in its earliest days, though, Islam was interpreted in diverse ways, with *santri* Muslims closely following traditional Islamic rituals, and *abangans* adapting Islamic traditions to their Hindu beliefs. Aceh was one of the first parts of Indonesia to covert to Islam, and to this day Acehnese are known for their relatively strict interpretations of Islamic traditions and for the strength of their convictions.

European influence in the region began in the fifteenth century. The first Portuguese ships sailed into Malacca in 1509, in search of inexpensive spices to preserve meats. The Portuguese eventually took over Malacca, only to hasten its downfall. Throughout the 1600s, Dutch Protestants established the Dutch East India Company (in search of a monopoly over the spice trade), and gradually increased their territory of control as it fit their economic interests, beginning with the "spice islands" of Maluku and the northwestern coast of Java. They consolidated their rule by expelling other colonial aspirants, including Spain and England (although the English maintained their colonies on Borneo). Even after the collapse of the Dutch East India Company, the Netherlands defeated the English to gain control over their colonies in Southeast Asia by 1816. Despite serious indigenous challenges to their authority, the Dutch prevailed in establishing control.

As Dutch colonial rule over the archipelago increased, and they began to integrate native Indonesians into their administrative structure, the growing sense of discrimination fostered much discontent. As we have observed in revolutionary leaders elsewhere, in the context of rising expectations, those native Indonesians who were afforded the opportunity to pursue higher education and serve in colonial officialdom as physicians, engineers, and other professionals chafed at the rigid subordination they faced compared to their European rulers. Although the nationalist movement was just beginning to form, many voices were calling for change, including the Javanese princess Raden Adjeng Kartini, who championed the emancipation of Indonesian women.[53] As discussed above, this situation of choosing a select few for opportunities produced extremely difficult identity struggles among the chosen few.

The nationalist independence movement was launched in the early years of the twentieth century, and was given an added spark by ironic celebrations by the Dutch of their own centennial of liberation from Napoleonic rule—which they commemorated in the midst of occupied Indonesia.[54] It all began to come together under the leadership of a young engineer named Sukarno (following the Javanese custom, he had one name). Sukarno founded the Indonesian Nationalist Party in 1927. In response to their independence rhetoric, the Dutch exiled Sukarno, Mohammed Hatta, and other nationalist leaders. World War II provided them an opportunity to return, reorganize, and lead their country to independence.

Indonesia's formal colonial era ended with the Japanese occupation of

1942–1945, during which time the Japanese plundered the region's oil fields to support their imperial navy. Ironic in hindsight, many Indonesians initially welcomed the Japanese, believing they would help in their fight for independence, and that the Japanese would not stay long. Instead, the Japanese sent Indonesians to work as forced laborers in Japan's territories. Those Indonesians who had been recruited and trained by the former Dutch colonial powers were again used as pawns during the Japanese occupation, as they became enforcers of the harshest Japanese policies on their neighbors and compatriots. But it was the Japanese defeat at the end of World War II that spurred Indonesia's independence movement into full gear. Prior to that time, Indonesian nationalists Sukarno and Hatta had begun to campaign for independence. Yet the movement was hindered by disagreement, rectified mostly by Sukarno's *pancasila* proposal, which emphasized the five principles shared by all Indonesians regardless of ethnic, religious, or political beliefs. These beliefs remain today, enshrined in the preamble to the modern Indonesian constitution.

Indonesia declared its independence in Sukarno's garden the morning of August 17, 1945 (two days after the Japanese surrendered), but struggled with the Netherlands for over four years before the Dutch recognized its independence, only after bloody battles and intense international pressure. Sukarno embarked on a program euphemistically referred to as "guided democracy" for most of his rule, from 1949 to 1965. As a world traveler, Sukarno eloquently espoused the needs of the third world, especially in the Bandung Conference of Asian and African States in 1955. He was also stridently anti-Western, taking over British and U.S. businesses, expelling Dutch nationals, and withdrawing from the United Nations. A 1965 coup, supposedly masterminded by the Communist Party of Indonesia (PKI), led to much bloodshed—as many as 400,000 were killed in fear of communist insurgency. The Chinese minority in the country suffered devastating losses in the attacks that followed the change of government.

Out of the ashes of the 1965 coup, the military commander Suharto rose to power. Suharto, who himself had attended a Dutch-run military academy and fought against the Dutch in Indonesia's war of independence, knew well the importance of military strength in maintaining his rule, a principle he applied fiercely throughout his "new order" government from 1966 to 1998. Although dramatic social improvements were achieved in the first years of his leadership, including declining poverty and increasing literacy rates, his government increasingly became a repressive state, complete with a gulag system used to enforce religious and political oppression. He was forced to resign from power in May 1998, in the face of widespread protests against his handling of the Asian economic crisis and international pressure to resolve the country's economic woes. A caretaker government led by interim president B. J. Habibie, a close associate of Suharto's, was in power for thirteen months before the groundbreaking elections of June 1999, the first free and fair elections to take place in four decades. In this election, the Indonesian Democratic Party–Struggle (PDI-P), led by Megawati Sukarnoputri, scored a resounding majority once the voting results were finally ratified in August 1999. The Indonesian legislature, the People's Consultative Assembly, in October 1999 met and chose Abdurraham Wahid—who was supported by an unprecedented Islamic alliance—as the state's fourth president.[55] Megawati, a critic of Suharto and daughter of Indonesia's founding father, was named vice president. Wahid, the Muslim cleric who was partially blind and in frail health, led the country for approximately twenty months before he was voted out of office by the legislature in July 2001, capping off a six-month impeachment process. Shortly after Wahid agreed to leave the presidential quarters, Megawati and her vice president, Hamzah Haz, took power in a country dizzied by political upheaval, internal violence, and a reeling economy.

Now It's Your Turn

As you move on to more contemporary considerations of these eight countries, keep in mind their diverse and rich histories. In what ways can you see their contemporary experience driven by their past? From the brief overviews provided, what traditions or values do you believe should be revitalized or adapted to serve the peoples of these countries? In what ways do you see legacies of Western domination continuing to play out in these countries?

Suggested Readings

General

Hattori, Eiji. *Letters from the Silk Roads: Thinking at the Crossroads of Civilization.* Trans. Wallace Gray. Lanham, Md.: University Press of America, 2000. Nonfiction, emphasizes the land-sea connections through Eurasia, highlighting silk and spice routes that transported goods and culture.

Africa

Achebe, Chinua. *No Longer at Ease.* New York: Anchor Books, 1994. Nigeria: fiction, sequel to *Things Fall Apart,* a young man torn between tradition and modernity becomes part of the corrupt colonial elite.

———. *Things Fall Apart.* New York: Anchor Books, 1994. Nigeria: fiction, Ibo society and one man's struggle against European invasion.

Emecheta, Buchi. *The Bride Price.* New York: George Braziller, 1980. Nigeria: fiction, gender relations, culture, and traditions in Ibo society.

———. *The Slave Girl: A Novel.* New York: George Braziller, 1980. Nigeria: fiction, domestic slavery in the early twentieth century.

Fuller, Alexandra. *Don't Let's Go to the Dogs Tonight.* New York: Random House, 2001. Zimbabwe: nonfiction, on growing up white in colonial Rhodesia.

Marechera, Dambudzo. *The House of Hunger.* London: Heinemann, 1978. Zimbabwe: nonfiction, on growing up black in colonial Rhodesia.

Ngugi, Wa Thiong'o. *The River Between.* London: Heinemann, 1965. Kenya: historical fiction, Christian missionary education and how its attempts to outlaw female circumcision affected two Kikuyu communities.

———. *Weep Not Child.* London: Heinemann, 1964. Kenya: historical fiction, the impact of the Mau Mau war for liberation on one family.

Okri, Ben. *The Famished Road.* New York: Anchor Books, 1993. Nigeria: fiction, a spirit-child in an impoverished community at independence.

Oyono, Ferdinand. *Houseboy.* London: Heinemann, 1966. Cameroon: fiction, a young man's diary illustrates the workings of racism in French colonial Africa.

Soyinka, Wole. *Ake: The Years of Childhood.* New York: Vintage Books, 1989. Nigeria: memoir of a childhood.

Tutola, Amos. *Simbi and the Satyr of the Dark Jungle*. San Francisco: City Lights Books, 1988. Nigeria: fiction, Yoruba myth and religion serve in a modern fable.

Vera, Yvonne. *Nehanda*. Harare: Baobab, 1993. Zimbabwe: fiction, life during British colonial rule.

Asia

Baum, Vicki. *A Tale from Bali*. Hong Kong: Periplus Editions, 1999. Indonesia: historical novel examining resistance and daily life in colonial Bali, with attention to the impact of Dutch imperialism.

Buck, Pearl S. *The Good Earth*. New York: John Day, 1931. China: historical fiction following one peasant man and his family through the end of the Chinese imperial period.

Chang, Jung. *Wild Swans: Three Daughters of China*. New York: Anchor Books, 1992. China: personal memoir told through the life experiences of three generations of Chinese women, from the collapse of the last dynasty to the reform era of Deng Xiaoping.

Feng, Jicai. *The Three-Inch Golden Lotus: A Novel on Foot-Binding*. Trans. David Wakefield. Honolulu: University of Hawaii Press, 1994. China: historical fiction, focuses on the evolution of modern China through the eyes of one family, with a special focus on the daughter with bound feet.

Lu, Xun. *Diary of a Madman and Other Stories*. Honolulu: University of Hawaii Press, 1990. China: satirical examination of life in late imperial China written by one of China's most celebrated authors.

Spence, Jonathan D. *Treason by the Book*. New York: Viking, 2001. China: historical fiction, early-eighteenth-century Manchu China.

Tan, Amy. *The Bonesetter's Daughter*. New York: G. P. Putnam's, 2001. China: historical fiction, Chinese mother relays her life experiences in a rural Chinese village during the warlord period of the 1920s.

Toer, Pramoedya Ananta. *Child of All Nations*. Trans. Max Lane. New York: Penguin, 1996. Indonesia: historical fiction, continues the story from *This Earth of Mankind* as the young Indonesian man fights for his rights against colonial Dutch rule.

———. *This Earth of Mankind*. Trans. Max Lane. New York: Morrow, 1991. Indonesia: historical fiction tracing the coming of age of a young Indonesian man who is educated by the Dutch toward the end of the Dutch colonial empire.

Latin America and the Caribbean

Chamoiseau, Patrick. *Texaco*. Trans. Rose-Miriam Rejous. New York: Vintage Books, 1998. Martinique: fiction, a family's chronicle of 150 years, starting with slavery on a sugar plantation.

Fuentes, Carlos. *The Years with Laura Díaz*. New York: Farrar, Straus, and Giroux, 2000. Mexico: fiction, the life of one woman through twentieth-century Mexico.

Garcia Marquez, Gabriel. *One Hundred Years of Solitude*. Trans. Gregory Rabassa. New York: Harper Perennial Library, 1998. Latin America: fiction, magical realist account of the Buendia clan over a 100-year period in the mythical village of Macondo.

Leon-Portilla, Miguel, ed. *The Broken Spears: The Aztec Account of the Conquest of Mexico*. Boston: Beacon Press, 1992. Mexico: nonfiction, the Spanish conquest of the Aztecs from the perspective of the conquered.

Matto de Turner, Clorinda. *Birds Without a Nest*. Austin: University of Texas Press, 1996. Peru: fiction, Indian life and the role of the Church.

———. *Torn from the Nest*. Oxford: Oxford University Press, 1998. Peru: fiction, colonial legacies and the exploitation of indigenous people in Peru.

Middle East

Ali, Tariq. *The Stone Woman*. London: Verso, 2000. Turkey: historical fiction examining the Ottoman Empire.

Daneshvar, Simin. *Savushun: A Novel.* Trans. M. R. Ghanoonparvar. Washington, D.C.: Mage, 1990. Iran: translation of the famous Persian novel originally written in 1969 by one of Iran's most famous fiction writers, chronicles a family during the Allied occupation of Iran in World War II through the eyes of a young wife and mother.

Farmaian, Sattareh Farman. *Daughter of Persia: A Woman's Journey from Her Father's Harem Through the Islamic Revolution.* New York: Crown, 1992. Iran: memoir, traces the personal struggle of one woman experiencing great personal and political turmoil.

Kazan, Frances. *Halide's Gift: A Novel.* New York: Random House, 2001. Turkey: fiction, examines relations between mothers and daughters in Istanbul, focusing on 1878–1909.

Pamuk, Orhan. *The White Castle: A Novel.* Trans. Victoria Holbrooke. New York: George Braziller, 1991. Turkey: historical fiction set in the seventeenth century, highlights Western traveler's experience in Constantinople.

Yarshater, Ehsan. *The Lion and the Throne.* Trans. Dick Davis. Washington, D.C.: Mage, 1998. Iran: stories from the Shahnameh of Ferdowsi; national epic of ancient Persia from the creation myth to the Arab-Islamic invasion of the seventh century.

PART 2

THE INTERNATIONAL ECONOMIC SYSTEM

Next we will be looking at the economies of the third world and considering whether the international economic system is contributing to the development or the underdevelopment of much of this world. The following chapters focus on INTERNATIONAL POLITICAL ECONOMY (IPE), or how economic and political issues interface. As an area of study, IPE's interest in the politics of economics includes a broad array of topics and concerns. In this part of the book we will focus on the gap in wealth and material well-being that exists between developed countries and less developed countries. The existence of such often massive inequality is a major source of friction between rich and poor; it is the source of what is sometimes referred to as the North-South conflict. People belonging to two dominant but diametrically opposed schools of thought, NEOLIBERALISM and STRUCTURALISM, have very different ideas about why this gap exists and how to bridge it. Procapitalist neoliberals are highly optimistic about the ability of the market to work its magic. On the other hand, structuralists characterize capitalism as exploitative. To varying degrees structuralists are pessimistic about the possibility of authentic development happening under the existing system. As you will see in the following chapters, the two schools of thought offer widely divergent answers for the questions we will consider: Why is the gap between rich and poor widening rather than narrowing with time? And why do the majority of the world's countries continue to suffer from underdevelopment? Is this underdevelopment due to poor decisions made by the countries themselves? Or is it due to the position of these countries in the international economic system, a capitalist system that is dominated by rich countries and the organizations working for them?

6

Globalization: Cause or Cure for Underdevelopment?

> The combination of extreme poverty and inequality between countries, and often also within them, is an affront to our common humanity.
> —Kofi Annan, UN Secretary-General[1]

Humor us for now and treat this chapter's title as a genuine question for analysis. Before you make up your mind, it is important to become familiar with two concepts fundamental to any discussion of INTERNATIONAL POLITICAL ECONOMY (IPE): GROWTH and DEVELOPMENT. Growth and development are generally considered to be desirable occurrences, and the terms are often used interchangeably to describe economic progress. However, growth and development are actually two very different things. While proponents of NEOLIBERALISM would argue that one needs growth to fund development, structuralists point out that one can certainly have growth without development, as has been the case in many less developed countries (LDCs). And, as the case of Cuba has demonstrated, although it is not easy, it is possible to have development without growth. That being said, let's clarify the differences in these two concepts.

Growth refers to an expansion in production, output, and perhaps income. The 1990s were largely a time of rapid economic growth; the annual output of the world economy grew from $31 trillion in 1990 to $42 trillion in 2000. Many less developed as well as developed countries experienced growth during that decade, but not all. For example, between 1990 and 1998, Brazil's economy grew by 30 percent, India's by 60 percent, and China's boomed, expanding by an astounding 130 percent.[2] Neoliberals argue that maximized economic efficiency produces growth, which is associated with rising profits. A common indicator of growth is gross domestic product (GDP) per capita, which is obtained by dividing the GDP by the population. GDP per capita (or the newer term, gross national income [GNI] per capita) supposedly gives one an idea of how much income the average citizen earns in a year (see Figure 6.1). However, keep in mind that income is only one, albeit important, measure of economic well-being, and GDP or GNI per capita assumes that income is divided completely equally—a situation that exists nowhere on earth. In fact, you can assume that in most cases, a few people will make much more than this figure and the majority will earn far less.

Figure 6.1   GNI per Capita for Rich, Middle Income, and Poor Countries (2001)

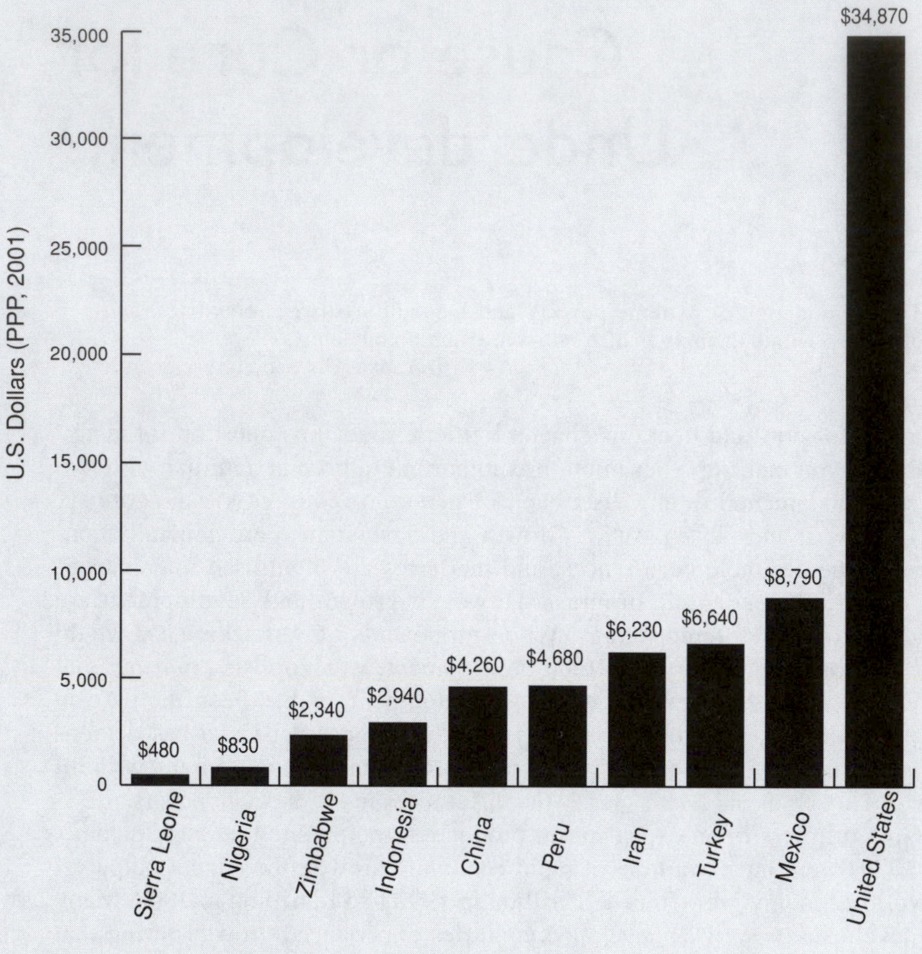

Sources: World Bank, World Development Indicators Database, 2002.
Note: Adjusted for purchasing power parity (PPP), a common index used to adjust income figures to reflect cost of living.

Whereas growth describes an increase in volume or output, development is generally understood to mean human development and pertains to issues of distribution. Development is a broad concept that is measured by composite indices such as the Physical Quality of Life Index (PQLI) and the Human Development Index (HDI) (see Figure 6.2). Both indices offer a more detailed picture of the economic well-being of a population. Growth rates alone tell us little about how people are doing. A state's economic growth rate does not reflect how wealthy the country is. It is not unusual for citizens of the fastest-growing economies to live in some of the worst conditions in the world (e.g., Mozambique in the late 1990s). For the past several years China has had one of the fastest growth rates on the planet, and a significant number of its citizens have seen their standards of living rise. Yet it would take another century of constant growth at these rates before average Chinese incomes would reach current U.S. income levels.[3]

As opposed to measures of growth, development indices give us a much clearer idea of people's overall quality of life. Three essential capabilities are commonly associated with development: the ability to lead a long and healthy life, to be knowledgeable, and to have access to the resources needed for a decent standard of living.[4] Take a look at Figure 6.3. Because it is comparable to the life expectancies of the citizens of many developed countries, a life expectancy of seventy-two years for Mexico suggests that the standard of living for Mexicans is relatively high. On the other hand, that the average Zimbabwean can expect to live to thirty-seven tells us that something is very wrong. The HDI and similar indicators tell us even more—not only in regard to life expectancy, but also about infant and child morbidity and mortality rates and maternal health, access to social services such as healthcare and education, and illiteracy (see Figure 6.4 and 6.5).

Development indices also include attention to other aspects of well-being: caloric intake, access to clean water and sanitation—access even to telephones

---

Figure 6.2 Human Development Index, 2001 World Rankings, Selected Countries

Norway	1	China	87
Australia	2	Jordan	88
United States	6	Iran	97
Italy	20	Vietnam	101
Spain	21	Indonesia	102
Israel	22	Tajikistan	103
Bahrain	40	Zimbabwe	117
Costa Rica	41	Myanmar	118
Bahama	42	Ghana	119
Mexico	51	Nigeria	136
Panama	52	Congo, Dem. Rep.	142
Belarus	53	Sierra Leone	162
Peru	73		
Ukraine	74		
Turkey	82		

Source: UNDP, *Human Development Report, 2001.*

Figure 6.3   Life Expectancy (2000)

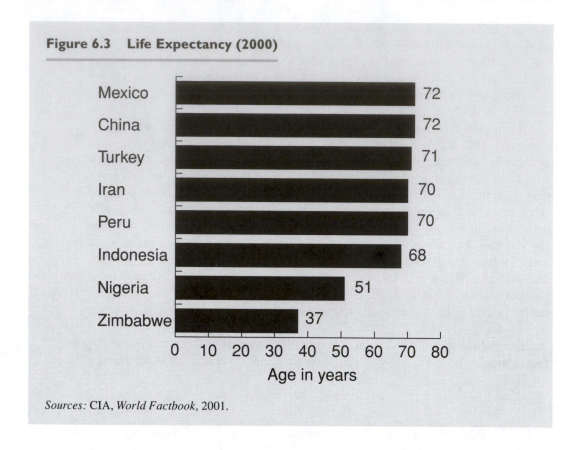

Sources: CIA, *World Factbook*, 2001.

and computers. Beyond traditional definitions that emphasize access, development has more recently been expanded to include considerations of people's range of choice. This dimension of development includes concerns such as political empowerment and participation, human security, protection of the environment, and gender equality. In this sense, human development clearly includes but goes beyond material needs. This understanding of development recognizes people's need to be creative and productive, to live in dignity, and to enjoy the sense of belonging to a community. Increasingly human development is being conceptualized as a development of the people, for the people, and by the people. It must therefore be understood as a process as well as an end; a process in which those targeted for development are participants in deciding how they will pursue it. In other words, human development is ultimately about freedom. It is as much about the process of enlarging people's choices as it is about people being free to access the things valuable to their well-being.[5]

The rate of advancement in every category of human development varies among countries. By some measures, such as a sense of community belonging, it could be argued that generally speaking, the citizens of less developed countries are far ahead of those living in developed countries. There has been some overall progress in terms of other, more widely recognized aspects of human development across the third world. For example, in these regions in the 1950s,

Figure 6.4   Infant Mortality Rate (2001)

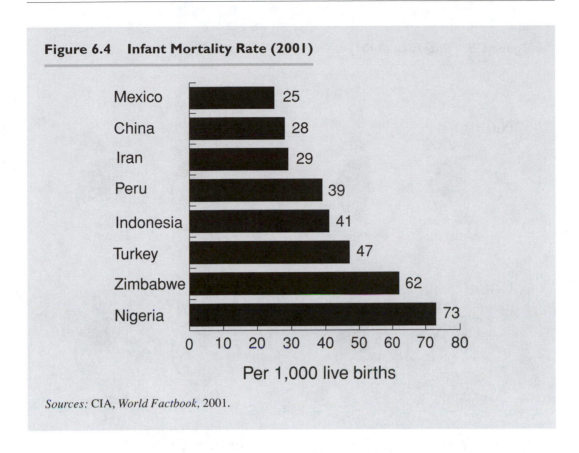

Per 1,000 live births

Sources: CIA, *World Factbook*, 2001.

15 percent of all children died before their fifth birthday (now 4 percent over-all).[6] However, not all have benefited from these improvements. Among LDCs, some are making faster progress on certain aspects of development (e.g., China on infant mortality rates, Peru on reducing the mortality rate of children under age five). For others, progress is much slower (e.g., Zimbabwe, where because of HIV/AIDS, life expectancy has actually regressed).

By comparing the information in Figures 6.1 through 6.5, you can see that growth and development are often very uneven. For years now, it has been widely recognized that developed countries control more than 60 percent of the world's income, whereas the poorest 20 percent of the world's population con-trol about 1 percent of the world's GNI.[7] Some non-Western countries, especial-ly those known as the newly industrializing countries (NICs), have made impressive progress in improving their citizens' standards of living. Neoliberals claim success even in communist-controlled China, where the number of des-perately poor people has dropped dramatically since the country began opening up to capitalism in 1978.

While we might assume that with time more countries will experience CON-VERGENCE, that they will eventually develop and "catch up" with developed countries, the fact is that the gap between the rich and poor is growing. The gap is largest in Latin America and it widened worldwide in the 1990s. In 1987 the

Figure 6.5   Illiteracy (2001)

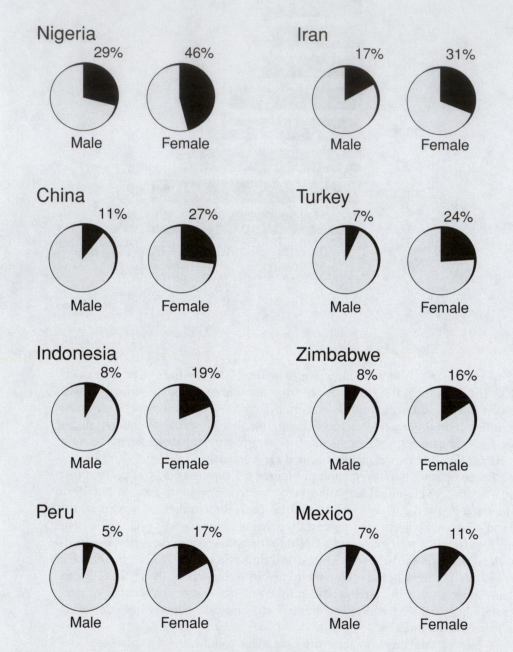

Sources: World Bank, World Development Indicators Database, 2001.
Note: Illiteracy is defined as the percentage of the population over age 15 that cannot read or write.

number of people living on less than one dollar a day was 1.2 billion. In 1999 that number was estimated variously between 1.2 billion and 1.5 billion. Raise that to two dollars a day and you are talking about the income of half of the world's population. While some analysts argue about whether the number of desperately poor has actually increased or declined slightly (see Figure 6.6), it is clear that a problem remains and it began long before the latest phase of GLOB-ALIZATION. The ratio of average incomes for the richest and poorest countries in the world grew from 9 to 1 in the late nineteenth century to 60 to 1 today. Even though there are serious pockets of poverty found throughout the developed world, the vast majority of the desperately poor live in non-Western countries. To think of it in another way, the average Ethiopian earns in a year what the average Swiss citizen earns every twenty-four hours.[8]

Yet even within the third world there are major differences in the levels of income and economic development. There are some significant economic differences between our case studies. China, Turkey, Iran, Peru, and Mexico are considered middle-income countries, while Indonesia (since its economic collapse in the late 1990s) and Zimbabwe are low-income. Although Nigeria is a major

Figure 6.6   Percentage of the Population Categorized as "Desperately Poor," by Region

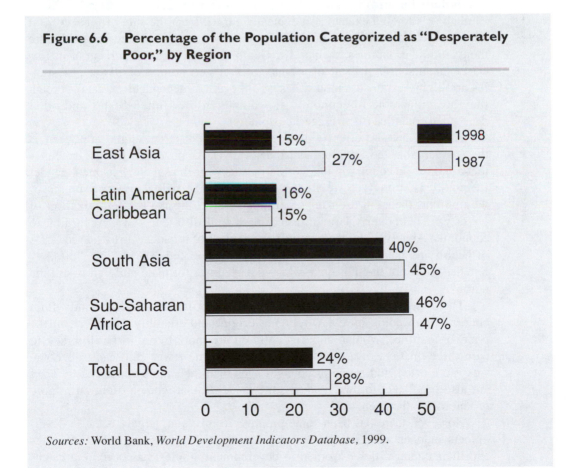

Sources: World Bank, *World Development Indicators Database,* 1999.

oil exporter (95 percent of exports), it is also one of the poorest countries in the world. Indonesia, Iran, and Mexico are also to varying degrees dependent on petroleum exports. For example, Mexico's economy is much more diversified than Nigeria's, spread between the agricultural, industrial, and service sectors. With the proliferation of MAQUILADORAS, or border assembly plants, its economy is increasingly based on the export of manufactured goods, as are the economies of China, Indonesia, and Turkey. Although the Indonesian and Turkish economies were faltering at the start of the twenty-first century, Mexico's recovery and China's phenomenal growth were largely based on the success of this sector.

China is still a low-income country, but it is also the third largest economy on earth (behind the United States and Japan). It enjoys regular trade surpluses and absorbs the vast majority of foreign investment going to LDCs. China, Mexico, and to a lesser extent Indonesia would qualify as emerging markets or NICs. With a few notable exceptions that we will discuss later in this chapter, these countries have sustained high growth rates for several years now. On the other hand, Peru and Zimbabwe are in somewhat less fortunate positions, in that they are exporters of less lucrative raw materials. Peru's economy is heavily dependent on mining and exports of fish products, and 30 percent of Zimbabwe's foreign exchange is typically earned from the sale of tobacco. But the relatively diverse base of their economies makes them the envy of more monocultural economies, such as The Gambia, which earns 90 percent of its foreign exchange from the sale of peanuts. Still, the economies of all the case studies are highly export-oriented. Because they are so dependent on sales abroad, they are vulnerable to economic slowdowns in the United States and other developed countries (their biggest customers).

Another measure offering a closer look and a different angle on poverty is the Gender Adjusted Development Index (GDI). Among other things, it tells us that although no country in the world treats its women as well as its men, gender inequality is strongly correlated with poverty. The rising impoverishment of women and their children is sometimes referred to as "the feminization of poverty." This poverty is manifested in several different ways. According to economist Amartya Sen, the comparative neglect of females worldwide in terms of health and nutrition has contributed to an estimated 100 million "missing" females—most of them in Asia, where a preference for male children is still the norm.[9]

There are certainly differences in the status of females between and within countries depending on class, regional origin, and ethnicity. However, in the poorest countries, women and girl children are more likely to be illiterate, to earn three-quarters of a male's wages, to consume fewer calories, to become sick more often, and to die at younger ages than their male counterparts. They are also less likely to own land, despite evidence that women often farm more productively than men.

However, there has been some progress in this area, largely because development planners now recognize that when women benefit, so do their families and their communities. "Women in development" (WID) has become a catch-phrase since the early 1970s. Prior to this time development planners largely neglected women. If they were included at all, it was mostly for instruction in home economics and family planning. Although WID projects continue to have their problems, the best ones are designed keeping in mind how women contribute to the overall development of their countries. Thanks to such a change of focus, female literacy rates have improved in several regions (although in 2000, two-thirds of the world's 876 million people who cannot read or write were female). In some countries the gender gap in primary and secondary education appears to be closing, and women have made impressive gains in attaining university educations.[10] We know now that the investment in education for females pays off with healthier children and smaller families. Research in several countries shows that the money women earn is more likely to be spent on their families, whereas men are often more likely to spend it on themselves.

Since the 1960s larger numbers of women in developed and less developed countries have been propelled into the paid work force by a number of factors, most notably economic necessity. Female participation in the labor force is up in China, from 7 percent in 1949 to 45 percent in the late 1990s. Increasingly employers are recruiting women because they are desperate enough to accept work and pay that men reject. Consequently, the feminization of poverty can occur even as more women are entering the FORMAL SECTOR. Women have a higher incidence of poverty than men and female poverty tends to be more severe than male poverty, despite the fact that around the world, women often work more hours than men. Female poverty is often intergenerational; overworked mothers may find that they must depend on the assistance of their daughters to make ends meet and to help them with childcare responsibilities. This situation helps to explain why on average globally, one in four girls who enter primary school drop out within four years.[11] For example, Turkish girls, especially those from poorer families, are twice as likely as boys to drop out of school, even before they reach the official compulsory level. Girls in rural China and many other countries face the same dilemma.[12]

Many of these girls leave school to help out on farms. Although women are crucial agricultural producers in much of the world, producing the food crops that ensure their families' survival, women rarely get equal access to appropriate technologies. Instead, women must rely on manual techniques that are heavily labor intensive, wasting time and energy. Part of the reason women lack access to tractors, fertilizers, and other inputs is because they lack credit. In Nigeria and elsewhere, women are often unable to obtain credit because they have no independent access to land. Where most of the population is employed in some capacity or another as agriculturists, access to land is the single most important factor determining well-being. But it is by no means the only one.

Although it should be viewed as being rooted in the denial of resources and opportunities to women, the feminization of poverty is often associated more than anything else with an increase in the number of female-headed households. It is important to remember that female-headed households are not a new phenomenon, yet their numbers are rising: it is estimated that 15–35 percent of all households in Africa, Latin America, and Asia have female heads. And whether or not there is a male present in the household, in more cases around the world women are becoming the main providers for the family. Although female-headed households are overrepresented among the poor, it is now recognized that homes headed by females do not always exist at a material disadvantage. Whereas we have tended to treat families headed by women as the poorest of the poor and the most powerless, clearly income and status vary among these households as they do in others. Women become heads of households for a variety of reasons, on permanent or temporary bases. Their husbands may migrate periodically in search of more lucrative work and leave them behind to farm. Some women head households after they are abandoned or widowed (this is especially common where young women marry much older men). The vast majority of the world's refugees are women and their children—often unaccompanied by a male relative. Still, it is important to recognize that in some cases, women *choose* to be household heads. Although women alone were once assumed to be powerless, a growing body of evidence now indicates that female heads of households employ a variety of coping mechanisms, and that such households may actually be more resourceful than those headed by males.

However, in general, rural women are the poorest of the poor, and the gap between their quality of life and that of the rest of the world is not narrowing in the way that it should—if what was being promoted in these countries was truly "development." Gender bias is a large part of why development initiatives have so often failed. Even where there has been impressive growth, we now know that economic growth alone will not eliminate inequality: societies must promote women's rights in order to reduce gender disparities.

When faced with these arguments about the underdevelopment of much of the world, neoliberals admit that yes, the gap between rich and poor is getting wider, but argue that the floor under the poor is rising steadily in much of the world. The gap between the rich and poor, known as RELATIVE POVERTY, may be growing. But, they emphasize, thanks to the spread of global capitalism, what is more important is that ABSOLUTE POVERTY is falling. Neoliberals are optimistic that an unequal concentration of wealth will eventually trickle down. As mentioned earlier, they believe that the concentration of wealth serves as a spur to investment, bringing faster economic growth. They maintain that all states reap benefits from the international economic exchange of goods and services. International cooperation is facilitated through the development of trading relationships. This is good for everyone, in that it promotes not only economic stability but also political stability. For the neoliberals, who dominate the governments of developed countries, the boardrooms of MULTINATIONAL CORPORATIONS (MNCs), and the international economic organizations and commercial banks known as INTERNATIONAL FINANCIAL INSTITUTIONS (IFIs), growth is everything. Countries cannot make reductions in poverty and they will not develop unless they raise growth rates first.

Globalization

The best way to raise growth rates, according to neoliberals, is to embrace globalization. In other chapters globalization is discussed more broadly, in terms of its sociocultural and political aspects, or how it has spilled over to affect just about everything: social relations (including class, race, and gender relations), culture, politics—even climate. In this chapter, we focus on globalization as an economic phenomenon. Globalization should be understood as the spread of capitalism worldwide. It is an all-embracing multidimensional force based in ECONOMIC LIBERALIZATION, or the adoption of capitalist, market-based reforms. Neoliberals are proponents of this economic liberalization, who argue for open markets and laissez-faire economics. The French term *laissez-faire* translates as "let it be." By this neoliberals mean that government's proper role is to withdraw from economics as much as possible and to "let economics be"—or allow the "invisible hand" of supply and demand to work. Market forces allowed to operate unimpeded by government interference maximize efficiency, according to these analysts.

Consequently, neoliberals regard globalization as a positive force that helps to further integrate the economies of the world into the international marketplace, often referred to as the international economic system. This system is capitalist, and it is supported by a number of very powerful institutions and organizations, most notably the INTERNATIONAL MONETARY FUND (IMF). Both the IMF and its counterpart, the WORLD BANK, were founded in the years after World War II, initially to assist in the reconstruction of Europe. Each of these multilateral institutions has its own mandate, but over the years their roles have changed and today there is some overlap in their functions. Both organizations are dominated by developed countries, since decisions in the international governmental organizations (IGOs) are made through weighted voting (that is, based on each member country's financial contribution). Structuralists describe this as a system based on "the golden rule" (whoever has the gold makes the rules). Whereas the World Bank's primary mission is to provide development assistance to the world's poorest countries, the IMF serves in a number of capacities, including the promotion of global economic stability. One way the IMF promotes stability is by serving as the lender of last resort to countries in economic crisis. It distributes loans to countries whose economies are failing.

According to the dominant players in this system, further integration into the world economy is exactly what underdeveloped countries need. LDCs should embrace globalization and raise growth rates by trading more in the international marketplace and competing to attract foreign capital. Created to update the GENERAL AGREEMENT ON TARIFFS AND TRADE (GATT), the WORLD TRADE ORGANIZATION (WTO) works to promote free trade by providing a forum for discussion of the unresolved issues that cause friction between states. Established in 1995, the body has some influence, since its 145 members (now including China) account for approximately 97 percent of the world's trade.[13] Neoliberals contend that because global capitalism is the best hope for the development of the third world, the WTO provides an invaluable service. The free flow of technology, capital, and ideas is raising living standards higher, faster, and for more people than at any other time in history. To take part in the feast, they argue that LDCs need only make a few necessary adjustments to liberalize their economies.

Part of what makes globalization such a fascinating process to study is that it can have positive as well as negative effects. It can contribute to increased cooperation and unity while at the same time creating conditions for fragmentation and conflict. As Thomas Friedman has pointed out, globalization is everything and its opposite. It can be both incredibly empowering and incredibly coercive. Both proponents and critics of globalization agree on its overwhelming force. Neoliberals contend that when it comes to LDCs' absorption into the international economy, the question isn't so much "When?" as it is "How?"[14]

Yet structuralists maintain that the majority of LDCs already share a common position within the world economy. They are relatively powerless within it. LDCs as a whole have very little influence in setting the agenda or making decisions for the international economic system. Through its enforcement of the existing rules of trade, the World Trade Organization further marginalizes LDCs. Although LDCs are lining up to join the WTO, in general developed countries are much more enthusiastic about the existence of the WTO than are LDCs, many of which view the organization as just another way for developed countries to protect their advantageous position within the existing system. For example, the WTO makes it very difficult for LDCs to protect infant industries and diversify their economies. Structuralists also accuse the organization of selectively dismantling trade barriers in a lopsided liberalization that is skewed in favor of industrialized countries and multinational corporations. In some cases, WTO rules that promote free trade in manufactured goods force LDCs to open up their markets to the products of developed countries, while the products of LDCs (especially agricultural goods, such as orange juice) are shut out of the former's markets.

Ironically, for all their talk about "free trade," it is subsidies and various protectionist measures by developed countries that are making it hard for much of the third world to earn an honest living through trade. According to the World Bank, if developed countries eliminated all barriers to imports from Africa, the region's exports would rise by 14 percent (an annual increase worth approximately $2.5 billion).[15] The free trade rules enforced by the WTO protect LDCs only as long as they remain producers of raw materials for export, particularly goods that do not compete with those of developed countries. According to a World Bank study, the average tariff that developed countries impose on manufactured goods from LDCs is four times higher than the average tariff they impose on each other's goods.[16] This kind of treatment is true of agricultural and other products as well, which are zealously protected by developed countries. In what have been called "the banana wars," the preferential treatment small Caribbean and African banana producers enjoyed in European Union (EU) markets was challenged by the U.S. government on behalf of U.S.-based MNCs operating in Central America.

Globalization's critics contend that non-Western governments are effectively immobilized by the combined influence of developed countries' governments, corporations, and international financial institutions. They argue that agents of globalization, such as the International Monetary Fund and the World Trade Organization, wield such power over LDCs that these countries are in effect being recolonized. Yes, LDCs can bring their complaints to the WTO, but they frequently cannot afford costly legal battles. Poor countries can't pay for the lawyers and lobbyists the MNCs and rich countries can hire to find loopholes in trade rules and buy the influence they need. The WTO's decisions are binding on members, and those that fail to comply with its rules risk potentially crippling sanctions. In sum, the SOVEREIGNTY of LDCs is steadily being eroded as governments give over to the IMF, MNCs, and developed countries their decisionmaking authority.

Trade

As you may have guessed by now, structuralists argue trenchantly against the economic orthodoxy, while neoliberals accuse structuralists of overstating their case and ask what feasible alternative they offer. This is the case for trade as well. According to neoliberals, the best way to jump-start growth rates is to adopt a strategy of trade liberalization or free trade. They maintain that the wealthiest countries have built their success on trade and (with a few important exceptions) by being open to competition. In fact, they argue that there is not a single example in modern history of a country successfully developing without trading and integrating with the global economy.[17] On the other hand, they point out, it is no coincidence that the poorest countries in the world are the ones that have been less than friendly to free trade. The countries that are worst off have adopted a variety of protectionist policies, artificially "protecting" domestic producers by slapping tariffs on imports. This kind of government interference with trade is notoriously inefficient, argue the neoliberals. LDCs that have adopted market reforms and opened their economies, such as China and Chile, have reaped the largest gains in terms of standards of living. Simply put, open economies grow much faster than closed economies.[18]

Neoliberalism's critics argue that openness does not guarantee wealth; a country's wealth depends less on ease of trade than it does on what is being traded.[19] Openness involves great risk, and the countries experiencing relative success are few and far between. Structuralists recognize that the impetus toward trade liberalization and embrace of globalization is nothing new. In fact, they argue that the reason why so much of the third world is underdeveloped today is because of the position it was assigned during colonialism or within the NEW INTERNATIONAL DIVISION OF LABOR (NIDL). What is new about the international division of labor today is that a handful of LDCs are moving in to fill voids in manufacturing that are left as developed countries mature into service-based economies. The textile and steel mills that were once so important to the U.S., British, and German economies have since moved south, creating this new division of labor.

However, there are aspects of the NIDL that are actually not so new at all. The expansion of regional and product specialization in this NIDL is based in the principle of COMPARATIVE ADVANTAGE. Seeking to increase efficiency through specialization in production, the colonizers created monocultural economies throughout the third world. This principle, widely revered by liberals for hundreds of years, is based in the assumption that countries differ in their ability to produce certain goods based on their natural resources, labor, and other factors. In order to maximize wealth, countries should specialize in producing goods for which they have a comparative advantage. Today the vast majority of LDCs continue to produce many of the same goods assigned to them during the days of colonialism—unprocessed primary goods for export. This makes good business sense, according to neoliberals. By concentrating on a few goods for export, LDC economies can become more fully integrated into the world economy. With the hard currency they earn from the sale of their raw materials, LDCs can pay their debts and import everything else they need (including food, fuel, manufactured goods, etc.). Moreover, if all countries liberalize their economies and open up to trade, it will mean that businesses will have to work harder to be competitive. The result will be improved and less expensive products—a benefit to all.

However, neoliberalism's critics argue that it isn't quite that simple. Although many people have given up and left for the cities, the majority of the world's population continue to live in rural areas and work as farmers. However, during colonialism rural communities were disrupted, many subsistence farmers were forced off the land, and small plots were consolidated into large plantations. People living in the third world today work plots of various sizes; most people are small holders or are landless. The landless often drift around the countryside looking for seasonal work, and are employed as tenant farmers or as migrant laborers on much larger farms or plantations. Small farmers in developed and less developed countries are rapidly being displaced as they find that they can no longer support themselves through farming and are increasingly forced to sell their land to huge agribusinesses. For example, until recently in Zimbabwe, large commercial farms produced more than 40 percent of the country's exports. What small farmers had in common is that they once practiced subsistence farming. Farmers ate what they produced and sold the surplus. However, today the vast majority of countries have moved away from food production and can no longer be considered subsistence economies. Rather, these are export-based economies, increasingly centered on the production of commodities known as cash crops. Coffee, flowers, sisal, and bananas are just a few examples of cash crops, which are produced for sale abroad (mostly to consumers in developed countries). Mines producing bauxite, copper, and diamonds, and aquaculture and ranches producing salmon and beef are also sites for the production of cash crops. What these commodities have in common is that they are raw materials, or unprocessed goods that will most likely be sent elsewhere for manufacture into finished goods.

Critics of this situation argue that as producers of raw materials, LDCs are assigned a disadvantageous position in the world economic system, and not only because most raw materials are vulnerable to sometimes dramatic price fluctuations, which make it extremely difficult to plan or budget from year to year. Any introduction to economics tells you that labor adds value. Because raw materials are unprocessed, they will always fetch a lower price than they would once processed into a finished good. The prices of exports by developed countries (mostly finished goods) have risen, while those of most of Africa's raw materials have been falling (by 25 percent in 1997–1999).[20]

The "terms of trade," or the overall relationship between the prices of exported and imported goods, are therefore inherently disadvantageous to LDC economies. Producers of raw materials must struggle to turn out larger volumes just to earn the hard currency to pay the higher-priced finished goods they must import. The laws of supply and demand simply work against the LDC. For example, Ghanaian farmers can work harder to produce more cocoa for sale on the world market, but the harder they work the less they will earn, since an oversupply of cocoa will drive down its price. Worse, prices are driven down even further as farmers inadvertently add to the problem of oversupply. They produce even more when prices are down, since it takes a bigger crop to scrape by. There is very little producers of most raw materials can do about this situation as long as their economies remain centered around the production of cash crops for export. No single country can demand higher prices for its goods, since there are many other producers competing for the sale. And demand for most raw materials is relatively elastic. Even if producers of any single raw material could form a producer's club or cartel to obtain a stronger bargaining position, consumers could turn to substitutes. They could increase their own domestic production of the good, or simply adjust their consumption of it. It is only because demand for oil is relatively inelastic that the oil producers' cartel, the Organization of Petroleum-Exporting Countries (OPEC), has been able to raise oil prices by slowing down production and restricting oil supplies.

Therefore, structuralists argue that the world economic system as it currently exists works to reinforce LDCs' dependence and leaves them vulnerable to a variety of problems. Having an undiversified economy is like putting all your eggs in one basket. LDC economies are vulnerable not only to swings in the world market price for their goods (the prices for many raw materials have fallen continually since the 1960s), but also to blight, drought, and other causes of crop failure. For example, Peru's fishing industry, a crucial sector of the economy, is only now recovering from the effects of El Niño in 1998. Moreover, over-reliance on one export has left countries that were once self-sufficient in the production of food crops, like Nigeria, now dependent on food imports. Even worse, some countries with hungry populations produce food crops for export. Instead of ensuring that its own population is fed, Brazil produces soybeans to feed livestock. Brazil and several other South American countries are famous for their cheap and tasty beef, which is sold on the world market to MNCs such as Burger King. Whereas the IMF and donor agencies urge LDC economies to hang in there and continue to develop their export-based economies, critics maintain that such a path will never produce healthy economies that can support their populations.

Until now, most LDCs have had little choice but to accept this advice. And although many countries have attempted to diversify their economies, it is easier said than done. There may be entrenched elites within the country who profit from having the economy structured as it is. Governments that are willing to open up new sectors are limited in the funds available to change things. It takes

A petty trader on his way to the fish market (UN Photo)

time and capital to diversify an economy. Moreover, the skills of local inhabitants are likely to be concentrated in the production of what are now traditional cash crops, and the infrastructure may only tie together existing points of production to points of exit.[21]

Even more debilitating than a monocultural economy is no economy at all. Many of the very poorest LDCs have little or nothing to sell on the world market. Some governments are so desperate to earn hard currency that they have joined the booming business of refuse disposal. As the citizens of developed countries become more aware of the dangers of pollutants to human health and comfort, they have organized into NIMBY ("not in my backyard") movements. For years, more affluent communities have actively searched for other places to dispose of their refuse. And for years poor neighborhoods in developed countries had become the sites of dumps and landfills. However, mounting pressure from these communities and regulations about containing wastes in developed countries have produced an international trade in refuse removal. Meanwhile, many LDC businesses (and some governments) that find it difficult making ends meet from the sale of cash crops are now competing to house the garbage and toxic wastes of developed countries. This practice of wealthy (predominantly white) populations dumping their often-poisonous wastes into poor (predominantly black or brown) communities is known as "environmental racism."

Burgeoning industries such as refuse removal are only the latest examples of how LDCs have attempted to cope with their weak position within the international economic system. While some initiatives are best understood simply as coping mechanisms, others were undertaken with the aim of changing the place of LDCs within the system. IMPORT SUBSTITUTION INDUSTRIALIZATION is an example of one such effort. In an attempt to follow the developed country path to development through industrialization, many LDCs have sought to break out of the mold as exporters of unfinished goods and lessen their dependence on imports. However, for a variety of reasons, most notably their inability to break into the markets of developed countries or compete with multinational corporations, this experiment often failed. Turkey adopted this model in the 1930s, but its STATE-OWNED ENTERPRISES (SOEs) were never efficient. As late as the 1970s Turkey was still overwhelmingly dependent on the export of agricultural products. However, since then its SOEs have been sold off to private interests that have had more success in building a textile industry. Still, most countries of Africa, Latin America, and the Middle East remain locked in their position as producers of cash crops in export-based economies.

Interestingly, until recently it was East Asia that liberals pointed to as evidence that capitalist development worked. The export-driven economies of the FOUR TIGERS, Hong Kong, Singapore, South Korea, and Taiwan—the most successful NICs—were based in the production of light manufactured goods. For decades, growth rates regularly exceeded 5 percent per year. Per capita income grew more rapidly in these NICs than anywhere else in the world. Between 1960 and 1990, for example, real per capita income in South Korea grew from $900 to $6,700. There were similar gains in life expectancy, literacy rates, and an overall reduction in poverty in South Korea and the other NICs. Most impressively, on average, the percentage of South Koreans living under the poverty line during this period was reduced from 60 to 20 percent.

However, analysts have always disagreed about whether the experience of the Four Tigers could be replicated elsewhere. Since the Asian economic crisis of the late 1990s, more serious questions have been raised about the use of the model. Neoliberals attributed the success of the NICs to their open economies, embrace of capitalism, and export-oriented approach as well as their well-educated, disciplined, and hardworking labor force. In addition, the NICs were credited with having an innovative entrepreneurial class, a high rate of savings, and relatively well-developed infrastructures.

Still, the NICs were hardly examples of success based on less state involvement in economies. This was not laissez-faire capitalism at work. Under the Asian model of STATE CAPITALISM adopted in the 1950s, governments were heavily involved in nurturing and protecting industries and businesses until they were globally competitive. Although there is some heterogeneity among the East Asian NICs, in most cases these states undertook what is called an export offensive. Throughout the region, governments manipulated nationalist interests to promote economic mobilization. Under this policy, the state became a driving force directing the economy with the aim of improving international competitiveness. The South Korean, Taiwanese, and other NIC governments directed economic growth through their allocation of credit to priority sectors. Scarcely a case of the invisible hand at work, these governments played an active, catalytic role in guiding investment strategies. They offered incentives and disincentives to prod the economy toward particular exporting industries. Most of these industries were initially light manufacturing and labor intensive but gradually became higher tech. These infant industries were nurtured and protected; the state intervened aggressively and employed protectionist practices to ensure that domestic firms could compete with foreigners.

At the same time that the governments of NICs were insulating their infant industries from foreign competition, they avidly sought to attract foreign investment. Decades ago South Korea and Taiwan successfully lured investors by offering tax incentives, keeping unions weak, and doing away with minimum-wage legislation. For many years, these East Asian governments could only be characterized as dictatorships determined to modernize. These authoritarian regimes manipulated nationalist identities to mobilize the population to work and sacrifice for the good of the nation. The government provided little in terms of social welfare. Air and water pollution soared. Political and civil rights were forsaken for economic growth, and the NIC governments used repressive mechanisms to resist popular pressure for change.

It is important to note that incomes in Taiwan, South Korea, and the other "emerging market economies" of Asia did gradually improve, as have quality of life indicators and (with the notable exception of China) respect for political and civil liberties. But it is primarily because of this policy of aggressive government intervention in the economy that the NICs were able to capture the market on certain goods. Today the East Asian NICs make up the world's largest source of electronic components. The NICs based their success on the partnerships that their governments made with businesses to raise productivity and capture an increasing share of the world market. Although this close relationship has been characterized as "crony capitalism" because it is associated with corrupt practices, it has also resulted in the creation of huge economic conglomerates. These economies were so competitive and their performances so strong that in some cases they dominated the market in certain goods. By the mid-1990s many of the NICs enjoyed trade surpluses with developed countries. As a result, the NICs provided the exception in a pattern of non-Western underdevelopment.

Foreign Investment

Since the days of colonialism (and often predating it), multinational corporations have been active throughout the third world. In LDCs these businesses have dominated the agriculture and mining sectors. Until thirty years ago, relatively few of the world's manufactured goods were produced in LDCs. However, that has been changing, as some non-Western countries have industrialized, and as more and more MNCs are looking to lower the costs of production by creating assembly plants overseas. MNCs are highly influential non-governmental actors in the process of globalization; their investment decisions often mean the difference in whether a country is increasingly drawn into the global economy, or marginalized by it.

Neoliberals and their critics agree that MNCs are extremely powerful eco-

Figure 6.7 The Asian "Flu"

What began as a currency crisis in Thailand in 1997 quickly spread through the rest of the region and became known as the Asian crisis or the Asian "flu." Actually a multifaceted problem, the collapse is most commonly attributed to the euphoria over the high and sustained growth rates enjoyed by the East Asian NICs. This euphoria gave rise to over-confidence and excessive speculation and risk-taking, resulting in overborrowing and overlending, as well as other poor economic decisions. For years banks protected cronies and hid bad investments. However, once it was suspected that the banks had overextended themselves, there was a rapid loss of confidence in the East Asian economies. Currencies quickly devalued, banks called in their debts, and panic spread as foreign investors fled. These once highly touted "emerging market economies" fell into a downward spiral, stock markets crashed, and the bubble burst. Once the economic miracle upheld by neoliberals for the rest of the developing world to emulate, the NICs had sunk into near zero growth rates and recession.

This dramatic downturn translated into substantial economic hardship for the majority of people living in these countries. The impact was not felt evenly. As NICs accepted AUSTERITY PLANS in return for emergency bailout loans from the IMF, formal-sector jobs available to them dwindled, while women's responsibility for their families soared. Now-unemployed locals put migrant laborers out of work. In Indonesia during this period, per capita income was cut in half and inflation jumped from the single digits to 80 percent. The depreciation of the rupiah was the worst since the Great Depression, and the number of Indonesians living in poverty rose from a relatively impressive low of 11 percent to a disturbing high of 25 percent. A host of repercussions came on the heels of the economic crisis, and hit the other countries of the region as well: the number of school dropouts climbed, as did the rates of crime, prostitution, and other social problems.[22]

nomic entities with an enormous scope and range of activities, including banking, pharmaceuticals, industrial goods, oil, foodstuffs, service—virtually any consumer item or need. Coordinating production on a global scale, they are hardly newcomers to the global economy; their precursors, such as the Dutch East India Company, were at the forefront of colonialism. Then and now, as economic units the largest MNCs easily dwarf the vast majority of LDC economies. For example, based on the company's revenue, the world's largest MNC, General Motors, is also the world's twenty-second largest economy. The economic power of MNCs is growing rapidly and although the number of MNCs is estimated at 10,000, their power is becoming more concentrated in a few huge firms. The world's 500 largest MNCs now account for more than half of the world's trade and 80 percent of all foreign investment. Analysts have been predicting for years that soon the vast majority of the world's production will be controlled by a handful of MNCs. Such predictions seem to be coming true, as nearly every day one learns of another acquisition, merger, or buyout between these corporate behemoths.

MNCs are headquartered in what we call parent countries (although some LDCs are the headquarters for these businesses, Japan, the United States, and the EU countries are the big three), and it is in parent countries where decisions are made, and to which profits return. Yet because of their size some predict that in the not-too-distant future the power of MNCs may overtake that of the nation-state. Our primary identity may change as we come to view ourselves more as employees of the company for which we work, rather than as citizens of the country in which we live. In many ways the power of MNCs already rivals that of the nation-state. While MNCs have been accused of being agents of their national governments, the governments of their parent countries are often put to work for the corporation's interests. U.S. interventions to protect MNCs in Iran, Guatemala, and Chile are just a few examples of where political meddling, including the overthrow of LDC governments, has occurred when MNCs and developed countries have perceived a government's politics as threatening to the economic status quo.

However, today it is increasingly common to hear that the once cozy relationship between corporations and their parent countries is over. Multinational because of their international operations, MNCs are truly stateless entities, not obligated to any particular country. For years, the U.S. and other governments have bemoaned their inability to force MNCs to comply with their foreign policies (such as sanctions against Iran, for example).

As you may already be sensing, the role that MNCs play in the development of LDCs is extremely controversial. However, stripped of all the politics, MNCs are simply for-profit corporations with activities abroad stemming from foreign investment. Through their investments these businesses establish subsidiaries or branches in what are known as host countries. In the third world, the vast majority of MNC activity is concentrated in a few big emerging markets such as Mexico, China, and Brazil. Leading the pack is China, which attracts more than one-third of all foreign investment in LDCs. There and elsewhere, MNCs are just managing the production cycle as they cut costs by hiring smaller firms as subcontractors. For example, the Gap markets tee shirts with the Gap label made by small, no-name factories in El Salvador and elsewhere.

As for-profit enterprises, MNCs are constantly seeking to improve their profit margins. Two of the easiest ways of doing this are to lower overhead costs and expand markets. That is precisely what MNCs are doing, whether they are investing in LDCs or in other developed countries. So much foreign investment goes to China because MNCs want access to the potential spending power of the country's 1.3 billion consumers as much as they want the ultracheap labor. According to Kathleen Schalch, at the turn of the twenty-first century some workers in China averaged a wage of three cents per hour.[23]

Although some would argue that until these workers are paid a decent wage, they are unlikely to become the market the MNCs so look forward to, neoliberals urge us to take the long view and consider the presence of MNCs around the world generally as a positive force. They contend that MNCs are an important agent for growth, generating wealth through their ability to invest freely around the world and their efficient use of the world's resources. To quickly sum up the pro-MNC argument: when these corporations invest abroad by opening factories, mines, or plantations, they are moving forward the development of the host country in a number of ways. First, MNCs create jobs, hiring people who are now earning a wage. Frequently employees of MNCs earn more than they could elsewhere in the economy. Chinese factories with U.S. investors are said to pay more generous wages than state-owned enterprises.

And there may be other benefits. Where Americans have invested in joint ventures with Chinese firms, workers are said to have more rights, more institutionalized procedures for filing grievances, and so on.[24] Western and non-Western proponents of foreign investment maintain that labor and other activists living in developed countries who call for international standards (such as an international minimum wage) are actually just trying to protect the jobs of workers living in rich countries. Neoliberals argue that activists critical of free trade and foreign investment are "the well-intentioned but ill-informed" led around by "the ill-intentioned but well-informed (protectionist unions and anarchists)."[25] Neoliberals maintain that consumer boycotts of the goods made in these factories are actually hurting workers in LDCs because such boycotts mean a loss of jobs. They offer examples of assembly-line workers in El Salvador, China, and Vietnam who are horrified that the United States would try to "help" them by putting them out of work. The MNCs are the ones "helping" them, by giving them a chance to earn a wage.

And by offering people the opportunity to work for a wage, MNCs may be assisting in the development of the community as well. The creation of jobs has a spin-off effect for the larger economy, as MNC workers will spend their earnings on rent, food, and so forth in the local economy. In addition, the wages earned will create more demand for imported goods, including goods produced by other subsidiaries of the MNC. Furthermore, MNC employees will become skilled workers, familiar with the new technologies the MNC brings in with it when it sets up shop. MNC employees and host countries in general are said to benefit from the corporation's presence, in that by simply being there, MNCs alter "traditional" attitudes. They are said to stimulate the spirit of innovation and entrepreneurship, teach important lessons about competitiveness, and create marketing networks that can extend into and benefit the local economy.[26]

On the other hand, critics of globalization and MNCs in particular contend with virtually every argument the neoliberals put forward. Instead of being the beacons for change, the structuralists are joined by others who maintain that these corporations are actually predatory monopolies that compound an already skewed distribution of wealth. MNC activities widen the growing gap between rich and poor—not only between developed and less developed countries, but also within them. A local elite, known as the COMPRADOR class, dominates LDC economies and political systems, and makes sweetheart deals with these corporations to exploit their own people. In return for kickbacks, a series of Nigerian dictators and their cronies have nurtured a very special relationship with Royal Dutch/Shell and other oil companies, to join in the exploitation of the country's riches for the benefit of a few. Theirs is a reciprocal relationship in which compradors work to maintain a climate conducive to MNC interests, and the corporations in turn use their wealth and political clout to help keep local aristocracies in power. If the relationship falls apart, or the population elects a government less compliant and willing to accede to MNC prerogatives, MNCs have been known to "help create" a government more to their liking (as in the case of Iran).

Moreover, critics argue that even ordinary citizens of developed countries are at the mercy of these giants, not only as workers to be displaced in the constant quest for ever-cheaper labor, but also as consumers who are overcharged for goods made for a pittance. Over the last couple of decades, MNCs have sought to lower the costs of overhead even more by setting up shop in EXPORT PROCESSING ZONES (EPZs) around the world, in countries such as Mauritius and Sri Lanka. Corporations are attracted to EPZs because there they can pay minimal taxes and operate without being held to the environmental standards they would find at home. Countries (including developed countries) have been accused of taking part in a "race to the bottom," diluting environmental regulations and labor laws in order to attract investment. And it is working: corporations are finding it profitable to relocate for all of these reasons—especially for guarantees of cheap and controllable labor.

Once there, they set up assembly plants where much of the work is labor intensive and low skilled. In recent years EPZ employers have become notorious for hiring females and paying them too little to live on, with the rationalization (true or not) that there is a male breadwinner—a female worker's wages are mere "lipstick money"—and need be only supplemental. In addition, corporations base their preference for female labor on stereotypical ideas about females being "naturally" patient and better suited for the mind-numbing tedious labor demanded by MNCs. Female workers are assumed not only to be more dexterous (important for sewing operations and in microprocessing computer chips, for example), but also to be more docile than men, more accepting of male (managerial) authority, and less likely to join unions.

However, now another class of workers is joining the labor force—one with more nimble fingers who are even more likely to submit to fatherlike authority. Increasingly child labor is replacing female labor as the most desired labor pool. According to the International Labor Organization, nearly 250 million children under age fourteen are working full time in the third world. The states tolerating the worst child labor practices are India, China, and Morocco. One of the most publicized tragedies resulting from the exploitation of children was the explosion of a Chinese school that was doubling as a fireworks factory in 2001. Although the government at first vehemently denied such a cottage industry existed, more than forty people (most of them children) died in the blast, where third graders were mounting fuses on fireworks as part of a "work for study" program. In Peru, where that country's president once worked as a shoeshine boy, the legal minimum age for child workers is twelve—the youngest in Latin America. Still, it is estimated that more than half a million children under age twelve work in Peru, particularly in rural areas. Child labor is especially common in the gold-mining regions of the Amazon, since their small size enables eight- and nine-year-olds to work deep in the mines in narrow shafts. Child labor is also increasingly common in Nigeria and elsewhere, and it is likely to continue to grow as long as corporations seek to remain competitive while increasing profits—and as long as consumers demand ever-cheaper goods.

In addition to paying wages that can only be described as exploitative, MNCs are criticized for cutting corners and ignoring abuses, exposing their workers to SWEATSHOP conditions. These corporations have long been associated

Figure 6.8   Child Labor: A Benefit to the Child?

The issue of child labor may be more complex that it seems. Some advocates for children argue that it can actually be a good thing. There are many different types of child labor, and the image many of us associate with it—of children working in dangerous conditions for a pittance—is truly horrific. Yet just 5 percent of the world's child workers are involved in the production of exported goods. Most of the rest are working (as generations of children did before them) for their families on farms, in cottage industries, or as apprentices to artisans. Some advocates for children argue that Western indignation and efforts to ban all child labor only throw the poor into greater misery.

Moral outrage can be counterproductive. For example, when it was reported that Wal-Mart was selling clothes made by children in Bangladesh, a boycott forced factories to fire child workers, who ended up going into more dangerous industries, including prostitution. In addition, the Western uproar may close a few factories, but it does precious little to address the root of the problem—poverty. In fact, these well-meaning interventions often wind up increasing families' hardships, without addressing the global inequities that create mass suffering. In some cases, such "human rights activism" is injurious not only to economic well-being, but social and cultural rights as well, as traditional art forms handed down through generations are lost.

Yet traditions are not always benevolent. In many parts of the world, child labor is the last vestige of modern slavery. And there are those who argue that if children are working, they aren't attending school or aren't left with the freedom to simply be a kid. Therefore, some advocates for children are coming up with ingenious ways of validating the argument that work in itself can teach important lessons, while creating more opportunities for children to learn in formal settings as well. In Morocco, where some argue that the abolition of child labor would mean the loss of traditional arts and handicrafts, the UN International Children's Fund (UNICEF) is trying to speak to the concerns of all by bringing teachers into the workhouses. In India, parents are being taught to adjust their labor needs so that their children can also attend school. Increasingly, children's advocates are moving away from an absolutist stance that views all child labor as abuse. They are coming to realize that working with the family and community can help to shape children's identities and give them a valuable sense of responsibility and belonging.[27]

with abusive practices such as forced overtime and corporal punishment, and "sweatshop belts" run through parts of Asia and Latin America. In China and Mexico, it is not unusual for workers to live and work in compounds behind locked gates and high walls surrounded by barbed wire. In many parts of the world, forced labor and prison labor are routine. Relatively speaking, the lucky ones are those working in effect as indentured servants, often from 7 A.M. until 11 P.M. seven days a week, with only one day off each month.[28] In factories around the world, workers must handle adhesives and other toxic substances with their bare hands, in brightly lit, poorly ventilated, and sometimes deafening environments. Of course, there is variation in practice, but it is not uncommon for workers to be subjected to an astonishing array of rules and corporal punishments. There are often strict guidelines limiting bathroom breaks and talking. The punishment for violations can be quite creative. Vietnamese subcontractors working for Nike were exposed for the practice of "sun drying": forcing workers to kneel for hours prostrate in the hot sun. Elsewhere, distractible children are kept at their work by the requirement that they hold a matchbox under their chins—with the promise that they will be beaten if they drop it to talk or even look around the room. Women in particular are subjected to sexual harassment and humiliation, such as the compulsory pregnancy testing that is policy in *maquiladoras* in Mexico and elsewhere in Latin America.

Moreover, MNCs' critics dispute the inference that host-country populations benefit from exposure to the technologies the corporation brings. Nor do most workers learn a skill: the vast majority remain unskilled or low skilled and very few local people ever make it to the ranks of management (a position often reserved for nationals of the parent country). Instead of raising productivity by promoting the use of labor-intensive technologies that are relatively cheap, simple to use, and labor enhancing, the technologies these companies do introduce are often inappropriate and capital intensive. Such technologies are not well suited to the needs of LDCs, since they are acquired at a significant cost. Not only are they expensive and sophisticated (requiring fossil fuels, costly imported spare parts, and highly skilled technicians for maintenance), but worse yet, these machines serve as devices of labor replacement. They replace the need for human labor and add to already high unemployment rates.

Another topic for dispute concerns MNC claims about the transmission of values such as modernity and entrepreneurship. Many people are disturbed by such claims because they smack of ethnocentrism. Too often people say "modernity" when they mean "Westernization." By implication then, whatever is non-Western becomes lumped into the category of "backward." Neoliberals assume that this modernity is a universally desired goal, when in fact what most of the world's people want is an escape from their material poverty. People of the third world may want the comforts and choices many Westerners enjoy; this doesn't necessarily mean that they want to become Western. Furthermore, what MNCs are selling isn't modernity, it is the image of modernity. These firms are actually creating dependence by aggressively marketing their products and seeking to alter consumer tastes and attitudes through glossy and often deceptive advertising campaigns.[29]

The worst example of how MNCs prey on the desperation of the poor is the Nestlé baby formula scandal of the 1970s. In an attempt to create an even more profitable market for its powdered milk products, Nestlé undertook a massive advertising campaign of misinformation. Targeting countries with appallingly high infant mortality rates, the company designed slick advertisements that strongly suggested that their infant formula was preferable to breast milk. While such claims are patently false on a number of counts, Nestlé was not satisfied with taking the money of desperate parents. In some countries, it went even further to guarantee itself a market. Ostensibly offered as a welcoming gift, the company went about providing two weeks' worth of baby formula "samples" to mothers leaving clinics with newborns—without informing them that if they used the formula for two weeks, their milk would dry up. The UN GENERAL ASSEMBLY condemned Nestlé for these actions, but less dramatic forms of abuse by other MNCs, such as the sale of adulterated baby food in poor countries, have continued to occur.

Under fire for ethical, environmental, and other lapses, many of today's

MNCs are fighting negative publicity and working hard to appear to be humanizing big business by promoting philanthropy and adopting a posture of corporate responsibility. In recent years, several companies have sought to deflect criticisms by hiring monitors to meet with employees to hear complaints and investigate problems. As mentioned earlier, corporations are increasingly subcontracting out parts of the production line to smaller firms that work in greater obscurity. When these abuses are exposed, corporations claim that they have limited power or leverage over these independent contractors or that host governments should be blamed for inadequate labor laws. However, as long as the neoliberals' staunch advocacy of deregulation prevails, the most that can be expected from MNCs is voluntary compliance with ethical norms and self-monitoring.

MNCs and neoliberals argue that voluntary codes are good enough, since it just isn't good business to misbehave anymore. In response to a newly recognized aspect of consumer preference, some companies have changed the way they do business, and are going further to treat workers well than often-weak regional laws require. For example, whereas they were once part of an alliance that lobbied hard against taking the threat of global warming seriously, now Shell and BP Amoco advertise with calls for reductions in carbon dioxide emissions. Nike has pressed its suppliers to open their factories to independent inspections, to remove child laborers from its lines, and to provide a better environment for its workers. Although there are still reports of sexual and verbal abuse of workers in its Indonesian factories, Nike says it is acting in good faith to remedy the problems. In another example, it appears that a group of nine pharmaceutical corporations are willing to stop blocking LDC efforts to buy anti-AIDS drugs at a more reasonable price (as of 2001, only 1.75 percent of the world's 40 million people infected with HIV were receiving such treatment).[30]

Many MNCs add that they abide by the laws of their host countries and if anyone should be blamed for a lack of standards, it is LDC governments. But often the only comparative advantage many LDCs have is cheap labor and the lack of government regulation, including environmental protections. If LDCs were to upgrade their working conditions to the standards of developed countries, they would lose business. Even those who agree that at least there should be some minimum standards necessary to keep people (wherever they live) from being exploited have a hard time agreeing on what those standards should be, let alone how to enforce them.

Aid and Debt

Although it played a much larger role during the COLD WAR, foreign aid of one form or another is still of critical importance to most non-Western economies. The vast majority of foreign assistance is distributed as bilateral aid, commonly defined as the transfer of concessional resources from one government to another. Multilateral aid is the transfer of resources from a group of donors (such as the UNITED NATIONS or the Organization for Economic Cooperation and Development) to a recipient. In either case, aid is very definitely a tool of diplomacy, employed in such a way as to manipulate the behavior of possible recipients. Aid is used as a carrot to encourage or reward loyalty or desirable behavior. Or the withholding of aid can be a stick used to punish those deemed undeserving. In actuality, the majority of U.S. aid does not go to the world's poorest people. With the current "war on terrorism," as during the Cold War, U.S. foreign aid is not provided on a needs basis, but rather is based on strategic calculation. Two countries, Israel and Egypt, receive the lion's share of all U.S. bilateral assistance.

For years, aid had been welcomed by LDCs as a spur to development. Then, in the 1990s, the popular slogan among developed countries became "trade not aid." Some, however, such as French president Jacques Chirac, say that this slogan should now be "aid for trade."[31] As with nearly every other topic raised in this chapter, there is a great deal of disagreement about the effectiveness of aid. Both neoliberals and their critics agree that more aid is not necessarily better at promoting development. Nearly everyone, even those who call for increased funding for foreign aid, have problems with the ways in which aid packages have been designed and managed. Neoliberals contend that aid can promote development if it is used as part of a larger package of reforms. Some, such as UN Secretary-General Kofi Annan, view aid as only one element in a development strategy that can be more effective if it is offered to help recipients run their own economies.[32] Critics argue that aid should not be used to benefit the economic or strategic interests of donor countries. Yet many radicals maintain that this is impossible, since aid is used as a tool of capitalism that actually increases dependency and contributes to the further underdevelopment of states. Conservatives, such as President Bush's former treasury secretary Paul O'Neill, argue that foreign aid is too often simply a waste of good money.

Foreign assistance comes in a variety of forms: cash, food, clothing, medicine, arms, or just about any other commodity. Contrary to popular U.S. belief, the United States is not a major donor of aid. Most Americans believe that the United States is much more generous, even overly generous with the aid it offers LDCs. Consequently, it is highly unlikely that U.S. politicians will campaign for larger aid budgets. However, relative to the size of its economy, the United States donates less in foreign assistance than any other developed country. Even measured in total dollars, it now gives less than Japan, France, and Germany. However, since September 11, 2001, certain poor countries again have some strategic value, as aid is increasingly being linked to the war on terror. And thanks in part to high-profile activism by Irish rocker Bono, even conservatives like Jesse Helms are beginning to view the fight against poverty as a moral obligation. Still, even though President Bush has pledged to ask Congress to increase the foreign aid budget from $10 billion to $15 billion by 2006, the total allocated to foreign aid actually makes up less than one cent out of every dollar in the proposed U.S. budget for 2003. In other words, each year, the average American pays a grand total of four dollars in taxes toward helping the world's poorest people. This is a fraction of what other nations think the richest country in the world should be offering.[33]

Worse, it can be argued that the United States is the principal beneficiary of the vast majority of U.S. aid, since so much of the aid it gives is "tied." Tied aid is aid that comes with strings attached that helps to guarantee a market for the donor country's goods. For example, the United States might extend a loan to Nigeria to buy tractors. This is a loan that the United States fully expects Nigeria to repay with interest, yet Nigeria has no choice but to use that money to buy U.S. tractors, even if Japanese or French tractors are less expensive, or preferred for some other reason. Aid activists point out that such packages should be recognized for what they are: subsidies of donor economies. LDCs argue that development should not be a profit-making enterprise for the rich at the expense of the poor. Britain is one of the few developed countries that have bought this argument, and is beginning to untie some of strings attached to the aid it offers. On the other hand, the United States (and many other developed countries) insist that it is becoming increasingly difficult to persuade their constituents of the need for foreign aid—and at least they can show that tied aid offers a reciprocal benefit, creating hundreds of thousands of jobs for the citizens of donor countries.

It is true that since the end of the Cold War there has been enormous pressure in the United States and other developed countries to cut foreign aid, as part of the "peace dividend" (or the monies saved now that the Cold War is over). As a result, the vast majority of foreign assistance provided comes not in the form of a grant or gift, but as a loan. Although most people's definition of aid would seem to call for the concessional terms offered by soft loans, with their low interest rates and long repayment periods, a substantial number of these loans are hard loans, bearing high interest rates and short repayment periods. Many of these loans are taken out to service debt (or make the scheduled payment on the debt accrued from past loans).

Therefore, a great deal of the assistance that developed countries offer is in the form of loans meant to pay the interest on an outstanding debt. This only adds to that debt, which may exist for a variety of reasons. In some cases, the monies owed are Cold War debts; the West lent to its anticommunist allies knowing that the resources would wind up in the hands of irresponsible, wasteful, or kleptocratic governments. Or LDCs lost money in failed (but expensive) attempts at industrialization. In other cases, world recession or unexpected changes in the global economy (such as sudden jumps in the price of oil or food) contributed to deficits that put countries into debt. Most LDCs have sunk into debt because they have consistently faced shortfalls in their balance of payments (again, due to their disadvantageous position in the international economy).

Clearly, external factors beyond these countries' control have played a large part in creating the crisis. However, to some extent, each country's debt grows out of its own particular combination of problems. Whatever the source of the debt, it only became a crisis as far as the IMF and donors were concerned in the early 1980s, when Mexico and other debtors declared their inability to pay and threatened a moratorium (or temporary halt) on servicing their debts. Such threats were widely regarded as amounting to an emergency, since banks had eagerly overextended themselves for years, making loans to LDCs without worry as to their creditworthiness. Banks and donors feared that if other countries had joined Mexico in the formation of a debtors' cartel, their collective default could have led to the collapse of the international financial system.

Since the debt crisis of the 1980s, IFIs and donors have recognized how vital it is that the vast majority of debtors be willing and able to pay. Donors are working with international financial institutions and are determined to manage the system to better protect it. There have been a variety of attempts to manage LDC debt over the years, but nothing has changed in the sense that the debt burdens of LDCs are still very real. In 1970, total LDC foreign debt was less than $100 billion. It rose to $600 billion by 1980, and by 1990 it was up to $1.6 trillion. As of 2000, the total foreign debt for all LDCs was over $2 trillion. Most of the increase in debt in the 1990s was because countries had to take out more loans to pay the interest on their existing debt. Two trillion dollars of debt equals about $400 of debt for every man, woman, and child living in LDCs (remember, the average income in the poorest countries is less than one dollar per day). This debt is as debilitating for the countries with the largest total debts, such as Mexico and Brazil, as it is for countries with lower total bills, but much smaller economies, such as many of those in Africa. For some low-income countries like Mozambique and Sudan, their debt ratios, or the portions of their total income that they must spend to service their debt, are 400–1,000 percent.[34]

When countries are in this position, scraping by, just making the minimum payments on their bills, this leaves precious little to spend on education, healthcare, or other aspects of development. Countries wind up literally choosing between food and debt. In making what has been called "the cruel choice," countries like Mozambique allocate four times more for debt repayment than healthcare—this in a country where one out of every five children dies before the age of five.[35] For many countries, these cuts are coming at the absolute worst time. According to Peter Piot, HIV/AIDS is like no other single factor in the world today in that it is so systematically undermining the gains made over decades of investment in human resources, education, health, and well-being. Piot argues that it is time that we make the connection between debt relief and epidemic relief. The countries hit have little money left to spend on AIDS prevention because too much of their budget goes to servicing their debts and rich countries are not coming forward with the funds necessary to combat the epidemic.[36]

Although Latin America is the region hit hardest by debt service, paying nearly a third of its entire export earnings to the banks, some poorer countries with smaller debts are actually in even worse predicaments (see Figures 6.9 and 6.10). To put this in some perspective, the World Bank defines countries as severely indebted if their debt to GNI ratio is over 50 percent. As of mid-2002, of our cases, Indonesia, Nigeria, and Peru are "severely indebted," Turkey and Zimbabwe "moderately indebted," and Iran, China, and Mexico rank as "less indebted."[37] Here's an easy way of making this a bit more concrete: in the late 1990s, Liberia and Guatemala, for example, were expected to spend nearly sixty cents of every dollar they earn servicing their debts. During this same period, Brazil's debt interest payments amounted to 75 percent of its government revenues.[38] It doesn't take an accountant to see that at a certain point payment becomes impossible, and countries fall even further behind. When this happens, donor response tends to vary, as it frequently hinges on the donors' political interests. Oftentimes the response tends to be stern: the World Bank suspended disbursements to Zimbabwe in 2000 because it was more than six months overdue and tens of millions of dollars behind in servicing its debt. Although the publics of developed countries largely regard such countries as deadbeats, unwilling or unable to meet their debt obligations, the major debtors are actually net exporters of capital. For example, Nigerian officials maintain that their country has repaid much more than it has borrowed. Economist Susan George, who contends that the sums LDCs have paid to service their debts amount to unprecedented financial assistance from the poor to the rich—an amount George estimates to be equivalent to six Marshall Plans—supports this view. She says that we should not worry about the banks going hungry—they've made back the original principal and more through high interest rates. And the banks continue to make tidy profits from the interest earned on this debt. In six of the eight years between 1990 and 1997, LDCs paid out to developed countries a total of $77 billion in debt service (interest plus repayment).[39] As in Nigeria, many of the governments that accumulated this debt and misappropriated these funds are long gone. However, the citizens of their countries are left holding the bag, responsible for repaying a debt they never asked for, from which they derived no gain. Eduardo Galeano likens this system to an open artery: LDCs are being bled dry. Rather than being healed by the IMF, the veins are kept open for the

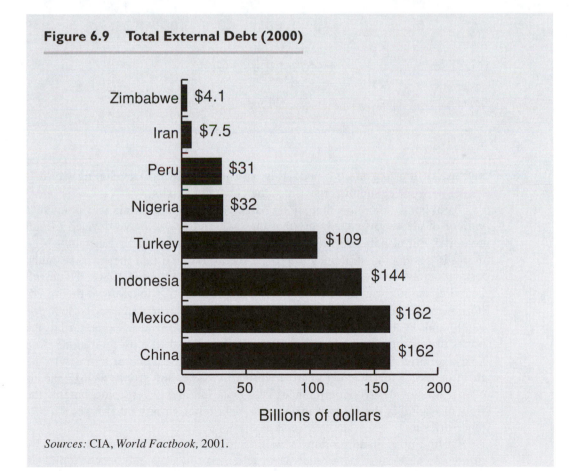

Figure 6.9   Total External Debt (2000)

Billions of dollars

Sources: CIA, *World Factbook,* 2001.

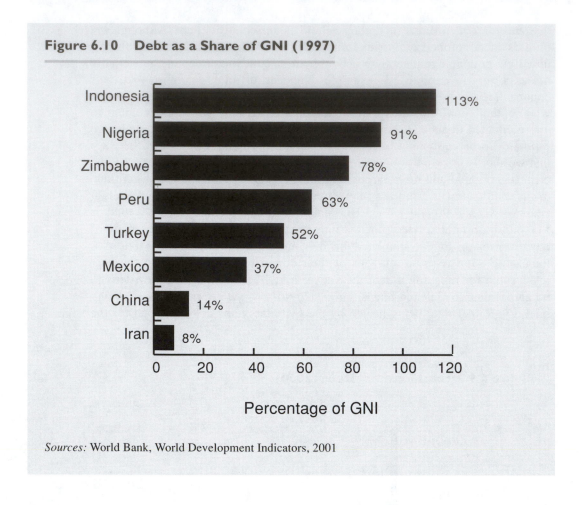

Figure 6.10   Debt as a Share of GNI (1997)

Indonesia — 113%
Nigeria — 91%
Zimbabwe — 78%
Peru — 63%
Turkey — 52%
Mexico — 37%
China — 14%
Iran — 8%

Percentage of GNI

Sources: World Bank, World Development Indicators, 2001

purpose of drawing more blood—this, at a time when the developing world is facing its worst economic crisis since the Great Depression.[40]

Neoliberals maintain that such characterizations are unfair and point to a variety of efforts over the years that the IMF and donors have devised to pull countries out of debt. Yet their critics argue that what IFIs have actually been doing is developing strategies to protect themselves, so that they will be much less vulnerable to the kind of pressure they experienced in the 1980s. The result is divide and rule: debtors now have a harder time uniting to confront their creditors because each country must meet with the IFIs to restructure its debt privately and on an individual basis. The terms of each deal are secret, and in the hopes of more preferential treatment, countries know they must go it alone. And this is an offer they cannot resist, since countries must come to terms with the IMF, or risk being deemed uncreditworthy. A bad rating from the IMF means economic suicide. Noncompliance risks isolation and severe punishment: the flow of capital in the form of investment, debt relief, or any other type of assistance dries up.

On the other hand, countries willing to accept IMF demands are usually offered some form of debt relief. Debt relief may involve debt rescheduling or, more rarely, debt forgiveness. Rescheduling of debt defers payment to a later date; it is a temporary reprieve, allowing for an extension of the period of repayment of the loan. Rescheduling is considered crucial for many countries because it makes their debt burden more bearable. However, critics maintain that rescheduling just disguises the actual inability of countries to pay off their debts, while ensuring that the banks continue to collect interest. In some cases, by rescheduling debts, countries are compelled to accept even higher interest rates than those originally paid.

As opposed to rescheduling, forgiveness means reducing or writing off part of a debt. While in the past this has usually been the option of last resort, a global campaign for forgiveness has developed since the late 1990s. That program, put forward by an unusual collection of personalities and religious figures such as U2's Bono and Reverend Billy Graham, became an international movement, known as Jubilee 2000. It called for the forgiveness of debt as part of a biblical mandate (the Book of Leviticus sets down that every fifty years all debts should be canceled, land returned to the dispossessed, and slaves set free). The time of liberation was known as "Jubilee," and its namesake movement pressed during the millennium year for a one-time full debt forgiveness for the world's poorest countries.

However, the closest the IFIs have been willing to come to this is a program for HIGHLY INDEBTED POOR COUNTRIES (HIPC), defined as having GNPs per capita of less than $675 and debts amounting to more than 80 percent of their GNPs. Under the program, developed countries promise to expand and accelerate debt relief measures, and to share a token of their prosperity with the poor. As of 2002, the United States, Canada, Japan, and several Western European countries pledged to provide the funding to forgive part of the debt of twenty-four of the world's poorest countries (all in Africa and Latin America). The argument for forgiveness goes as follows: in countries where the majority of the population lives on less than one dollar a day, it is not only wrong but also inefficient to require them to spend so much of their revenue paying back their creditors (plus, relatively speaking, we're not talking about a lot of money here, since HIPC currently only accounts for about 8 percent of the total external debt of LDCs). To be considered for the HIPC program, a country must be desperately poor and be willing to divert all the money it would have paid on its debt to programs promoting education, healthcare, and economic development. For countries that qualify for the HIPC program, or any future assistance, just one more string is attached: applicants must be willing to faithfully accept all the conditions set for them by the IMF.

Jubilee 2000 (now called "Drop the Debt") has so far failed to win its demand for full debt cancellation without preconditions. The amounts of relief offered have been tiny compared to the need, and are still not enough to make debt repayments more manageable, or help countries achieve what is called "debt sustainability." Most of the countries eligible for the HIPC program are like Niger, dependent on the sale of one or two raw materials (in Niger's case, uranium), the prices of which have taken a dive in recent years.[41] Consequently, some activists argue that even if the debt had been canceled, there would still need to be a fundamental change in the position of developing countries in the world economy, or the poorest would fall back into debt. The advocates of Jubilee 2000 recognize that debt cancellation in itself will not bring about far-reaching change, but they argue that it would offer those so burdened by debt the new beginning that they desperately need.[42]

7

Structural Adjustment: Prices and Politics

> I feel like I am trapped in hell.
> —Emanuel Seuger, Nigerian truck driver[1]

> The "wretched of the earth" want to go to Disney World—not to the barricades.
> —Thomas L. Friedman, writer[2]

As mentioned in Chapter 6, the conditions attached to the program for highly indebted countries (or any debt restructuring, for that matter) are based in NEOLIBERALISM, in a set of ideas known as the Washington Consensus. The Washington Consensus sums up the position of INTERNATIONAL FINANCIAL INSTITUTIONS (IFIs) and the donors that dominate them (the United States, Canada, the European Union, and Japan)—that underdevelopment is due to the domestic failings of the underdeveloped countries themselves. In other words, it is argued that less developed countries (LDCs) need internal structural reforms to stabilize their economies. Just as the diagnosis of the problem is universal, so is the cure. A fairly uniform prescription is proposed for dealing with any economy's ills: an opening up (or liberalization) of their economies to foreign competition, and the adoption of a series of market-based reforms, including privatization, deregulation, and an embrace of GLOBALIZATION. According to the Washington Consensus, economic crises wherever they occur should be approached in the same way and treated with a consistent dose of economic liberalization and fiscal austerity, or belt tightening. The prognosis for LDCs is quite optimistic: if countries will only take their medicine, they will experience healthy growth rates. Healthy growth rates will provide for the growth of a middle class, and then more stable, viable democracies are sure to follow.

It is the INTERNATIONAL MONETARY FUND (IMF) that administers the cure. The IMF plays several highly influential roles in the world economy, one of which is the promotion of global economic stability. The IMF promotes stability by serving as the lender of last resort to countries in economic crisis, distributing loans to those whose economies are facing temporary shortfalls. By shortfalls, we are referring to an imbalance in payments, or a situation in which a country is spending more than it is earning. When this occurs, a country is said to experience a deficit, and countries must find ways to finance or cover their deficits. This is how many countries go into debt: compared to the unpopular alternatives of raising taxes or cutting spending, governments prefer to take out loans to cover the shortfall. When countries run into serious financial trouble, it is often the IMF to which they turn for "rescue packages": emergency loans or bailouts. Again, countries get "rescued" only after they have agreed to the IMF's cure. Obviously, this makes the IMF an extremely powerful institution, with tremendous influence over the decisions of governments.

So what is the cure, exactly? What are the conditions attached to the provision of new loans so necessary for the servicing of old debt? The first thing to understand is that there is a regimen associated with the cure, known as STRUCTURAL ADJUSTMENT PROGRAMS (SAPs). Also called AUSTERITY PLANS, SAPs are premised on the neoliberal consensus that the world should be run like a business. The IMF argues that its goal is debt reduction. That means getting countries to follow what neoliberals would characterize as more sensible economic policies. According to this view, countries need to adopt progrowth policies and get their revenues to exceed their expenditures—in order to get out of the red. At its core, any adjustment program is based in the adoption of market reforms, which are believed by neoliberals to lay the basis for future growth. What countries need most is to keep their eyes on the bottom line. Short-term consumption should be curtailed in order to promote long-term investment. Beyond this, the particulars of each SAP vary. Politics very definitely comes into play, since the IMF is willing to tolerate misbehavior by some states that it would not permit from others. For example, the IMF has been willing to overlook Russian non-compliance with loan conditions, when such noncompliance by a less strategically important country would be punished.

While the list of conditions varies somewhat by country, SAPs share a number of common elements, all based in the idea that debtor countries need to undergo a series of adjustments to promote growth, get themselves out of debt, and foster DEVELOPMENT. The first order of business for SAPs is reducing deficits, or attaining a balance of payments. One way to do this is to cut spending. After meeting with the IMF, governments are to go back home and cut the "fat" from their budgets, most commonly spending on social welfare programs. Such cuts are likely to take even more of a toll than they do in developed countries, since in many LDCs, private income is so low that public provisioning is crucial. Even the middle classes are hit hard by SAPs; since Argentina's economy has gone into a tailspin, teachers and other professionals have joined the poorer classes in looting to help make ends meet.

Moreover, cuts in social welfare programs mean reduced government funding for education, healthcare, sanitation, the provision of clean water, price controls and subsidies for food, as well as nutritional supplements for young children and nursing mothers. In China, budget cuts have meant the dismantling of the once hugely popular and widely emulated "barefoot doctor" program. One of the greatest successes of the Cultural Revolution, the free rural healthcare provided by the Chinese government had greatly improved the quality of life for millions of people. However, the end of this program resulted in a 400–500 percent increase in health costs from 1990 to 1997. Where the bill for a hospital stay is more than the yearly income of most peasants, a lack of barefoot doctors

Figure 7.1 Military Budgets and Adjustment

Until the end of the COLD WAR, many third world governments (both civilian and military) received much of their foreign aid in the form of military assistance. With the tacit if not outright approval of the West, many of these governments also spent the lion's share of their budgets on the military. In less-than-democratic regimes, the armed services played a large part in keeping these governments in power. However, many people living under authoritarian rule hoped that with the end of the Cold War and the rise of new democracies around the world, the military's influence would wane. They looked forward to a DEMOCRACY DIVIDEND, in which money would be cut from military budgets and reallocated to long-neglected social services such as education and healthcare.

Unfortunately, this democracy dividend has been slow in coming in many countries, for reasons that are sometimes perplexing. Five years after independence in South Africa, the government was still spending nearly as much on defense as it did on health.

The Turkish government has decided in recent years to increase military spending rather than invest more in educational resources. This isn't unusual; newer democracies, worried about keeping the military satisfied with its retirement, often continue to spend scarce funds in an attempt to placate this still powerful actor. The hopes for a democracy dividend are being realized in some countries in Latin America that have had long histories of military rule. In Argentina, Haiti, and Brazil, for example, militaries are rapidly losing their privileges and their budgets have been cut. However, in Bolivia, Guatemala, and other new democracies where there are sharp ethnic or other divides, the military's budget and role have been expanding. In Mexico, the military budget has continued to rise, in part because of pressure from the United States to continue cooperating in the war on drugs. This mixed picture is representative of the other regions as well, and is due to a variety of factors unique to each country.

means that people simply go without care—often until it is too late. The toll this is taking is already reflected in startling statistics: the number of tuberculosis cases has quadrupled in China in the last fifteen years. Although the government has not released official figures, it is widely believed that the gains made against infant mortality are rapidly disappearing.[3]

In addition to the revenues saved by cuts in spending, austerity plans often require governments to increase their income by raising taxes, and by increasing export earnings. One way of doing the latter is to focus on export promotion, which for most countries means an intensification of the production of raw materials for sale on the world market. Working in tandem with this effort at export promotion is the devaluation of one's currency, which a government undertakes by changing its official exchange rate. A currency devaluation is prescribed because it promises to accomplish two goals at once. It should spur increased export earnings, since one's goods will be cheaper (and therefore more competitive) on the world market. At the same time, devaluation means that because its currency is worth less, the cost of imports will rise, putting goods out of the reach of most of the population, and therefore conserving scarce hard currency. Again, the idea is to achieve a balance of payments (or even a surplus) where there has been a deficit. According to neoliberals, deep cuts in spending combined with a jump in revenues from export sales will help

Figure 7.2   Paying Taxes: An Especially Unpopular Idea in Mexico

In a move that cost him some popularity, President Vicente Fox proposed a radical idea—that Mexicans pay their taxes. Tax evasion appears to be a tradition in Mexico; it is estimated that one-third of the economy operates off the books, and many rich people pay no income taxes at all. Yet to satisfy his creditors and demonstrate his commitment to fiscal reform, Fox set about finding a way to increase government revenues. Because a thorough overhaul of the tax collection system would take too much time, the president lobbied to add a 15 percent sales tax to necessities such as food and medicine. However, this plan has been widely denounced by virtually everyone in Mexico as extreme—and especially devastating for Mexico's 40 million poor. In one of his first major losses, Fox failed to pressure the Mexican Congress into accepting his proposal. The president could only get a watered-down version of it passed—taxing cigarettes, alcohol, and luxury goods.[4]

countries accumulate the hard currency to get out of debt and on the path to prosperity.

The path to prosperity is predicated on the acceptance of some other conditions as well. Here the emphasis is on the adoption of policies that will enhance productivity and encourage capital flows based on foreign investment rather than aid. The way to accomplish these goals, according to the IMF, is to privatize the economy. Privatization means selling off STATE-OWNED ENTERPRISES (SOEs), which are notorious for being wasteful and inefficient. Although SOEs were originally created to reduce foreign dominance of LDC economies, neoliberals argue that these government monopolies over the delivery of public services, such as water and electricity, should be put on the open market and sold to the highest bidder, whether local or foreign. While neoliberals admit that privatization of utilities has often meant higher prices for water, electricity, and telephone service, they argue that private investors have made improvements and dramatically expanded services, increasing the poor's access to those services.[5] In cooperation with the terms of its SAP, Mexico has sold off hundreds of state-owned enterprises, including its control over the seaports, railroads, and telecommunications industry. However, most Mexicans strongly resist the privatization of PEMEX, the state-owned oil and gas monopoly, despite IMF pressures. China has been slow to sell off state industries, fearing the creation of social unrest due to mass unemployment. A stagnating economy in the countryside has contributed to pressures that have already resulted in Chinese villagers clashing with police over rising taxes and fees. Since 70 percent of its industrial work force is employed by the state, full compliance with market reforms could result in layoffs of 100 million Chinese workers. Although it has faced similar hardship on a smaller scale, Peru went ahead with privatizations in 2002 that resulted in such violent strikes in the south that President Alejandro Toledo felt compelled to call for a state of emergency. Similar programs are now under way in Nigeria and Turkey, although they are proceeding slowly.

In addition to privatization, neoliberals argue that governments must work harder to attract foreign investment of all kinds. They must make themselves attractive to MULTINATIONAL CORPORATIONS (MNCs) for all the reasons neoliberals have put forward as benefits associated with their presence in host countries. Governments should work aggressively to lure more foreign investment in a variety of ways, including a policy of deregulation (the removal of legal constraints on the operation of businesses, such as an end to health and safety or environmental regulations). Critics remark that it also helps if the country can advertise having a large pool of labor, willing and eager to work with little interference by unions or other activists. This is the case in Peru, where the Fujimori government chose not to enforce the labor code meant to protect workers against anti-union discrimination. For years, employers have been free to restrict collective bargaining rights—and this is likely to go on there and elsewhere, as long as economic times are tough. In Nigeria, unions are only now resuming their work after years of repression. Nigerian trade unions have led countrywide protests and strikes that have stalled government attempts to deregulate and raise the price of subsidized fuel. For many years in Mexico, the largest unions were in the pocket of the Institutional Revolutionary Party (PRI) government and promoting the interests of employers. Critics of Fox maintain that he continues on with this tradition and independent labor activists live with the threat of violence.[6] However, governments are not always so successful at controlling unions. Despite recent attempts to curtail them, in Zimbabwe unions are powerful and active.

To understand the impact of conditionality, take the case of Indonesia. In 1997, in return for $43 billion in emergency funding, Indonesia agreed to an adjustment that had more than 100 conditions attached. Among them was the requirement that the government close its clove monopoly and eliminate price subsidies on basic foodstuffs. Similarly, Ecuador's 1999 SAP included 167 conditions, including a requirement that the government allow a steep rise in petrol prices and a doubling of the price of cooking gas. Ecuadorians recognized the hardship this would cause and went out into the streets in protest.

By the early 1990s the IMF and donors had added another condition. With the COLD WAR over, the neoliberals began admonishing LDCs to go beyond "getting prices right" and to also work at "getting politics right." Based in the view that democracy is a natural complement to capitalism, donors argued that the hardship associated with SAPs and their seeming failure to deliver on promises of growth and development are due to the failures of government, not the model. As we will discuss in more detail in Chapter 14, the West became convinced that a lack of "good governance" was to blame—not the neoliberal model itself.

When the economies of the East Asian NEWLY INDUSTRIALIZING COUNTRIES (NICs), which had for so long been upheld as models for development, stumbled in the late 1990s, neoliberals blamed the Asian "flu" on the lack of political liberalization in these countries. For more than a decade, Western donors had ignored rampant corruption in Asia and elsewhere as long as governments embraced neoliberal reforms. However, by the late 1990s corruption, cronyism, and the "incestuous" relationship between government and business in Asia were deplored as the cause of the region's ills. The NICs had gotten prices right, but they had suffered from a lack of regulation, supervision, and transparency—

in effect, they hadn't "gotten politics right." The problem, as identified by neoliberals, was one endemic not only to East Asia but also to much of the third world: political reform had lagged behind economic reform when, from a neoliberal perspective, the success of either reform would be inextricably linked to progress in the other.[7]

Neoliberals maintain that in the long run, perseverance in economic and political liberalization will pay off. It just takes time and patience. They point to a number of countries, such as Mexico and South Korea, that have taken this sometimes harsh medicine in return for emergency loans, and whose growth rates now indicate a recovery. Moreover, Mexico and South Korea have undergone extensive political reforms at the same time that they have adopted economic reforms. Just a few years ago they were authoritarian systems, but both countries today have made substantial progress in their transitions to democracy.

How "Getting Prices Right" May Be "Getting Development Wrong"

Critics of the neoliberal model don't mince words when they argue that globalization is the new colonialism. Its aims and outcomes are remarkably similar to those of colonialism in that the "development" it promotes is not one that improves the lives of LDC citizens. Rather, from a critical perspective, free trade and globalization are about ensuring markets for Western goods and retaining the third world as a source of cheap labor and raw materials. They leave the destiny of non-Westerners in the hands of their former colonizers. Structural adjustment amounts to a financial coup d'état in that SAPs undermine the SOVEREIGNTY of the state and deny people the right to economic self-determination. Even if the model may one day prove effective in promoting economic development, it is certainly antidemocratic in that enormous decisions affecting people's lives are made behind closed doors, without their participation.[8]

The conditions attached to a continuation of aid amount to blackmail, according to the critics. The restructuring of debt has resulted in a system of international peonage. According to this argument, LDCs fell deeply into debt because of their position in the INTERNATIONAL ECONOMIC SYSTEM, and SAPs effectively force them to remain in that position. The IFIs appear to be more interested in the business of business than in the business of development. Described as a debt collector for commercial banks, the IMF is so busy making sure LDCs continue to service their debts that to promise development will be the outcome is a cruel joke. The critics point out that Ghana was until recently the poster child for IMF reforms in Africa. It began implementing an SAP nearly twenty years ago, but its total debt has quadrupled and even the IMF admitted in the late 1990s that at its current growth rates it would be decades before the majority reaches the poverty level.[9] Thus the economic reforms imposed on LDCs are entrenching the very development model that caused their original problem.

Whereas neoliberals emphasize the positive benefits of globalization and maintain that adjustments are necessary to promote long-term economic health, critics argue that structural adjustment serves the interests of the powerful. Globalization is contributing to a grotesque and dangerous polarization between those who benefit from the system and those who are passive recipients of its effects.[10] The combined effect of the reforms imposed on LDCs is devastating. SAPs throw the middle class into poverty, but they take their hardest toll on the poorest of the poor. There are good reasons why adjustment is known as shock therapy. Shock waves ripple throughout countries, with multiple consequences. In Zambia, for example, the direct impact of IMF-imposed reforms was a 16 percent drop in the gross national product (GNP), a doubling of the mortality rate of children under age five, and 60,000 workers laid off within two years.[11] In the following sections, we will briefly describe some of those consequences and how the millions who are worse off because of SAPs are seeking to cope with their effects. Globalization is contributing, both directly and indirectly, to a series of interconnected problems that vividly illustrate the downside of interdependence. Neoliberal reforms have often been promoted by developed countries with little thought to the human and environmental impact on LDCs.

Migration

In a variety of ways, globalization and structural adjustment are adding to a series of large and growing human migrations. These migrations occur within countries, from rural to urban areas, and between countries, from underdeveloped to developed countries. Structural adjustment often makes what was a subsistence living now unbearable. With lower prices for their cash crops and no food security in rural areas, people are desperate. People have always been drawn to the cities (in developed and less developed countries) for the opportunities they are believed to hold. Not only do people come hoping for work, but they also come for the chance to improve their lives, through access to education, healthcare, and other government services. For many years, it has been a common practice for governments to try to keep urban populations satisfied and stable by providing subsidies that ensure that the populations surrounding them are fed and the lights are on. As much as there is a pull factor drawing people to the cities, there is also a push factor: the hardship of rural life.

Not all farmers unable to make a living in the countryside pack their bags and leave. In response to the demands of developed countries, increasing numbers are finding it lucrative to turn to the production of alternative crops. Where farmers have realized that they can't make a living producing bananas or coffee, many are planting opium poppies, marijuana, and coca. Such work means survival for tens of thousands of people living in LDCs. The production of these particular cash crops also means a great deal for the overall economies of countries such as Colombia, Bolivia, and Afghanistan. In the late 1990s, cocaine generated $3 billion in annual revenues for Colombia (surpassing the proceeds from coffee and oil).

Others attempt to cope through a variety of different activities—legal or not. Although millions of immigrants are estimated to have illegally entered developed countries, the majority of LDC migrants do not cross international boundaries. Rather, they are setting up residence in São Paulo, Nairobi, Shanghai, and Manila. The flight from rural areas has had a number of consequences, among them over-urbanization and the rapid creation of megacities, or cities with populations of over 8 million. The largest of these, Mexico City, at the turn of the twenty-first century had a population of over 21 million. The crush of bodies in this and other cities contributes to a number of health problems. It also raises a number of serious political, economic, and social dilemmas.

Hastily erected shantytowns house most of these new residents. It is common for a thick fog from coal cooking fires to hang over these cities. Without adequate sanitation or waste disposal, the cities emit poisonous gases that make one's eyes water and make it difficult to breathe. In the Philippines a shantytown built on a hill of garbage outside Manila collapsed in 2000, smothering hundreds of squatters. Most of these people had been poor farmers who had gone into bondage to moneylenders and lost what little land they had.[12]

Yet newcomers are met with other disappointments as well. Not only are there no places to live and few government services, there is no work. The shutdown of state-owned enterprises associated with structural adjustment often means mass layoffs, adding to unemployment and underemployment rates. Where the unemployment rate is high, as in Zimbabwe, where over 50 percent of the population is without work, many displaced workers make their living scavenging. One more way of coping, people survive by picking through the endless filth of the cities to sell in junk shops that specialize in plastic bottles, cardboard boxes, pieces of aluminum, glass, and the like.

In recent years hundreds of Nigerians have died in explosions caused by "scooping," another form of scavenging. When one of the many gasoline pipelines that run unattended for miles throughout the country develops a leak, accidentally or not, the poor scoop up the flowing gasoline into cans and buckets. They then haul it away and sell it on Nigeria's thriving black market. Always a dangerous practice, it has worsened in recent years as organized crime cartels have joined this part of the scavenging business. Now it is believed that gangs recruit children to scoop pipelines that are deliberately punctured. When you get a lot of excited people around a gas leak, all it takes is for someone to light a cigarette, or for a motorbike to backfire, and you have an inferno. The result is bodies burned beyond recognition, many of them poor women and children eager to earn a bit of money.[13]

Such tragedies create tremendous pressures on governments that have resorted to increasingly aggressive attempts to reduce urbanization and the press of impoverished populations. Yet even the most stringent policies have failed to contain the growth in urban populations. For example, it is estimated that there are 1 million illegal residents in Shanghai alone (a city of 14.7 million). Millions of rural Chinese residents leave their home villages to travel from city to city in search of work, sending their earnings home to their families. They have become known as the "floating population," and while Chinese government estimates place their numbers at 110 million, most observers increase the estimate to at least 200 million people.

The Informal Sector

With little hope of employment in the formal sector, large numbers of city dwellers turn to the underground economy, also known as the INFORMAL SECTOR. Although it is the single largest employer in many LDCs, the informal economy is a shadow economy of sorts. It is composed of semilegal or illegal activities that are under the table, and therefore not included in the calculation of a country's gross domestic product (GDP). Given the characteristics of the work, there are no accurate estimates of the numbers of people involved, although analysts agree that worldwide the number of informal-sector workers runs into the millions and is growing much more rapidly than the formal economy. It is estimated that 30 percent of the urban labor force in Latin America works in the informal sector. In Peru and many Latin American countries, where underemployment is vast, women who recently migrated from rural areas compose the backbone of this labor force. Latin America's experience is by no means unique; the informal economy provides an important cushion against austerity. It is a central means for survival in Africa, Asia, and the Middle East.

Although informal-sector work is often viewed as independent self-employment, it is also work performed semilegally or illegally for an employer (such as pieceworkers making lace from their homes for subcontractors). In the informal sector there are no explicit, written labor contracts, and no state regulation of wages or working conditions. Much of the informal sector, such as the microenterprises of female petty traders selling the equivalent of fast food along roads and sidewalks, amounts to what are known as male-dependent enterprises: they replicate in the public sphere work that is often traditionally within the reproductive realm. This is true of the other major sources of work for women in the informal sector, as domestic labor and as sex workers. As you might imagine, much of this work is highly dependent on disposable income, and during times of austerity these sectors are especially hard hit.

Yet there are benefits of this work as well. As opposed to formal-sector jobs, which rarely provide for childcare, many women working in the informal sector bring small children to work with them, as they find ways of making petty trading, knitting and selling sweaters, hairdressing, and catering compatible with their childcare responsibilities. Petty trading is an important part of informal-sector activity for men and women, and sexual divisions of labor often exist within the market, whether it falls into the formal or informal sector. For example, in the Dominican Republic, women are disproportionately represented as vendors of less lucrative goods such as clothing and food, whereas men tend to be involved in the sale of legal and illegal commodities that generally earn a higher income. Although the majority of women working in this sector just barely make ends meet, some jobs are more lucrative than others, and some women make relatively impressive incomes.

Violence Against Women

The rapid economic change associated with globalization has created opportunities for some women, but it has exposed them to a rising backlash. This backlash is expressed in a number of ways, including dramatic growth in the range, incidence, and intensity of gender violence. Where populations are undergoing rapid change and economic hardship, newly autonomous women become an easily identified threat. Women are caught between neoliberal policies that propel them into the work force and a traditionalist backlash that seeks to drive them back into their homes. In many parts of the world, men experience what some analysts call status inconsistency, or anxiety associated with changes in gender relations, the structure of the family, and the position of women. As Valentine Moghadam argues, the WORLD BANK wants women to assist in population control, and it wants them to work outside the home and earn enough to feed their families. But it isn't doing much when things get ugly. Thus globalization is related to a backlash of sorts, one manifested in a rising incidence of violence against females. For example, Peruvian activists recognize close links between rising rates of domestic violence and economic disarray. There the economic reform has contributed to massive unemployment, low wages, and troubling insecurity. People are described as living in a constant state of frustration, and women have often borne the brunt of this frustration.[14]

Where there is mass unemployment, women's entry into the labor force is sometimes viewed with hostility by men, who see women as displacing them. In cases around the world, women are finding themselves more often to be the targets of individual attacks as well as attacks by conservative social movements. Women are blamed not only for taking jobs from men, but also for the loss of traditional cultures (another byproduct of globalization). Often considered the keepers of tradition, their growing visibility and their perceived competition with men in the labor market angers and terrifies traditional elements, both male and female. The autonomy that comes with work outside the home is often believed to make women immodest, decadent, cultural traitors. Conservatives uphold tradition as providing a secure base in a scary world and argue for a world in which men and women know and accept their proper place. They acclaim virtues of traditional womanhood, and the dress and behavior of women become paramount. Those who accept this role as wife and mother are honored and exalted; those who resist are deemed traitors who must be punished. As a result, working women are held morally accountable and subjected to a broad variety of assaults and affronts, both public and private. When it was the government of Afghanistan, the Taliban's policy of restricting women to the home and denying girls an education was in part a response to fears associated with a growing visibility of women in the work force. As we mention in Chapter 14, such fears have contributed to public attacks on females worldwide. The result has been a variety of "cleanup campaigns," which include mass arrests of women, punishment for violations of dress codes, a rise in honor killings, as well as sexual harassment and other forms of discrimination against females.[15]

Rape (and the threat of rape) is another way of "putting women back in their place." In many countries, rape and other forms of sexual assault can only be committed against "honest" women—women of "good moral character," whose chastity can be vouched for. Women who work outside the home, who live without a father or husband, are especially suspect and rarely afforded the protections of society.

When rape is used to target particular groups, it is also used to humiliate men and to undermine communities. Although we usually think of mass rape as a weapon of war, it is also utilized in other types of conflict as well. For example, because they were identified as prosperous and foreign, ethnic Chinese women living in Jakarta were singled out for sexual assault as part of the violence that rocked Indonesia in 1998. The Indonesian government asserts that nothing happened and not one rape was reported. However, human rights activists estimate that more than 100 such rapes occurred. Some speculate that the security forces were directly involved. And many human rights workers believe the attacks were not spontaneous, that the government and military encouraged anti-Chinese sentiment to divert hostility over price hikes (directly resulting from the government's devaluation of the rupiah) toward individual retailers.[16] Similar attacks have targeted women in Rwanda, Kosovo, and elsewhere.

The Environment

The assault on the environment is another negative consequence of globalization. Urged on by the IMF, the World Bank, and other donors, newly industrializing countries have followed the path of developed countries: for years they placed a higher premium on growth than on environmental protection. In the early 1990s Mexico City had the worst air pollution of any city on earth; the air quality was so bad that simply breathing was like smoking two packs of cigarettes a day.[17] Yet in other ways as well, the results of a policy of "growth at any price" are long-term and devastating. China's economic boom, based on the use of coal and fuel-inefficient technologies, is rapidly creating pollution problems of unparalleled magnitude. Although developed countries are currently the biggest polluters and consumers of the world's resources, China and India are already the fourth and fifth largest producers of greenhouse emissions. According to the World Health Organization, seven of the ten most air-polluted cities in the world are in China. Twenty-seven percent of all deaths in China are due to respiratory diseases. Lung cancer in city dwellers has increased by nearly 20 percent just since 1988. China's situation is unique only because of its extremely rapid growth and large population; most countries, especially developing countries, are pursuing economic growth without concern for long-term environmental damage.[18]

However, the blind pursuit of growth at all costs is the approach taken by the exporters of raw materials as well. Structural adjustment programs that encourage export promotion result in intensified pressures on the land and other resources. The deforestation and desertification associated with the overexploitation of the environment have accelerated with neoliberal economic reforms. Globalization is directly related to environmental devastation in a number of ways. Structural adjustment programs urge countries to increase their growth rates by increasing productivity. Often this is defined as an opening up of untouched areas and exploitation of one's resources to their fullest extent. What this means is that land is stripped of its resources, and fragile ecosystems such as rainforests are destroyed. In the early 1990s, of the twenty-four largest debtors, eight never had or no longer had significant forest reserves. Of the sixteen major debtors remaining, all of them are recognized as major deforesters. In other words, the top non-Western debtors are all on the list of the top ten deforesters: Brazil, India, Indonesia, and Nigeria, just to name a few. Hardly anyone would argue that debt is the exclusive cause of deforestation and the other problems described here. However, with few alternatives the landless of these countries push into the forests for their subsistence needs, or looking to work for MNCs.[19] In the drive to increase sales on the world market, land is needed and new mines and plantations are opened.

Poor management of the environment is costly in monetary terms as well. It is estimated that in Nigeria, the losses from ruined land and disappearing forests run about $5 billion each year.[20] As the world begins to recognize the global threat that environmental disasters pose, the IMF, World Bank, and other donor agencies have come under increasing pressure to appear more environmentally responsive, and have allocated larger staffs to address the issue. There is more funding for environmental projects, and environmental impact statements for development projects are now mandatory.

Environmentalists welcome this shift, yet some question the sincerity of such concerns, since the overall prescription creating environmental disasters remains unchanged. For every "green" initiative, there is another project that appears oblivious to the ecological havoc it causes. For example, the World Bank is continuing to invest in fossil fuel plants in India and China rather than pursuing the development of renewable forms of energy. Huge and expensive dam projects are built to irrigate plantations owned by agribusiness and to electrify cities. But these projects, such as the Sardar Sarovar Dam in India, are controversial because often it is only the urban rich who benefit from them. Moreover, big dams have forced the resettlement of millions, creating what are known as "development refugees." In some cases this form of "development" has resulted in damage to fragile ecosystems, or the loss of irreplaceable archaeological treasures.[21] Similarly, since its green conversion the World Bank has approved of several other highly controversial projects, such as construction of an oil pipeline to run from Chad through Cameroon and out to the Atlantic Ocean. This enormous construction project is backed by a group of oil companies that promise to boost desperately impoverished Chad's revenues by 50 per-

---

Figure 7.3   China's Development Refugees Along the Three Gorges Dam

Leaders of the People's Republic of China (PRC) are on the verge of completing a project that has been envisioned by leaders for centuries: controlling the swells of the world's third largest river, the Yangtze, and building the world's largest hydroelectric power plant, named the Three Gorges Dam. This dam, which will flood most of the legendary Three Gorges region in south-central China, is being built in an effort to reduce the country's reliance on coal, which currently supplies 75 percent of the PRC's growing energy needs. The dam, scheduled to be completed in 2010, will provide hydroelectric energy (producing an estimated 10 percent of the country's total demand), and will increase river transport into China's central regions. But these gains come at a huge cost. Over nineteen cities, and 115,000 precious acres of farmland along the banks of the Yangtze, will be flooded. Additionally, approximately 1.6 million residents will be permanently displaced. Already, tens of thousands of residents have been forced from their homes for the construction of this project, which many deem structurally unsound. The resettlement process has been anything but smooth: monies set aside to assist in the transition have been siphoned off to well-placed officials, who use the relocation funds to finance trips abroad and lavish homes.

cent. However, critics argue that the average Chadian has little to gain and much to lose from this project. Meanwhile, the pipeline will run through protected areas, it will poison ecosystems, and even a small oil spill could wipe out fisheries and ruin local economies.

Structural adjustment is linked to environmental devastation in other ways as well. For example, cuts in fuel subsidies have pushed more people to the forests in search of fuel wood. People are turning to the forests to cushion the blow of shock therapy in other ways as well. In parts of Southeast Asia, Central Africa, and Latin America, commercial hunting in tropical forests has boomed as the hungry have pushed into the forests. There has always been hunting in the forests, but never on this scale. People are eating much more wild meat now, as the cost of meat from cattle and chickens is out of reach. Moreover, the international market for wild meat, desired by some for its novelty, by others as a luxury, is huge and growing. As a result of these combined consumer pressures—and the logging industry, which is building roads that make access to the rainforests even faster—in parts of tropical Africa, hunting for "bush meat" is considered out of control. In just ten years or so, the world's second largest tropical forest (in the Congo Basin) could be emptied of large mammals. Gorillas and chimpanzees could become extinct. In Indonesia, wild pigs are already very rare. This situation is called "empty forest syndrome." This is just another example of how economic hardship is forcing the adoption of coping strategies that are detrimental to the environment. It is also an example of how "development," as it is currently being pursued, is in direct conflict with conservation programs.[22]

Figure 7.4 A Zero-Sum Game?

Whether the question is saving the rainforests or the Arctic National Wildlife Refuge, the relationship between growth and the environment is often posed as a winner-take-all ZERO-SUM GAME. For purists on both sides, there can be no compromise. On the one hand, there are citizens of non-Western countries who will tell you that they want these projects, that they desperately need them—and the income that might trickle down from the construction of roads, dams, pipelines, and other projects. Of the over 1 billion people earning less than one dollar a day, most of them live in rural areas with the most biodiversity.[23] With so many people living in poverty, it is argued that environmental protection is a luxury that they cannot afford. Many non-Westerners point out that the United States and Europe did not adopt environmental protections when they were developing, and that it is hypocritical of rich countries to impede LDC development because of pollution and other environmental concerns. Some analysts offer the "Environmental Kuznets Curve" in validation of this argument. According to the curve, the environmental quality in a country initially deteriorates as the economy begins to industrialize, but then improves as citizens reach a certain standard of living. Economists disagree about exactly when it is that countries turn this corner, but contend that by the time a country has a per capita income of $8,000, it has made significant improvements against a variety of forms of pollution.[24] With so many countries falling far below that mark, we can expect it will be some time before the majority will be willing to make this shift in priorities. Perhaps in the meantime we should move away from treating the promotion of development and the protection of the environment as an either/or choice.

Disease

The massive population movements both back and forth within countries and across international borders have a number of effects, including the spread of disease. Any number of dangers to human health can be aggravated by the changes associated with structural adjustment and globalization. Shifting rainfall patterns linked to global warming, and the movement of populations into previously forested areas have been linked to an unprecedented jump in the incidence of malaria, which afflicts more than 400 million people.[25] As we just discussed, economic hardship has added not only to political instability but also to pressures on the environment. In a vicious circle, economic and environmental pressures are contributing to the emergence of resistant strains of malaria, as well as to the surfacing of new diseases such as the West Nile virus and Ebola. Austerity has contributed to rapid urbanization, which means that health workers must deal with a host of public health nightmares—just as the budget cuts necessitated by SAPs have left them profoundly ill-equipped to deal with these problems. Per capita medical spending in many African countries is less than five dollars a year. The meager sanitation systems that may or may not have served city populations a decade or two ago simply cannot handle the massive influx of people now fleeing the poverty of rural areas. Budget cuts mean that the public health sector is drained: it is not uncommon for clinics and hospitals in the poorest countries to lack not only electricity and running water, but also sterile equipment and protective gear. The health delivery system in Zimbabwe, for example, has been described as paralyzed, as vital life-saving equipment at government clinics has broken down and there are no spare parts. The hospitals are avoided and considered as places one goes only to die. The healthcare system itself becomes a vehicle for the transmission and spread of disease.

The combination of overcrowding, lack of adequate sanitation, and lack of clean water is adding to the death toll for common killers of children under five, such as dehydration from diarrhea. It is also contributing to a resurgence of old killers such as tuberculosis and measles, not to mention more virulent and drug-

---

Figure 7.5   A Small Investment with a Huge Payoff

According to a 2001 study conducted by the Commission on Macroeconomics and Health, if rich countries spent an extra one-tenth of one percent of their economies on the health of the poor, it would add $38 billion a year to health spending by 2015. If this money went to poor countries determined to improve their healthcare systems, these countries would see at least $360 billion a year in economic gains. In other words, investment in healthcare is sound economics; if the United States doubled what it currently spends on health assistance, the cost would amount to about $25 per citizen per year. If the United States were joined by other developed countries, millions of people worldwide would be lifted out of poverty and 8 million lives each year would be saved. However, as long as Americans continue to consider foreign aid to be a waste of money, even the easiest and least costly health improvements (such as curing a case of tuberculosis for $15) will remain out of reach.[26]

resistant strains of diseases such as malaria. While everyone recognizes that ill health is highly correlated with poverty and a major impediment to development, in a variety of ways it could be argued that structural adjustment is ensuring continued underdevelopment. After twenty years of structural adjustment, despite all the promises of science, life expectancy for the majority of the world's people has stagnated, or even reversed, and nearly 11 million children, most of them infants and toddlers, die each year of preventable causes.[27]

The diseases most devastating throughout much of the third world are preventable, curable illnesses that incapacitate and kill, such as malaria, tuberculosis, and acute lower respiratory diseases. For example, the World Health Organization estimates that the death rate from measles, which kills 900,000 children every year, could be cut in half with just one dose of vaccine (which costs twenty-six cents per child). Although it is not yet the world's most effective killer (it is the fourth leading cause of death worldwide), AIDS has the capacity to make a mark on the world unrivaled since the Black Death of the fourteenth century. This is a coming crisis and it is worse than early forecasts estimated: it has already killed more than 27 million people, most of them in the prime of life. Another 42 million people worldwide currently have HIV or AIDS—and 5 million more people are infected each year. At this rate, AIDS is now expected to produce the largest death toll in human history. Even worse, AIDS is hitting areas of the world least prepared to deal with it.

As it is with other diseases, poverty is intricately connected to the perpetuation of HIV/AIDS as well. AIDS was once most common among truck drivers and soldiers; incidence ran highest where there were well-developed roads and bridges. Yet increasingly it is found in all occupational groups and classes. It is aggravated by the extreme hardship associated with austerity, which is not only promoting male outmigration but also leaving many women little alternative but to enter the informal economy as sex workers. Likewise, people who cannot afford antibiotics and medicines to treat other sexually transmitted diseases live with genital sores that make them more vulnerable to HIV infections.

The rapid transmission of disease (including HIV) in southern Africa and many other LDCs is facilitated by a migrant labor system that dates back to colonialism. Unfortunately, the separation of families created by male outmigration in search of work is hardly an historical artifact. This situation, in which men (and some women) leave their families behind to work in the cities, in mines, in factories, and on plantations, is common today in many non-Western countries. Men away from home for months at a time commonly form liaisons with local women who may have seen other partners come and go. These men become infected with HIV and when they return home, pass it on to their wives, who then pass it on to their babies.

Screening for HIV is physically and financially inaccessible for many people worldwide. Too often a woman is already pregnant before she becomes aware of her HIV status, since many women are only tested when they come to clinics for prenatal care. Without wider programs the children born to many of these women will soon be orphans, as AIDS spreads to rural areas and even extended families find it difficult to support the rapidly growing burden on them. In the meantime, many of the children of weakened and ill parents leave

Figure 7.6   How Other Coping Mechanisms Are Linked to the Spread of HIV

In China, individuals who sell their blood to so-called blood heads are contracting the disease at enormous rates. Some people donate blood as often as five times in three days—well beyond the recommended rate—using contaminated needles and reused tubes. Not all of these people are volunteers looking to earn extra cash. Similar to reports elsewhere of people being abducted and their organs sold on the world market, people in China (even children) report being forced to give blood after being kidnapped and beaten by gangs. Health screenings are sometimes administered, but even those who "fail" the exam donate—they just get paid less for it. In India the spread of HIV has also been linked to blood donation. The government outlawed payments to blood donors once it recognized that nearly 10 percent of the country's AIDS infections were being transmitted through tainted blood, often sold by intravenous drug users.[28]

school to assume greater household responsibilities. It is estimated that by the year 2010, one in seven children under age fifteen in sub-Saharan Africa will have lost one or both parents. What to do with them, and what will become of the estimated 14 million children already left behind is yet another problem also unrivaled in human history.[29]

Thus, in addition to the dislocations felt by their families, the cuts imposed by structural adjustment have a variety of direct effects on children. Rising food prices and government cuts affecting food subsidies and nutrition programs have taken their toll. Several countries in Latin America have reported sharp increases in infant mortality rates since the cuts in social services. In the months after Peru's implementation of its SAP in 1988, poor children temporarily stopped growing due to malnutrition. In Thailand too, malnutrition among children worsened noticeably. After the 1997 crisis 10 percent of Thai children were found to be underweight. In addition to health concerns, rising school fees have made it is less likely that all children will receive an education. And the quality of education is eroded by budget cuts, as schools are overcrowded in dilapidated buildings, with classes often taught by overworked and underpaid teachers. Because of the pressures on their families, today children spend more of their time working in a variety of capacities to help make ends meet. It is estimated that there are 17 million children worldwide now working in slavelike conditions. Of that number, approximately 15 million indentured child laborers in South Asia have been sold into slavery by their own families because they are so deeply in debt.[30]

While we have mentioned the problems associated with the growing numbers of orphans created by AIDS in several parts of the world, the stress associated with SAPs has also been linked to higher rates of child abandonment and abuse, resulting in growing numbers of street children worldwide. For example, bigger cities in Turkey face a growing population of children, mostly homeless, who make a living on the streets. Current estimates claim that 6,000–7,000 children are on the streets of Istanbul alone. As families become displaced, children

A boy carries bricks for a living in India (UN Photo)

leave home at younger ages to join the paid work force, beg, or steal, either as a source of support to their families or entirely on their own. Often these children exist in utter destitution, living homeless or in packs in abandoned buildings, surviving on very little and spending what they have on drugs, or paint thinner and glues to dull hunger pains.

Perhaps just as troubling is the fact that around the world, social attitudes about children are changing. It is increasingly common to hear of the mistreatment of these children by ordinary people. In a well-publicized case in Turkey, a McDonald's manager nearly froze to death a ten-year-old tissue vendor who operated outside his store by putting her in a hamburger freezer. Around the world, street urchins are often viewed as a threat or an eyesore; in the worst situations they are targets of attack by "social cleansing squads" of vigilantes and police. In the 1993 Candelaría massacre in Brazil, for example, eight children were beaten to death on the steps of a cathedral.

Is Globalization Entirely to Blame?

Although the single-minded pursuit of the neoliberal paradigm has unleashed an array of problems manifested in various forms of social disintegration and economic dysfunctionality, there is no one cause of all of the troubles described in this chapter. While the spread of HIV, the destruction of rainforests, massive human migrations, and the exploitation of labor are based in social and economic institutions and systems of relationships that predate globalization, these processes are argued by some to be accelerated by the adoption of the neoliberal reforms that provide the momentum for globalization. Perhaps it is an overstatement to suggest that such tragedies are due to structural adjustment, but growing evidence suggests that the variety of problems identified here are associated with growing economic hardship. Structuralists assert that in many ways—economically, socially, culturally, politically, ecologically—the neoliberal approach has been a disaster for the world's poor. It is not working, it has cured nothing, and the IFIs have had plenty of time to impose their plans.[31]

Neoliberals reject such assertions. When presented with the above arguments they counter that if their way appears to be failing in many LDCs, that failure is due to irrational or inefficient domestic policies, not LDCs' irretrievably inequitable position in the world economy. The problem is poverty. It isn't globalization that is contributing to disease, emigration, and the like—it is the poverty that results from a *lack* of integration into the world economic system. Too many countries have undertaken needed economic reforms too slowly or halfheartedly. They warn that economic liberalization is like riding a bicycle: you either move forward, or you fall off. It is this hesitancy, or lack of full cooperation, that explains why so few have yet to see improvement in their standards of living.

Neoliberals go on to contend that many of these problems are rooted in individual behaviors: people *choose* to work for the wages they are offered, they make the decision to have unsafe sex, they deplete the forests in search of firewood. Therefore it is individuals and their choices—not structures—that should be blamed. However, others contend that more often than not, each of these so-called choices should be understood as a coping mechanism. For most of the world's population, the behaviors condemned are not so much about "choice" as they are about survival.

The Neoliberals Make an Adjustment

Perhaps the IMF and donors have been caught off-guard by the "IMF riots," the dislocation and hardship associated with structural adjustment. The collapse of the East Asian economies, followed by tepid growth rates in Latin America and the rest of Asia, plus a decline and negative performances in Africa and the Middle East, have forced a broader reassessment of the model by even its most ardent advocates. Poor economic performance throughout much of the third world, combined with the added pressure of the highly visible antiglobalization protests in Seattle, Prague, and Genoa, has the IMF and other IFIs now arguing that they are changing. Increasingly, as is illustrated in the *World Development Report 2000,* neoliberals are making an adjustment of their own. In an effort to salvage the economic reforms by taking off their hardest edges, the World Bank became the leading player charged with helping countries construct safety nets to carry them through the period of adjustment. Adopting the slogan "DEVELOPMENT WITH A HUMAN FACE," neoliberals approved the creation of poverty alleviation programs (PAPs) to provide populations undergoing hardship with short-term, temporary relief. They have borrowed a line from their critics and are now declaring that there is no single recipe for all the world's ills. In an interesting turnabout, the IMF now says it recognizes that every country is different and a "one-size-fits-all" solution is unlikely to suit each country's particular needs.

Does this mean that the Washington Consensus has frayed over the events of the late 1990s? Is there a crisis of legitimacy now, for the neoliberal model and its prescription? The answer, according to neoliberals, is a resounding no. The lesson learned is not that the Washington Consensus is wrong, but it is incomplete. There are some serious divides between neoliberals over the question of how to handle future meltdowns like those seen in Asia in the late 1990s. However, it is probably safe to assume that the Washington Consensus isn't declining; rather it is adapting, shifting in response to perceived needs. As part of this shifting strategy, some neoliberals argue for the creation of a "new" IMF. Horst Köhler, the managing director of the IMF, admitted that in Indonesia the SAP went too far. He said that he now recognizes that the adjustment ended up alienating the population and contributing to the disintegration of the country. As a result, the new, more flexible IMF has begun reconsidering the issue of conditionality: some conditions will continue to be necessary, but countries will now be allowed more of a voice in helping to identify what those conditions should be. In the new IMF, LDCs will be allowed to play a greater role in defining the terms of their adjustment and their reform path. This is quite a departure from the old IMF, in which decisions were made by donor countries, for aid recipients.

The IMF's very disparate group of critics differ in how seriously they take these promises, or over whether such promises should be made. Some neoliberals have even split with the IMF over the question of its proper role. They insist that the organization is already doing too much, that it needs to get out of the antipoverty business. These more conservative analysts maintain that the IMF's RESCUE PACKAGES for Asia and Mexico were mistakes because they give NICs and lenders the idea that they will always be bailed out. As a result, governments and investors are never forced to recognize the consequences of their mistakes. They will continue to be reckless with their lending and this will only mean future crises. On the other hand, many others, especially in Asia, reject such an analysis. Many Asians feel that they were let down and taken advantage of by the West during the crisis. They resent the reforms forced onto them as a precondition to assistance, and argue that it amounts to Western imperialism.

Left-leaning critics, who are critical of the new IMF for other reasons, join these voices. They say that they see through all this talk about change and insist that for neoliberals, there is still only one road to development. But some analysts view the neoliberal shift as having some potential, if it means that countries might be able to travel the road at different speeds, or even at their own pace. One shift likely to be welcomed by LDCs is the promise that the IMF would no longer urge LDCs to adopt policies promoting trade liberalization that the rich developed countries have yet to undertake. As mentioned earlier in this chapter, it is common for SAPs to force LDCs to open their economies to foreign trade, while developed countries continue to protect their domestic producers from LDC competition with subsidies and tariffs. LDCs argue that they would have a much better shot at benefiting from free trade if everyone played by its rules. Moreover, Köhler promised in 2000 that the IMF's loan portfolio would look radically different in a few years. Some analysts interpret such statements as an implicit promise of debt relief. Whatever the case, it appears that in its effort at "getting politics right," the IMF may have to accept some of its own medicine. It will have to work harder at good governance, becoming more transparent and more accountable to the public, as well as to all of its 184 member states.[32]

8

Alternative Approaches to Development

Poverty is not created by poor people. It is produced by our failure to create institutions to support human capabilities.
—Muhammad Yunus, founder of the Grameen Bank of Bangladesh[1]

Both the proponents and critics of GLOBALIZATION argue that it is faceless, emerging everywhere at once. Like the view that promotes and seeks to perpetuate it, based in NEOLIBERALISM, globalization's overwhelming dominance verges on the hegemonic. By hegemonic, we mean that something is so dominant, so powerful, that there are no apparent rivals. When it comes to globalization and the neoliberal approach to development, less developed countries (LDCs) are told again and again to remember TINA—"there is no alternative." Yet critics of the orthodoxy struggle to provide other choices; they demand a counterhegemonic approach that includes considerations of justice. These analysts seek to put development on an equal par with growth, if not ahead of it. Instead of "getting prices right" or "getting politics right," they argue for "getting institutions right for development."

Over the years a variety of alternative paths to development have been proposed—some reformist, some more revolutionary—but few of them have met with much success. Many of these proposals urge the creation of indigenous models and self-reliance, such as Tanzania's Afrosocialist *ujamma*. Others, such as China's Great Leap Forward, centered on a rejection of the capitalist world system and instead proposed autarchy. Still others, such as the NEW INTERNATIONAL ECONOMIC ORDER (NIEO), attempted to reform the international economic system to make it fairer. Among other things, they called for developed countries to increase their foreign aid allocations, and to invest in research and development of technologies appropriate to non-Western needs. Proponents of an NIEO asked that more soft loans be made available to developing countries. They called for debts to be renegotiated or forgiven. The NIEO's architects agreed that there should be less conditionality on loans; developed countries should not be so eager to impose adjustments on others that they themselves would be loath to accept. MULTINATIONAL CORPORATIONS (MNCs) should be regulated to create a fairer system that fosters development. LDCs should be allowed more of a voice at the INTERNATIONAL GOVERNMENTAL ORGANIZATIONS

(IGOs) that dominate their lives, especially the International Monetary Fund (IMF) and the World Bank. In addition, using the Organization of Petroleum-Exporting Countries (OPEC) as a model, LDCs should create cartels or producer clubs for other raw materials. These cartels could then negotiate on the world market with buyers of their goods, to set a price range acceptable to all—in order to achieve a more stable and fairer price for their products. As you can see, the proposals of the NIEO are wide-ranging and comprehensive. They date back to the 1960s, and various aspects of the NIEO are periodically resurrected for consideration. However, thus far, even the most moderate reforms have failed, mostly because LDCs have so little power with which to renegotiate the terms of their incorporation into the world economic system.

Today, a variety of activists concerned about the continued underdevelopment of much of the third world are facing the same fundamental problems that earlier generations did, when they call for the creation of a counterhegemony. Although there is plenty of disagreement among the critics of corporate-led globalization (or "globalization from above"), they generally agree on the need for "globalization from below," or grassroots-based efforts to prioritize sustainable human development and security. In short, sustainability considerations are based in the belief that the welfare of present generations should not be pursued at the expense of future generations. In its broadest sense, even the World Bank and World Trade Organization (WTO) have embraced the term "sustainability," calling it one of their principal objectives. Yet critics argue that sustainability means much more, and that it directly runs counter to neoliberal values that place a premium on greed, the profit motive, and consumerism.

Human security, on the other hand, is based in an entirely different set of values, such as cooperation, compassion, economic democracy, and decentralization. It speaks to individual and collective perceptions of present and potential threats to physical and psychological well-being. Human security is a relatively new term that takes understandings of security beyond issues of armaments and territorial security. The counterhegemony maintains that security against direct violence is just one form of human security. These analysts have extended the concept to include the security of people, not just nations. Human security is defined as the absence of structural violence such as poverty and other forms of economic, social, and environmental degradation.[2]

Efforts to promote human security center on the eradication of extreme poverty and take a holistic approach. This definition of development views it as a process and an end, the result of a complex set of interactions between political, economic, social, environmental, and cultural factors.[3] For example, one aspect of human security is the promotion of gender equality, which seeks to end discrimination against females in all areas of life. Such initiatives are proactive as well, focused on creating choices and opportunities for women and ending all forms of violence against them. Human security is also promoted through projects that target investments to benefit low-income groups. One example is agrarian reform, which includes land redistribution, the building of infrastructure such as rural roads and clinics, as well as increasing accessibility to credit and appropriate technologies. In order to get the maximum benefit from such policies all aspects of the reform (including land titles) need to be made available to women. Other "pro-poor" economic growth policies expand employment opportunities by upgrading skills in traditional and untraditional occupations, so that businesses and other enterprises can be more competitive.

One aspect of development that inspires intense disagreement within the counterhegemony is the question of whether it might be possible to promote human security through globalization. The pragmatists argue that they aren't fighting globalization as much as they are resisting its worst features. They believe that a fairer globalization can be created. These labor and human rights activists, joined by environmentalists, consumer advocates, and others, are working to replace the corporate view of liberalization with a more democratic, participatory model. Such a model would allow countries to escape externally imposed conditionality and redefine their own development directions.[4]

There are divisions among critics of globalization and the neoliberal approach, some of whom have been participants at the recently formed World Social Forum. One bloc rejects any kind of globalization and seeks to stop it in its tracks. Others believe the question is not whether we globalize, but how we globalize. They are seeking to adapt or manage globalization. Groups such as Oxfam and Drop the Debt are offering credible alternatives for the way in which we think about debt relief, labor standards, and other issues. As a whole, those who seek to adapt globalization are defining a goal. They are calling for more choices, for a people's globalization movement that eliminates inequalities between rich and poor, between the powerful and the powerless, and that expands the possibilities for self-determination.[5]

Most of these activists generally acknowledge that there are some benefits of globalization, but they want to blunt its negative impact. The majority agree that integration into the world system is inevitable and possibly even desirable, but they call for stricter labor and environmental regulations to minimize the system's exploitative potential. In other words, participants in this largely reformist forum favor engagement with the global system on terms and conditions carefully selected and coordinated by a state committed to social interests and accountable to its citizens. They seek to rewrite the rules of globalization, to make it work for people and not just profits. Such ideals are summed up by its slogan, "Another world is possible."[6]

Many of these counterhegemonic activists consider themselves to be "experimentalists," such as Ravi Kanbur and Joseph Stiglitz, who want an alternative model, but who don't offer a single replacement for the neoliberal model. Rather, they join Amartya Sen, who offers a new set of values to guide development, including a respect for traditional societies, a celebration of community over consumption, and grassroots organization. Such an approach represents a direct challenge to the neoliberal model in which growth is the primary goal. The experimentalists recognize that growth is important, but they contend that the priority to which it is accorded should be reconsidered. In other words, growth is a necessary but insufficient condition for the elimination of poverty. They argue for what they consider to be a more evenhanded perspective, in which concern with growth is balanced with equity and quality of life issues.

Likewise, the experimentalists are critical of the neoliberal model that promotes a replication of the experience of developed countries, setting each coun-

A young Pakistani student practices her letters (UN Photo)

try on the same path with the same goals. They point out that the developed countries that have been the most successful in eradicating poverty (the Scandinavian countries) have not left it to the market to sort out—rather, governments have intervened with antipoverty measures. In LDCs today, social investments in areas like education and healthcare must accompany any economic reform.

In addition, experimentalists argue that local people should be encouraged to evolve development solutions that are self-governing and in conformity with their own cultural norms and practices. They contend that projects should begin on a small scale. Community successes can then be scaled up to regional and even national levels, but remain reflective of local cultures and prioritize social responsibility. Experimentalists suggest that in some cases the end result may be a hybrid, or a fusion of two or more approaches that may even still include aspects of the neoliberal model. For example, the experimentalists recognize the necessity of a free market, but argue for a more flexible one in which governments set their own path and pace for reform. Some experimentalists offer China as a model for the flexible approach. Its gradual installation of economic reforms, including the creation of rural industry to employ displaced farmers, has resulted in high, consistent growth for over twenty years.[7]

Other experimentalist initiatives include a variety of successful grassroots-based projects that exist throughout the third world. Whether they come in the form of cooperatives, microenterprises, or the like, grassroots-based projects are the purest expression of the idea of "development of the people, for the people, by the people." Advocates of this approach insist that a participation that includes the poor and previously excluded groups is key to human security. Sustainable development is a people-centered development. This approach values local knowledge and wisdom as the basis for an authentic development. While the government can play an enabling role, providing people with the opportunity and environment for self-development, a just and sustainable development is based in inclusiveness—it is a people's movement, not a foreign-funded initiative.[8]

Such a line of attack demands a fundamental shift away from the majority of development thinking, which takes a highly centralized TOP-DOWN APPROACH. We shouldn't be treating targeted populations as victims to be "saved." This only winds up patronizing and ultimately alienating the very people agencies are trying to help. Instead, a participatory, grassroots approach is decentralized and bottom-up: it views the targeted population as a rich source of information, as experts on the environment in which they live, as conveyors of a culture that has sustained them for thousands of years.

Democratically determined development is manifested in a variety of forms. Among other things, it may involve land reform, enhancement of the role of women as agents of change, the satisfaction of critical needs, investment in human capital, or any variety of self-help programs.[9] Founded in Bangladesh in 1976, the Grameen Bank is an example of how powerful a seemingly novel, indigenous-based, BOTTOM-UP APPROACH can effectively alleviate poverty. The opposite of a trickle-down approach, the Grameen Bank offers small loans (often $40) to the landless, poor, and others without collateral. Most of the landless and poor targeted for assistance by the Grameen Bank are women, whose only other choice would be to turn to moneylenders or loan sharks. But these microcreditors do much more than provide credit to those without collateral. They foster entrepreneurship and emphasize self-employment over wage labor. Loans are not extended for immediate consumption needs, but as seed money to encourage the startup of small businesses. For example, a woman might borrow just enough money to buy a few hens and then sell the eggs in the market. Or where telephones are a luxury, she might buy a cell phone and charge for its use.

The bank, actually a network of village-based franchises, is self-sustaining. It is run like a club. Members demonstrate their reliability by initially taking out very small loans and repaying them. Gradually they become eligible for larger amounts of credit. In addition, members are educated about the value of credit. They are obliged to follow the bank's code, which among other things calls upon members to grow vegetables to eat and sell the surplus, to look after the health and education of their children, and to be ready to help each other. Peer pressure in these tightly knit groups keeps defaults rare (at about 1 percent—a much lower rate than for commercial banks). Because of the success of the program in Bangladesh, microlending coalitions such as the Microcredit Summit Campaign have a near-term goal of serving 100 million of the poorest families in countries worldwide, including the United States, China, Peru, Indonesia, and Nigeria.[10] While microlending programs are too small to effectively address the larger internal and external barriers to development, they have made a tremendous difference in the lives of individuals. Donors are coming to realize that when the poor have access to the institutions the rich enjoy, they can become self-reliant and prosper. Even lenders such as Sogebank, Haiti's leading commercial bank, are recognizing the untapped potential of small entrepreneurs and aggressively expanding into microfinance.

With a view to making change on a larger scale, many countries are hoping to emulate the success of the European Union (EU) and the North American Free Trade Agreement (NAFTA). For several decades countries have fashioned a variety of attempts at promoting regional INTEGRATION. As we discuss in greater depth in Chapter 16, many of the most successful efforts began as initiatives aimed at economic integration, which later developed into political and security alliances as well. Regional trade accords proliferated in the 1990s, and every region has undertaken a number of attempts to build strength in numbers and harness its economic energies in order to create economies of scale and to lessen dependency on developed countries. In this effort to gain strength from numbers, these experiments have varied widely in their ability to produce any leverage within the international economic system for developing countries.

In Asia, one of the most promising exclusively regional efforts at integration is ASEAN + 3, of the Association of Southeast Asian Nations. Composed of ten Southeast Asian states plus the three relatively gigantic economies of China, Japan, and South Korea, ASEAN + 3 is considered one of the most active regional groupings outside of Europe. Although the protectionist sentiments of some members have derailed hopes of a regional free trade area, the group is considering other proposals, including the creation of a common currency. The South African Development Community (SADC) is often named as one of the most promising of Africa's attempts at regional integration. Although South Africa is now a full member of the organization, the SADC was originally founded during the apartheid years to help South Africa's neighbors hold strong against that country's economic dominance of the region. One lesson of the various experiments with integration is that without built-in protections, smaller and weaker economies tend to lose out and be overshadowed by joining with a more powerful neighbor. The people of Latin America, for example, are busy sorting out this issue as they consider whether the culmination of their efforts at regional integration should include the world's largest economy, the United States.

The members of the Andean Community of Nations (CAN), the oldest of the South American attempts at regional integration, fear that the region's closer integration with the United States and Canada will allow it to be overrun by countries with stronger free market economies. Similarly, a more recent attempt at regional integration is also threatened by initiatives such as the Free Trade Area of the Americas (FTAA). Together composing approximately half of South America's gross domestic product (GDP), the countries of Brazil, Paraguay, Uruguay, and Argentina have sought to harness their economic strength through the creation of Mercosur, also known as the COMMON MARKET of the South. Created in 1991, Mercosur has made some progress as a free trade area and a customs union that seeks to protect its producers with a common external tariff

Figure 8.1   The Free Trade Area of the Americas: An Alternative Route to Development?

While some characterize it as an attempt to take globalization and make it more beneficial to LDCs, others view the proposed Free Trade Area of the Americas as simply business as usual. In fact, some see the rise of the FTAA as another step toward further regionalization of the world, in which the world is divided into three major blocs: the United States dominating the Americas; Europe dominating Africa and the former USSR; and China or Japan dominating Asia. These blocs are already lining up for battle. President George W. Bush has argued hard for the closer integration of regional economies in order to make the Americas more competitive against the Far East and Europe. According to a 2001 poll, over 70 percent of Latin American respondents favored the FTAA and the economic integration of the region.[11]

Not due to be formally established until 2005, the FTAA is conceptualized as a hemispheric extension of NAFTA. If the thirty-four members to the negotiations come to terms, the FTAA could create a hemispheric free trade zone (excluding Cuba) that would run from Alaska to Tierra del Fuego.[12] Neoliberals throughout the hemisphere are excited at the prospect of dropping trade and investment barriers to create a vast commercial bloc (worth $7 trillion). Many Latin American countries are eager to join such a partnership, to get access to the rich markets of the United States and Canada. Proponents of the trade pact want to benefit from free trade in the way Mexico has. Its critics worry about the negative side effects Mexico has suffered, including a loss of culture and exploitation of labor and the environment.

against nonmember imports. Sales from energy-rich Bolivia and Venezuela to energy-hungry members such as Brazil have contributed to a quadrupling of trade between members, but as a customs union, Mercosur has faltered.

In part this is because the region's economy as a whole appears to be in a meltdown, in part it is because Mercosur's common front toward outsiders is falling away. In an apparent shift of strategy, instead of deepening ties with existing members, Mercosur is expanding its reach to include new members—beyond Latin America. Members are seeking to make Mercosur a strong regional body and to reduce their traditional dependence on the United States by liberalizing trade with what is now Mercosur's single largest customer, the European Union. While some have their doubts about the plan (given the current economic difficulties), efforts at the integration of Latin American and European economies have moved at a pace unthinkable a few years ago. There are plenty of sticking points that may still derail the initiative, but the EU has indicated a major change in its own common external tariff—a policy that for years has protected its agricultural producers from foreign competition. This is what many LDCs have been waiting for, since such a policy has until now effectively shut them out of the highly lucrative European market. Analysts suggest that the European shift may be based in its fear of losing markets if the United States pulls Latin America closer through the FTAA. If globalization is indeed the only game in town, Latin America—and all LDCs—can try to strengthen their position by diversifying their trading relationships.

Conclusions: Must We Accept TINA?

In this chapter we have discussed a variety of issues central to the study of the international economic system. By now you should have a sense of some of the economic diversity that exists within the third world. You should recognize some of the differences, but also similarities in the range of LDC experiences. We have discussed globalization as an economic force that is accelerating the integration of non-Western economies into the international economic system. Throughout the chapter we have debated the pros and cons of this integration, and considered how globalization has opened opportunities but also created problems for LDCs. Yet repeatedly we are reminded by neoliberals that "there is no alternative." Even critics of globalization agree that it can seem unstoppable. Non-Western economies are expected to conform to the rules and accept the adjustments pressed upon them by donors. With very few exceptions, LDCs are operating within the constraints of a global capitalist system. It is important to recognize that while they are not powerless, the political leaders of non-Western countries are limited in their capacity to make decisions. To some degree, of course, this is true for the leaders of rich countries as well. With a total national debt of more than $6 trillion, the United States has three times the combined debt of all the LDCs.[13] However, because of the advantageous position of the United States within the international economic system, and because it is a leading member of the international economic organizations calling the shots, even the world's largest debtor is not held accountable to the rules in the same way that less powerful debtors are.

Linking Concepts and Cases

As we turn now to a discussion of how our eight case studies are faring in the international economic system, try to identify some of the various ways in which these countries are coping with the economic pressures on them. They are also having varying degrees of success in this endeavor. It may be helpful or instructive for you to do some research to update this material.

How are our cases doing in terms of GROWTH and DEVELOPMENT? Have there been any significant changes in their economic fortunes since this book was published? Which countries do you consider to be better off? Which are performing the worst? Why have some countries been more successful in their adoption of NEOLIBERALISM than others? How do you define "success"? How do you see the struggle between growth and development playing out in these countries? What are these countries' experiences with HIV/AIDS? To what can you attribute the difference in priority that governments accord to fighting the disease? In which countries has the pursuit of economic growth meant environmental devastation? How dependent is each of these countries on the export of raw materials? How diversified are their economies? What kind of support do you think the United States should be willing to offer these countries? Why?

Case Study: Mexico

At the start of the twenty-first century, Mexico was considered by the West to be a model of economic reform. However, twenty years earlier the country was at the epicenter of a debt crisis. Its economic problems can be traced at least as far back as the 1970s, when it was one of the world's largest oil producers. Oil prices had reached an all-time high and governments of the Institutional Revolutionary Party (PRI) borrowed large sums and spent lavishly. Unfortunately for Mexico, oil prices had dropped by the early 1980s and Mexico was left with one of the largest debts in the world—$80 billion. The government had borrowed far beyond its means, was being charged exorbitant interest rates, and could not keep up with its payments.

After Mexico rocked the international financial system by threatening to default on its debt, the country was compelled to adopt a series of AUSTERITY PLANS throughout the 1980s. However, Mexico's economic problems continued and its debt piled up. By late 1994, in order to win U.S. support for Mexico's membership in the North American Free Trade Agreement (NAFTA), Mexico agreed to the terms of another round of economic reforms. Mexico had little choice but to faithfully meet the conditions outlined by the INTERNATIONAL MONETARY FUND (IMF). Then-president Ernesto Zedillo announced a series of measures, including a 40 percent devaluation of the peso that went into effect literally overnight. The combined effect of the reforms proved a shock to the system. The peso collapsed and the economy took a nosedive. Growth rates plunged into the negative digits. Inflation and interest rates soared. The effect on the middle class and the poor has been compared to that of a financial neutron bomb: it destroyed the population, leaving only the real estate standing. People couldn't afford basic necessities. Instead of milk, some parents had to feed their children coffee just to put something in their stomachs. Although the suicide rate had been steadily rising in Mexico since the crisis began in the early 1980s, it peaked as the economy hit bottom in 1995.

The gravity of this crisis (and the fear of wider repercussions resulting from it) spurred the United States to press the IMF to provide Mexico with a $40 billion emergency bailout package—at the time the largest rescue ever. This intervention prevented Mexico from defaulting on its debt and enabled it to continue on with its economic reform. By the late 1990s the country appeared to have made it through its period of austerity and surprised many with the speed of its recovery. Mexico is now a major exporter, and although its gross domestic product (GDP) fell by 0.3 percent in 2001, it enjoyed healthy growth rates of 6–7 percent from the late 1990s through 2000. It is the second largest economy in Latin America, and second only to Canada as a trading partner with the United States.

While some of Mexico's recent growth is also related to higher oil prices, much of it is due to Mexico's membership in the North American Free Trade Agreement. Since 1994 NAFTA has established a free trade zone between the United States, Canada, and Mexico. Because goods produced in Mexico can be exported to either of its partners in NAFTA duty-free, MULTINATIONAL CORPORATIONS (MNCs) such as General Motors, Sony, Sanyo, and Goodyear have poured into Mexico. Foreign investment has tripled, as businesses were eager to move to Mexico, with its low wages and lax enforcement of environmental regulations. Since the passage of NAFTA the numbers of MAQUILADORAS have mushroomed, with devastating results for rivers, rank with industrial byproducts and raw sewage. This is especially a problem for towns unable to keep up with the rapid growth in population along the U.S.-Mexican border. Still, most businesspeople consider NAFTA to have been a boon for the Mexican economy; *maquila* goods now compose nearly half of Mexico's exports.

While during the go-go years of the 1990s the export enclaves of the north were described as thriving, the south offered—and continues to offer—a very different picture. Although Mexico's GDP per capita at the turn of the twenty-first century was $3,840, one would never know it after examining the human development indicators for southern Mexico. Literacy rates, life expectancy, and infant, child, and maternal morbidity and mortality rates there are much worse than in the rest of Mexico and rank with those of the world's poorest countries. Mexico's official minimum wage is about four dollars a day. Yet one-third of the working population earns even less than the minimum. In 2001, 40 percent of the population lived below the poverty line.[1]

President Vicente Fox plans to close the development gap between Mexico's north and south by extending the north's relative *maquila*-based prosperity southward. Although neoliberals on both sides of the border have expressed some interest in this plan, others are more skeptical. The critics argue that the *maquila* model is one that Mexico should not embrace; instead of bringing development, GLOBALIZATION has further marginalized the poor and increased the country's dependence on the United States. Small farmers are having a very difficult time competing against highly subsidized U.S. farmers and agribusiness, as their prices are undercut by cheap imports from the United States. If the current trend continues, the country could soon even be dependent on imports of corn, a traditional Mexican staple. However, placing his bets on the long-term benefits of globalization and closer integration with the United States, it seems likely that President Fox will continue on the neoliberal path of economic reform.

Whatever its future, Mexico's market is now one of the most open in Latin America. This country's experience illustrates both the benefits and the risks of globalization: Mexico's recovery coincided with an economic boom in the United States, but the recession in the United States was quickly felt in Mexico. Even before the U.S. slowdown was officially pronounced a recession, the Mexican government slashed its projections for economic growth in 2001 from 4.5 to 2.5 percent. By late 2001, *maquiladora* operators such as DaimlerChrysler had shut down plants and cut hundreds of thousands of Mexican jobs. In a country that once prided itself on having the lowest unemployment rates in Latin America, it is estimated that 20 percent of the population is unemployed or underemployed—and the government offers no unemployment benefits. Still, Mexico is the only Latin American country whose economy has remained relatively stable during the latest global economic slowdown. Like his northern counterpart, President Fox remains optimistic that the current economic crisis will be a short one. However, to gird itself against more fallout, the government is aggressively pursuing expanding its economic partnerships with several European, Asian, and Latin American countries. But with nearly nine-tenths of its exports going to the United States, for now at least Mexico's economy is inextricably linked to and dependent on its northern neighbor.[2]

Case Study: Peru

Since independence Peru has struggled through fifty-year cycles of debt, dependence, and default.[3] Its economy was based on the export of raw materials such as guano and nitrates in the nineteenth century and it has been dependent on the sale of agricultural goods and mineral products for much of the last hundred years. Here is a country where the gap between rich and poor has not improved substantially over time. As you read in Chapter 5, a tiny elite of landowners and merchants have long controlled the country's wealth. In the 1960s, a leftist military government attempted to redistribute wealth by nationalizing several foreign-owned firms and attempting one of the region's most ambitious land reforms. However, for a variety of reasons the reforms failed to benefit the majority of farm families and the government was unsuccessful in asserting itself against the more powerful MNCs.

In the 1970s, prices for Peru's exports plummeted while its expenditures rose, and the country fell deeply into debt. Peru was in crisis. By the 1980s, its creditors were demanding that the country pay half of all the hard currency it earned each year to service its debt of $16 billion. Unable to keep up with its payments, Peru fell $1 billion into arrears. In what has been described as a "brave but dumb" strategy, President Alan García declared a moratorium on servicing its debt, limiting payments to 10 percent of its export earnings. The international financial community responded by making Peru ineligible for credit. Peru became a pariah—desperate for cash, forced to dramatically cut imports, and living day by day. Not surprisingly, by the late 1980s the country suffered from a deep and prolonged plunge into recession. Between 1985 and 1990, the percentage of Peruvians living below the poverty line grew from 17 to 44 percent. Economic trends in Peru in the 1980s were among the worst in Latin America—and the region as a whole was struggling with what is often called "the lost decade."[4]

By the end of García's term many Peruvians were frantic for another approach. Although as a presidential candidate Alberto Fujimori had campaigned against IMF reforms, after his inauguration he promised that he could get results from an ambitious program of neoliberalism. With the backing of business elites, the new president undertook one of the most radical privatizations in Latin America and opened Peru up to foreign investment. The displacement of workers associated with the sale of STATE-OWNED ENTERPRISES (SOEs), combined with drastic cuts in social spending, was likened to a form of shock therapy (so named for an invasive medical procedure in which the patient is nearly killed in order to be saved). This policy became known in Peru as "Fujishock."[5]

In this case the patient reacted by going into a deep recession. The sudden lack of government services, including sanitation and potable water, paved the way for a reappearance of cholera, a poverty-related disease that had been unknown in Peru since the 1800s. Some parts of Peru had never before known such economic distress. Yet because Fujimori was willing to push through the reforms, Peru was able to resuscitate its relationship with the IMF and obtain debt relief. By the mid-1990s foreign investment was up and the country was registering impressive growth rates. Most important for Peruvians, inflation was brought down to the lowest levels in forty years. Despite the hardship associated with Fujishock, the end to hyperinflation bought the president enormous goodwill.[6]

Yet events beyond Fujimori's control soon brought that brief period of recovery to a close. The weather phenomenon El Niño and the Asian financial crisis hit the agriculture and fishery sectors hard in 1997 and 1998. Although it now appears that the Fujimori administration attempted to cover it up in its official economic reports, Peru suffered a recession in 1998 and growth remained stagnant through the turn of the century. Peru was rocked by strikes against low wages, the privatization program, as well as the possibility of a third term for Fujimori, who was forced to step down in 2000.

As a candidate for president in the 2001 elections, Alejandro Toledo's campaign slogan was "More Work." Peruvians suffer from extensive underemployment—nearly three-quarters of the population can only find part-time work. This is widely considered to be the central economic issue for Peruvians. Half the population lives below the poverty line and 15 percent live in extreme poverty. Unable to subsist on what they could earn as farmers, now even young women are leaving the countryside to find work. This urban crush has been exacerbated by the impact of economic reform: in the last few years tens of thousands of working-class industrial jobs have been lost through privatization, and middle-class bureaucrats were put out of work by government cuts. For those that were able to hang on to their jobs, Peru's STRUCTURAL ADJUSTMENT PROGRAM (SAP) dismantled regulatory legislation protecting workers. Peru has successfully attracted foreign investment, but mostly in sectors such as mining and oil, which do not generate many jobs. In the meantime, the businesses that are hiring have made the most of this situation, demanding "flexibilization." The result has been a growing class of temporary workers, unrepresented by unions and operating under extremely precarious conditions. They have joined the ranks of the INFORMAL SECTOR, which is believed to employ more Peruvians than any other part of the economy.

Toledo hopes to make good on his campaign promises by promoting intensive farming, food processing, and tourism. However, it will be difficult for him to deliver on his pledge to create 400,000 new jobs, since the country has been in a severe recession and was just projecting a modest 4 percent growth in 2002 (although this was higher than just about every other country in the embattled region). To help encourage that recovery, this former economist for the WORLD BANK adopted a centrist economic policy. Toledo recognized that globalization is a reality; he has made it very clear that Peru needs international aid and investment (this may be soon in coming, since in 2002 the U.S. Congress renewed the Andean Trade Preferences Act, which lowers tariffs for Peruvian goods sold in the United States). Similarly, Toledo attempted to move forward with IMF-sanctioned privatizations in 2002. However, the effort was met with such violent protests that the new democracy experienced its first governability crisis and the president was forced to call a state of emergency. This incident seems to have shaken Toledo; as of early 2003, he appears less eager to push this and other market reforms, widely perceived in Peru to be a foreign-prescribed remedy. Toledo campaigned insisting that the state would take the sharp edges off of the free market reforms. He said that he believes it is the government's job to provide some public assistance and to protect Peruvians from the extreme hardship associated with adjustment. The president is known as much for his indecision as his big promises; consequently, Peruvians and donors alike are eager to see if Toledo can actually produce "capitalism with a human face."

Case Study: Nigeria

As the world's sixth largest exporter of oil, Nigeria would seem to be the envy of much of the third world. One might expect that at least its standard of living would hover near that of other oil producers. However, Nigeria is one of the poorest countries in the world. Oil didn't guarantee Mexico's development, and it is often said to be a curse of sorts for Nigeria.

Part of the problem is that one Nigerian government after another has stolen a large portion of the hundreds of billions of dollars in revenue generated by oil. And what hasn't been stolen has been misspent. Windfalls from the days when oil prices were high were wasted on white elephants, such as a steel mill that was initiated more than twenty years ago. At a cost of $8 billion, the Ajaokuta steelworks was the biggest industrial project in Africa. It has never come into operation, and few believe that even if it does, it can never operate efficiently.

But before all the blame goes to corrupt or incompetent policymakers, a word needs to be said about the role of MNCs in Nigeria, especially Shell Oil. The Niger Delta, site of most of the country's petroleum and natural gas reserves, is not only an environmental basket case (at least 2.5 million barrels of oil have been spilled into the delta—equal to ten *Exxon Valdez* disasters).[7] It is also one of the country's poorest areas, as little of the wealth created by the extraction of 2 million barrels of oil per day has been returned to its residents.

Nigeria's rank on almost any level of human development is especially tragic because Nigeria is a country of such tremendous potential. GDP per capita was just $310 in 1999. Its vast resources could provide a diversified economic base, its huge population could create an economy of scale. Its resilient small farmers have tenaciously hung on for years—even as the government has doggedly shifted its focus from agriculture to oil. Yet Nigeria is a classic monocultural economy today. Approximately 95 percent of its foreign exchange is earned from the sale of petroleum and petroleum-based products, but the industry fails to serve or employ many Nigerians. Ironically, Nigerian motorists routinely spend hours of their workdays waiting in some of the longest gas lines in the world.

In the mid-1980s, heavily in debt, a military government negotiated Nigeria's first SAP with the IMF. The adjustment contributed to resumed economic growth, but at a high human cost. The dictatorship that followed basically thumbed its nose at the IMF and proceeded to rob the country blind. Nigeria became an international outcast and fell into economic decline. Democratically elected president Olusegun Obasanjo found the treasury empty when he took office in May 1999. In arrears in repayment of a nearly $30 billion debt that exceeded 75 percent of the country's GDP, Obasanjo came into office desperate for debt relief. Servicing the debt would account for more than 30 percent of the budget.

To pay it, Obasanjo attempted to raise revenues by quickly increasing Nigeria's output of oil by 50 percent. But he needed foreign investment to pay for technological improvements that would make this possible. To do this he had to combat the view widely held among investors that there are big opportunities in Nigeria, but also big risks. Eager for international assistance of all sorts, early in his term Obasanjo declared himself a neoliberal reformer. However, he was under heavy pressure to accept an austerity plan that would include privatization of SOEs, deregulation of government price controls on basic goods, and devaluation of Nigeria's currency, the naira. In addition, the IMF wanted the president to implement a wage freeze while simultaneously deregulating prices. A deal was struck in 2000 in which the IMF promised $1 billion in loans and a restructuring of the country's $35 billion debt. Consequently, the Nigerian president was expected to cut government subsidies of food, likely to result in a 50 percent increase in the prices of basic foodstuffs such as oil, rice, and flour. When he did the same for popular fuel subsidies in early 2002 (resulting in an 18 percent price increase), labor unions launched a general strike to which police responded with tear gas and bullets. As the government moves forward with its austerity plans, it can expect to see more mass violence, as people cannot afford basic necessities. The number of Nigerians earning less than one dollar a day jumped from 34 percent of the population in 1992 to 70 percent in 1999. And user fees have been introduced for all public services, including education and healthcare. As elsewhere, it is women who must find ways to make do for their families and who will bear much of the burden of structural adjustment.

And all of this—just as Nigerians were expecting things to get better. Instead of a DEMOCRACY DIVIDEND, Nigerians are feeling the impact of the adjustment: life expectancy has fallen to age fifty-one; infant mortality has risen to 74 per 1,000 live births (compared to 6 per 1,000 in the United States). In addition, there are new epidemics of cholera, yellow fever, and meningitis—all associated with rising poverty. Even in the southwest, which should be food self-sufficient, hunger and malnutrition are widespread. The pressure the president has been feeling from the IMF is likely to be matched by the heat he will feel at home—if he actually has the stomach for the reform. It should then come as no surprise that in what is widely viewed as a politically calculated move (just a year before the 2003 presidential elections) Obasanjo went off the prescribed diet. In fact, there are a number of signs that Obasanjo has gone on a binge: instead of rebuilding the country's crumbling infrastructure, the government spent $93 million on a space program and over $330 million on a new soccer stadium—more than it allocated to health or education.[8] Excessive spending could jeopardize Nigeria's line of credit with the IMF. Yet the strict regimen prescribed by donors is likely to produce the kind of political turmoil that could buy Obasanjo an early retirement.

Case Study: Zimbabwe

In 2000, Zimbabwe held the dubious title of "Africa's fastest-shrinking economy."[9] That must have come as especially hurtful news to its citizens, since with its comparatively diverse base, Zimbabwe's economy should be better off than that of many other African countries. It is relatively more industrialized than much of Africa, with its sugar refineries and textile industry. Although tobacco dominates its exports, Zimbabwe also sells gold and other minerals on the world market. Until recently it was not only able to feed its population, but it was also a food exporter. It once enjoyed a healthy tourist industry based around Victoria Falls, often listed as one of the wonders of the world. Most impressively, under the Robert Mugabe government Zimbabwe was making significant strides in human development. Upon independence in 1980, the Zimbabwe African National Union–Patriotic Front (ZANU-PF) had made its antipoverty campaign a priority. It invested heavily in schools and healthcare, undoing the years of neglect that had been policy under white minority rule. Such programs succeeded in attaining for Zimbabweans one of the highest literacy rates on the continent.

However, the majority of its citizens could never be called wealthy, and their standard of living declined precipitously through the late 1990s. Although they differ in emphasis, most analysts agree that several factors explain Zimbabwe's suffering. Some argue that the steady impoverishment of the country is due to government mismanagement. Others agree but blame it on the effect of the region's many civil wars, including Zimbabwe's participation in the Congolese War, which is estimated to have cost $1 million per day. Climatic disasters such as drought are also identified for the misery they have caused. But the austerity associated with structural adjustment must also be recognized as a major factor in this equation.

Deep in debt for many of the reasons mentioned earlier in this chapter and needing to attract foreign investment and promote trade, the Mugabe government had little choice but to accept the terms of an SAP in 1991. But the government backed away from structural reform after 1998, as the prescribed devaluation failed to boost exports and chronic fuel shortages shut down factories. Fuel prices rose by nearly 75 percent in 2001, and rising bus fares left many people walking. Growth rates hovered around zero. The annual income of the average Zimbabwean was estimated to have dropped from $620 in 1998 to $437 in 1999. By 2001, 60 percent of the population was living below the poverty line, and 60 percent of the adult population was unemployed. People found that they could not afford basic necessities such as cornmeal, as inflation grew from 22 percent in 1995 to 80 percent in 2000 to over 100 percent by 2002. The IMF predicted 522 percent inflation for 2003. Those who managed to find the money to pay higher prices often found staples periodically unavailable. It was not uncommon to come across long lines for gasoline, kerosene, cooking oil, and even bread. Because the government didn't pay peasant farmers for their maize crop in 2000, there was no money (or incentive) to plant for the next year. Combine that with two seasons of unusually bad weather, war, and political instability, and it is no wonder that cereal production in 2002 was down by 67 percent since 2001. Most worrisome is that hunger looms now even at harvest time. The World Food Program estimated in late 2002 that more than 15 million people in southern Africa urgently needed food aid (approximately 8 million of them in Zimbabwe—more than two-thirds of the country's population). And famine is something many Zimbabweans had thought was a thing of the past.[10]

With the famine not yet into full swing there were already rumors that Zimbabwean schoolchildren were fainting of hunger in their classrooms—and there is little of a government safety net to catch them.[11] Certainly the Mugabe government shares a good portion of the blame for the state of the economy, but it is because of budget cuts required by the SAP that the government's "Growth with Equity" program was reversed and conditions for the majority have worsened. Two years into the reform adopted more than a decade ago, the country was losing the impressive gains it had made in terms of infant and child mortality and literacy rates. Ten years into the SAP, there were such serious shortages of basic medicines and supplies like soap that it was not uncommon to hear of patients buying their own medicines from a pharmacist before going to the hospital. Per capita spending on public health plummeted below levels seen in the 1980s—this in a country where one in three adults are infected with HIV/AIDS. By 2002 life expectancy in Zimbabwe had dropped to age thirty-six.[12] The disease has already wreaked havoc on the country. One can only imagine its long-term effects on Zimbabwe.

In much of Zimbabwe "SAP" has come to stand for "Suffering for African People."[13] Even the World Bank expects that things will get worse before they get better, but it and other INTERNATIONAL FINANCIAL INSTITUTIONS (IFIs) blame the Mugabe government for the country's woes. In 1999, faced with upcoming parliamentary elections and sporadic riots over shortages, Mugabe chose a course that many have described as self-defense. He appealed to the 70 percent of the population who live in rural areas, resurrecting the long-neglected issue of land reform with his slogan "The Land Is the Economy, the Economy Is the Land."

For over 100 years, land has been a central issue in Zimbabwean politics. Because the vast majority of Zimbabweans earn their living from agriculture, it is also a key economic issue. As of mid-2002, white Zimbabweans composed 1 percent of the population. Yet more than two decades after independence, hundreds of thousands of blacks were still on waiting lists while 4,500 whites still owned 70 percent of the country's best land. Make no mistake about it: land reform is an issue the government absolutely must deal with. However, in what many inside and outside Zimbabwe consider a thinly veiled attempt to save his political career, Mugabe adopted a more radical approach. He urged the seizure of white farms without compensation. Hundreds of squatters congregated on 1,000 farms since 2000 and the president consistently refused to remove them, despite court orders and international outcry. By early 2003, 95 percent of the country's commercial farmland was scheduled for redistribution. The redistribution proceeded in stages. White farmers were given ninety days to leave and those who refused were rounded up and arrested (in an interesting turn of events) for illegally occupying the land. In the meantime, despite predictions of a massive famine, the Mugabe government ordered these farmers to cease work on the land.[14]

As this book went to press, the reform was ongoing. Only the effect on the economy was clear. Production had virtually ground to a halt at the country's white-owned farms, which normally account for much of Zimbabwe's food supply, as well as approximately half of its exports and foreign exchange earnings. Not only did this jeopardize the jobs of 400,000 farm laborers, but business confidence was in tatters, investors were scared off, and tourism declined by 60 percent between 2000 and 2001. There was no rule of law. Even many of those who agreed that a massive land reform was long overdue argue that this particular approach was the last thing Zimbabwe needed. The economy was at its lowest point since independence. Worse yet, as Zimbabwe continued its free fall, it threatened to pull many of its neighbors down with it.

Case Study: Iran

Leaders of the Islamic Republic of Iran have long struggled over many issues related to political economy. The current economic system combines central planning (complete with five-year plans and projections), state ownership of key industries (namely oil), village farming, and the rise of small-scale private industries. Since the 1990s the country's financial problems have intensified—exacerbated by an import surge that began in 1989—and Iranian leaders have experimented with openings to the West, especially in their attempts to exploit the country's chief export, oil, and balance the state's role in moderating commerce and economic well-being. As Iran increases its integration with the rest of the world, these struggles are likely to intensify.

One of the central issues facing Iran is its dependence on Western countries, especially through the preeminence of oil in Iran's political economy. Sometimes referred to as "black gold," oil has dominated all aspects of life in Iran since its discovery in the early 1900s. For many years, Iran's identity in the world economic system was as a provider of cheap oil and a consumer of Western goods and services. Economic self-sufficiency was a goal elucidated by the post-1979 leadership, largely in vain. Despite these concerns, which prompted attempts to diversify, Iran continues to be plagued by such dependence and by the fluctuations endemic to such an export. At times this has worked in Iran's favor, such as in the early 1970s and mid-1990s, but at other times, when oil prices are low, this reliance has caused many problems. For example, from 1977 to 1989 the economy hit a downturn and income per capita dropped nearly 45 percent.[15] Profits are needed in the oil business—the state plan is to double output by 2020—in order to finance other sectors of the economy. To promote this growth, the Islamic Republic has purchased ten new oil tankers, built in China and South Korea. Iran's economy was hobbled by its war with Iraq in the 1980s. Natural disasters (the 1990 earthquake caused $7 billion worth of damage), combined with the flood of immigrants who fled to Iran throughout the 1990s (the refugee population is estimated to be as high as 4 million), have stretched the economy to its limits.[16] Additionally, attempts to produce growth through rapid industrialization and virtually unlimited urbanization have wreaked havoc on the Iranian natural environment, attention to which is only belatedly being given.

As an Islamic state, Iran has attempted to integrate the teachings of the Quran in all aspects of life, including the financial sector. Iran and Sudan are the only two Islamic countries that have attempted to incorporate the Quran's condemnation of earned interest (*riba* in Arabic) through the establishment of special Islamic banks (although other countries, including Turkey, Malaysia, and Kuwait, offer Islamic banks as an option to conventional, interest-bearing banks). Even though Islamic banks avoid traditional interest calculations because they are exploitative, other profit arrangements, based more on future profits of borrowers, are used in many Islamic banks throughout the world.[17] Yet under Ali Akbar Hashemi Rafsanjani's leadership, the Iranian economy has become increasingly integrated, and the rial is now fully convertible.

Similar to other non-Western countries, Iran promoted free trade zones (FTZs) in the early 1990s, with tax exemptions, customs duties, and other incentives to promote economic growth and foreign investment. Such moves have come at great cost: unemployment is high (officially reported at 33 percent, although it is likely much higher), and the gap between the rich and the poor is growing. Attempts to privatize formerly nationally owned companies and corporations threaten to put even more people out of work. An occasional Mercedes can be seen in the streets, and the ultimate sign of affluence is a cell phone. Yet poverty remains endemic for over 50 percent of the population. While women are increasingly integrated into the work force, they tend to have the strongest presence in fields such as education and healthcare, and their employment can be curtailed by the wishes of their husband.

Rebuilding an economy damaged by war and international strife and crippled by international debt is becoming a priority of the current Iranian leadership, even if leaders insist that the correct political and cultural environment must exist in order to ensure economic development in the long run. The competing aspects of this goal are even more intense in the urban areas, where social services for a growing population are already strained. Attempts to limit population growth have been less than successful, as the Iranian population has experienced the highest population growth in the world, 3.7 percent. President Mohammed Khatami has launched many efforts to promote closer economic relations with Iran's neighbors, including hosting an Organization of the Islamic Conference (OIC) economic summit in Tehran in 1997—which the United States unsuccessfully tried to sabotage by hosting a rival conference in Qatar at the same time.[18] Iran has also sought relations with European countries, including Italy and France, searching for new trading partners and welcoming foreign textiles and other goods into the country. But such moves will be seen as a weakness by many in the government and society, and may only increase Iran's economic, social, and political vulnerability.

Case Study: Turkey

Turkey is a state rich in natural resources. One of the most productive of these resources is its geography; ancient Anatolia was a main crossroad between East and West on the famed Silk Road between Xi'an (China) and Rome. Yet its location at this intersection of East and West, and its fragile relations with neighboring countries, pose both challenges and opportunities to the Turkish people today. Demonstrative of the vulnerabilities of many non-Western economies, which rely on export-oriented growth, Turkey suffered a great deal as a result of the UN embargo against Iraq, one of the country's major markets for export. The war in Bosnia also impacted Turkish exports, largely due to increases in freight expenses. Currency devaluation throughout Asia and in the Russian Federation also hurt Turkish exports to those regions, as the imported Turkish products became increasingly expensive for consumers to purchase. Each of these events, occurring outside Turkey's borders, signify some of the more problematic aspects of its attempts at global integration and indeed the contradictions experienced by states attempting modernization.[19]

In many ways, though, the Turkish economy has much dynamism, combining both modern industry and traditional crafts. It also has a history of mingling state control with private, entrepreneurial enterprise. State intervention in the economy was largely curtailed in the 1980s, except for the industrial sector. Unlike Iran, for example, Turkey's primary export of textiles and clothing remains under private rather than governmental control. Yet this dynamism has been weakened, as all types of disasters have hit home in Turkey as well, including natural, political, and economic crises. For example, the devastating Izmit earthquake of 1999, which claimed an estimated 20,000 lives, struck the region that accounts for over 35 percent of the state's GDP, just when leaders of the country were negotiating a $5 billion loan from the IMF. Because of the government's delayed response to the crisis—a natural disaster exacerbated by shoddily constructed apartment buildings that were greased with corrupt payoffs—public confidence in the government plunged. As inflation continues to soar, many local officials attempt to supplement their meager state salaries with bribes, eroding public sentiment even further.

Since the end of World War II, Turkey's leaders have increasingly looked to the West for economic markets and trade. Much of this "glance West" has surrounded Turkey's attempts to become a member of the European Union (EU), a complicated effort that we will discuss in later chapters. Turkey became an associate economic member of the EU's precursor, the European Community, in 1963, and is the only country to have concluded a customs union agreement (forged in 1996) without being a full member.[20] In December 2002, much to the disappointment of many in Turkey, EU leaders failed to set a firm date to begin formal negotiations for Turkey's membership. In fact, such discussions will not commence until December 2004. A combination of domestic human rights concerns (especially related to Turkey's treatment of the dissident Kurdish population) and tensions with EU member Greece, help explain this dichotomy of economic ties without political acceptance. Adding insult to injury, former French president Valéry Giscard d'Estaing publicly stated that, in his opinion, inviting Turkey to join the EU would mean "the end of Europe."[21] He verbalized what many in Turkey have long believed—that the EU is a "Christian club" that is unlikely to welcome them with open arms.

Continuous struggles with routinely double-digit inflation, inadequate investment in technology and manufacturing, unceasing unemployment, and widespread income disparity have become the norm rather than the exception. Increasingly, Turkey's debt burden, especially to multilateral institutions, takes a toll on any signs of progress. Each challenge is often made worse by publicly pitched battles between politicians, including high-ranking leaders such as former president Ahmet Necdet Sezer and Prime Minister Bülent Ecevit. Following the financial crisis of 2000–2001, launched by a series of bank failures (linked to corruption), the IMF proposed granting Turkey nearly $15 billion worth of credit, demanding that leaders increase the privatization of telephone, airline, and power services, and improve the famously corrupt and moribund banking system. Few are confident that the government will be able to adequately rise to the demands, which include privatizing state-owned companies, and capping wage increases for government employees, hardly a move that will boost morale. In addition to the threat of widespread unemployment from the restructuring of state-owned companies, these painful SAP demands risk endangering already weak political coalitions. In a ringing endorsement, the World Bank and IMF cite Turkey and Argentina as "two of the world's most perilous developed economies."[22] The Argentine prediction has rung painfully true—will Turkey follow? Now that the charismatic Kemal Dervis has resigned as vice president of the World Bank in order to return to Turkey and guide it through such crises, maybe the prognosis will brighten, although many Turkish citizens express their doubts. To some extent, Turkish citizens have grown to tolerate the endemic inflation and fluctuating economic policies of their governments.[23] Yet the social and economic drain of Turkey's SAPs were prominent themes in the 2002 parliamentary elections. The leader of the Youth Party, popular multimillionaire Cem Uzan, promised to "kick out the IMF" and teach the United States and the West "a good lesson."[24] (In the end, his party failed to cross the 10 percent threshold required to gain seats in parliament.) Even though Recep Erdogan, the leader of the victorious Justice and Development Party, officially backs the SAPs, he campaigned on the need to soften the hardships endured by ordinary Turks.

Case Study: China

It is ironic that a state that once prided itself on autarky and self-sufficiency in the 1960s is now one of the most rapidly growing and interconnected economies in the world. It is often stated that if all of China's provinces were counted as individual countries, the twenty fastest-growing countries in the world between 1978 and 1995 would all have been Chinese. Yet bookies would have a hard time determining the odds of China's future economic situation. The World Bank foresees two dramatically different scenarios for China's future. One is that China could be the East Asian exemplar of rapid growth followed by stagnation, an outcome they have come to call "Sinoclerosis" (with *Sino* meaning "China"). We have witnessed such downturns elsewhere, but what makes China's case different is the dizzy pace of its change, which could lengthen any recovery efforts as well. The second outcome that global observers posit is the long-term development of a fully integrated yet strong Chinese economy, able to provide for its own population and come to the assistance of others as well.[25] At this juncture, the latter seems optimistic, although not impossible.

China's leaders have adopted multiple economic models, some disastrous, and some potentially successful. In the late 1950s, Mao Zedong launched the so-called Great Leap Forward as a way to economically modernize the country and catch up with the West. Through intense agricultural and industrial programs that included encouraging farmers to construct "backyard burners" in their fields in order to melt down pots and pans to make steel, Mao proclaimed that the Chinese people could surpass Western production totals in less than fifteen years. The results were disastrous: as many as 20 million people are believed to have died of starvation because of the misguided agricultural policies of the period—and some estimate this total could be as high as 30 million.[26] The man to follow Mao, Deng Xiaoping, took economic growth and prosperity as his primary goal. Touting such non-Marxist phrases as "to get rich is glorious" and "it is all right for some to get rich first," Deng launched a new economic revolution of sorts in the 1980s. Ordinary people could start up their own companies and trade their agricultural products with local governments, and even foreign firms such as Atlanta-based Coca-Cola were invited to produce, market, and sell their products on the mainland. The results, the full ramification of which we will not know for some time, have been astounding.

As we have discussed throughout the preceding chapter, compared to the recent performance of other non-Western countries, China is an anomaly, particularly in its ability to lift people out of poverty. Yet considerable struggles remain, in large part because of the uneven direction of China's economic change. Today the Beijing government officially recognizes more than 60 million poor people, mostly in the central and western regions of the country. Most believe that this number is far too low, and that it is increasing rapidly. Leaders have promoted a domestically run, collaborative program to assist rural women in supporting themselves and their families. This "Program of Happiness," coordinated by the China Population Welfare Foundation, the Chinese National Family Planning Association, and the Chinese Population Gazette, provides microloans for Chinese mothers to start their own businesses. After each recipient gets on her feet, her repaid loan goes to the next local woman who is eligible. Most feel that the local peer pressure helps keep the program growing and successful.[27]

Yet the Chinese economic situation today is sprinkled with contrasts. On one hand, it has the world's best-performing stock market (with double-digit growth), wildly popular with China's growing middle class.[28] Start-up Internet companies in Chinese cities launch a new class of "dot-com" aspirants. And although homeownership remains a rare novelty, more and more younger couples are able to purchase their own apartments, and Sweden's Ikea and other international furniture companies are opening stores along the Chinese coast. Yet today many Chinese face the prospect of widespread unemployment due to restructuring efforts of moribund SOEs. This practice, under which the government refuses to finance unprofitable companies, threatens to throw millions of Chinese citizens, many in the poorer northeastern section of the country, out of work. The so-called iron rice bowl, in which the government provided a guaranteed job for life, is being smashed. China's factory workers fear not only the specter of unemployment, but also the near absence of unemployment insurance in a state where employment used to be a guarantee. Farmers in the countryside are receiving fewer subsidies from the government (indeed they are often paid with near meaningless "IOU" cards), and are facing an increasingly competitive global agricultural market for their goods. Peasants are already mounting protests against government leaders who tax them heavily and fail to follow through on government contracts for commodities. These problems are likely to get worse, rather than better, in China's early years of membership in the WORLD TRADE ORGANIZATION (WTO).

China's rapid economic changes are taking a huge toll on the physical environment, especially on its forests and native panda population. Even though China currently bans commercial logging in its own forests, Chinese companies along the border of Burma have been contracting with legal and illegal loggers to help reach the country's growing demand for wood products. Logging and population growth combine to threaten one of China's great natural resources, the giant panda, which now unsuccessfully competes with humans for land to live upon. Scientists estimate that only 1,000 pandas remain in the wild in China, and even on national reserves set aside for panda habitats, humans compete with endangered animals to eke out a living. Government attempts to move families out of the thirty-three panda reserves have been unsuccessful, and even international programs designed to help residents establish a new life in apartments outside the reserve have been shunned by many.

Case Study: Indonesia

In the early 1990s, Indonesia was hailed as one of the successful "Little Tigers" of Southeast Asia. Yet just over a decade later, the smoldering Indonesian economy continues to falter from its precipitous collapse. Indonesia has long been searching for a viable economic model that fits the needs and resources of the people. Even after its hard-fought political independence from the Dutch, the Indonesian economy continued its dependence on primary crops introduced by the Netherlands (primarily pepper, coffee, rubber, and sugar). Under the so-called Guided Economy of 1959–1965, Sukarno nationalized all plantations: a move that led to widespread stagnation and capital flight. The president and his economic cronies concentrated on prestige projects, paying scant attention to day-to-day management of financial matters. Inflation and poverty were widespread after the government defaulted on its foreign debt and the resulting halt of foreign assistance. Indonesia's second president, Suharto, attempted to turn the Indonesian economy around, especially by mending ties with other countries. As a staunch anticommunist (who came to power under the guise of overthrowing a communist plot in 1965), Suharto received much aid from Western countries. His model of economic development was a familiar one in Asia: promote industrial and business growth under the tutelage of government sponsorship and support, with political control to limit unionization, citizen protests, and the expression of dissent.

After Indonesia's oil boom, Suharto began to shy away from the so-called Berkeley Mafia free market advice of the 1960s (Indonesia's own version of the Washington Consensus). Throughout the 1970s the president pursued increasingly restrictive trade and investment policies, favoring the steel, shipbuilding, and aircraft industries. The oil collapse in 1985 and 1986 wreaked havoc throughout the country, as prices fell below ten dollars per barrel, and, returning to "Mafia" advice, Indonesia increased its exports of textiles, clothing, footwear, and wood. This system was marred with corruption: contracts were traded for regime support and the families of high-profile politicians did famously well. The Suharto family held a monopoly over the control of some spices, including cloves, and other prosperous domestic industries, such as the processing of citrus fruit. Because of back-scratching financial arrangements, few cautioned against (or even noticed) trends in poor loans, increases in short-term external debt, and other ill-conceived projects, including Suharto's children's scheme to build a "national car," which was later abandoned.[29]

The gains of the 1990s came to a screeching halt as the crisis of 1997 hit—no Asian country fared worse than Indonesia. The economy contracted nearly 14 percent in 1998. Inflation topped 65 percent and the national currency lost 70 percent of its value, producing what the World Bank referred to as one of the most dramatic reversals of fortunes ever. In January 1998, Indonesia's rupiah was named the "world's worst-performing currency." Even though consumer confidence is beginning to return, the Indonesian economy remains plagued by problems in the banking and financial sectors, especially problems with debt and loan problems. Indonesia's international debt is crushing. The government's ability to maneuver solutions to these problems is limited by a history of corrupt deals in which friends and family pocket the goods. Foreign investment has yet to return, as the country remains embroiled in political and religious turmoil.

In subsequent chapters, we will discuss Indonesia's regional discord and the possibility of fragmentation. Although much of this strife is highlighted by cultural and religious differences, there are clear economic components to Indonesia's regional battles as well: the restive areas of Aceh and northern Sulawesi have long been economically oriented to the outside world, and when economic constriction hits, these relatively prosperous regions tend to fare the worst. Additionally, disparities in economic well-being between Indonesia's myriad of ethnic groups are more pronounced compared to the relatively prosperous ethnic Chinese community—a group who are always targeted for attack when the economic situation sours. As we see in so many other situations, a debilitating economic environment tends to exacerbate other conflicts into crisis.

Similar to many of the countries we discuss, Indonesia was rocked by the demands of lending institutions to make dramatic changes. IMF conditions for the $45 million aid package in 1998 included a requirement to redirect funds away from assistance programs and social spending, and sparked a fury of unrest throughout the country. Initial runs on banks led to street riots. Demonstrations against Suharto, who was viewed as impotent in the face of outsider demands, eventually toppled the longtime president. In the post-Suharto period, Indonesia has experienced some debt forgiveness, and a gradual restoration of assistance programs. Corruption and poor governance, though, have curtailed monies from multilateral institutions (especially the World Bank and the Asian Development Bank) as well as individual governments. Indonesia's collapsed economy is only made worse by continued wrangling among the leadership and by outsider demands for change. President Abdurrahman Wahid inherited a country mired in economic crisis—his inability to improve the financial woes of Indonesians is only partially to blame for his short-lived tenure. His successor, Megawati Sukarnoputri, knows all too well how important the financial card is, but few believe she will be able to withstand the struggles that lie ahead. Much hope is placed on Indonesia's continuing status as a net oil exporter, but even oil, as we have seen elsewhere, can be an unreliable asset. As society painfully realizes the empty promises of growth and development, many may lose faith in the ability of government leaders and the world community alike.

Now It's Your Turn

Perhaps as the neoliberals tell us, the experience of a handful of countries should be a lesson to all the rest. However, after two decades of sacrifice and deteriorating conditions for the majority, is it right for developed countries to continue to insist that the neoliberal model is the only feasible path to development? Are neoliberals correct about TINA—is there really no alternative?

Should the leaders of less developed countries simply press for a more flexible approach to further integration into the INTERNATIONAL ECONOMIC SYSTEM as it currently exists? Will the managers of the system (Western donors and the international organizations they control) allow alternative paths to be forged? Or can a combination of strategies that utilize indigenous experience and culture create a system more beneficial for all? What does "independence" mean in a globalized world economy?

Suggested Readings

General
Sen, Amartya. *Development as Freedom.* New York: Knopf, 1999. Nonfiction, the Nobel laureate on the relationship between political freedom and economic well-being.

Africa
Dangarembga, Tsitsi. *Nervous Conditions.* Seattle: Seal Press, 1989. Zimbabwe: fiction, postcolonial description of the many forms of oppression experienced by a young girl.

Emecheta, Buchi. *Joys of Motherhood.* New York: George Braziller, 1980. Nigeria: fiction, describes the responsibilities of a wife and mother.

Lessing, Doris. *A Proper Marriage.* New York: HarperCollins, 1995. Zimbabwe: fiction, on violence and married life.

Uwazurike, P. Chudi. *Yesterday Was Silent.* Princeton: Sungai Books, 1994. Nigeria: fiction, describes city life during the oil boom in Lagos.

Vera, Yvonne. *Without a Name.* Harare: Baobab Press, 1994. Zimbabwe: fiction, describes the difficulties of a young woman's move from the country to the city.

Asia
Boomgaard, Peter, Freek Colombijn, and David Henley, eds. *Paper Landscapes: Explorations in the Environmental History of Indonesia.* Leiden: KITLV Press, 1997. Indonesia: nonfiction, long-term perspective on environmental degradation.

Croll, Elisabeth J. *Endangered Daughters: Discrimination and Development in Asia.* London: Routledge, 2001. Asia: nonfiction, discusses the discrimination faced by females throughout Asia, especially young girls.

Li, Ang. *The Butcher's Wife and Other Stories.* Boston: Cheng and Tsui, 1995. Trans. Howard Goldblatt. China: fiction, stories about an abused wife who kills her husband.

Lingard, Jeanette, trans. *Diverse Lives: Contemporary Stories from Indonesia.* New York: Oxford University Press, 1995. Indonesia: fiction, collection of fifteen short stories expressing a range of experiences from different walks of life in Indonesia in the 1980s and 1990s.

Tong, Su. *Rice.* New York: William Morrow, 1996. Trans. Howard Goldblatt. China: fiction, set in the 1930s, the journey faced by a starving refugee after the rice paddies are flooded.

Qing, Dai. *The River Dragon Has Come.* Trans. Yi Ming. Eds. John G. Thibodeau and Phillip B. Williams. Armonk, N.Y.: M. E. Sharpe, 1998. China: collection of essays about China's controversial Three Gorges Dam project compiled by an outspoken investigative journalist who was imprisoned for speaking out against the world's largest hydroelectric dam.

Yan, Mo. *The Republic of Wine: A Novel.* Trans. Howard Goldblatt. New York: Arcade, 2000. China: fiction, profoundly bizarre book satirizing corruption and greed in a mythical province of Liquorland.

Yan, Mo. *The Garlic Ballads.* Trans. Howard Goldblatt. New York: Viking, 1995. China: fiction, traces the disastrous effects in the Chinese countryside when the government orders farmers to grow garlic rather than rice.

Latin America and the Caribbean

Galeano, Eduardo. *Upside Down: A Primer for the Looking Glass World.* New York: Metropolitan Books, 2000. Latin America: nonfiction, on Yanqui capitalism and the North-South conflict.

Montero, Mayra. *In the Palm of Darkness.* Trans. Edith Grossman. New York: HarperCollins, 1998. Haiti: fiction, a herpetologist travels the devastatingly poor countryside and sees how poverty combines with ecological collapse.

Poniatowska, Elena. *Here's to You, Jesusa!* New York: Farrar, Straus, and Giroux, 2001. Mexico: nonfiction, the *testimonio,* or survival story of a campesina.

Middle East

Daneshvar, Simin. *Savushun: A Novel About Modern Iran.* Washington, D.C.: Mage, 1991. Iran: fiction, set during the Allied occupation of World War II.

Friedl, Erika. *Children of Deh Koh: Young Life in an Iranian Village.* Syracuse, N.Y.: Syracuse University Press, 1997. Iran: nonfiction, the experiences of girls and boys in a poor rural area.

Tekin, Latife. *Berji Kristin: Tales from the Garbage Hills: A Novel.* Trans. Ruth Christie and Salina Paker. New York: Marion Boyars, 1996. Turkey: fiction, based on the stories of rural migrants to Istanbul who built a shantytown in a garbage dump.

PART 3

POLITICS AND POLITICAL CHANGE

Ideas are among the most powerful forces that we possess. All people hold opinions and viewpoints about the world around them. Should income be equally distributed? Should political leaders provide moral and religious guidance? How should citizens respond to perceived corruption and abuse of power? Thoughts about authority, society, gender relations, economic resources, the environment, and other values help shape the general perspectives that people hold about their role in the world. Ideas about the way things should be often impel people into action, sometimes in violent ways, and this will be the subject of the chapters that follow.

Also in this section of the book we will consider the impact of ideas and their translation into action in terms of the "third wave" of democratization, which hit much of the world toward the end of the COLD WAR. (The "first wave" of DEMOCRATIC TRANSITIONS is commonly identified with the expansion of democracy in the United States and Western Europe [1820s–1926]. The "second wave" [1945–1962] is associated with independence and the experimentation with democracy in much of Asia and Africa.) As we will see, the result for governments around the world has been a crisis of sorts. We will explore the various ways in which different governments have handled this crisis. In doing this we will consider, implicitly at least, the chances for democracy in the third world. As you might have guessed, the odds vary by country. While several countries do not appear to be headed in the direction of Western-style democracy at all, there are some well-established democracies in the third world. On the other hand, some fragile democracies have already broken down. Many countries are at varying stages in the process of reform. Others just appear to be making this transition, as their democratization is more "virtual" than real. In more than a few cases political liberalization has been precluded by instability, due to fundamental problems such as disagreements concerning whether the state should continue to exist intact. In most but not all cases, carefully crafted negotiations, pacts, and other agreements have at least temporarily resolved some problems. But even when contested SOVEREIGNTY is not an issue, both democratic and nondemocratic governments struggle to grapple with other demands. Any new democracy faces a host of challenges. In the chapters that follow, we will discuss these tests and assess the nature of political transitions in the third world.

10

From Ideas to Action:
The Power of Civil Society

There is no freedom of thought without the press.
—Chant by Iranian students at a rally commemorating
the third anniversary of President Mohammad Khatami's election[1]

In this chapter we explore a range of perspectives held by ordinary citizens, activists, and leaders. These viewpoints derive from many sources, including history (both ancient and recent), practical experiences of daily life and policy, and leadership cues and demands. Additionally, worldviews are framed by a combination of more seemingly subtle influences, as varied as educational systems, entertainment opportunities and institutions, and basic information sources that are made available to the public. We examine belief systems that both unite and divide people, and focus on ideas as sources of conflict and cooperation. Passion is a major part of the story. Yet our emphasis goes beyond simply the beliefs that people hold: we examine the forums in which these views are expressed, the ways that other groups attempt to curtail people's ability to express opinions, and how crafty activists subvert limits on expression.

Ideas merge theoretical, often fuzzy concepts of the way the world "should be" with the necessarily concrete actions that people take on a day-to-day basis to try to implement their visions. The sheer multiplicity of ideas invites controversy: When one person or group's ideas conflicts with others, how can these differences be reconciled? Why do some people's ideas seem to count, at least in the public realm, more than those of others, and how is this negotiated (or not)? We often think of leaders holding a monopoly on creating the ideas that "count," but this is certainly not always the case. When groups of people begin to identify with a different value or idea system than that of their leaders, they may organize and challenge the status quo. Sometimes they are successful, and sometimes their efforts meet a pain-filled failure.

Ideologies

Ideas that are free-floating, unattached to a more general perspective or value system, are not very likely to have tremendous impact. Yet when connections between sets of values and perspectives are recognized as interconnected, and when these views impel people to action, they literally have a force that may change the world.

When people share a similar set of ideas linked to programs for action, we refer to this idea set as an IDEOLOGY, literally the "science of ideas," although such beliefs are hardly described with scientific precision. At their most fundamental level, ideologies are sets of ideas that describe the world or current state of affairs, help people understand their role within society, and arouse people to take an action, either to preserve or to change the existing situation. Ideologies consist of loosely connected systems of ideas: few traditions propose a strict laundry list of beliefs one must hold in order to subscribe to a given ideology. Rather, people notice common tendencies in beliefs, and often unite together with others who share similar perspectives.

Ideologies attempt to simplify complex problems and point toward potential solutions. They tend to be the foundation of most policies and actions, even if they are not identified as such. Most of the major systems of ideas that have been at the forefront of the non-Western world were formulated in response to experiences with colonialism and dependence, especially the economic struggle to survive. Leaders and ordinary citizens alike turn to ideologies to help them cope with civil unrest, grinding poverty, and international humiliation. Ideologies often provide deceptively clear-cut answers to complicated realities, especially during times of instability. Frequently, groups of people who share an ideological worldview get together to form a political party as a way to implement the ideas that they feel are important. Yet while political parties appear and disappear, and quite often adopt varying and misleading names, political ideologies endure.

Common in discussions about ideologies are the terms "conservative" and "liberal." These concepts represent two major schools of ideological thought. They are relative terms, meaning that what is seen as conservative in one country or social situation might not be so in another. Liberalism is often considered the first coherent political ideology, which developed throughout European societies in the early 1800s. Liberals emphasize the freedom of the individual, limits on governmental interference, and the equality of all human beings. The idea that all people possess inalienable rights to life, liberty, and the pursuit of property, for example, is a classical liberal idea derived from the writings of John Locke. Liberals hold optimistic beliefs about what individuals and groups can achieve, and they often fight for progressive (forward-moving) changes.

Because of liberalism's high value on freedom, this ideology had a tremendous impact on the wars of liberation that we discussed in Chapter 4. If all people are created equal, as liberalism contends, then individuals should be able to rule themselves, rather than having decisions made for them by colonial leaders in a faraway land. Liberal beliefs encouraged the fight for self-governing peoples who had been subjugated to foreign rule, some for centuries. This movement was particularly pronounced in the post–World War II environment. The outcome of many of these wars of national liberation, however, was the perpetuation of political control and limits on freedom. Liberalism also has influenced the desire by some ethnic groups to pursue their own homeland, often distinct from the government in which they live. We discuss these ethnonationalists in

Chapter 12. Yet the desire for cultural representation and self-expression does not always lead to the fight for a new state. Owing to the influence of liberalism, some ethnic groups have staked a claim to greater public expression of their culture and ways of life, achieving rights to use their native language, educate their children about their history and culture in public schools, and demand greater representation in public life.

Liberal ideas have also been responsible for many revolutions throughout the world, especially popular movements to overthrow monarchies, dynasties, and other forms of hereditary rule that precluded individuals from power. Some liberal revolutions attempted to redistribute land and economic resources that had been taken away from people. One example is found in President Benito Juarez's La Reforma program in Mexico in the mid-1800s, which stripped the Catholic Church of much of its property and power and formally granted civil rights to indigenous peoples. Juarez's liberal program was also popular for its staunch resistance to French invaders. Other liberal movements fought to bring voting rights and other participatory freedoms to groups, including women, minorities, and youth. Liberal proponents today in the non-Western world attempt to advance greater respect for human rights and individual freedoms, and they often lead the vocal charge toward democratic institutions. Fundamentally, liberals agree that the power of government needs to be limited, although they disagree over the fine lines of state involvement, especially in the realm of economics.

If liberals agree that governmental power should be limited and that individuals should have a say in decisions that are made about their lives, there is disagreement about matters of degree. Debates about the role of government in people's lives have led to two major types of liberals. One group, often called positive liberals, argues that government ought to shoulder some level of responsibility for people's lives, calling for diminishing the inequality among groups, fostering greater participation, and in general promoting the well-being of citizens. Positive liberals are often the strongest supporters of welfare-state policies, including childcare, healthcare, education, unemployment insurance, and pensions. People often assume that welfare policies are designed only for the needy in society, but actually many welfare programs, including public education and public pensions, are distributed to all citizens, irrespective of need, and they are present in most states of the world. Negative liberals believe that there should be minimal government involvement in the economy, arguing that the free market, regulated only by the forces of supply and demand, should operate. This group argues that government involvement often has the unintended consequence of limiting individual freedom by creating patterns of dependence and perpetuating cycles of poverty. These debates can become quite heated. Yet in the non-Western world, the degree of governmental assistance is often framed not by ideological but rather economic concerns.

Ideas rarely exist in a vacuum. They often are formulated, expressed, and modified in response to other views of the world. This explains the development of the other major school of thought, conservatism. As you are probably aware, conservatives are known for attempting to preserve the status quo, and sometimes for encouraging a return to values and traditions of the past. As conservatism began to develop, it challenged each of the major premises of the liberal way of viewing the world.

Traditional conservatives emphasize an organic view of society, in which the needs of the whole society, the so-called social fabric, are more important than individual freedom. In contrast to the liberal emphasis on the equality of all people, conservatives emphasize that every person is born with natural inequalities, thereby contradicting the liberal notion of the fundamental equality of all people. They emphasize the talents and skills that some people have at birth that others do not. Conservatives advocate a slower approach to change, emphasizing the utility of existing institutions and patterns of behavior and reviling the dangerous passions and actions of revolutionaries. They lament the liberals' pace of rapid change, and believe that revolutions tend to bring about more harm than good, because they damage key traditions and hierarchical structures that serve as the basis for social traditions and identity. Many of the conservative persuasion prefer familiar patterns of relations, rather than the uncertainty that comes from progressive change. It is from this belief that we tend to associate conservatives with the status quo; in fact, the label derives from the Latin word *conservare,* which means "to save or preserve." Conservative parties and groups today, while they often support democratic institutions, urge caution in the pace of transitions and cast a wary eye toward liberal causes.

One modern manifestation of conservative ideas today is found in religious fundamentalism, including Christian and Islamic variants, the adherents of which promote the value of religious institutions and authority, often placing great emphasis on traditional family structures and gender roles. Much of the debate surrounding fundamentalists and their detractors relates to the adaptations of religious institutions to the modern world. Adherents to fundamental traditions often promote a stricter, sometimes literal interpretation of religious texts, whether they be the Torah, Bible, or Quran. Not all faith-based movements, though, are conservative, as we discuss below. Islamic fundamentalism has become an increasingly important mobilizing force for some adherents, especially since the establishment of the Islamic Republic of Iran in 1979 and the signing of the Camp David Peace Accords that same year. Islamic movements have often been motivated by the perception of increasing Westernization, concomitant with the rise of individualism and secularism, which are viewed as threatening to traditional lifestyles. Following the civil war in Afghanistan, for example, the Taliban promoted a rigidly conservative approach to Islamic religious beliefs that included strict gender segregation based on a belief that men and women are fundamentally unequal. It also justified the public execution of criminals, including women accused of infidelity to their husbands, as a necessary aspect of social control. The Taliban's actions were couched in the refutation of Western standards of behavior.

Christian fundamentalists share this hostility toward individualism and secularism, objecting to the liberal separation of church and state that made religious values and practices a private rather than a public matter. Conservative evangelical Christians have been very active in many parts of the non-Western world, including Latin America (especially Guatemala and Brazil), Africa (chiefly South Africa and Zimbabwe), and some Asian states (notably the

Figure 10.1   Do All Muslims Agree?

At the turn of the twenty-first century, followers of the Muslim faith were second in number only to Christians. While estimates vary, most agree that Muslims compose approximately 20 percent of the world's population—it is the fastest-growing faith tradition in the world. With so many adherents, it is logical to assume that there are varying levels of agreement and disagreement among the Muslim faithful. The biggest source of lasting division originated in a succession struggle launched after the prophet Mohammed's death in 632. Today, the majority of Muslims, approximately 90 percent, characterize themselves as Sunni Muslims. The name *Sunni* derives from "Sunna," meaning "the tradition of the prophet Mohammed." The primary schism is Shiite Islam, meaning the "Party of Ali."

Immediately following Mohammed's death, his cousin and son-in-law, Ali ibn Abi Talib, claimed to be the leader of all Muslims. But most believers followed Abu Bakr, who was reputed to be the first outside Mohammed's family to convert to Islam. Abu Bakr became the first of the four caliphs, or successors, in the Sunni tradition. Twenty-three years after Mohammed's death, Ali was named the caliph. His rise to leadership was controversial and not recognized by many. Syria's leader, among others, refused to recognize Ali, and he ruled from Kufah, Iraq, facing much dissension.

A series of succession crises, including the murder and torture of disputed leaders, led to the creation of Shiism, the first major schism within Islam. The Shiites replaced the caliphate with imams, claiming that their leadership was hereditary from Mohammed. After the schism, Shiites were persecuted and acted in secret, during which time they devised their own teachings on the implementation of the word of Mohammed. One change was the designation of an authoritative figure to interpret divine will, rather than placing the onus on the community of believers, as Sunnis taught.[2] The Shiites believed that as religious leaders, imams possess knowledge of which the masses are incapable. This view complicated the challenges of rival successors, since imams were viewed as infallible leaders. Although most Turks are Sunnis, the Shiite minority in Turkey is known as Alvis.

The major Shia sect is named the "Twelvers" for the twelve imams following Mohammed. Twelver Shiism is the state religion in Iran, which is the only Muslim country that is overwhelmingly Shiite. Developed in the sixteenth century, this sect of Shiism highlights the twelve legitimate imams, beginning with Ali and ending with the twelfth or "hidden imam," who went into concealment in 941 but who will reappear to finish the triumph of Shiism some day in the future. Between the sixteenth and the eighteenth centuries, Twelver Shiism merged with Persian tradition, forging a tight bond with the development of Iranian identity and nationalism.[3]

In the eighth century, the mystical movement of Sufism developed, in protest to the formalism of Islam. The title comes from the Arabic word *suf,* meaning "wool." Many Sufis wore coarse woolen clothes, imitating the Christians from Syria. Although both Sunni and Shiite fundamentalists reject it, Sufism has appeal among those who were frustrated by the power-seeking ulamas, or clerics, and against those who view Islam as a religious experience rather than a call to political action.[4]

Philippines). While there is great variation among followers, in general evangelical Christian churches advocate conservative sexual and gender mores, economic discipline, as well as a greater role for some newer church institutions. In Brazil, for example, evangelical leaders in government publicly contested the role of the Catholic Church in society. In Guatemala, fundamentalist Protestant groups rally in opposition to unions and against LIBERATION THEOLOGY, a left-leaning perspective on Catholicism that we discuss below. Many of the fundamentalist traditions in Africa trace their origins to the anticolonial movement. In Zimbabwe, the Pentecostal Assemblies of God is believed to include approximately 10 percent of the population.[5] Disparate groups of fundamentalist Christians in Africa, believed to number in the tens of millions, have joined together in opposition to abortion, feminism, and the rights of homosexuals.[6]

But conservatism and liberalism are only two of many traditions of like-minded ideas. The other major world ideologies that have affected social, political, and economic life include socialism, communism, fascism, and anarchism. Each of these ideological systems developed in response to liberal views of the world, and promotes its own ideas on the value of individualism, governmental involvement in the economy, and the structure of society. It is important to understand the basic definitions of each of these distinct ideologies. But it is also necessary to keep in mind that the underlying components of any ideological system are manipulated, changed, and adapted by people to fit their particular circumstances and to match their goals. Nonetheless, a fundamental understanding of the common characteristics of these views provides an important starting place for this inquiry of the role of ideology in the non-Western world.

Socialism is an ideological tradition that has had tremendous impact throughout the entire world, either in its application or in its opposition. Because of the centrality of economic matters, socialism, in multiple variants, has been a particularly important ideology in the non-Western world. Historically, socialism was critical of private property and the uneven distribution of wealth. It is an idea that significantly predates one of its most famous adherents, Karl Marx, who adapted early socialist ideals and melded them onto a revolutionary framework. Marxist socialists argued that fundamentally there were two types of people in the world, making up the dominant CLASSES of society. First are the few who own property and therefore exert much influence in economic, political, and social affairs. They are known as the BOURGEOISIE. Yet the bourgeoisie could not exist without the MASSES, who in a Marxist framework are forced to work at the mercy of the powerful, and labor tirelessly without proper compensation or protection against abuse. This second class, who always outnumber the first, is known as the PROLETARIAT. Writing in the midst of the European industrial revolution of the late 1800s, Marx argued that once the workers of the world were made aware of their uneven plight caused by the powerful property owners, inevitably they would rise up in anger and overthrow their oppressors. Marx predicted that after the revolution, which was likely to be violent, proletarians would rule in their self-interest, attempting to eliminate the bourgeoisie. During this stage of initial socialism, economic inequalities would persist, but they would be eradicated in the final stage of the revolution, when communism would be achieved.

While Marx's ideas may seem particularly appropriate for individuals living and working in the non-Western world, it was really only after the innovations of another revolutionary activist that his ideas were applied in the effort to promote wide-scale change. In imperial Russia, hardly a paragon of the industrial battlefield that Marx predicted would bring his revolutions to life, the activist later known as Vladimir Lenin took up the ideas articulated by Marx and his collaborator, Friedrich Engels, and from them crafted a plan to implement a Marxist revolution by an ELITE, highly disciplined VANGUARD PARTY. This Leninist party would not wait around for electoral victories that Lenin believed would never come. Rather, it would seize state power and implement a Marxist revolution from above. Revolutionary hopefuls throughout the non-Western world found a solution in Lenin's model, which ran counter to Marx's initial focus on worker-led mass revolutions. Lenin's ideas on the connection between imperialism and capitalism seemed especially relevant to many at a time when capitalism was rapidly becoming a global movement. Lenin taught that richer capitalist countries used the poorer countries of the world in order to finance their growth and prosperity. Capitalism, by definition, would promote uneven development, as the rich countries would get richer on the backs of cheaper labor in the non-Western world, which was increasingly becoming dependent on trade with the imperialist powers. These ideas strongly resonated with citizens in non-Western countries who recognized their exploitation, especially in countries with formal imperialist governing structures. Communist movements, following the Leninist model, were integral in independence movements in Vietnam, Indonesia, Angola, Mozambique, and Guinea-Bissau.

Even though Karl Marx believed that communist revolutions would be conducted in the advanced, industrialized countries of Europe and North America, his ideas were most vigorously applied to countries in the non-Western world. In fact, some would argue that the perceived failures of communism since 1989 were predictable from the beginning: a Marxist revolution simply was not tailored to a non-Western, nonindustrial country. Yet even today, the world's largest communist party, with approximately 60 million members, can be found in the People's Republic of China (PRC), a country that remains predominantly agricultural. Chairman Mao Zedong's application of Marxist communism in a nonindustrialized setting spawned similar revolutionary attempts in other countries, including Peru's Sendero Luminoso (Shining Path), which we discuss in Chapters 12 and 13. In the countries where a full-fledged Marxist-Leninist revolution was undertaken, however, the leadership has never moved beyond the stage of initial socialism, during which time a single party can rule, theoretically, in the name of achieving final communism. It is because of this connection, some would say deviation, of Marxist socialism that many people associate socialism with one-party rule. This correlation, however, is not wholly accurate.

Democratic forms of socialism have also influenced SOCIAL MOVEMENTS in the countries we are studying. Fabian socialists argue that the original goal of socialists has been distorted by its revolutionary application by Marx and his adherents. They argue that democratic, peaceful means are the only viable way to promote the socialist cause. These democratic socialists attempt to promote greater equality (especially economic) among citizens, and they advocate a strong role for government in promoting the needs of society. Democratic socialism was especially influential during African wars of independence in the 1970s, when leaders encouraged the government to be proactive in citizens' lives, especially in the areas of literacy and education. From the mid-1960s until the recession of the 1970s, President Julius Nyerere of Tanzania, for example, promoted a socialist model of economic development under the *ujamma* model, which roughly translated from Kiswahili means "familyhood" or "pulling together." Nyerere not only collectivized agriculture and factories, but also, under the leadership of a single party, mandated major investments in primary schools and social services. In general, socialist leaders are critical of unbridled capitalism, pointing to often disastrous effects of the market on the environment, family and social relations, and culture. They tend to be leading the charge against international economic institutions such as the WORLD BANK and the INTERNATIONAL MONETARY FUND (IMF), although they are certainly not alone in their critiques. Socialism in the non-Western world, though, emphasizes NATIONALISM and local traditions, rather than the international and universal working-class IDENTITY promoted by initial socialist activists.

If liberalism emphasized people as individuals, conservatives urged a focus on society and its traditions, and socialists viewed the world in the framework of classes. In response to each of these ideologies, another combination of ideas was formed that found fault with each of the preceding characterizations of the world. Similar to the other ideologies, its basis was found in historical tradition, including linguistic interpretations of history, so-called scientific understandings of race and racial identity, and an elitist prescription for political power and governance. Ideas that would form the core of fascism existed long before the ideology was named. Fascism emphasizes that which unites people as a way of segregating individuals into homogeneous groups in order to promote unity and strength. Because of its opposition to most of the systems of ideas that developed before it, and because of its negative proscriptions on life in general, it may be argued that it is clearer to understand what fascists are against than what they are for.[7]

Fascists believe that the class focus of socialism is too divisive, especially because it emphasizes status as either a worker or an owner over a person's national heritage. "Fascism," a term first coined in Italy, comes from the Latin word *fasces*, alluding to a set of reeds tightly bound together. Fascist leaders emphasize the importance of race and nationality, promoting in many cases a racially pure community of individuals who work together without division. Fascism also teaches that it is necessary to have a strong leader who will provide guidance and direction to the masses, and that the all-powerful leader understands the needs and the interests of the people better than they themselves do. In this sense, fascism is clearly an elitist ideology, which openly concentrates the majority of the power among a small minority of seemingly qualified individuals.

Fascists emphasize the fundamental inequality of humans and have a clear hierarchy, often based on biological conceptions of race, of "superior" and "lesser" peoples. While fascists are not the only group to deny the universal equality of all people, they go a step further in openly advocating the use of violence for handling contradictions that exist between people. While the most destructive fascist dictatorships were promoted in the European countries of Italy (under Benito Mussolini) and Germany (under Adolf Hitler), fascist authoritarian movements have also been strong in the non-Western world as well, especially Chile under Augusto Pinochet. Fascism is an authoritarian ideology of exclusion, and regimes that adhere to it promote division and hierarchy, violating the fundamental human rights of those deemed inferior and preventing individual liberties for all except the few deemed worthy of holding power. Fascists deny the desirability of a multicultural society, arguing to violent extremes that multiple ethnic groups cannot coexist within a single society. This ideology called for a strong government that would organize and lead the masses, as well as a developed propaganda system that would educate and motivate them into action.

In recent years, groups adhering to neofascist beliefs have gained prominence in many parts of the world, especially in economically troubled regions where immigrants, refugees, migrant workers, and other groups seen as outsiders can be scapegoated for a wide range of social and economic problems. Contrary to its antecedent, neofascist violence is aimed at particular ethnic communities rather than the state. Neo-Nazi attacks in Germany, for example, have targeted the immigrant Turkish, African, and Vietnamese populations with firebombs and other violent attacks. Similar to their ideological predecessors, these activists condone the use of violence and segregation in order to promote the cause of their own, self-defined group.

Ideologies develop as a way to capture the relationship between leaders in government and ordinary citizens. Anarchists challenge the desirability of hierarchical power structures, emphasizing voluntary cooperation and free association over power and control. Anarchism is difficult to characterize as a single school of thought, as its adherents' beliefs straddle those of almost all groups along the ideological spectrum. Noam Chomsky defines anarchism as a "historical tendency" or a "tendency of thought and action" rather than an ideology per se. Anarchists are often known for their acts of disobedience. They share a concern about the concentration of power, whether that is governmental power over ordinary citizens, patriarchal power of men over women, or global corporate power exercised by business conglomerates. Most anarchists promote the values of democratic participation, decentralization, and opposition to bureaucracy. While some anarchist groups condone the use of violence to further their cause, this is a point of disagreement among those adhering to this ideological perspective.

Anarchist movements have been especially popular among youth. In major Turkish cities, for example, Anarchist Youth Federations protest against sexism, capitalism, gerontocracy, and nuclear proliferation. Conscientious objectors of required military service have also aligned with antimilitarist anarchist youth groups. Anarchists claim that no one should have authority or control over another. In this they often challenge basic rules of behavior. Puerto Rican feminist and labor activist Luisa Capetillo is perhaps Latin America's best-known anarchist; she gained notoriety by becoming the first woman to wear pants in public in Puerto Rico. Through her work to encourage labor unionization in Puerto Rico, she worked to redefine women's freedom. The 1994 Zapatista uprising in Mexico and student strikes have been particularly influenced by anarchism, challenging especially the power of governments over minority ethnic groups. This movement, which has been viciously repressed by authorities, has awoken indigenous activists across Latin America and in other regions as well.

Because of their disdain for governing structures, anarchist movements tend to reach across borders and geographic limitations to embrace a global audience. The environmental movement Earth First confronts government and corporate behavior, especially its disregard for ecological concerns and its anthropocentric, or human-centered, bias. Additionally, diverse movements against transnational corporations and seemingly supranational organizations such as the WORLD TRADE ORGANIZATION (WTO) and the IMF have mobilized activists of all stripes who challenge the authority and actions of large bureaucracies. Protests organized to disrupt WTO meetings around the world united environmentalists, farmers, students, intellectuals, feminists, and union activists. Although all of the participants were not necessarily anarchists, the focus on the negative aspects of global capitalism went right to the core beliefs of anarchism. Many terrorist groups, which we discuss in Chapter 12, base their actions in the ideology of anarchism as well.

We have presented a series of often competing ideological systems to help you see the variety of worldviews that exist in our world at the beginning of the twenty-first century. Yet any true understanding of the power of these views can only be found in comparison. To examine systems of ideas, it is helpful to visually align beliefs on the POLITICAL SPECTRUM. We commonly use the terminology of "left, right, and center" to place beliefs in comparison with each other. The terminology we use comes from seating arrangements in the National Assembly of France during the revolution of the late 1700s. Moderates sat in the center, those who favored DEMOCRACY and rapid change congregated on the left side (or wing), and those who supported the monarch and the Church, arguing against change, sat on the right. We continue to use this linear system today to compare belief systems, although it is helpful only as a general guideline. People and groups cannot be placed on the spectrum with clear precision (few of us hold completely consistent views and opinions), and all discussions about the spectrum in a particular country or society must be understood as relative to particular circumstances.

Ideas are placed along the political spectrum according to views on the importance and desired direction of change, the role of government in the economy, and the perceived value of church and religious institutions. To the left of center, beliefs focus on the positive value of change (especially forward-moving developments), a larger role of government in economic matters, including the promotion of greater equality, and a smaller public role for religious institutions in the lives of people. To the right of center, church and religious institutions serve a more important role in both government and society. Advocates of these ideologies are more suspicious of change, and the government tends to be less involved in economic affairs generally. To the right of center, people tend to emphasize the decline of society and advocate a reevaluation of social, political, and economic structures, often returning to values of an earlier period. Because anarchist beliefs usually complement other ideological traditions, and because of the great variety of perspectives embodied within anarchism, it is difficult to clearly place it on one side of the spectrum or the other. As the language of this explanation suggests, there are few absolutes in the characterization of ideologies, but these general patterns capture the most important ideas. Keep in mind that an understanding of the dominant ideological leanings in a particular society or governing administration will only provide limited information in the policies of the regime. For example, we highlighted the role of government and political intervention as a point distinguishing some ideological traditions. But state interventionist economic programs have been used by regimes characterized as both rightist (Juan Peron's Argentina and Getulio Vargas's Brazil) and leftist (Salvador Allende's Chile).

How and why do people develop particular opinions and views? We are all products of a lifelong process generally referred to as socialization, by which individuals acquire their beliefs and values. Some of this socialization is accidental. Other aspects of socialization are deliberate attempts to pass on values and belief systems from generation to generation. Beliefs about government, politics, economics, and the role of the military are all influenced by some of our earliest life experiences. Educational and religious institutions, the media, peer groups, and the family each influence the development of beliefs. While much of the process of acquiring attitudes about society is implicit and somewhat taken for granted, such as family relationships between women and men, governments and social groups may also explicitly influence people's sense of values, especially as they relate to the governing system. For example, in China, primary school students attend compulsory moral education classes once a week, in which they learn obedience and deference to authority, as well as the "five loves": love for country, people, science, work and workers, and socialism. Institutions of the media are often overlooked as sources of socialization, yet newspapers and television programs can be people's sole source of information about civic and political life.

The media both inform and persuade. Recognizing the power implicit in controlling access to information, it is common for governments to exercise some level of control over communications media, often through a monopoly over news and publishing outlets. Sometimes two versions of media are produced, an official version for public consumption, which downplays the tensions existing in society, and a version meant only for viewing by government leaders, which expresses a more accurate account of pressures and hot spots. Government regulation of the media, which makes the expression of unofficial opinions problematic and even dangerous, often forces dissident groups who express views in opposition to the leaders to publish underground, in the so-called gray media or second channel.[8] These unofficial communication avenues,

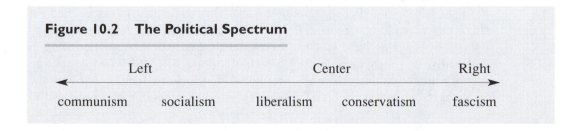

Figure 10.2   The Political Spectrum

	Left		Center		Right
	communism	socialism	liberalism	conservatism	fascism

which straddle the permissible and the forbidden, have been especially lucrative in environments where entrepreneurship and risk-taking are encouraged. In China, for example, simply stamping a book "for internal consumption only" meant that there would be a huge market on the side for bootlegged copies. Arguments over controlling the media are front and center in contemporary Iran, as the press has been caught in the factional struggles between Khatami's reformist faction and the more conservative faction, backed by the judiciary, which announces a symbolic "red line" that editors and publishers are not to cross if they want to continue their work.[9] Editors who challenge the boundary of the permissible have been shut down, jailed, and even flogged.

Looking at the world around us, we observe similarities and differences among groups of people. It is oftentimes difficult to put our finger on the source of differences, when they exist. Much of it has to do with the processes of socialization. When we compare political attitudes across multiple societies, people commonly speak of a POLITICAL CULTURE that exists among a defined group of people, such as "Mexican political culture" or "Turkish political culture." This concept was developed to capture the commonly shared understandings and basic assumptions that people in a common experience tend to exhibit.

To say that a group of people share a particular political culture does not mean that they agree on all of the important issues of politics and governance. Rather, it means that they are likely to share a common perspective about their public surroundings, including their political leaders, governmental structure, and the enduring symbols and values of public life.[10] Political culture includes citizens' general feelings toward government, including their desire (or lack thereof) to participate in political issues. It also captures a sense of people's understanding of the decisionmaking process, including attitudes about its merits. Understanding that people have different social, political, and economic experiences than our own helps us avoid assumptions that the way relationships and institutions operate in one setting is the way that they exist elsewhere. The concept of political culture helps us recognize the long-term impact of social, historical, and economic circumstances.

A classic study on political culture attempted to use these ideas to compare cultures throughout the world. The *Civic Culture* study of 1959, based on survey research, was conducted by a group of leading U.S. political scientists.[11] It identified three dominant types of political culture throughout the world. First, Gabriel Almond and Sidney Verba classified a "participant culture," in which most people exhibit pride toward their country's political system, feel that they should participate in it, and have a sense that their participation makes a difference. They also generally understand the way the system works. Second, the study identified a "subject culture," in which people tend to discount their ability to participate in and change politics; rather, they view themselves as obedient subordinates of the government. People in these societies tend to be aware of the operations of the political system, but overall are cautious about participating in it. Finally, the study identified a "parochial culture," in which people tend to identify almost exclusively with their immediate locality, feeling that national political issues have very little to do with them. In such cultures, people tend to speak little about political affairs, because in their viewpoint such matters rarely touch their lives.

What did Almond and Verba conclude about political culture from this study? The only one of our cases that was included in this original study was Mexico, which was characterized as the prototypical parochial culture. While recognizing that each country contains people with a mix of views, the leaders of the study generalized about each society as a whole. This was a pivotal attempt to make broad statements about many countries at once, in a comparative framework.

Yet there are serious limitations to such an approach. For one, it invites the potential for discriminatory assumptions, or at the very least, establishing a hierarchy of favored characteristics. It was clear by the way the findings were presented that a participatory, aware, and active population should be the ultimate goal for each society. Yet there was little recognition that the standards for the study were based on Western traditions and cultures, which promote civic duty and activism as a virtue. The *Civic Culture* study and others that have followed in its footsteps are indicative of the wide-eyed optimism of many Americans in the late 1950s and 1960s. The implicit hope was that Western-style democracies were going to flourish around the world, and that there was a single model of the so-called developed, democratic state. In fact, the guiding assumption of the study was that the "participant" culture is a precondition to stable democracy.

In addition to being ethnocentric, this approach tended to emphasize the changes that were not taking place, presumably because people did not exhibit characteristics found in other Western cultures, rather than the realm of the possible, or what could take place. Also, such an aggregated view of single political cultures oversimplifies complex societies. The assumptions of national culture make grandiose claims that are difficult to substantiate. For example, in a state like Nigeria, with over 250 different ethnic groups, does it really make sense to talk of a singular "Nigerian" political culture? There is also a problem of translation: concepts such as EFFICACY, duty, and participation do not always translate very clearly, and people have differing images in their mind as to the precise meaning of these terms. Political culture is useful to explain differences among groups, but it is less helpful when used to explain so-called national traits, as David Elkins and E. B. Simeon identified.[12] While it is clear that culture is important, it is less clear how to measure it. At best, the concept of political culture is useful for understanding general orientations, but it is important that we not make assumptions much beyond this.

Identities

When individuals make assessments about the world around them, they make decisions based on a self-perception of who they are, or their identity. Increasingly, we understand that people's self-perception influences their behavior and attitudes. It affects whom we define as potential collaborators or competitors, and it impacts the outcome that we seek. The traditional ideologies that we discussed above are largely devoid of an explicit awareness of self-identity: they aim to provide an outlook based on larger issues often irrespective of individual attributes. Yet a growing trend in social thought and action revolves around identity issues that fundamentally get at the question of who we are. They tend to be very personal ideologies that encourage people to fight for recognition of the joint needs and preferences of particular groups, often those that have been denied expression in the past. Identities are extremely complex concepts. For one, we each have multiple individual characteristics: one individual embodies the identities of friend, daughter, Asian, worker. We choose to emphasize a particular trait based on the context in which we are involved. For example, at a sporting event, people are usually defined as either athletes or spectators. At an international sporting event, it becomes even more complex, with the characteristic of national identity becoming important. Yet at other gatherings, such as some religious meetings, one's categorization as a female or male is the defining character.

Individual and group identities are quite closely related; in addition to describing themselves individually, people group with others. This involves the development of a collective, or shared, identity. Groups of ordinary people mobilize around a common self-definition, usually as a way to achieve a common goal. Additionally, leaders attempt to rally their citizens around an identity related to their own power. Leaders who are defensive about their own ability to maintain power are particularly adept at rallying people around a shared sense of belonging, often making promises to varied groups as a way to lock in their support. Robert Mugabe provides a good example, with his promises of land and "Africa for Africans." Such POPULIST attempts can be particularly strong in countries undergoing dislocation or change. The Peronists in Argentina exemplified populism by forming coalitions of the urban poor and parts of the organized working and middle classes, promising greater economic equality, and independence (especially economic) from foreign countries. In the 1930s, Mexico's Lázaro Cárdenas similarly promised a better life through land reform and industry nationalization, under the leadership of a single dominant party. Peru's Alejandro Toledo is also considered a populist president. The 1979 Iranian Revolution was a populist movement that rallied the common people against the West, personified in opposition to the Shah. Populist movements are fundamentally about identity: they attempt to rally groups to action in the name of the self-described "people": they may be left or right in orientation, but their motivation is nearly the same. The difficulty with populism on its own, however, is that "the people" rarely fit into one category. Populism is usually combined with other movements. Nationalist movements, for example, have been common bedfellows for populist leaders.

For over 200 years, the idea of nationalism has been used promote the interests and needs of a particular nation, or group of people. Usually, nations are identified as sharing a common history, culture, language, ethnicity, or religion, although the actual components of national identity can vary widely. Nationalist movements have been a potent uniting (and dividing) force throughout many of the countries that we are studying. The initial struggle faced by many of these countries was to establish a common identity after the colonial period. National identities were therefore defined more in opposition to the colonial rulers than in composition of shared characteristics. The concept of "Indonesia," for example, was an entirely novel identity for the disparate ethnic groups who had operated a vast trading network from the islands of Java and Sumatra for centuries. Yet especially between the two world wars, the notion of a single, independent Indonesia was created and promoted, mostly by students and young professionals, in opposition to Dutch rule.

Throughout the non-Western world, indigenous nationalist movements developed as a way to honor unique local traditions and ethnic identities. After a sense of identity was mobilized against the occupying powers, nationalist movements sometimes turned to violence as a means of expelling foreign influence, as in Vietnam, Algeria, Indonesia, Zimbabwe, Mozambique, and Angola. Some nationalist leaders propelled their movement with socialist ideology, such as Ho Chi Minh in the Vietnamese struggle against France and later the United States. Other nationalist leaders turned to socialist policies to help reconstruct their country after achieving independence, including Algeria, India, Guinea, and Zimbabwe. In its opposition to capitalism, socialism presented a means for national self-sufficiency and economic independence.[13]

Today, nationalist movements of identity are on the rise, but they certainly are not new—as we discussed in our study of war of national liberation in Chapter 4. We identify two types of nationalist mobilization: one calls for independence from larger political units that attempt to incorporate multiple national groups, and the other tries to bring attention to their identity in the face of global homogenization. Most of the countries that we are studying are richly multinational, made up of people with diverse linguistic, religious, historical, and cultural traditions. For some, this has not been an issue of great division, either because the leadership suppresses such discussion (as in the case of Tibetan identity in China), or because the groups themselves fail to see a need to challenge the status quo. For others, the expression of diverse national identities can be dangerous business. For example, the Kurdish people, many of whom identify as a nation with a common language and culture, have increasingly challenged their incorporation within the political entity of Turkey. Turkish leaders have defined the "Kurdish question" as a terrorist threat, and have until very recently outlawed any independent expression of Kurdish identity, including their native language, a restriction that continued until the early 1990s. The arrest of Kurdish leader Abdullah Öcalan has lessened separatist tensions somewhat, but the potential for aggression, in both separatist action and state response, remains. We will return to the question of the role of violence in irredentist movements in Chapter 12.

Second, with increasing economic interdependence and trade, the rise of GLOBALIZATION motivates some national groups to emphasize their unique characteristics in the face of the commercial and cultural homogeneity. While there are many positive aspects of a global economy and the conveniences it brings, many feel that it inhibits indigenous cultures and traditions in the name of modernity. In response to the perceived growth of Western values and goods, many groups increase their expression of microidentities. Some of this has been in response to global corporate developments. For example, there was much resistance in China when Seattle-based Starbucks opened a coffee shop in the cherished Palace Museum, the former residence of the emperors and empresses

Figure 10.3 Tibet and the Tibetan People

Located in southwestern China, Tibet is a great example of a region in which people exercise multiple identities. Living on the world's highest plateau, the Tibetan people have fought against conquest by many peoples, including the Mongols, the imperial Chinese, and the British. Shortly after the declaration of the People's Republic of China in 1949, troops of the Chinese Communist Party (CCP) marched into Tibet, attempting to enlarge their rule over the important border region. Their suppression of the Tibetan uprising was fierce: thousands of Tibetans were killed and hundreds of sacred monasteries were destroyed. While the CCP was nominally successful at establishing its rule, many, including the main spiritual leader of the Tibetan people, the Dalai Lama, fled to India in 1959, where the government in exile remains today.

Buddhism was declared the official religion of Tibet in the eighth century. Yet Tibetan Buddhists are not all unified in their expression of religious tenets or doctrine—in fact a fierce rivalry has long existed between two groups, the "Yellow Hat" sect (known as the Gelugpa) and the "Black Hat" sect (Kagyupa). Until the 1600s, the Black Hats, led by the Karmapa Lama, dominated Tibetan affairs, but for the last 400 years the Yellow Hats, under the leadership of the Dalai Lama, have persevered. The current Dalai Lama, believed to be the fourteenth reincarnation of the spiritual leader, received the Nobel Peace Prize in 1989 for his advocacy of peace and environmental concerns. Not all Tibetan Buddhists, though, share his passion for nonviolence.

Residents of Tibet today include native inhabitants of the region, as well as Chinese migrants from other regions of the country—including many of the Han Chinese majority, who moved to Tibet in search of economic opportunities promoted by the government in Beijing. Many native residents of the territory fear they are losing their indigenous culture, religious traditions, and way of life, which are challenged not only by Han migration to the region but also by the modernizing ways of young Tibetan residents.

known outside China as the Forbidden City. Many Islamic groups decry the pervasiveness of Western standards in areas of fashion, gender relations, and entertainment. One scholar, Benjamin Barber, has named the tension "Jihad vs. McWorld."[14] Since September 11, 2001, though, Barber and others have quickly cautioned us not to make the easy and inaccurate assumptions that the world can so neatly be characterized in a binary fashion, grouping people in tight categories as either in favor of Western-style modernization, or not. Rather, the image that Barber attempted to convey in the provocative title of his study is more accurately viewed as a means of capturing the diverse opposition that has formed to the proliferation of mass markets, technology, and Western-dominated popular culture.[15] For many groups on the receiving end of this new culture, it forces a reevaluation of their fundamental identity.

People also emphasize their class identity, which is based on their status within the economic structure. For example, people who consider themselves "working class" tend to identify with others who receive hourly wages for their labor. Although the origins of class awareness are largely Marxist, people who speak of a class identity are not necessarily Marxist revolutionaries. Income is unevenly distributed in every society. Guillermo O'Donnell and others have argued that a middle class, which is without the extremist tendencies of either wealth or dire poverty, is critical in transitions to democracy, as we discuss in Chapter 14. But especially in societies where there is a sharp divide between the rich and the poor, such as Peru, identity as a member of the working class or the upper class is extremely important, a lesson that feminist mobilizers took some time to learn. Class identity has been an often-cited rallying cry to stand in opposition to the status quo.

Another source of identity that is often masked by the dominance of the government is a regional identity. This shared identity among residents of a particular region, such as a north-south distinction, or the type of region, such as urban or rural, is heightened when governments pursue economic reforms that promote regional disparities. For example, regions in Mexico may be differentiated by the prevalence of export industrialization in the north, leading to relative prosperity as compared to destitution in the south, where the economy is more dependent on domestic sales. Northern Nigeria, which is predominantly Muslim, has since independence dominated political power and decisionmaking, but most of the money is found in the southern, predominantly Christian and animist part of the country. Indonesia is another country with pronounced regional differences, compounded by linguistic and religious differences that are geographically concentrated. The westernmost province of Aceh, deemed the most "Islamic" of any region in the state, is sometimes called "the front porch of Mecca" because it points toward Saudi Arabia. It also has great natural wealth in its possession of liquefied natural gas, which distinguishes it from other provinces. On the other geographical extreme, easternmost Papua (formerly Irian Jaya), lags behind the rest of Indonesia in infrastructure and economic development, and three-fifths of the population are Protestant.[16]

In many countries of the third world, a majority of the population lives in the countryside, often making their living off of the land. Contrary to popular belief, rural dwellers are not necessarily conservative in their political views nor are they passive recipients of the status quo. In some cases, peasants may be the forerunners to democratic processes. For example, one scholar counters popular belief by demonstrating that voter turnout in African rural areas tends to be higher than in the cities.[17] Peasants around the world are known as crafty political entrepreneurs who know how to work the system to their maximum advantage. In 2002, villagers outside Mexico City held a long standoff with the government, protesting the loss of their land to the state. At about the same time Nigerian women staged a takeover of an oil terminal and held hundreds of oil workers hostage (many of them Westerners) until ChevronTexaco agreed to build schools and electrical and water systems. There is also much evidence of mass protests by Chinese peasants against leaders who are perceived to be corrupt. These demonstrations, which tend to leak to the Western media weeks after the fact, can have tens of thousands of participants at a time. But the picture is complex, and clientelism, or the maintenance of PATRON-CLIENT RELATIONSHIPS that reinforce the status quo, can persist in rural areas. Mexico's Institutional Revolutionary Party (PRI) relied on rural support for years, and rural dwellers fearful of change have been a crucial base of support for the Mugabe regime in Zimbabwe.

Throughout the world, religious affiliations also serve as an important sense of identity. It is not surprising that one's basic values and assumptions about human beings, morality, and justice color opinions on issues of politics, economics, and culture. In the United States, a separation of church and state tends to be promoted, meaning that religion is often viewed as a personal matter, and that religious beliefs should not become too closely involved in matters of politics and governance, although the dividing line is increasingly being challenged. The separation of church and state is a contested concept in many regions of the world. In fact, in some of the countries that we are studying, a greater fusion of religion and politics is desired not only by the political elites, but by ordinary citizens as well.

When contemplating religious issues and their importance in politics and governance, many think of the Middle East, the birthplace of the world's three major monotheistic religions: Islam, Judaism, and Christianity. While religious issues are indeed important in this region, religious values and beliefs are difficult to separate from events in other parts of the world as well. Our two Middle Eastern cases place religious principles front and center in public affairs. These two predominantly Muslim countries present an interesting paradox. In Turkey, where the population is approximately 98 percent Muslim, the government fiercely fights to retain its SECULARISM, established since the beginning of the modern republic in 1923. In 1997, Turkey's first (and only) Muslim prime minister, Necmettin Erbakan, was forced to resign under pressure from the military, the institution in Turkey that most wants to limit religious influence in Turkey's public affairs. It is a crime punishable by death to attempt to replace Turkey's secular government with an Islamic regime. Iran, however, is an official Islamic republic, established by the revolution in 1979, making it a theocracy. For example, Iran's highest court, the Council of Guardians, bases its decisions on the sacred Muslim text, the Quran, rather than the country's 1979 constitution. Currently, some groups within Iran, buoyed by the support of President Mohammad Khatami, are attempting to move away from Islamic fundamentalism toward political and religious pluralism. This movement faces fierce opposition from religious clerics, who hold much of the power within the country.

The role of formal church institutions has long been an issue in Mexican politics, especially since the leadership of President Juárez in the mid-1880s. For example, Mexicans have fought two civil wars to decide the Church's role. The country is overwhelmingly Roman Catholic but fiercely anticlerical. The 1917 revolution sought to limit the Church's involvement in politics. Religious schools were closed, and church property was seized. Priests were prohibited from voting or wearing the collar in public. But the election of the socially conservative National Action Party (PAN) in 2000 has emboldened the Church and reignited a number of controversies.

In some countries, governments construct a specific doctrine to explain the role of religion in politics and society. Political and military leaders in Indonesia, for example, continue to promote the importance of the *pancasila,* literally the "five principles." These pillars of Indonesian life are monotheism, national unity, humanitarianism, representative democracy by consensus, and social justice. Sukarno, the first president of Indonesia, created the *pancasila* creed as a way to unite the diverse peoples of Indonesia. Today the *pancasila* doctrine continues to appear in Indonesia's constitution, and a symbol of it appears in the national coat of arms.

Another example of the importance of religious identity in the non-Western world comes from a Christian tradition. Liberation theology is a movement that started within the Catholic Church, and it has had an especially powerful impact in Latin America. It is by definition an action-oriented ideology that calls on its followers to promote social justice, focusing especially on the most economically poor members of society. As a system of thought, it is intriguing because of its combination of Marxist revolutionary ideas (which are explicitly hostile toward organized religions) with Christian teachings. While its origins were within Roman Catholicism, it is increasingly an ecumenical movement, including other Christian churches and institutions, especially since the mid-1980s.[18] And although many of its leaders received training in European religious institutions, liberation theology is increasingly becoming an indigenous intellectual and ideological movement addressed by native theologians to the social ills plaguing the less developed world.

In 1988, Peruvian theologian Gustavo Gutierrez published *The Theology of Liberation,* considered by many to be the definitive statement.[19] In it he stressed social praxis (practice), with a commitment to critical reflection and a renewed dedication on the part of the universal church to the disenfranchised poor and destitute. Gutierrez argued that too many Christians, especially Catholics, focus on the orthodoxy (correct teachings) rather than on the orthopraxis (correct practice) of a Christian life. Liberation theology activists maintain that people need to move beyond doctrine to focus on the economic, political, and social issues that affect ordinary people on a daily basis.

We emphasize two teachings of liberation theology. First, advocates contend that poverty is caused by structures (such as the international economic system) rather than individual, idiosyncratic characteristics, including laziness, bad luck, or other sources of blame. Therefore, the "liberation" of the poor is more than an act of individual charity; it is a demand for a new social and economic order in order to promote the universal humanity of all peoples. Second is the idea of collective sin, articulated by Brazilian theologian Leonardo Boff. Boff argued that people who support unjust regimes, even if they themselves do not personally exploit the poor, are collectively responsible for the result.[20] Boff's statements implicated not only leaders and citizens in the Western, developed world, but citizens of poorer countries as well. Liberation theology has impacted many of the countries we study here. A 2000 pastoral letter in Mexico, for example, criticized political and economic systems as "poverty generating structures," and called on people to fight to build a more just society. The South African Council of Churches applied the principles of liberation theology through black theology to end apartheid. Several ecumenical organizations, including the Zimbabwean Catholic Bishops' Conference and the Zimbabwe Council of Churches, played important roles in the struggle against white minority rule, and continue to condemn human rights abuses. They argue that poverty is due to oppressive structures and call for activism, primarily through the development of base Christian communities who work to educate, evangelize, and empower the economically poor. Movements inspired by liberation theology have met with harsh repression by governments (backed by military force) and institutional churches as well, especially in El Salvador and Guatemala. This has provoked an increase in violence by adherents.

Mobilization around issues of gender has been particularly strong throughout the non-Western world, especially since 1975, when the UNITED NATIONS held its first international women's conference in Mexico City. Similar to other groups, women have mobilized in response to repression, exclusion, and other crises, both on their own behalf and in the interest of others, especially children. As we discuss below, there is no single brand of feminism, but rather many different viewpoints commonly united around the desire to advance the voice of women in today's world. Some view feminism as a solely Western idea, although many women in the non-Western world disagree.[21]

Feminism is a complex worldview that includes many perspectives, and there are vigorous debates about what defines a "feminist." One school of thought distinguishes feminists who work primarily for civil equality that recognizes the fundamental equality between women and men. Such groups, often called liberal feminists, have been at the forefront of suffrage movements as well as civil rights movements that fight for gains in equality before the law. This view is contrasted with another school of thought that emphasizes the dif-

A mural in Namibia urges grassroots participation (UN Photo)

ferences that exist between women and men. Commonly known as radical feminists, they argue that liberal feminists fail to recognize the unspoken assumption that women should perform the same as men. In contrast, radical feminists fight for the equal recognition of women's standards as well as men's; they argue that women's ways need to be given equal recognition. It is a question of standards and assumptions; while radical feminists agree that men and women are equal, they contend that stopping there fails to challenge the continued dominance of a male-centric society.

Feminists have actively challenged notions of "correct" female (and by association, male) behavior that are rooted in custom and tradition. In a related fashion, many women openly confront the notion that politics is the exclusive domain of men. Mexico, for example, has a long feminist history. Some analysts argue that it is Mexico, not the United States, that has been the cradle for feminism in the Western Hemisphere. Sor Juana Inéz de la Cruz, who lived in the 1600s, is said to be the first feminist of the Americas. In large numbers, Mexican women joined the revolutionary armies of Villa and Zapata. Benita Galeana led the first land takeovers by squatters during the Great Depression. She was arrested sixty times and lost her eyesight while on a hunger strike fighting for women's suffrage. Since the 1980s, *MAQUILADORA* workers have claimed an unusual degree of freedom for themselves, despite the low pay and sexual harassment they continue to face in the factories. Mexican feminists today are fighting for reproductive rights, for better working conditions, and to have violence against women (especially sexual assault and wife battery) taken more seriously. However, in Mexico and in Latin America as a whole, women have not fully harnessed their potential as a political force compared to other interest groups such as labor movements and church groups.

Similar to other sets of activists, groups working to further women's causes disagree about the point of focus for their actions. Some groups accuse others of reinforcing gender distinctions by focusing on issues of family, motherhood, and children, replicating traditional political roles. Mothers' groups in Latin America, for example, were challenged by radical feminist leaders because their work focused on practical interests, such as providing meals to deprived children, rather than on more "strategic" issues, including sexual freedom and domestic violence.[22] Yet the mothers' groups, in their emphasis on seemingly practical needs, rallied tens of thousands of activists against military regimes, revealing that the emperor had no clothes.

Another debate centers on the relationship between culture and feminism. This has definitely been a theme of contention and division among Latin American, African, and Islamic feminists. Women who work within the system, or within the structure of prevailing religious norms, are accused by others of replicating traditional views that subordinate women, rather than challenging the status quo.

Non-Western variants of feminism have argued that "practical" concerns, including providing meals and healthcare to families, can be just as feminist as the political concerns of other feminists, such as demanding access to political decisionmaking. Adherents to the latter focus, which is considered to be more "strategic" than practical, claim to be working for larger structural changes that would ultimately transform gender relations. But non-Western women do not hold a monopoly on this desire: in Latin America, for example, feminism was central to the effort to delegitimize military rule and re-create civil society.[23] Yet other feminist groups, in the face of the same struggles, adopted an explicitly human rights character to their activism. Economic crises and the imposition of STRUCTURAL ADJUSTMENT PROGRAMS (SAPs) impelled women to organize and demand relief, filling in the gaps of what government could not (or would not) provide. Maybe some viewed this as practical and too "traditional," but to the women who were organizing, it was feminism at its best.

To be successful, people plan their strategies within existing contexts—sometimes this means radically challenging the system, and other times it means reforming it along the edges. Patriarchy and social conservatism are so pervasive, for example, that many women in northern Nigeria believe that reform within Islamic law is the only hope for promoting gender equality. The issue of the Islamic veil captures some of this controversy. Many Westerners associate the traditional headscarf or veil with women's oppression and submission to male authority. Yet for many Islamic women, the decision to wear a headscarf is a conscious choice; the veil, or *purdah,* provides them an avenue of expression and even opposition. For some, wearing the veil literally creates a wall that allows women to move through the male world of school and work; it allows a quiet insubordination. In Tunisia, donning a religious veil is forbidden, and many challenge this rule. In Turkey, the Islamic veil is a source of fierce controversy; secular feminists are against it and religious women march for their freedom to wear it. For example, in 1999, Merve Kavakçi, a newly elected member of parliament, was denied her seat because she wore a headscarf to her inauguration ceremony. Some women have refashioned traditional styles into a modern fashion of headscarf, granting them expression and individuality. In this sense, women have reappropriated Islamic admonitions for modest dress as a means of heightening their presence and voice.

Clearly, not all women are feminists. In fact, some ardently oppose mobilization and action in the name of equality or women's causes. Some groups, self-proclaimed antifeminists, reject the importance of feminist issues and often agree with gender segregation and clearly defined family roles. They often advocate a culturally conservative position, reaffirming the notion of a predetermined place for women at home, rearing the family, rather than in the marketplace or other public domains of men. Key issues of antifeminists include opposition to abortion and women's employment outside the home. Some antifeminists even support outright subordination to men, as can be found in women's support for the Taliban movement in Afghanistan.

The Taliban Islamic movement, which formed the Islamic Emirate of Afghanistan in 1996, advocated an extreme form of Islamic fundamentalism. Even prior to the 2001 war in Afghanistan, the Taliban and its administration were isolated from most of the world, including the leading Islamic countries. Iran, joined by Russia and India, backed the main opposition group, the Northern Military Alliance. The Taliban condoned public stoning, flogging, and amputation for the violation of its laws; in fact, it held weekly punishment sessions in a Kabul stadium. Its treatment of women was especially harsh. In the name of protecting the honor, life, and property of Afghani women, Taliban law required that they be fully veiled in a chador, and they were forbidden from most education and employment. Additionally, no social mingling or communication was permitted between women and men outside the family. Non-Muslim women were required to wear a yellow dress with a special mark to further segregate them from society, since Muslims and non-Muslims were forbidden contact. Taliban leaders, schooled in a particular version of Islam, justified that their standards derive from traditions in Afghanistan's tribal culture and adhere to Islam. They rejected universal norms of human rights that derive from a liberal, secular approach. Taliban leaders, and many citizens, especially peasants and members of the working class, were frustrated at what they perceived to be intrusion by outside organizations and governments and their attempts to contravene local cultural mores that they argue have existed for more than a millennium. Their actions inspired debate about cultural values and standards that continues even after their demise. Are there universal norms, applicable to all people irrespective of culture, level of development, or social system, or is there merit in an approach referred to as cultural relativism, in which standards are dependent on relative circumstances?

Elites, Masses, and Legitimacy

It has been implicit in our discussion to this point that power is distributed unequally. Usually in public life, some people hold power and other people are influenced by it. In this chapter, we have emphasized that all people possess ideas about the world around them. It is obvious that in many areas of life, the ideas of some matter more than the ideas of others. In every society around the world, people can be divided into two categories, either the elites (possessing power and influence) or the masses (lacking power and influence relative to the elites). There are always more of the latter. Even though the so-called elites may exercise more influence and authority in economics, politics, culture, or other areas, they are not able to maintain this status indefinitely.

An important term that conveys one of the most fundamental political relationships between elites and masses is LEGITIMACY, sometimes viewed simply as "rightfulness."[24] All leaders, no matter the level, need to be concerned about their legitimacy. Legitimacy can be viewed as a sense that an individual or group who has power holds such power properly. Individuals or groups can possess power or influence, but if the people over whom they have influence do not view them as legitimate, their power and influence will likely be short-lived.

Sociologist Max Weber identified three primary sources of legitimacy: tradition, charisma, and legality. Traditional legitimacy is based on cultural precedents established for recognizing authority and power. A tribal chief, for example, bases his legitimacy on this source. Hereditary monarchies, in which some people receive their influence because of membership in particular families, are other sources of traditional legitimacy. The "Mandate of Heaven," possessed by members of the Chinese imperial leadership, is another example of legitimacy that is traditional in nature. Charismatic sources of legitimacy are based on personal attributes that command attention, respect, and oftentimes obedience. Charisma is both something that people are said to exhibit, as well as something given to them in the eyes of ordinary people. For example, Ayatollah Khomeini, the former religious leader of the Iranian Revolution, was viewed as a mythical hero to many. Before the 1979 revolution, while he was living in exile (mostly in Turkey, Iraq, and France), people in Iran insisted that they could see his face in the moon.[25] The third source of legitimacy, according to Weber, is legality: establishing seemingly impersonal rules and procedures to determine the recipients of leadership and authority. In this example, elections and laws transfer a sense of legitimacy to individuals and groups.

Legitimacy is what makes political systems last. It transforms raw power into a sense of authority. Without legitimacy, rulers' mandates are enforced out of a sense of fear, rather than a sense of duty or obligation.[26] A lack of legitimacy can cause a government to crumble. In some cultural traditions, there would be signs from the ancestors or the spirits that a leader had lost his or her legitimacy. In imperial China, for example, natural disasters were perceived to be signs that the emperor had lost the legitimacy to rule. In many modern democracies today, legitimacy is based on the popular mandate. Although elections are increasingly being viewed as the legitimizing tool of modern leaders, this has not always been the case, nor do many leaders maintain their legitimacy based on legal means alone.

Do powerful elites really need to be concerned about their legitimacy? Simply put, they do. It is difficult to survive on coercion alone, and leaders need authority in order to accomplish the day-to-day tasks of governing. Coercion and the violence it entails are costly, not only in a crude financial sense, but in terms of morale as well. Certainly, some authoritarian leaders have made extensive use of threats and coercion as a means of maintaining their power. But it is extremely difficult (although not impossible) to maintain power in this manner for long. Leaders in all areas of public life need to develop connections with the masses, and must be able to foster a sense that they are legitimately empowered to make decisions. When citizens no longer feel that the leadership has legitimacy, they are often impelled to act. As we will discuss below, ordinary citizens, even in the face of dire constraints on their behavior and threats of coercive responses from leaders, attempt to challenge circumstances that they feel are unjust and illegitimate. While some of these attempts face anguishing defeats, others are successful at challenging the state of affairs and bringing about desired change.

Leaders maintain their legitimacy in a variety of different ways. Ideology plays a key role, as members of the elite attempt to craft views and actions to their liking. The manipulation of ideologies by leaders is particularly acute in totalitarian systems, in which the government has control over most aspects of people's lives. The use of important symbols, such as buildings, images, linguistic phrases, and historical heroes, is another means by which leaders attempt to promote and increase their legitimacy. In societies that have experienced revolutions, or have had a recent history of revered leaders, paying homage to and noting a lineage from these leaders can be a powerful source of legitimacy, especially in uncertain times. On the fiftieth anniversary of the founding of the

People's Republic of China, for example, then-president Jiang Zemin, who was also general secretary of the Chinese Communist Party (CCP), ordered large pictures of him to be carried on high behind the traditional posters of Mao Zedong and Deng Xiaoping. This rather blatant attempt of demonstrating the source of his authority is not unlike other public relations campaigns in which leaders engage. In your examination of legitimacy in the non-Western world, be careful to avoid connections between legitimacy, stability, and popular content. Just because you observe a pronounced sense of legitimacy in a particular country does not mean that citizens agree with all (or even most) of the actions that their government takes.

Leaders may also promote their legitimacy by providing material gains to the population. Indonesia's former president Suharto based much of his legitimacy, especially in the later years of his rule, on promises to the people that their economic lives would improve. When the futility of this promise was painfully realized in the spring of 1998, however, his legitimacy plummeted, and he was forced from office. This example provides another lesson about the importance of stability. When leaders are successful at maintaining it, for the most part life is stable. When they fail, it can often lead to popular mobilization or other forms of participation, a topic to which we now turn our attention.

Ideas in Action

If they are not acted upon, ideas remain a possibility, rather than an expression of will. In the remainder of this chapter, we examine the next step: when individuals and groups decide to take action based upon their beliefs. We examine forms of political participation, which we define simply as efforts by ordinary people to influence the actions of their leaders.[27] Sometimes activists work within the bounds of legal activity, although oftentimes they attempt to change or break the conventional rules. While in some systems, especially totalitarian regimes, citizens are forced to participate in governmentally sponsored demonstrations, rallies, or protests, for our purposes we only examine participation that is voluntary. Fundamentally, political participation is about communicating preferences to the people who have power and influence (elites).

Certainly, not everybody, even in the most developed democracies, participates. One important characteristic that participants tend to exhibit is a sense of efficacy, which is a sense that one's participation can make a difference. If you feel that by writing a letter to an elected official you are likely to influence her or his point of view, you have a strong sense of efficacy. On the other hand, if you do not vote because you are of the mind that it does not make a difference, you have a low sense of efficacy. Oftentimes, a sense of efficacy also correlates with levels of education, as well as socioeconomic security. It takes time to be active and engaged in public life, and few people can afford to take time off from work or be away from family in order to speak at a neighborhood assembly or picket against an unjust action.

How do people participate in their political, social, and economic world? We often think of voting in elections as the primary means of political participation, but in fact, this is just one of four primary ways that people can participate in public life: (1) explicit communication, both spoken and written; (2) regime action, including voting and joining political parties or legal organizations; (3) mobilizational action, including demonstrating in social movements or rallies or participating in boycotts or other forms of group resistance; and (4) inaction, by refusing to vote or obey authority, or utilizing the so-called WEAPONS OF THE WEAK. These categories are not necessarily mutually exclusive. In fact, individuals and groups who feel dissatisfied with one type of action, such as normal constituent communication, often decide to pursue another strategy, such as joining a protest.

Spoken and Written Communication

Many citizens decide to communicate with their public leaders, often using simple means such as telephone calls, public speeches, letters to officials or to the media, or public signs and posters. Most officials establish some form of channel to foster communication between themselves and their constituents. In some cases, these official channels are very explicit. For example, ever since the earliest years of the People's Republic of China, party and government offices have designated receiving rooms for citizen communication, which are functionally called "letters and visits" offices. Letters to the media can be an extremely useful way to communicate dissatisfaction with a leader or policy. Even in the most totalitarian systems, government-controlled newspapers are designated as receiving points for citizen letters and complaints. Even if the letters themselves are not published in the "official" media, they are often collected and distributed for the leadership to read. Petitions, often presented by groups of people rather than individuals, are another common form of participation in many countries. Publicly displayed posters and graffiti can also be an effective way to communicate problems or concerns. Chinese society has a long-established tradition of posting *dazibao,* literally "big character posters," in public areas for citizens and leaders alike to read. In times of political turmoil, most of these displays remain anonymous or are signed with pseudonyms, but in times of particular openness, people confidently sign their names to their commentaries.

Regime Action

The second major category of participation is regime action, or participation that is overtly designed to support the functioning of the larger political, social, or economic system. This is the type of participation with which most people are likely familiar. In many countries, democratic and nondemocratic alike, citizens are called on to elect representatives to make decisions in their name. The difference in nondemocratic systems, though, is that there is little if any choice of candidates, or the candidates who are elected fail to exercise power or influence. Citizens are also called on to vote in referenda about issues that affect them, such as the Mexican vote on whether or not the Zapatistas should become a national opposition party.

Political parties stand out as one of the most common vehicles of participation. These organizations develop as groups of similarly minded individuals organize so that they can influence policy decisions. Parties help individuals identify with issues in public life, and they organize people into action. They also promote a common identity among participants, in some cases helping to bridge ethnic or cultural divides. In democratic and nondemocratic systems alike, political parties form so that the elites can appeal to ordinary citizens. In some countries until very recently a single party dominated public life, and citizens have had few choices but to belong to the ruling party. In others, a meaningful PARTY SYSTEM has developed in which competing groups of people openly vie for attention and power. Parties often rename themselves (as the Muslim parties in Turkey), craft new coalitions (with other parties as well as constituent groups), and shift power balances, all in the attempt to maintain dynamic links between elites and masses.

Maurice Duverger classified three main types of political parties, based on their style of organization and operation.[28] In the CADRE PARTY, PERSONALIST REGIMES, often based on friendships and favors, and factional groupings made up of people with similar approaches who try to stick together, dominate the relatively small group of elites involved in political matters. Often in systems where cadre parties prevail, the right to vote is limited, meaning that political parties do not face the need to justify their ideological positions or policies to many beyond groups already possessing power or influence. A second type is the MASS PARTY, which attempts to reach out beyond the walls of power to appeal to less politically engaged individuals and groups. Mass parties have open membership, but often leaders target specific segments of the population to whom they plan to pitch their ideological appeal: factory workers, intellectuals, peasants, or other groups. In order to maintain their interest and support, mass parties develop local branch offices that provide services and information to their likely constituents. Duverger's third type is the DEVOTEE PARTY, which is dominated by a charismatic leader and a small elite united in forging a revolutionary path. The Chinese Communist Party during Mao's leadership is an exemplar of such an elitist party, even if its rhetoric attempted to cater to a mass audience.

How important are political parties within the non-Western world? In single-party states, such as the PRC, they are the primary venue through which the elite exercise their power. In transforming states, such as Indonesia, the nascent political party system is dominated by personalities and crowded with minute fractions. In other countries, including Peru, traditional parties have become virtually extinct. Many leaders sense they are better off without a party than with one. In states where personal relations continue to dominate politics, elections tend to be centered on candidates rather than parties. These systems are marked by extreme electoral volatility, and can easily open the door for populist antisystem candidates who have few qualms about dissolving democratic institutions once they capture the seats of power.

Another type of institution that facilitates the participation of ordinary citizens is the employment organization or union. Independent unions attempt to provide a collective voice to workers. They work to promote workers' rights and interests, including sick leave, access to healthcare, and the right to strike, which is restricted in many areas of the world. Unions played an important role in civil rights movements in South Korea and South Africa. In some countries, unions work closely with elites; left-leaning political parties tend to develop strong ties with labor and trade unions. Unions may also serve as the launching pad for oppositional movements and parties. The Movement for Democratic

Change (MDC) in Zimbabwe, for example, which nearly unseated the Zimbabwe African National Union–Patriotic Front (ZANU-PF), grew out of labor unions. In other countries, governments attempt to co-opt independent expression through the establishment of official, state-sponsored unions. If Chinese workers attempt to organize independently of the CCP-run federation of trade unions, they face almost certain jail time, or are sent to camps for "rehabilitation through labor." In fact, independent unionization is dangerous business throughout the third world.

Latin America remains an extremely risky place to organize for workers' rights. According to statistics from the International Confederation of Free Trade Unions (ICFTU), ninety people were killed in one twelve-month period for union activity, more than twice as many as on any other continent.[29] In countries reliant on exports, including Nicaragua, El Salvador, Guatemala, Mexico, and Honduras, trade unionists face many restrictions on their ability to strike. Repression is also common in Africa, where 80 percent of worldwide arrests for union activities take place. Finally, in the Middle East, independent trade unions are virtually nonexistent. In this region, the situation is particularly bleak for foreign workers, who make up approximately two-thirds of the labor force in many countries. In most countries in the region, foreign workers are not permitted to join or form any type of workers' union.

Union organizing can also be found among the youth. Children's labor unions, whose origins are found in the New York newsboy strikes against Joseph Pulitzer and William Hearst at the turn of the twentieth century, are vying for a stronger voice in national and international debates about child labor. According to the International Labour Organization (ILO), there are more than 250 million children workers worldwide, only a fraction of whom have banded together to form unions in support of their cause. Brazilian street children formed the first modern children's labor union in 1985.[30] Similar groups can be found throughout Africa, Southeast Asia, and India. Children's labor unions are becoming increasingly organized (some now hold international meetings), and they are united in the voice that child labor should not be abolished, but rather reformed.

Mobilizational Action

Mobilizational action is the third category of participation, which includes social movements and other forms of collective action by aggrieved groups of people. By definition, this form of participation involves more than one person. People around the world understand the strength that can be found in numbers. When a group of like-minded individuals forms to influence the turn of events around them, they are said to have formed a social movement. We often think of participants in social movements as attempting to change the status quo and bring about a new state of affairs, but in fact many participants in social movements are fighting instead to maintain the current state of life. Social movements form when there are grievances, either because people sense that they are being unfairly singled out or that they are not doing as well as other groups (relative deprivation), because they feel that promises, either implicit or explicit, were not kept (rising expectations), or because they perceive a threat of some

Figure 10.4 China's "Cultural Revolution"

Not all forms of regime action are so organized or peaceful—nor are they designed to promote stability and harmony in the regime. In a utopian attempt to "continue the revolution" that brought victory to the Chinese Communist Party, Chairman Mao Zedong launched the "Great Proletarian Cultural Revolution" in 1966—his goal was to fight against bureaucracy and create nearly constant struggle. What followed was a virtual civil war, in which it is estimated that 10 percent of the population (nearly 100 million people) were singled out as targets for revolutionary disciplining and struggle. Mao and his devoted "Red Guards" (middle school and high school youth who attempted to implement his directives throughout the country) publicly humiliated specific groups who were deemed harmful to China's progression as a revolutionary socialist society. Being labeled an intellectual, expert, bureaucrat, or some-

one with a foreign connection was the greatest curse of life during the Cultural Revolution: Mao and his supporters despised these groups. During the ten years of the revolution, a virtual cult developed around Chairman Mao, as Red Guards and others attempted to commit his most important sayings—captured in the famous "Little Red Books"—to memory. After 1969 the Red Guards were disbanded and sent into China's remote rural areas to educate the peasants about Mao's revolutionary ideas. Most Chinese today refer to the period as the "ten dark years"—it is believed that at least 400,000 people were killed in the violence that marked the period, and almost everyone else was affected by the revolutionary fervor. Life was turned upside down—especially in the cities—schools, universities, and most offices set up to manage day-to-day living were closed for much of the ten-year period.

sort. There is also a sense that the "time is ripe" for change, providing an opportunity structure for action. There are seemingly favorable times for groups of people to engage in collective action, often because of a political or economic transition, unexpected access to power, divisions among leaders, or a decreased likelihood of repression.[31] Changes in the international environment and movements with "spillover effects" also inspire action. For example, the MDC in Zimbabwe models itself on the Serbian experience: activists threatened massive street demonstrations to bring down "Africa's Milosevic."

Savvy activists develop expectations of the likelihood of success, and act accordingly. For example, in the Iranian student demonstrations of 1997, the so-called Prague Spring of Iran, young students and women who had not benefited from the policies of the earlier regime decided to exploit the opportunity available to them when President Khatami took office in August. Even if their movement ultimately experienced limited success, some activists decided to exploit the door that was opened to them during the transition. This is not always the case, however. Opportunities are in the eye of the beholder. As levels of success are achieved, the need for mobilization often decreases. For example, the weakening of Mexican feminism ironically coincided with gradual accession of women to full political rights in the early 1950s.[32]

Social movements can be defined by an issue, such as civil rights or environmental protection, by a core group, such as women's movements or students' movements, or by a common target, such as antiglobalization protests or antimilitary demonstrations. One of the most common characteristics of social movements is that they often begin with a narrowly defined issue, and then rather quickly blossom to include other complaints and interests, broadening their appeal to a greater number of groups. Rarely are social movements confined to a single issue, and alliances between sets of activists are common. A group of students begins a protest ostensibly about economic corruption. Then they are joined by unemployed workers angered by layoffs, and state employees frustrated at the inattention of their government-controlled union. The widespread protests then attract others at odds with the regime, including mothers who are confined to the home because of factory cutbacks, migrant peasants who cannot find work for more than a week at a time, and high school dropouts wanting to get in on the action. This situation is part of the story of the widespread demonstrations in China in the spring of 1989.

University students wanting to pay homage to a fallen leader sparked the movement. After other groups joined the students in Beijing and 300 other cities, and after the international media picked up on the unlikely protests, a prodemocracy movement formed. As participants multiplied, the task of the protest organizers increased exponentially. Disagreements about tactics increased, such as whether or not protesters should stage a hunger strike, whether they should openly confront the regime by blocking Tiananmen Square during an international summit, and whether they should negotiate with other protesting groups. We now know, thanks to extensive documentation and interviews with exiled protest leaders, that a serious factional split developed early on in the movement. Disagreement among movement leaders is common after a protest gets off the ground.

Participants in social movements often disagree about the scope of their protest actions. Do they want to provide a wakeup call to the regime and then return to life as usual, or do they want to bring regime leaders to their knees, attempting to cripple the economic and diplomatic base of the state? Some protesters view dialogue (especially with governments) as "selling out," while others view it as a strategic tactic. Some activists want to forge alliances with other organized social groups, uniting in their common cause of increasing regime transparency and accountability. Movements to extend political freedom and promote environmental protection are often linked, either in formal coalitions or because activists cross lines. Concern for the survival of indigenous peoples is often linked to environmental concerns, as in Nigeria in the Movement for the Survival of the Ogoni People (MOSOP), and in Mexico with the Zapatistas. In China, many of the same activists who supported the movements in 1989 are the harshest critics of the regime's attempts to complete the Three Gorges Dam by 2011, which many international groups and Chinese scientists alike fear will be a huge ecological disaster once put into operation.

Economic concerns have been a major mobilizing force throughout the non-Western world. For many years, people unable to cope with AUSTERITY PLANS (discussed in Chapter 7) have protested against SAPs, most visibly in what has come to be known as an "IMF riot." IMF riots, which often involve looting and burning, are a form of protest that has broken out in Jamaica, Egypt, Indonesia, and Argentina, as people find that they can no longer manage with such devastating hardship. Less dramatic but sometimes more deadly versions of IMF riots take the form of mass demonstrations, such as those in Bolivia motivated by fatigue over fifteen years of adjustment.

In addition to achieving a desired goal, social movements are also important because they provide a sense of identity and belonging to participants. In her studies of Peruvian women's movements, Maruja Barrig argues that by participating in democratically organized programs such as communal kitchens and milk distribution programs, women develop a sense of solidarity and model behavior that could be extended into other areas of life.[33] To better understand the organization and impact of social movements, we examine two subtypes: women's movements and youth mobilization.

People often think of women's movements being involved in suffrage, or the right to vote, and little more. Women's mobilization, though, has gone well beyond this single cause, and in fact women activists refused to be held back by the absence of the right to vote. For example, even though Mexico had some of the most vibrant and developed women's networks throughout Latin America, as early as the 1930s, it was among the last countries in the Southern Hemisphere to grant women the right to vote.[34] Women's movements, especially in the third world, have been particularly strong at demonstrating that personal issues are indeed political issues. As we discussed in Chapter 7, NEOLIBERALISM has contributed to crises and poverty, and women have been channeled disproportionately into low-paid and transitory work. This has led many women to seek participation in community-based and neighborhood organizations to survive as they struggle to fill the gaps created when the state cuts services. Already struggling to support a family, these women face a huge burden without social services to rely on. Yet it sometimes seems that the most burdened and desperate people can mobilize to accomplish huge tasks. For example, women spearheaded the Madres de Plaza de Mayo movement in Argentina, which brought attention to the "disappeared" husbands and sons of the participants, ignited human rights protests, and launched similar movements throughout Latin America. Another example of activism by women directly affected by official state violence can be found in China following the crackdown on the students in Tiananmen Square. Ding Zilin, whose son was killed on the last evening of the demonstrations as he attempted to vacate the square, and others have staged an international movement to publicize the plight of their children and the brutality of the Chinese government. Mothers go to the front lines supposedly for defense of family and morality. But often they are subjected to STATE-SPONSORED TERRORISM, sexual abuse, and humiliation. They face similar discrimination within other participatory channels, including parties and unions that co-opt women into auxiliary chapters. Whether in traditional parties or social movements, women must prove themselves against visible and invisible obstacles. Women in many countries form their own organizations because their demands for equality and justice are viewed as divisive or frivolous.

Women throughout Latin America, especially in Peru and Chile, established communal dining programs to pull resources and feed the economically poor. During the 1980s, one of largest social movements in Latin America was the

Vaso de Leche, or Municipal Milk Program. Based in Lima, Peru, its participants distributed at least a single serving of milk a day to more than 1 million children in the mid-1980s. While the military concentrated on progressive and radical rural reform, popular social programs initiated by women attempted to incorporate new groups into public affairs, especially the urban lower class and peasants. Their mobilization was especially critical because of the disastrous economic crises that battered the region throughout the 1980s. In the end, though, they maintained some reliance on government, especially at local levels, for funding. They also received support through international donations, mostly from the United States. These activities were important not only for the services they provided to needy people, but also for the linkages they established between women's groups. They helped many women feel a sense of belonging and empowerment, which helped promote active involvement in public affairs that otherwise seemed "off limits." The challenge they face for more long-term impact, though, is to be able to organize when not in the face of crisis.

Additionally, college and university students tend to be at the forefront of protests and social movements. Why is this the case? Students tend to be skeptical of the norms of government and society, yet optimistic about their ability to make a difference. Many Latin American youth argue that their role is to offer sorely needed answers for the new situations their countries are facing. The traditional model of the party is exhausted; the youth need new organizations capable of responding to demands for a new more participatory and flexible POLITICAL CULTURE. Students tend to be risk-takers, willing to sacrifice time, money, and sometimes their lives in order to make a point. Some have noted a correlation in the location of major universities in capitals, as well as a connection between social movements and this geographical fact (Tehran, Mexico City, Beijing). University campuses also can be ideal locales for communication networks. The National University–San Cristobal of Huamanga Peru, for example, served as the launching pad for one of the most violent movements in Latin America, Sendero Luminoso (Shining Path). Some student movements to unseat leaders have been successful, such as Indonesia in 1998 and Iran in 1979, and others have been painfully unsuccessful, notably Mexico in 1968 and China in 1989.

University students also have a history of political activism in Iran. In November 1979, in the early days of the Islamic Revolution, students were one of the groups leading the seizure of the U.S. embassy in Tehran when fifty-two American hostages were captured. Twenty years later, in July 1999, student-led demonstrations for press reform broke out at Tehran University, spreading to eighteen cities. Sensing an open opportunity caused by widened rifts between Iran's conservative Supreme Leader, Ayatollah Khamenei, and the popularly elected but lower-ranking president, Mohammad Khatami, students staged five successive days of protest for democratic reform and press freedom. Students mobilized after the legislature passed a restrictive press law and after conservative leaders ordered the closure of a popular left-leaning Islamic newspaper, *Salam*.

In response, police forces raided the university dorms while students were sleeping, pushing some from multistory windows. In response, even more students joined the protest, using updated twists of slogans from the 1979 revolution. The chant "Independence, Freedom, Islamic Republic," was altered to "Independence, Freedom, Iranian Republic." Most accounts claim that the police killed one student, and approximately twenty more were seriously injured. In addition, nearly a thousand students were arrested for participating in the unrest, and at least four people were sentenced to death, in secret trials, for inciting violence. In July 2000 a military court acquitted the Tehran police chief whom most blame for leading the charge to violence the year before, inciting a muted but audible outcry from many in Iran and abroad.

Weapons of the Weak

The final type of participation that we discuss is powerful in its ability to cause disruption through inaction or (on the surface) seemingly inconsequential acts of individual resistance. If the traditional spaces to which people can turn are denied (unions, political parties, media, protest channels), they learn to turn elsewhere to express their sentiments, especially their grievances. Anthropologist James C. Scott identified "weapons of the weak" as a way to categorize concealed, disguised, individual resistance. These actions, such as concealing a pig from state officials or falsifying income records, may not garner the same amount of attention as a revolt in the national capital, but they can be extremely effective tools against injustice, nonetheless. People pursue less obvious and less explicitly confrontational forms of resistance when open challenge to authority is too risky. In varied contexts, Scott and others draw our attention to "everyday forms of resistance" pursued by dominated groups, such as women, peasants, or other disenfranchised individuals. As we discussed in Chapter 4, weapons of the weak were common forms of resistance in struggles for national liberation.

Some analysts have sought to explain why women and other repressed groups in some parts of the world appear to be aloof from politics and less likely to participate in democratic struggles. They argue that in many cases women's political power and participation has declined since the precolonial period. Women's initial response to being politically marginalized during colonialism was resistance. However, this resistance often proved ineffective and was followed by a disengagement from formal politics or withdrawal into a consciously apolitical stance. Instead, women have come to favor private, extralegal channels and institutions including families, secret societies, spirit cults or prayer groups, and traditional women's associations. Additionally, women tend to be more active in regard to socioeconomic issues at the local rather than the national level.

But part of the reason why some groups appear complacent to outsiders is that observers fail to recognize acts of resistance that do not utilize more conventionally recognized channels of protest. Many actors employ weapons of the weak in the face of power, accomplishing in subtle acts what might never be achieved in more traditional routes. Individuals feign support for a cause, while subtly putting a cog in the wheel to block it. Actors can drag their feet, pretend compliance, and organize others to break rules through acts of civil disobedience. As Célestin Monga argues, outsiders often lament the absence of civic participation in African societies, because they overlook the long tradition of indigenous activism, what he terms the "anthropology of anger."[35] People get angry when systematically oppressed, and they develop ways of escaping repression. They pretend to accept the rules imposed by authoritarian groups, and are constantly adjusting to escape domination and circumvent coercive strictures. Such participation is grassroots-based and highly creative. Activists subvert the rules by not confronting power directly. These informal methods of participation and protest may be what truly pushes change.

Subversive music is a common form of political expression. For example, one of Africa's most famous Afrobeat musicians, Fela Anikulapo-Kuti, considered music a weapon. While praise singing is a tradition associated with greats such as King Sunny Adé, Fela invented a new art: abuse singing. In the late 1970s, Fela took on Olusegun Obasanjo, the military dictator of Nigeria, arguing that Afrobeat was the only music where you could say what you feel and tell the government what you think. For upholding the rights of the powerless and taking the military on in his songs, Fela was beaten and jailed. His seventy-eight-year-old mother was thrown from a second-story window and later died of her injuries. He is followed in these pursuits by his son, Femi Kuti, whose Afrobeat songs attack corrupt politicians and warn about AIDS. Another highly influential political forum for dealing with real-life issues such as corruption, drug trafficking, AIDS, and sexism is the *telenovela,* or soap opera, a favorite form of entertainment for millions in Latin America. The *telenovela* is much more influential than the newspaper in Mexico; it is said that writers are using this art form the way Thomas Paine used the pamphlet. As dictatorships have been retired, a flourishing independent medium is taking advantage of the political openness to tackle once-taboo subjects. A Venezuelan *telenovela* dealing with corruption prompted street protests that helped bring down a president in 1993.[36]

Music may also be a subversive tool linking exile communities to their homeland by openly challenging behavioral limits. The Persian pop sensation Googoosh Faegheh Atashin, said to be as famous in Iran today as Elvis in the United States, was wildly popular before the 1979 revolution. After the establishment of the Islamic Republic, though, she was barred from the public stage on religious grounds, because women's voices were viewed as "demonic." Yet in the swell of reforms following Mohammad Khatami's election, Googoosh received her passport and launched a world tour, much to the excitement of the exiled Iranians abroad, especially in Los Angeles and other large expatriate communities.[37] But the shows are not only for Iranians living away from their country. Concerts (and Western movies) are routinely illegally copied for a prosperous bootleg network in Iran. Iranians abroad shoot movies and concerts using small hand-held cameras, then send the tapes off to Iran, where they are copied en masse and sold within days of their release.[38] The ban on decadent Western rock music and films remains in place, but it becomes impossible to check every compact disc and videotape that enters the country.

Weapons of the weak are seemingly invisible and unthreatening, yet they convey a strong message about the grievances and power of dominated people. Mass abstention can be another discreet weapon of last resort. In expectation of massively fraudulent elections in Peru, the main opposition party encouraged people to stay away from the polls, to spoil the ballots, or to write "no to fraud" on them. Dissidents slip an encrypted missive into a newspaper article, the true meaning of which becomes clear when the last word of each sentence is read vertically up and down the column. In the middle of a photograph portraying an abundant harvest, "down with dictatorship" is subtly carved in the wheat. By the time these tricks are discovered, it is too late for authorities to pull thousands of magazines or newspapers from the shelves. Another example is found among the women of Iran, who boldly challenge traditional Islamic customs of modesty by requesting cosmetic improvements (including rhinoplasty performed by doctors trained in Cleveland) on the bit of their face that is exposed. Similarly, women dye their eyebrows and purchase nonprescription contact lenses to challenge societal norms and express their individual identities. Iranian newspapers have carried accounts of teenage girls in Iran who chop their hair and dress as boys as a way to refuse submission.[39] While these actions may not seem forceful, or overtly political, each is an expression of voice and power in its own right.

Some find their situation so egregious that they perceive their only option to be that of "exit."[40] Increasingly, analysts recognize suicide as an explicit political choice by individuals who feel they have no other option. Women in southeastern Turkey, caught in a rapid and forced migration to the urban areas, attempt suicide at record rates.[41] Women who feel trapped in arranged marriages, or torn between the modern world of the city and their desire to return to more traditional patterns in their rural homes, gain a sense of control over their fate in suicide that they cannot find in life. Unprecedented numbers of Mexicans took their own lives after the devaluation of the peso and the resulting crash of the Mexican economy in 1994. While suicide is usually conducted in private, these cases were unique in their public display; young men, believing they had no chance under the existing economic circumstances to establish a family, threw themselves in front of subway cars. In the Chinese countryside, we observe alarming statistics. From 1991 to 1997, suicide was the number one cause of "accidental" death for young women aged fifteen to thirty-four (23.80 per 100,000), while traffic accidents (18.79 per 100,000) were the top cause of death for young men. Other leading categories were drowning, falls, and poisoning. The author of the article citing the statistics, the president of the Chinese Academy of Preventive Medicine, called for these so-called accidental injuries to be studied as a public health problem.[42]

The management of information is another classic form of everyday resistance. For example, rumor is especially popular and effective in Africa, where oral traditions are highly valued. Rumor has been described as a potent brew of what is not known in the here and now, linked to what may or may not be known by those able to manipulate the supernatural. Rumors are hypotheses; in places where there is no authoritative news or information source, rumors don't just titillate, they are currency.[43] In the last days of Mobutu's reign in Zaire, rumors about prophecies of his impending doom greatly undermined what was left of the regime's credibility and contributed to its ultimate demise.

Conclusions: Civil or Uncivil Society?

To what can such varied forms of citizen participation and activism lead? Some speak of the potential emergence of a civil society in which citizens are able to enjoy some level of autonomy, or independence, from the government, and a multiplicity of voluntary associations are permitted to form. The belief is that if citizens are able to seek membership in independent associations, absent of government control or influence, this promotes an actively engaged citizenry who adopt a moral sense of obligation to participate in civic causes. With a multiplicity of groups and voluntary associations, people have an increased opportunity to express themselves as well as competing viewpoints and perspectives. This leads many to connect civil society with democracy. This straightforward connection, though, can be misleading.

In many regions of the world, the development of an independent merchant class is viewed as part of a nascent civil society. If people have an area in their life over which the government has no influence or control, this is said to foster an independent, civic identity above political divisions. For example, after the 1985 Mexico City earthquake, the urban poor worked through neighborhood organizations to force the government and World Bank to alter their recovery plans. Similar civic action groups have formed to fight crime and corruption in Mexico and Nigeria. In Nigeria, vigilantism by groups of young men known as "area boys" has widespread approval from people fed up with government inaction.

High literacy rates and access to independent media promote an independent sense of society, as citizens can educate themselves about alternative ideas and approaches to issues. For example, once the Turkish government's monopoly over radio and television broadcasts was abolished in 1993, citizens suddenly had a huge proliferation of options for information and leisure. The Internet revolution, spawned by changes in communications technology, also has the potential to change people's sense of self, state, and society. These changes are important not only for the options they make available for citizens, but also for the increase in accountability that they foster. Some view the development of an increasing space for civil society as a potential birthing ground for democracy, because it promotes the existence of diverse competing groups and encourages citizens to take an interest in and participate in government.

Yet civil society will not automatically be more benign or democratic; given the increased space for organization and mobilization, it is just as likely for anti-democratic groups to form. This is especially although not exclusively the case in regimes with a recent history of political and social violence, in which individuals were socialized into accepting coercion and repression as a regular mode of behavior. The proliferation of competing groups is not a silver bullet against repression. Observing groups like the Carapintada military leaders in Argentina, and the Inkatha in South Africa, Leigh Payne referred to the proliferation of "uncivil movements" that promote exclusion and violence as a means of competing and gaining power within a democratic system.[44] Such groups are common in a variety of countries, with or without past experiences of authoritarianism. They gain influence through the use of threats, legitimating myths, and coalition formation, and no system is immune. Exclusionary movements are capable of securing their demands within the democratic system, so they face no pressing need to overthrow it. But these groups provide an insidious threat to an inclusionary, vibrant democratic society. They use democratic language, institutions, and strategies toward their own uncivil ends. They can transform themselves into political parties with undemocratic goals. The Odua People's Congress in Nigeria, a Yoruba militia that once played a big part in the prodemocracy movement, transformed its message into a hard-line ethnic supremacist agenda. Given the elitist, antipeasant rhetoric common among student demonstration leaders in China, many wonder whether the 1989 movements, had they been successful, would have resulted in a more or a less democratic outcome than exists today.

The presence of these "uncivil groups" highlights the value-laden approach many use to the civil society debate. David Rieff argues that many have used the concept of a civil society, correlated with increased tolerance, expression, and diversity, to welcome groups of whom we approve.[45] Yet if civil society merely refers to groups who are able to operate independent of the reach of the state, their ideology about mode of action or inclusion of minority groups has nothing to do with it. In this estimation, Serbian war criminal Radovan Karadzic is just as civil as Czech human rights leader Vaçlav Havel. The National Rifle Association, which the United Nations refused to admit as a legitimate non-governmental organization, is as much an agent of civil society as is the International Campaign to Ban Landmines, which has received considerable international financial and emotional support. Rieff, Payne, and others cause us to question the mere proliferation of organizations as a desirable consequence linked to the weakening of political power. As Alison Brysk reminds us, constituents participating in free and competitive elections returned authoritarian leaders to power in Guatemala, Bolivia, and elsewhere.[46]

Linking Concepts and Cases

Now that you have a sense of the variety of views and actions that are taken in the third world, we present you with evidence from our eight case studies so that you can explore these ideas further. As you look at issues of voice and participation in these countries, try to observe patterns of similarity and difference between and among them. What is the impact of history on the development of POLITICAL CULTURE? To what do you attribute differences in the frequency and volatility of expression? In which of these cases can you see generational-based clashes—what is their source? Which countries have more mobilized civil societies, and which cases appear to be less vibrant? Why do you think this may be the so?

Case Study: Mexico

Fifty years ago, poet Octavio Paz described Mexico as trapped in a labyrinth—with a political culture of cynicism and suspicion deeply rooted in the country's history.[1] Part of the explanation for this is that under the Institutional Revolutionary Party (PRI), the Mexican government actively sought to preempt all meaningful citizen participation. Through its use of CORPORATISM, the government attempted to incorporate or co-opt all potentially influential groups in society. Yet today in Mexico civil society is fighting to change that relationship and let Mexico's leaders know that it should be society that dictates and the government that obeys.

What explains this dramatic shift in political culture, and how far-reaching is this change? As you will read in Chapter 14, Mexico began in earnest in the 1980s a protracted political liberalization that may date back to the late 1960s. A crucial part in the transition to DEMOCRACY was played by civil society. Citizen groups like Alianza Civica fought hard (and continue to fight hard) for the DEMO-CRATIC TRANSITION. Others, too fearful to speak out, have used WEAPONS OF THE WEAK, accepting handouts or attending rallies, but still voting their consciences. Many people mobilized after the 1985 earthquake in Mexico City, after the government's ineffective response left civil society to organize to save their neighborhoods. This disaster was an important watershed event, and since then Mexicans (perhaps simplistically identified as "parochial" in classic civic culture studies) have agitated for change in a variety of ways. Some Mexicans worked as observers in the elections and are now serving as watchdogs monitoring the new government. Teachers and pensioners have clogged traffic in Mexico City, demanding better pay and more of a voice in the decisions that affect their lives. Environmentalists battle for monarch butterflies in the Lacandón forest, and against some of the worst smog on earth. Farmers fought being evicted from their land for the construction of a new airport (and won). Feminists continue their work to make violence against women a public, not a private concern. In the late 1990s Mexican bishops issued their most important pastoral letter in thirty years, calling for changes in Mexico's political and economic systems, which they characterized as "poverty generating structures." Students striking at the National Autonomous University of Mexico over tuition increases went further and took on the global economy. Thirty years ago, these voices would have been tolerated only under the most restricted of circumstances.

Still, it is not like freedom is ringing out all over. There are still political prisoners in Mexico, and the PRI government has yet to answer for taking some very heavy-handed actions in Chiapas (also known as "the Mississippi of Mexico") against people believed to be sympathizers of the Zapatistas.[2] The Zapatistas, which we discuss as a GUERRILLA movement in Chapter 13, have evolved over the years into an unusual phenomenon of civil society. They first came to the world's attention on January 1, 1994, with an attack on the Mexican government deliberately timed for the day the North American Free Trade Agreement (NAFTA) went into effect. But since then the Zapatistas have been fighting a very different kind of war. They are said to have "revolutionized revolution" by giving up violence in favor of a global media campaign. The term "Zapatismo" now describes a grassroots political movement based in local activism that is multiracial, multiparty, classless, and ageless. Words are now their weapon, and the Internet is their intercontinental delivery system.

Dignity is an important recurrent theme for the Zapatistas, who argue that they are fighting for all Mexicans, but in particular for the indigenous people of Mexico, who have been dispossessed by 500 years of oppression. The Zapatistas support the continuation of indigenous life against NEOLIBERALISM and the assault of GLOBALIZATION. They are fighting for the Indians' right to be different, to speak their language and be educated in it, to preserve their culture, and to have some control over the land they live on.[3] In the presidential elections of 2000, Zapatista communities registered to vote in historic numbers, helping to bring an end to seventy-one years of PRI rule. The number of civilians who consider themselves Zapatistas has risen into the tens of thousands, and includes a broad range of civil society.

Such groups are more likely to be heard in a democracy, where there is tolerance for dissent as well as government accountability for its actions. However, some Mexicans argue that the difference between the old regime and the new is about as significant as the difference between Coke and Pepsi. Still, others maintain that Mexicans have reason to be hopeful.[4] For the first time in over seventy years, Mexican citizens were permitted to elect another party into the presidency. That president is Vicente Fox and his party is the National Action Party (PAN). Center-right, probusiness, and religious, the PAN has a socially conservative agenda. In contrast, the PRI is currently considered center-left, although its IDEOLOGY has fluctuated over time in what is described as the "pendulum effect." A much smaller third party, the Party of Democratic Revolution (PRD), was created by Cuauhtémoc Cárdenas (son of former president Lázaro Cárdenas) when he split with the PRI. However, the PRD is weakened by factional bickering and by the fact that it shares much of the same ideological terrain as the PRI. Both parties suffered electoral shocks in the 2000 presidential elections, as the PRI lost the presidency and the PRD lost its cause, democratization.

Immediately following the 2000 elections, the PRI went into a tailspin and some analysts predicted that the party was dead. Yet a year later, the PRI had righted itself and was doing fairly well in local elections. Most important for the PRI, it remained the largest party in both houses of Congress. Seeking to take back the executive's office in the next elections, the party's strategy is to leave only the far left to the PRD and the far right to the PAN. The PRI has claimed for itself a spot at the broad center, which can accommodate everything from socialists to Christian Democrats. The still male-dominated PRI toyed with the idea of having a female face. Beatriz Paredes, candidate for party president and architect for a changed PRI, maintained that as an opposition party the PRI must embrace the call for change rather than be threatened by it. The PRI is attempting to reconnect with women and young voters (more than 60 percent of Mexicans are between the ages of fourteen and twenty-eight)—but in the end the good old boys' network went with Roberto Madrazo, a former governor of Tabasco state suspected of stealing more than one election. However, the PRI insists that it is renovating and has sought to find creative ways of broadening its appeal by reaching out to a highly prized group of constituents; it has proposed a "youth law" that would improve the way in which the state deals with the needs of young people, as well as a dating service on the party's website (www.pri.org.mx), which encourages singles to "find love in the PRI"—regardless of one's political affiliation.[5] The PRI has received a lot of attention for all this, but analysts suggest that this facelift does not amount to the overhaul the PRI needs if it is ever to break its tradition of corruption.

Unlike past Mexican presidents, Fox does not have a political machine backing him in his dealings with the legislature. In fact, the president is said to have a difficult relationship even with his own party. He is said to be the most openly religious president in recent history. However, in terms of social policy at least, the divorced and remarried president is more social democratic than conservative. The president's cabinet, composed of business leaders, academics, and politicians from across the POLITICAL SPECTRUM, has been described as a debating society. Meanwhile, Fox struggles to get laws passed through an obstinate PRI-led Congress flexing its newfound power, as well as through an entrenched bureaucracy in which very little has changed since the old days.[6]

Case Study: Peru

If any generalizations can be made about Peruvian political culture, they are few in number and quickly outdated. It has often been said that Peruvians, traditionally identified as having a strong civil society and a weak state, value decisive leadership over institutional checks and balances.[7] Some analysts suggest that this tendency to favor authoritarians goes back to the days of the Inca Empire and centralized rule. Such traditions continued under colonialism—as did militarism—which has been a constant in Peru.

There is a long history of military intervention in Peruvian politics; most of the country's nearly 200-year history has been spent under military rule. During much of the 1990s, large numbers of Peruvians supported President Alberto Fujimori's growing authoritarianism as a necessity in the country's wars against terrorism and inflation. However, by the end of the decade this justification no longer rang true for most people. Peruvians became increasingly divided over what they valued more highly—security or freedom. Although the president still had his supporters, more Peruvians were impatient with his excesses. They resisted Fujimori's efforts to overturn the constitution and destroy the integrity of the electoral process.

It was not the international community, but primarily (though not exclusively) an urban, middle-class civil society who rallied to prevent *continuismo,* or the open-ended continuation in office desired by Fujimori. Each Friday during the prodemocracy rallies in early 2000, groups of women gathered in front of the presidential palace with washtubs, scrub brushes, and aprons to protest how dirty Peruvian politics had become by symbolically washing the Peruvian flag. Around the palace each night, women carried large plastic needles to "vaccinate" Peruvians against the Fujimori administration. Many deeply religious Peruvians were elated when the usually conservative archbishop Juan Luis Cipriani spoke of a "dark power" that had to be removed from the government. An independent cable television station exposed that dark power when it broadcast a videotape of a congressman on the take and unleashed the scandal that eventually brought Fujimori's resignation.

Because of the ground swell of activism at the turn of the twenty-first century, it can no longer simply be said that civil society in Peru is weak or antidemocratic. In 2001, Peruvians turned out in large numbers to vote in an election extraordinarily free of fraud and other electoral abuse. Yet it does appear that people have lost faith in their leaders and institutions.[8] Ten candidates entered the 2001 presidential contest, including former president Alan García, who made a remarkable comeback. By the time of the runoff election in June the field had narrowed to two: García and Alejandro Toledo. However, the race was not about party platforms or the candidates' proposed solutions for the country's problems (which were actually quite alike). García and Toledo had similar programs: they both promised jobs, cheap credit for farmers, and a social welfarist agenda that appealed to those intensely frustrated with the status quo. Similarly, their alleged public and private transgressions dogged both candidates along the campaign trail. García's problems were mostly public; the former president faced charges of corruption and is responsible for human rights abuses committed during his first administration. Toledo, on the other hand, was constantly working to dispel rumors about a stormy marriage, a child born out of wedlock, and parties with prostitutes and cocaine.

At least part of the reason García was able to make it to the runoff was because of the weakness of the competition. Back after nine years in exile, García is a charismatic and skilled POPULIST whose speeches can pack houses. Once known as Latin America's "premier social democrat," in the 2001 campaign García declared that he had learned from his mistakes. He condemned the material hardship associated with Fujishock but claimed to be a leftist willing to practice market-friendly policies.[9] García promised that he would seek to negotiate rather than decree lower debt payments, something he had tried in the past. Perhaps even more important than his message was that García was the only candidate who had a real party base. He was backed by the American Popular Revolutionary Alliance (APRA), a well-established political machine and the strongest of Peru's weak parties.

As opposed to the more radical APRA, Toledo's Peru Posible party was a relatively new catchall movement of the center-left. This was no traditional political party—such things are virtually extinct in Peru. Instead, many if not all of the contenders in the presidential race were part of candidate-centered movements. They are called "flash parties": because they are so closely identified with a single personality, they are considered disposable, vanishing almost as quickly as they appear.[10] For example, Toledo rose to power without the support of a powerful party. Rather, he was the favorite throughout the campaign for leading the fight to bring Fujimori down. Just as interesting a character as García, Toledo attempted to make race an issue in this country so highly stratified along ethnic and class lines. He built his image around his Indian blood and humble origins more than any presidential candidate in Peruvian history. The eighth of eighteen children (seven died in infancy), Toledo worked from an early age as a shoeshine boy. After a couple of Peace Corps volunteers helped the obviously gifted Toledo get a scholarship to the University of San Francisco, he went on to Harvard and Stanford before working as an economist for the WORLD BANK. "The Cholo from Harvard" as Toledo calls himself, likes to be compared to the fifteenth-century Inca emperor Pachacutec. Yet as much as he tried, Toledo failed to appeal to Indians and mestizos on this basis. In the 2001 elections Peruvians did not vote by ethnicity. And it was García who won over more poor and working-class voters.[11]

By the time the election came around, voters were so tired of the mud slinging and so disillusioned with both candidates that nearly 10 percent of them spoiled their ballots or cast blank ballots to show their disgust. In such a climate, Toledo came out the winner—but without a strong mandate. To make the country governable, Toledo is working to make cross-party alliances and particularly with another party, Somos Peru (We Are Peru). But Toledo needs to be able to work with the APRA and the independent parties as well, since in 2001 his Peru Posible party had only 45 of the 120 seats in a Congress badly divided along party lines.[12]

Since taking office President Toledo has been under constant attack—even by his own party. The left criticizes him for his neoliberal economic policies while the right condemns his "neopopulist" style of governance and longs for Fujimori's return. The result of regional elections in late 2002 was widely viewed as a vote of no confidence in President Toledo and his policies, as his party fared badly compared to the APRA and the smaller, independent parties.

Many Peruvians reported that they did not trust the president. Toledo, for his part, blamed his rapid decline in popularity on a concerted campaign to undermine him. Although he refused to identify who he thought was behind this conspiracy, some of his aides accused the press of being "Fujimorista." It is not surprising that he is a bit paranoid given the fact that since moving into the presidential palace, Toledo has faced constant problems. The government appears to be in disarray. Street protests in Lima and other cities have become more aggressive, as protesters demand that Toledo make good on his promises. In one of the most audacious attacks, civil servants wanting their government jobs back pushed into Congress and ransacked it. People in the countryside want the roads Toledo promised them built; victims of STATE-SPONSORED TERRORISM want compensation. There were three prison uprisings within six months of Toledo taking power. The list goes on. As much as they may be true, what is clear is that Peruvians are in no mood to hear Toledo's pleas that real change will take time.[13]

Case Study: Nigeria

It is in large part due to the unceasing efforts of a vibrant civil society that Nigeria began in 1999 its first experimentation with democracy in nearly twenty years. However, once propelled by a common enemy, today Nigeria's civil society lacks a common vision.

Often described as a "conglomerate society," Nigeria is composed of more than 250 different ethnic groups and these divisions are complicated by regional, religious, and linguistic identities, some of which were described in earlier chapters. For most of the years since independence in 1960, political power, both civilian and military, has been largely under the control of northern Muslims, who resent the southern domination of commerce. On the other hand, many southerners feel that they have never had a government that represented their interests. In 1993 they turned out to the polls and celebrated the presidential victory of Moshood Abiola, a Yoruba businessman from the southwest. When a military dictatorship unhappy with the results voided the elections, Nigerians from around the country joined forces to show their support for Abiola and the democratic process. The Sani Abacha dictatorship responded to such demands by imprisoning Abiola as a traitor and made every effort to decimate Nigerian civil society. During this period, hundreds of Nigerians joined the president-elect as political prisoners. The list of activists martyred includes his wife, Kudirat Abiola, who was run down in the streets by unnamed assassins for having the "audacity" to demand that her husband be given decent medical care while in prison. Moshood Abiola also died in detention, just before he was to be released in 1998, apparently of natural causes (although many Nigerians believe that there was foul play). Perhaps the most famous Nigerian martyr is Ken Saro-Wiwa, the writer and filmmaker who took on Shell Oil and the Abacha government. For threatening to publicize the abuses of the oil industry and the oppression of the Ogoni people, Saro-Wiwa and seven other activists were arrested on trumped-up charges, tried without DUE PROCESS in military courts, and executed—despite international pleas for mercy.

Such actions explain why Nigerians danced in the streets at the news of Sani Abacha's sudden demise. However, burned more than once, many people were skeptical when the military pledged to hand over power to a civilian government. Citizen coalitions such as the Transition Monitoring Group worked hard to keep the military out of politics and lay the groundwork for the democratic transition. Several political parties were hastily formed to put up candidates for political office, yet few of them had much of an ideological base. Rather, many Nigerian politicians continued a tradition of manipulating IDENTITY to achieve political power. Fearing loss to a rival, they mobilized populations by asserting their cultural distinctiveness. In this oil-rich country, where political power translates into access to economic resources, politics is viewed as a winner-take-all gamble. Politicians from all regions have propagated myths of irreconcilable differences, while working hard to blur the glaring disparity between the rich and poor. This explains why elections in Nigeria and many other countries are fought as mortal combat.[14]

Identity politics were certainly at play in the 1999 elections. Although the ideological differences between the candidates were negligible, the presidential race came down to a fierce contest between Olusegun Obasanjo of the People's Democratic Party (PDP) and Olu Falae of the Alliance for Democracy (AD). Both candidates were southwestern and Yoruba, and both were stronger than their parties. It is widely suspected that the parties owed their loyalty to the former military leaders who created and provide them with financial support. In the end, Obasanjo was elected, largely because northerners believed that he was someone with whom they could work.

The sense that Obasanjo has been bought and paid for by the northern military ELITE has created a surge in religious and ethnic tensions since 1999. There is a great deal of populist frustration at the grassroots—among all groups in Nigeria. This includes northerners, who don't believe the president is sufficiently under control. Organizations such as the (Yoruba) Odua People's Congress and the Muslim Brothers (an Islamist group popular in the north and closely associated with Iran) have proven especially attractive to young people. Marginalized by economic hardship, with little political voice, students from the north and south vie with each other but actually share much in common as they take on the establishment. Such groups have become an extremely powerful political force; these militant civic organizations are explosive and violent.[15] Here is an illustration of how civil society is not always a progressive force for democracy; some groups that once played large roles in the prodemocracy movement are now pursuing supremacist agendas.

As a result the country is fracturing along ethnic, religious, and regional lines. Much of the killing is occurring in attacks and counterattacks between people deemed "indigenous" and "not indigenous" to areas throughout the country. Yet one of the greatest areas of conflict since the transition to democracy in 1999 concerns initiatives by one-third of the country's thirty-six states to impose SHARIAH (or what some consider to be Islamic law) over the objections of the non-Muslim community. Since the imposition of shariah, several Nigerians have received what some consider cruel punishments, including death sentences. For example, after failing to prove that four men had raped and impregnated her, in 2001 a still-breast-feeding teenage mother was flogged 100 times for adultery. That same year a pregnant woman was sentenced to death by stoning for having had premarital sex (the man with whom she allegedly had sex was set free because of lack of sufficient evidence to prosecute him for adultery). Many people, particularly non-Muslims but even some Muslims, consider such actions to be abusive and fear that the northern states are seeking to create an Islamic theocracy in Nigeria.

On the other hand, the embrace of *shariah* does speak to some very real concerns of Nigerians. Islamic radicalism has spread in the north as people have become more and more disappointed with democracy. Many ordinary people want to live under RULE OF LAW and argue correctly that this is something the government has not provided. Justice is much swifter and reportedly crime has dropped in some states with *shariah*. This is a welcome turn of events that some attribute to Islam's bans on alcohol and prostitution and its efforts to separate the sexes and to encourage modest dress for females. Proponents of *shariah* argue that every system Nigerians have ever known has failed—colonialism, military rule, and so-called democracy. Yet there was a system that worked in the north that existed prior to colonialism, and it was the religious state. Consequently, for Muslims (and Christians as well) in Nigeria and in many other countries, religion has come to serve much more than just spiritual needs. The mosques and churches play an important social welfare role, providing assistance because the state is not addressing people's fundamental requirements. This attempt to return to models of the past is not unheard of in Nigeria. In the late 1970s the Maitatsine movement, led by an Islamist prophet, appealed to Nigeria's poor and taught lessons of positive social justice and self-help. When it began to challenge police brutality and, influenced by the success of the Iranian Revolution, sought to overthrow the secular state, the revolt was put down. In the struggle the prophet was killed, and thousands more were murdered, injured, or imprisoned.[16]

In its latest incarnation, just since the democratic elections in 1999, fighting over the imposition of *shariah* has claimed over 10,000 lives and displaced many more people throughout the country. Obasanjo has been condemned for doing little to prevent the unrest or to intervene to stop the killing and destruction associated with it. For nearly three years, the president treated the violence as something that would eventually wind down on its own. However, in early 2002, after a mysterious explosion on an army base that killed more than 1,000 and a week of communal violence that followed, Obasanjo's tone changed dramatically. As if awakened from a deep sleep, the president for the first time publicly stated that the country was sliding into anarchy and that democracy was facing its greatest challenge. Meanwhile, the president is beset by critics on all sides and distracted from the very real issues he must deal with—if democracy, let alone the country of Nigeria, is to remain intact.

Case Study: Zimbabwe

Despite the risks involved, Zimbabwe has a flourishing urban and rural civil society. Zimbabwe's urban civil society had (until recently at least) largely come together to support the Movement for Democratic Change (MDC), the greatest threat to the Zimbabwe African National Union–Patriotic Front (ZANU-PF) and its monopoly on power in more than two decades. The grievances that have contributed to the MDC's once meteoric rise have been festering for years. Austerity had turned many people, who don't normally think of themselves as political, into activists. At the turn of the twenty-first century, almost all Zimbabweans disapproved of the government's handling of the economy, and three-quarters of those surveyed wanted President Robert Mugabe to resign.[17] The MDC capitalized on this sentiment with its election slogan "Change Everything, Everything Changes." With a focus on political and civil rights, this liberal party called for an end to government corruption and for greater transparency, the reduction of poverty, and the rule of law.

The multiracial MDC has enjoyed a remarkably broad base of support. Although the party grew out of Zimbabwe's trade unions, which are very male-dominant, it includes a feminist plank in its campaign.[18] The MDC's core supporters are young urban dwellers (the so-called Born Frees), who were either children at independence or born soon after. Too young to remember the humiliation and suffering blacks experienced under white rule, Mugabe's appeals to black nationalism fall flat with much of the younger generation, who compose one-third of Zimbabwe's voters. Interestingly, voting in the 2000 and 2002 elections was not so much by ethnicity as it was based on an urban/rural split (although the MDC is very popular in predominantly Ndebele Matabeleland, whereas ZANU-PF has never been well-liked there).

Yet there are very real divisions in the country that cut across ethnicity. As opposed to the younger, urban generation of Born Frees, older and rural people have a hard time ignoring the fact that even twenty years after liberation, whites continue to hold on to disproportionate amounts of Zimbabwe's most fertile land. Older, rural blacks are more likely to support the land occupation movement in Zimbabwe, which is finally forcing the land issue to be taken seriously. This activism, which has at times taken the form of organized and spontaneous rural movements, is often treated outside the "civil" framework because of its use of violence and because it seeks more radical, transformative change—as opposed to the liberal agenda usually associated with civil society and more characteristic of the MDC.

Land occupations have long been a primary source of advocacy for radical land reform in Zimbabwe, and in many other countries as well. Over the years the ZANU-PF government has managed the sporadic, spontaneous occupations that have occurred by promising that it would address the land question. In the 1980s the government did redistribute some land (3 million of a targeted 8 million hectares of land were allocated to 70,000 families). However, for various reasons the program slowed down, its targets were never met, and farmers who did receive land did not get access to credit and other forms of badly needed support. As we discussed in Chapter 9, grossly inequitable landownership patterns continue to prevail in Zimbabwe—nearly a quarter of a century after independence. From the perspective of many Zimbabweans this is because Britain, which denies that it has a historical responsibility for the land problem, has not offered the financial assistance that they expected. Yet the Zimbabwe government maintains that reparations are due and that it cannot compensate white farmers for the loss of their land without British assistance.

Therefore, what is happening today in Zimbabwe is a good example to the world of what happens when crucial questions are left unresolved for decades. The latest wave of land occupations is based in a very old grievance aggravated by the deepening poverty associated with neoliberal reforms. Although the media have largely used the negative terms "land invasions" or "land grabs" to describe recent efforts to keep the land issue on the agenda, it must be recognized there is broad participation in this movement. It includes not just the Zimbabwe National Liberation War Veterans Association but also traditional leaders and spirit mediums, who seek to reclaim people's historical rights to the land and its resources. For these activists, land has sacred and cultural value as well as productive potential. The effort to reclaim the land (now backed by a government that has evicted white farmers) is for them not just a development issue but also a restitution and justice issue.[19]

For Zimbabweans it may be a restitution and justice issue, but the land occupations and government orders have been widely portrayed in the Western media as sheer political opportunism. It is true that Mugabe has been attempting to protect himself by drawing the rural poor closer with promises of land. And there is an opportunistic element to the land seizures, in that some individuals claiming to be war veterans have used the occupation movement to intimidate farmers, extort money, and poach. However, analysts disagree about how much of this behavior ZANU-PF controls, including some of the political violence occurring throughout the country. On the one hand, there are many reports of police standing by and even participating in attacks on farmers and MDC supporters. On the other hand, Sam Moyo contends that ZANU-PF is following behind this SOCIAL MOVEMENT, not leading it. It may be that the party tried to co-opt it, but has been forced to accommodate what soon became a mushrooming land occupation movement. Sure, Mugabe may have been cynically using the movement for short-term political gain. But Moyo counsels us not to forget the very real needs asserted by this social struggle and to recognize that the anger we see stems from past injustices and deprivation. The reconciliation model promoted by the West and once accepted by Mugabe has not resulted in justice or reparation. From the point of view of many rural people in Zimbabwe, the neoliberal, laissez-faire approach to land reform, as it has been pursued, must be challenged.[20]

Because this model is not being challenged by the MDC, the government has been able to portray its opposition as the lackeys of white farmers and Britain. Against these charges the MDC has accused Mugabe of taking too long to bring about meaningful reform, and using it only to enrich his cronies. As you might guess, the environment leading up to the 2002 presidential elections became very tense and hostile. As the ruling party imposed a series of "security" laws making campaigning and criticism of the government nearly impossible, the MDC struggled to find ways to get its message heard, including using weapons of the weak. For example, since government repression precluded the public rallies favored by men, MDC women launched a "chitter-chatter" campaign in which they held informal meetings disguised as tea parties to allow discussion of the issues.[21] However, despite its best efforts, the MDC lost the March 2002 presidential elections, which are widely considered to be illegitimate. Although the opposition party has called for fresh elections and threatened mass action, as of early 2003 the streets had stayed mostly quiet. This may be due to any number of factors. However, now, in addition to restrictions on civil liberties, the government is finding other ways to punish its detractors. In a time of massive food shortages, ZANU-PF is accused of using food as a political weapon. Although the government denies that the practice is widespread, the United Nations has confirmed numerous instances of MDC supporters seeking assistance being turned away by government officials.[22] Years of harassment appear to be taking their toll on the opposition. There are signs the MDC is in disarray. For example, the party couldn't field candidates in hundreds of wards in local elections in 2002, as many MDC hopefuls were intimidated out of running for office. Apathy also seems to be setting in; people ignored MDC calls for a strike in late 2002.

Although MDC leaders have threatened to take President Mugabe down in much the same way that Yugoslavian dictator Slobodan Milosevic was finally ousted, Mugabe has held on to power tightly. Perhaps this is because Zimbabweans were remembering the lessons of China's Tiananmen more than those of Yugoslavia.[23] In fact, many analysts believe that the only way Mugabe will fall will be at the hands of his own party. This is a possibility, since ZANU-PF is beginning to show signs of wear and may be splitting over questions of loyalty to its leader. One of the clearest signs of this was in January 2002, when Edison Zvogbo, a senior ZANU-PF member of parliament, publicly criticized the new "security" laws restricting freedom of speech. Analysts say Zvogbo would not have dared do so unless he had support within party and government circles. Some go as far as to predict that it may well be Zvogbo who succeeds Mugabe when he goes—one way or another.[24]

Case Study: Iran

Iranian civil society, long stifled by its rulers, is cautiously beginning to emerge from the ashes. Much of this development is fueled by Iran's internal struggle between groups who want to forge a uniquely Islamist path to a modern state and society, and those who envision a modern Iran less hostile to secular demands and more open to Western traditions. While the struggle between these two dominant views has helped carve room for the action of independent groups, especially students and the media, it has also increased the danger under which such groups operate. Leading the reformist cause, President Mohammed Khatami has put much energy toward promoting a freer press (his experience throughout the 1980s as head of the Ministry of Culture and Islamic Guidance made him familiar with such issues), and he initially sanctioned many progressive journals and newspapers. This provoked a sharp reaction from clerical leaders. In the spring of 2000, for example, over twenty newspapers and journals were closed down by the judiciary. Authors have also been imprisoned. After publishing her work *A Short History of Human Rights in Iran,* Shirin Ebadi was jailed for violating Iranian publishing standards. Even individuals speaking at conferences far away from Iranian soil have returned home to tough trials and jail terms for allegedly insulting the Islamic Republic abroad.[25]

The integration of religious values and rules with everyday life has long been a struggle among the elite of Iran, especially following the colonial influences of Russia and England. After the Islamic Revolution of 1979 established Iran as a theocracy, this debate was muted. Ayatollah Ruhollah Khomeini often declared that "politics and religion are one" and that Iran's theocracy is "God's government." The implication of this conception puts dissenters in a dangerous space: opposition to the government is opposition to God. Some of today's leaders, including President Khatami—in power since 1997—challenge this view.

Modern reformers in Iran, campaigning for increased political pluralism and religious flexibility, tasted victory in both the 1997 presidential election and the parliamentary election of February 2000. They were particularly popular with intellectuals, women, youth, and business groups. Yet holding the presidency and majority of seats in parliament does not necessarily translate into real power. Conservatives dominate the judiciary and the appointed Assembly of Experts, which can veto any legislation passed by parliament, and have attempted to reverse some of the changes that have taken place. For example, a special Press Court charged newspapers and journalists with trampling on revolutionary and Islamic principles. In August 2000, Ayatollah Ali Khamenei, Khomeini's successor as the country's Supreme Leader, ordered reformist members of parliament to kill a bill that would have helped revive some of the banned newspapers. The Ayatollah's public intervention in the legislative process was unprecedented. He stepped in, he said, to "save the revolution and the faith." Many conservatives fear Islamist disintegration has been launched by reformers, especially Khatami, whom they hope will be "no Mikhail Gorbachev." An exhibition in Tehran just before the 2001 presidential elections openly declared as much, including a message that a vote for Khatami could be a vote to end the Islamic Revolution.[26] Conservatives take issue with the accusation that they are trying to go backward. They state that they, too, are interested in reform, just not Western-style reform. In their view changes in Iran must fit within the context of "Islamic-style" democracy, in which clerics still hold political power befitting of an Islamic and not a liberal republic. For the conservatives, Khatami and other proponents of the "culture of liberalism" are only bankrupting the Islamic Republic.[27]

Of the many groups pushing for greater change in Iranian politics and society, women and youth stand out. Women were prominent during Iran's constitutional revolution of 1906–1911, and they are once again returning to the public forefront. For example, in 2001 for the first time in the republic's history, a woman ran for president. Farah Khosravi, who holds a master's degree in management and planning, announced her candidacy well in advance of Iranian norms. Her decision to run challenged the orthodox interpretation of Article 115 of the Iranian Constitution, which states, "The president should be elected from among spiritual and political men." Younger citizens, especially university students, have also become more active in politics. This is a significant development, as some estimate that approximately half of the Iranian population is under twenty-five years of age. Students were some of the most vocal supporters of the reform movement headed by President Khatami, and they have taken to the streets multiple times to demand faster change than other social groups are willing to stomach. With these protests, they carry on a tradition bequeathed to them by their elders from the 1979 revolution, many of whom now suppress student actions out of concern that they are moving too fast.

Open struggle is not yet possible in all areas of modern Iranian life. For example, many young girls are leaving home—where they are often beaten and sexually abused—and attempting to establish a new life for themselves in recently established shelters in Tehran (the only Iranian city to take this bold step). These girls are taking huge risks—aggrieved family members sometimes show up at the shelter planning to behead the girls as punishment for publicly embarrassing the family.[28] The stories of these runaways—boys and girls alike—reveal a society increasingly strained along the edges. Drug addiction, divorce, and abuse were viewed as "nonproblems" in the 1980s, but children hanging out at bus terminals and walking city streets reveal the growing complexity—and challenges—of Iranian life in the twenty-first century.

Case Study: Turkey

The expression of opinion in Turkey is a relatively open enterprise, although some limits on dissent and independent identity have yet to be dismantled. These restrictions are particularly acute when it comes to the two hot topics of modern Turkish life: political Islam and Kurdish nationalism. Openly expressing even a mildly sympathetic perspective toward either of these two causes can land a person in jail, get her or him banned from public life, or worse. These two topics, and the manner in which the government (and sometimes the military) treats them, present the two main obstacles to free expression and the development of a vibrant civil society in Turkey today.

Religious SECULARISM was vividly enshrined in the birth of the republic by Mustafa Kemal Atatürk, the self-ordained "Father of the Turks." Since that time, most government leaders and military elites have ardently guarded against the political expression of religion. Just in case the government errs in this regard, the military has clearly expressed its willingness to take matters in its own hands. Plotting to replace the country's secular government with an Islamic regime is a crime punishable by expulsion from politics, or in the most extreme cases, death. In 1997, for example, Turkey's Muslim premier, Necmettin Erbakan, was forced to resign after barely a year in office, under heavy pressure from the prosecular military. Even if some claim that Erbakan has maintained his influence outside his office, despite his banishment from politics for five years, his departure was a strong signal to others who want to mix politics and religion. Leaders of the Virtue Party, largely made up of the remains of Erbakan's disbanded Refah movement, claimed a new moderation in their stances in an attempt to gain ground with both citizens and government leaders alike, but they were unsuccessful. In June 2001 they too were banned by a decision of the Constitutional Court, even though, as the largest opposition group in parliament, their representatives occupied 102 of the 550 seats.[29] Representatives were permitted to remain in parliament as independents, although many were being wooed by the far-right National Action Party. Inciting religious hatred can also lead to a ban on politics. When the Justice and Development Party, led by banned politician Recep Tayyip Erdogan, won a majority of seats in the legislature in November 2002, parliament overturned President Ahmet Necdet Sezer's veto to allow Erdogan to serve as prime minister. Erdogan was banned from holding office because he read a poem that courts accused of inciting religious hatred.

In the struggle to balance the role of Islam in the modern republic, several women have helped expose the extremes to which some groups are prepared to push the issue. For example, Merve Kavakçi lost her seat in parliament over her donning an Islamic headscarf. Later, her Turkish citizenship was stripped, because she had acquired a U.S. passport to travel (Turkish law does not allow dual citizenship). Even young girls who want to publicly express their religious modesty have faced official pressure: security forces have been called into Turkish schools to fight against "antisecular propaganda," refusing to allow students wearing headscarves to enter the school.

Many of the gains that have been made in free expression in recent years have been the result of international and regional pressure placed on the country. Turkey's desire to gain full admission to the European Union (EU), for example, is at least partially contingent upon the government's renunciation of the death penalty as a political tool. This presents a dilemma for Turkish leaders, particularly in the handling of the other sensitive issue in political life today, Kurdish nationalism. The Kurds are the only large linguistic minority in Turkey, composing approximately 15 percent of the national population. In 1999, Turkish officials captured Abdullah Öcalan, the leader of the Kurdistan Workers' Party (PKK), and sentenced him to death for murder, terrorism, and treason. In an attempt to win the support of the EU, the Turkish parliament banned capital punishment during peacetime. For the medium term, at least, this action failed to persuade European decisionmakers, who, despite the urging of the United States, decided to delay further talks on Turkey's EU membership until at least December 2004. The PKK, which is strongest in southeast Turkey, only speaks for a minority of ethnic Kurds—most favor peaceful solutions espoused by groups including the Kurdish-identity People's Democracy Party, which also faces a possible ban from politics.[30] Despite the attention Turkey received for this controversial case, some openings have been made for the Kurds. In 1991, for example, the ban on speaking Kurdish in public was lifted, and many Kurdish-language publications appeared. Article 8 of the restrictive Anti-Terror Law, which made separatist propaganda a criminal offense, was modified in 1995. Yet fears of separatism and desires for revenge against the violence surrounding the Kurdish question (37,000 have died in the conflict between the Turkish military and PKK forces alone) make gains in the open discussion of Kurdish issues difficult to foresee in Turkey's near future.

The future of Turkish civil society—attempting to accommodate the diversity of Turkish identities highlighted by secular-minded Kemalists and their weighty generals, Western-oriented entrepreneurs and business owners, Kurdish nationalists, and Islamists—remains unclear. Clearly, multiple points of views exist, but all too often some voices attempt to ostracize and condemn others. Many limits on expression—including the ban on speaking Kurdish—have been lifted, and since 1993 the state has relinquished its monopoly over radio and television broadcasts. But when push comes to shove and sensitive topics are raised, there is little room for Turkish civil society to maneuver.

Case Study: China

The expression of ideas, especially political ideas, within modern China is limited by the continued dominance of the Chinese Communist Party (CCP), founded in 1921. Even though competing parties do exist, decisions within China today need the approval of CCP officials, and attempts to launch an opposition party have met with severe resistance. China continues to abide by the Leninist principle of mandating a singular, elitist, unchallenged party. For example, since the summer of 1998, at least thirty members of an attempted opposition party, the China Democracy Party, have been imprisoned, usually under the veil of "subverting state power." Most received sentences of eleven to thirteen years. Yet there is a strong tradition of dissent and disagreement within China, dating back to the first student demonstrations against the government in the May 4th Movement of 1919. This movement, which most people christen as the beginning of modern Chinese politics, developed in response to public dissatisfaction with the Treaty of Versailles. As most protests do, the movement quickly took on other issues, including reflection on the source of China's condition relative to other countries. Ironically, some of the same leaders who gathered in Beijing to denounce the Chinese government were responsible for violently ending student demonstrations in the nation's capital in 1989. The demonstrations in Beijing's Tiananmen Square that spring and summer attracted global attention as university students protested against inflation, corruption, and the absence of reform. As the world's television cameras captured the dynamic events taking place in Beijing and other Chinese cities, the government prepared to send tanks to crush the movement, which it ultimately did on the nights of June 3 and 4, 1989.

In addition to explicitly political demonstrations and protests against corruption and the abuse of constitutionally guaranteed rights, increasingly Chinese citizens organize around other collective identities, especially rural farmers and varying religious affiliations. Chinese peasants were the backbone of the Communist Revolution of 1949, yet they have benefited the least from the policies of the government. With alarming frequency, Chinese peasants wage protests against illegal levies and fees in the countryside, as well as the issuance of IOUs, a persistent problem since the mid-1980s. Also, in defiance of state limits on religion, Chinese citizens seek membership in underground Christian churches. The government officially recognizes 12 million registered Christians throughout the country, although most missionary organizations put the total at nearly 60 million. Chinese leaders are particularly irritated with the Roman Catholic Church, especially after Pope John Paul II canonized 120 Chinese Catholics on China's National Day, October 1, 2000. Additionally, large numbers of Chinese are joining spiritual self-help groups who draw their heritage from traditional breathing exercises. The Chinese government has viciously disbanded Falungong practitioners because they appear to challenge the CCP's monopoly of power. In response to the government crackdown on its activities, Falungong adherents increased in numbers, organizing large and well-coordinated demonstrations in Tiananmen Square. In January 2001, five alleged Falungong adherents set themselves on fire in the midst of the square, attracting domestic and international attention to their movement. A year later, after the government had made a significant dent in their membership, Falungong practioners from over ten countries were arrested for violating the Chinese government's ban on their expression.

As we discussed above, the effects of development on gender in China are very uneven. Communist leaders inherited a dismal record of attention to women in 1949, and although the situation has improved greatly (baby girls, for example, are no longer forced to have their toes broken to create a small foot through binding), women in China today continue to face many struggles. Traditional attitudes toward girls have been reinforced by the one-child-per-couple policies implemented since the 1980s. Although many Chinese citizens recognize the need to limit the country's population growth, there is little doubt that the implementation of this policy has had detrimental effects on women and girls. Economically, one of the most disturbing trends affecting the mobility of women is toward the feminization of agriculture, as women are left behind in impoverished rural areas while the men in the family go to the cities in search of more lucrative employment. Recognizing some of these seemingly unintended consequences of the population control policy, the Chinese government announced a general loosening of the plan in December 2001, permitting two children per couple in the major urban areas. Such exceptions had already been permitted in the Chinese countryside, where families with a firstborn girl were permitted to have a second child within the confines of local policies.

If we measure civil society in terms of independent organizations, there is not much to be found in China today—most organizational life is corporatist, permitted only if it serves the interests of the state. Yet once we include levels of education, literacy, and the proliferation of media sources, the picture looks quite different. Currently, the national literacy rate is approximately 82 percent, representing an astonishing accomplishment by the CCP regime in just over fifty years. While newspapers and magazines continue to operate on the official sponsorship of the CCP, most observers note a qualitative change in the types of stories covered by the media, as well as the increasing investigatory powers of newspaper and magazine journalists. Access to the Internet is also creating a wealth of options for Chinese citizens, although the government attempts to limit access to "hostile" websites of other countries. And art, long utilized by the government's propaganda machine to convey appropriate messages to the people, is becoming more edgy and daring. "Shock art" and "action art"—displays that are designed to create a response by the viewers—are becoming more common, both in the underground and in officially sanctioned exhibits.[31] China is the site of many global influences, from Kentucky Fried Chicken just off Tiananmen Square, to multiple McDonald's in every major city—as well as the opening of Wal-Marts in China's biggest cities. Recently, the People's Literature

Publishing House completed its largest initial print run for a work of fiction, publishing the tales of *Ha-li Bo-Te* (Harry Potter) for literature enthusiasts young and old. The long-term effects of such access on a society who only decades ago memorized the sayings of Mao Zedong remain to be seen.

Case Study: Indonesia

Indonesia is a country rich in diversity. Rather than viewing linguistic, cultural, and religious diversity as a strength, however, Indonesian leaders and to some extent ordinary citizens view it as a threat. Especially during the thirty-two-year-reign of General Suharto, any identity that contradicted national unity was squelched. The two biggest offenders were the expression of religious division and communism. In fact, until very recently, any printed materials containing Chinese characters could be confiscated, on the suspicion that they might promote communist infiltration. Yet during the spring of 1998, months of protests by Indonesian students led to Suharto's resignation. The demonstrations, ignited by the enduring economic crisis that had crippled the country since 1997, quickly evolved into a referendum on the continued leadership of Indonesia's second president. Throughout the streets of Indonesia's major cities, Suharto was vilified for his corrupt, heavy-handed rule of the country. After they were successful in toppling the president, however, diverse groups of demonstrators faced a dilemma familiar to other activists protesting authoritarian leaders: since organized opposition had been illegal for so long, there were few available networks through which opposition groups could communicate and mobilize. After the fall of Suharto, opposition groups remained segmented and disunified.

During Suharto's "New Order," the only viable electoral force—not technically a political party—was Golkar, a federation of army-sponsored associations and trade unions that served as an umbrella for anticommunist associations and a government-fabricated identity. Opposition parties existed and ran candidates in the People's Consultative Assembly, but their acceptance was always at the disposal of government leaders. Opposition candidates were often refused the right to be seated in parliament, even after their election, and they were rarely permitted to staff cabinet positions in Suharto's government. Additionally, governmental employees were open to charges of disloyalty for joining any party that may challenge Golkar—the source of their bread and butter.[32]

In the summer of 1999, in the first open general elections since 1955, Muslim cleric Abdurahman Wahid became president. Wahid was chosen as a compromise candidate, as was his vice president, Megawati Sukarnoputri, to whom he had actually lost in the popular election (once seated, parliament members chose the president and vice president). Megawati, the famously aloof daughter of the country's first president, Sukarno, had become the virtual lightning rod for opposition forces during the decline of the Suharto era, especially after her popular party, the Indonesian Democratic Party–Struggle (PDI-P), had been temporarily banned in 1997. Many Indonesians looked to their unusual alliance as a way to mend the deep rifts that have developed throughout Indonesian society—a task that proved too difficult to handle. A six-month impeachment process culminated in Wahid's dismissal in June 2001 and his replacement by Megawati.

One of the most prominent cleavages in Indonesia today is expressed in widespread religious tension. Indonesia is unique in Southeast Asia because of the prominence of Islam as a belief system among its people. In fact, Indonesia is the country with the world's largest Islamic population (87 percent of citizens identify themselves as Muslim). Until recent years, the most serious religious-based conflict had been within Islam, between parties representing variations on adherence to Islamic law. More recently, violence between Indonesia's Christians, who make up the second largest grouping of religious believers, has broken out. Since the beginning of the economic crisis in 1997, Indonesia has been plagued by bloody fights between Christians and Muslims, which have claimed thousands of lives in Ambon, the Moluccas Islands, West Kalimantan, and elsewhere. Simmering discord that was latent during the economic prosperity of earlier decades has exploded since Suharto's exit in 1998. Ethnic rioting in many major cities has included the systematic rape of Indonesian-Chinese women, a group often targeted for violent attacks whenever there is a crisis (especially economic). Indonesian women have been caught in the midst of much of this turmoil. Even prior to being targets for violence during the economic upheavals, women (especially younger women) experienced great hardship during the push for economic development in the 1980s. It was not uncommon for young girls to leave their rural homes and set off for the big city in hopes of earning big money doing sweatshop labor.

Indonesia is beginning to develop a civil society made up of semiautonomous groups (truly competitive political parties were first allowed in January 1999) and more liberal media. Yet while there have been fewer media closings during the Wahid and Megawati administrations than during those of their predecessors, when intelligence officers were known to routinely dial up media organizations to demand that particular stories not be printed, concerns about the genuine freedom of expression remain. The impetus for a widespread crackdown does not always come from Jakarta—book-burning attacks by an anticommunist alliance of right-wing and Muslim groups in the spring of 2001 were reminiscent of earlier purges of perceived communists in the mid-1960s. The choice of targeted books is interesting—including the works of Indonesia's most famous novelist (and hardly a communist), Pramoedya Ananta Toer, and the famous *Chicken Soup for the Soul* series.[33] More recent bloody attacks and threats against Westerners and their areas of influence, especially in light of the U.S.-led war on terrorism in Afghanistan, also demonstrate the potentially uncivil nature of the growth of independent spheres of society.

Now It's Your Turn

Why do you think people turn to political ideologies to achieve their causes? How can ordinary citizens and leaders alike be manipulated by ideologies? Why do you think youth are attracted to particular movements? After reading about some of the forms of activism and expression discussed in this chapter, do you view any actions, such as wearing an Islamic headscarf, differently than you had before? Why or why not? What are some of the seemingly unusual ways in which people are making their concerns known? Why do they choose these methods? How much do you think people's economic, political, or cultural situations have contributed to their activism (or lack thereof)?

Suggested Readings

Africa

Ba, Mariama. *So Long a Letter*. London: Heinemann, 1981. Africa: fiction, in the form of a letter to an old friend, a widow's reminiscences of her struggle for survival after her husband rejects her for a second wife.

Emecheta, Buchi. *The Wrestling Match*. New York: George Braziller, 1983. Nigeria: fiction, discusses generational divides, coming of age in a rapidly changing culture.

Hove, Chenjerai. *Bones*. London: Heinemann, 1990. Zimbabwe: fiction, on the civil rights movement.

Nwapa, Flora. *One Is Enough*. Trenton, N.J.: Africa World Press, 1992. Nigeria: fiction, life as a single woman in the city.

Veal, Michael E. *Fela: The Life and Times of an African Musical Icon*. Philadelphia: Temple University Press, 2000. Nigeria: biography, discusses the music and politics of the father of Afrobeat.

Wiwa, Ken. *In the Shadow of a Saint: A Son's Journey to Understand His Father's Legacy*. South Royalton, Vt.: Steerforth Press, 2001. Nigeria: nonfiction, a son's reflections on his father as a private and public man, the martyred writer and activist Ken Saro-Wiwa.

Asia

Chang, Pang-Mei Natasha. *Bound Feet and Western Dress*. New York: Doubleday, 1996. China: personal memoir that chronicles one woman's life from before the Communist Revolution to becoming vice president of China's first women's bank.

Ha, Jin. *The Bridegroom: Stories*. New York: Pantheon Books, 2000. China: short stories, based on modern challenge of being Chinese while wanting to be more Western.

Hong, Ying. *Daughter of the River*. New York: Grove Press, 1998. China: personal memoir of a girl born during China's famine in the late 1950s, telling her life story through Tiananmen and beyond.

Kepner, Susan Fulop, ed. *The Lioness in Bloom: Modern Thai Fiction About Women*. Berkeley: University of California Press, 1996. Thailand: anthology and novel excerpts discussing everyday experiences as well as controversial topics in Thai society, including sexuality, gender relations, and abuse.

Lockard, Craig A. *Dance of Life: Popular Music and Politics in Southeast Asia*. Honolulu: University of Hawaii Press, 1998. Various countries: highlights connections between popular music and politics.

Stewart, Frank, ed. *Silenced Voices: New Writing from Indonesia*. Honolulu: University of Hawaii Press, 2000. Indonesia: short stories, poetry, and a play from Indonesian authors.

Tapontsang, Adhe. *Ama Adhe: The Voice That Remembers the Heroic Story of a Woman's Fight to Free Tibet*. Boston: Wisdom, 1997. China: nonfiction, details Adhe's years of torture in the People's Republic of China as a result of organizing efforts in Tibet to combat the Chinese invasion of 1959.

Zha, Jianying. *China Pop: How Soap Operas, Tabloids, and Bestsellers Are Transforming a Culture*. New York: New Press, 1995. China: nonfiction, highlights cultural changes in China since the 1980s—interviewing movie producers, television script writers, authors, and others active in the modern culture scene.

Latin America and the Caribbean

Paz, Octavio. *Sor Juana Or, The Traps of Faith*. Trans. Margaret Sayers Peden. Cambridge, Mass.: Belknap Press, 1988. Mexico: biography of the Mexican poet and feminist.

Powell, Patricia. *A Small Gathering of Bones*. London: Heinemann, 1994. Jamaica: fiction, the experience of a gay man in Jamaica in the 1970s as he confronts the hostility of his family, church, and society while a mysterious illness threatens the gay community.

Middle East

Accad, Evelyne. *Wounding Words: A Woman's Journal in Tunisia*. Trans. Cynthia T. Hahn. London: Heinemann, 1997. Tunisia: autobiography, considers the role feminism can play in the Arab world.

Buchan, James. *The Persian Bride*. Boston: Houghton Mifflin, 2000. Iran: fiction, Englishman falls in love with the daughter of a general in the Iranian air force and learns to see the world through her eyes.

Green, John, and Farzin Yazdanfar, eds. *A Walnut Sapling on Masih's Grave and Other Stories by Iranian Women*. Portsmouth, N.H.: Heinemann, 1993. Iran: collection of stories with emphasis on gender disparities.

Khorrami, Mohammad Mehdi, and Shovich Vatanabadi, eds. and trans. *A Feast in the Mirror: Stories by Contemporary Iranian Women*. Boulder: Lynne Rienner, 2000. Iran: collection of short stories written by modern Iranian female authors.

Parsipur, Shahrnush. *Women Without Men: A Novella*. Trans. Kamran Talattof and Jocelyn Sharlet. Syracuse, N.Y.: Syracuse University Press, 1998. Iran: follows five individuals who have the opportunity to decide their fates—the stories present a strong commentary on Persian mores on gender relations.

Tekin, Latife. *Dear Shameless Death*. Trans. Saliha Parker and Mel Kenne. New York: Marion Boyars, 2001. Turkey: fiction, migrant woman who moved to Istanbul with her family returns to and reflects on life in the village where she grew up.

The Call to Arms:
Violent Paths to Change

A revolution is not a dinner party, or writing an essay, or painting a picture, or doing embroidery; it cannot be so refined, so leisurely and gentle, so temperate, kind, courteous, restrained and magnanimous. A revolution is an insurrection, an act of violence by which one class overthrows another.
— Chinese revolutionary leader Mao Zedong[1]

Here we are, the dead of all times, dying once again, but now in order to live.
— Subcomandante Insurgente Marcos, leader of the Mexican Zapatistas[2]

On September 11, 2001, Americans faced violence in a way that most in this country had never experienced. When planes were crashed into the towers of the World Trade Center in New York City, the Pentagon just outside Washington, D.C., and a field in rural Pennsylvania, we witnessed the power of organized violence. As the United States and the world struggled to understand the reasons for these actions, we contemplated a force that has long been used by individuals and groups who feel they have few other ways to express their opinions. In Chapter 10 we discussed people's option of "voice," focusing on ideologies and participation. In this chapter we focus on a particular type of participation that engages the use of violence. We examine a variety of means of violent expression, especially highlighting the individuals and groups behind the actions, emphasizing the role of governments and militaries, terrorists and revolutionaries. This is an extremely important area of inquiry for the third world, as it is estimated that of the 200 or so wars and other violent conflicts that have taken place since the end of World War II, the vast majority (all but twelve) occurred in the less developed, third world.[3]

Some view violence as the breakdown of politics, but we encourage you to view it instead as a tool used by actors to accomplish their goals. Violence is a powerful weapon, used by terrorists, governments, GUERRILLAS, militaries, militias, and activists canvassing the whole gamut of ideological persuasion. While many commonly view the use of violence as a means of gaining territory, as we will see in this chapter, such tactics are also often used to exact responses including fear, intimidation, surrender, and subjugation. The psychological force of violence (or the threat thereof) is perhaps the greatest source of its potency.

Violence can take many forms, and its perpetrators justify it in a variety of ways. Behind violent acts are a myriad of motivations, aspirations, and justifications—all open to competing interpretations. As students of the third world, we attempt to classify types of actions taken by ordinary people and political elites alike: but these labels are often reductionist (overly simplified) and they may imply judgment. Take one form of violence with which we have all become more familiar in recent years: TERRORISM. As analysts, we can come up with a clear-cut definition of what we mean by the term, involving purposeful acts against innocent civilians in order to provoke fear and insecurity. Clearly, some individuals and groups engage in these acts in ways consistent with this view, and they take action without apology—proud to be listed among the world's most renowned terrorists. Yet there are other times when the term is inaccurately used as a political label to characterize a seemingly unjustifiable action by a group of people. In discussions of this topic, watch carefully the labels that are tossed around: tagging a group to be terrorist can oftentimes fulfill one's political agenda more than anything, and it can be used to delegitimize a group's perspective. Classifying acts of political deviance is a subjective enterprise.

Terrorist violence is used in many different types of conflict and by many activists of all stripes. Below, we will observe terrorism at work, including during warfare, revolutions, and times of peace. The designation of terrorist acts can sometimes be a puzzle; dependent upon one's perspective, the task of defining what exactly "terrorism" is has befuddled many social scientists.[4] As Noam Chomsky once stated, "what is terrorism to some is heroism to others."[5] Sometimes the fiery debate has taken on the language of "freedom fighters" versus "terrorists"—it should not be surprising that groups of people using violence believe that the ends justify the means.

Rather than trying to argue for or against a particular definition, we highlight key components: terrorism is a deliberate organized act, with the goal of inspiring fear. Usually, innocents are victimized, although the definition of who is "innocent" can be manipulated. Terrorists have shown devastating flexibility in both their targets and their tactics, which include bombings, kidnappings, hijackings, and the threats of such actions. They want to gain an audience—attention, even negative attention, is what they seek to publicize their causes. They want to alter opinion and policy. Contrary to popular belief, they're not all after land or material resources. Rather, they sometimes fight bigger, more seemingly abstract issues, such as GLOBALIZATION. The September 11 attack on the United States pointedly targeted two of the greatest symbols of Western wealth and military power: the World Trade Center and the Pentagon. Since attention is what these groups are after, CNN with its "around the clock news" is the greatest thing since sliced bread. Terror tactics evolve based on the response of societies and governments. In a scenario that seems almost quaint by today's standards, planes used to be commandeered by hijackers to go to Cuba. Nowadays groups are creating weapons of mass destruction out of airplanes. Why? The flexibility of terrorism requires relatively few people to pull it off, and at the beginning of the twenty-first century it is not as hard to get your hands on adequate materials to invoke terror. Maybe the world has become jaded and it takes more to get our attention—which is precisely what advocates of terror and other forms of violence desire.

As we discuss various manifestations of violent expression below, watch for the use of threats by perpetrators and for the use of labels by victims. What surprises you about the conflicts that we explore? As you read, try to understand the motivation behind competing sides of the issues.

Conflict and War

Why do people, especially in groups, turn to aggressive acts of defiance? There have been many theories used to explain when and why people turn to violent means.[6] To some, resorting to violence is a way of dealing with their dissatisfaction over a state of affairs. When facing frustration and unmet expectations, it is argued, people are likely to turn to aggression. Conflict is also likely in societies that experience great change, whether political, economic, or cultural. This can be especially true if that change is uneven, as the fits and starts of life often are. Promises of dramatic improvement are often unfulfilled, leaving some, particularly those who feel they made the most sacrifice in the name of the cause, expressing betrayal. People who believe they have limited options to make their voices heard try to challenge each aspect of security and comfort.

Another explanation, known as the RESOURCE MOBILIZATION approach, emphasizes agents' ability to commandeer leadership and political opportunities for expression. In this view, collective action is taken when the time is right and when the necessary connections between resources and people can be crafted. Because of the power of human agency, though, no single approach can be used to help explain the rise of violent action.

Significant differences, also known as CLEAVAGES, can almost always be found in societies and groups of people. These are based on a variety of factors, including the myriad of idetities we discussed in Chapter 10, as well as perceptions of well-being and fair treatment. Yet these differences are not always viewed as relevant, and they may remain latent for long periods of time. What sparks the change? In other words, what are some of the factors that make cleavages important enough differences for people to act on, even in violent ways?

One of the issues that alters a situation from low to high priority is the perceived extent of differentiation between and among groups. Many argue that the perception of stark differences between the rich and the poor in a given region or society can often be a source of violence. In the literature on social movements and mobilization, this view is referred to as RELATIVE DEPRIVATION. It is one thing if everyone is poor, but if some people are poor and others are very rich compared to others, the likelihood for action is much greater. If there is a strongly held perception that the difference between those who have benefited from a particular policy or program is great, a sense of indignity may impel people to act. As we saw in Chapter 7, the general state of the economy is an important factor influencing individuals' and groups' perception of their well-being and their decisions about action or inaction. In times of economic hardship, especially if policies are perceived as unevenly harming some groups of people, we have observed that some groups will turn to crime, violence, and other disruptive forms of behavior. China, for example, reports a large rise in crime, secret societies, triads, and gangs, accompanied by a rise in unauthorized gun ownership, although official statistics are not collected.[7] This has especially become a problem in the Western reaches of the country, which have benefited less from China's economic boom than southern and coastal regions.

Expectations about changes in lifestyle are also important. If people have little reason to expect anything from society or government, they often remain passive and largely inactive. But if they are given reason to expect more, especially through sacrifice, their hopes increase. Expectations sometimes end up being dangerously unfulfilled. Sometimes there is an ASPIRATION GAP between what one expects and what a person or group can actually achieve or acquire. Exposure to the international media that portray a variety of lifestyles and norms, increased interaction with other members of society who live in different circumstances, and especially elite cues about the way life can be help create circumstances in which this chasm can widen. A related idea is the REVOLUTION OF RISING EXPECTATIONS, which people experience as they begin to believe in the possibility and likelihood of positive change, for either themselves or their families. People naturally develop expectations about their future life. For example, many students attend college with the expectation that they will be able to get a good job to support themselves after graduation. Expectations often have a way of increasing in scope, and it is common for people to believe that with hard work and effort, life will get better. If this cycle is broken, and quality of life decreases rather than improves, it can be followed by frustration and disappointment.

Yet the motivation for action is not always as it appears, and people sometimes use unexpected public forums such as sports events and funerals to vent their frustration. For example, riots among young people in Iran, ostensibly expressing their frustration with the national soccer team, were really about groups frustrated with unemployment and poverty. An event later termed "part street party, part riot" followed a particularly sensitive series of national soccer matches in Tehran. People took to the streets, urged in part by the son of the late Shah, who now lives in the United States and has access to television and radio communications technology. Protesters vented their frustration with the slow pace of reform throughout the country, directing their anger at the conservative Council of Guardians. Complaints were also voiced about arrests of reformist deputies who had spoken out against the council, as well as a recent spate of seizures of illegal satellite dishes. The soccer match provided an impetus and the emotion for sources of genuine frustration to be expressed.[8]

Others, led by political scientist Arend Lijphart, have assigned importance to the patterns of division existing within society, distinguishing between crosscutting or coinciding cleavages.[9] These expressions are used to characterize whether or not the significant conflicts and areas of difference in society are diffused among varying groups, or are concentrated among particular sectors of society. For example, if the economically poor in a given country also tend to be the religious minority, employees in the service sector of the economy, and predominantly women, this would be an example of coinciding cleavages. In all aspects of differentiation, a particular group of people seem to be getting the short end of the stick. Coinciding cleavages are more volatile, as all of the conflicts are stacked up into tidy groups, and it is clear who does not agree with whom. In contrast, crosscutting lines of division help diffuse the conflict: the significant points of difference are spread among multiple groups in society, keeping any one group from perceiving any tremendous amount of injustice. Although real life never conforms to neatly crafted categories, Nigeria is often cited as an example of coinciding cleavages, where differences in religion, ethnicity, and region line up. Yet not all Yoruba are Christian, and of course the regions are not entirely homogeneous. Some Ibos, for example, live in the north. Another example can be found in Mexico, since the south is much poorer, less industrial, and more Amerindian than the rest of Mexico. Again it is an imperfect categorization, since the southern region of Chiapas contains some interesting divisions between Indians who are Protestant and those who are Catholic. The point remains, though: more pronounced divisions can invite greater potential for conflict along these lines. They certainly invite an "us versus them" distinction that can significantly hinder consensus building.

Another factor that influences the potential for violent action relates to the availability of meaningful avenues of expression. Protests and riots are sometimes designed to be turbulent from the outset, but other times they turn violent when participants feel they are being ignored or that it is only through destructive action that their voices will be heard. Yet violence is not always an act of desperation. Ironically, some groups have engaged in violent tactics just as they were about to become successful and achieve their goals.[10]

In our discussion of the relevancy of differences, we have concentrated mostly on groups smaller than governments and STATES. We now turn to a discussion of types of war, which is usually one of the first categories of violent conflict that comes to mind. Since the eighteenth century, war has been defined as violence between states or between organized groups, with the explicit goals of gaining territory, seeking revenge, or conquering recalcitrant groups of people. The twentieth century has been called the "century of war" because of the dominance of hostile conflict—three times as many people died in war during this century than during all of the prior nineteen centuries combined.[11] Wars produce scarred soldiers, lonely widows, traumatized victims of torture and rape, and political prisoners. Increasingly, the casualties of war are civilians rather than combatants.

There are many different types of wars, and the number seems to keep increasing as a variety of conflicts are now categorized as wars or warlike situations, including "nonconventional" wars such as the war on terrorism. In our discussion, we highlight some of the main types of warfare, including interstate, civil, guerrilla, and proxy wars. We discussed another significant type of warfare, wars of liberation waged by ethnonationalists, in Chapter 4. Yet we return to some themes related to this type of combat in our discussion of separatist conflict below.

Interstate and Separatist Wars

Interstate wars are the most conventional type of modern warfare, even if today they are no longer in the majority. Wars between states mostly involve traditional militaries, and commonly occur over border disputes, contested landholdings, and perceived threats to security. The legacies of colonialism have often been the source of wars in the third world, with conflict over borders that fail to recognize significant historical, ethnic, and cultural continuities, and the creation of MULTINATIONAL STATES and stateless peoples. China, for example, has fought border wars with India in 1962 and the Soviet Union in 1969–1978, and invaded Vietnam in 1979.

One extremely volatile border situation can be found between two South Asian giants, Pakistan and India, in the region called Kashmir. It has been a point of conflict since the departure of the British in 1947, and over 30,000 people have died in the crossfire. A UN cease-fire in 1949 provided both India and Pakistan a portion of the region rich in resources and historical connections, but this compromise barely held—and it is rarely viewed as little more than a temporary solution. The Indian territory, India's only Muslim-majority state, is referred to as Jammu Kashmir, while the Pakistani-controlled territory, also predominantly Muslim, is named Azad ("Free") Kashmir. Complicating matters even further, the People's Republic of China (PRC) established claims to part of the region in the 1950s, even building a road to assist military transport. China still occupies the northernmost part of the territory, known as Aksai Chin. Part of the reason for the enduring conflict in the region is that inhabitants themselves are not united in their desire for the future, a dilemma common in border wars. Plans to hold elections in 1995—with the hope of resolving the territorial dispute forever—were abandoned after an attack on a Muslim mosque. Nuclear tests by both Pakistan and India in 1998 escalated tensions even further, and an attack on the Indian parliament in December 2001 again brought these two Asian states to the brink of war.

One of the most devastating interstate wars in the third world was the eight-year war between the Middle Eastern giants, Iran and Iraq. Claiming over 500,000 lives, it was the longest war in the recent history of the Middle East.[12] Although the conflict began when Saddam Hussein ordered Iraqi forces to invade Iran during a perceived time of weakness for the young Islamic Republic, its origins can be found in historic, territorial, and ideological differences. Even though Iraq initially welcomed the Iranian Revolution of February 1979, it broke relations with the regime in October of that year, branding the regime "non-Islamic" for inciting Shiite communities throughout the Gulf to rebel against their regimes.[13] Hussein and many Iraqis feared that the Islamic Revolution would embolden Iran and challenge contested waterway claims and the Gulf region in general. At one point during the war, Iran demanded Hussein's ouster as a precondition for peace talks, flaming internal opposition within Iraq. Iraq's capture of Kharg Island, Iran's principal Gulf oil terminal, in December 1985, quieted anti-Hussein movements within the country.

The war itself was one of the most brutal in the region, as Iran launched so-called human wave attacks in which hundreds of thousands of civilians, including boys as young as nine years old, were sent to their death in assaults on Iraqi artillery positions. (This has been a strategy used by combatants with large populations, employed by China in the Korean War and by both sides of the Ethiopia-Eritrea conflict.) Religiously motivated troops joined the war in their attempt to seek martyrdom; some were even given symbolic keys to a paradise that was promised to martyrs. Iraq responded with mustard and nerve agents.

Iraq was surprised that the initial attacks didn't make Tehran crumble, and by 1982 began to seek peace. Iran refused these initiatives and attacked across the border, significantly weakening the Iranian military and leading to a long stand-off with Iraq. After a prolonged war of attrition, an UN-brokered cease-fire was accepted in 1988. The only border crossing between Iran and Iraq was reopened in 1999 to allow Iranian pilgrims to visit Shia holy sites in Iraq.

Wars are also fought over contested definitions of states—questioning what amount of territory should be included in internationally recognized borders. In Chapter 10 we introduced the notion of the NATION-STATE and the existence of areas of tensions in some, although by no means all, multinational states. The preservation of borders and territorial integrity is an essential function of states. Yet the modern state has "deterritorialized" many national groups, sometimes because of the artificial demarcation of boundaries, often at the hands of imperial powers. Groups challenge their incorporation into a particular state for a variety of reasons, often relating to issues such as religious expression, ethnic disputes, or pressures relating to natural resources. Of course, few of these issues stand alone. Some indigenous groups, such as the Dayaks and Igorots in Southeast Asia, seek to maintain a traditional, nonindustrial, nonurban life that conflicts with national economic development plans of many states. Other groups take issue not with the industrial or economic goals of the government, but rather want to have their own homeland or government. This phenomenon is also known as SECESSION. For most, the goal is either to achieve national liberation from political occupation or to create a new political state. For others, the struggle is for humane treatment, more autonomy, and the right to the free expression of their cultural traditions. Sometimes, though not always, this can lead to violent conflict, either in the suppression of the movement (such as China's response to the expression of an independent Tibetan identity), or in the expression of the need for a new identity. The Sikh community in Punjab, India, seeks a homeland called Khalistan, the "Land of the Pure." To date, India has been hostile to calls for this homeland, which geographically stands at the strategic intersection of India, the PRC, and Pakistan.

The results of separatist conflict can be disastrous, including displacement, genocide, and ethnic cleansing. The third world is riddled with the tragedies of such conflict, including the murder of Armenians by Turks (1915), of Kurds by the Iraqis (1984–1991), of Hutu and Tutsi in Burundi (1993–1998), of Tutsi and moderate Hutu in Rwanda (1994), and of Hmong by Laotians and the Chinese (1975–1979). Yet some caution against viewing these conflicts as rooted in "ancient tribal" or even distinctly religious rivalries.[14] Such conflict, rather, has been stoked by modern power plays or by rivalries that were introduced by outside, often colonial powers. Yet it remains true that more groups of people are actively fighting today for new forms of political independence and expression than in decades or centuries past. Muslim rebel groups have been campaigning for SELF-DETERMINATION in the south of the Philippines, a predominantly Christian state, for more than three decades. One group of Malaysian Muslims, the Moro National Liberation Front (MNLF), recently broke a five-year peace agreement and attacked army positions, resulting in the deaths of one hundred guerrillas, four soldiers, and seven civilians.[15] A more famous group of armed

Figure 12.1   The Kurds

Another important example of separatist conflict can be found in the diverse Kurdish population, approximately 30 million people who are considered the largest group of stateless people in the Middle East. At least one-fifth of the Kurds live in Turkey, with significant populations also found in Iran, Iraq, the former Soviet Union, and Syria. Facing widespread persecution since the late 1980s, many Kurds have immigrated to Germany (where they faced much neo-Nazi violence) and the Netherlands. Contrary to popular perception, the Kurds are not a single, homogeneous group. Kurdish people speak several different, often mutually unintelligible languages and espouse different forms of Islam. Even in a similar fight for autonomy, two separate entities have emerged: the rival parties of Masoud Barzani and Jalal Talabani.[16] War broke out between their rival factions in 1994, over the proceeds of transborder trade. Thousands of Kurds on both sides of the internecine battle died.

Turkey is the Kurds' main path to the west. Yet depending on the mood in Ankara, one can be sent to jail for broadcasting in Kurdish, teaching Kurdish languages in schools, or running a political campaign on the basis of ethnicity. Since 1984, war between the Turkish government and some Kurds has claimed at least 30,000 lives and driven several million Kurds from their homes. Common interpretations of Turkish law hold the promotion of "hatred between ethnic groups" to include any mention of a Kurdish problem. One human rights campaigner, Akin Birdal, was jailed for two years for speaking of a "Kurdish identity" in public. Parents are even prevented from giving their children Kurdish names. Approximately 1.4 million Kurds live in Iran's remote northwestern province of Kurdistan; about twice that many live elsewhere in Iran. Iranian Kurds are predominantly Sunni Muslim. Facing oppression from the Shia regime in Tehran, the Kurdish Nationalist Movement in Iran was driven into Iraq. The Iranian government has been making gradual concessions to the Kurds, including increasing the number of print publications in Kurdish, supporting Kurdish classes and television programming, and supporting Kurdish dress.[17]

The Kurdish problem has been particularly acute in Iraq. Following the 1991 Gulf War, most Iraqi Kurds (approximately 2.5 million) live in a semiautonomous northern district, protected by a no-fly zone enforced by the United States and Great Britain. Violence against them, though, began long before the Gulf War. U.S. intelligence estimates that from 1987 to 1988, Saddam Hussein's government used chemical agents to gas to death 50,000–100,000 Kurds.[18] Iraqi Kurds have faced forced migration away from major oil-producing regions with obvious strategic importance. There have been reports that some have been forced to sign forms renouncing their ethnic identities and declaring themselves to be Arabs.[19]

Muslims in the Philippines is the Abu Sayyaf Group (ASG), known for kidnapping foreigners and Christian Filipinos, including the murder of a prominent Catholic bishop in 1997. Formed in 1991, it is a splinter group of the MNLF and is rumored to have ties with Al-Qaida. The primary goal of the ASG is to create an "Iranian-style" Islamic state on Mindanao, the southernmost region of the Republic of the Philippines.

Indonesia has also faced much secessionist conflict. The state leadership following independence from the Dutch vigorously pushed nationalist assimilation policies. Aceh, a northwestern province on the island of Sumatra with a population of 4 million, is home to the longest-running and most violent separatist conflict in Indonesia—war has been waged intermittently for over fifty years. The Acehnese are considered to be more orthodox Islamic than residents in other regions of Indonesia. The region is also a major oil and gas producer, and there is a bitter sense by many Acehnese that Jakarta skims off much of the revenue of the region.[20] The area has been rife with conflict, with murder of innocents by both the Free Aceh (Aceh Merdeka) guerrillas and the Indonesian security forces alike. A more recent troubling development has been the proliferation of gangs operating under the guise of the Free Aceh movement.

Civil Wars

Although interstate conflicts are obviously important, an increasing number of battles in the world today are internal. Even some of the major cross-border wars, including those between India and Pakistan and Eritrea and Ethiopia, trace much of their origin to civil conflict. The third world has been beleaguered by civil wars, including conflict in Algeria, Angola, Cambodia, Chad, China, Laos, Nicaragua, Nigeria, Rwanda, Somalia, Sudan, Uganda, Yemen, and Zimbabwe. Civil wars, which occur within a single country, are known to be the most brutal and damaging type of conflict, inflicting particularly heavy tolls on civilian populations. Families are often separated in civil wars, either by the outcome of the war or along lines of allegiance. Because of the brutality of the conflict, ill will and the scars of war often continue long after the official warfare is complete. Sometimes the estrangement can last for decades or longer.

Civil wars are fought for a variety of reasons. Oftentimes, battles rage over which leader or group should rule a country. Such was the nature of the Chinese civil war from 1945 to 1949, which ended with Nationalist Party (KMT) forces fleeing to the island of Taiwan and the Chinese Communist Party (CCP) proclaiming the People's Republic of China. Other civil wars are fought between rival leaders or groups. Colombia is a country that was torn apart by civil wars throughout much of the nineteenth century, waged between rival Liberal and Conservative party leaders, guerrillas, drug traffickers, and other entrenched interests. The ongoing war in Colombia was launched in the mid–twentieth century by a conflict now referred to as *la violencia*.[21] This war initially started out as a street riot in Bogota, following the assassination of a Liberal Party leader and candidate for president. It has worsened as Colombia's problems have mounted: continued elite conflict over the future direction of the country, the deepening and professionalization of the drug trade and the concomitant development of a police force that rivals the military in many ways, and the development of paramilitary groups throughout the country. A war that began between two rival political parties has devolved into an ideological struggle including Marxist-Leninist guerrillas, the military, narcotraffickers, and militias, with significant regional and international involvement.[22]

From 1967 to 1970 a civil war was fought in Nigeria in which more than 1 million people died. The declaration of war was the culmination of a series of events, most immediately a pogrom directed against Ibos in the north. Led by Odumwegwu Ojukwu, the Ibo sought to create "Biafra," an independent and sovereign state carved out of their traditional home in Nigeria's southeast.

Figure 12.2   Taiwan—Renegade Province or Independent State?

The controversy surrounding the status of Taiwan, just off the southeastern coast of China, demonstrates that in some ways the Chinese civil war of the 1940s still rages. After the Chinese communists defeated the Chinese nationalists in the fall of 1949, Chiang Kaishek and his supporters completed their transfer to Taiwan, much to the chagrin of the indigenous population. (An uprising in 1947, prior to the complete arrival by the Nationalists, is believed to have claimed over 20,000 lives.) From their base in Taipei, the Nationalists pledged to "retake" mainland China, up until the death of Generalissimo Chiang in 1975. Major combat was averted largely by the positioning of the U.S. Seventh Fleet in the Taiwan Straits, which separate the two lands. Owing to anticommunist sentiment in the 1950s and 1960s, most of the world, with the exception of France and later Great Britain, refused to recognize the newly minted CCP regime as the legitimate government of China—they recognized the Nationalist regime on Taiwan instead. This continued until the early 1970s, when Taiwan exited the UNITED NATIONS and most countries of the world completed normalization with the PRC.

Both groups involved in the dispute purported to support "one China," but both the nationalists and the CCP viewed themselves as the legitimate government of all Chinese people. Former president Lee Tenghui and his successor, Chen Shuibian, began to challenge the meaning of Taiwan being part of "one China," much to the consternation of Beijing.

However, for a variety of reasons, including concern over the loss of the substantial oil revenues coming from the region, the north and west combined forces to resist secession by all conceivable means. Biafra became Africa's most internationalized war in the 1960s, as the countries of the world lined up on one side or the other. When the much larger and better-equipped federal army found that it could not prevail against the Ibo forest fighters, it resorted to a policy aimed at starving the Ibo into submission. The blockade had devastating consequences, particularly on women and children. Although they eventually lost the war, the Ibo won international sympathy, as the Biafra conflict was considered by many to be a genocide led by the largely Islamic north against the Christian east.[23]

Guerrilla Warfare

Guerrilla, deriving from the Spanish words for "little war," is a term used for troops operating independently of state militaries, and often in opposition to them, following a relatively loose set of methods that are designed to deceive enemy forces and overcome deficiencies in equipment, force size, and location. In their attempt to damage the LEGITIMACY of a government, guerrilla forces target civilian populations for recruitment. Women soldiers have participated in this form of combat more than other types of warfare.[24] Additionally, there is often an extensive effort, through propaganda, terror, and policies, to win the support and fighting power of peasant populations. Guerrilla groups are known for setting up successful pilot projects, including schools and clinics, to provide services to groups often ignored by the state and to win their support.

In guerrilla warfare, conventional rules of engagement, especially concern-

Figure 12.3   Zimbabwe and Africa's World War

Since the ouster of its long-standing dictator, Mobutu Sese Seko, the Democratic Republic of Congo (formerly Zaire) has been mired in civil war. There are at least three rebel movements fighting the Kabila government, and six African countries have lined up on one of the many sides in this war. No one knows how many people have been killed; estimates range from 100,000 to 3 million. Zimbabwe is one of those countries weighing in on the side of President Laurent Kabila, Zimbabwean President Robert Mugabe's old friend. Mugabe entered the war hoping that his country's participation would give him the international stature he craves. He also hoped for a badly needed public relations boost and that Zimbabweans would rally around the flag—something that did not happen. The war has been popular with high-ranking officers in the Zimbabwean army, who have made their fortunes from Congolese mining concessions. However, many in the lower ranks have not seen any benefit. And the appalling conditions back home have made this adventure look to many Zimbabweans like the estimated $1 million a day the country was spending there was a huge waste of money.[25] Since peace deals were brokered by most of the major parties to the war in 2002, the president says he is ready to bring his 8,000 troops home. As a July 2002 cease-fire between the Congolese government and the external parties to the war continued to hold and foreign armies dispersed, the government also signed a peace agreement with rebel forces on December 17, 2002. UN peacekeepers plan to oversee the power-sharing agreement, known as the Pretoria Accord, as rebel armies are expected to transform into political parties and vie for seats in parliament.

ing noncombatants, are largely ignored. Policies, both psychological and concrete, are designed to exhaust and demoralize the enemy while recruiting civilians either through fear or persuasion. Battles tend to center around long, protracted campaigns, often from a rural base. Guerrilla tactics are mobile, necessitated by their smaller troops sizes, and when successful use the element of surprise to make gains. Revolutionaries who perceive the unorthodox methods of fighting to be their only shot at victory often use guerrilla warfare. Examples include the Chinese civil war and revolution, Fidel Castro's 1959 revolution in Cuba, and Ho Chi Minh's battles against the Japanese, French, and later U.S. troops in Vietnam.

The modern Chinese state was founded largely upon the principles of guerrilla violence. Mao Zedong, the leader of China's 1949 revolution and one of the modern world's leading revolutionaries, was a man of contradictions. He was a poet and librarian, which is how he first encountered Marxist and Leninist theories on revolutions. Mao came of age in a China that was on the brink of collapse, worn down by the imperial wars of the late 1800s, the infighting of the warlord period following the collapse of the Qing Dynasty, as well as the economic misery and political uncertainties that follow the end of an empire. Although Mao was a relatively insignificant participant in the founding of the Chinese Communist Party in Shanghai in 1921, he grew to lead it throughout the revolutionary war with KMT forces, and was the man who proclaimed the beginning of the PRC in Tiananmen Square on October 1, 1949. Throughout the revolutionary war and in wars that followed the establishment of the PRC, Mao advocated a type of warfare known as "people's war," which combined guerrilla tactics with Mao's emphasis on China's "human factors," highlighting the importance of the masses and the need to motivate and organize them. Mao often stated that "if our hearts are pure, we will fight with the strength of 10,000 men." The so-called people's war from 1927 to 1949 combined elements of social revolution with a war for national SOVEREIGNTY. From their base in China's northern rural areas, the CCP successfully employed guerrilla tactics to conquer cities, win the support of the population, and reign victorious.

Proxy Wars

Another type of conflict, sometimes referred to as "warfare by substitutes," involves surrogate fighters who are recruited to fight battles that other, often more powerful groups do not want to get involved in directly. Such proxy wars were especially common during the COLD WAR, when the United States and the Soviet Union acted as patrons for wars that were in their interest. The United States propped up anticommunist governments, including Indonesia, South Korea, South Vietnam, and Chile, while the Soviet Union did what it could to support Marxist-Leninist regimes throughout the world, including China (initially), North Korea, and North Vietnam. Recognizing that even the most powerful states or richest groups cannot afford to be in constant war with their enemies, these countries choose instead to support dissenters, separatists, and other potential clients of a rival to avoid mutually assured destruction. During the Cold War, proxy conflicts were used to avoid direct opposition between the superpowers.

The goal of this type of conflict is to wear down the enemy, weakening it by encouraging the waste of resources, without expending a tremendous amount of resources or energy. Surrogate conflict can also include the assassination of political leaders or individuals. It often includes direct sabotage. In the early 1980s, for example, the United States "unofficially" provided support, buttressed by a special operations manual of the Central Intelligence Agency (CIA), to Nicaraguan Contra rebels who were fighting the leftist Sandinista government. Similar efforts were taken by the Soviet Union to encourage North Korea to attack South Korea in 1950.

Some turn to this substitute conflict as a way of improving their own image and to place some distance between themselves and the seemingly unsavory battles at hand. It has been argued that a group known as Islamic Jihad, an offshoot of the military wing of Hamas, was used as a proxy to carry out executions on behalf of the government of Iran, which attempted to improve its international image following its isolation during the 1980s.[26] In proxy conflict, nationals are involved usually in training and support, employing private armies in a country to put down revolutionary movements, assassinate critics of the regime, and maintain control. Fidel Castro's Cuba was relatively unusual in sending large numbers of soldiers abroad; since many of the fighters were nonwhite, they were welcome in many places that the Soviets and the East Europeans were not, including Guinea, Mozambique, and Angola.

Proxy wars permit the sponsoring agent to focus on "big picture" events and strategy, while others do the "grunt work" on the ground. For example, the U.S.-

led war in Afghanistan was considered by most to be a proxy war, using Northern Alliance and other anti-Taliban forces to do the dirty work while the United States led the air campaign and provided intelligence. The elusiveness of Osama bin Laden thus far has been attributed to the use of Afghan, Pakistani, and other ground forces who might have succumbed to bribes from bin Laden's associates to permit him to escape the country. In a majority of proxy wars, there are often very real regional conflicts or domestic divisions at the heart, which are greatly amplified by the patronage of outsiders.

Faces Behind the Disruption

So who is responsible for acts of violence? As you can imagine, there is great diversity in the types of individuals and groups who believe their use of destructive means is justified. In this section, we discuss some of the major types of groups involved in belligerent activities. The faces behind the disruption can be as diverse as the forms of violence that are employed. For example, even though men make up the majority of individuals who engage in terrorism, women have frequently joined terrorist groups. Some argue that participation in violent groups provides women a rare outlet for gender equality, an argument that is used to explain women's participation in terrorist organizations and revolutions.[27] In Peru's Sendero Luminoso (Shining Path), large numbers of women participated as equals in the group's apparatus, overcoming the subordinate role and status historically ascribed to them in Peruvian society. And some made it to top positions in the regional command and the National Central Committee, including Abimael Guzman's wife, Augusta la Torre, who has been described as "a major force" in the movement.[28] Women have been active leaders in the Kurdistan Workers' Party (PKK) in Turkey, the Palestinian uprising (INTIFADA), and many other movements. It is believed that as many as one-fourth of Russian revolutionaries in 1917 were women.[29] It was a woman who was sent to assassinate India's prime minister, Rajiv Gandhi, in 1991. In 1970 one female Palestinian refugee, Leila Khaled, almost single-handedly hijacked a commercial plane, evacuating all passengers before she blew it up. The participation and leadership of women cannot be reduced to ideology or level of restrictions imposed on them. In Bahrain, where women enjoy some of the most liberated circumstances in the Gulf, young women and girls have joined in arson attacks at local stores, seemingly as a way to belong or to overcome the doldrums of daily life.[30]

Young people have also long been attracted to violence—often drawn to the idea of belonging to a meaningful group that provides direction and identity. We discuss one of the most famous sets of twins—the Htoo brothers from Myanmar—below. But there are others. Shining Path, which was born in a university setting, appealed especially to students. The most violent stages of China's CULTURAL REVOLUTION employed the use of middle and high school–aged "Red Guards" to terrorize those labeled enemies of the CCP and to foment revolutionary fervor throughout the country. In Zimbabwe, both the Zimbabwe African National Union (ZANU) and the Zimbabwe African People's Union (ZAPU) mobilized entire classrooms of kids, who left with their teachers to train as guerrillas. Participants in the Palestinian intifada are believed to be particularly young. Research puts the median age of terrorists in the third world at approximately twenty-two years old. Youth have been active in arson attacks, hand-to-hand combat, sabotage, and suicide missions. Some postulate their involvement can be explained by the lack of outside commitments that would limit their availability for activities, while others point to youths' propensity for risk-taking, their passion for causes, and their mobility.

Militaries and Militias

In any discussion of the major groups that sponsor violence as a means to achieve goals, we would be remiss if we excluded governments themselves. As sociologist Max Weber highlighted in his classic definition of the "state," one of the greatest powers of governments is their monopoly over the right to use force. This does not mean, of course, that states are the only groups that hold coercive power, nor does it imply that all use of government force is proper or legitimate, but it does accurately imply that governments tend to have the most organized, well-financed, and effective means of making their preferences known. By engaging forces in wartime combat, adopting domestic policies that include executions and punishment, and supporting abductions, assassinations,

Figure 12.4   Legality as a Tool of State Terror

Governments possess many means to craft seemingly "legal" means by which they can impose their will and limit opposition voices. Perceived troublemakers, for example, are often forced into exile: either to remote parts of the country, or outside of the state altogether. In China some dissidents have been released from prison, but they are provided a one-way ticket out of the country and often depart without being able to send notice to their families. Others, like Myanmar's Aung San Suu Kyi, are placed under house arrest or sent to remote areas to stay out of trouble. Police brutality is another overt form of state violence; outright abuse at the hands of the Turkish police is listed as one of Turkey's worst human rights abuses—the issue was again in the spotlight during prison riots throughout 2001. Other governments use executions (state-sanctioned murder) as part of routine public policy. Amnesty International reports that China executed more people in three months of 2001 than all other countries in the world in three years.[31] Iran has also increased its use of capital punishment in recent years.

Leaders also manipulate judicial channels in order to achieve their goals. In its war against terrorism, Alberto Fujimori pushed through the creation of special military courts to try those suspected of terrorism or treason. Often secret, these were faceless courts in which the judges were hooded, or in which the defendant sat alone in front of a one-way mirror.[32] The president argued such courts were necessary because too many terrorists were slipping through the civilian courts because of constitutional restrictions on prosecution. It should come as no surprise that the conviction rate in these special courts was virtually 100 percent, as trials often lasted less than twenty minutes, there was no DUE PROCESS, and convictions were often based on phony evidence or confessions extracted with torture.[33] As a result, several hundred people known as "the innocents" were wrongly imprisoned after being railroaded through these courts. Most of them have since been pardoned or absolved of wrongdoing, but the experience has done them irreparable harm.

and forced relocations, it is clear that governments all around the world use violent means to achieve their ends.

As an institution of government, the state military wields tremendous power. Militaries consist of disciplined, organized, and well-funded groups of people with great influence: official armed units are used to implement key directives of governments, often using force. Militaries are found in almost every country of the world. The major exception is Costa Rica, which dissolved its military in the 1950s, even though it still has a small paramilitary force.

Young men under the age of twenty-six nearly exclusively carry out military acts. In World War I women first donned military uniforms and received military ranking. Yet today in Benin, Israel, and Myanmar both sexes are formally required to enroll in military service, and increasingly women participate in noncompulsory military training and combat as well. Just as it is wrong to assume that all women are mothers, it is also a mistake to think that all mothers are peaceniks and opposed to the use of violence to effect change. African women trained with men and fought alongside them in Zimbabwe's war for liberation. In the mid-1970s approximately one-third of the soldiers fighting for ZANU were female, and some of these women held positions of authority over men. In addition, civilian women provided assistance to the guerrillas as their way of fighting. They cooked for the rebels, and because for a while at least women could better avoid the attention of Rhodesian soldiers, they sometimes disguised their bundles as babies and smuggled supplies to guerrilla bases. Just as women participated in the war effort in various ways, so too did they have different expectations about what the coming change should mean for them. ZANU recognized how important women's support was to the struggle and challenged local norms during the war by making an explicit commitment to women's liberation. However, for various reasons since taking power the liberation government's position has been described as ambivalent at best. ZANU did push through some significant reforms of benefit to women, but there has been no transformation of gender relations.[34]

Increasingly in modern combat, civilians, especially children, are often the group most victimized by warfare. Since 1945, 90 percent of the casualties in war have been civilians.[35] The statistics are even more telling when they are viewed not as raw numbers, but as a trend. Prior to the early 1990s, the ratio of military to civilian casualties was eight to one. In the wars of the 1990s, the trend was reversed: for every military fighter that died in combat, eight civilians perished.[36] Some of this can be attributed to the "civilianization" of war, as noncombatants are increasingly targeted for attack or are innocently caught in the crossfire.

Another development of late-twentieth-century warfare that highlights the changing face of violence has been the inclusion of large numbers of children as active protagonists of warfare. It has been estimated that more than 300,000 children (under the age of eighteen) fight today as soldiers with government and armed opposition groups in over fifty countries. It is estimated that underage fighters are currently used in thirty conflicts. Most child soldiers are between ages fifteen and eighteen; the youngest age recorded by the Coalition to Stop the Use of Child Soldiers is seven. The presence of children in combat has become a critical problem in Africa and Asia, although youth are used as soldiers, porters, cooks, messengers, checkpoint guards, sexual slaves, and spies throughout the world. Myanmar has the highest numbers of child soldiers in the world, within both governmental armed forces and nongovernmental groups, and the fighters are often under fifteen years of age. Because of their agility and fearlessness, children have also been employed to do much of the more dangerous work in battle zones, including mine-clearing operations. The proliferation of "small arms" (discussed in Chapter 17) has also increased the use of child soldiers, as the ease of modern combat has made strength, size, and experience less important. The Russian AK-47, which flooded markets after World War II, weighs less than seven pounds in its modern versions—it is something an eight-year-old can maneuver with relative confidence.[37]

Even if they are not formal "soldiers" per se, children have been combatants in some of the world's bloodiest conflicts. In the Palestinian uprising, for example, children are active agitators against Israeli forces, throwing stones and sabotaging units, and they have paid dearly, often with their lives. Some children are forced to take up arms, but others are given little choice in the face of poverty, discrimination, and the pressure to conscript. Pregnancy, often the outcome of gang rape by comrade or enemy soldiers, isn't enough to keep young girls out of combat, either. Human Rights Watch estimates that in some conflicts, namely El Salvador, Ethiopia, and Uganda, as many as 30 percent of child participants are female. Young girls have been used as suicide bombers in Sri Lanka and Lebanon, and many girls are allocated to soldiers as rewards, as "wives." In Uganda it is estimated that most of the girls taken by the opposition Lord's Resistance Army (LRA) have sexually transmitted diseases, including AIDS.[38]

Young soldiers receive little or no training. In warfare, children are also subjected to severe punishment, sometimes even harsher than what adults would receive. There have also been reports of widespread juvenile disappearance, extrajudicial execution, and torture—orphans and street children are particularly vulnerable to recruitment. Perhaps because they have a less developed sense of right and wrong, children (in some places known as the "lost generation") are said to commit the worst atrocities. Drugs are also used to make children effective killers. Children want approval, and sometimes they find acceptance in the most violent groups. Often, child soldiers are orphans, desperately eager to please adults (even if the adult is responsible for them being orphaned). Most have been traumatized themselves, as witnesses to murder of their families, sometimes even forced to participate in ritualized killings. The Revolutionary United Front (RUF) in Sierra Leone, for example, trained its child soldiers by ordering them to kill other children or even their own parents or someone they knew so that they wouldn't fear death or try to escape.

In that civil war, all sides used children as frontline troops. When Charles Taylor's National Patriotic Front of Liberia invaded Sierra Leone on Christmas Eve in 1989, it was estimated that 30 percent of the soldiers were boys less than seventeen years old. The RUF has forced children into service, kidnapping them and administering drugs to them against their will. The UN International Children's Fund (UNICEF) has worked with over 1,700 children in Sierra Leone (out of a possible 6,000 underage soldiers), attempting to demobilize and demilitarize them, many of whom have become hardened to brutal conflict by cocaine addiction. Children have also been targeted as willing suicide agents. During the Iran-Iraq War, thousands of patriotic Iranian children were sent to the front lines, holding the symbolic key to a paradise as martyrs. In Sri Lanka, young Tamil girls (often orphans) were recruited by opposition forces and trained as suicide bombers, known as the "Birds of Freedom."[39]

Child soldiers are not always fighting for their own country or ethnic group. In the conflict in the Democratic Republic of Congo, for example, children from Namibia and Rwanda were brought into the fray. Children have also been recruited into terrorist and separatist groups. Peru's Shining Path is believed to have forcibly recruited several thousand indigenous children. Child soldiers have also been common in Colombia's nearly fifty-year-old civil war.

One of the most famous recent cases of children rebels surrounded the teenage Burmese twins Johnny and Luther Htoo, leaders of the Burmese rebel group called "God's Army." Many of the children who fight with this group are orphans of the war in Myanmar. The twins claim mystic powers, including being invulnerable to the personal devastation of land mines and bullets, which are said to "bounce off" the young commanders. They are also said to have invisible soldiers who assist them, and are rumored to have black tongues. Johnny Htoo is said once to have jumped into a stream, after which he was transformed into an old man. He returned to his teenage self after convincing his fellow fighters of his prowess. One of the unique aspects about the group is that these young boys, who became soldiers before they reached the age of ten, have led grown adults into battle. The belief among their followers is that they are not as young as they seem. Rather, in fitting with Karen animist teachings that messiahs will be sent to lead the people through difficult times, they are reincarnations of past revolutionary and legendary heroes. Working in concert with the Vigorous Burmese Student Warriors, God's Army rebels seized hostages throughout Thailand, including once capturing more than 800 patients and staff at a hospital. In the winter of 2001 the twins turned themselves in to police in Thailand, at the tender age of fourteen.[40]

In Figure 12.5, we present comparative data on militaries in the third world. While we believe this information is a useful starting point, we urge you to consider that countries are notorious for underreporting both the size of their formal military force strength, as well as the amount of budgetary resources committed to the military. One way that governments get around full reporting of their troop strength is by creating paramilitaries and other semimilitary units that are not counted in the final troop total. For example, the PRC, which has undertaken dramatic troop reductions since the mid-1990s, does not include the 1.3 million members of the People's Armed Police (PAP) in its final troop count. This ambiguity is one reason why the CIA, in its *World Factbook,* reports the portion of the population available for military service and the portion fit for military service, rather than actual troop numbers. Additionally, the average worldwide national expenditure for the military, expressed as a percentage of gross domestic product (GDP), is 2 percent. As you can see in the figure, some of the states we focus on in this study, notably Nigeria and Turkey, dramatically exceed this figure.

Figure 12.5 Militaries in the Third World (2001)

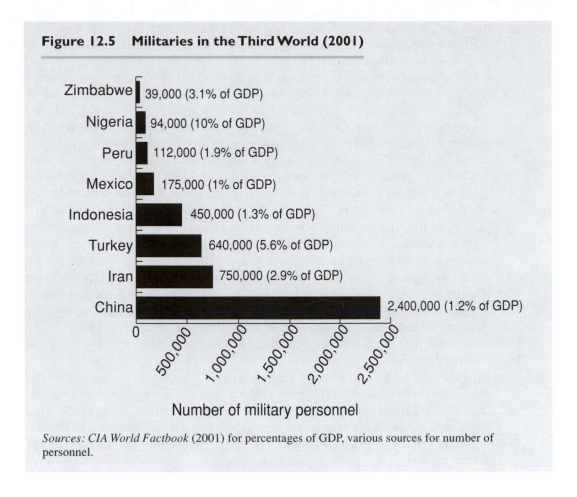

Number of military personnel

Sources: CIA World Factbook (2001) for percentages of GDP, various sources for number of personnel.

Despite relatively generous expenditures for militaries—when compared to spending for healthcare and education, for example—soldiers in the third world tend to be compensated very poorly. As a result, it is common for groups to turn to extortion at roadblocks, kidnapping, bribery, and other malfeasant forms of behavior to supplement their income. Paramilitary police in the restive Indonesian province of Aceh, for example, received sixty cents a day in compensation from the government, which is less than the cost of a pack of cigarettes.[41] This problem has also been identified with the Chinese police force, which is famous for forcibly collecting bribes in the Chinese countryside, a dilemma that other countries face as well.

The declared goal of the modern military is to provide defense and security for a country. Civilian leadership over the military is recognized as a common value in the world today. In this model, the military is simply one of many interest groups lobbying for its own priorities. This norm is known as civilian rule, which has been violated in many countries, and not only in the third world. So-called professional militaries act on the authority of governments and possess restricted powers to challenge civilian political leadership. They develop particularized areas of expertise, such as challenging external enemies, and keep out of areas beyond their purview, such as political infighting. No military is completely professional in this sense, but we can observe varying degrees of professionalism using this metric.

The polar opposite of this civil-military duality—military rule—often begins when elements within the military sense a crisis. The manifestations of this perceived crisis are varied, but can include societal cleavages, leadership controversies, economic malaise, tensions within the military itself, defeat in war, contagion effects from neighboring countries, external intervention, personality conflicts between the military leadership and political leaders, or simply an easy power grab.[42] In the interest of providing stability, the argument goes, a disciplined, professional military would often be the best candidate to lead an interim transition. Unfortunately, in many situations the perceived "crisis" lasts longer than most civilian leaders originally envisioned and the so-called transition becomes standard operating procedure. Chile, for example, experienced military rule for eighteen years. Military rule is often precipitated by a government overthrow, or a coup d'état, when the governmental leader or part of the leadership is replaced by violence or threat. After a coup, which is usually quick, the military government is often referred to as a junta, or council. Military commanders have then been known to take control of schools, train new soldiers in their own doctrine, and take elaborate measures to silence the masses.

Military coups and military rule have been a common occurrence in the third world. In Iran, the 1921 coup ushered in a "new order," only to be followed by another coup in 1935. Sometimes coups are initially welcomed by the population, such as the Nigerian coup against corruption, fraud, and economic mismanagement in 1983–1984. Many people applauded the military as saviors of the country. Some coups appear to be contagious, following in line one after the other. Nigeria experienced nine military coups in thirty years and has spent most of its independence under military rule. Military coups are not necessarily violent—in fact most are bloodless, although a particularly brutal coup occurred in Chile in 1973, in which at least 2,000 people died. Turkey is another country with quite a scorecard of coups.

The Ottoman Empire was founded by warriors, and to many, this tradition of military dominance rightly continues in the modern Turkish state. Modern Turkey was born of a military coup by the Kemalists in the 1920s, who claimed to be protecting Turkey from Islamic rule (Atatürk himself was a war hero). Turkey has become famous for military interventionism, often "in the name of DEMOCRACY." Ever since, the military has perceived itself as possessing a special role to defend Atatürk's secular republic. Three more coups followed in 1960, 1971, and 1980. In the 1980 coup, a six-man military junta suspended parliament, arrested leaders, and closed the doors on all parties and independent associations, including unions. The junta also instituted mass arrests and oversaw the drafting of the 1982 constitution, considered to be one of Turkey's most repressive. This power of military regimes to craft democracies that garner favor for themselves, including AMNESTY for their actions after they leave office, is a common occurrence in countries facing activist militaries.[43]

A different type of coup took place in Turkey in February 1997, when the military "encouraged" the resignation of Islamist prime minister Necemettin Erbakan. The prime minister had ruffled many feathers during his tenure, with perceived overtures to Iran, Iraq, and Syria, hosting Islamic shaikhs at his formal residence during the Muslim holy month of Ramadan, and (unsuccessfully) attempting to end the ban on headscarves. After seemingly flagrant Islamic activities in a small town near Ankara marking "Jerusalem night," the military presented Erbakan a list of measures to limit Islamic expression in Turkey, including the closure of intermediate-level religious schools, to which he eventually signed his name. One military officer even called the prime minister "a pimp" for going on the pilgrimage to Mecca as a guest of Saudi Arabia. When Erbakan urged sanctions against the officer, the military refused.[44]

Even in the absence of outright military rule, there are circumstances when militaries wield a tremendous amount of influence, even in the selection of the prime minister or other executives of government. Such persuasion is often made in threats not to support or protect a leader if he violates the wishes of the military. The term PRAETORIANISM is used to characterize states where civilian authorities face such intimidation. Some more simply call it blackmail. The concept derives from the praetorian guards who protected the Roman emperor. Often they would threaten to withdraw their crucial support if they did not get to choose who would be in power. Similarly, through their threats of vetoes and departure, militaries can shape policy.

Unlike most of its neighbors, Mexico has succeeded in establishing an unwritten deal between civilian and military leaders, as long as the military polices itself for human rights abuses and stays out of politics. However, Mexico had a long tradition of military intervention in politics; much of the nineteenth century was known as the age of CAUDILLOS. After the Mexican Revolution, several military figures vied for power. From 1917 through the 1930s, citizen-soldiers ruled, as all of Mexico's presidents during that period had started their careers as officers in the revolutionary army. The military continued to play a very important role in the Institutional Revolutionary Party (PRI) and therefore the government throughout the 1930s. By the early 1940s President Lazaro Cárdenas began to demilitarize politics by dramatically reducing military expenditures and limiting the military's representation in the party. Since 1943, candidates for president have been automatically disqualified if they had a military background. Over time, the military was pushed to the margins of decisionmaking in Mexico, and unlike armed forces elsewhere, the Mexican military has never since been able to exploit periods of crisis to expand its influence. Most analysts do not consider the military to be an independent political "wild card" in the way that it is in other countries. It is possible that continued instability in Mexico could draw the military into the political arena, but for sixty years the state has been largely under the control of civilians.[45]

In many countries of the third world, militaries have a mixed record of achievements and failures. They have been good at providing order and economic growth. Yet they have also racked up a miserable record of human rights protection, especially in circumstances where they rule outright or where they are temporarily installed as an interim government. Some military regimes are characterized as caretaker governments, preoccupied with law and order and

Figure 12.6 Argentina's "Dirty War" (1976–1983)

In a frightening display of military might, the Argentine military junta that took power in 1976 launched a devastating attack against "leftist terrorists" and other perceived enemies of the regime. During the junta's seven-year reign, 10,000–30,000 people were "disappeared." Its criteria for "known terrorists" continuously broadened, eventually including journalists, politicians, priests, nuns, actors, and teachers. In an attempt to maintain their international reputation, junta leaders—many of whom had been schooled in U.S.-led communist counterinsurgency programs—tried to keep the abductions quiet. People from all walks of Argentine life suddenly were "disappeared" in the middle of the night, without any official record. Some were put in secret jails, others were buried in mass graves, and still others were drugged and forced to walk off the planks of ships. Yet some refused to remain silent: the fourteen women who marched on the Plaza de Mayo in Buenos Aires in 1977, known as the "Mothers of the Plaza," were later followed by the "Grandmothers of the Plaza." Many continue their weekly pilgrimage to bring attention to the disasters brought to their society by the Argentine military coup.

less concerned with implementing social changes. Corrective regimes attempt to create a national identity and promote orderly economic development. Most Nigerian military regimes in the 1980s and 1990s fit this category. Revolutionary military regimes promote the most radical changes of all, highlighting dramatic land reform that is never fully implemented.

Rape has been used as a deliberate military tactic, especially within the strategy of ethnic cleansing, but in other forms of violent warfare as well. It has been common in Rwanda, Kuwait, Haiti, and Colombia, among other wars. Women and girls are frequently victims of gang rape committed by soldiers. The Khomeini regime in Iran set up so-called residential units to suppress female dissidents. The elite Revolutionary Guard used these outposts to continuously rape women who refused to submit to the regime.[46] Rape has also been used as a form of genocide, as male soldiers and paramilitaries have been ordered or allowed to impregnate "enemy" women. Sexual assault has long been part of a purposive strategy to sever women's ties to the community and to strip them of their dignity and pride. Because it so often leads to the ostracism of these women, rape has been likened it to "genocide in slow motion." These trends point to the overall sexualization of war in the modern world.[47]

One example of an entrenched, long-running military government is that of Myanmar, ruled by the military since 1962. In the late 1950s, the Burmese army gained prestige and importance during the country's struggle for independence. In fact, prior to the beginning of its latest crackdown in the late 1980s, it was the police, not the military, who were the most hated institution in the country. But that changed when the military brutally suppressed popular demonstrations against its rule in 1988. Most estimates claim that 3,000–8,000 people were killed in this assault. Popular disgust with the army increased after it was overwhelmingly defeated by the National League for Democracy in the 1990 elections and refused to step aside. The leader of this political party, Aung San Suu Kyi, served most of the 1990s under house arrest. In the face of widespread distrust, the army has virtually doubled in size since 1989. In 1997 the ruling junta changed its name from the State Law and Order Restoration Council to the State Peace and Development Council, reiterating its oft-stated pledge to restore democracy. Few jumped at the pronouncement, which has shown little likelihood of becoming a reality. In a small stride toward normalcy, though, in the summer of 2000 universities, which were closed for approximately twelve years, were permitted to reopen.

In many countries, regular military units are declining in numbers, prestige, and the support they receive. Some cannot escape their tarnished reputation; others appear to be bureaucratic beasts lumbering over sick economies. They are being replaced, especially in areas of conflict, by paramilitary units, or relatively autonomous armed groups often in charge of security for an individual person, political party, or institution. To avoid the stigma of the appearance of military rule, some governments are turning to civilian militias to handle their security tasks. These can sometimes be virtual death squads, as we have seen in both Rwanda and East Timor. Their funding comes from the government (although often through covert channels) and they usually report directly to military officials. In some cases, including Colombia, paramilitaries are made up of off-duty soldiers and policemen hoping to pocket some extra cash. Paramilitary units are often launched in an attempt by governments to wash their hands of violent acts.[48] Mexican paramilitary units have been used in Chiapas to try to deflect the blame from the state military. Similarly, in the early 1980s, China created the PAP, a unit that surged in growth after the crackdown on students in Tiananmen Square in 1989. The PAP, unlike the regular police force in China, is fully armed—it guards government offices, patrols borders, and quells riots and uprisings.

The power of military units can become extremely dangerous in transitional circumstances, such as after the fall of powerful leaders or a change in power, as rogue groups, still possessing weaponry and the desire for influence, attempt to maintain their power and voice. In Indonesia, a paramilitary group formed from former police cadets who failed the four-year officer course. Some believe this unit—named Gunung Tidur—was responsible for a fatal series of fires during the May 1998 riots that led to Suharto's downfall.[49] Retired generals, upset at their loss of prestige and patronage, were also blamed for bombing a mosque outside of Jakarta in 1999.[50] Similar episodes have been reported in Tajikistan, Nigeria, and elsewhere. In Nigeria, it is believed that a paramilitary group was behind the late 2001 assassination of a high-ranking official close to Olusegun Obasanjo.

One case in which the power of militias was highlighted was the chaos following the positive referendum on independence in East Timor in 1999. Violence between rival civilian groups, mostly instigated by the government-backed militias, claimed the lives of thousands and destroyed much of the region. The problem continues in West Timor, where tens of thousands of refugees remained for over a year after the referendum. Militias in West Timor continued to intimidate the refugees to keep them from returning to the independent East Timor. As one scholar put it, once the refugees depart, the militias no longer have a reason for existence—they provide job security to a group hungry for employment.[51] The increased numbers of people fleeing sectarian violence in the Molucca Islands exacerbated the refugee crisis, where clashes between Christians and Muslims have claimed thousands of lives.

In addition to traditional government militaries and militia groups, privately employed soldiers, or mercenaries, play an important role in wars in the third world. Mercenaries are as old as war itself, but in today's world their recruitment, deployment, and action is a multimillion-dollar business. Often, these soldiers-for-hire travel from country to country to earn a financial profit. For example, Serb and Ukrainian soldiers trained fighters in Zaire. In fact, foreign mercenaries fueled both sides of the conflict in the Congo. In the Congo and Angola, over eighty companies were used to funnel soldiers into the battlefield. The most famous is the South African–based company Executive Outcomes, which was hired to provide fighters in both Angola and Sierra Leone to guard mines that are the source of "conflict diamonds," precious jewels that are illegally sold on the regular market and used to finance conflict. The government of South Africa has attempted to pass legislation making it illegal for citizens to fight as mercenaries in other countries. Of course, it is not an issue confined to Africa; in Colombia, British Petroleum hired a battalion of soldiers to protect its interests, and mercenaries have been hired to protect Firestone's rubber plants as well. Mercenaries have also been active in a separatist conflict that has been fought in Papua New Guinea since the late 1980s. To put down the insurrection, the Papuan government hired soldiers, euphemistically called "military advisers," from the Bahamas-based corporation Sandline.

Governments may possess a monopoly over the right to use force—which states use both to change circumstances and to promote the status quo—but by no means are they the only promoters of violent change. We now turn our attention to some other groups that advocate or promote aggression to achieve their cause.

Terrorists

Who are terrorists? In the mid-1970s, terrorist expert Frederick Hacker argued that terrorists are usually characterized as criminals, crazies, or crusaders, and that sometimes they are characterized as all three.[52] As we discussed at the beginning of this chapter, labeling individuals or groups as terrorists can be fraught with difficulty and inaccuracies. Why do people turn to tactics that target civilians? Some trace it to feelings of hopelessness, or the belief that there is no other avenue through which they can express their opinion. Terrorism often involves groups who are struggling for resources. In fact, it has been argued that terrorism takes place because modern war, which requires large militaries, advanced weaponry, and the like, has become a luxury tool of rich countries. All in all, terrorism can be a monetarily cheaper alternative to conventional warfare, and yet, due to its ability to fester fear and insecurity, it can be extremely effective in achieving political objectives. Many different types of terrorist groups can be identified. Terrorists may be associated with political revolutionary movements (including the famed "Carlos the Jackal"), national liberation (or separatist) causes (such as the Philippines' Abu Sayyaf and Mexico's Zapatistas), or single-issue campaigns (such as the Animal Liberation Front). Such groups are found along all points of the ideological spectrum, but tend to

Figure 12.7   Peru's Shining Path

A political movement on the extreme left, Shining Path became notorious for its brutality. As a result, it is without equal in Latin America in terms of its use of violence. At the center of the organization was Abimael Guzmán, a professor of philosophy at the University of San Cristóbal de Huamanga. Under the nom de guerre "President Gonzalo," Guzmán led what he viewed as a revolutionary war to delegitimize the Peruvian government. To accomplish this, Shining Path adopted a campaign of sabotage, harassment, intimidation, and assassination. Because of its use of unconventional tactics and the cold-blooded nature of their execution, Shining Path is widely recognized as a terrorist organization. Inasmuch as this might be a valid characterization, the label was used to justify the Peruvian government's own use of terror in fighting terrorists. Ironically, the government's repressive policies created the very conditions the rebels claimed they were fighting—playing into the hands of Shining Path.

congregate especially on the extreme left (e.g., Peru's Shining Path) and the extreme right (e.g., Al-Qaida).

Terrorist violence is used in many kinds of political activity. Some distinguish forms of terror by categorizing the targets of such activity. Domestic terrorism is used to delineate those terror acts that are based in a single country without significant support from outside sources. Actions by the Free Aceh movement in Indonesia would qualify as ethnonationalist domestic terrorism. The 1996 attack on the Japanese embassy in Lima, staged by the Marxist Túpac Amaru Revolutionary Movement (MRTA), is another example.

Although Shining Path has received the lion's share of attention, the MRTA—sometimes called "Shining Path Lite"—captured world attention in 1996.[53] Claiming they were fighting for democracy and on behalf of the poor, fourteen MRTA fighters (many of them in their teens) made international headlines when they took 500 members of Peru's elite hostage at a cocktail party at the Japanese ambassador's residence in Lima. The rebels released most of the hostages, but kept seventy-two people for months of negotiations until in an equally stunning raid on April 22, 1997, Peruvian commandos stormed the residence, successfully ending the siege. According to some of the former hostages, the young kidnappers attempted to surrender but were executed on the spot—a charge the Fujimori government denied. Since the raid the movement appears to have been significantly weakened; one of its most important leaders was killed in the fracas and nearly all the armed rebels associated with the group were rounded up and imprisoned shortly thereafter. Fujimori won international and domestic praise for his government's crackdown, although the record of abuse and torture is only now beginning to emerge. Its methods included killing entire families and torturing acquaintances in order to get a targeted rebel. If the allegations ring true—over 4,000 tortured and killed in the 1990s alone—Fujimori will be placed among the region's worst human rights abusers.

In contrast, international terrorism includes terror activity that is not limited to one state. The deep pockets of international terror networks reach into many different societies as a way of evading detection—transferring funds through the use of promissory notes or other underground methods that require minimal paperwork and are therefore difficult to trace. It's not all about unmarked Swiss bank accounts, either. One arrangement is known as *hawala*—which is Hindi for "in trust." This system allows people working in one country to deposit payments (often in currency or gold) in a local office, so that a third party can have virtually instantaneous access to the money in another country, in a paperless transaction that is conducted through phone calls and e-mails.[54] Some have described it as the Western Union of the non-Western world.[55] Based in the United Arab Emirates, *hawala* offices are found throughout the Middle East, North Africa, and Asia. Some banks operating under this system have been accused of funneling profits from customers' fees to terrorist leaders, including Osama bin Laden and other high-ranking members of Al-Qaida.

Prior to September 2001, few Americans had heard of Al-Qaida (meaning "The Base"), even though many were familiar with the name of its leader, Saudi fugitive Osama bin Laden. Al-Qaida, formed in 1988, is a deeply embedded international network of terrorists based in many countries, supporting extremist Muslim fighters in conflicts around the world, including Chechnya, Tajikistan, Kashmir, and Yemen. But as we have learned since mid-2001, many Al-Qaida operatives live and work in other countries around the world, with significant bases in Germany, the Philippines, Pakistan, and the United States, among others. Some of the stated goals of this network include the overthrow of nearly all conservative Muslim governments, to be replaced by a more virulent form of Islamic governance and to drive Western influence from the Muslim world, especially the U.S. presence in Saudi Arabia. Even though Al-Qaida members often mention freedom for the Palestinians in their rhetoric, it seems to always take a back seat to their other concerns. In addition to funding its own terrorist activities, Al-Qaida is believed to be the premier funding source for Islamic extremist activities in the world. In 1996, bin Laden publicly issued his "Declaration of War" against the United States, which he and other members of Al-Qaida view as the chief obstacle to change in Muslim societies. It is important to note that while bin Laden and this group claim to speak on behalf of Muslims around the world, Muslims have nearly universally denounced their calls for violence and extremism, before and after September 11.

Terrorist groups combine multiple grievances to craft their own unique expression of rage against the status quo. These groups often present a combination of ideologies and demands and then fit their actions to their strengths and circumstances. For example, Uganda's Lord's Resistance Army formed in the 1980s, following the "Holy Spirit Revolt Movement," led by then twenty-eight-year-old cult leader Alice Lakwena, and later by her cousin, Joseph Kony, a former Catholic choirboy who is said to be possessed by spirits. First Lakwena (from the mid-1980s) and then Kony (from the late 1980s) promoted the proliferation of gangs, murderers, rapists, and sheer terror, especially in northern Uganda. They fought the Ugandan army, telling young recruits to smear botanical shea butter on their bodies to repel bullets and to sing Christian hymns as they march straight toward the enemy. They also told recruits that the rocks they threw at soldiers would turn into grenades. After suppression by the Ugandan army, Lakwena fled to Kenya, where she was imprisoned until 1987. The LRA aims to re-create the kingdom of God and establish a state based on the Ten Commandments. In addition to Christian precepts, the group incorporated both aspects of indigenous religions and minor tenets of Islam—Kony announced that Fridays would be a second sabbath, largely as a way to appease his financial sponsors in Khartoum, Sudan. Sudan's sponsorship of this group is largely designed to counter Uganda's support of separatists in southern Sudan. Some of the LRA's more unusual tenets though, including the ban on eating the meat of a white-feathered chicken or riding a bike—a primary form of transportation in Uganda—cannot accurately be traced to any of these belief systems. Kony claims that he is instructed by God, and that the LRA is very strict about enforcement: one man was killed for violating the bike ban. LRA soldiers forced his wife to eat one of the man's feet or be killed. LRA agents are famous for abducting many young teens: UNICEF estimates that the group has taken in as many as 10,000 boys and girls. Not surprisingly, the LRA does not receive much support from the local population, but the Ugandan army has been unable to put down the resistance for over ten years.[56]

Even though terrorism by independent groups is most common, terrorist methods are also advocated by clandestine agents of governments, through government-sponsored or -supported groups designed to intimidate and repress individuals and groups within society. They often use death squads to threaten and eliminate their enemies. States risk being ostracized by the international community as they engage in terrorist acts; however, this is a gamble that some are willing to take. Increasingly, even if groups are not acting on the orders of a government, they are often acting with its support (ideologically and oftentimes financially), giving rise to the term STATE-SPONSORED TERRORISM. Because of the passion groups are able to drum up for their causes, attempts to isolate state-sponsored terrorists have been incomplete at best.

There is a growing list of known governments that are active in supporting groups beyond their shores: the usual suspects include Iran, Iraq, Cuba, Libya, Sudan, North Korea, and Syria. Cuba, Yemen, and North Korea, who have been accused of providing safe haven to hunted terrorists. With the insecurity that follows in the wake of terror attacks, it is tempting to divide the world in two, placing countries that cooperate with the U.S.-led "war on terror" on one side and those that do not on the other. As we discuss in Chapter 19, the BUSH DOCTRINE implicates any country that supports terrorists as terrorists themselves. Such clarity, though, can be misleading. True, there are some countries that invoke sovereignty—the right to control what happens within one's borders—and argue that they will not cooperate in this war on terror, which they claim is just another attempt by the United States to impose its will on others. Yet there are other countries, including the Philippines and Somalia, that are plagued by weak governments and cannot control their own territory; therefore their assistance would be impotent at best.

Iran is viewed in the West as a large-scale sponsor of terror violence—a charge that leaders in Tehran vehemently deny. The country is suspected of having committed or sponsored assassinations in northern Iraq, attacks against the Kurdish Democratic Party of Iran, and other policies of liquidating the regime's opponents who live outside the country. Iran also stirs the coals with neighbor-

Figure 12.8   The Israeli-Palestinian Conflict

Perhaps few situations are more enduring than the ongoing conflict between Arab Palestinians and the Israeli government. This dispute has been the source of five major wars, and it has contributed to numerous other regional upheavals, claiming thousands of lives—including children, teenagers, and entire families. The outbreak of conflict, especially following the 1967 Six-Day War, has created millions of Palestinian refugees, scattered across multiple states and refugee centers in the region. Terrorist violence has marred all sides in this clash, rife with border disputes, intense religious symbolism, and security concerns. It seems no one's hands are clean—but each side claims it has been provoked by the other, and both the Israeli government and the Palestinian Authority claim that the injustices of the situation make it difficult for them to control those under their rule. In fact, one of the dangerous turns in the dispute has been the willingness of individuals to take actions into their own hands, sometimes wrapping themselves in nail-studded explosives and taking their own lives—along with the lives of many others—in crowded urban areas. In early 2002, Wafa Idris, a volunteer medic with the Palestine Red Crescent Society, was identified as the first female suicide bomber to attack Israel within its borders (she has since been followed by several more). Some noted the irony that one who devoted so much time to preserving life would take her own, but others spoke of the anger she exhibited after attempting to medically respond to so many who had been injured during the uprising against Israel.[57] While police attacks and the bulldozing of homes have been commonplace on the Israeli side, suicide bombings have proven to be a weapon of choice for some Palestinians—even though Palestine Liberation Organization (PLO) president Yasir Arafat formally renounced terrorism and suicide attacks in 1988.

ing Iraq by providing safe haven to some PKK operatives. Following the attacks of September 11, the United States argued that it would welcome Iran's support in the war on terror if it withdrew support from perceived terror groups. In fact, the United States needed the support of Iran to avoid the appearance that the war in Afghanistan was a war against Islam. Sudan has condoned many activities of Iran, and has also shown increased cooperation with Iraq. Yet we contend that its most serious ties to terrorism are domestic—including attacks against its own people in southern Sudan. Libya has been accused of being an active sponsor of terror since the early 1970s. Once behind the wheel of government, Colonel Muammar Qaddafi's goal was to launch an Arab-Islamic revolution, for which he trained thousands of foreign terrorists each year in Libyan camps. Among the most famous was Carlos Ramirez Santos, also known as "Carlos the Jackal," who operated on behalf of Libya, Syria, and Iraq until his extradition from Sudan and deportation to France in 1997.

Yet as we have discussed before, the view from within each of these countries diverges from the account we are familiar with in the West. Remember that groups engage in violent actions because they believe it is the best way—and sometimes the only way—to be heard. Although Sudan has been accused of assisting or planning much terror activity in the West, the Sudanese leaders and citizens alike contend that they have suffered at the hands of Western terrorism as well. Public sentiment in Sudan turned strongly against the West after the

1998 U.S. bombing of the only medicine factory in the country following the Al-Qaida attacks on U.S. embassies in Kenya and Tanzania. Many international organizations (including the United Nations) and leaders in both the Western and the non-Western world have challenged the evidence that was used to justify the attack on this factory, which the Clinton administration argued was being used to produce chemical weapons. UN analyses of the wreckage and the soil around it found no signs of chemical weapons production. Many people, not just in the third world, considered the timing of this attack—the week of the president's appearance before a grand jury—as an attempt to divert attention away from Clinton's own political difficulties. This prompted many to compare the saga with the movie *Wag the Dog,* which had coincidentally been released at almost the same time.

Another way to categorize types of terrorism is by focusing on the tools used to provoke fear or cause damage. While nuclear weapons and their delivery tend to be cost-prohibitive and technologically problematic for many countries of the world, bioterrorism is more within their reach. This leads some to refer to biological and chemical weapons as the "poor man's nuclear bomb" and "the great equalizer." Biological weapons, including anthrax, the plague, and smallpox, are viewed as an ideal tool for many terrorists today because their effects

A UN weapons inspector in Iraq takes a sample of nerve agent from a container (UN Photo)

take days to appear, making an elusive escape more likely. Yet it can be extremely difficult to contain any outbreak resulting from a biological attack, meaning that the perpetrators may themselves be harmed as well. Such weapons remain dangerous because of their availability and potency: small amounts can wreck havoc on large groups of people. They have already been used as weapons of mass destruction—most destructively by Saddam Hussein's forces against the Kurds in Iraq. Iran, victimized by Iraq's use of chemical weapons during their war in the 1980s, is also known to be producing (or preparing to produce) biological and chemical weapons.

Chemical weapons, in the form of mustard gas, tabun, sarin, and VX, are believed to be the easiest-made weapons of mass destruction. Their ingredients, including pesticides and fertilizers, are readily available. The main difficulty in their deployment comes in the delivery of the agents, because in most cases they must be miniaturized in order to be potently delivered. Most of the seven countries included in the U.S. State Department's list of state sponsors of international terrorism (Iran, Iraq, Syria, Libya, Cuba, North Korea, and Sudan) are known to possess chemical weapons.[58] Perhaps Western countries are not in the best position to condemn such action, though, as the United States and Russia possess the two largest stockpiles of chemical and biological weapons in the world. In fact, the scourge of these terror agents was introduced by the Western powers, which used them widely in World War I and in the Vietnam War.

Even if complete nuclear weapons may be out of reach for many states, some believe the world faces an increased threat of nuclear terrorism due to the quantity of materials relatively unaccounted for—including plutonium and highly enriched uranium. Even if an individual cannot piece together enough material to build a nuclear bomb, it is believed that a group could still build such a device—widely referred to as a "dirty bomb"—to spread radiological contamination. Widespread destruction can be achieved by wrapping radioactive material (including spent fuel rods) around conventional explosives. Once detonated, in the form of a car bomb, suitcase nuke, or other device, the intense radiation will be far more destructive than the blast itself. As of yet, there are unconfirmed suspicions that Iran received or smuggled nuclear materials out of the Soviet Union. It is extremely difficult to know if Al-Qaida or other known terror groups have access to such materials, although it is highly plausible.

Figure 12.9 Narcoterrorism

The idea of narcoterrorism captures the symbiotic relationship between drug cartels and terrorists that began in the 1970s. Many terrorist groups, including the Sunni Taliban regime, which formerly ruled Afghanistan, and some extreme Shiite groups in Lebanon, are believed to have financed their operations from the sale of illicit drugs, especially opium.[59] Shining Path agents are known to offer protection to local peasants and coca growers. So-called taxes on coca growers and levies on traffickers' flights out of the region have been a primary source of revenue for Shining Path, whose income is estimated to range between $10 million and $100 million a year.[60]

Revolutionaries

We opened this chapter with a quotation from one of China's great revolutionaries, Mao Zedong, who emphasized the violence and uprootedness of revolutions. To elaborate on Mao's famous prose, a REVOLUTION may be defined as a change in regime, with the desire to achieve extensive, relatively quick, and often concurrent changes in economic, political, and social structures. Even though many countries claim to hold a revolutionary heritage, if we adopt the conventional definition of revolutions as fundamental transformations in everyday way of life, they are actually fairly rare events. The classic revolutionary states, in which such dramatic changes were implemented, are China, France, and Russia.[61] Revolutions such as these are unlike other changes of power because their goal is to destroy the existing system, often through the use of charisma and violence. In the Chinese and French revolutions, for example, people even changed their names and ways of referring to others. Following China's 1949 revolution, it was common for people to refer to each other by the egalitarian "comrade" rather than by surname or title.

That being said, there have been many attempts to promote revolutions and revolutionary change beyond the three traditional "grand" revolutions. Many countries in the third world claim a revolutionary heritage, including Iran, Mexico, Turkey, Cuba, Peru, and Zimbabwe. Revolutions are often launched from remote regions where governmental groups have less control, and their leaders build their power base through ideological persuasion. Those at the forefront of the revolutionary effort often employ guerrilla tactics, especially the element of surprise, such as the Zapatistas marching into San Cristobal unexpectedly on New Year's Day 1994. In a nutshell, revolutions are about change.

Revolutions bring new people to power, incorporating groups such as peasants and workers who were otherwise left out of the process. In this sense, they attempt to "liberate" people—a term that is commonly associated with revolutionary endeavors. Many revolutions are class-based, arising from structural changes that pit one group of people against another. Revolutions can also be born of crises manifested in territorial expansion, economic reorganization, international dislocation, or population expansion. Situations ripe for revolution include those with widespread misery, oppression, and injustice, combined with either a weak government that is unable to solve problems facing it or a significant crisis. In these situations, when "push comes to shove," groups who perceive themselves on the losing end of the bargain concentrate their resources and attempt to overthrow the oppressive system. In revolutionary situations, groups demand some role in decisionmaking, whether facing down military rulers in Mexico, Bolivia, or Cuba; colonial regimes, such as Vietnam and Algeria; or monarchies, such as imperial China and Russia. In each of these cases, the entrenched elite was unable (or unwilling) to incorporate the new voices without a fight. Revolutions can also follow the collapse of an empire or regime, as happened with the collapse of the Qing Dynasty in China, the Ottoman Empire in Turkey, and the Qajar Empire in Iran (then known as Persia). A crisis situation unites otherwise disconnected groups to rebel against the status quo and claim power. Successful revolutions often coalesce around a single leader (or small group of leaders) who is able to harness discord into a potent political force.

Sometimes leaders of revolutions are (or become) military leaders as well, including Turkey's Mustafa Kemal Atatürk, Burkina Faso's Thomas Sankara, and Algeria's Houari Boumedienne. Yet not all revolutionary leaders have a military background: Iran's Ayatollah Khomeini was a religious leader, China's Mao Zedong was a librarian, Guinea Bissau's Amilcar Cabral was a census taker, and most people believe that the Zapatista's Subcomandante Marcos was once a professor. Revolutionary leaders tend to have charisma and they come from the relatively privileged classes—many were leaders of the intelligentsia, among the most educated members of society, who are accustomed to having their say. Yet the harbingers of revolutionary movements often suffered some sort of major setback, experiencing failed expectations or suffering from the aspiration gap we discussed above. Many leaders of revolutions faced a tumultuous history in their own countries—difficulties they often rectify with a vengeance against their former suppressers.

For example, Khomeini was exiled to Iraq from 1964 to 1968 for criticizing the Shah and allegedly sparking riots. He was later evicted from the Shiite holy city of An Najaf, by Saddam Hussein. Khomeini viewed himself as uniquely fit to avenge the problems of the West, especially the humiliations wrought on Muslims in the Middle East. Following his victorious return to Iran in 1979— after mass protests against the Shah's regime had long festered—he quickly acted on these ambitions, transforming the Iranian Revolution into an Islamic Revolution.[62] Mustafa Kemal Atatürk, leader of the 1919 Turkish Revolution, also viewed himself as distinctively able to lead his country down a new path. The difference in their approach was the role of religion in the revolution: Khomeini believed an orthodox version of Islam and a rejection of all things Western was the best corrective to Iran's problems, while Atatürk prescribed an unyielding form of secularism to overcome Turkey's challenges. Both rode the rising wave of NATIONALISM in their respective societies.

Another revolutionary who capitalized on nationalist themes was Ho Chi Minh, leader of the modern revolution in Vietnam, whose name means "Bringer of Light." At the end of World War I, when he was a student in France, Ho approached President Woodrow Wilson with the hope that Wilson's doctrine of self-determination would be applied to Vietnam. Wilson turned Ho away. Ho later founded the Viet Minh, an acronym for the Vietnam Independence League, but died before his dream of a unified North and South Vietnam was realized, at tremendous cost. Affectionately known by many Vietnamese as "Uncle Ho," he repelled French attempts to regain their Asian empire in the 1950s, and later frustrated U.S. attempts to defeat them in the 1960s and 1970s.

Some revolutionary leaders are already incumbent rulers who overthrow their fellow leaders to establish a new governing system. The Turkish Revolution of 1919 is one such example. Some have called it an ELITE REVOLUTION, or a revolution from above—defined by the swift overthrow of the elite by other members of the elite, limited mass participation, and limited violence.[63] Ellen Trimberger argues that the specific characteristics of elite revolutions, especially their restrictions on the involvement of the masses, can lead to situations in which the military may regularly intervene, which certainly holds true for the coup-riddled experience of Turkey.[64] The Peruvian revolution by coup, led by General Juan Velasco Alvarado, may also be described as a revolution from above. Despite these examples of elite revolutions, it is important to note that most are made "from below," incorporating the masses or other disenfranchised groups in an overthrow of the power structure. In fact, the Velasco revolution failed in part because it didn't incorporate the participation of other groups, including the people it meant to serve—the peasants.

Women have been active participants in revolutionary struggles and wars: harboring rebels, moving weapons and intelligence around the country and through war zones, staffing health organizations, and carrying the rifle. Women served key roles in revolutions in Nicaragua, Palestine, South Africa, Zimbabwe, Mexico, and the Philippines. In the Philippine Revolution of 1896–1902, known as the first anticolonial independence movement in Asia, women gained prominence. As one example, Teresa Magbanua was known as the Filipina "Joan of Arc" for her battles against the Spaniards in the late 1800s. In the Mexican Revolution, both Emiliano Zapata's and Pancho Villa's armies included women revolutionaries, called *soldaderas*. They were originally camp followers who fed soldiers and provided services that the government did not. Gertrudis Bocanegra organized an army of women during the Mexican War of Independence in 1810: she died in 1817 after being arrested and tortured. Women often organized their own units, armed themselves, and fought as soldiers equal to the men. In unprecedented numbers, women participated in every aspect of the anti-Somoza effort in Nicaragua; in fact, they made up 30 percent of the Sandinista army and occupied important leadership positions, commanding full battalions. They were mostly young women, and the men with whom they shared units appeared for the most part to accept them. But after the revolution, women were largely ignored, even betrayed by the Sandinistas.[65] And although there were female soldiers in Namibia, women never rose to officer status. In Namibia and Zimbabwe female soldiers were often stigmatized after the war for being "mannish" by carrying guns. When Sam Nujoma thanked the Namibian people for their contribution to the country's liberation, he mentioned women specifically but did not recognize them as fighters.

Despite proclamations of great change, revolutions fade away—they are difficult to sustain for very long. Revolutions require resources (personnel, coercion, money), energy (charismatic leaders and committed followers), and a level of ideological zeal and commitment that few societies can maintain for very long, much to the chagrin of both those who led the revolution and those who suffered losses during it. China's Cultural Revolution is the best example of one leader's attempt to literally "continue the revolution" and maintain its legacy.

Terror often plays a large role in revolutions and revolutionary societies. Because revolutions attempt to achieve dramatic changes, there is little room for dissent or discussion. As with much violent conflict, clear sides are chosen by combatants and bystanders alike. Individuals and groups who are viewed to be against the regime are labeled "counterrevolutionaries," a charge that carries great danger, often tantamount to a death sentence. Especially after it is perceived that there has been some setback to revolutionary progress, terror methods, including torture, isolation, and forced labor, are commonly employed as a means of holding on to power and keeping the revolution alive. For example, resisters and suspected police informants in South Africa were subjected to "necklacing," in which a flammable, long-burning automobile tire was placed around their necks, and they were doused with fuel and burned to death. Campaigns promote insecurity, as new enemies are defined in rapid and often changing succession. With crackdowns on the press, harassment and imprisonment of opponents and their supporters, and calls for land invasions, Mugabe was an example of this as he headed into the 2002 elections.

One of the most problematic legacies of revolutions is the selection of leadership beyond the revolutionary generation. Succession is an issue in many countries of the non-Western world, but especially those with a revolutionary heritage. Leadership transition in nondemocratic states is rarely orderly. Leaders tend to seek to rule for life, and few mechanisms are put in place to choose their replacements until a crisis precipitates change—which means that leadership turnover happens during times of instability. Plato predicted that such circumstances, often deriving from chaotic mass rule, produce authoritarian despots. Deng Xiaoping's death in 1997 passed with barely a hiccup, because Jiang Zemin had been given almost eight years at the helm under Deng's steady hand and continued hold on (informal) power. The formal transfer of power from Jiang Zemin to Hu Jintao in 2002–2003 was similar in some ways, masking the fact that Jiang still controlled the reins, albeit from behind the scenes. Even though the titles of leadership were conferred to Hu Jintao, the leader of China's so-called fourth generation, analysts agree that Jiang and his protégés continued to exercise real power. Many express uncertainty about life in Cuba after Fidel Castro, and his uncharismatic brother Raul is often discussed as the leader in waiting. Even though there was plenty of worry in South Africa as Nelson Mandela neared retirement, the country has remained more stable than many feared, although the African National Congress (ANC) has taken a noticeable slide in the polls.

Do revolutions often accomplish what their leaders set out to achieve? Since revolutions claim to promote fundamental transformations in power relations, it is important to assess their gains. Few revolutions are total failures, but few accomplish most of their explicit goals, either. In the early years of a revolution, it is common to observe significant attempts at land distribution and social change, employing at least the rhetoric, if not the reality, of equality. Castro, for example, appeared to have taken on *machismo* with laws requiring men to pitch in with domestic responsibilities—but the laws were rarely enforced. Most revolutions also produce at least some form of leadership change, sometimes replacing tyrannical leaders, at times swapping them with more despotic individuals.[66] The ruling groups in power after the revolution rarely deliver on the grand pledges used to mobilize people to join the revolution.

Social stratification is rarely decreased in postrevolutionary societies—rather, the bureaucratic malaise and the expansion of state power that tends to follow revolutionary conflict often increase the gap between rich and poor.[67] Revolutions in the third world have an especially poor record of promoting equality and increased freedom, even if there was actually some redistribution of wealth or land reform, such as in China and Cuba. In China, Cuba, and

Nicaragua, one form of inequality was simply replaced with another, as the for-mer landlords became poor and party leaders became more comfortable. Pledges to promote sexual equality, as well, were often relegated to lower status after the revolution was won, leading many to argue that the goal had been formulated only to secure support of women in the revolutionary fight. In Namibia and Zimbabwe, the promises for gender equality were "postponed" in order to appease still-powerful traditional (patriarchal) interests that the vulnerable revo-lutionary governments needed as allies. In the dangerous attempt to create "new" societies and new cultural foundations, and to do this quickly, huge groups of people often get caught in the crossfire. Although the statistics remain hotly debated, it is estimated that 2–3 million people died during Pol Pot's dis-astrous communist revolution in Cambodia, and at least 1 million died during the revolutionary fervor in Vietnam. Mao Zedong went to the grave with many deaths on his shoulder: some estimate that as many as 60 million people died in China as a result of his rule.[68]

Due to these broken promises, postrevolutionary societies often face great difficulty dealing with the revolutionary heritage they inherit, and governing groups in these societies tend to be defensive and reactionary. For example, in Iran in 1981, two years after the Islamic Revolution, the government crushed the so-called Marxist mujahidin after they purportedly bombed the Islamic Republic's office in Tehran. The mujahidin had been part of the coalition that overthrew the Shah in the first place, but they quickly fell out of favor with Khomeini and his supporters. The new government executed 6,000 of its mem-bers and supporters, and thousands of ordinary people answered the virulent call to attack "enemies" of Islam. Training camps were established, including one camp in Tehran that was reserved for women trainees only.[69] Especially in Mexico, Cuba, Peru, and China, the complex legacy of the revolutionary leaders has proved a formidable challenge to the ruling regime that follows it, especially when groups ruling in the name of a revolutionary heritage seem to abandon prior goals and pledges.

To conclude our discussion of revolutions and revolutionary heritage, we compare two revolutions that continue to shape life in the third world. Both the 1979 Iranian Revolution and the 1949 Chinese Revolution were extremely pop-ular with the population. In China, this support was sustained, for the most part, until the crackdown on the students in 1989. In Iran, the "grand coalition" quickly collapsed. Even though it was estimated that approximately one-fifth of the Iranian population demonstrated against the regime of Mohammad Reza Shah Pahlavi in December 1979, the euphoria ended shortly after it toppled the Shah's regime.[70]

The execution of the 1979 Iranian Revolution was rapid, while the Chinese Revolution was drawn out over twenty-two years of warfare before the PRC was established in 1949. Both revolutions took time to consolidate. In fact, most issues in both societies today emanate from the struggle of trying to be "mod-ern" and relatively integrated without losing the hard-fought gains of the past. Both revolutions replaced imperial eras, even if there was a thirty-eight-year interim period in the case of China. The Iranian Revolution rid society of an unpopular monarch who had already once been deposed, ending 2,500 years of dynastic rule. In China, the Qing Dynasty had collapsed in 1911, but rival groups and factions, including political parties, warlords, and millennial cults, sparred over the country's future throughout most of the transition.

In their attempt to shoot the moon, revolutionaries sometimes create new problems for themselves and those who follow them. Leaders in both Iran and China, for example, realized that their calls for "revolutionary" families to have many children as a way of prolonging the revolutionary spoils soon created a painful drain on public resources. Mao encouraged population growth throughout the 1960s and early 1970s, yet mandated limits on family size in the late 1970s. In the 1980s Iran's population jumped from 34 million to more than 50 million. As a result, Iran has introduced one of the world's most comprehensive family-planning programs, making every form of birth control free of charge and requiring couples to pass a family planning course before they can legally marry. This initiative prompted Health Ministry officials to go door to door, with clerics issuing FATWAS to approve intrauterine devices and vasectomies.[71]

Both postrevolutionary societies are now evaluating the modernization of their regime and the ways that they can continue revolutionary rhetoric while reaching out to other countries. The Iranian Revolution is undergoing an "Islamic Reformation"—defining the proper relationship between Islam and the modern world.[72] Iran leads the Islamic world in this debate, publicly challenging precepts everywhere from the courtroom to editorial pages to the cinemas. And clerics convicted of taking the debate too far have become celebrities among the ordinary population. Ever since the death of Mao Zedong in 1976, Chinese leaders have rethought their revolutionary saga, once even stating that Mao was 80 percent correct and 20 percent wrong in his handling of Chinese affairs. After Deng Xiaoping pushed China to open its doors to the outside world, Chinese began to question their revolutionary rhetoric more than ever. Few communist cadres had considered rehearsing their memorization of Mao's quotations while sitting at a Starbucks or Kentucky Fried Chicken.

What was accomplished by these two revolutions, grand in scale if not in achievement? In both China and Iran, literacy rates increased dramatically, especially among the youth. Between 1970 and 1990, literacy in Iran topped 90 percent, even as the population itself had doubled.[73] China also achieved dramatic improvements in literacy and healthcare between the 1940s and the 1970s, especially in the countryside. Revolutions in both countries provoked fearful responses from nearby states. Turkey blames the rise of PKK terrorism and separatist claims on the Iranian Revolution, and many of China's Southeast Asian neighbors, led by Indonesia, formed the Association of Southeast Asian Nations (ASEAN) as a way of combating a possible domino effect of communism throughout the region. Obviously, new cadres of leadership entered the ranks in both countries as a result of their revolutions. As the postrevolutionary generation gives way to the post-postrevolutionary leadership, the combination of pragmatism with the revolutionary legacy that is used to justify their rule may become increasingly difficult.

Conclusions: Whither Violence?

Is the world more violent today? Those who argue that it is point to the end of the largest military buildup the world has ever seen, the Cold War, and the resulting widespread availability of weapons—to governments, individuals, and organized groups alike. They also find evidence in the renewal of latent issues, such as separatist movements and ethnic violence, that were earlier suppressed by totalitarian regimes—as we have witnessed in Yugoslavia, Congo, Nigeria, and Indonesia. There are those who maintain that the world today is no more violent than it used to be. They point to the violent nature of governments throughout time, the determination of violent revolutionaries and terrorists in other time periods, and highlight the current moves toward strengthening regional and international norms against the use of violence by governments and groups of people. It is up to you to weigh the evidence to decide: Do you think the turn of the twenty-first century is more or less violent than centuries before it?

As we have shown in this chapter, the use of violence as a means of implementing change is not always ideologically, religiously, or culturally based. Nor is it always the usual suspects ("criminals, crazies, or crusaders") who are the perpetrators of violence. State-sponsored violence, domestically and internationally, makes up a large proportion of violence in the world today, Western and non-Western alike. Our discussion has also highlighted that it is not only so-called extremists who engage in violent acts. Some groups and individuals feel that it is only through hostility and aggression that they can get the respect, attention, and credence they deserve.

On a concluding note, it is tempting when looking at these issues and actors to be reductionist: to claim that the tactics of revolutionaries, terrorists, and government fighters are evil, that actions are always based in fanaticism, or that violence is always irrational. One does not have to condone the use of violence to take such actors on their own terms and attempt to understand why they take the actions that they do.

While many see violent actions as the only way to solve a situation, it is difficult to make the transition beyond violence. The use of violence often, although by no means always, is self-perpetuating. People are forced to take sides, defining "enemy" groups and dehumanizing neighbors, colleagues, and fellow citizens. Following times of discord and disruption and attempts to move beyond it, there is a great sense that past "scores" need to be settled.

Linking Concepts and Cases

As we have discussed, violent expression can take many forms and derives from many different motivations. In what ways is conflict expressed differently in the countries that we are studying? What are the main sources of discord and how are they expressed? Do you observe any significant differences between the states that were established via revolutionary or liberation wars and those that were not? How do you think the power and role of the military in each of these states impacts the operation of government or the expression of dissenting opinion? What legacies of past conflict can you observe in these states at the beginning of the twenty-first century? Based on what you already know about each of these cases, what type of situation do you expect to find in each of these countries? For example, given what you learned about civil society in Chapter 10, what expectations do you hold for the expression of violence in each of these states?

Case Study: Mexico

As you will recall from Chapter 5, armed uprisings are central to much of Mexico's history. And Mexico is once again caught up in REVOLUTION— although this one is of a different type.[1] On New Year's Day 1994 in the relatively isolated southern state of Chiapas, the Zapatista National Liberation Army (EZLN) suddenly appeared on the international stage and declared war on the Mexican government.[2] Calling themselves the Zapatistas, these rebels took up the image of Emiliano Zapata, one of the fallen heroes of the Mexican Revolution. The Zapatistas claimed they were fighting "not to usurp power, but to exercise it," to restore the LEGITIMACY of the government and reassert the promises of the revolution against a seventy-year dictatorship led by a clique of traitors. The Zapatistas maintained and continue to maintain that their struggle adheres to the Constitution of 1917; they are fighting for justice and equality, work, land, housing, and other basic human needs, as well as freedom, DEMOCRACY, and peace. This constitution is their Magna Carta, and the most sacred part of it is Article 27, which guarantees land rights to the indigenous peoples of Mexico. The Zapatistas contend that their interest is not in creating an imagined utopia. Rather, they seek to restore the lost democratic agrarian ideal that

Zapata died for, which was betrayed by the Institutional Revolutionary Party (PRI).[3]

Instead of the stock vocabulary of most revolutionaries, the Zapatistas speak of Enlightenment values such as democracy, justice, and liberty. They call for a new political relationship between Mexicans and their government, one in which people exercise power through new types of political leadership, and new types of political parties. The revolutionaries argue that they are not advocating socialism, capitalism, social democracy, or any particular ideology. For the Zapatistas, a people's most fundamental right is the right to choose, to decide what form their government will take.[4]

But in Chiapas there have been no choices, since politics has long centered around a feudal relationship between wealthy local bosses who are pro-PRI and a majority poor (but heterogeneous) population. Inasmuch as the Zapatistas want to change that relationship, the PRI government joined local elites in trying to maintain the status quo. In response to this new and threatening "internal enemy," the government began a massive invasion of Chiapas. To destroy the nearly 3,000 EZLN fighters, the government initially sent in 60,000 soldiers (approximately one-third of the Mexican army). Although it claimed to be there to defend public order, the government has been accused of complicity in systematic, brutal persecution committed by paramilitary groups subordinate to and dependent on the PRI. These "armed groups" are composed of civilians willing to do the dirty work of suppression while settling other scores. Not only do they attack, rape, and murder people suspected to be Zapatista sympathizers, but there are religious and ethnic elements behind many attacks, as Catholics and evangelical Protestants have clashed. One of the worst atrocities was the 1997 massacre at an open-air Catholic church in Acteal. At Christmas in this place of sanctuary, progovernment paramilitaries killed forty-five people, mostly women and children.

Although the war has been enormously destructive for the people living in Chiapas, the Zapatistas have never posed a military threat to the government. Rather, they have been fighting a very different kind of war. Said to be the first insurgent group to understand and effectively use the power of the Internet, under the leadership of media GUERRILLA and poet Subcomandante Marcos, the Zapatistas have attracted world attention. In part this is due to the mystery surrounding Marcos, whose identity is unknown, always hidden behind a black ski mask. The most-wanted man in Mexico, his persona has become a catalyst for this new kind of revolution. Attracting more attention because he cannot be seen, Marcos has become an icon, considered by many to be the most extraordinary revolutionary figure since Che Guevara.[5]

Over a short period the Zapatistas have evolved from a guerrilla army into a nonviolent political movement pursuing a radical democratic dialogue. Early on in his administration President Vicente Fox boasted that he could solve the problem in Chiapas "in fifteen minutes." Many people scoffed at this bravado, noting that Fox didn't have a clue as to the complexity of the conflict. Yet Fox resuscitated the San Andres Accords, which served as the basis for a bill compared to the U.S. civil rights reforms of the 1960s. The Zapatistas very much wanted this bill to become a law. However, the president could not control the

Mexican Congress, which passed the bill in 2001—but only with last-minute changes that significantly watered down the reforms.[6]

Some expected the Zapatistas to lose their momentum, since the guerrillas had lost their main symbolic enemy with the transition to democracy. However, as far as many people are concerned, the struggle continues because the same groups are still in power.[7] Even on Fox's watch, tortures, rapes, disappearances, and murders continue in Mexico as they have for years—and for years police and soldiers have operated with impunity because the military polices itself. Although Fox promised to subject the security forces to greater scrutiny and to establish a TRUTH COMMISSION to investigate past abuses, he has since backed away from that pledge. One of the topics to be discussed if such a body were ever formed would be an event the government has never been willing to fully explain: the "Tlatelolco massacre," the shooting of hundreds of student demonstrators just before the Mexico City Olympics of 1968. The government has always claimed that students fired on the police; however, in 2002 this became more questionable as one of Mexico's leading newspapers published photographs, which had been hidden for more than thirty years, showing the corpses of students shot and cut open with bayonets. In response to the shock associated with the release of the photos, Fox appointed a special prosecutor to investigate what could be Mexico's Watergate as well as its own "dirty war" of the 1970s. In an attempt to destroy the two dozen antigovernment guerrilla groups that operated across Mexico during that period, the army is accused of having killed more than 1,000 and "disappeared" hundreds of people. The president at the time, Luis Echeverría, denied that anyone was killed but characterized the opposition as "terrorist" (until his death three decades later he refused to speak with the special prosecutor). His silence was not unexpected; in all the years since Tlatelolco, PRI governments never openly discussed these events and Mexico's official history books have ignored them. Even though there are some indications that with Fox's appointment of a special prosecutor's office to investigate past abuses, the issue may be opening up a bit, many Mexicans doubt there will ever be a full accounting of what happened. And because the military has long been the least democratic and most secretive of Mexico's governmental institutions, it is highly unlikely that Fox will risk provoking the army by attempting to punish it.

Critics argue that if Fox backs down on this, it will show that his government is no different than that of his predecessors. Years ago, in a quid pro quo deal struck in 1946, Mexican officers agreed to stay out of politics as long as the military was placed beyond scrutiny. As a result, this military has been unique in its willingness to let civilians rule. This is one record few Mexicans want broken.[8]

Case Study: Peru

Like so many others, the Peruvian military was originally created to protect the country against foreign challenges. As we will discuss in Chapter 18, over the years since independence most of these challenges have come from its neighbors and concerned IRREDENTIST claims. According to Cynthia McClintock, the

Peruvian military was not traditionally allied with landowning elites. It did make common cause with the ruling class from time to time. But for most of its history the Peruvian military has been conservative in ideology, and for generations its officers came mainly from the upper classes.[9] However, by the early 1960s the military itself had undergone a transformation; more of its officers had a lower-middle-class background and the institution had become more progressive in its politics. In 1968, in a preemptive move aimed at halting the advance of the radical left, General Juan Velasco Alvarado led a "military revolution." This revolution proved short-lived, since by the mid-1970s the military continued to rule but had shifted back to the right. When it finally bowed out, turning responsibility for the government over to civilians in 1980, the military remained one of the most powerful institutions in the country, protective of its prerogatives and autonomy.[10]

Yet as described in Chapter 5, a horrendous civil war was heating up just as civilians had resumed power. A leftist insurgency movement, Sendero Luminoso (Shining Path), began its attacks that same year.[11] Some time earlier, in the remote, impoverished region of Ayacucho, an obscure philosophy professor, Abimael Guzmán Reynoso, had begun to command a following. A personality cult developed around Guzmán; "President Gonzalo," as he was called, considered himself to be the "Fourth Sword of Marxism" (after Marx, Lenin, and Mao). To his followers this philosopher king was incredibly charismatic. His first supporters were university students and recent graduates—young people from the middle and upper-middle classes seeking social mobility and frustrated by the country's prolonged economic crisis. What became a fanatical guerrilla movement was in many ways more a religion than a political entity; Guzmán's followers were true believers, remarkably devoted to the cause.[12]

Although Shining Path's ideology drew from Marxist philosophy, it was unlike other Latin American revolutions in that Guzmán disdained the Cuban model and rejected Soviet assistance. Rather, Guzmán studied in China and claimed his movement to be orthodox Maoist.[13] Like Mao, Guzmán sought to mobilize the peasantry for a rural revolution. However, the comparison pretty much ends there. Nor did Shining Path duplicate earlier Peruvian uprisings that had extolled the Inca Empire and sought to recover a lost paradise.[14] Rather, according to Guzmán, Peru's social order had to be destroyed to make way for a new one, and this required killing 10 percent of the civilian population. The guerrillas fought a vicious war in the countryside and the cities, killing not only soldiers and government officials, but also development workers and popular community leaders, whom Shining Path considered sellouts. The more violence the better, argued the rebels; it was only after purification through bloodshed that Peru would become a Maoist utopia. In this effort these true believers did their best; it is estimated that Shining Path killed 25,000 Peruvians in the 1980s and early 1990s.[15]

But the military did its part to add to the death toll as well. The Fernando Belaúnde (1980–1985) and Alan García (1985–1990) governments adopted similar responses to the insurgency. They declared states of emergency, suspended constitutional guarantees, and to varying degrees turned the war over to the military. Thousands more civilians were killed in the crossfire between Shining

Path and the security forces. Gross human rights violations were committed on both sides. In the military's zeal, anyone suspected of being a member of Shining Path was subjected to torture and harsh treatment. Unable to ignore what was happening, President García made a few feeble attempts at controlling the military, but without much success. In part this is because both Belaúnde and García alternated between two approaches to the insurgency. They never could decide whether to fight an Argentine-style dirty war, or whether to pursue a developmentalist solution, offering massive social assistance and promoting economic development to root out the fundamental causes of the insurgency and win over the population.[16]

On the other hand, President Fujimori (1990–2000) was very clear on this point. This president favored a no-holds-barred, draconian approach. After his self-coup of 1992, Fujimori effectively became a dictator in a civil-military regime. One of the first things he did was to expand the military's legal prerogatives to match its actual prerogatives. In return for its loyalty, Fujimori gave the military absolute control over the counterinsurgency program. As a result, in 1992 Peru was identified as having the highest rate of disappearances of any country in the world (some estimate that over 4,000 people were "disappeared," killed, or tortured by the military since 1980). The 1992 La Cantuta kidnapping and execution of nine students and a professor at a teachers' college is just one of the most heinous examples of human rights abuse committed by government forces.[17]

It was this free rein that Fujimori credited with his victory over TERRORISM. In September 1992 not only was Guzmán captured in a hideout above a Lima dance studio, but so were the master computer files for the entire organization. This amounted to a bonanza; police rounded up more than 1,000 suspects within a few weeks. Yet even more crucially, the government succeeded in totally destroying Guzmán's mystique. Placed in a cage and dressed in a striped prison uniform, "President Gonzalo" was revealed on television as a meek, paunchy, middle-aged man with thick glasses.[18] Because so much of Shining Path's power was based in the personality cult centered on Guzmán, this dramatic change in persona proved devastating to the movement—at least for a while.[19]

Peruvians overwhelmingly approved of Fujimori's authoritarian approach and reelected him to office in the mid-1990s. However, by the late 1990s they turned against him, as the president was still using repression, only now against his "legitimate" opponents. Determined to hold on to power, Fujimori virtually declared war on the opposition. As is discussed in Chapter 11, through civic action Peruvians eventually forced Fujimori out of power and demanded new presidential elections. They breathed a sigh of relief as the military stood by quietly.

Since his election in 2001, President Alejandro Toledo has begun working to reassert civilian control over the military. This will be quite a task since during Fujimori's tenure even mild criticism of the military was taboo. The former president not only promoted generals with notorious human rights records, but he was generous with the armed forces as well; at nearly 300,000 men, Peru's armed forces are nearly twice the size of Colombia's (and Colombia is a larger country and caught up in a massive civil war).[20] Given Peru's financial straits, it can't be surprising that Toledo has promised to cut the military budget by 15 percent. The government has accepted the retirement of more than 100 officers caught up in the corruption scandals associated with Vladimiro Montesinos, former spymaster and Fujimori's right-hand man. As of early 2003, eight high-ranking officers had been imprisoned and a truth commission was holding hearings on government and guerrilla abuses.

Slowly so far, out of fear that it might provoke a coup, the Toledo government has continued with the military reform begun by the caretaker Valentin Paniagua administration. These reforms seek to depoliticize the military and assert civilian control without antagonizing it.[21] However, just one year into Toledo's term there was talk about low morale and rumors of an "undeclared strike" by the military. When it comes to the military, the president knows that he must tread carefully. Peru enjoys an advantage in that it has more of a tradition of civilian control over the military than many other countries, but at best the civil-military relationship is one of "conditional subordination."[22]

Case Study: Nigeria

For over forty years Nigeria has suffered under several cycles of civilian and military rule. Since its independence in 1960, two government leaders have been assassinated and there have been six successful coups, with many more failed ones. The military has spent more time in power than civilians, and when civilians have ruled, it has mostly been at the discretion of the military.[23] As of early 2003, no civilian leader has left office voluntarily. Both previous experiments with civilian government were overthrown by the military.

Without a doubt, the military has been the dominant political actor in Nigeria since it first took power in 1966. Lacking any sense of professionalism, the military does not serve civilian authority; rather it considers itself to be above all other institutions. Instead of being apolitical, the military has morphed into an armed political party.[24] Even if the military is "above" all other institutions, it is hardly isolated from the country's myriad social and economic divisions. Rather, the military itself has a long history of internal disputes and is factionalized, with cliques taking power to promote the interests of one particular ethnic or regional group against another.

For years the military has been divided into a series of personal loyalty pyramids led by corrupt senior "military godfathers" who manipulate identity politics to their own ends. Multimillionaires obsessed with power, senior officers vie with each other for their own personal aggrandizement. These "militicians" have found that the surest route to controlling the country's vast oil wealth is through coup to political office.[25]

Nigeria's second military government demonstrated its determination to hold on to the country's oil wealth. Much of this fortune is concentrated in Nigeria's southeast. When the Ibo, the largest ethnic group indigenous to the region, declared their intent to secede and create their own independent country—Biafra—Nigeria was at war. This civil war raged from 1967 to 1970. Despite the overwhelming force of the Nigerian military, it was frustrated in its efforts to put down the insurrection. It reacted with stunning brutality, quarantining the southeast to starve out the rebels. Nearly 1 million Ibo died before it was all over—most of them civilians, many of them women and children. Although in the end the military government prevailed, Nigeria had come perilously close to breaking up. The Biafran War was used to rationalize giving the military even more power, and it grew dramatically in size and strength, starting in the 1970s. While the money coming into the country after the oil shock of 1973 helped to soothe old wounds, it also opened the way for rampant corruption and clientelism. As Basil Davidson put it, the Nigerian military behaved "like pirates in power."[26] As an institution it was a parasite, eating up scarce resources without contributing to the economy.

Yet compared to the harsh authoritarian rule Nigerians would come to know in the 1980s and 1990s, the generals who ruled Nigeria in the 1970s were relatively sober and honest (Olusegun Obasanjo willingly transferred power to civilian rule). But after the failure of a second attempt at democracy in 1984, military corruption reached unprecedented levels. In the early 1990s, despite their claims to the contrary, it became clear that the officers in charge wanted to hold on to power indefinitely.

By the time they annulled the long-delayed 1993 presidential elections, General Ibrahim Babangida and his cohorts had realized that a civilian government could interfere with their ability to steal the country's resources. The rightfully elected Moshood Abiola or another civilian president might attempt to punish former leaders for their abuses. Therefore, instead of a transition to democracy, what followed was the most predatory rule the country had ever seen, under General Sani Abacha. In terms of despotism, Abacha outdid all others. With no vision and no ideology, the government became an instrument of repression, its legitimacy based on fear. Under Abacha all institutions were subordinated to the military. The police did not exist to serve and protect, but to kill those who protested and to collect bribes. Abacha's own paranoia even contributed to substantial discord within the military throughout most of the 1990s. There were frequent rumors of coups, and the officer corps was repeatedly purged and reshuffled. By the time of Abacha's sudden death in 1998, the Nigerian armed forces were completely discredited. Whereas in the past they had sometimes welcomed the generals' leadership, after fifteen years of misrule the Nigerian public was disgusted and disillusioned with the military.[27]

Yet the military was not entirely ready to return to the barracks. It began looking for ways to impose control without resorting to coup. Although a caretaker government made a good show of initiating new elections and the long-awaited transition to democracy, it is suspected of having had a strong hand in deciding who would take the reins of power. Some analysts contend that the generals were determined that Nigeria's next president be a former military officer and that they handpicked Obasanjo for the job. Many Nigerians suspect that the military bankrolled his campaign. The only thing that is unclear is how much their support had to do with his victory.[28]

Since taking office it appears that Obasanjo is treading carefully, seeking to placate a domestic and international public who want justice without alienating his powerful backers. In more than one instance, the president has acted like a general, ordering military operations that turned into massacres in 1999 and

2001. On the other hand, the president surprised many by firing or retiring several generals in his first few months in office. As part of an anticorruption campaign, he has ordered leading members of former military regimes to return property misappropriated while in office (as of early 2003, the government has recovered more than $1 billion from the Abacha family). Moreover, Obasanjo says he is determined to professionalize the army. In what is to be the biggest reform of the armed forces since the Biafran civil war, he has joined with the United States to rebuild and retrain the military. Remarkably, Obasanjo has been willing to take on some powerful officers who criticize the U.S. military role in Nigeria as imperial. Still, the president must be concerned about the military's proclivity to coup. No one knows better than Obasanjo how entrenched the military is and that he can only push so far those who may have helped return him to power.

Case Study: Zimbabwe

Chimurenga is a Shona word that has great salience for all Zimbabweans. It has a number of meanings, but it generally refers to revolution, war, struggle, and resistance. As we discussed in Chapter 5, in the First Chimurenga War, in the 1890s, the Shona and Ndebele fought against the loss of their land to white settlers. Also in that chapter, we described how Zimbabwean nationalists came to the conclusion that the racist colonial government would never step down peacefully. The result was the Second Chimurenga War and its focal point for Africans also was land—in this case reclamation of what was theirs. This second war was what most people consider to be Zimbabwe's war for liberation, and it was revolutionary in its aims, although not necessarily in its outcome.

Two nationalist movements led the liberation war, the Zimbabwe African People's Union (ZAPU) and the Zimbabwe African National Union (ZANU), an offshoot of ZAPU formed in opposition to it. In 1963 the armed wing of ZANU, the Zimbabwe African National Liberation Army (ZANLA), sent its first group of soldiers to China for guerrilla training. China continued to support ZANU throughout the liberation war, and the Soviet Union provided assistance to ZAPU's armed forces, the Zimbabwe People's Revolutionary Army (ZIPRA). Whether through acts of commission (as was the case with the United States) or omission (as was the case with Britain), the West had for years largely stood behind the white governments—in effect leaving the Africans little choice but to turn to the communists. This was perfect for white Rhodesians, who joined white South Africans in portraying themselves as the last bulwarks against black communism. Consequently, with the involvement of external actors, Zimbabwe's struggle became for many outsiders a COLD WAR PROXY WAR.

Justified as a necessary response to "the communist threat," the white government put the country under a state of emergency that would last fifteen years. ZAPU and ZANU were banned and their leaders, including Nkomo of ZAPU, as well as ZANU's Robert Mugabe and others, were held in detention for nearly a decade. Lacking its senior leadership, both guerrilla armies were fairly ineffectual in the 1960s.[29] However, once they realized that the conflict would be protracted, they knew that they would need a strong base of support and set about mobilizing the masses for it. At outdoor all-night mobilization meetings, or *pungwes,* the guerrillas lectured their civilian audiences in a revival-like atmosphere. It was not difficult to raise peasant consciousness—the loss of their land was an issue of great importance for most people. Also crucial to the guerrillas' success was the legitimacy they enjoyed from their association with a strong sense of cultural NATIONALISM. This was largely due to the backing of spirit mediums, who because they provided a vital connection between the living and their dead ancestors were extremely influential in much of the countryside. However, ZANU and ZAPU were disadvantaged by their inability to create "liberated zones" inside the country, where they could win over people by running schools, clinics, and other pilot projects. By the late 1970s civilians had spent years in the crossfire. As many communities began to tire of the drain of war, conflicts between the guerrillas and their hosts became more common.

All of this was a problem for both ZIPRA and ZANLA, which most analysts today consider more alike than different. While the two groups had their disagreements, both armies were led by nationalists who appealed to Africans as Zimbabweans rather than as Shona or Ndebele speakers. Neither liberation army was ethnically homogeneous, but because they tended to recruit from their different areas of operation (ZIPRA in the north, from bases in Zambia; ZANLA through two-thirds of the country, from bases in Mozambique), they became identified in that way—ZANU as primarily "Shona," ZAPU as "Ndebele."[30] Despite the rivalry between them, in 1976 the two parties joined forces in an uneasy alliance known as the Patriotic Front (ZANU-PF).[31] With this and other factors working in their favor, the guerrillas escalated their assault. By 1979 the white government was so weakened that it was forced to negotiate a peace. The Patriotic Front was ready for an end to the carnage as well; although approximately 1,000 whites died defending Rhodesia, it is estimated that some 30,000–80,000 people—mostly black civilians—died in the war for liberation.[32]

However, not long after independence Zimbabwe was back at war—this time caught up in a struggle between the victors. For years there had been tensions between ZANU-PF and ZAPU, but relations became hostile after the 1980 elections in which ZANU-PF won control of the government. Although each blamed the other for provoking the violence, the four-year civil war that followed clearly had an ethnic dimension. The Fifth Brigade, an entirely ZANU and Shona-speaking elite military unit trained by the North Koreans, was set loose to find dissidents in Matabeleland, a heavily pro-ZAPU region. The countryside was ravaged as the military used scorched-earth tactics. By the time the Unity Accord was brokered in 1987, between 8,000 and 30,000 more people had been killed, most of them Ndebele civilians.[33]

So soon after one civil war, Zimbabwe may be headed toward another. In what some are calling the Third Chimurenga War, the struggle appears to be over land, a topic we have discussed in several previous chapters.[34] As experts predicted, the government did crack down in the weeks before the 2000 and 2002 elections, imposing a fresh series of highly restrictive "security" laws that give the government even greater powers than it had under the last years of white rule. Political violence spread, as journalists were arrested, opposition legislators were kidnapped and tortured, and a newspaper office and a factory with a contract to print election materials for the Movement for Democratic Change (MDC) were bombed. The government's newly created "youth militias" roamed the countryside intimidating anyone even thinking of supporting the MDC. Many people feared that the country would fall into civil war if Mugabe stole the elections. By early 2002, there were indications that ZANU-PF loyalists were preparing for war. Weeks before the vote, the government sent troops to pro-MDC Matabeleland in what must have been a frightening déjà vu. There were rumblings that if ZANU-PF lost, its supporters would go back to the bush to resume what they saw as the struggle for liberation.[35]

What has the military had to say about all of this? The Zimbabwe National Army was formed in 1980 by integrating the three rival armies (ZANLA, ZIPRA, and the Rhodesian security forces). Although in many ways it remains a revolutionary army, Zimbabwe's 40,000-person military has until lately been considered relatively professional. For that reason it is a wild card. Members of the military hold powerful positions in the cabinet, the parliament, and state agencies. No one is sure how the military is lining up or what it will do in the future. Some Zimbabweans believe that Mugabe is losing the army's support, as there were rumors of coup in 2001 and since there has been talk of a split between officers and rank-and-file soldiers (a divide based on who made their fortunes and who did not in the Congo war, the lack of accommodations and decent pay for lower-ranking soldiers, and the fact that Mugabe has consistently favored ZANLA officers with the highest-ranking posts). Although the MDC insists that a coup is not what the country needs, such a shift would open the way for significant changes if, for example, the military refuses to fire on opposition protesters.

However, in a statement that even jaded analysts called stunning, Zimbabwe's chief military officer, General Vitalis Zvinavashe, announced in early 2002 that the military would decide if a new elected president was fit to serve and warned that the army would not accept a leader who had not fought in the liberation war. Clearly, this threat was directed at Morgan Tsvangirai, the opposition's candidate for president (who chose to continue his studies rather than fight in the liberation war). As this book went to press, the military had not yet made good on that threat. Still, even if Tsvangirai (or anyone, for that matter) does somehow manage to win the presidency one day, he or she may never be able to take power from such an unabashedly politicized military—especially one that does not relish the idea of being held accountable for years of corruption.[36]

Case Study: Iran

Iran's history of coups, revolution, and violence runs deep. The country's periods of major strife and unrest were each propelled by similar issues: opposition to a corrupt, unjust king, and resentment against the intrusion of foreign powers. Legacies of these struggles linger today, manifested especially in the pronounced policy differences between the moderate president Ayatollah Mohammad Khatami and the more conservative spiritual leader Ayatollah Khamanei, as we discussed in Chapter 11. The debate over Iran's revolutionary legacy and the meaning of its status as an Islamic republic in the modern world, however, is far from an elite-dominated CLEAVAGE. It is a debate central to most public disputes in Iranian society today.

The Iranian military has always been a patron to the powerful. In 1925, after the fall of the Qajar Dynasty, Reza Khan took the historical title for Iranian kings—"Shah"—adopting the name Reza Shah Pahlavi. With Turkey's Atatürk as his model, the new monarch promoted secularization and limited clerical powers. Pahlavi alienated several groups—especially the religious clergy—stripping the clerics of land and control of schools, ending polygamy for women, and giving women the right to vote, work, and have abortions. He led from 1925 to 1941, ignoring constitutional limits and using his creation, the modern military, to suppress any unrest that threatened to challenge his rule. His son, Mohammed Reza Pahlavi (Shah from 1941 to 1979), continued absolute power, much to the resentment of ordinary citizens and clerical leaders alike. In the early 1950s there were attempts to challenge the Shah, but with assistance from the United States and Britain he regained full power in a coup d'état against the extremely popular prime minister Mohammed Mossadeq. Even though the military remains important in Iran today, the military is an instrument of policy, and it takes a back seat to the elite Revolutionary Guard.[37]

Despite his tyrannical rule, most argue that Mohammed Reza Pahlavi led Iran into an era of growth, as Iran's economy became one of the largest in the Middle East by the mid-1970s. Yet there were many failures of the Pahlavi regime. Tensions arising from policies that benefited the rich failed to incorporate unions, intellectuals, and religious leaders, leading to failed expectations and increasing perceptions of RELATIVE DEPRIVATION. In particular, there was the revolution of rising expectations with the higher prices for oil in the 1970s, and then an ASPIRATION GAP—as only the Shah and his cronies saw the proceeds. Frustration and aggression simmered and began to hit a breaking point with widespread inflation in 1975 and strikes throughout 1978. Facing increasing calls for reform that would incorporate larger segments of the Iranian population the Shah buckled down: in 1975 he formed the Resurgence Party (Hizb-I Rastakhiz) from his military connections. Citizens were given the choice to join the party or depart the country. In an attempt to rein in the clerics, the Shah then declared that he was both political leader of the state and spiritual guide of the community, complete with the announcement of the coming of a new civilization that would surpass Sweden by the year 2000.[38] The Shah replaced the Muslim calendar with a new royalist calendar, disregarded the *SHARIAH* by raising the age of marriage, and ordered universities not to register women who insisted on wearing the Islamic chador. Each of these moves enraged religious leaders and increased their cries against the moral laxity of the country.

The Shah further provoked Ruhollah Khomeini—a cleric experiencing rising public support whose given name means "Inspired of God"—and his followers when the government published an article ridiculing Khomeini in January 1978. Religious demonstrations in the holy city of Qum followed, and the violent government response left many demonstrators dead. The Shah attempted to frighten potential demonstrators and other challengers to his rule by creating his own personal security force, SAVAK. The government's response in Qum launched a cycle of demonstrations every forty days, concurrent with the ritual in Shia Islam for a religious ceremony to take place for forty days after a death.[39] The continuation of demonstrations, a major movie theater fire exacerbated by a slow state response, and Khomeini's inflammatory speech commemorating the end of the holy month of Ramadan coincided to lead the country to revolution. By November 1978 the Shah—who at this time was very ill—placed Iran under military rule. His demise was hastened by his appeal for assistance from the West, and the quick collapse of his own military creation. Because the system was corrupt to the core, it fell apart easily. What followed was nearly a spontaneous revolution that included many diverse groups from Iranian society. Women took on the veil to show protest against the Shah and the debauchery of the West. It was an unusual revolution in several ways: urban, with relatively little bloodshed, it created a rightist THEOCRACY that was retrogressive in nature.

In fact, one of the biggest surprises of 1979 was the departure of the Pahlavi military after the Shah left for the United States in January. Islamic revolutionaries provided security for when airports reopened to allow the exiled Khomeini to return from Paris. Khomeini was able to capitalize on popular discontent—especially among the youth—and successfully urged the military to wholly desert the monarch. The Ayatollah then proceeded to purge the military of monarchists loyal to the Shah by dismissing 12,000 military personnel, most of whom were officers, in an attempt to "Islamicize" the military.[40] He then created the Pasdaran, or Revolutionary Guard, an elite military force whose influence continues today. As a capstone to the revolution, Khomeini activated traditional claims inspired by seventh-century political philosophy giving religious leaders divine right of protection, and established their supremacy over both political and spiritual matters. It had been the Shah's secularism that most aggravated Khomeini and his followers, and their revolution called for a new role for Islam in the political state—the establishment of a theocracy. The legitimacy of clerical leaders, while increasingly questioned by some segments of Iranian society today, has been a stronghold of the Islamic Revolution.

Iran's sponsorship of international terrorism, as we discussed above, is a major source of strained relations with many powers, especially Turkey, which accuses Iran of supporting the Kurdish Workers' Party (PKK). Again in its 2001 report, the U.S. State Department ranked Iran as the leading state sponsor of terrorism, especially for its support of Hezbollah and other groups fighting against a nonviolent resolution of the Israeli-Palestinian conflict.[41] Iranian support for the Shiite Hezbollah organization in Lebanon, the "Party of God," a radical Lebanese Shia Muslim group fighting Israeli occupation of southern Lebanon and responsible for attacks against the U.S. military in the 1980s (notably the attack on the Marine barracks in Beirut), is a sore spot for U.S.-Iranian relations. Iran also has ties with Hamas, the mainstream Islamist organization in Palestine, and with the "marginal" Islamic Jihad organization. Yet few countries—apart from the United States and Israel—consider Hezbollah to be a terrorist organization. Hezbollah supports other Islamist resistance groups, including Hamas and Islamic Jihad in Palestine. Yet contrary to popular perception, it is not affiliated with bin Laden's Al-Qaida and its spiritual leader, Shaikh Mohammed Hussein Fadlallah, was one of the first Muslim clerics to condemn the September 11 terrorist attacks.[42] Even if Iran no longer has monetary ties with these organizations—as it claims—it almost certainly maintains political ties with them.[43]

Because of Iran's theocratic rule, enemies of the regime are defined to be enemies of God. One of the Iranian regime's most famous announcements of decided enemies was Khomeini's 1989 *FATWA* (or religious injunction) declared against Salman Rushdie, author of the seemingly sacrilegious *Satanic Verses*. This decree provided a sum of over $2 million (plus expenses) for killing Rushdie. Attempts on Rushdie's life have failed, although attacks on his collaborators have had mixed success; a suicide bomber sent to London accidentally blew himself up in a hotel room, the book's Japanese translator was stabbed to death, and attempts on the lives of the publishers were made as well. Other enemies include political dissidents, such as Shapour Bakhtiar, the last prime minister under the Shah, who was murdered in Paris in August 1991. As many as 200 émigrés are believed to have been abducted, from many countries of the world.[44] Violence has played an integral role both in the collapse of the Pahlavi Dynasty and in the commencement and continuation of the Islamic Republic. As cleavages within society and between elites and masses continue to deepen, rather than to ameliorate, the possibilities of the politics of disruption remain.

Case Study: Turkey

Modern Turkey is a state supported (and some would say sustained) by an activist military. In fact, military interventions have become so common that some Turks have come to call them "soft, postmodern coups."[45] As we discussed in Chapter 11, the primary source of discord in Turkey concerns the expression of religion: in both society as a whole, and specifically in the presence of the separatist Kurdistan Workers' Party, the PKK.

Mustafa Kemal Atatürk, the founder of the Turkish Republic and its first president, is viewed as a military hero who put the final nail in the coffin of the theocratic Ottoman Dynasty, which had lasted six centuries. Mustafa Kemal, as he was known before 1923, was a decorated military commander in the Ottoman army, enraged, like most Turks, by the Greek (and other foreign) occupation of Anatolia, or Asia Minor. After winning the Turkish War of Independence against the Greeks in 1922, the new, nationalist, secular republic was established. Atatürk, or "Father of the Turks," as he was later known, left a legacy of national pride, republican government, and secularism—a legacy that the Turkish military has adopted as its organizational duty to maintain.

The military has a dark history in Turkish politics, and its influence, autonomy, and power are unique among the world's democracies. (We assess the characterization of Turkey's political regime in Chapter 15.) Concerns about the Turkish military and its yearning to intervene in the face of perceived crises mar the country's application to join the European Union (EU). Following the latest coup in 1980 (and period of military rule from 1980 to 1983), the military rewrote the Constitution of 1982, which still governs Turkey today. This document enshrines the unique role for the nation's military as guardians of Turkey's secular government and territorial integrity. Calls from the Turkish executive to rewrite the constitution to assist the country's acceptance into the EU, and lessen criticism from the INTERNATIONAL MONETARY FUND (IMF), have largely been ignored, at best, by the military establishment.[46]

The clout and reach of the military are also seen in a yearlong class on the principles of Atatürk and political events that every tenth-grader in Turkey must attend. This course, taught only by military officers, uses a textbook written by the military forces.[47] There are, however, some signs that the unchecked influence of the military in Turkish affairs may be weakening. Recently, in a significant statement that seemed to depart from prior policy, a party leader and deputy prime minister stated that Turkey's "national-security syndrome" was the main obstacle to democratic reforms in Turkey and ultimately to Turkey's EU membership. Yet public opinion polls continue to rank the armed forces as Turkey's most popular institution, a long-standing tradition.[48]

In addition to responding to internal threats from the perceived rise of radical Islam or Kurdish separatism, the military, not surprisingly, is used for external threats as well. The greatest of these, as viewed from Ankara, is the threat from Greece. Turkey boasts a 100,000-man Aegean army, first deployed in 1975 to face down offshore Greek units only miles away. Disputes over sea-lanes, air rights, and mostly barren islands have brought the two countries to the brink of war, most recently in 1996. Following improved relations between Greece and Turkey in 1999, a retired admiral recommended disbanding the Aegean force, attracting overwhelmingly negative attention in the domestic media and in Turkish security circles.[49]

Turkey's most dominant issue of state-sponsored violence is its response to the volatile issues of the Kurdish Workers' Party, founded in 1974 as a Marxist-Leninist insurgent group. While some, including Iran, view the PKK as the legitimate representative of an ethnic group, the Turkish government, and especially the military leadership, argue that the PKK is a terrorist guerrilla organization that threatens the existence of modern Turkey. In its struggle with the PKK, the Turkish government has forcibly moved noncombatants, turned a blind eye to extrajudicial killings and torture, and limited freedom of expression, including cultural and linguistic expression. Regional governments close to PKK concentrations have often declared states of emergency, allowing security forces to exercise semi–martial law powers, including restrictions on the press and the forced removal of anyone deemed in the way of public order.

The PKK, whose goal is to establish an independent Kurdish state, has responded in kind, murdering innocent civilians, terrorizing Turkish cities and tourist sites, and attacking Turkish targets abroad, especially in Western Europe. In execution style the PKK has murdered entire families (including infant children) who are viewed as collaborators, and they have attacked schools in Kurdish regions, burning buildings and executing village teachers. Often posing as women, with weapons concealed under their chadors, they set about killing PKK rivals by the hundreds. Their targets have also included more moderate Islamists and other Turks—especially Kurds who do not agree with PKK aims—who refused to give money to their cause. It may seem ironic that most of the civilians murdered by the PKK are themselves Kurds, whom the PKK accuses of acting in complicity with the Turkish state. This points to a central conundrum faced by Kurds throughout the Middle East: intense rivalries between competing groups have prevented any unity of action.

Similar to the fate of Shining Path after Guzmán's capture, the dramatic arrest of Abdullah Öcalan in February 1999 limited—but did not curtail—the activities of the group. Öcalan went on the run after the PKK was expelled from Syria in October 1998. He was captured in February 1999 in Nairobi, Kenya, and renounced the armed fight for Kurdish independence six months later. PKK advocates insist that Öcalan's statement was the result of police coercion and they refuse to give in. Tensions between Iran and Turkey increased after the Islamic Republic placed Öcalan's brother, Osman Öcalan, under the protection of the Iranian government.[50] Nevertheless, the PKK has experienced a general decline as a viable challenge to the Turkish state since Öcalan's detention.

Other groups challenge the secularism of the Kemalist regime. First active in the 1960s, Islamic subversive activity increased in the 1980s with the growth of a Turkish branch of Islamic Jihad. Iran is viewed by leaders of this group as "an example and a guide" for much militant antisecular fighting in Turkey since the early 1990s.[51] Turgut Özal's rule in the 1980s and early 1990s reduced opposition to Islam in Turkey and relations with Iran benefited from it. Yet in 1999, Prime Minister Necmettin Erbakan was accused of having direct connections with terrorist organizations, including Hezbollah (both Lebanese and Turkish) and the Japanese Red Army. Erbakan was deposed for his Islamist views and banned from politics for five years. Again the military demonstrated its prerogative in protecting (in its view) the Kemalist legacy of modern Turkey.

Case Study: China

Similar to many of the countries we have studied, China has had multiple revolutions rather than a single revolutionary moment. Yet strangely enough, especially for their fervently anti-imperial character, both of China's major revolutions incorporated Western ideas, only later adapting the "Chinese characteristics." The first revolution took place in 1912, after the last dynasty of China, the Qing Dynasty, collapsed. Sun Yat-sen, a Christian medical doctor known as the father of modern China, planned the revolution from Tokyo, Honolulu, Vancouver, and London. Yet the revolution, led by the Nationalist Party (KMT), failed to consolidate their rule, due partly to the focus on establishing a limited republic, and partly to Sun's illness and premature death in 1925, after which China descended into regional chaos. Warlords, individuals who had accrued military and political power over small regions of the country during the unrest that accompanied the collapse of the dynastic period, engaged in violent attempts to regain control over their fiefdoms. Out of this, another nationalist leader, Chiang Kaishek, rose to the fore. Twice the nationalists worked together with the younger, inexperienced, and ill-equipped Chinese Communist Party (CCP), and twice the nationalists betrayed them, to dire consequences. In the second United Front, as their alliances were called, the KMT and the CCP worked together, some would say in a halfhearted manner, to expel the Japanese, who had invaded the north of China. It was during this conflict—

in which the nationalists gained the reputation as a corrupt band of soldiers who would quickly flee from the advancing Japanese—that the CCP gained the support of many of China's ordinary people. This was especially true in the countryside, which was the main recruiting ground for the fledgling CCP. Even though Mao Zedong was hardly a key member at the first party meetings in Shanghai in 1921, by the late 1920s he began to emerge as a revolutionary hero and cultural icon who would impact China, and all of Asia, like no other man. Yet victory over the nationalists in China's civil war (1945–1949) was not enough. In Mao's attempt to "continue the revolution," he launched the country into a state of virtual civil warfare during his so-called CULTURAL REVOLUTION. Even though the main campaigns of the ten-year movement, designed to promote absolute equality and cleanse China of foreign and Confucian influence, were primarily confined to China's major cities, the period is referred to as the "ten dark years" that no Chinese living on the mainland escaped. This decade of civil unrest—a "planned revolution" of sorts—was rife with purges, public denunciations, propaganda, and ideological fervor.

In the relative calm of the post-Mao period, when economic reform took precedence over ideological expediency, societal conflict, suppressed by earlier campaigns and a near-complete lack of choice, began to resurface. Societal violence is also on the rise, in ways and numbers not seen since the last years of the imperial periods. Abduction, robbery, drug smuggling, and sex industries—often involving young girls kidnapped from the countryside—are all on the rise. In Beijing alone, a former paragon of order, police seized 100 hand grenades and 1,500 guns between April and August 2001—statistics startling in both their admission and their magnitude.[52]

The role of China's People's Liberation Army (PLA) in governing is difficult to discern, because the institution is so closely intertwined with the CCP. In fact, the PLA, founded in 1927, follows in a long line of military involvement in politics: military commanders established many Chinese dynasties. It is common to hear that the CCP commands the gun, meaning that the PLA is subordinated to the party. Mao himself argued in 1927 that "all political power grows out of the barrel of a gun," and later that "the party commands the gun, while the gun shall never be or must never be allowed to command the party." Leaders since Mao, though, have attempted to limit party influence over the military, even though Deng Xiaoping, as chair of the Central Military Commission, effectively utilized PLA units to clear Tiananmen Square in 1989. Jiang Zemin, his successor, came to office with weaker ties to the PLA, a fact that caused many observers (Chinese and foreigners alike) to question his likelihood of staying in power. Yet Jiang successfully courted military clients and was careful to avoid alienating PLA commanders in his policy decisions. It is a matter complicated even further by the phenomenon known as "wearing multiple hats"—important political figures holding several posts at the same time (the best example was President Jiang Zemin, who concurrently held the posts of general secretary, chairman of the Central Military Commission, and president). Yet not every soldier or even military officer is a member of the Chinese Communist Party.

The PLA, in true guerrilla fashion, had won over the "hearts and minds" of the Chinese people during the postimperial struggle, especially in response to the Japanese invasion in the 1930s. As its name suggests, it was the PLA, whose lifeline was the CCP, that broke China's painful cycle of international humiliation at the hands of the imperial powers. Yet to many today, the Chinese military is synonymous with the crackdown on the students in Tiananmen Square, which we discussed in Chapter 11. For those who were outside the situation, it is difficult to convey the profound sense of shock that most Chinese citizens experienced when the army, "their" army, turned so violently against unarmed students in the square that June in 1989. Leaders in Beijing had to activate PLA units from north-central China to clear the square, since the original troops, who had trained near Beijing University in the summers, were persuaded by the protesters to avoid firing their weapons.

Owing to China's vast size and regional distinctions, the PLA at the beginning of the twenty-first century remains both factionalized (along ideological lines) and regionalized. The attempt has been made to promote officers from all over the country, a Maoist concept known as "five lakes and four oceans."[53] In 1985 the Central Military Commission had seven military regions, reorganized again in 1998 to five "war-zone regions" (Nanjing, Guangzhou, Jinan, Shenyang, Chengdu)—at one point there were twelve.[54] These attempts at reorganization buttress China's attempt to completely modernize its forces, giving rise to concerns in Asia and abroad over its growing military strength. Yet while the PLA boasts the world's largest standing military—approximately 2.7 million troops—it remains encumbered by a top-heavy bureaucratic apparatus and by sorely outdated equipment, much of which it had purchased from the former Soviet Union.

Case Study: Indonesia

Since the late 1990s, Indonesia has been a state nearly torn apart by violence of almost all the types discussed in this chapter. Paramilitary groups with the alleged backing of Suharto's military forces responded brutally to the independence vote in East Timor (discussed in Chapter 18). Indonesia has engaged in a four-year national debate on the past and future role of its armed forces, known as ABRI (Angkatan Bersenjata Republik Indonesia), which has traditionally filled in when there was a vacuum of civilian leadership. Separatist guerrilla groups on many of the archipelago's islands, especially Aceh, have increased the tenor and the intensity of their actions. The fragile religious balance in many regions of Indonesia, held together before by the regime's *pancasila* doctrine, which accepted all monotheistic faiths, has begun to unravel—to disastrous outcomes. Riots, led by discontented students and angry middle-class Indonesians, broke out as Suharto first clamped down on political expression, closing media outlets and political party offices throughout the mid-1990s, and later, as the military was called in to quell economic riots in 1998. Suharto's successors, numbering three in less than as many years, have failed to demonstrate that they learned any valuable lessons about the instability caused by relying on the military to put down civic unrest; Habibie, Wahid, and Megawati each made it clear, in statements and actions alike, that they put much trust in the military apparatus as a means of preserving the stability of the Indonesian state. Habibie's close ties to the Suharto-era military blemished his record with the populace, who wanted a clean break from the "New Order" era that Suharto had initiated. Wahid struggled with the military's legacy, attempting to root out corruption in the midst of national debates over whether or not to pardon Suharto. His successor, Megawati, inherited this problem as well.

Indonesia is the world's most populous Muslim nation. Although Muslims in Indonesia are overwhelmingly moderate, Muslim extremism in Indonesia has been on the rise since the collapse of the Suharto regime in 1998. Although most of these groups existed prior to the late 1990s, the Suharto government, in the name of preserving national unity, harshly repressed demonstrations. Democratic openings and international events have combined to encourage such groups to speak out. The country has been rife with anti-American protests since the war in Afghanistan began. One of the leading anti-Western voices is the hard-line Islamic Defenders Front (FPI). FPI raids on bars known for seemingly "inappropriate" female dancing and gambling, though, engender dislike more than support from the majority of Indonesia's Muslims.[55] Another radical Islamic group, Jemaah Islamiah ("Islamic Community"), is believed to be behind the October 2002 attack on a nightclub in a resort area of Bali, which left nearly 200 people dead. This group, which is known for its desire to establish an Islamic state combining Malaysia, Indonesia, Singapore, and parts of the Philippines, is purported to have links to Al-Qaida, a charge its leaders deny. The Bali attacks, which killed many foreign tourists and severely curtailed the dominant industry in the area, tourism, again raised the possibility that Indonesia, marred by instability in recent years, could become a haven for terrorist activity.

Since 1999, sectarian violence has been particularly deadly in Indonesia. Some attacks were based on news and rumors of Muslims or Christians being murdered in one city or village, which prompted vengeance in another.[56] The island of Sulawesi has long been a flash point of religious violence. This island, just west of Moluccas, has a history of violence between Christians and Muslims, deriving largely from the prominence of Dutch missionary campaigns prior to independence. Violence returned to the area in a three-year vigilante war, fought with spears, bows and arrows, and homemade guns. Ostensibly, it was a conflict based in religion, sparked by Christian youths drinking alcohol near the mosque in town. Yet, similar to most cleavages, it was exacerbated by widespread job disparities and leadership opportunities (or lack thereof) in the town. After death sentences were handed out only to Christians, and not to Muslims, further violence ensued.[57]

Oftentimes the conflict goes beyond what police are willing or able to handle, as a recent incident between native Dayaks and immigrant settlers from the island of Madura on the Indonesian portion of Borneo (also known as Kalimantan) highlights. After they received promises from security forces that they would be protected in their attempt to board ships and flee, the Madurese attempted to cross the island. Angry Dayak residents cornered the migrants, and shepherded the 118 Madurese, including 20 children, to a soccer field, where they were brutally murdered. Six victims were beheaded and 112 were hacked to death with machetes, spears, and knives.[58] Rumors persisted that security forces had demanded expensive bribes to "protect" the migrants, but they immediately fled when the native Dayaks threatened them.[59] Because of its inaction the government is now accused of assisting this ethnic group in its desire to clear Madurese from portions of Borneo. As this incident demonstrates, militaries can be brutal both in their execution of force as well as in their incompetence.

Yet the most famous case of separatism in Indonesia occurred on August 30, 1999, when East Timorese voted for their independence. Turnout was outstanding—98.6 percent of those eligible, out of whom 78.5 percent rejected integration with Indonesia. Roadblocks set up by militants to intimidate voters complicated the balloting. Prior to the election, violence was a tool used by both sides; prointegrationists were murdered, as were proseparatists—often killed with machetes. The Indonesian military had instigated groups and encouraged anti-independence sentiment since the 1970s.[60] Pent-up anger burst onto the scene when the vote actually took place.

After the elections, violence became rampant, with government-sponsored militias engaged in "political cleansing."[61] The situation was complicated further by competition between multiple regionally based militias. The United Nations estimates that the death toll from the violence could be as high as 7,000, and that up to 300,000 people had been displaced in the postelection violence (all of this in a population of 850,000). Many express concerns about a domino effect of separatism following the East Timor transition. Indonesian scholar Donald Emmerson argues that these concerns are unfounded because East Timor had never been part of the homeland that Indonesian nationalists claimed from the Dutch.[62] East Timor was a former Portuguese colony invaded by Jakarta in 1975. Women have been extremely active in independence movements in Aceh and East Timor, even though there are very few women members of the explicitly nationalist movements, Free Aceh or RENETIL (Resistencia Nacional dos Estudantes de Timor-Leste).[63]

Another flash point is Irian Jaya, on the Indonesian half of the island of Papua New Guinea. This is a classic example of the forced incorporation of a culture that has been sustained because of economic interests (the region has the world's largest copper and gold mines). Although the region was incorporated, as was the rest of Indonesia, by the Dutch, many of the indigenous Papuan people, who are distinct from the dominant Javanese in Indonesia, believed they would achieve their independence after the Dutch left. Irian Jaya declared independence in 1961, but Indonesian forces occupied the land in 1963. The separatists have maintained their own flag, the Morning Star, as a unifying symbol. In fact, thirty people were once killed in a dispute when someone tried to remove the Morning Star flag: Indonesian law states that only the Indonesian flag (known as the Red and White) is permitted to fly over its territory.[64] Despite the absence of any significant armed rebellion, former president Abdurraham Wahid reneged on his promise of moderation and cracked down on separatists, killing at least ten people.[65] In November 2001 a leader in the Papuan separatist movement known for his desire for a peaceful solution to the independence crisis was kidnapped and murdered as he returned home from an event held by the army's special forces branch, Kopassus—and not surprisingly, the government in Jakarta was suspected.[66] Tensions are not limited to the chasm between

Papuans and the military. A new rift has developed as Indonesians from overcrowded Jakarta and individuals fleeing violence-marred Ambon have moved to the region.

Now It's Your Turn

What has been the effect of catastrophic violence in the countries that have experienced it? What do you think it takes to become a revolutionary leader? Why are some leaders more successful than others at rallying others to implement change? Do you believe any of the countries that we are studying are ripe for revolution? How would you compare governments' responses to revolutionaries or perceived insurgents? How do you explain why some people believe violence is the only solution to their dilemmas? What would it take for you to adopt violent means of expression?

Suggested Readings

Africa

Achebe, Chinua. *Girls at War.* New York: Bantam, 1991. Nigeria: fiction, short stories about the Biafran War.

Chinodya, Shimmer. *Harvest of Thorns.* London, Heinemann, 1991. Zimbabwe: fiction, a young man caught between two worlds living during Zimbabwe's liberation war.

Marinovich, Greg, and Joao Paulo Silva. *The Bang Bang Club.* New York: Basic Books, 2001. South Africa: nonfiction, photojournalism and South Africa's struggle for liberation.

Sithole, Ndabaningi. *Roots of a Revolution: Scenes from Zimbabwe's Struggle.* New York: Oxford University Press, 1977. Zimbabwe: fiction, stories from the battlefield.

Yvonne, Vera. *Under the Tongue.* Harare: Baobab Press, 1997. Zimbabwe: fiction, life in war-torn Rhodesia.

Asia

Jin, Ha. *Ocean of Worlds: Army Stories.* New York: Vintage International, 1998. China: fiction, stories of Chinese soldiers as they sit on the border between Russia and China, at the brink of war.

———. *Waiting.* New York: Pantehon, 1999. China: fiction, romance and forbidden love set against the backdrop of the 1949 Chinese Revolution and beyond.

Kohen, Arnold S., and Paul Moore Jr. *From the Place of the Dead: The Epic Struggles of Bishop Belo of East Timor.* New York: St. Martin's, 1999. Indonesia: nonfiction, an account of one of the leaders of the East Timorese independence movement.

Margolis, Eric S. *War at the Top of the World: The Struggle for Afghanistan, Kashmir, and Tibet.* New York: Routledge, 2000. Various countries: nonfiction, explores competing claims to territory and security in these contested regions.

Min, Anchee. *Red Azalea.* New York: Pantheon, 1995. China: fiction, memoir of growing up in Shanghai during the first two decades of the Communist Revolution.

Sun-Childers, Jaia, and Douglas Childers. *The White Haired Girl: Bittersweet Adventures of a Little Red Soldier.* New York: Picador. China: nonfiction, biographical coming-of-age account written by one Red Guard who embraced Mao's revolution and later felt betrayed by it.

Taring, Rinchen Dolma. *Daughter of Tibet.* London: Wisdom Books, 1986. China: nonfiction, biography of a Tibetan Buddhist woman detailing the Chinese occupation.

Latin America and the Caribbean

Alvarez, Julia. *In the Time of Butterflies.* New York: Penguin, 1995. Dominican Republic: historical fiction, based on the true story of the Mirabel sisters, murdered for their association with a 1960 plot to overthrow the Trujillo dictatorship.

Benitez, Sandra. *Bitter Grounds.* New York: Picador, 1998. El Salvador: fiction, the effect of the long-standing civil war in El Salvador on three generations of women.

———. *The Weight of All Things.* New York: Hyperion, 2001. El Salvador: fiction, innocents caught in the crossfire between guerrillas and death squads.

Dandicat, Edwidge. *The Farming of Bones.* New York: Penguin, 1999. Haiti and the Dominican Republic: fiction, a young woman's story of survival and the 1937 massacre of Haitians in the Dominican Republic.

Limon, Graciela. *Erased Faces.* Houston, Tex.: Arte Publico Press, 2001. Mexico: fiction, the life of a young woman as a rebel leader in Chiapas.

Ponce de Leon, Juan, ed. *Our Word Is Our Weapon: Selected Writings.* New York: Seven Stories Press, 2000. Mexico: nonfiction, a collection of the writings of Subcomandante Marcos.

Vargas Llosa, Maria. *Death in the Andes.* Trans. Edith Grossman. New York: Farrar, Straus, and Giroux, 1996. Peru: fiction, contemporary terrorism as experienced in Peru.

———. *The Feast of the Goat.* Trans. Edith Grossman. New York: Farrar, Straus, and Giroux, 2001. Dominican Republic: fiction, thirty years of state terrorism under Trujillo.

———. *The Real Life of Alejandro Mayta.* Trans. Alfred Mac Adam. New York: Farrar, Straus, and Giroux, 1986. Peru: fiction, the life of a revolutionary in a futuristic battleground.

———. *Who Killed Palomino Molero?* Trans. Alfred Mac Adam. New York: Farrar, Straus, and Giroux, 1987. Peru: fiction, the torture and murder of a young man in a corrupt society.

Middle East

Arat, Zehra F., ed. *Deconstructing Images of "The Turkish Woman."* New York: St. Martin's, 1998. Turkey: nonfiction, examines gender in Turkey from the late Ottoman era to today, looking at literature, culture, labor, and religion.

Hiro, Dilip. *The Longest War: The Iran-Iraq Military Conflict.* London: Routledge, 1991. Iran and Iraq: nonfiction, accounts of the most devastating war in modern Middle Eastern history.

Kanafani, Ghassan. *Palestine's Children: Returning to Haifa and Other Stories.* Trans. Barbara Harlow and Karen E. Riley. Boulder: Lynne Rienner, 2000. Palestinian territories: fiction, short stories reflecting on Palestinian desires for a homeland.

Laird, Elizabeth. *Kiss the Dust.* New York: Puffin Books, 1994. Iraqi Kurds: fiction, a Kurdish family's travels from a comfortable life in northern Iraq, to an Iranian refugee camp, to England.

Moin, Baqer. *Khomeini: Life of the Ayatollah.* New York: St. Martin's, 2000. Iran: nonfiction, biographical account of Khomeini both before and after the 1979 revolution.

Paidar, Parvin. *Women and the Political Process in Twentieth-Century Iran.* Cambridge: Cambridge University Press, 1995. Iran: nonfiction, traces the gains and setbacks of women in recent Iranian political history.

Pakravan, Saïdeh. *The Arrest of Hoveyda: Stories of the Iranian Revolution.* Costa Mesa, Calif.: Blind Owl Press, 1998. Iran: fiction, short stories focusing on the demise of the last Shah's regime.

Ballots, Not Bullets: Seeking Democratic Change

A country without free elections is a country without a voice, without eyes, without arms.

—Octavio Paz, writer[1]

As you read in Chapter 12, violent conflicts and the military's tendency to assume political power pose a variety of problems for many countries. This certainly has an effect on political performance and the prospects for DEMOCRACY in all of the regions we discuss. Ethnic and religious strife, as well as other divisions, create very real problems for governments—both democratic and nondemocratic. In the most difficult cases even SOVEREIGNTY, or the state's right to exist, is contested. As in the cases of Israel and Somalia, there are often profound differences over who should be part of a political community or what should be its territorial boundaries. In a democracy, citizens agree that the government can make legitimate claims to their obedience. However, if the military or another powerful group of people does not accept these demands as legitimate, this poses serious problems for the viability of the government. Until such claims are resolved, democracy is imperiled, if not impossible.

What Is Democracy?

But before we can talk about how difficult to sustain it is, we should first ask ourselves, what is democracy? What makes a country democratic? Let us first say that there is wide disagreement over what should be emphasized when defining democracy. There is no single archetype for democracy, no single, unique set of institutions characteristic of democracy. In this chapter we will limit ourselves to a discussion of political democracy, as opposed to social or economic conceptions of democracy. As you will soon see, within political democracy there are different kinds of constitutional systems, and democracies vary widely in levels of citizen participation, access to power, checks and balances, governmental responsiveness to popular demands, party strength, and political pluralism. Therefore, in defining democracy we need to be as general as possible to allow for the many systems that are differently democratic.[2]

However, for all its variations, certain minimal criteria must be met for a political system to be considered democratic. Although governments satisfy these criteria to different degrees (and none of them perfectly), three conditions are commonly named as essential to any democracy: the existence of competition, participation, and respect for civil liberties. With the identification of these common denominators we can begin to define democracy. Democracy is one type of political system. As opposed to AUTHORITARIAN systems in which decisionmaking power is concentrated in the hands of a few and authority is unchallengeable, democracies are based in the decentralization of authority. In democracies citizens take part in making the decisions of government. More simply put, democracy is a system of governance in which citizens hold their leaders accountable for their public actions. Accountability is ensured through open competition for office. Democracy institutionalizes competition for power through elections that are free, fair, and held on a regular basis.[3]

But another important part of competition is inclusiveness, which demands a high level of political participation in the selection of leaders and policies. Where government makes room for people to add their voices, the political process has been opened up to promote effective political participation.[4] In a democracy, citizens should be able to influence public policy. At its core, democratization entails the accommodation of a wide range of opinions. For a country to be considered a democracy, there must be room for a lively and vibrant civil society, with active parties, trade unions, and religious and cultural groups that operate independently of the regime. Of course, it is also expected that people will be free to organize and express themselves without worry of harassment or imprisonment. This is necessary to satisfy the democratic requirements of both participation and competition.

Therefore, participation is expressed as the right of all citizens to take part in the democratic process. "Taking part" can mean any number of things, but it must at the very least include the right to political equality. In democracies there should be very few restrictions on the citizen's right to vote or run for office. No one should be excluded because of gender, ethnicity, religion, class, or sexual orientation. Neither should there be a property or literacy requirement for citizens to participate in the process. The greater number of people who are denied citizenship and whose opportunities are hurt by such denial, the more unlikely states will be able to achieve a CONSOLIDATION of democracy, or make it durable. Democratic governments will take pains to be inclusive, to ensure collective as well as individual rights, to ensure that minority and traditionally oppressed groups have equal representation, and to ensure that the votes of all citizens are weighted equally (one person, one vote).[5]

The term *free* is often used synonymously with the term *democratic*. According to the human rights organization Freedom House, the number of countries defined as "free" has nearly doubled—from 69 in 1989, to 120 in 2000. Countries, or to be more precise, political systems, that are termed "free" generally allow for a high degree of political and civil freedoms, but they do so to varying degrees. Some people offer up the sheer number of elections held in the late twentieth century as evidence that a democratic REVOLUTION has taken place. They identify elections as the watershed event marking the DEMOCRATIC TRANSITION and treat democracy as an event rather than a process. This is prob-

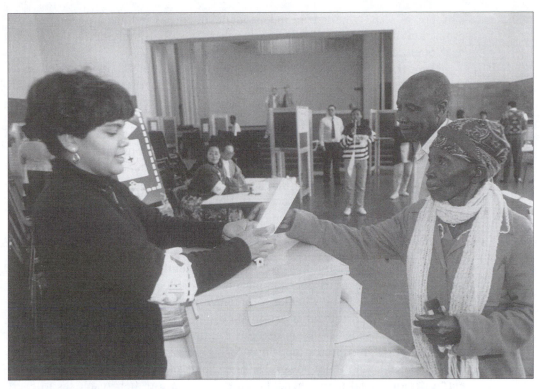

A voter casts her ballot in South Africa's first democratic elections, in 1994 (UN Photo, by C. Sattleberger)

lematic for a variety of reasons. Elections can sometimes result in a setback for democracy, especially if antidemocratic candidates are elected or if divides are deep and the election is perceived as a win-or-lose event. This is why democracy must be rooted in a political culture that promotes popular participation, one that tolerates differences and accepts the consensus.[6]

In some ways it is remarkable that between 1990 and 2002, forty-two of forty-eight countries in sub-Saharan Africa held multiparty elections, since at the start of the 1980s only four countries were doing such a thing. However, elections alone do not make a democracy. Rather, democracies have electoral and nonelectoral dimensions. Be careful not to fall for the FALLACY OF ELECTORALISM, or the tendency to focus on elections while ignoring other political realities. Many countries have gone through the motions of elections, yet power has remained in the hands of an oligarchy or the military (e.g., El Salvador in the 1980s; Zaire/Democratic Republic of Congo in the 1990s). Even Indonesia and Nigeria were in many ways at the turn of the twenty-first century examples of ELECTORAL DEMOCRACIES, because they had not yet made much progress with other crucial areas of political reform. How rulers come to power is important, but just as important is the strength of democratic institutions and whether they can hold elected leaders accountable for their actions. In determining the success of a democratic transition, it is more important to ask whether the RULE OF

LAW prevails and whether an independent, impartial judiciary guarantees the protection of political and civil rights, rather than simply relying on the "litmus test" of elections.[7]

Democracies that pass a more comprehensive test are commonly known as LIBERAL DEMOCRACIES. As opposed to the minimal framework of electoral democracies, liberal democracies are based on a deeper institutional structure that offers extensive protections for civil and political rights, individual and group liberties such as freedom of thought and expression, freedom of the press, and the right to form and join assemblies or organizations, including political parties and interest groups. Where civil rights are protected, people feel that they have the freedom to participate in the political process. Democratizing societies will encourage civil society to flourish, and political parties and interest groups to organize without constraint. Again, there are no perfect democracies. No country completely lives up to all the standards listed here. And what can start as a major political transformation can turn out in a variety of ways.

What do we mean by this? Transitions frequently become sidelined by disputes between democrats over the meaning of freedom, the best constitutional and electoral system, or whether to organize as a unitary or federal state. All democracies, even the most established ones, must continuously work to improve their democratic practices. For example, the economic inequality that exists in the United States (and in every democracy to some degree) has the effect of skewing political power. Despite claims of political equality, the affluent are "more equal than others" because they can use their resources to exert disproportionate influence over policy.[8]

Because of problems with democratic practice, often the line between democratic and nondemocratic regimes is unclear. Several countries are hard to place because they may satisfy some requirements of democracy but not others. For example, Turkey's formal structures may be democratic, but in practice its constraints on free political activity complicate the issue. Governments that are characterized as "free" or "democratic" commonly experience isolated violations of civil liberties or occasional electoral malpractice. However, they are considered democratic because they meet certain minimal standards (e.g., it

---

Figure 14.1 Respect for Political and Civil Rights: How Our Cases Rate

Freedom House is a highly respected NON-GOVERNMENTAL ORGANIZATION (NGO) monitoring democratization and human rights worldwide. As part of this work the organization rates every country based on its respect for political rights and civil liberties. Here is a quick look at how the following countries were ranked in the 2000–2001 report:	Mexico	Free
	Peru	Partly free
	Nigeria	Partly free
	Zimbabwe	Partly free
	Iran	Not free
	Turkey	Partly free
	China	Not free
	Indonesia	Partly free

Source: Freedom House, "Freedom in the World, 2000–2001," www.freedomhouse.org.

must be possible for the ruling party to be turned out of power; people generally expect that a fair electoral process and basic freedoms will continue into the future; etc.). New democracies differ markedly from one another, with varying strengths and weaknesses. Contrary to popular belief, there is no end point at which a country can be said to have "attained" democracy.[9] It should be expected that it will take some time for appropriate political systems to be created, and that they will evolve at least partly in response to political failures.

Therefore, democratization is something that should be understood as an ongoing, dynamic process instead of a singular achievement. Just as we recognize that some countries may come closer to fitting the democratic ideal than others, we must recognize that a similar continuum exists for their less-than-democratic counterparts. In the end, most governments fall somewhere in between the two poles of democracy and TOTALITARIANISM, which is an extreme form of authoritarianism. Many governments allow for more freedoms than do rigidly totalitarian regimes, but these freedoms are so few that such governments cannot adequately qualify as democracies. As you will see in the next chapter, there is an unusually large array of names for those systems that fall somewhere in between. For example, many third world governments, including those of Turkey, Indonesia, and Iran, are termed DELEGATIVE DEMOCRACIES: they are neither liberal democracies nor full-blown dictatorships. Delegative democracies are sometimes called democratic because they have a similar outward appearance to that of their more democratic counterparts. However, delegative democracies are led by elites whose commitment to democracy is contingent and instrumental, not routinized, internalized, and principled.[10] Delegative democracies are a peculiar form of democracy; through clean elections a majority empowers someone to become the embodiment and interpreter of the nation's interests. No, this doesn't sound very democratic, but as Guillermo O'Donnell contends, delegative democracies are more democratic than they are authoritarian. What is important to remember is that even though some governments are doing a better job of promoting certain aspects of democracy than are others, the success is relative and the work is ongoing.[11]

Background to the Transition

As mentioned earlier, starting in the 1970s and accelerating through the 1990s, a number of what were sometimes characterized as stunning political changes occurred throughout the world, including the third world. The winding down of the COLD WAR coincided with a period of what some called a global democratic revolution, as a "third wave" of prodemocracy movements rose up not only in Europe, but also in Asia, Africa, Latin America, and to a lesser extent the Middle East. Some analysts have characterized the last twenty-five years as a critical historical moment, "the greatest period of democratic ferment in the history of modern civilization."[12] Much of this commotion grew out of an ABERTURA, or a political opening associated with a mix of reforms. Countries undertaking such reforms are often described as experiencing a POLITICAL LIBERALIZATION. Periods of political liberalization are generally associated with a variety of changes such as greater press freedoms, greater freedom of assembly, and the introduction of legal safeguards for individuals. People living in countries experiencing a political liberalization witness the release of most political prisoners, the return of exiles, and perhaps most important, a growing tolerance of dissent.

At the turn of the twenty-first century, nearly 50 percent of the world's population are living in countries that can claim to be broadly democratic. And with a few exceptions, the full-fledged dictatorships so common during the Cold War have virtually disappeared.[13] However, not all governments that have made way for a political liberalization are necessarily headed toward democracy. As O'Donnell has noted, not all processes culminate in the same result. For example, China and Iran are said to have liberalized politically, but this does not mean that they are democratizing or are in the process of a democratic transition. China and Iran do not appear to be on their way toward adopting the kind of political system that the West usually considers democratic. On the other hand, what is remarkable about the last quarter of the twentieth century is not only the sheer number of countries that made political reforms, but also the number that began a democratic transition of one kind or another. In understanding how so many countries arrived at this point it is important to recognize that each country's situation is unique; its citizens are responding to a particular set of historical challenges and socioeconomic problems. Consequently, no single set of determinants can satisfactorily explain the origins and evolution of democratic transitions throughout the third world.[14]

As you will recall from Chapter 10, some analysts emphasize the significance of internal factors in understanding change. Their interest is the roles played by domestic actors, whether elites or masses, in the dramatic political

Figure 14.2 Is Democracy Universally Desirable?

Operating under the assumption that "all good things go together," starting in the late 1980s donor countries began pressuring aid recipients to show that they were making political as well as economic reforms. The targets of these reforms frequently criticized such interference with domestic politics for a variety of reasons. One problem was that developed countries, with their emphasis on political and civil rights over economic and social rights, were arbitrarily assigning certain values as democratic. Advocates of what is called the "Asian values" argument contend that democracy is a Western concept not traditional to most of the world's cultures. Just as cultures that contain a democratic tradition have a better chance of making democracy work, those with little or no experience with democracy face significant disadvantages. These analysts argue that democracy has failed to take root in much of the world because it is not generally accepted there. They contend that it is ethnocentric to assume that democracy is a universal value, because under this definition democratic values (such as individualism) are unique to the West.[15] Moreover, the West's insistence on respect for democracy, political and civil human rights, and environmental concerns is hypocritical, since its own progress in these areas leaves much to be desired. Such an argument is difficult to dispute. Democratic principles are hardly unique to the West, just as the authoritarian impulse is scarcely restricted to the non-Western world.[16]

events we've been describing. The preceding chapters have demonstrated how people around the world are being mobilized by a variety of pressures. Citizens have demanded the opening of political space in which a variety of new relationships can be crafted. Not all of these groups are mobilized by democratic interests, yet whatever their goals, new forms of social mobilization and patterns of state-society relations are emerging in which relationships of power and accountability are redefined. Yet just as often it has been political elites that have initiated a political transition. Frustrated over their inability to govern effectively or faced with a crisis of LEGITIMACY, civilian and military leaders have on occasion stood aside to allow for democratic change. Once the transition is under way, elite commitment to democracy (or the lack of such commitment) has often played a large role in its success or failure.

Other analysts emphasize the role played by economic forces in promoting political change. They contend, for example, that the industrialization and economic success of South Korea and Taiwan created in these countries an environment conducive to democratization. There and elsewhere, as the middle class has grown, these citizens have become more politically conscious and vocal in demanding political and civil rights. However, around the world it is more common to find that political change has occurred as people have struggled to cope with devastating economic crises. There are cases from all four regions we study in which the hardship associated with austerity incited popular protests that nearly brought down governments, democratic and nondemocratic. In the immediate post–Cold War period often such demonstrations persuaded authoritarians to initiate political reform—or at least to affect the appearance of reform.

Although the political liberalization of some countries predated the end of the Cold War, external pressures associated with its demise (such as the withdrawal of superpower support for authoritarians) are recognized as another factor driving reform. Yet even now the governments of many third world countries continue to be highly extroverted; their survival depends on foreign patronage. As you read in Chapter 7, since the 1970s, in return for aid, international organizations such as the INTERNATIONAL MONETARY FUND (IMF) have directed developing countries to impose economic reforms on their increasingly disgruntled populations. However, after the Cold War ended, donor countries began to insist that third world governments initiate political reforms aimed at promoting "good governance"—increasing the accountability and transparency of government.[17] This is the "all good things go together" argument that we discussed in Chapter 7: proponents of NEOLIBERALISM tend to assume that economic growth and democratization complement each other and are mutually reinforcing (although there is still disagreement about which comes first). However, the developed countries have never been consistent in their demands for political liberalization; the vigor with which such calls were made varied depending on the target of reform (for example, for strategic and economic reasons, most Middle Eastern countries were largely exempt from donor attention).[18]

A variety of other external factors have also been used to explain the recent political changes experienced in so much of the world. Some analysts credit the dramatic events of the late twentieth century to a zeitgeist, or a "spirit of the times," unique to the immediate post–Cold War era because at that moment in

Figure 14.3   When Islamists Win Elections

Algeria's experience has been a lesson for many people seeking change in predominantly Muslim North Africa and the Middle East. Under a variety of pressures for political liberalization, Algeria's authoritarian government allowed democratic elections in 1991. A number of parties organized to participate in these elections, among them the Islamic Salvation Front (FIS), an umbrella party representing many smaller Islamist groups. When the FIS was poised to win a strong majority of seats in a second round of parliamentary elections in early 1992, the Algerian government (with the tacit backing of France and the United States) voided the elections, declared the FIS illegal, and set out on a campaign to portray all Islamist contenders for power as a threat to democracy in Algeria and to the West. Supporters of this policy argued that Islamists were totalitarians in disguise, adopting the rhetoric of democracy only to gain power. In a way, these arguments became a self-fulfilling prophecy, as what happened in Algeria confirmed views of the West as hypocritically only supporting democracy when it is in its own interests. Not only in Algeria, but also throughout much of the region, democracy is at an impasse, and Islamists have since come to view it as corrupt, elitist, and morally bankrupt. The Islamist appeal has grown and exists in all Arab countries, and this may be as much due to sympathy for the Islamist program as it is based in resentment of corrupt government and Western hypocrisy.[19]

history democracy appeared to be breaking out all over and democratic ideology had no serious contenders.[20] This zeitgeist is believed by some to have contributed to a snowballing or demonstration effect, as authoritarian governments toppled like dominos.[21] Analysts interested in this facet of change argue that among states closely linked by culture, geography, or some other shared experience, the more successful a transition in any one country in the group, the more likely we are to see similar political change occur among the other members of that group. This effect has been magnified by the revolution in communications, in particular satellite television, which allows outsiders to watch events literally as they unfold. The intriguing role that this technology plays in political change is only one part of an "international diffusion effect," which can change leaders' expectations, affect crowd behavior, and even alter the balance of power almost overnight. Although such effects have mostly been associated with the military coups and the collapse of civilian rule, during the last twenty-five years the information revolution has also worked to support a resurgence of democracy.[22]

After the Transition:
Consolidating and Deepening Democracy

One way to understand the resurgence of democracy is to think of it as occurring in phases. Of the political systems that are democratizing, some are just making the transition from authoritarian rule and beginning to establish democratic regimes, such as Mexico and Nigeria. On the other hand, South Africa and most of Latin America are well into a second phase of democratization, known as consolidation. When is a democratic transition complete? According to analysts Juan Linz and Alfred Stepan, it is complete when there is sufficient agreement about the political procedures to produce an elected government. It is complete when a government comes to power as the direct result of a free and popular vote, and when this government has the authority to generate new policies. Finally, a democratic transition is complete when we can be sure that the executive, legislative, and judicial power generated by the new democracy is not subservient to other bodies such as the military. Most important perhaps, all politically significant groups agree to abide by the procedural rules of the game. In effect, a democracy has progressed from transition to consolidation when no significant political groups are seriously trying to overthrow the democratic regime or secede from the state.[23] These are the democratic rules and procedures that must be established before one can begin to speak of consolidation.

Even when a transition can be described as complete, there are still many tasks that must be accomplished, conditions that must be established, and culture (or attitudes and habits) that must be developed before democracy can be considered durable, or consolidated. How do we know when a democracy has been consolidated? Analysts admit that it is easier to recognize consolidation by its absence. Unconsolidated regimes are fragile, unstable, and plagued by signs of disloyalty. Beyond this it is hard to define consolidation, because no single indicator other than general stability serves as its marker. We know that the road to consolidation is a long and complicated one. Perhaps the simplest way of telling if consolidation exists is if democracy has become "the only game in town." The majority of people believe that the system is a good one, and that it is the most appropriate way of governing collective life.[24] When this is the case, the regime enjoys broad and deep levels of popular legitimacy.

When a democracy is consolidated, the issue for government is no longer how to avoid democratic breakdown. You know you have a consolidated democracy when, even in the face of extreme economic or political hardship, the overwhelming majority of people believe that any political change must occur through the democratic system. All political actors have become used to the idea that political conflict will be resolved according to the established rules, and convinced that violations of these rules will be ineffective and costly. In other words, when it is consolidated, democracy becomes a habit; it is routinized and widely accepted. This takes years of practice—some political scientists argue that two generations of uninterrupted democratic rule must pass before the rules of the game are refined, tested, and strengthened.[25]

How do we ensure that democracy lasts that long? Democratic stability is promoted when the rights of the political opposition and minorities are safeguarded. That may sound counterproductive, especially where divisions are deep, but analysts tell us that conflict becomes less intense as it is contained within institutional channels. Most important, over time there is a change in the political culture of elites and masses, as commitment to the democratic framework is no longer simply instrumental but rather a commitment based in principle. As democracies consolidate, we gradually see within them the development of what some analysts call a "civic culture." Although mutual trust between potential opponents, willingness to compromise, and cooperation between political competitors are all identified as key components of civic culture, the particulars of any democratic political culture will vary by country. In general, though, as consolidation proceeds, political elites and the masses gradually internalize democratic values and develop habits of tolerance and moderation. Rights become realities and there is an agreed standard of fairness. Of course, this balanced political culture is only likely to occur where inequalities are relatively low and people can afford not to care too much about politics—and such circumstances do not yet exist in most new democracies. As one analyst put it, "The trick, then, is for democracies to survive long enough—and function well enough—for this process to occur."[26]

In other words, consolidation is another breakthrough of sorts. It is fostered through a combination of institutional, policy, and behavioral changes and it is an important achievement for any budding democracy. Yet just because a regime is consolidated does not mean that it is immune to future breakdown. Any number of crises could occur to make a nondemocratic alternative attractive and undo even a consolidated regime. One way of avoiding such breakdown is by recognizing the intimate connection between consolidation and the deepening of democracy. This qualitative shift is sometimes described as a third phase of democratization. Democracies are deepened as they improve, by promoting equality and extending to more citizens the opportunity for participation in political life. By this definition, even older, more established democracies may still become more democratic. All democracies can be improved, made more responsive and representative.[27]

At this stage countries are often caught in a catch-22 situation. In what is sometimes called "the democratic dilemma," democracies need to be deepened to fully consolidate. However, the deepening of democracy can undermine the prospects of consolidation. Deepening democracy means addressing social and economic inequalities, and this is likely to threaten elite interests and provoke an authoritarian reaction. Consequently, in the short term at least, the most stable democracies are also often the most superficial ones—the ones that forestall necessary changes to minimize the risk of coup. Ironically, because they are "shells of what they could be," these democracies ultimately fail.[28] Incapable or unwilling to deal with the problems of massive inequality, they are vulnerable to "reverse waves" or democratic breakdowns. Such democratic breakdowns should be expected, just as they followed the first and second waves of democratization earlier in the twentieth century. These reverse waves have been traumatic times for human rights and international peace; they gave rise to fascist and communist regimes in the period between World Wars I and II, as well as military dictatorships in the 1960s and 1970s.[29]

Is there any indication that we are headed in that direction again? By the start of the twenty-first century there were troubling signs that support for democracy in some less developed countries (LDCs) was eroding. The expected reverse wave may already be hitting Latin America, the region furthest along in its transition. For example, a 2001 survey of seventeen countries conducted by the highly respected polling organization Latinbarometro found an unprecedented and sharp decline in popular support for democracy throughout much of the region. The numbers continued to decline in 2002. Mexico and Peru were two of the only Latin American countries polled in which optimism about democracy remained high (perhaps due to the relatively recent revivals of democracy in those countries). In a similar poll conducted in 2000, also by Latinbarometro, only 37 percent of Latin American respondents claimed to be satisfied with the way democracy worked in practice. This may be related to their dissatisfaction with market reforms, not just democracy. Popular support for democracy was lowest in Paraguay (12 percent) and Brazil (18 percent). This was quite a plunge for Brazil, where 62 percent of the population had described itself as very prodemocracy in 1995. In a stunning admission, a majority of Paraguayans revealed their disillusionment with democracy and nostalgia for authoritarian rule. And Latin America's experience is hardly unique. Although Latin America's level of support for democratic rule is low compared to other regions, the same questions posed in Asia and Africa elicited similar responses. In 1998 and 1999, for example, one-third of the South Koreans surveyed agreed that in certain circumstances authoritarian government might be preferable to democracy. While 70 percent of the public surveyed in twelve African countries said democracy was always preferable to other forms of government, people expressed their frustration over the failure of democracy to deliver economic benefits.[30]

With good reason, given the pressures weighing on them, the post–Cold War era has been a time of crisis management for the leaders of non-Western states. This crisis was (and is) being managed in a variety of ways, and the result, however loosely defined, is a fascinating array of variations on democracy. Catherine Boone identifies the most common manifestations of this crisis management as REFORM, RECONFIGURATION, and DISINTEGRATION. In the sections below and the next chapter we will describe these forms of crisis management as practiced in the third world. However, the particulars vary by country and whether a political system has reformed, reconfigured, or disintegrated can at least in part be explained by the structural differences among states. Individual decisions must also be factored in, as people worldwide make choices and take actions in response to the unique predicaments they face. In other words, just as the extent of the crisis each country faces is a function of the relative weakness of the regime and the strength of the pressures bearing on it, so too is the outcome.[31]

Reform

To review the fundamentals, for a political system to be considered a democracy it must be based in certain principles such as participation, representation, accountability, and respect for human rights. No government has a perfect record in this regard; however, some countries have made more progress in certain areas than in others. Long-standing, well-established democracies exist in India, Costa Rica, Botswana, and a handful of other non-Western countries. Given the diversity of these countries, it should come as no surprise that no single set of institutions, practices, and values embodies democracy. Similarly, various mixes of these components produce different types of constitutional systems. However, most democracies operate under some variant of the PARLIAMENTARY SYSTEM or the PRESIDENTIAL SYSTEM. Although U.S. citizens are most familiar with the presidential system, also found in much of Latin America and scattered throughout Africa and Asia, the largest democracy in the world, India, has a parliamentary system, and parliamentary systems are the norm in Europe.

This is significant, since some analysts argue that the choice of constitutional design and electoral system may impact the quality and stability of democracy. There are pros and cons to each constitutional system, and each system involves some trade-offs. Analysts disagree about which is best for developing countries. One group, led by Juan Linz, argues that although the presidential system has worked well for the United States, its record in LDCs is more problematic. The presidential system tends to concentrate power in the executive branch, perhaps making the president too strong and (where there is little commitment to democratic values or practices) facilitating the abuse of power. In Peru, Zimbabwe, South Korea, and elsewhere, presidential systems have been associated with executive coups (self-coups) and executive strikes against democracy.

This is one of "the perils of presidentialism," based in the tendency for executives in presidential systems to view themselves as having authority independent of the other branches of government. Even when they have won by the slimmest of margins, presidents are more likely than prime ministers to find opposition in the legislative branch irritating and to consider it an interference with their mission. Not all presidential systems suffer from this problem, but where presidentialism exists, whoever is elected president believes he or she has a mandate, or the right to govern as he or she sees fit. Under such circumstances, the executive is constrained only by the "hard facts of existing power relations" and the constitutionally limited term of office.[32]

It might appear that such an approach does not build a strong basis for the development of democratic institutions. Not only does presidentialism adversely affect the quality of democracy, but it is commonly viewed as a major factor contributing to democratic breakdowns. Part of the reason for this is lack of capacity: while a strong executive is capable of making rapid decisions, it is often less proficient at coping with crises. Still, some presidential regimes have survived extremely difficult challenges. But where there is presidentialism, gridlock (resulting from the mix of a domineering president and a newly assertive legislature) is more likely. And some analysts contend that presidencies tend to be more rigid and are less likely to avail themselves of the creative approaches demanded by most crises.[33]

Still, fearful that mounting problems will overwhelm a weak or inexperienced government, voters tend to create presidentialist regimes, as they frequently flock to candidates who promise to save the country. Such leaders appear to be strong, courageous, and above partisan interests. This image is very seductive, especially for people who have lived through difficult or uncertain times. Consequently, we should not be shocked by the frequency of presidentialism. It is important to remember that democratic elections are not an end unto themselves. Newly democratizing countries can be expected to continue on in a transition that is not necessarily linear in its progression. There is rarely a simple trajectory from authoritarian to democratic rule; transitions are often longer and more complex than that. This is in part because the values and beliefs of officials are embedded in a network of inherited power relations and do not change overnight. This helps to explain why elections in newly democratizing countries can be such an emotional and high-stakes event. Oftentimes the candidates compete for a chance to rule virtually free of all constraints. After the elections, voters are expected to become passive cheerleaders for all of the president's policies.[34]

For these reasons, parliamentary systems are described by Linz as better suited for most countries. According to Linz, parliamentary systems are more stable and more representative than presidential systems. In parliamentary regimes the only democratically legitimate institution is parliament. The executive's authority is completely dependent upon parliamentary confidence. As opposed to presidential systems (in which the executive is usually selected through direct popular elections), in parliamentary systems there is no worry about executives reaching out to appeal to people over the heads of their representatives.[35]

However, Donald Horowitz argues that parliamentary systems can actually end up more polarized and coalitions can end up more unstable than they are in presidential systems, and that this can impede the business of governance. Unlike presidential systems, parliamentary governments risk periodic crises (known as a "vote of no confidence") that can result in the ousting of executives and the disruption caused by new elections. On the other hand, Linz argues that what appears to be instability in parliamentary governments can actually be a benefit: since parliamentary systems are more flexible, they are self-correcting. Moreover, Linz contends that fragmentation is not a problem unique to parliamentary systems. Because there are fewer incentives to make coalitions in a presidential system, gridlock is a persistent problem and the legislative and executive branches end up competing against each other rather than working together. Yes, coalitions and power sharing are possible under such systems, but more often the institutional rivalry associated with the separation of powers in a presidential system can be extremely destabilizing, especially for unconsolidated democracies.[36]

The tendency of presidential systems toward majoritarianism (in which majorities govern and minorities oppose) makes politics a winner-take-all ZERO-SUM GAME. Because it creates a sharp divide between the government and the opposition, majoritarianism aggravates divisiveness in countries where it is already a problem. What one wins, the other loses. However, the zero-sum nature of majoritarian politics is also associated with parliamentary systems such as those of Britain, India, Jamaica, and Sri Lanka. In parliaments dominated by a single majority party, this party controls both the executive and legislative branches. Consequently, the prime minister may end up having more effective power than that of the typical president.

Still, not all parliamentary systems are majoritarian. Some forms of parliamentary government tend to be multiparty and to create governments built on what is called a consensus model. As opposed to the sharp divides of majoritarianism, the consensus model found in Turkey and most of continental Europe attempts to share, disperse, and restrain power in a variety of ways. For example, under the consensus model a parliamentary government can promote the creation of broad coalition cabinets and an executive-legislative balance of power. According to Linz, in such parliamentary systems the executive is more accountable before the legislature. This is important, since in deeply divided societies it is crucial that particular groups not be excluded. Government must work to build consensus and give everyone a stake in the system by encouraging coalitions. Yet in presidential systems gridlock is not always the rule and conciliatory practices are not unknown. Actually, some analysts argue that the mode of election (i.e., single member versus proportional representation) is more important in fostering conciliation and consensus building than whether the constitutional system is parliamentary or presidential.[37]

An additional factor considered in these debates concerns another aspect of rigidity versus flexibility. The proponents of presidential systems argue that rigidity of fixed presidential terms is an advantage as opposed to the uncertainty and instability characteristic of parliamentary politics. However, there are also disadvantages to the inflexibility of presidential systems. Not only is reelection possible only on a fixed term, but it is very difficult to impeach or remove a president from power before his or her term is over. As a result, the country may be stuck with a "lame duck" government that has lost public confidence and support. Or, because of fixed terms and limits on reelection, experienced and capable leaders must step down at the end of their terms.

Conversely, advocates of parliamentary systems say that such systems are advantaged by their greater flexibility and adaptability. With a vote of no confidence, in which the majority of the members of parliament vote to "censure" the prime minister, the legislative branch can force new elections to be called at any time to turn out an executive who has lost popular support—without regime crisis. And popular, effective executives can be retained indefinitely, whereas a president may be required to retire just as he or she is becoming an adept leader. Moreover, because in presidential systems the executive is both head of government and head of state, there is no constitutional monarch or ceremonial president who serves as a moderating influence on the executive (as there is in parliamentary systems). Although it is increasingly the case in parliamentary systems as well, presidential systems tend to place a heavy reliance on the personal qualities of a single political leader. Again, Linz argues that this is risky, especially in countries where there is an authoritarian tradition.[38]

In the end, consideration of a country's history and culture is crucial in the selection of a constitutional system, since the issue of "fit" is so important. Lack of synergy between a country and its constitutional system can greatly undermine popular support for democracy. Some countries have switched from one type of constitutional system to another in an effort to get it right: Zimbabwe and Nigeria have replaced parliamentary with presidential systems, while many Latin American countries suffering from presidentialist politics have considered adoption of parliamentary forms of government. Still, some analysts argue that the constitutional system matters little, since the differences between the two types of systems are exaggerated—both systems have succumbed to military coup and single-party rule. They add that perhaps other factors, such as political culture or the economy, are more important than institutional choice in promoting durable democracies. The one thing these political scientists seem to agree on is that any system involves some trade-offs.[39]

As you will see in the sections that follow, no matter if it is presidential or parliamentary, democratization must be based on certain bedrock principles: DEMOCRATIC INSTITUTIONALIZATION, political competition, and various forms of vertical and horizontal accountability. Beyond this, there is room for an enormous variety of formal and informal rules and institutions within what we broadly recognize as democracy.[40]

Democratic Institutionalization

Political systems are classified as democratic as long as they have made or are making observable progress toward what is often referred to as democratic institutionalization. In order for democratic systems to be long lasting and meaningful, democratic institutions must be crafted, nurtured, and developed.[41] When democratic institutions are strong, the processes of government are established and less vulnerable to nondemocratic intrusions (e.g., military takeover). Under such circumstances, citizens and leaders alike can develop reasonable expectations about the rules and procedures of government, which are "above" the whims of individuals or groups. In other words, the rules should be stable and formalized—they should not vary dramatically based on which particular leader is in office. This development of regularized processes is often referred to as institutionalization. Through their various functions, institutions ensure participation, representation, accountability, and respect for human rights.

Democratic institutions are often thought of as the formal, concrete organizations (such as the executive, the legislative, and the judicial branches of government, as well as political parties and civil society) that are the principal means through which citizens select and monitor democratic government. Yet other democratic institutions are more procedural, such as regularized patterns of interaction that are widely accepted and practiced, like electoral rules, the checks and balances of presidential systems, or the rules governing the transfer of power. Whatever their form, democratic institutions promote in one way or another the individual's right to participate in the political life of the community. In their particular capacities, each institution in a democracy serves a critical function.[42]

Political Competition

Political competition is a procedural part of democratic institutionalization. It involves much more than the right to form parties or to take part in elections. For example, in order for parties and candidates to freely compete for political office, they need access to the media, just as citizens need independent sources of information. Individuals and parties seeking power know that positive press and advertising are crucial to any campaign. For example, most analysts of Mexican politics agree that television coverage of the 2000 presidential campaign in Mexico was a deciding element in the vote. Now media-savvy parties enlist public relations firms to create commercials full of slick images. They hire U.S. spin-doctors to manipulate sound bites so as to put their candidate in the best light. However, the live airing of the Mexican presidential debates was historic, because it gave the population an unprecedented chance to see the candidates stripped of their Madison Avenue sheen.

Figure 14.4 Image Is Everything

Here are examples of some of the images created for successful political campaigns in 1999 and 2000. Consider the basis of these candidates' popular appeal:

Mexico. The strapping Marlboro Man lookalike Vicente Fox was sold as a macho Harley-driving challenger who would run Mexico as a CEO rather than as a politician. He broke with polite convention to call his challenger a "sissy." Famous for his foghorn voice and cowboy boots, Fox is known for his off-color jokes and boisterous, blunt style.

Nigeria. His handlers worked hard to make Olusegun Obasanjo popularly known as a snooker-playing teetotaler. Born again (in more ways than one) he is both a "born again" Baptist and his political career has come back from the brink. By the late 1990s Obasanjo had distanced himself from his past as a military dictator, exchanged his general's uniform for traditional dress, and spoke often of the years he spent in prison for his support of the prodemocracy movement. He campaigned as a southerner with experience who could work with the north and bring unity to the country.

Beyond access to the media, political competition is based in the principle that political parties must be free to organize, present candidates for office, express ideas, and compete in fair elections. To help safeguard the process from undue influence of elites, more democracies are developing rules concerning campaign finance, including ceilings on how much private individuals and groups can contribute to political parties and candidates. Strict enforcement of limits on donations and other aspects of party financing is a necessity. Prior to recent Mexican reforms, one candidate reportedly spent twenty times the legal campaign limit.[43]

Campaign finance reform is just one aspect of a number of procedural elements meant to safeguard democracy. Although governments vary widely in terms of these procedural elements (such as when elections are to be held), in democracies the procedures for holding government accountable are well established and respected. Regular, free, and fair elections are taken for granted in democracies. While elections are often upheld as an indicator of freedom, and they can be an important part of a democracy, in and of themselves they hardly guarantee that a country is democratic. Remember the electoral fallacy: even nondemocratic states may hold elections.

Whether it is the first election or the fiftieth, the orchestration of free and fair elections is a complicated undertaking. The investment of a great deal of time, money, and effort is necessary long before election day to lay the basis for a legitimate result. Free and fair elections require the creation of an independent electoral commission. The reputation of such a commission must be beyond reproach, as it undertakes the tedious and painstaking work that is critical to the honesty of any vote. As you might imagine, this can be quite difficult in a country without reliable transportation and communication facilities, or with an enormous population (India has 600 million voters). Where no good census exists, just the registration of voters is an enormous task. However, throughout the third world, more electoral commissions are developing computer programs to

Figure 14.5   Elections in China

While it should be clear from the above discussion that elections are an extremely important component of democracy, the existence of competitive elections alone is not sufficient evidence of the stirrings of a democratic transition. In the People's Republic of China, for example, truly competitive elections at the local level have taken place since the mid-1980s, although these have been confined to villages and to county-level people's congresses. At the village level, citizens now elect members of "Villagers' Committees" every three years. These committees are officially nongovernmental organizations, since villages are not a formal level of government. They manage public affairs and social welfare, help maintain public order, and promote economic development, primarily through job creation. As early as mid-1992, 80 percent of China's approximately 950,000 villages had completed at least two rounds of elections.[44] International observers, many under the auspices of the Carter Center, have followed election campaigns, and they have consistently noted a level of competition and campaigning that was previously unknown in China. Political parties other than the Chinese Communist Party (CCP) are not allowed, but candidates are able to run as independents. During this period approximately 40 percent of the elected candidates were not in fact running under the CCP banner.

Observers have noted concerns about voter privacy: people normally marked their ballot from their seats, rather than using a private booth. As this is common practice, people who would attempt to use the more private polling booths might raise suspicion among their fellow villagers. Most analysts believe that these elections were implemented less to promote democratic sentiment and more to facilitate control over unruly agents in the countryside. Giving peasants the opportunity to vote out corrupt communist officials enhances their sense of legitimacy for the regime overall. And while there is some debate about extending village committee elections to the township level (the lowest official level of government in China), it is proceeding slowly.

---

organize electoral rolls and prevent fraud. But even these computer programs must be strictly monitored. To protect against fraud and to demonstrate his dedication to democratizing the process, former Mexican president Ernesto Zedillo adopted reforms to ensure that his country's electoral institute was truly nonpartisan. Billions of dollars were spent to compile a reliable list of eligible voters in Mexico. The adoption of national identity cards for the first time afforded millions of women (and others who were less likely to have a driver's license or other form of official identification) the opportunity to vote. In Nigeria, President Obasanjo proposed that national identity cards be used to register voters in that country's 2003 elections to help prevent fraud. However, the idea had to be scrapped, since regions with large illiterate populations feared this was a ruse to disenfranchise their voters and tilt the balance of power.

Where citizens have had little or no experience participating in clean elections, voter education is a necessity. Beyond ensuring that they have access to the information required to make an informed decision, voters must understand the ballot and be able to indicate their choices. Where a large proportion of the population is illiterate, this requires designing a ballot using symbols or photographs of the candidates as well as the written word. Furthermore, there are a number of practices democracies use to help ensure that there are no irregularities at the polls or with the count. Voting in most of the world is low-tech; ballots are marked by hand or with fingerprints. Voting with fingerprints helps to cut down on fraud, since the ink stains the skin for a few days and helps deter anyone who might wish to vote twice. Steel ballot boxes with padlocks made a certain statement and were the fashion in the 1980s in most Latin American countries. For symbolic and practical reasons, transparent ballot boxes are favored today in Mexico and throughout the region. As Mexico democratized, it invested in new voting booths. Outfitted with curtains, these booths were a break with the past in that they were designed to accommodate only one person at a time and ensured the privacy of the vote. The impact was enormous: for the first time in their lives, Mexicans could be sure they were voting without someone looking over their shoulders. Similarly, Haiti boasted of its first free and fair election in 1990 with the Creole slogan "As clean as a knife through a potato."[45]

Beyond efforts to guarantee privacy, local and international election observers must be trained and posted to help ensure the fairness of the process. A large part of this involves things like making sure that the process is orderly, that there is no intimidation at the polls, and that no one who is registered to vote is turned away. People often wait for hours to vote in mile-long lines, as turnout for elections is much higher in many third world countries than it is in the United States, where it is not unusual for fewer than 50 percent of registered voters to cast their ballots—even in presidential elections. The voting process itself must be clean; the electoral commission must ensure that there are enough ballots at the polls, and there must be sufficient numbers of observers to ensure that the process is free and fair. In addition, the commission is usually responsible for collecting and tabulating the vote, which is done by hand in most countries. Once the count is final, the results must be reported in a timely manner. As a good faith measure, a new computer system in Mexico allowed the manual count of the 2000 presidential elections to be rapidly posted in public on big screens and the Internet.

Taken together, these procedures help to ensure that an authentic democratic transition is under way. For countries experiencing them, the first democratic elections, or FOUNDING ELECTIONS, are historic events. They often symbolize a departure from authoritarianism, and dramatically demonstrate the power of a mobilized citizenry. Although the conduct of elections had improved greatly since 1997, in many ways the 2000 presidential vote in Mexico symbolized such an event. Virtually everyone agrees that this was the freest and fairest vote ever. The result serves as an indicator of its authenticity: the governing party allowed itself to lose the elections. It was a surprise for many; the victory by challenger Vicente Fox put an end to over seventy years of uninterrupted one-party rule. There was similar jubilation in 1999 over democratic elections in Nigeria after fifteen years of military dictatorship. Likewise, people celebrated that the parliamentary elections in Indonesia in 1999 were the freest since 1955.

While founding elections mark an important watershed event, most analysts agree that it is the second round of elections that are a more vital step toward consolidation, especially if they result in an orderly transfer of power. Many Nigerians know that the transition of 2003 will pose the greatest challenge for their new democracy. Nigerians recall from their experience in 1993 that an incumbent unhappy with the result can quickly end a democratic experiment. Nearly two dozen parties were slated to compete in Nigeria's 2003 general elections. Just months ahead of the vote, some parties had not yet selected their candidates for president and none of them were talking much about platforms. This is not unusual in Nigeria, where politics is said to be more about personality and style (not to mention money and ethnicity) than about ideology or issues. As this book went to press, President Obasanjo was favored to win reelection. But he was facing some serious challenges from within his own party as well as from some of the powerful figures who had had a lot to do with Obasanjo's win in 1999. By the time you read this, whatever the outcome of the elections, it is likely that Nigeria's president is a former soldier or military leader.

Although there are "dominant-party democracies," such as Botswana, in which there has never been a transfer of power because one party has always won elections, these countries are still widely regarded as democracies. For as long as the possibility of change exists, the system is democratic. Still, for most countries the transfer of power from one party to another is a crucial part of the transition and an essential turning point in the development of a democracy.

Beyond these procedural elements and general principles, there are a number of other qualities we expect to see in countries making a democratic reform. Some analysts focus on the recruitment of candidates and argue that the people's representatives be drawn from an "open" political elite. Candidates for office in democracies are often sensitive to accusations of being part of an "old boys' club" and portray themselves as part of a new "breed" of leaders, capable of making real change. For example, Fox is said to be an untypical Mexican politician. Of immigrant descent, the former Coca-Cola executive campaigned as a businessman rather than a politician. Still, he once served as governor of the state of Guanajuato and although he was not a member of the ruling party, he could be considered part of the political elite. Ahmet Necdet Sezer was the first president in modern Turkish history who was neither an active politician nor a military commander (he was chief justice of the Constitutional Court). And during Alejandro Toledo's campaign for the Peruvian presidency, much was made of his rise from shoeshine boy to Stanford-educated economist. Toledo embraces his identity as an outsider and makes the most of the fact that he is the country's first Amerindian president.

Whereas the idea of any elite dominating politics is perhaps antithetical to the democratic ideal, the fact remains that the economically rich have a disproportionate hold on power in both democratic and nondemocratic governments. Yet by "open," it is hoped at least that democratic systems will be more accessible to newcomers, more concerned with the interests of the general public, and more likely to work for the interests of the majority. At the very least, because in democratic systems the political elite can be held accountable to the voters, we can assume that those who are elected will try harder to make good on their promises.

Vertical Accountability
One of the cardinal rules of democracy is "you can't stay in power by doing nothing." No democracy is likely to be consolidated without high levels of sup-

port offered by legitimacy, and no democracy will garner high legitimacy rates without some degree of effective governance. As mentioned earlier in this chapter, one of the two most commonly understood components of good governance is accountability. But there are two kinds of accountability: horizontal and vertical accountability. By vertical accountability, we refer to a government's relationship with its citizens. The more responsive a government is to popular demands, the more satisfied people will be with the way government works and support it through hard times. The better government is at promoting the general welfare, the more people will trust their government, believe the system to be a good one, and be committed to it.[46]

Capacity building. The ability to strategize, prioritize, and carry out state functions to improve people's lives, or capacity building, is a crucial test for most new democracies. One measure of its capacity is the government's ability to deliver public services. Yet although people commonly cite effectiveness as a highly valued attribute of governments, democracies don't necessarily make for the most efficient of administrations. And decisive action is even more difficult for democracies under economic strain. As you read in Chapters 6 and 7, undemocratic governments have sometimes proven to be quite capable of delivering not only services, but also economic growth. It could be argued that when it comes to capacity building, democracies are disadvantaged in that by definition in this type of political system a variety of actors must be consulted in decision-making. Consequently, democracy tends to be a messy and slow business. New democracies certainly have a lot on their plates, and one of the first things their leaders must learn is to restrain expectations. New democracies are often expected not only to stabilize economies and promote economic development, but also to make good on promises of political freedoms and representativeness. They are to be accountable to their citizens, establish order, and promote the rule of law.[47] Beyond that, there are more mundane expectations of new democracies as well. The problem is that often these governments do not inherit usable bureaucracies and they therefore lack the administrative capacity to make progress in providing services, implementing policy, and so on. Elected government should at the very least be capable of performing what are commonly regarded as essential functions: collecting taxes, enforcing the law, and designing and implementing policies responsive to the majority. Some analysts expand the definition of essential functions to include a concern with the population's economic and social well-being. This typically includes demands for the supply of public goods (such as the rehabilitation of a communications and transportation system, or the provision of sanitation and electrification). Unless democracy can provide these things, it is unlikely to be viewed favorably for long. But for economic reasons if nothing else, this is out of reach for many governments.

Newly elected governments (such as Obasanjo's in Nigeria in 1999) not only face economic shortfalls, but also often find it extremely difficult to put back the pieces after years of mismanagement and abuse. It is extremely difficult to increase governmental capacity when the infrastructure has decayed beyond the point of viability. People are bitter about long lines for gasoline in a country that is one of the world's largest exporters of oil, where the electricity and telephone systems are off as often as they are on. Newly elected democratic governments know that they don't have much time to prove themselves. Where citizens have spent years under wasteful authoritarian rule, many expect to see a DEMOCRACY DIVIDEND, or a general improvement in the quality of life and standard of living in just a few years' time. Fox promised before his inauguration that within 100 days Mexicans would see results. Yet turning around an economy often takes longer than that, and although some populations have demonstrated impressive patience, sooner or later they are likely to become frustrated after waiting so long to see the benefits of change and fighting so hard for it. Under such pressures to perform, communication with the masses is of the utmost importance, and leaders who lose touch with their constituencies soon find themselves out of work. In much of Latin America as well, the appeal of POPULIST authoritarians may grow as more people sense that democracy isn't meeting their expectations.

Analysts suggest that democratic transitions are greatly affected by economic factors in a variety of ways. Certainly other factors come into play, but several consecutive years of negative economic growth lessen the chance of survival for a democratic regime (or a nondemocratic regime, for that matter). Poverty and economic inequality are key obstacles to democratization, and more than one country experiencing economic misery has fallen to what is called "the totalitarian temptation" in the search for alternatives. However, poverty does not guarantee failure. Some poor countries such as Uruguay have completed their transitions and consolidated their democracies despite hardship. The oldest third world democracy, India, is often characterized as a puzzle in that it retains democratic governance against all odds—poverty, entrenched caste and religious divisions, and problematic regional issues. Certainly such hardship makes these democracies more risk-prone, but a few cases show that it is possible for democracies to survive. To a great extent the ability to do this depends on whom the population blames for the economic problems, and the perceived desirability of political alternatives. Even where democratic government appears to be getting off to a slow start, as long as most people believe that democracy is the best political system for them, it can survive even under difficult economic conditions. If, however, people and their leaders believe democracy itself is compounding the problem, or that it is incapable of remedying the situation, democratic breakdown is likely.[48]

One of the first initiatives of any new leader (democratic or not) is to attempt to bond with the masses by blaming the country's problems on the previous administration. It is quite common for candidates to be elected promising to fight CORRUPTION, or the abuse of power for private gain. Corruption is a problem shared by all forms of government in virtually every country in the world, including the oldest democracies. Both Obasanjo and Fox came into office saying that fighting corruption would be their first priority. Obasanjo began implementing anticorruption legislation, which was touted as the toughest in Africa. He needs all the help he can get, since Nigeria was identified by the organization Transparency International in 2001 as the most corrupt country in the world (Indonesia was close behind). It is said that Nigeria's national treasury was empty when Obasanjo took office. To rectify this problem, he is attempting to find and recover funds illegally transferred by Nigerian politicians and soldiers to accounts abroad. Switzerland has already frozen more than $600 million in illicit funds. Yet this is only the tip of the iceberg; it is estimated that the last dictator alone, Sani Abacha, looted the treasury of $8 billion.[49]

Fighting corruption by promoting accountability and transparency is crucial if democracies are to progress. In old and new democracies alike, pervasive official misconduct can contribute to democratic breakdown. Bribery, extortion, influence peddling, and other scandals can greatly damage political legitimacy and disillusion people, alienating them from the political process.[50]

How can corruption be reduced? Most experts recommend a broad strategy based around the idea of increasing TRANSPARENCY, which can be understood in a number of interrelated ways. In one crucial sense, it means openness, particularly in terms of spending and budgetary matters. During Mexico's liberalization, the government began declassifying information and publishing the federal budget in full (something that had traditionally been cloaked in secrecy). The Obasanjo government came in promising to make the process of awarding government contracts transparent. Peru's democratically elected president Alejandro Toledo pledged to fight corruption by creating government websites and providing toll-free information numbers for people to report official misconduct. Likewise, in countries improving their transparency, it is common for presidential discretionary or "secret" funds to become not so secret, and to be cut or abolished altogether.

Accountability is not only about punishing wrongdoers but also about reducing the incentive to steal by raising the risks and costs associated with it. It means that officials who treat the state treasury as a private source of wealth, down to police and petty officials who supplement their meager incomes with *una mordida* ("a bite") or *bakshish* ("a gift"), will no longer be allowed to violate the law with impunity but will be prosecuted for it. Governments must improve the ability to detect extortion and other abuses so as to better expose, punish, and disgrace those guilty of misconduct.[51] In Mexico, which is said to have a culture of graft, Fox has proposed a "Transparency Commission" to investigate the abuses of previous governments and to serve as a government watchdog. Programs like this one are popular but potentially problematic. They tend to be political and can wind up as witch hunts. In Mexico a number of unsolved mysteries, including the assassinations of a presidential candidate, an archbishop, and a leader of the Institutional Revolutionary Party (PRI), who was also the former brother-in-law of the sitting president, may never be solved. Not only would it involve the indictment of literally thousands of people, but the records may no longer exist.

Similarly, in Indonesia there have been multiple attempts to hold Suharto and his family accountable for abuses. During Suharto's thirty-two-year reign his family accrued a personal fortune estimated at $40 billion. The former president, with great fanfare, was placed under house arrest, but the charges against him were later dropped, ostensibly for health reasons. His youngest son, Hutomo (Tommy), who held a monopoly on clove processing and controlled many key national industries, was sentenced to eighteen months in prison for a corrupt land deal. This was the first time a member of that family had ever been convicted of a crime, but few Indonesians were satisfied with the light-handed treatment of the Suharto clan.

The rule of law. There are important distinctions between the rule of law and rule by law. Rule by law is commonly employed by authoritarian regimes to repress populations. Dictators pass a series of laws as a way of cracking down on "enemies of the state." On the other hand, one of the core functions of a democracy is guaranteeing the rule of law. Whether that means making it safe for people to walk around their neighborhoods at night or a policy of zero tolerance for official corruption, strengthening the rule of law is a tremendous challenge for many democratizing regimes. Although there have been some high-profile arrests since Fox became president, it is estimated that 95–98 percent of the crimes committed in Mexico still go unpunished. Public frustration with the Nigerian government's inability to impose the rule of law has led to vigilantism. Groups such as the Yoruba nationalist Odua People's Congress (OPC) have lynched suspected armed robbers and others designated as "undesirable," including innocent Hausas. In response, President Obasanjo ordered the army to shoot troublemakers on sight. Such an order illustrates the president's frustration with his inability to guarantee the rule of law, but the rule of law also means that legal systems in democracies should be able to guarantee predictable and impartial treatment from governmental agents, including the police, the military, and judges. This poses a major challenge for many governments, especially where such agents have long traditions of acting with impunity. Within Mexico, the culture of corruption within the police force (and the military, which serves as a national police) is so institutionalized, so ingrained, that many people consider the police to be the worst criminals. In 1997 the army general appointed to head Mexico's war on drugs turned out to be on a drug cartel's payroll. Moreover, the alarming crime rates in Mexico were and continue to be very much an election issue. President Fox knows that fear of kidnapping, robbery, and other crimes also affects investment and tourism. One important way of promoting public security would be to curb the power of the Ministry of Interior, which, as the agency supposed to police the police, has earned the nickname "Ministry of Fear."

People need to be able to trust the police as public servants and they need to have confidence in the administration of justice. Recent reforms in Mexico's military have led to some impressive gains against that country's drug mafias. A strong, efficient, and independent judiciary is another decentralizing institution crucial to the success of both parliamentary and presidential systems. A powerful judiciary, professional, depoliticized, and largely free from executive or other partisan interference, can be the greatest protector of a democratic constitution and source of democratic legitimacy. It is the ultimate guarantor of the rule of law.[52] Yet analysts recognize the judicial branch to be one of the democratic institutions it takes longest to create, and progress is probably most accurately measured by degree. For example, until very recently, judges in China were purely political appointments. Judges lacked even the cursory legal training that lawyers received. In Turkey, the judiciary is nominally independent, but the Constitutional Court is mostly regarded as within the purview of the military. The Mexican Constitution allows for a separation of powers between the executive, legislative, and judicial branches: the president nominates justices, who are confirmed by the legislature and given lifetime appointments. However, under the PRI, incoming presidents were guaranteed a court of their liking, since it was understood that the entire bench would retire along with each outgoing president.

Reconciling group conflict. As Robert Dahl notes, at its basis the exercise of democracy is the institutionalization of conflict.[53] Democratic leaders must spend a great deal of their time at least appearing to be responsive to the interests of groups with conflicting interests. States are not independent of ethnicity, class, gender, and other interests, but the legitimacy of democratic governments is partly derived from their ability to appear to be independent of these interests, to modify conflict, and to build consensus. Yet democracy has an inherent paradox: it requires both representativeness and conflict, but not too much of either. Democracy must allow for competition, but only within carefully defined and accepted boundaries. Reconciling group conflict is at the heart of democratic politics, but the ability to do this doesn't happen overnight. New democracies must work to promote understanding and contain conflicts so that CLEAVAGES don't tear their countries apart. As mentioned earlier, democracy is institutionalized competition for power. However, if that competition is too intense, the system can break down entirely. It is therefore crucial that new democracies find mechanisms to mitigate conflict and promote consensus. They must do this in a way that works successfully to pull together all the core principles of democracy: participation, representation, accountability, and respect for human rights.[54]

Cleavages are found in every country in the world. They tend to run along lines of class, ethnicity, religion, region, and party. Because it is wrapped up in issues of identity, ethnicity is often listed as the most difficult type of cleavage for a democracy to manage. In MULTINATIONAL STATES, compromise is difficult, and in deeply divided plural societies, ethnicity is often thought to predetermine access to power and resources. What one group wins, another group fears it will lose—and fear of exclusion is not an unreasonable concern, given the experience of many countries. Elections become a desperate struggle between parties, as well as ethnic groups, regions, even religions. The rules matter little, since to lose political power is to lose access to virtually everything that is important. Under these circumstances the potential for polarization is such a real threat that some analysts hold out little hope for democracy where divisions are deep and identity has been politicized.[55]

Democratic governments must therefore attempt to manage or soften this conflict in a variety of ways. As described in more detail in Chapter 12, they can attempt to generate crosscutting cleavages, or find common ground between groups, can work to moderate political views, and can promote tolerance and cooperation. Another way of mediating these pressures is through institutional designs that encourage the decentralization of power. Federal systems of government may be crucial to the survival of democracy where cleavages are deep, since they allow for more autonomy and responsiveness at the local level. They also diminish the winner-take-all character of politics by facilitating the greater representation of minorities and other marginalized groups. Conflict may be reduced and interethnic accommodation promoted through other efforts to reconcile historical differences. The protection of minority rights may go a long way toward managing deep divides—for instance, through the recognition of more than one official language, respect for a variety of legal codes, and toleration of parties representing different communities. A number of countries, such as South Africa, have been relatively successful in managing tensions by skillfully crafting democracies that take into account the particular mix of cultures and identities contained within their territory. Some analysts suggest designing coalitions, like Bosnia-Herzegovina's, that allow for a sharing or rotating of power. More commonly such efforts ensure that all have equal rights to citizenship and protect the rights of minorities to use their own culture, religion, and language. Ethnic groups who are allowed to share power are much more likely to view the democracy as legitimate.

Yet this is not always the case, and some politicians actually encourage "tribalism" and manipulate issues of ethnicity to their own political advantage. It may not be possible to generate crosscutting cleavages where there is a close coincidence between them (as in Nigeria, where people are often united by region, ethnicity, and religion).[56] As a result, reconciling group conflict often poses a nearly impossible task for many newly elected governments.

In addition to political cleavages concerning ethnicity and religion, there are also often deep divides over matters concerning women's equality. Although for various reasons women have also been known to support authoritarians, they have often been at the forefront of prodemocracy movements, in part because they expected that democracy's emphasis on human rights would include them and their children. In some cases they were correct in this belief. As the *abertura* has unfolded, political space has gradually opened to women in several countries. As Bahrain moved toward a tentative democratic transition in 2002, women were permitted to vote and run for office for the first time (thirty-one women did run, and all of them lost).[57] The lesson here is that simply allowing previously disenfranchised groups the right to participate in elections as candidates and voters is not enough to result in a true *abertura*. Affirmative action to guarantee women's representation in political bodies may be one way of prodding such an opening. Taiwan has an electoral system that reserves 10 percent of the seats for women. India, Venezuela, and several other countries have adopted quotas as well. Although these rules often go unenforced, in general women's representation in government (especially at the local, but also at the state and federal levels of government) has increased remarkably. In the late 1990s females held 18 percent of the seats in the Peruvian Congress, making Peru a leader in the region, which averages less than 15 percent female representation. However, in South Korea (and much of East Asia except Taiwan), where the lack of such a system combines with patriarchal pressures to restrict their participation in politics, women's representation remains very low.[58]

Still, increasing the formal representation of women doesn't guarantee that the distribution of political resources will change, and women politicians (who need to conform to succeed) are not usually in a good position to challenge the existing system, which is resistant to change.[59] In even what appear to be bold

Figure 14.6   Shattering Stereotypes

Some of the first female heads of government and heads of state in the modern era have come from the third world:

• Sirimavo Bandaranaike of Sri Lanka is considered to be the "dean" of women's leaders. She was the world's first elected female prime minister, serving in that post from 1960 to 1965, 1970 to 1977, and 1994 to 2000.

• Indira Gandhi was prime minister of India from 1966 to 1977 and 1980 to 1984, when she was assassinated.

• In 1988, at the age of thirty-five, Benazir Bhutto became Pakistan's elected prime minister, the first woman to head a modern Islamic state (she has also faced corruption charges on more than one occasion). As of early 2003, Bhutto was a self-exiled party leader preparing for a political comeback.

• In 1993, Turkish voters elected Tansu Çiller as their first female prime minister. She led the country for four years, until 1997, and remains a government adviser.

• In 1997, Janet Jagan, age seventy-seven, won election as Guyana's first female president, succeeding her husband in office.

• Khaleda Zia was selected as Bangladesh's prime minister in 2001, when her coalition won the majority in parliament. She replaced a female incumbent, Sheik Hasina Wazed.

• In 2001, Indonesia's Megawati Sukarnoputri and the Philippines' Gloria Macapagal Arroyo became the presidents of their countries, replacing men ousted for incompetence and corruption.

Certainly some third world women have come to office by making a name for themselves. But Hillary Clinton and Elizabeth Dole are not unique: in developed as well as less developed countries (and for men too), the family name has sometimes opened doors for women and served as an important entrée into politics. Many female presidents and prime ministers have risen to prominence at least partly because they were the widows or daughters of male political leaders (Corazon Aquino, Indira Gandhi, Violeta Chamorro, and Benazir Bhutto are just a few examples).

political reforms, such "progressive" legislation is mostly a formality that has meant very little change in the lives of women. Liberalizing governments have also been known to extend women's economic rights, such as the right to own property, or the right to equal pay for equal work. But these reforms as well have often disappointed because of a government's failure to implement the new laws or to put resources into programs promoting equality. Democratic and nondemocratic governments commonly include a ministry or department specifically established to deal with "women's issues." However, it is rare for such offices to hold much power; in most cases they are marginalized, and the women heading them are mere tokens in otherwise overwhelmingly male cabinets. Although it could be argued that women's status has generally improved in most regions, that progress has come very slowly. Moreover, there continues to be great unevenness in women's experience of gender equality, both between and within countries, based on regional, class, ethnic, and other divides.

As you can see in Figure 14.7, the UN Development Programme (UNDP) has developed a composite measure to examine the opportunities that are made available to women in countries around the world. This index, called the Gender Empowerment Measure (GEM), provides a detailed look at the prospects women face in the professional aspects of life, including serving in government,

Figure 14.7   Measuring Gender Empowerment, 1999

	GEM Rank	Seats in Parliament Held by Women	Female Administrators and Managers	Female Professional and Technical Workers
Mexico	33	16.9%	19.8%	45.2%
China	40	21.8%	11.6%	45.0%
Zimbabwe	58	14.7%	15.4%	40.0%
Peru	63	10.8%	20.0%	39.4%
Indonesia	71	11.4%	6.6%	40.8%
Turkey	85	2.4%	8.6%	33.0%
Iran	88	4.9%	3.5%	32.6%

Source: UNDP, *Human Development Report 2000.*
Note: In 1999, the GEM was calculated for 102 countries. Index for Nigeria was not calculated.

holding managerial office, and serving in a professional or technical capacity. An examination of the GEM rankings for over 100 countries shows that high levels of income are not necessarily required to create opportunities for women. As the UN's 1999 *Human Development Report* asserts, some developing countries "outperform much richer industrialized countries in gender equality in political and professional activities. . . . Costa Rica and Trinidad and Tobago are ahead of France and Italy."[60]

A look at our case studies in the GEM chart shows that even Mexico, which has the most favorable score, still has far to go in promoting gender equity. Men dominate virtually all governments (including democratic ones), and despite claims to the contrary, most governments are not representative of all "the people." Even relatively progressive governments have broken their promises to women (not to mention other historically marginalized groups) for a variety of reasons, most notably to avoid challenging traditional patriarchal interests.[61] Sonia Alvarez points out that states are slowest to work on particular types of issues defined as private, outside the "proper" realm of politics. It is only in the last thirty years that well-established liberal democracies have begun to deal with social relations, including spousal rape, sexual harassment, and other forms of violence against women. Most newly established democracies would rather delay dealing with such issues because of the controversy surrounding them. In Asia, for example, Malaysia is one of only a handful of countries to even recognize that the possibility of rape in marriage exists.[62] Therefore, while the *abertura* offers a range of possibilities perhaps once unheard of, the window of opportunity has only partially opened. Interestingly, sometimes it is the less-than-democratic regimes that can push through policies promoting gender equality. In democracies, through a process that is supposed to foster inclusion and consensus building, the promotion of human rights, especially women's rights, may get put on a back burner—in the interests of "unity."

Horizontal Accountability

Any number of obstacles can interfere with a leader's ability to make good on his or her promises. Ironically, the democratic process itself is likely to be identified as one of those obstacles. For example, although he appears to have a clear mandate, in reality Fox has extremely limited powers. As of 2002, the PRI still had a slight majority in the legislature and it controlled many state governments. Indonesia's Wahid faced an even greater struggle trying to bring together disparate groups. He was selected president even though an opposition party, the Indonesian Democratic Party–Struggle (PDI-P) won a plurality of seats in the legislature. As a result, he chose that party's leader, Megawati Sukarnoputri, as his vice president. This compromise, however, did not satisfy many groups, who almost from the beginning began to call for the president's impeachment. This eventually occurred in July 2001, and Megawati assumed the reins of power. Although this all may sound very frustrating, it is important to remember that democracy centers on the decentralization of power. In presidential systems decentralization produces a separation of powers, allowing for checks and balances on the executive.

Separation of powers.   Part of the reality for democracies worldwide is that power sharing between legislative and executive branches has the potential for gridlock. When the PRI lost its majority in the legislature in the historic elections of 1997, it became clear that this body would no longer serve as a rubber stamp for the president. At first the scene was described as somewhat chaotic, as legislators were forced to learn how to negotiate. Similarly in Nigeria, Obasanjo was constantly at odds with a fractious National Assembly. Although his party controlled both houses, the president was known to refer derisively to the young, ambitious lawmakers dominating that body as "children" who were causing him no end of trouble. Deadlock over the budget resulted in policy paralysis; disbursements were put on hold and salaries went unpaid. For their part, the "children," who campaigned for Obasanjo, soon felt excluded by him. They accused the president of being more the authoritarian than democrat, a "my way or the highway general."

Of course the social and economic crises this and other governments have inherited from their authoritarian predecessors reinforce certain practices and ideas about the proper exercise of political authority. Moreover, dominant political cultures may value decisive leadership over institutional checks and balances. As mentioned earlier, presidentialism is likely to develop where a state of constant crisis has generated a strong sense of urgency. A parentlike figure, the president tends to become the embodiment of the nation, benevolent guardian and defender of its interests. There is no horizontal accountability. Because of his or her stature, other institutions such as the legislature and courts are seen as nuisances that interfere with the full authority the president has been delegated to exercise.[63] In Turkey, controversial executives such as Turgut Özal and Tansu Çiller were at times vertically accountable to the electorate, but they lacked any sense of horizontal accountability to other institutions, including the legislature. Few democracies can count on this luxury. Because elected governments are vertically accountable, they are more hesitant to make unpopular decisions.

While the executive in delegative democracies can often move faster because of the relative lack of horizontal accountability, the lack of an autonomous legislature or judiciary places immense responsibility on the president. It is up to the executive to shoulder the burden of a country's tremendous problems—and it's entirely the president's fault if he or she fails.

Civil control over the military. As you read in Chapter 12, in the face of growing instability, civilian leaders have often sent in the police and even the military to restore order among unruly crowds. Unless they find some other way of building legitimacy, these leaders become heavily dependent on the support of the security forces. However, the military often views itself as the supreme arbiter of the national interest. Its concern over civilian inability to impose calm in the midst of a political or economic crisis has on occasion prompted the military to take matters into its own hands.

A government that must continually look over its shoulder out of fear of an army takeover is in an extremely precarious situation. Many new democracies find themselves coexisting with powerful militaries by being careful not to challenge their prerogatives. Ideally, freely elected democracies would not be constrained or compelled to share power with other actors, including the military. Democratically elected governments should have unquestioned and full authority to generate new policies or carry out their core functions. Therefore, it is crucial that militaries be removed from politics and firmly subordinated to civilian control. MILITARY PROFESSIONALISM, or the military's depoliticization and recognition of civilian supremacy, is absolutely critical to the survival of democracy. The military must view itself as serving the civilian government, not as the definer and guardian of the national interest.

Unfortunately, few countries experiencing a democratic transition can rest fully assured that the military accepts this role. Where the transition was preceded by a military regime (or a military-dominated regime), unless it is eliminated by foreign intervention or by revolution, the security forces will still hold a powerful place in government during and after the transition. The military is a crucial part of the government that the new democracy must attempt to manage. Many new regimes have made efforts to establish civilian supremacy, with varying degrees of success. Although ultimately the goal is for military decisionmaking to be subject to civilian control, because of the military's power, leaders must know when and how far to push reform. This is the dilemma President Fox is facing, since the Mexican military has rejected civilian oversight and insists on maintaining its tradition of answering only to the president.[64]

Analysts agree that Nigeria needs to reduce military prerogatives, although they disagree whether Obasanjo is the man to do it. Wary of other former military leaders who might stage a comeback, Obasanjo has purged some army officers associated with the Abacha regime. However, many Nigerians suspect that Obasanjo owes his presidential win to military financiers and doubt he has the will to make significant reforms in civil-military relations. Since Obasanjo has been in office, soldiers have committed massacres without worry of prosecution, in part because the president doesn't want to provoke a coup. In Nigeria as in several other countries, getting the military out of power may necessitate an amnesty deal that would excuse its members from ever facing punishment for their abuses of human rights.

Conclusions:
When the Transition Turns Out to Be the Easy Part

President Wahid of Indonesia also struggled to gain control over not only the official military units but also the (oftentimes more reckless) militia units throughout the country. Wahid is now gone, but the military continues to run a parallel government in Indonesia, which has become greatly destabilized in recent years. This is not uncommon; during political transitions the military is often in a position to negotiate the terms of its withdrawal so that it retains non-democratic prerogatives. Ironically, such deals may be a political necessity—to get the military out of the presidential palace—but in the long run it greatly limits the possibilities for consolidation.[65] Because this is one of the limits of Turkey's democratization, it is frequently categorized as a delegative democracy. Consequently, until the possibility of coup d'état is remote, no system can be considered durably democratized.

Where democratic experiments have been attempted and failed, it is impossible to identify a singular cause for their failure. The lesson is that we cannot assume there will be a simple unilinear advance to democracy in the third world, given the heterogeneities and inequalities that exist there. While we celebrate the number of countries embarking on their democratic transition and look forward to their consolidation, perhaps our interest should be the substance of these institutions, at least as much as it is their sustainability. If this is the case, it is crucial then that instead of undermining it, we find ways to support the deepening of democracy, to improve the chances of its consolidation.

Political Transitions: Real or Virtual?

Elections in Peru have never been a ballroom dance.
—Rafael Roneagliolo, election monitor[1]

I do not enjoy power, but I have not achieved my objectives yet.
—Ali Akbar Hashemi Rafsanjani, former Iranian president[2]

Given the difficulties associated with the DEMOCRATIC TRANSITIONS described in the last chapter, it is important to recognize that transitions can be tough, protracted, and inconclusive. Many countries that began a POLITICAL LIBERALIZATION have already returned to authoritarianism, while others hang on precariously, under serious threat. The so-called transition we see in many countries may be more virtual than real. Transitions can be co-opted, controlled, or aborted.[3] As is discussed in the sections that follow, it is not unusual for AUTHORITARIAN governments to seek to legitimize their rule through elections. They are not above affecting the appearance of reform and will go to any lengths to hold on to power. However, with some important exceptions, authoritarians have tended to perform poorly. In Somalia and a handful of cases, years of authoritarian rule have aggravated various divides to such an extent that the state itself has disintegrated or collapsed. As we will see near the end of this chapter, more than a few states today are at risk of imploding or becoming virtually "stateless."

What Is "Virtual Democracy"?

You could say that there are as many different types of authoritarian systems as there are democracies. They can be right-wing and conservative, seeking to maintain the status quo or even turn back the clock to an idealized time, or they can be left-wing and radical, promoting transformative change. What we see among communal dictatorships, THEOCRACIES, and populist dictatorships (to name only a few) is that even governments that reject the democratic transition are scrambling to preserve their positions. They are under varying degrees of pressure from donors to at least affect the appearance of reform. Although these nondemocratic regimes share some important qualities with DELEGATIVE DEMOCRACIES, their leaders are solidly authoritarian. Whereas executives in delegative democracies dominate the other branches of government, the authoritarians described in this section subvert the entire democratic process. They may not appear quite as repressive as old-style authoritarians. The levels of repression today may not rank in terms of severity and magnitude with what occurred during the height of the COLD WAR. Still, in reconfiguring systems there are significant restrictions on participation, competition, and civil liberties. They may have elections, but they are patently unfair. For example, when it appeared that the "wrong party" was about to win, the Algerian government canceled the 1992 elections. Reconfiguring regimes ban parties at will, and restrict most political organization and competition. Sure, Egypt's President Hosni Mubarak was elected for a fourth time, but he ran unopposed. They are repressive of civil and political freedoms. Reconfiguring incumbents interfere with the campaign process and seek to further their political goals by establishing control over television, radio, and newspapers. Authoritarian governments have routinely imprisoned and tortured journalists critical of their policies. Prior to and following the presidential elections in 2002, Robert Mugabe placed tough curbs on the media. In much of the world it is not uncommon for journalists to be arrested, imprisoned, and tortured. "Preventive measures" including torture and assassination have been used in Egypt and Algeria against all those opposed to the government, including Islamists—both those directly implicated in violent action as well moderates committed to nonviolent means for change.[4]

And their leaders are frequently quite unabashed about it. They often make exceptionalist claims that the rules don't apply to them. When he was president of Peru, Alberto Fujimori admitted that his country was "an imperfect democracy," but insisted that any reforms would go "at Peru's pace."[5] Conservatives in Iran argue that they want reform, but that it must be in the context of an "Islamic-style" democracy in which clerics still hold political power, befitting of an Islamic, not a liberal, republic. Although these leaders deny the impact international pressure has on them, most are sensitive to their image overseas and few can face down the threat of sanctions. In effect, what many leaders have created is what has come to be known as "donor democracy." In order to keep the flow of aid open, these "democratic authoritarians" must look like they're making respectable progress at "getting politics right." From their point of view, getting politics right may actually mean putting stability first, especially where experiments in democracy have been associated with corruption, inefficiency, instability, and economic chaos. This is the government's point of view in China, and it, along with Iran, is one of a handful of countries that does not need to be much concerned with appearances.

Both Iran and China claim to be pursuing their own versions of democracy. In China's case it is socialist democracy "with Chinese characteristics." Iran's theocracy is in many ways more democratic than the governments of its neighbors (and Western allies) in the Middle East. Leaders in the People's Republic of China insist that their country is exceptional and will not follow the path of other countries. They continue to buck trends toward democratization, writing off experiences in the Western world as "bourgeois liberalization," which they hope to keep far from Chinese shores.

Yet only a handful of countries have been able to ignore or contain Western pressures for reform. Because of its size and perceived power, China can scorn

Western advice on good governance and still rest assured of the continuation of benefits such as most-favored-nation status and membership in the WORLD TRADE ORGANIZATION (WTO). Because there is always someone eager to buy its oil, Iran is similarly well placed to evade Western pressures for democratization (although how well it can handle pressures from within may be another story). Most Middle Eastern governments do not have to bother reconfiguring, because of their oil and because they are relatively pro-Western. Out of fear that democracy might produce governments not so compliant, the West has done little to pressure Saudi Arabia and the other Gulf states to democratize. They may be corrupt and unpopular, but because these governments provide their people with relative economic and political stability, most analysts agree that there are no serious challenges from within.[6]

However, the majority of authoritarians do not have this luxury. Instead, through the use of manipulation and deception, these impostors are making what can only be called a pseudotransition. The result is the creation of virtual democracy or semidemocracy, in which formal democratic political institutions exist to mask the reality of authoritarianism. Again, what they are doing is in effect crisis management. Authoritarians must come up with new survival strategies because the old ones are no longer viable. They cannot portray themselves as new democrats and meanwhile fall back on the old strategy of mass repression. They can no longer afford to co-opt the opposition with pork barrel items because of STRUCTURAL ADJUSTMENT PROGRAM (SAP) requirements. Instead, they try to create new friends, mobilize old ones, and find new ways to channel and control participation. Often this results in only the most superficial changes. Of course, each government varies in the degree to which it is using these strategies. The mix of strategy reflects each country's unique historical context as well as donor response, and this combination of factors explains the variation in result.[7]

Reconfiguration

Perhaps more remarkable than the reforms described in the previous section is the story of how less-than-democratic leaders have scrambled to hold off pressures for real change by simply appearing to be more democratic. According to Catherine Boone, this scramble can be described as a RECONFIGURATION, which can play out in any number of ways.[8] Reconfigurations are not in themselves necessarily bad things or nonevents. Even the most incremental steps or alterations can accumulate into substantial reform, if not transformative change. Simply the fact that regimes are squirming to renovate or reconfigure is evidence that the pressures on them offer the potential for more substantive change. Reconfiguring systems may become more democratic or authoritarian. The outcomes will vary because they will be shaped by the choices made by individuals and groups operating under the constraints unique to each country.[9]

Despite the fact that they can come in many different shapes and sizes, there are certain qualities associated with reconfiguring regimes. As we will see in the sections that follow, reconfiguring regimes centralize power in the hands of one or a few. They are personally appropriated states, in which the leader becomes interchangeable with the government. With little or no ACCOUNTABILITY, such governments easily fall prey to the temptations of corruption. To ensure that they retain their position and affect the appearance of LEGITIMACY, they practice what we characterize as "low-intensity democracy." When they can't win elections fairly, they are not above drawing from a bag of tricks—even resorting to various means of repression. Because of their overreliance on the military, reconfiguring regimes often end up as "hard states," which may work to keep them in power in the short term, but ultimately leaves them vulnerable to collapse.

Centralization of Power

Ironically, authoritarians justify their centralization of power as a way to secure their countries from collapse. Their leaders argue that the country is in crisis, and therefore they need to control every institution that might interfere with the effective exercise of power. For example, during the Cold War, dictatorships kept judiciaries weak and submissive—so as not to be distracted with questions of constitutionality. However, some courts appear to be taking all this talk about democracy seriously, rendering decisions that proclaim that they cannot be bought or repressed into submission. Yet in virtual democracies, this is often a thankless task. Although Zimbabwean courts have continually attempted to demonstrate their independence, the president's policy has been to disregard court orders. President Mugabe even refused to intervene as his supporters stormed the Supreme Court and made threats against judges. As a result, most independent judges in Zimbabwe have resigned. In Iran, a shadow judiciary exists parallel to the civil judicial institutions.

Authoritarians typically demonstrate a similar predilection toward forcing the legislative branch of government into line. For years the parliaments and congresses serving such regimes have in one manner or another become rubber stamps for executive initiatives. There is a dual track of power in Iran and China. In both countries there is a government hierarchy of executive power. But running parallel to most institutions and often trumping the government is the true locus of power in each country. In Iran, the clergy and its institutions are supreme. In China, it is the branches (and "small groups") of the Chinese Communist Party.

Occasionally, however, governments playing at democracy have made the mistake of allowing their hold over the legislature to get away from them. In the 2000 elections in Zimbabwe, Mugabe's party for the first time lost its outright control of the parliament. What happens in such cases is that either the executive has deluded himself into vainly believing that popular support would continue his party's domination at the polls, or he has simply proven unable to control the outcome in the way he could in the past.

Personally Appropriated States

As you will recall from the first chapters of this book, most (but not all) third world countries have long histories of authoritarian government that go at least as far back as the colonial period. The result is now a tradition of arbitrary and unchecked power operating in both civilian single-party states and military dictatorships. Whether headed by a civilian or military leader, such governments can best be described as PERSONALIST REGIMES or "personally appropriated states." By this we mean that there is such a consolidation of power in the hands of one individual that this leader comes to personify the nation. Personality is a big part of being able to pull this off. A personalist leader tends to be exceptionally charismatic, or at least have a talent for making people believe that he or she has a near-mystical ability to know what is good for the country. To prove it, such a leader will try to portray him- or herself as a populist, "a man of the people." For example, "El Chino" (as former Peruvian president Fujimori liked to refer to himself) perfected his image as someone who was not afraid to get his boots dirty. In one especially amusing turn, he even donned a black leather jacket and was televised running all over Lima, helping the police root out a crook (who happened to be a former confidant of the president).

Although this and other attempts by elites to appear to be "regular guys" (former president Jiang Zemin of China reportedly liked to put on a cowboy hat and sing karaoke) frequently wind up comedic, such regimes are more often characterized by an extreme centralization of executive power. During the Cold War, many of these leaders literally appointed themselves "president for life." Or, as in the case of Iraq and Syria today, they have groomed their sons to succeed them in "hereditary republics." Others haven't gone quite that far, but have constructed a system that guaranteed their personal control in perpetuity. Zimbabwe's Mugabe has enjoyed more than twenty years of uninterrupted power. Fujimori had the constitution changed to allow his "re-reelection." Such actions do not sit so well with most developed countries, now that the Cold War is over; for the most part, those willing to abide by such behavior in allies they could count on before are less patient today.

Corruption

What sustained such long-standing regimes, besides superpower support, was often a combination of co-optation and repression. In these neopatrimonial regimes the leader plays the role of the benevolent but stern father. Under the continuation of a very old tradition in much of the world, PATRON-CLIENT RELATIONSHIPS are based on reciprocity. The patron allocates resources and in return the client owes the patron his or her political loyalty. For example, Fujimori established the Ministry of the Presidency to give himself control over one-third of Peru's total national budget. His administration did work hard to reduce extreme poverty; it built more schools, roads, and health clinics than that of every other Peruvian president combined. But Fujimori expected much in return. A prime example of the power of personalism is that for many people in Peru, the person was more important than the office—and the president was the government. The poor came to view government services not as something the government owed its citizens, but as a gift from Fujimori himself. Such policies frequently achieve their aims; Peru's poor became the most dedicated "Fujimoristas."

Another example of how this patron-client system works is illustrated by the relationship between potentially politically relevant interest groups (such as trade unions or peasant organizations) and the government. CORPORATISM is most associated with fascism in Nazi Germany, but it has several different meanings. Usually associated with some form of authoritarianism, its conservative advocates claim that it offers an alternative path to LIBERAL DEMOCRACY and socialist TOTALITARIANISM. In many of the highly personalist regimes in Latin America in the 1960s and 1970s, corporatism took the form of "bureaucratic authoritarianism," in which the military joined with technocrats to promote order and growth. Whatever its variant, corporatism is unique to no single part of the world; it tends to grow wherever there are long traditions of powerful state rule. Corporatism describes the behind-the-scenes relationship between a governing party (or state) and various organized interests or sectors. It is built around a relationship of reciprocity in which the party seeks to control interest groups by recruiting, partially including, or co-opting them. The interest group affiliated with the state gets recognition as an "official" organization, the only one with the right to speak on behalf of a specific group. Although the state defines the powers of these organizations, the organizations do attain some of their objectives, and the state gains a new base of support. While part of the deal is that the interest group must drop at least some of its demands, some groups argue that they are being pragmatic in embracing such relationships, since the only alternative may expose them to massive government repression. Those who place a premium on stability and maintenance of order view corporatism as a benefit; however, under corporatism the masses are left out, and change, if it comes at all, is likely to be slow.[10]

Not only does this kind of co-optation swing elections, but patronage networks often result in gross governmental excess and a distortion of priorities. In the worst cases, they amount to kleptocracies, in which leaders and their cronies help themselves to the nation's treasury and resources. ELITES benefit materially as sweetheart deals with MULTINATIONAL CORPORATIONS (MNCs) create a windfall—and a class of multimillionaires. For example, the chair of a state-owned industry too cash-strapped to pay its bills was rewarded by the Zimbabwean government with a Mercedes reportedly worth $127,000 (the beneficiary also happened to be President Mugabe's brother-in-law). Such nepotism is hardly a post–Cold War phenomenon. But it has proliferated since the 1980s, as political leaders distribute valuable assets and lucrative state contracts to key allies and clients through the privatizations called for by SAPs. Of course, the extent of corruption varies widely by country. It is important to remember that no government in the world is completely clean. In some countries the corruption can be characterized as "the politics of the belly," in reference to grossly underpaid civil servants who moonlight or take bribes in order to make ends meet. Elsewhere, there may be a long tradition of gift giving or nepotism, but the government still manages to function. However, in the most predatory states, corruption is so pervasive that the system is rotten. Ultracorrupt states are often notorious not only for their private use of public resources, but also for their lack of capacity and incompetence.

Low-Intensity Democracy

Yet despite these failures, reconfiguring regimes are hard to overthrow. Their leaders operate under what Phillip A. Huxtable calls "the universal law of politics": those in power strive to stay in power.[11] Few authoritarians willingly relinquish the reins of government to anyone but a handpicked successor. Instead of caving in to Western pressures, the "reform" they seek to initiate is entirely on their own terms, with their own timetables, and within the constraints they impose.[12] One common sleight of hand is to rush elections through before the opposition can organize or unify quickly enough to compete against the incumbent. The result is what we call "low-intensity democracy," in which there may be great fanfare about the coming democratic reforms. A new constitution may be created, opposition parties may be legalized, and elections may be held—but the reform process itself is hijacked. Elections are carefully calculated to produce the victory of the incumbent, who can then resist further change by claiming the popular mandate.[13]

There are a variety of ways of accomplishing this besides garden-variety practices such as stolen or stuffed ballot boxes, or turning away registered voters while allowing unregistered voters to cast their ballots (often more than once). Although many U.S. voters were alarmed to learn in 2000 that many of these irregularities have occurred in their own elections, the United States isn't the only place where entire graveyards have voted. Many people around the world vote under the watchful eye of a party functionary. In Indonesia under President Suharto, people were required to vote at work. Their ballots were opened on the spot and tallied on a large board visible to all.[14]

Moreover, the national electoral organizations established by governments are often biased, funded by (and working for) incumbents. It is not uncommon for international and domestic election observers to be hindered or frustrated in their work. In Zimbabwe, monitors from the European Union and other international groups were denied visas to oversee the 2000 parliamentary elections and the 2002 presidential vote. In Peru, observers sent by the Organization of American States left in protest over the Fujimori government's handling of the 2000 elections. In the first round of voting, for example, the number of ballots cast reportedly exceeded the number of voters by 1.4 million. Such elections cannot be considered free and fair—especially where there is no independent scrutiny of the count. In Peru it is said that the Fujimori government administered the results in a "step-by-step" coup. There and elsewhere, the collection of ballots can only be described as chaotic, as computer systems were said to break down for hours or even days, resulting in highly suspicious delays in the count.

Mobilization Through Repression

Not only do reconfiguring regimes interfere with their opponents' ability to campaign for office, but they themselves run campaigns that are divisive and polarized. In a climate of economic hardship incumbents can successfully portray democratic politics as a ZERO-SUM GAME and play up fears, accentuating divisions along ethnic, religious, and other lines to mobilize the public. In the 2000 campaign, President Mugabe and the Zimbabwe African National Union–Patriotic Front (ZANU-PF) aggravated divisions between urban and rural dwellers to mobilize support. Increasingly under assault from liberal, prodemocracy movements identified with the cities, reconfiguring regimes like Mugabe's fall back on their long-established networks of rural support. Despite the fact that they too have been affected by budget cuts, systems of patronage (alliances with local and regional power brokers in the countryside) are often more institutionalized and therefore slower to break apart. Because poverty is often most pronounced in rural areas, the people living there fear losing what little state support they receive. As a result, rural areas are often major bastions of support for governments attempting to reconfigure. And in this sense, Mugabe has played his cards well, since it will be difficult for his opponents to win power without the support of the countryside, where more than half of the population lives.

Besides manipulating rural-urban divides, reconfiguring governments may encourage a resurgence of ethnoregional or religious ideologies in order to mobilize populations. As a result, ethnic conflict often worsens under authoritarian rule. Over the years Mugabe has cynically manipulated ethnic and racial divides to maintain his power base. Nationalism may also be used to divert attention from the government's failings by identifying scapegoats as the source of the country's problems. For example, leaders may exaggerate the threat by certain out-groups, either foreign or domestic. Fujimori attempted to rally nationalist support behind his antidemocratic policies by proclaiming that outsiders would not dictate to Peru. Playing on Peruvian sensitivity over a long history of U.S. interference in the region, Fujimori declared, "My country is not a banana republic . . . how dare they demand a second round regardless of our independent voting results! It is totally uncalled for, and it is a great insult to Peru that I will personally never, ever, forget."[15] In Zimbabwe, Mugabe originally blamed white farmers for the country's problems. Now Britain and the opposition Movement for Democratic Change (MDC) are scapegoated. In speeches, Mugabe corrupts his main challenger's name to "Tsvangison," making it English-sounding to Zimbabweans, and calls him a "tea boy," insinuating that Morgan Tsvangirai is a British stooge. In fact, Mugabe blames the British government for all of Zimbabwe's current political and economic problems. He has renounced the long-standing policy of reconciliation and declared that the former colonizers should be tried for genocide.

In terms of enemies at home, it is not uncommon for women, homosexuals, immigrants, or minorities to be blamed for economic hardship, political instability, or a "decline in values." To legitimate their rule, reconfiguring regimes lash out at all kinds of enemies—real or invented. In an effort to appeal to conservative traditional and religious elements, authoritarian leaders commonly call for a reassertion of identity. For example, authoritarians are notorious for manipulating "family values" and reinforcing traditional conceptions of women's proper role. Whereas some women are mobilized by conservative appeals to their "innate" commitment to the family and morality and have even supported military coups against democratic governments, those women who do not or cannot conform to "traditional" roles are designated as traitors. In countries around the world women are stigmatized and even attacked for their inability or unwillingness to stay within the boundaries set for them by the patriarchal order.

Even in supposedly progressive regimes, women often face a remasculinization of politics as reconfiguring governments make appeals for restoring "cultural authenticity." For example, in the 1970s and early 1980s, Mugabe recognized the important roles women served during the struggle for independence.

Upon independence the new ZANU-PF government declared an unusual commitment to feminist goals. There were high expectations, as the government not only ended women's status as perpetual minors, but also introduced legislative reforms that challenged bridewealth and other traditional practices deemed by some to be harmful to women. But in response to an uproar of unanticipated complaints, ZANU-PF took an abrupt about-face. By the mid-1980s Mugabe was blaming "feminist extremism" for a variety of social evils and was calling for a return to "authentic African cultural values." This resulted in "Operation Cleanup": mass arrests of urban women and schoolgirls suspected of everything from "baby dumping" to prostitution.

Similar crackdowns have occurred in several countries for many of the same reasons. Whether it is the imposition of "protective legislation" that denies women access to employment, or reproductive controls that refuse them access to contraception or abortion, what reconfiguring leaders are doing is building political alliances, more specifically partnerships with traditional and conservative elements. Taken altogether the politics of exclusion practiced against women, homosexuals, or particular ethnic or religious groups only work to heighten social tensions and violence. As we can see in the worst cases of this, such as Rwanda, the politics of exclusion deepen already existing divides and undermine the prospects for a more authentic democratization at some point in the future.

Hard States

As states weaken and cleavages resurface, the possibility of state collapse grows. Where leaders stubbornly refuse to stand down, the ensuing instability is used as a justification for a more repressive authoritarianism. For example, Zimbabwe's MDC promises mass action but fears the government will use it as an excuse to declare martial law and lock up the opposition. Worse yet, Mugabe might order a massacre like the ones that killed tens of thousands of people in Matabeleland in the 1980s. Governments that commit such atrocities are described as "hard states." In such cases, authoritarianism itself becomes the cause of state collapse. Not to be confused with strong states, hard states such as Algeria, Yemen, and Egypt become totally dependent on the military for their survival. In many of these countries the government may have a civilian façade, but the armed forces have an overwhelming influence.

As we have seen in this chapter, the civil and military spheres in much of the world are not as separate as they are in the United States. Howard Wiarda and Harvey Kline argue that such a separation is not traditional in much of Latin America, whereas alternation in power between military and civilian rule is the norm. Many countries' constitutions give the military the right, even the obligation, to intervene in the political process under certain circumstances. Similarly, executives are often constitutionally afforded extensive powers to bypass the legislature, and until recently judicial review was not part of the Latin American legal tradition.[16] Consequently, it can't be surprising that considering what the country was going through, by the early 1990s Peru was rapidly becoming a hard state. The powers Fujimori claimed for himself were not unusual given traditional state-society relations. Fujimori was widely applauded for his efforts against inflation and TERRORISM—and he was returned to office by a landslide. However, by the late 1990s his base of support was wearing thin, and many experts argue that Fujimori never would have resigned had he had the backing of the military, which has been known for issuing its own political proclamations and has periodically sent tanks into Lima to reinforce its positions. Even with Fujimori gone, Peruvians were fearful of what might happen in the 2001 presidential election. And they remain cautious. Although the military stood aside in the Peruvian case, under these and similar circumstances it is not unusual to see militaries step in to fill the political vacuum, and to establish order—if nothing else.

While it is common for military leaders to promise a transition to democracy, most coups should be viewed as nothing more than yet another reconfiguration. There are some cases, such as Nigeria, where it appears that the promised transition did finally take place. But some people are skeptical about Nigeria, and doubt the military will ever truly turn over power to civilians, because in most cases such transitions are delayed, incomplete—or temporary. More often military leaders reconfigure themselves as civilian candidates for president, hold staged elections, limit the ability of the opposition to compete, and then fix the results.[17] Or, as is feared in Nigeria, the military continues to govern from the wings. If this is the case, it should fool no one. It amounts to just another manifestation of virtual democracy.

Disintegration

When the reconfiguration gets out of control, when the government will not budge in the face of overwhelming opposition and divisions within the military render it unable or unwilling to prevent a breakup, the result is DISINTEGRATION. So far, outright disintegration has been the least common outcome associated with this period of crisis management. Yet several states have collapsed because they have proven incapable of meeting the challenges reconfiguration has raised. This phenomenon has occurred most frequently in Africa, but it is a risk in a few other places as well, including Indonesia. Facing internal and external demands for substantive change, weak states (such as Somalia) have quickly eroded. Others are in the process of decay and appear to be sliding toward disintegration. According to I. William Zartman, disintegration is best conceptualized as a long-term degenerative disease. Countries in decay are in varying stages of decline, but what they have in common is state paralysis: they can no longer perform the functions required for them to pass as states. Under such circumstances government retracts and the countryside is left on its own. The state becomes a shell; there is no sovereign authority. Power is up for grabs and warlord politics, or rival power centers, play increasingly larger roles in people's lives. There is a breakdown of law and order and organized violence becomes generalized. The effect is societal collapse. People retreat into ethnic nationalisms or religious affiliations as a residual source of identity and organization where no single institution can claim to receive the support or exercise control over the people living there.[18] Under such circumstances, even the firmness of national borders becomes vulnerable, and the fracturing or breakup of states becomes even more likely. Analysts tell us not to be surprised if such a pattern emerges over the next few years, as the previous waves of democratization have been followed by reverse waves of democratic breakdown.[19]

But the degenerative disease so many states are experiencing does not always prove fatal. A cure or more likely a remission is possible. Some states may survive political turbulence of the kind described, exist on the brink of collapse, and still emerge with new vigor. More analysts are arguing that given the arbitrary boundaries demarcating states, perhaps in some instances fragmentation is not a bad thing. Juan Linz and Alfred Stepan make the interesting point that in order to have a democratic regime, there must first be a viable state.[20] While we must never forget the human tragedy so often associated with disintegration, for some countries disintegration is increasingly being thought of as a necessary first step—before democratization can even be considered. Given the foundation of a more viable state, democratic forces may then regroup and substantive reforms can begin. Although external actors need to be kept in mind for the considerable role they play in shaping outcomes in weak states, what may prove to be more crucial to their recovery is the ability of civil society to rebound. The inhabitants of a territory must come together to restore faith in government and to support the successor government. If they can do this, what is left of the state may recover its balance and return to more or less normal functions. However, if the pieces do not come back together, warlord politics is a likely fate of many weak states. Still, nothing is preordained. Even weak states evolve differently and no outcome is inevitable.[21]

Conclusions: Is a Reverse Wave Ahead?

From the preceding discussion, it should now be clear that leaders have acceded to internal and external demands for political liberalization not only in a variety of ways, but also to varying degrees, depending on the intensity of the pressures they face. Some leaders have been willing to make the reforms necessary to build the base for a still-fragile democratic system. And while a strong economy is an asset, despite all odds democracies even in some of the poorest countries have proven to be impressively resilient. Elsewhere leaders have made partial changes, or reconfigured the political system in such a way as to maintain their own power bases. To varying degrees authoritarians of varying stripes have affected the appearance of change. During this period of intense reconfiguration and reform, there are some states that appear to be explicitly bucking the liberal democratic trend. In the case of China, for example, one specialist calls democratic attempts in the twentieth century "the lessons of failure."[22] Certainly, China is not alone in this category, even if we are living in a "democratic age."

Still other political systems have disintegrated (or may yet still disintegrate) under the cumulative effect of the pressures already described. Because they are so fragile, some democracies will struggle and eventually fail. Ironically, given the current climate, it is the reconfiguring regimes that are more likely to prove successful, at least in the short term. They are certainly the ones best placed to enforce the economic reforms the donor countries so desire. The point is that in the post–Cold War period, many governments (democratic or not) that would have once been propped up by external powers will now likely be allowed to fall. In the end it is important to remember that there are a wide variety of possible outcomes to the transformations under way.

Perhaps the worst thing for democracy is for developed countries to accept an incumbent's portrayal of political reform as destabilizing and dangerous. Unwilling to budge on SAPs, too often donors lower the threshold for their political expectations. They back off from demands for reforms such as respect for civil rights, agreeing with authoritarians that perhaps the people "aren't ready yet." Yet as Larry Diamond and Marc Plattner observe, it is certainly in our interests to do everything we can to nurture and support these fragile governments.[23] There is nothing inevitable about the triumph or persistence of democracy. Even consolidated democracies can decay if there is a long period of incompetent leadership. In the case of authoritarians, we know from history that the more repressive a government is, the more likely it will threaten its neighbors, as well as its own people. International pressure alone did not create this third wave of democratization, but if international support for it should wane, the viability of already frail democracies will be further diminished. It is therefore crucial that the international community provide the support necessary to preempt a third reverse wave, by assisting these democracies in their deepening and CONSOLIDATION.[24]

Linking Concepts and Cases

As you are well aware from your reading of previous chapters, great variation exists among our eight case studies in terms of history, economy, and society. In the following pages we will briefly review each country's recent political history, using examples from our cases to illustrate some of the concepts just discussed. As you read these case studies, look for the major similarities and differences in experience in the various countries—especially in regard to their REFORM, RECONFIGURATION, or DISINTEGRATION. Keep in mind that because of the dynamic nature of politics, it is likely that some things have changed since this book was published. See if you can answer these questions from the reading that follows, or research further to provide an updated response.

Where is each case located on the continuum from consolidated liberal democracy to AUTHORITARIAN REGIME? Why do you place it where you do? Why do you think some countries are taking the reformist route while others reconfigure? What are some of the ways in which government leaders attempt to hold on to power? To what extent have the military, economic hardship, and the existence of pluralism complicated transitions, or CONSOLIDATION?

In which cases has the population appeared to choose the order provided by authoritarianism over the instability associated with democracy? What are the major supports and constraints for democracy in each country? Where have the constraints become crises, and which are the most prone to disintegration? Which governments are suffering from the worst crises of efficacy? Have they been able to overcome these problems? What are some of the ways countries have attempted to undo decades of CORRUPTION? Of those that have made the most progress toward democracy, what was the secret of their success? Conversely, how are the reconfiguring regimes faring now? Which of the case studies have made progress at deepening democracy? In what ways are they accomplishing this?

Case Study: Mexico

Over the last few decades, Mexico embarked upon one of the world's longest and most dramatic DEMOCRATIC TRANSITIONS. Until 2000, Mexicans had lived for seventy-one years under a government controlled by the Institutional

Revolutionary Party (PRI). Politics in Mexico was for generations a ZERO-SUM GAME in which all formal power was centralized under the control of one party. Although this was no democracy, many Mexicans appreciated the relative stability their country enjoyed under the PRI. Still, since the 1970s certain factions in the PRI recognized the need for political reform, which occurred in fits and starts. By the mid-1990s it had become clear to many Mexicans that the relative stability provided by one-party rule could not make up for the excesses that came with it. Mexico was experiencing a series of legitimacy crises, most notably associated with an economic collapse in 1994 and a civil war in the south. In addition, Mexicans were rocked by a number of major scandals and were no longer able to overlook the pervasive corruption within the government. Many Mexicans felt threatened by a growing lawlessness in the country, much of it linked to Mexico's newly prominent position in the international drug trade. Moreover, Mexico's economic difficulties and growing inequalities especially in the rural south were contributing to a situation in which stability could no longer be ensured.

At about the same time that all this was happening, the United States, Mexico, and Canada were moving toward the creation of the North American Free Trade Agreement (NAFTA). Yet its passage was held up in the U.S. Congress because of a number of concerns, including questions regarding the antidemocratic character of the PRI government. In the end, a combination of internal and external pressures convinced PRI technocrats (so named because of their foreign-trained expertise in economics and careers built in the bureaucracy rather than the party or politics), including President Ernesto Zedillo, to move forward with a "silent revolution," or gradual democratization of Mexico. It is remarkable that Mexico made its transition without many of the hallmarks of transitions elsewhere: there was no collapse, no national conference, and no constitutional assembly.[1] In fact, the biggest fight Zedillo had on his hands was with entrenched elements within his own party, known as the "dinosaurs," an old guard who wanted to maintain the PRI's absolute control of power.

Despite the internal struggles, political and economic reform proceeded. The legislative elections of 1997 marked a watershed event, in that for the first time the PRI lost its majority in the Mexican Congress. Yet it was President Zedillo's dramatic break with the tradition of the *dedazo* (or "the tap of the finger," in which the outgoing president handpicks his successor) that opened up the political space for Mexicans to take part in truly democratic elections. Mexico is known for the important role leadership has historically played in building viable civilian systems out of weak political rule. Although previous leaders were mostly either indifferent or hostile to democracy as being too risky, Zedillo and the technocrats realized early on that the greatest risk to the PRI would be the postponement of reform.[2] The party did put up a determined effort to hold on to power by winning the 2000 election outright. There were some irregularities (including intimidation and attempts at vote buying: in one state the PRI attempted to win loyalty by giving away washing machines). Yet in many ways this election amounted to Mexico's second revolution—after seven decades of uninterrupted rule, the PRI lost and actually allowed itself to be removed from power.

The personality dominating this "electoral revolution" was Vicente Fox of the conservative National Action Party (PAN). Fox campaigned hard on the average Mexican's dissatisfaction with politics as usual. He appealed to young and middle-class voters, the turnout for the election was relatively high (64 percent), and Fox won by a clear margin. Just as surprising as the result of the vote was that the transfer of power was remarkably smooth. However, Fox soon realized that his work was cut out for him. Although he came in riding a wave of popularity, with a term limit of six years Fox has precious little time to demonstrate to Mexicans that he can make good on his big promises, most notably to fight corruption and expand economic growth. As a candidate, Fox was ebullient with his promises; some of his proposed political reforms in terms of energy, labor, and taxes would have been unimaginable under the PRI. Although progress in these areas has been characterized as very slow, the government has begun to make some inroads against corruption, and there have been some high-profile drug arrests. Another remarkable change is that the press is now much freer to criticize the government.

Yet after all the boasting of his campaign, the president is having a hard time following up on his domestic agenda. In part this is because Mexico's democracy is working—it is stronger, more accountable, and more transparent. It is also because this president has less power than any of his predecessors. His relationship with Congress has been a test for Fox, since the PRI has a plurality of seats. Fox knows that he needs alliances in Congress if he is to see any major legislation passed. However, these alliances have not come easily, as the PRI and the much smaller Party of Democratic Revolution (PRD) prefer their role as the opposition. In addition, the president already has developed some significant differences with his own party. There is a new and more equitable balance of power between the executive and legislative branches, which is being pursued by the latter energetically. Congressional elections in 2003 may give the opposition a majority. And the judiciary is now showing signs of a new independence. Consequently, many of the president's big plans have been dropped or put on hold. Perhaps it was due to inexperience, perhaps it was because he was too sure of himself, but by his second year in office the president was learning that long-standing, complicated problems could not be corrected in his predicted "fifteen minutes." The president's own record so far has been mixed; but in many ways Mexico has progressed in its transition and begun the work of consolidation.

In some ways then, it appears that the Mexican democracy is faring better than the Mexican president. Before he had even finished his first year in office, it was looking like the honeymoon was over. Fox's once-impressive popularity had slid in the polls to less than 70 percent and by the end of 2002 it was at 50 percent.[3] But it would be a mistake to write this president off too soon. It is not uncommon for the initial euphoria associated with elections to pass. In Mexico's case Fox's drop in the polls is perhaps coincident with the country's economic slowdown. Still, some are concerned that cynicism and disillusionment have set in so soon—especially if in the minds of Mexicans the president and the democracy become too intertwined.

Case Study: Peru

Whereas most of the rest of Latin America has continued on with a POLITICAL LIBERALIZATION dating back to the early 1980s, Peru reversed course—and has since reversed itself again. Although it wasn't a smooth ride, until 1992 Peru was undergoing a democratic transition and was on the same path as many of its neighbors. Not exactly a liberal democracy, most analysts agree that it had made some progress toward democratic institutionalization. Still, Peru's leaders had not done enough to successfully reform the country's long-standing authoritarian practices and institutions.

In his war on drugs, two guerrilla insurrections, and hyperinflation Alberto Fujimori, the democratically elected president of Peru, determined that democratic dialogue was inefficient. Extraordinary circumstances called for extraordinary actions. Frustrated with the limitations placed on him by the checks and balances of Peru's democratic institutions, in 1992 Fujimori assumed for himself the powers of a military dictator to take on the country's problems. Supported in his efforts by a military that was always just behind the scenes, Fujimori ruled by decree. With the assistance of the National Intelligence Service (SIN) and the military elite, he concentrated power in his own hands, declared a state of emergency, and dismantled democratic institutions by closing Congress and purging the judiciary. By 1995 he had vanquished his enemies, turned the economy around—and was reelected by a landslide. Although there is room for disagreement as to why Peruvians were willing to surrender their hard-earned but still somewhat restricted democratic liberties to Fujimori, even his enemies admit that the president was able to provide Peruvians with a sense of stability relatively unknown in the Andean region—albeit the kind of order that can only exist in the short term.

While appreciative of the order he provided, many Peruvians became concerned when the extraordinary powers Fujimori accrued to himself to fight these wars continued to amass—even after the wars were ostensibly over. The government became even more heavy-handed and abusive. By the late 1990s Fujimori was the longest-sitting head of state in Latin America, second only to Fidel Castro. Because some of the trappings of democracy were maintained, analysts describe his government as "hybrid authoritarianism."[4] Until the attempted "re-reelection" of 2000, there was room for disagreement over whether the government had crossed the line from DELEGATIVE DEMOCRACY into authoritarianism. However, Peru could no longer meet even the minimum qualifications of democracy once Fujimori determined that there was no one else capable of running the country. So that he might run for a third term, in 1998–1999 the president trashed the constitution, fired judges who disagreed with him, and held a massively fraudulent referendum. Fujimori pulled out all the stops and ran what is widely agreed to be the dirtiest campaign and elections in the country's history. Although it is still unclear who was calling the shots, the SIN was turned loose on all that opposed him. Candidates for president risked harassment, intimidation, and blackmail. In the end, the world and large numbers of Peruvians refused to recognize the results of the 2000 elections against Alejandro Toledo, in which Fujimori declared himself the winner.[5]

Peruvian politics continued to take several more interesting turns soon after the 2000 elections. A scandal involving Vladimiro Montesinos, the president's closest adviser and Peru's equivalent to former F.B.I. strongman J. Edgar Hoover, eventually brought them both down. Although mysteries abound concerning who actually held power in Peru and the military's role in what some call a "clandestine coup," crowds celebrated the president's faxed resignation in November 2000 and the promise of new elections in early 2001. In the meantime, an interim government led by the respected and able Valentin Paniagua took the first important steps toward a democratic transition and the reconstruction of democratic institutions.

Most experts agree that the initial transition went unexpectedly well. The 2001 presidential campaign was marred by mud slinging, particularly between candidates Alejandro Toledo and Alan García. Still, under the supervision of a reformed electoral authority, nearly 15 million voters registered their choice for president with virtually no violence or fraud. Consequently, international observers declared the June 2001 elections to be free and fair. Toledo came out the victor, narrowly winning a five-year term as president with 45 percent of the vote (to García's 40 percent).

As the leader of this new democracy, it is crucial that Toledo do everything he can to avoid the pitfalls of the past and work to rebuild democratic institutions, restore the credibility of the judicial system, and establish the RULE OF LAW. However, he will have to strengthen his position to pull this off. Toledo didn't have a strong mandate coming out of the elections; a year into his term the president had one of the lowest popularity ratings (about 18 percent) of any elected leader in the region. Furthermore, Toledo is confronted with several problems at once. Not only are the poor and middle classes showing their impatience with Toledo, but the broadly based unity that once bound those opposed to Fujimori has rapidly evaporated. In part this is due to the economic hardship so many Peruvians are experiencing; it is therefore urgent that the government demonstrates itself capable of improving the economy. However, whatever his promises the president is restrained in his efforts by the Congress, where his party only had 45 of 120 seats. And the media, which are relishing the return of its independence, have battered Toledo. Due to a number of gaffes and a newly free press eager to publicize them, from the start of his term Toledo has had an image problem—and a loss of confidence in the president could easily translate into a lack of confidence in democracy.[6]

As if this weren't enough, Toledo is the one who must clean up the mess Fujimori left behind. The country was still reeling from corruption scandals made public when Vladimiro Montesinos's collection of videotapes, exposing many of the country's power elite taking bribes, were shown on nationwide television. It will be on Toledo's watch that extensive investigations into misconduct and abuse will come, as well as the arrests and trials of "untouchables." This list includes Montesinos, who after fleeing the country was captured and sentenced in 2002 to nine years in prison after being found guilty on one of the more than seventy charges pending against him. Yet even behind bars, Montesinos is still widely considered a powerful man, and from Japan Fujimori is actually talking about a political comeback. Despite the risks it entails, it is crucial that Toledo continue the interim government's restructuring of the armed forces and reassert civilian control of the military. Clearly, Toledo has some formidable tasks ahead of him. The changes set into motion now will need time to take off, since a real transformation will take years. Already there are some improvements: there are more freedoms under this government, there is more rule of law, Peru's institutions are showing signs of more independence and more accountability, and the country is believed to be inching toward an economic recovery. However, the most difficult challenge this government faces is to build political institutions and restore Peruvians' faith in politics. According to one analyst, "Peru is like a spouse who has been cheated on: there is a lot of hurt and mistrust."[7] It is up to this government to show Peruvians that democracy is a relationship worth saving.

Case Study: Nigeria

As you read in previous chapters, Nigeria has come through a nightmare to begin its democratic transition. And in what is surely a case of truth being stranger than fiction, a born-again former military dictator is leading the way. Until this latest experiment with democracy, in 1999 Nigeria had only spent ten of its nearly forty years of independence under civilian rule. Earlier experiments with democracy failed in the midst of intense political crises, polarization, incompetence, and a lack of economic development. Nigerians have endured incompetent and corrupt civilian governments; they suffered worse through a civil war and through coup after coup, but the country hit bottom the five years it spent under the dictatorship of Sani Abacha (1993–1998).

It is difficult to briefly relate just how venal this government was. Nelson Mandela put it into perspective when he characterized the Abacha regime's atrocities as ranking with those of apartheid South Africa. Racism is not institutionalized in Nigeria, but the country is plagued with a variety of other divides. For decades the north has dominated the military (and therefore the government). Those with political power amassed enormous fortunes from the country's oil wealth to such a degree that Nigerian political culture has been described as "prebendal," or based on the systematic abuse of state office and resources for individual and group gain. This is hardly a fair characterization of the Nigerian people, since most of them received nothing from these transactions. Under both civilian and military rule, the majority of Nigerians have been permanent outsiders.[8] For years, those who dared speak out against the government and its abuses were harshly repressed.

Yet in what has been described by many Nigerians as divine intervention, in June 1998 Sani Abacha suddenly dropped dead (reportedly of a massive heart attack). By that time the military had tired of the exercise of government and was willing to give civilians another shot at it. To create what would become known as the Fourth Republic, Nigerians poured into the voting booths in February 1999. They elected representatives at all levels of government, including the presidency. And although observers cited many electoral abuses, they accepted the results because the irregularities did not appear to be systematic. Olusegun Obasanjo won with 62.8 percent of the vote, the military remained in the wings, and Nigeria began its fourth experiment with democracy.

Although not all Nigerians accepted the result, most observers agree that Obasanjo and his People's Democratic Party (PDP) won imperfect though basically free and fair elections (the PDP easily dominated the legislature, occupying 237 of 415 seats in the National Assembly). Yet from the outset there were serious challenges to Obasanjo's ability to govern. Although he is Christian and Yoruba, many in his own community view him as suspicious because of his long ties to powerbrokers in the north. As regional, ethnic, and religious divides deepened over many northern states' attempts to impose *SHARIAH*, Obasanjo increasingly found himself torn in opposite directions. The country itself appeared to be fragmenting, and the population was becoming increasingly frustrated with the government's lack of capacity. Long lines for gasoline and power outages were still common for Nigerians; unemployment and inflation were still high.

The country has been wracked by what has been called the worst cycle of violence in more than thirty years. Over 10,000 people have died in riots since the return to democracy in 1999. Rising crime rates, vigilantism, and police corruption and abuses indicate that the rule of law does not exist. This is a critical moment for the Obasanjo government; it appears that people have not accepted the desirability of waging their conflicts through peaceful and democratic means.

Consequently, 2003 is being widely hailed as a "judgment year," an important test for democracy in Nigeria as the first civilian-run elections in twenty years will be held in March and April. This is a general election, so there will be a series of elections for local, state, and legislative office, culminating in the presidential election. People are right to be nervous, since the other two times civilian governments organized elections, they were so blatantly rigged that the military took over power. Some Nigerians are arguing that this round of elections is already doomed, since voter registration in 2002 was such a mess. In addition to complaints about a shortage of materials and the pace of registration, officials were caught hoarding registration cards with plans to sell them to politicians looking to improve their numbers. It is clear that a long tradition of discord, suspicion, and cynicism continues in the Fourth Republic. Even the usually unflappable Obasanjo has warned that political violence and lawlessness are undermining democracy. Although in one poll three-quarters of Nigerians said they never wanted another military government, just a few years into the democratic transition larger numbers of people, especially northerners, were beginning to call for a return to military rule.[9]

Much public dissatisfaction with the government stems from the sense that the leaders of this democracy care more about themselves than about the people. From very early on, the president appeared more interested in positioning himself well for reelection than in earning votes. Soon after taking office the president began blaming others when things went wrong. Frustrated over deadlocks, Obasanjo tended toward presidentialism in his dealings with the other branches of government, especially the legislature. The president had a difficult relationship with lawmakers, and on several occasions even members of Obasanjo's own party have sought his impeachment. As of early 2003 there was very little evidence that consolidation had begun. There appeared to be little agreement on the rules of the game. Political elites were too busy bickering to exhibit behaviors aimed at building trust and cooperation. Already the Fourth Republic exhibited many of the attributes of a delegative democracy, as horizontal accountability had already eroded. This is a democracy that, for a variety of reasons, is not consolidating. If Obasanjo is reelected and continues to view democratic checks and balances as interfering with his mission, he may act to further centralize executive powers. The absence of democratic checks on executive power may enable the president to act more decisively, but it will not necessarily mean that he will be able to act more effectively. Unless this course is reversed, the Fourth Republic may soon be history, and the cycle will begin once more.

Case Study: Zimbabwe

Since the overthrow of white minority rule in 1979, Robert Mugabe and his party, the Zimbabwe African National Union–Patriotic Front (ZANU-PF), have effectively dominated the country's politics. To be fair, it should be pointed out that when he was first elected, Mugabe inherited from colonial Rhodesia a highly centralized state and powerful security force. As Jocelyn Alexander and others contend, in many ways Mugabe is Ian Smith's heir—both have made race an issue when it shouldn't be.[10] Over the years, the president, who fancies himself rivaling only Mandela as the continent's leader, has reconfigured in a variety of different directions. Mugabe has veered from left to right on the political spectrum. For years now he has claimed that the country is democratic, yet he has made a determined effort to undermine Zimbabwe's democratic institutions since the mid-1980s. Through alternating policies of co-optation and repression, Mugabe has been largely successful at controlling his opponents. Over time he has created for himself a one-party state.

Until recently Mugabe could count on the full cooperation of the legislature in this effort, since party loyalists held virtually all the seats in the House of Assembly. However, by the late 1990s, internal and external pressures forced Mugabe to undertake a reconfiguration. Mugabe is vain enough to want to be popular; he wants to appear to be law-abiding, and he does not wish to be seen by the world as a Sani Abacha or Slobodan Milosevic. The president very much wants the prestige of legitimacy, and believes he can get that with the pretense of democracy. However, at about this time a new opposition group, the Movement for Democratic Change (MDC), was rapidly gaining popularity in the cities. Meanwhile, the economy was in shambles and Mugabe, desperate for foreign aid, knew that parliamentary elections due to be held in 2000 had to at least appear to be democratic. Recognizing these realities, Mugabe met these expectations partway. As is his constitutional right (he has changed the constitution more than a dozen times), he rushed the date for elections, hoping the MDC would be caught off guard and without enough time to organize an effective campaign. He did not outlaw opposition parties, but he did not intervene in pre-election violence aimed against them. There were abuses on all sides, but human rights organizations report that ZANU-PF supporters were particularly active, beating, gang raping, and killing opposition candidates and their supporters. Women were frequently the main targets of intimidation; during some sexual assaults the victims were asked repeatedly if they were pro-MDC. If the right to campaign is as important as the right to vote, then clearly these elections were marred from the start.

Although domestic and international observers were impressed by the high turnout and orderly appearance of the process, they agreed that the results of the 2000 elections were in doubt. Yet here again is evidence of a reconfiguration: Mugabe permitted the opposition a partial success. The MDC made an impressive showing (winning 57 of 120 races), but it did not win enough seats to control the parliament. The MDC kept Mugabe from single-handedly changing the constitution, but it did not have the majority necessary to impeach the president nor did it have any real policymaking influence. Perhaps it is just part of the democratic façade erected to assuage donors, but the election outcome may prove to be significant because it means that for the first time in twenty years, ZANU-PF actually lost its two-thirds majority. Not surprisingly, the legislature came to an impasse; initiatives proposed by the opposition were buried by ZANU-PF and the most the MDC could do was attempt to stall the president's initiatives.

At home and abroad, it appears that President Mugabe is backed into a corner, but he is taking on all comers. His relationship with the opposition is one of marked hostility. Laws passed just months before the 2002 presidential elections effectively prohibited the opposition from holding rallies or handing out flyers without official permission. It became illegal to "use abusive language on the person of the president."[11] Mugabe has lashed out, threatening to ban the party and sending police to arrest MDC leader Morgan Tsvangirai for treason, a crime punishable by death. As this book went to press, Tsvangirai still moved about the country unharmed; however, the opposition leader was on trial, accused of trying to assassinate Mugabe.

The president's relationship with the judiciary was also quite chilly until the president intimidated the most independent-minded judges to resign and replaced them with ones more to his liking. Occasionally there are rumors that even the president's own party is split over allegiance to him; a handful of Mugabe's closest allies within the party died under mysterious circumstances in 2001. However, for now internal reform is unlikely, as Mugabe appears in control of the party. Still, the period preceding the March 2002 presidential elections was a historic moment for Zimbabwe. Despite the president's determination to win at all costs, the few opinion polls available in Zimbabwe just two months before the March 2002 elections suggested that Mugabe would lose heavily if the vote was free and if voters could cast their ballots in privacy. But that was not the case. Mugabe was returned to the presidency with 56 percent of the vote, although there were numerous reports of irregularities, including the disenfranchisement of thousands of Zimbabweans living in pro-MDC areas. The opposition promised mass action and civil unrest if it came to this, but months after the election all was mostly quiet. The president remained in control of the country, while Zimbabweans watched and waited.

Case Study: Iran

Iran is a country gripped by contradicting visions of its transitional goals. As a society built on revolution, it has undergone cyclical changes, especially in its relationship with the Western world. The 1979 revolution, which overthrew Shah Mohammed Reza Pahlavi, sought to overturn the attempts at "Westernization" and establish an indigenous Islamic Republic under the leadership of Ayatollah Ruhollah Khomeini. Former two-term president Ali Akbar Hashemi Rafsanjani is often credited with maneuvering Iran through a murky decade of economic struggles and international isolation, and concurrently launching the country in an *ABERTURA*-type direction. A reform movement embodying the desire to promote political pluralism gained prominence after Mohammad Khatami's election in 1997. Khatami campaigned on a reformist platform calling for relaxed social and cultural norms, mild regard for Western culture, and the inclusion of women in governance. Yet the prominence this movement achieved in 1997 has activated a powerful conservative reaction, from both leaders and some citizens. The resulting reconfiguration may be viewed as an attempt to build a modern "Islamic-style democracy"—led by clerics. Khatami's clear reelection in June 2001 seemed to solidify his position as a reformer, but also increased the stakes of his difficult platform. His support base—predominantly students and young professionals—has become increasingly disenchanted with his inability to push genuine reform past the clerics, but they know that their best hope, at least for the time being, remains in the embattled president. Khatami's lukewarm support for cultural change and freedom of expression risks splintering the reformists even more.

Power in the Islamic Republic has long been concentrated in a single leader or small group of leaders. Yet since the early 1990s elections in Iran have become increasingly competitive and participatory. Candidates for parliament have to cross a minimum 25 percent threshold of the vote, so it is not unusual to have runoffs between the front-runners. Political parties cannot participate in elections, although some "political groups" have won legal recognition since 1997. Yet candidates must first muster the support of the Council of Guardians, set up in 1979 to interpret legislation and ensure their conformity with the sacred law of Islam. This group approves all legislation before it becomes law. Additionally, the council determines whether or not candidates are eligible to serve in the parliament, before they withstand the public votes. This advisory group also rejected computer voting in elections, demanding that all votes be counted by hand. The task took approximately one week in Tehran alone.

A key issue in Iran's political development is the lack of separation of powers—Iran has virtually no horizontal accountability between institutions. The Supreme Leader, for example, is answerable only to God. Both the president and elected members of parliament are subordinate to the Supreme Leader, currently Ali Khamenei. The major organizations, including public security, military, and broadcasting units, are not accountable to the executive or legislature. Within the judicial system, there is not even an attempt to feign autonomy. Judges are held to both political and religious qualifications. Religious judgments (or *FATWAS,* such as the one issued by former Supreme Leader Ayatollah Ruhollah Khomeini against novelist Salman Rushdie) cannot be repealed by civil courts. The Supreme Leader has veto over everything. For example, Iran's Supreme National Security Council voted in favor of improved relations with the United States in 2000, but Ali Khamenei vetoed it.[12]

The Council of Guardians, whose members are all appointed to power (half by the Supreme Leader), continues to frustrate the reform efforts of Khatami and his supporters. Their actions make it clear that efforts to change life in the Islamic Republic need the support of top conservatives.[13] This will necessarily color both the degree and the type of reconfiguration in the regime for the foreseeable future.

The message of recent election cycles is that Iranian citizens are voicing a protest vote against the status quo. Yet it seems that the louder the voices of reform grow, the harder the advocates for conservatism become. Khatami's promise to advocate a free press has been largely stalled by clerical acts blocking such developments. Even though reformers hold both executive and legislative majorities, they are limited in what they can achieve. Conflicting voices, some calling for secular reform, others for Islamic reconfiguration, will continue to battle it out as Iran forges its way through the twenty-first century.

Case Study: Turkey

The Turkish Republic has undergone multiple phases of political development since its establishment under Mustafa Kemal Atatürk in 1923. Under his leadership, the country experienced dramatic change, especially in social life. Atatürk went to pains to foster a modern, secular state united under the singular leadership of the Republican People's Party (RPP). His successor, Ismet İnönü, permitted party contestation, largely in response to UN concerns, but the party system struggled for decades in order to become fully embedded within Turkish politics. Today, Turkey is raised as a clear example of a delegative democracy, primarily because of the dominance of personalism in its national politics, as well as irregular institutional relationships, including the decay of Turkey's political parties and their weak links with Turkish society.

Similar to many of the countries we are studying, leaders in Turkey are attempting to battle corrupt political actions that challenge regime legitimacy. Yet most cases fail to reach the courts because they are blocked by parliamentary action: court cases must first receive parliamentary authorization before they can proceed. Strong party discipline, in which party members refuse to "break ranks" and challenge one of their own, has usually brought such cases to a grinding halt. A 1998 attempt to amend the constitution and remove parliamentary immunity in corruption cases did not receive the majority it needed to pass. Especially problematic is the military's intervention in politics, which we highlighted in Chapter 12. The military-dominated National Security Council continues to be a key initiator and approver of major policy in modern Turkey.

It is possible that external pressure—namely European Union (EU) demands for membership—may have the greatest potential to promote genuine reform within Turkey. In December 1999 the republic was accepted as a formal candidate for membership in the EU, but it has been excluded from talks with the other twelve candidate countries because of its perceived stalled progress on democratic reform. In this regard, many looked to President Ahmet Necdet Sezer, who was sworn into office May 2000, as the most likely harbinger of change. Sezer, the former chief justice of Turkey's Constitutional Court, criticized the 1980 constitution (composed after the military coup) for being overly restrictive of human rights and freedoms. While such talk is welcomed by many outsiders, it has won him few friends among military leaders at home. The Turkish cabinet has made progress, though, in its promise to abandon the death penalty within the first five years of the twenty-first century and to lessen curbs on free speech.

Turkish leaders face two dominant struggles that challenge the regime's ability to handle opposition groups in a democratic framework. First is the lively debate between those who want to preserve Turkish secularism, enshrined in the Kemalist doctrine, and those who seek a greater role for Islam in national life. Even nationally elected leaders can be forced off the scene for the appearance of publicly promoting religious values. The second issue, potentially even more explosive than the first, is found in Kurdish NATIONALISM, as discussed in Chapter 11. Both the government's handling of this issue (outlawing discussion of anything remotely separatist and banning political parties associated with Kurdish identity) and its treatment of captured Kurdistan Workers' Party leader Abdullah Öcalan (including his death sentence) have demonstrated Turkey's difficulty with the institutionalization of conflict. These struggles are only exacerbated by the country's incessant struggle with its finances and economic reform. While Turkey has clearly moved out of the zone of authoritarianism that marks many countries in the region, it remains a country short of consolidated democracy.

Case Study: China

Life for ordinary citizens in China is freer than it has ever been since the commencement of the People's Republic. Yet the most accurate way to characterize the changes that are happening in this country would be to emphasize the leadership's reconfiguration of political and social life—changes mostly introduced by Deng Xiaoping in the 1980s. As a victim of Mao Zedong's ideological and personal purges himself, Deng set out to depersonalize Chinese politics and attempt to place the country again on the path of "normalcy." There is certainly a great deal of change taking place, and in many senses political relations in China are increasingly institutionalized. Some of the biggest developments are happening at the local levels, including elections for local committees and congresses. Yet the biggest hindrance to true political liberalization (on a national scale) is the dominance of the Chinese Communist Party (CCP), and especially the lack of separation between party and government in almost all public affairs. One of the best illustrations of this merger of power is the "multiple hats" syndrome: Jiang Zemin was concurrently the president of the country, the general secretary of the CCP, and the chairperson of the Central Military Commission. This pattern is replicated at lower levels as well. In the early 1980s there were attempts ostensibly to separate the party and government, but they were fully abandoned after the unrest in Tiananmen Square in June 1989. Chinese leaders continue to insist that their country is a socialist democracy, in which "the people are the masters of the country," whose will is expressed through the actions of the CCP.

Chinese politics has been and continues to be dominated by strong personalities. People commonly refer to generations of leaders: Mao led the first generation, Deng Xiaoping led the second, Jiang Zemin is the ordained beacon of the third generation. Although Jiang lacks the stature and revolutionary experience of his predecessors, he tries, even in semiretirement, to frame himself as a leader on par with the great Chinese heroes. His constant attempts to portray himself as worthy of such association belie his weaker credentials. Increasingly, his legitimacy risks being threatened by perceptions of ineptitude or behavior unbefitting a communist cadre. There is now much talk on the streets of Jiang's extramarital affairs, as he is seen around town with a popular female journalist and a well-known army representative to the national legislature. While some ordinary citizens were aware of Mao's now famous infidelities before his death, it would have been far too dangerous to openly talk about them in public, which is not the case today. In this sense, Jiang lacks the perception (held by Mao and Deng, to a lesser extent) of being infallible.

Government and party leaders vigorously emphasize the "unity of the Chinese nation" and the dangers of instability and chaos if this unity is challenged. Yet this harmony is not as prevalent as leaders would like their people to believe: China is an extremely decentralized country with a surprisingly weak central government that has a difficult time enforcing its mandate at the local levels. Until recently, the central government had difficulty even collecting tax monies from its provinces. Central leaders today battle the seemingly rampant corruption that challenges not only the façade of harmony but the precarious legitimacy of the regime as well. Jiang refers to the CCP's battle with corruption as the "life-and-death struggle" of the party (and therefore the state). Cases of increasingly higher-ranking leaders, including the former mayor of Beijing, are routinely publicized. Reports reveal thousands of cadres getting caught red-handed with unauthorized cars (often sedans or expensive Japanese imports), houses, and other signs of "lavish lifestyles" unfit for communist cadres. This includes cracking down on obvious displays of graft, including hosting elaborate banquets with public funds, illegally acquiring military and police vehicles, accepting credit cards, and speculating in shares. The regime faces a potentially dangerous task ahead, as accused party officials increase in number and rank. In a single-party state, where the public perception of corruption is so serious, how can the leaders avoid wholesale "guilt by association"?

Case Study: Indonesia

The politics of transition in Indonesia began with a bang: following the resignation of President Suharto in May 1998, the country embarked on an uncertain path of reform. The post-Suharto leadership inherited a series of grave problems, headlined by a great sense of betrayal, corruption, and hopelessness that followed the economic collapse of 1997. A key turning point in this reform effort was the 1999 parliamentary election, characterized by Freedom House as "reasonably free although not entirely fair." The rainbow of parties able to compete during this election was a vivid departure from the past, when Suharto's political machine, Golkar, dominated. Out of this election, a ruling coalition formed, led by a presidential team made up of leaders from two competing parties. Yet the least of the problems Abdurrahman Wahid and Megawati Sukarnoputri faced was their differing party loyalties, even though eventually it was Megawati's Indonesian Democratic Party that pressed Wahid's resignation. They needed to clean out a political system infested with corruption, tame a military accustomed to wielding considerable influence, and manage an economic recovery oftentimes made worse by international demands. With Wahid's forced resignation in July 2001, Megawati was elevated to president and faced the same struggles with less support from below.

Indonesia's political institutions are hobbled by past abuse: there was little institutional accountability or autonomy during the Suharto era, and practices encouraging transparency may be slow to crystallize. The Indonesian military, accustomed at the very least to an advisory role during previous administrations, faces constrictions to its political involvement. Yet it continues to hold seats in the legislature, even though the number was diminished from seventy-five to thirty-eight. Originally, these seats were assigned because members of the armed forces were not permitted to vote in elections—in an attempt to avoid politicizing the military.[14] Yet their influence in the People's Consultative Assembly remains largely unabated today. The bloody episode of paramilitary violence in East Timor after their independence vote demonstrated the difficulty civilian leaders face trying to muzzle the military. Judicial leaders, who used to be appointed and dismissed by the executive, now face the daunting task of processing corruption cases including Suharto's family. These trials, especially the dismissal of the former president's case, demonstrated the continuing need to promulgate and enforce impartial laws.

Indonesia is another country that has been dominated by strong personalities. In this unstable era, it is difficult to see any singular person surrounding herself or himself with as much power as Sukarno and Suharto achieved. "New" Indonesian leaders need to balance the need for international support and aid with the need to attend to domestic difficulties. President Wahid was abroad a good portion of his tenure, attempting to seek investment for the ailing economy as well as to bolster his image at home. Less than three months after her inauguration as president, Megawati Sukarnoputri was meeting with President George W. Bush in Washington and facing widespread protest at home for her support of the U.S.-led war on terrorism, which many viewed as a veiled war against Islamic civilization.

Since the end of the Suharto regime, Indonesia has been rocked by religious and separatist violence, coupled with a faltering economy and continued political instability. Some people contemplate whether or not the possibility of disintegration looms on Indonesia's horizon. As we discussed earlier, a national identity as an "Indonesian" is still a relatively new concept for most people, who are distinct from other Indonesians in terms of language, culture, history, and religion. As a government spokeswoman stated during the debate over East Timor in 1999, "Indonesia is an abstract concept, based on the former Netherlands East

Indies. If we start allowing different parts to break away, it will be dismembered before we know where we are."[15] Following the August 1999 vote for East Timor's independence, there has been a surge in both religious and sectarian activity, oftentimes demanding independence. In spite of these tremendous pressures on the Indonesian state, Donald Emmerson argues that if leaders would be able to rein in the military and make significant progress in the struggle against corruption, an Islamic democracy could result.[16] The two most likely candidates for secession are Aceh and Papua, formerly known as Irian Jaya. For largely economic reasons, though, their independence appears unlikely at this point. The citizens of Indonesia have struggled through a tremendously difficult path following the downfall of their strong-willed authoritarian leader. The problems that were masked during his reign now threaten to paralyze the leaders who follow him.

Now It's Your Turn

After considering the problems of democratization described in this chapter, how do you think democracy can be made more sustainable? In your view, what are the most important factors in determining the overall success or failure of a democracy? Given what you know of these cases, do you find the Western model of democracy's divisiveness appropriate for our cases? Could this model be applicable for much of the third world? What would you think are the challenges of having a democratic system during a crisis situation? What would be its benefits? Do you think that it is likely that political liberalization alone can address the needs of countries experiencing great economic and political instability? Are there any circumstances in which you believe disintegration might be a better outcome? Why?

Suggested Readings

Africa

Achebe, Chinua. *A Man of the People*. New York: Anchor Books, 1967. Nigeria: fiction, violence and corruption in a newly independent country.

Armah, Ayi Kwei. *The Beautyful Ones Are Not Yet Born*. London: Heinemann, 1969. Ghana: fiction, corruption and cynicism in the final years of the Nkrumah government, as experienced by a railway clerk and his family.

Ngugi, Wa Thiong'o. *Devil on the Cross*. London: Heinemann, 1982. Kenya: fiction, on "the Satan of capitalism" and political corruption in postindependence Kenya.

Soyinka, Wole. *The Open Sore of a Continent: A Personal Narrative on the Nigerian Crisis*. New York: Oxford University Press, 1996. Nigeria: nonfiction, a discussion of life under Sani Abacha.

Asia

Chan, Anita, Richard Madsen, and Jonathan Unger. *Chen Village Under Mao and Deng*. Berkeley: University of California Press, 1992. China: nonfiction, an examination of how life has changed under reforms.

Hefner, Robert W. *Civil Islam*. Princeton: Princeton University Press, 2000. Indonesia: nonfiction, examination of potential for Islamic democratic transition in Indonesia.

Liang, Xiaosheng, and Hanming Chen. *Panic and Deaf: Two Modern Satires*. Trans. James O. Belcher. Honolulu: University of Hawaii, 2001. China: fiction, satirical exploration of changes in "new" China written by a former Red Guard from the Cultural Revolution.

Xiao Di Zhu. *Thirty Years in a Red House: A Memoir of Childhood and Youth in Communist China.* Amherst: University of Massachusetts Press, 1998. China: Cultural Revolution narrative.

Xiaolong, Qiu, and Hsia-lung Chi'iu. *Death of a Red Heroine.* New York: Soho, 2000. China: fiction, murder mystery set in Shanghai highlighting problems of nepotism, corruption, and vice in China's most populous city.

Latin America and the Caribbean

Castañeda, Jorge G. *Perpetuating Power: How Mexican Presidents Are Chosen.* New York: New Press, 2000. Mexico: nonfiction, politics under the PRI.

Fuentes, Carlos. *The Death of Artemio Cruz.* Trans. Sam Hileman. New York: Farrar, Straus, 1964. Mexico: fiction, on the abuse of power and the failure of the Mexican Revolution.

Garcia Marquez, Gabriel. *The Autumn of the Patriarch.* Trans. Gregory Rabassa. New York: Avon, 1999. Latin America: fiction, uses a composite of dictators to describe authoritarianism in the region.

Paz, Octavio. *The Labyrinth of Solitude.* New York: Grove Press, 1991. Mexico: nonfiction, the Nobel laureate on the country's history and politics.

Middle East

al-Shaykh, Hanan. *Women of Sand and Myrrh.* Trans. Catherine Cobham. New York: Anchor Books, 1992. Nonfiction, focuses on four contemporary women in an unnamed Middle Eastern country who share the experiences of living in societies undergoing upheaval and change.

Cooper, Roger. *Death Plus Ten Years.* London: HarperCollins, 1993. Iran: nonfiction, personal narrative of the fates of journalists in their struggle with the regime.

Danishvar, Simin, *Danishvar's Playhouse: A Collection of Stories.* Washington, D.C.: Mage, 1989. Iran: autobiographical reflection after the death of the writer's husband.

Mottahedeh, Roy. *The Mantle of the Prophet: Life in Post-Khomeini Iran.* Oxford: Oneworld, 2000. Iran: nonfiction, political narrative embedded in rich survey of culture.

Rachlin, Nahid. *The Heart's Desire: A Novel.* San Francisco: City Lights Books, 1995. Iran: semifictional account of a trip by an Iranian American couple from the United States to Iran.

Reed, Fred A. *Anatolia Junction: A Journey into Hidden Turkey.* Burnaby, Canada: Talonbooks, 2000. Turkey: nonfiction, exploration of Said-I Nursi, founder of the Nurcu Movement in Islam.

———. *Persian Postcards: Iran After Khomeini.* Vancouver: Talonbooks, 1994. Iran: nonfiction, the country since Khomeini's death.

PART 4

BEYOND THE NATION-STATE

We the peoples of the United Nations determined to save succeeding generations from the scourge of war . . . and to reaffirm faith in fundamental human
rights, in the dignity and worth of the human person, in the equal rights of men
and women and of nations large and small, and to establish conditions under
which justice and respect for the obligations arising from treaties and other
sources of international law can be maintained, and to promote social progress
and better standards of life in larger freedom . . . have resolved to combine our
efforts to accomplish these aims.

—From the Charter of the United Nations

Today more than ever, we live in a global economic, political, and cultural
world, in which no country is an island completely isolated from the influence
of other regions. The impact of geographical dividing lines between governments is in many ways less important today than at the beginning of the twentieth century. This development has profound effects on the issues that face us, as
well as the institutions with which we handle these issues. In the chapters that
follow, we examine some issues that are decidedly multinational if not global in
scope, and discuss some of the institutions, both regional and global, that have
developed in response.

17

Sovereignty and the Role of International Organizations

Among many developments in the last fifty years, few parallel that of the increased interconnectedness of the world's states and of issues that affect citizens of the globe. We begin with a discussion of the role of states, acting not alone but rather in regional and global organizations, with special attention to the UNITED NATIONS. What are some of the issues that these organizations have tackled? Have they achieved much success? Next we talk about groups that have organized independently of governments, by highlighting the development on NONGOVERNMENTAL ORGANIZATIONS (NGOs) in the world today. We conclude with discussion of some of the major global challenges facing our world, and discuss the capacity of NGOs at the regional and international level to resolve these issues.

The rise of groups outside of the traditional NATION-STATE in part has led to a rethinking of the idea of national SOVEREIGNTY, commonly understood as government's autonomy or independence to act, especially within its own borders. The legitimate authority over any given territory, usually viewed as the entitlement of the state, includes the right to self-defense and the determination of its own destiny. The principle of sovereignty implies a degree of NONINTERFERENCE in one's affairs. Yet in recent years, many leaders, including former U.S. president Bill Clinton and UN Secretaries-General Boutros Boutros-Ghali and Kofi Annan, have argued that state sovereignty may be limited by the desire to promote seemingly UNIVERSAL humanitarian goals and human rights. This belief, alternatively known as the CLINTON DOCTRINE, places the suppression of crimes against humanity, which include ethnic cleansing, mass rape, and genocide (or the systematic decimation of people), above claims of state sovereignty. How can the international community respond to mass executions within other countries, or the systematic rape and torture of vulnerable groups? How should other countries respond? These are not new questions in international relations. Rather, they are reminders that the questions surrounding our past inaction in the face of mass violence, especially the Jewish Holocaust, have not all been answered, and that the controversy over how and when to intervene in others' affairs still haunts our world.

Despite all of the euphoric claims of globalism and our interconnected twenty-first-century world, systematic torture and the murder of specifically targeted groups of people continue to take place today, and we continue to struggle with our response. Does sovereignty mean that government leaders can violate the human rights of individuals and groups within their borders? As we discuss below, some now argue that humanitarian needs in countries or regions permit (or even require) the response of other countries, including a military response. Yet a central tension remains: Do problems that cross national borders demand an international response? What if the problem is confined within a single state? Are other countries justified to take action, in the name of promoting human rights? How should this response be coordinated, implemented, and monitored? This approach poses many other questions: What degree of suffering warrants a response from others? Under what conditions is international action justified? Who has the LEGITIMACY to carry out such actions, through what mechanisms, and with what precise objectives?[1] Is unilateral action, undertaken by a single state or group, justified as long as it is in the name of humanitarian needs? Does a multilateral approach, involving the coordinated effort of multiple governments, necessarily make an action more legitimate? The answers to these questions have the capacity to dramatically change the way in which nation-states and the governments that lead them view themselves and their roles.

To this point in the book, we have talked much about the role of state actors. Yet recognizing the principle of interdependence, supranational organizations that go beyond single nation-states have taken a more active role in international affairs. Some of this action is taken by groups of governments who willingly forgo some degree of their independent sovereignty in order to accomplish particular goals. Other action is taken by nongovernmental actors who organize not around their governmental identity, but rather around a particular cause or interest. Both types of organizations are increasingly prominent on the world stage.

International Governmental Organizations

INTERNATIONAL GOVERNMENTAL ORGANIZATIONS (IGOs) are made up of official representatives of states who gather to discuss responses to issues and conflicts that affect the world community. We have already discussed two prominent IGOs, the INTERNATIONAL MONETARY FUND (IMF) and the WORLD BANK, which were both established at the Bretton Woods Conference of 1944. In this section, we discuss the role of IGOs and other multilateral institutions in resolving global issues. We focus on both regional and global IGOs as a tool of fostering cooperation among governments. One important feature of IGOs is that their memberships comprise official governmental representatives, and their goals are to calibrate the policies of like-minded states as well as to solve contentious issues that arise between conflicting state policies and goals. These goals are different from those of the other major type of organizations that we discuss in this chapter, the nongovernmental organizations (NGOs).

Each of the organizations that we discuss poses different challenges for the third world. Often, less powerful countries are excluded from decisionmaking structures within these organizations, either explicitly or implicitly. This contradiction of universal membership is most stark with respect to the United

Nations, in which each state is guaranteed an equal voice in some chambers, most notably the General Assembly, but not others, including the much more powerful Security Council. The lack of TRANSPARENCY, or clear, publicly available decisionmaking processes, challenges both the participation of many states and groups as well as the perception that actions taken by these organizations are positive. Many of these organizations are undergoing reform to fix these drawbacks, but the obstacles remain formidable.

Regional Organizations

Over the last several decades there has been a proliferation of regional economic blocs, free trade areas, customs unions, and common markets. Since the late 1970s the impetus for this growth has come from both the desire to form regional trade organizations as well as a defensive response to GLOBALIZATION. We view regionalism as a framework of cooperation, with an indefinite duration, intended to include multiple issues, most often economic or security in nature.[2] The latter part of this explanation captures the transition that has touched many organizations in the third world; quite a few began with an initial focus on economics and trade within a defined (although not absolute) geographical space, and are now adopting other complementary agendas as well.[3]

A few observations on regional alliances focus our attention on some of the unexpected aspects of these organizations. Sometimes, former enemies (or countries with continuing hostilities) seek alliances as a way to formally move beyond their conflict. In Latin America, for example, Peru is a member of many regional organizations to which countries it has had past disputes with also belong, including Ecuador and Bolivia. The Association of Southeast Asian Nations (ASEAN) began largely in response to the regional perception of the growing communist threat in Southeast Asia. ASEAN's predecessor, the Southeast Asia Treaty Organization (SEATO), was distinctly strategic in focus. Member states within this organization continue to hold competing views on a variety of issues, including economic growth, environmental issues, and threats to security.

Another security-focused regional organization that brought together states in the larger interest of promoting stability and a common defense is the South African Development Community (SADC). The SADC originated in 1980 to provide political and economic protection against the apartheid regime in South Africa, which later joined after its independence in 1994.[4] From the start, members recognized the gains to be made in infrastructure and other assistance. Its initial focus was self-defense because of its shared vulnerability in the face of South Africa. Today its focus has shifted somewhat, offering a powerful challenge to the dominance of free market trade ideologies found in many regional associations. Leaders of the SADC have argued that the state must remain interventionist in economic as well as political-social affairs in order to promote investment, development, and holistic growth.

Part of the success of the SADC lies in its realistic priorities for regional planning.[5] Leaders have promoted small-scale irrigation over grandiose dams, as well as the use of appropriate technology, including attempts to combat widespread deforestation by developing more fuel-efficient stoves and alternative energy sources for cooking pots. As we find in other regional organizations, members have benefited from functionalist arrangements on technical matters, including efforts to sustain tropical forests, curtail the illegal trade in ivory and diamonds, promote the repatriation of refugees, and manage the distribution of limited natural resources, including through oil and natural gas pipelines. SADC members have expressed an interest in evolving a structure similar to that of the European Union (EU), but the SADC currently is dependent on external donors for 90 percent of its budget, and it has no teeth—no enforcement powers. Worse, its fourteen members have recently divided into blocs over the question of how to handle Zimbabwe. The Democratic Republic of Congo, Angola, and Namibia (all allies in the Congolese War) back Zimbabwe, whereas the governments of South Africa, Botswana, and Mozambique are more willing to be critical of their old friend Robert Mugabe.

Increased interaction and contact can have many unintended consequences. Just as regional organizations developed to promote greater economic integration or cooperation in security matters, less formalized interaction has helped to promote regional solidarity through personal and cultural exchanges. For example, South American member states of Mercosur, also known as the COMMON MARKET of the South, have begun exchanges of mayors, provincial governors, and students, and Spanish is now obligatory in Brazilian schools as a way to promote regional cohesion.[6] This regional organization (soon to include over 200 million inhabitants) formed in the absence of developed linkages among states, and is now considered one of the main economic blocs of the world.

Two regional actors, ASEAN and the Organization of American States (OAS), had their genesis during the COLD WAR, both forming as alliances to combat the rise of communist governments. Both organizations have moved beyond this ideological focus in the post–Cold War era, with ASEAN welcoming its former nemesis, China, on a consultative basis. Current member states of ASEAN, formed in 1967, are Brunei, Indonesia, Laos, Malaysia, Myanmar, the Philippines, Singapore, Thailand, and Vietnam, with consultative status held by the "dialogue partners," which outnumber the member states: Australia, Canada, China, the European Union, India, Japan, New Zealand, the Republic of Korea, Russia, and the United States.

With the commencement of the ASEAN Regional Forum in 1994, the noneconomic aspect of the organization has again been highlighted. This component of ASEAN was developed in order to promote peace and security in the Asia-Pacific region. It will need greater participation by China to bring more power to the association. A recent debate with far-reaching consequences is the discussion among members about potential regional intervention under the UN flag in Cambodia.

The OAS, the preeminent organization for the Western Hemisphere, began with an agreement among member states in 1948, and the organization was launched three years later. It includes thirty-five members (all countries in the region except for Cuba, which was suspended in 1962 at the demand of the United States). U.S. dominance of the OAS during the Cold War meant that the organization was focused on isolating Marxist governments and fighting against leftist rebels. Since the end of the Cold War, the emphasis has shifted greatly.

The priorities of the OAS today are to promote education in member states, to preserve and strengthen DEMOCRACY through the promotion of social justice, human rights, and civil society, and to provide solutions to the debt crises many member states face. Despite the presence of many regional economic organizations in Latin America, the OAS has also helped promote microenterprise and telecommunications trade, while shining attention on abuses of labor rights and the need to promote sustainable development throughout the region. The OAS has been a major diplomatic player in the region as well, most notably helping to cool tensions between Ecuador and Peru in the mid-1990s. It also was a leading regional voice challenging Alberto Fujimori's hijacking of the presidential elections in 2000. There is much talk among member states about the organization adopting a more hands-on approach as a "watchdog" of democracy, a controversial perspective that would call for intervention to limit political corruption and institutional decay, promoted mostly by Argentinean voices.[7] Member states agree much more readily with the call to increase institutional and social linkages.

In Africa, the premier regional organization, formed in 1963, is the Organization of African Unity (OAU). It was created during the era of Africa's independence, and has dramatically changed in the last four decades. Out of concern that its status quo approach had doomed it to irrelevance, the OAU has been retired and transformed into the more powerful African Union, which convened its first summit in South Africa in July 2002. Its architects hope that it will one day operate along the lines of the European Union, with a pan-African parliament, a central bank, and a common currency. With the same members and many of the same problems as the OAU, the African Union has a stronger charter (but not yet a larger budget) to promote integration between the fifty-three countries of Africa. Unlike the OAU, member states are to promise to hold free elections and the African Union has the right to intervene against genocide or gross human rights abuse. However, there are already divides that may prevent any of this from ever actually happening.[8]

One of the first comprehensive initiatives coming out of the region in this period, the New Partnership for African Development (NEPAD), was proposed by Presidents Thabo Mbeki (South Africa) and Obasanjo and other government leaders in 2001. The idea behind this ambitious recovery plan is for developed countries to reward African states practicing good governance (or transparency, accountability, and other reforms) with debt relief, but also increased aid, investment, and freer trade. Although some say they'll believe it when they see it, given African leaders' continued reluctance to criticize their cohorts, through independent "peer reviews" of performance, Africans will apply mechanisms aimed at encouraging other African governments to stick with a program of agreed standards aimed at remedying institutional deficiencies and promoting sustainable development.[9]

How can membership in a multilateral organization, with either a regional or global scope, change conduct within a country? Turkey's decades-long attempt to join the EU provides a good example. Turkish leaders submitted their formal application for full membership in 1987, but the EU did not accept Turkey as a candidate until December 1999. Turkish prime minister Bülent Ecevit announced his target of gaining EU membership by 2004, which most believe is extremely optimistic, especially now that discussions on Turkey's accession to the EU will not convene until late that year.

What is holding up Turkey's coveted membership? Its continued sparring over the divided status of Cyprus, with Greece, an EU member since 1981, exacerbates the tension. Fundamentally, though, the issue boils down to concerns about Turkey's human rights record, especially its treatment and execution of accused terrorists. Representatives from Reporters Without Borders, the international nongovernmental organization advocating the rights of journalists and media employees, claim that Turkey has almost as many journalists in jail as the rest of the world put together. The role of the military in Turkey's constitution and its civil administration also opens Ankara to problems. In an effort to acquire EU membership, Turkey's parliament has enacted some reforms that could have favorable outcomes for the respect of human rights: military judges have been removed from civilian courts, longer prison terms have been established for those guilty of torture, and barriers preventing prosecutors from easily muting unpopular voices within government have been removed. Most significantly, the parliament also banned the use of capital punishment during peacetime. Turkey provides a good case of how some domestic decisions are influenced by the desire to acquire membership in broader associations.

The United Nations

Among the myriad of international organizations that exist in the twenty-first century, the United Nations, founded in the immediate aftermath of World War II, stands alone as the most universally recognized. Its goal, as stated in the UN Charter, is intricately tied to the period from which it grew: to "save succeeding generations from the scourge of war." Its predecessor, the League of Nations, a product of World War I, was largely unsuccessful in reaching this goal, as World War II broke out within two decades of its establishment. While the cause of the failures of the League of Nations are still hotly debated, many have identified one of its key weaknesses as the granting of equal voice to every state. This, some argue, failed to accurately reflect differences in power and influence among states. Today's United Nations is designed to include all states of the world (although Yugoslavia's membership was suspended in 1992),[10] and its organizational structure gives greater influence to some countries than others— an issue we will return to below. The main headquarters of the UN are in New York City, with principal offices in Geneva (where special offices for human rights and disarmament are located), Vienna (the main offices for international drug abuse monitoring, criminal justice, peaceful uses of outer space, and international trade law), and Nairobi (the headquarters for offices on human settlements and UN environmental programs). Through its committees, agencies, assemblies, and related organizations, the United Nations gathers leaders to define policy objectives, set standards, and monitor compliance with internationally agreed policies and programs, and to promote the peaceful resolution of conflict throughout the world.[11]

The UN Charter, signed in 1945, outlines the principles of COLLECTIVE SECURITY, state sovereignty, and the equal rights of SELF-DETERMINATION of all peoples. Collective security embodies the concept that states will impede an aggressor state by binding together in a cooperative framework. The goal of such collective action is to prevent conflict, but if it does occur, such aggression is met with force. It is a tactic that combines the pooled resources and power of united countries, seemingly indicative of "world opinion," with the threat to use force if security and peace are threatened. During the Cold War, collective security took a back seat to the old power politics the UN was designed to replace. Without superpower agreement in the Security Council, collective security did not operate. During the Cold War, the only collective security action was that taken in Korea from 1950 to 1953, made possible only because the Soviet Union boycotted the Security Council to protest the exclusion of the People's Republic of China from the United Nations. The force was commanded by a U.S. general whose orders were from Washington rather than the United Nations per se. The operation of collective security was more evident in actions taken following Iraq's invasion of Kuwait in 1990, when the powerful veto-wielding permanent members of the Security Council all acquiesced in agreement to combat this force. Again, though, this action must be viewed only as a limited example of collective security, especially given the commanding role of the United States during the war. As Karen Mingst and Margaret Karns point out, the exclusion of non–Security Council voices from discussion of the operation rallied many UN members, including leaders of the third world, to decry their exclusion.[12]

The doctrine of self-determination, although incompletely applied, has been an important force for non-Western peoples within the United Nations. In a nutshell, the concept embodies the belief that all peoples of the world have the right to rule themselves, rather than to be ruled by outside, colonial powers. The processes of decolonization, spearheaded by African and Asian representatives to the UN, led to the peaceful independence of many states, especially in the 1950s and 1960s. However, as we discussed in Chapter 4, the remnants of colonialism, including the vestiges of imperial governments, continued well into the twentieth century. Chapter XI of the UN Charter establishes a pivotal role for member states regarding "non-self-governing territories." Members of the United Nations have a responsibility to assist in the establishment of self-government where it does not yet exist. The independence of Namibia in 1990 is one of the most unusual cases of UN-supervised decolonization. Formerly known as South West Africa, the territory was placed under the responsibility of the United Nations, rather than being given status as a member state, in 1950, after South Africa refused to administer the territory as it previously had under the League of Nations system. Today, this aspect of the charter enables the United Nations to assist in the development of newly self-governing states, such as East Timor. Currently, approximately eighteen non-self-governing territories remain under the tutelage of a United Nations member state, mostly in the Caribbean and Mediterranean (where the United Kingdom and the United States are the dominant administering authorities).

One of the most important General Assembly resolutions passed in the United Nations is the 1948 UNIVERSAL DECLARATION OF HUMAN RIGHTS (UDHR). The development and acceptance of this document has helped to promote a wide-ranging body of human rights law, including treaties that recognize economic, social, cultural, political, and civil rights. Articles 1 and 2 of the

Universal Declaration state that "all human beings are born equal in dignity and rights" and are entitled to rights "without distinction of any kind such as race, color, sex, language, religion, political or other opinion, national or social origin, property, birth or other status." Through its committee structure, fact-finding missions, international conferences, and advocacy, the UN attempts to promote these ideals in all of its work.

Organization of the United Nations. The main structures within the United Nations include the General Assembly, the Security Council, the Economic and Social Council (ECOSOC), and the International Court of Justice (ICJ), the principal judicial organ. The GENERAL ASSEMBLY, in which each member state is represented, makes recommendations in the form of nonbinding resolutions. Some committees of the UN write reports analyzing the implementation of standards and solutions, or propose new organizations to monitor situations. The main aim of the UN is to promote consensus, and this work is achieved through the laborious and detailed processes of drafting resolutions that have the support of a plurality of state representatives. Although all nonbudgetary resolutions are nonbinding, they highlight steps that governments should take to resolve conflict and promote peace and prosperity, and elements of resolutions are often incorporated into the national laws of the supporting countries. The General Assembly is the most procedurally democratic arm of the United Nations, since each state gets one and only one vote, irrespective of size, power, or prestige. From the speeches and debates within the General Assembly, we can ascertain a great deal about the voice of world opinion.

One of the most visible agencies of the UN is the SECURITY COUNCIL. The Security Council can initiate binding action, including final approval of the General Assembly's choice of SECRETARY-GENERAL, the chief administrative officer of the United Nations. Additionally, the Security Council recommends states for membership to the General Assembly. The Secretary-General is appointed by the General Assembly on the recommendation of the Security Council for a five-year, renewable term. Of the seven Secretaries-General since 1946, four have come from countries in the third world: U Thant, of Burma, who served from 1961 to 1971; Javier Perez de Cuellar, of Peru, from 1982 to 1991; Boutros Boutros-Ghali, of Egypt, from 1992 to 1996; and Kofi Annan, of Ghana, who has led the organization since 1997.

As the name implies, the Security Council is designed to deal with threats to peace and security. It convenes a meeting at the call of any member state that feels threatened or violated, and it often calls representatives of conflicting sides to present their case to the chamber. Representatives on the Security Council are often required to make very rapid and important decisions. In circumstances determined to constitute "threats to the peace, breaches of the peace, or acts of aggression," as defined by CHAPTER VII of the UN Charter, the Security Council can order binding action, including economic sanctions or the use of armed force. In the post–Cold War era, the Security Council has been more activist, especially in terms of peacekeeping and humanitarian issues, as we discuss below.

There are two sets of countries that sit in the Security Council. Reflective of their strength, the five post–World War II powers—the United States, the Soviet Union, the United Kingdom, France, and China—were given permanent, veto-power seats in the Security Council.[13] These countries are known as the permanent five (P-5). This privileged position was given to the powerful countries of the mid-1940s to recognize their importance at the time of the UN's birth, a lesson taken from the experiment with the League of Nations. Granting these countries a veto over substantive (not procedural) matters bestows on them a tremendous amount of power; a single no vote by any of these five countries will halt any action taken by the Security Council. Members' use of their veto power has fluctuated across time, with vetoes being used much more frequently to block action during the Cold War than since the 1990s. The most frequent invoker of the veto has been the Soviet Union, especially during the 1940s and 1950s (seventy-nine vetoes total). The United States ranks second in its use of vetoes, registering seventy-two since 1945. China has used vetoes the least, tallying only five since 1946.[14] Yet even if the veto is rarely used today, the threat of its action can certainly change policy proposals and influence the topics that are brought to the Security Council for discussion. It is a powerful tool that the vast majority of member states do not have, nor are they likely to have in the future.

The second group within the Security Council consists of ten other states, elected by the General Assembly on a temporary, two-year rotating basis, without veto power. Some voices, within both the Western and the non-Western world, argue that this structure is outdated and needs to be modified, both to more accurately reflect the balance of power in today's world, and to be more representative of non-Western countries. As one scholar expressed it, "To many nations, today's Security Council may seem more like a domineering Star Chamber than a fount of international jurisprudence."[15] China is the only non-Western permanent member of Security Council. UN Secretary-General Kofi Annan has on many occasions called for increasing the size of the Security Council to give it more diversity and a stronger voice for developing nations. An enlarged Security Council could include a permanent seat from each region of the developing world, including, for example, a permanent (nonveto) African, Asian, and Latin American position to be rotated among states in the region. Currently, there is a regional focus to the election of nonpermanent members; five are elected from Africa and Asia combined, one from Eastern Europe, two from Latin America, and two from Western Europe and other areas. Another proposal for a larger Security Council could include permanent states irrespective of regions. Brazil, Germany, and Japan are the states most often cited, because of their realized or potential economic strength. Germany and Japan also argue that they contribute more financially to the UN than Russia, China, Great Britain, and France.

Any change in the makeup of the Security Council will require an amendment to the UN Charter, and is likely to take much time. Gaining the approval of the current P-5 is only the first step, and an unlikely one at that, since it would leave their power diminished. Opposition to Security Council enlargement also comes from less powerful states that are not currently represented in the Security Council, but that fear the power such a change could give to their adversaries. Pakistan, for example, opposes any proposal that might give India a role. Iran, the current leader of the Group of 77 (a third world organization that seeks leverage in bargaining with developed countries), favors an increase in geographic representation, but wants to limit the exercise of veto power. Pakistan, Argentina, Bangladesh, Malaysia, and Egypt oppose any new members to the Security Council. The number of competing reform proposals, and the fierceness of both support and opposition for these plans, demonstrates the power of the Security Council as well as widespread distrust of a group who increasingly operate behind closed doors. At best, today's Security Council represents the world power structure as it was in 1945, heavily favoring the victors of World War II in an institution designed to give equal voice to all states. At worst, it is an enduring legacy of big-power politics that operates without systematic input from the majority of people whom it is designed to serve.

Another area of controversy within the United Nations surrounds its expanding mandate to take action in countries in the name of humanitarian relief. One of the fundamental questions plaguing UN strategies is the hot topic of intervention: When and how should a global body respond to crises in another state's affairs? Since the end of the Cold War, the United Nations has increased its activism, first in military opposition to the Iraqi invasion of Kuwait, and later with involvement in internal conflicts in the former Yugoslavia, Somalia, Cambodia, El Salvador, and East Timor, among others. Each state's fundamental right to sovereignty is enshrined in the UN Charter, as we discussed above, and sovereignty is treated as a sacred principle upon which the United Nations is based. State leaders who resist UN action in their countries predictably invoke this principle, which helps explain why there has been no UN response to humanitarian crises in Tibet (due to China's opposition) or Chechnya (over Russia's opposition).

As a large, global body consisting of representatives from almost every country of the world, what can the United Nations realistically accomplish, in addition to providing a forum for discussion and the diplomatic solution to problems? The primary modes of influence available to UN actors include economic sanctions, censure (losing the right to vote in the General Assembly), and intervention, either with or without military backing. These actions are permissible under Chapter VII of the UN Charter, which authorizes the Security Council to take enforcement measures to either maintain or restore international peace and security. During the Cold War, Chapter VII provisions were invoked twice: to impose economic sanctions on the white minority regime in southern Rhodesia in 1965, and to impose an arms embargo against the South African apartheid regime in 1977. The latter set of sanctions is now viewed as the most comprehensive package implemented under Chapter VII provisions. They were lifted with the end of the apartheid in 1994.

Sanctions imposed under Chapter VII authority have been a more common tool in the post–Cold War era. They have been invoked against Iraq, the former Yugoslavia, Libya, Haiti, Liberia, Rwanda, Somalia, Angola, Sudan, and Sierra Leone. Sanctions can be either mandatory (all member states face risk of punishment if they do not comply) or voluntary. Sanctions are always controversial, because they risk harming ordinary citizens more than powerful leaders. In their favoritism of one group over another, they can prolong and deepen existing conflict. In Bosnia, for example, the concern was that economic sanctions tied the hands of the Bosnian Muslims while Bosnian Serbs were rearmed by Serbia.

The human toll of economic sanctions has been especially brought to the light in view of the sanctions against Iraq. After the initial economic and transportation sanctions imposed following the invasion of Kuwait were seen as ineffective, the Security Council passed Resolution 678. This resolution authorized member states to use "all necessary means" to expel Iraq from Kuwait, which was ultimately used to justify the Gulf War. After the end of the war in April 1991, Iraq continued to face sanctions, as it was forced to destroy its weapons base and compensate victims of its aggression. Following the cease-fire, Iraqi leaders averted full inspection of their arsenal, invoking the principle of state sovereignty. Even the elaborate "oil for food" deal, under which the Iraqi government could earn revenue for basic humanitarian provisions for its people from the previously forbidden sale of oil, did not lessen the crisis. As the sanctions period passed the ten-year mark, members of the world community increasingly faced the devastating humanitarian toll of these measures. Malnutrition, extremely limited access to safe drinking water (piped water supply, devastated by the war, was down to 5 percent of prewar levels in Iraq's major cities), and the recurrence of infectious diseases that had previously been eradicated—each took a tremendous toll on the most vulnerable of the Iraqi population. Few of these outcomes have been caused by sanctions alone, but rather are a combination of the devastation of the Gulf War, the hoarding of materials by the Iraqi elite, and the limited flow of assistance that has trickled down to the Iraqi people. Doubts and controversies about the statistics of this crisis have been common, but few would challenge the assertion that, while the Iraqi leadership remains unchanged in its opposition to unfettered inspection of its weapons arsenals, the people of the country have paid dearly. Segments of Iraqi society, especially those associated with the military or with the ruling Baath Party, are seen with luxury cars, flat-screen televisions, and other amenities. This is not the way sanctions are designed to work.

France, Russia, China, Turkey, Egypt, and Saudi Arabia have led the campaign at the UN to lift Iraqi sanctions in order to end this suffering. Increasingly, countries are breaking them: up to 150,000 barrels of oil a day are transported through a Syrian pipeline, and as much oil is moved by truck via Turkey.[16] Increasing numbers of Arab leaders are formally received at the reopened Saddam International Airport in Baghdad, and voices calling for the end to sanctions are outlasting calls for continued isolation. Not all of this is about humanitarian concerns, of course, as countries want to compete for contracts to help rebuild a land that has been devastated from top to bottom.

The case of Haiti (1991–1994) demonstrates the success that can be had with multilateral, directed, and comprehensive sanctions. In this tiny island state, it was not the oil and arms embargo that had been launched in 1993, but rather the threat of military intervention by a U.S.-led force of 20,000 troops that finally forced the Haitian military government out. The traditional military response has been to send national armies under national command but claiming UN approval into a region to promote nonviolence in the wake of conflict. Yet the UN does not have any military or armed forces of its own to respond to crises. One of the more extensive initiatives of the UN was the 500,000-person international force under unified command sent to South Korea from 1950 to 1953, which eventually ended in stalemate and the continuation of partition along the thirty-eighth parallel.[17]

Peacekeeping operations. For some, the UN is made up of people who wear the famous "blue hats": the so-called peacekeepers. Yet the processes of "keeping the peace" in areas marred by conflict have fundamentally changed. Traditionally, soldiers participating in PEACEKEEPING OPERATIONS (PKOs) were supposed to keep warring parties separated, provide monitors between former combatants, or guarantee a cease-fire, as they did observing the Arab-Israeli truce in 1948. (Peacekeeping is a much more elaborate process than peacemaking, which is viewed as bringing the warring parties to agreement. Ideally, but not always, peacekeeping forces pick up where the peacemakers leave off.) Peacekeeping troops can only fight if attacked, and they can remain only as long as all warring parties agree to their presence. And while the PKO along the border of Ethiopia and Eritrea has been relatively successful, with both sides respecting the cease-fire and few peacekeepers or civilians having been targeted for violence, this mission is the exception rather than the rule.

Today we ask peacekeepers to do much more: enforce international law, police, contain violence, protect civilians, and arrest war criminals.[18] Peacekeepers have been placed in charge of disarmament operations as well, a mix of policing and military operations that is untenable at best. Where is the line between keeping the peace and quelling unrest? Increasingly, peacekeepers are forced to walk this dangerous line. Additionally, peacekeepers have been put in charge of reconstruction after wars, and have served as human rights monitors and election observers, as in Namibia and Cambodia.

There were more PKO missions in the 1990s than in all previous years of UN existence combined. Prominent PKOs throughout the 1990s included Mozambique (1993), Somalia (1993), and El Salvador (UN operations in each of these countries closed in 1995), as well as Rwanda (canceled in 1996) and Eritrea (2000). Peacekeepers have also been involved in the coordination of administrations in Kosovo (where they operate parallel to the North Atlantic Treaty Organization [NATO], which handles military matters) and East Timor. Yet in many cases, they seem neither equipped nor authorized to take such action. Many voices call for both strengthening and expanding UN peacekeeping forces to respond to foreign conflicts, especially civil conflicts that present the gravest possibilities for humanitarian disasters. Responsibilities placed on the individuals who don the blue helmets of the United Nations, a color explicitly chosen because it is not worn in combat, are likely to increase in the future.

Who are the peacekeepers? The UN Department of Peacekeeping Operations has 32 officers coordinating 27,000 troops.[19] Troops used to be drawn heavily from Nordic countries and Canada, but defense cuts at the end of the 1980s decreased the involvement of these regions. Today, third world countries have large armies searching for employment, but they tend to lack the training necessary for the duties they face. The solution, imperfect at best, was to give these armies something to do in a PKO. In fact, most PKO troops deployed in recent

Figure 17.1   The African Crisis Response Initiative

The idea for the African Crisis Response Initiative (ACRI) grew out of the need for a regional peacekeeping force, a multinational African force that would be sponsored by the United States and other donors. After the debacle in Somalia in the early 1990s, the United States in particular was determined not to send troops into Africa. In its determination not to be the world's policeman, the United States swayed the UN to opt against humanitarian intervention in Africa. This policy of disengagement, when it came to Africa, is now widely recognized as contributing to the Rwandan genocide. The ACRI was first proposed by the Clinton administration as a response to concerns that U.S. policy was not only immoral but destabilizing. The ACRI was designed to promote regional stability in Africa without turning to the U.S. military. Instead, selected African countries, such as Senegal, Uganda, and Nigeria, provide the troops. The United States, Britain, and France are providing the funding to train and equip these soldiers as peacekeepers, spending much less than typical peace operations carried out by the West. The result is Africans taking the lead in resolving African conflicts. For example, in one of its first efforts, under the ACRI a few hundred U.S. military advisers spent ten weeks training Nigerians to return to Sierra Leone as peacekeepers.

While the Bush administration and U.S. Congress are supportive of the ACRI and are likely to continue its funding, many Africans, including Nelson Mandela, have expressed their ambivalence about the program. They worry that once there is a peacekeeping force just for Africa, then the region will be forgotten entirely. Furthermore, some observers have questions concerning the ACRI's relationship to the UN, its mandate, and its command and control structure. They want more specific assurances about long-term external support for the program. Some Africans find the ACRI patronizing, as the program was designed by the United States with very little prior consultation of Africans. Many people are puzzled and annoyed at the U.S. failure to recognize or build on existing subregional organizations, such as the Economic Community of West African States (ECOWAS) and the SADC. One thing is clear—as it exists now the ACRI is no panacea. It is far too small to do the job; it needs more than the $20 million a year it receives, and it needs nearly ten times the number of trained troops it had as of 2002 (the ACRI was at that time comprised approximately 6,500 peacekeepers).[20] In addition, the ACRI will need at least ten years of consistent external funding before it can be mobilized anywhere in Africa. Just as important, it will need strong African leadership, or this peacekeeping force will be perceived as a puppet of the West.

UN operations have come from the developing world (India, Nigeria, Jordan, Bangladesh, and Ghana supply the most). PKO forces are also often drawn from regional groups, in the attempt to avoid aggravating conflict by inviting "outsiders" into local conflicts. Some have proposed increasing the contingency of so-called regional cops, funded internationally but sanctioned by the United Nations to enforce Security Council mandates. They could provide the legitimacy of the international community but place the onus on self-interested, local agents. For example, Australia led the troops in East Timor to patrol after the vote for independence. Nigerians led a West African force in Sierra Leone.

Richer countries rarely send soldiers on peacekeeping missions, preferring to finance the operations instead or send observers. Other countries shudder at the thought of their troops being under the command of another country, or a leader from another state. Members of the P-5 states are reluctant to send their troops into another country's affairs. President Clinton's views shifted over time. He started out as a strong multilateralist who was willing to intervene in other countries to complete a collaborative mission. But he began to back off after Somalia, and wrongly blamed the United Nations for a mission that was under U.S. command. During his campaign for president, George W. Bush stated, "I will never place U.S. troops under UN command." But if dominant countries command forces of soldiers, how multilateral is that? To the majority of the world's population, who live in the less powerful countries, this smacks of big-power politics all over again. Concerns about the imbalance in the burden shouldered by non-Western countries have caused some to argue for a permanent UN standing army to which all countries contribute.

Peacekeeping has become dangerous business, especially as the title has grown to include monitors, observers, and aid workers—seemingly innocuous titles in times of peace, but extremely dangerous roles following periods of unrest, where their presence is largely unwelcome. For example, following the 1999 election in East Timor, a UN-sponsored relief office in West Timor was stormed by angry crowds, and the bodies of three UN workers (from the United States, Croatia, and Ethiopia) were burned in the streets. The United Nations and international diplomats expressed disappointment in the outcome of the trials for these deaths, when the accused were tried for "mob violence resulting in death" rather than manslaughter. This was particularly disturbing after the defendants openly admitted complicity in the aid workers' deaths, expressing national pride rather than remorse.[21] In a humiliating episode, hundreds of peacekeepers were captured by rebels and held hostage in Sierra Leone.

A common problem is that the presence of peacekeepers can give citizens a false sense of security, while the peacekeepers themselves lack the real power to intervene. Additionally, the presence of peacekeeping forces is dictated by the powerful states (via the Security Council), which determine whether or not it is in their interest, broadly defined, to intervene. This also helps clarify why there have been so few PKO operations within P-5 states, which explains the international community's muted response to the crisis in Chechnya, for example.[22] And peacekeeping is not immune to the politics of individual states, by a long shot. Many observers believe that the French fear of an "Anglo-Saxon conspiracy" of U.S. and British influence spreading across parts of Africa that had long been considered within the French sphere of influence impelled them to action that only exacerbated the bloodshed. Paris attempted to maintain its influence by backing corrupt governments in resource-rich Rwanda and Zaire. Although the French exonerated themselves for their actions in Rwanda, they are believed to have violated the arms embargo, trained Hutu soldiers, and essentially blocked any international action except their own.

What challenges do PKOs face? First, peacekeepers' hands are tied. By 1995, Dutch peacekeepers stood helplessly by in Srebrenica, Bosnia, as Serbs murdered thousands of Muslim men and boys. And the mostly Belgian UN force pulled out of Rwanda at the start of the genocide in 1994, after a number of their own were killed. PKO missions are limited by financial constraints as well. Many states demonstrate a tremendous lack of commitment, especially financially, refusing to pay even when they vote to authorize a mission. The United

States shoulders much of the blame in this regard: it has refused to pay a portion of its PKO dues, arguing that the payment scale, designed in 1973, warrants reconsideration.[23] In the controversial area of peacekeeping, U.S. unpaid assessments total $930.2 million, nearly 69 percent of the arrears for PKOs.[24] In May 2001 the United States failed to be reelected to the UN Human Rights Commission, which it helped establish and of which it had been a member since 1947. While the reasons are complicated, more than a few leaders stated that their opposition to the United States was based on its failure to shoulder financial responsibility for UN programs.

Additionally, the UN and related agencies need better staffing and processes to collect information and respond to, and potentially prevent, outbursts of violence that require an international response. Following the crisis in Rwanda in 1994, Secretary-General Annan has repeatedly argued for the need for this department to have better intelligence gathering. While increased intelligence capacity might be necessary, many view this assertion by Annan (which Clinton supported) to be a halfhearted attempt to excuse the explicit decision not to take action in Rwanda even after evidence of the coming genocide was made available to the Secretary-General. If peacekeeping missions need anything, they argue, it is better equipment, common training for interoperability, and updated

A UN peacekeeping soldier is accompanied by a group of local children as he conducts a security patrol (UN Photo)

maps: UN troops got into trouble when they became lost in Sierra Leone's countryside and their radios did not work.

A comprehensive strategy suggested by Francis Deng is broken into three phases: monitoring developments to draw early attention to impending crises; interceding in time to avert the crisis through diplomatic initiatives; and mobilizing international action when necessary. Ideally, problems should be addressed and solved within domestic frameworks, with international involvement only after the failure of internal efforts. In some cases, the West should be involved because of the gravity of the humanitarian tragedies we're talking about. But crisis-induced reactions are more symbolic than effective in addressing the major substantive issues involved, as we learned in Somalia and elsewhere. Intervention is a major intrusion from the outside. Some elements inside will welcome it because of the promise of tangible benefits, but we should expect peacekeepers to encounter resistance on grounds of national sovereignty or pride, so the justification for intervention has to be reliably persuasive, if not beyond reproach. Deng says that the difference between success and failure is the degree of spontaneous acceptance or rejection by the local population.[25]

Another struggle in responding to crises is that the process needs to be streamlined so that it can respond more quickly and efficiently. Currently, the Security Council rules on sending soldiers to a conflict, then the Secretary-General puts together a collection of troops from countries that volunteer them. The General Assembly cannot even act on getting troops together until the Security Council agrees to the force. Theoretically, the United Nations has almost 150,000 personnel (military and civilian) from eighty-seven countries ready for "rapid deployment." Yet under the current budget, the Secretary-General has a $50 million reserve fund for "preventive action."[26] Many have highlighted the need for a trained standby army ready for emergency intervention.

Additionally, there is a growing sense among many that some issues, particularly the most egregious violations of human rights, require humanitarian intervention by the world community. The United Nations has been one of the most active organizations in coordinating the implementation of and transition beyond humanitarian response teams. No longer is the United Nations a neutral arbiter along buffer zones. The defining point it faces now is a clearer, more universal acceptance of its new role, particularly in response to emerging needs. Two of the most prominent examples of humanitarian intervention to which UN peacekeeping forces responded include Saddam Hussein's attempts to attack ethnic Kurds in his country, and Slobodan Milosevic's acts against the ethnic Albanians, a UN mission that was later abandoned after NATO launched a war campaign. Yet there is a disturbing pattern of neglect and inaction in other cases. UN actions in Sierra Leone, for example, are significant in terms of how long the conflict was ignored, in how the UN tried to broker a peace on the cheap and forced what is called the "see no evil" treaty down the government's throat. This plan, condemned by Mary Robinson and the UN Human Rights Commission, gave high-ranking cabinet positions control of the diamond fields and AMNESTY to the Revolutionary United Front (RUF), known for its "Operation Leave No Living Thing" and trademark mass amputations. To add injury to insult, the UN then sent in a handful of temporary cops, who managed to get themselves captured and held hostage by one of the parties to the peace treaty.

The need for a coordinated international intervention arises, according to one point of view, because powerful nations do not have direct interests at stake, and are therefore unwilling to get involved. There is often a delay, during which time rebel forces may try to "finish the job" before "outsiders" arrive. Humanitarian intervention, especially, requires distinguishing between the "good guys" and the "bad guys," and it is not always clear which side is the

Figure 17.2   The Rwandan Genocide

The clearest case of genocide in the 1990s took place in Rwanda, during which the international community made a deliberate decision not to intervene to halt the conflict. The UN pulled its limited troops out of the region in April 1994, after Belgian peacekeepers were killed, and just as the genocide was beginning. By the time it was over, over 800,000 people were dead. Within the United Nations, the United States blocked a proposal for further UN intervention, even though Nigeria, Tanzania, and Ghana each offered to send peacekeepers to the region. Clinton's response was that the United States would only send troops to peacekeeping missions if they were limited in scope: the UN could not get involved in every dispute.[27] This case is appalling not only in its numbers, but in the speed with which the mass murders were conducted; perhaps 250,000 of Rwanda's Tutsi were murdered in just over two weeks, in what may accurately be termed the "fastest genocide rate in recorded history."[28] One scholar estimates that the daily killing rate during the Rwandan genocide was five times that of the Nazi death camps.[29] The UN's commanding general in Rwanda claimed that the presence of 5,000 well-armed troops could have saved many of these lives. Or, had the UN Assistance Mission for Rwanda (UNAMIR), which was confined to the capital city Kigali, been reinforced and expanded, as the government of Belgium requested (and the United States and Britain blocked), many believe the genocide could have been averted.

The decision not to respond, even when the UN was presented with overwhelming evidence of plans for a massacre, is troubling at best. From an overwhelming number of accounts, the writing was on the wall, if only the world had wanted to see it. Four weeks before the massacre began there was evidence of targeted killings of ethnic minorities, an increase in weapons imports, and radio broadcasts of hate-filled speeches.[30] Individual countries, buoyed by a veto in the UN Security Council, blocked actions to prevent the genocide. Washington voted against sending a small contingent, largely because it had just lost eighteen soldiers in Somalia, and was weary of involvement in Africa. France has been convincingly accused of complicity in the murders by supporting the Hutu government, and then sending French soldiers on a peacekeeping mission that allowed many murderers to escape into the Congo to continue the carnage. Lieutenant-General Romeo Dallaire of Canada, the commander of the UN forces in Rwanda, consistently warned of the coming genocide. As he stated, "Soldiers witness crimes against humanity but are ordered not to interfere . . . there is enormous frustration in witnessing genocide and being powerless to do anything."[31] As Rwanda well illustrates, these situations threaten the peace and security of not only the site of the crisis, but also neighboring countries and the international order itself. The international community cannot wait too long to act decisively. A lesson that must be taken from the Rwandan genocide is the importance of preventive action, which, according to most analysts, is much more cost-effective than massive interventions.[32] This requires foresight, planning, and a willingness to act.

Former UN Secretary-General Boutros Boutros-Ghali stands before a shed containing the remains of scores of dead killed during the 1994 Rwandan genocide (UN Photo)

most deserving of support. Sometimes intervention can strengthen the weaker side, giving it little incentive to compromise and prolonging the conflict that troops were sent to end. As we have seen in many cases, noble intentions can lead to disastrous consequences, especially if they are not backed up with sufficient international will, including military force, finances, and the willingness to stay until the problem, sometimes intractable, is solved. To underscore the complexities surrounding these issues, we briefly discuss two cases of UN intervention in Figures 17.2 and 17.3: one in which the PKO was shut down precisely at the dawn of tragedy, and another mission that was sent in following a UN-sponsored referendum for independence.

Figure 17.3 The East Timor Referendum for Independence

Indonesia occupied East Timor for almost twenty-five years following its military invasion of the former Portuguese colony in 1975. In 1998 the newly appointed interim leader of Indonesia, President B. J. Habibie, indicated he might grant some flexibility in the consideration of a referendum on East Timor's status. Facing minimal pressure from Australian prime minister John Howard, Habibie announced in January 1999, much to the disdain of his military commanders, that the vote would take place sooner rather than later. His announcement was met with immediate opposition in his own country, on the part of military leaders and ordinary citizens alike. The UN supported the election, with a great deal of assistance from Portugal as well, during which the East Timorese voted overwhelmingly in favor of independence. The Indonesian militia response was brutal. Almost half (some say three-fourths) of the population was displaced, as many people were rounded up and sent to refugee camps in West Timor (400,000 of 825,000 residents). There were accounts of widespread rape and torture. Facing threats from the United States and the United Kingdom that they would halt future arms sales indefinitely, and block millions in IMF funds, Indonesia submitted to the presence of a UN PKO, under Australian command. The peacekeeping portion of the operation, which is attempting to create and sustain an entire civilian administration in a region that has long been unstable, has been marred with problems. In September 2000 three UN refugee workers were killed in West Timor, where over 100,000 refugees remained over a year after the referendum. This violence forced the evacuation of hundreds of other workers because of security concerns. Currently, the United Nations continues to be responsible for administering day-to-day operations in the region, and a tenuous peace remains.

Most of the problems with PKOs are exacerbated by the fact that we ask peacekeepers today to do much more than their original mandate—it seems they are rarely given an opportunity for success. This is challenged by both the financiers of the missions, but more importantly by the recipients of the action, who often have little if any say in operations in their own country. The other view is that humanitarian interventions smack of imperial intervention because of the particularistic politics that are involved in each case. "Humanitarian" may sound well and good, but these interventions are also designed to achieve political objectives.[33] Such actions for the international community are taken into uncharted territory, and often have unintended effects. Peacekeeping and humanitarian intervention can clearly make a bad situation worse.

Some interventions have exacerbated or prolonged crises, since they diffuse the specific interests that foreign powers, such as France or the United States, seek to project or protect. While participants ostensibly need to be impartial, the longer multinational forces stay, the greater the danger of loss of impartiality and therefore effectiveness in carrying out their mandate. Mission mandates need to be clear and achievable: an imprecise mandate is a recipe for confusion and a worsening of the crisis. Often the immediate purpose of humanitarian interventions is to deliver relief. But to have a lasting impact, such missions must move beyond Band-Aids to promote more substantive change, which can be a massive undertaking.

Lasting peacekeeping also includes state reconstruction, a focus that was ignored in Rwanda after efforts failed so miserably in Somalia. In a sense, peacekeepers are asked to engage in a complex process of engineering, including the preventive work that could be done by other agencies within the UN. Societies torn apart by strife need a comprehensive approach that pays more attention to the conditions that led to the crisis in the first place. Also, peacekeeping efforts especially need to encourage the rebuilding of CIVIL SOCIETY, which, as we discussed in Chapter 10, emerges rather than being created. The processes of peacekeeping need to provide protections for minority groups and individuals, as well as reassure people that it is acceptable to express opinions without fear of reprisal. The RULE OF LAW, or the impartial and universal application of legal norms, must gradually prevail. A mistake that we have learned from past operations is that we cannot rush to elections: nascent parties need time to consolidate, form platforms, and present them to voters. In addition there is a huge need to defuse armed movements, which is a controversial undertaking and difficult to implement. When major portions of the society feel unsafe, they are unlikely to surrender their sometimes only means of defense to outside intruders in the name of "making the peace." Otherwise it will be easy for disenchanted groups to reject election results, with or without violent means, and voters will have little choice but to vote on the basis of ethnic or religious identity. Elections held under the wrong conditions can be a real setback for democratization.[34]

The UN and social development. In recent years the crisis-response aspect of the United Nations has received much of the limelight, as we have discussed so far. It has been the lead voice of the world community, however conflicted, that governments (and agents acting in the name of governments) may be held accountable for actions within their own borders. The UN and its agencies have also been at the forefront of attempts to promote international law and universal principles. Since its inception in 1945, a key aspect of the United Nations has been its promotion of peace through programs designed to enhance the well-being and development of the world's population. One aspect of social development it has attempted to tackle is child neglect and abuse. Many children are forced to forgo daytime educational opportunities to make money on city streets, shining shoes, washing cars, or collecting recyclables. Educational programs under the auspices of the UN International Children's Fund (UNICEF) allow these street children to receive an education in the evenings. As we discussed in Chapters 6 and 10, child labor is a huge problem in the third world.

The Convention on the Rights of the Child (CRC), adopted in 1989 and now having 191 signatories, is perhaps the most broadly signed convention in the world (the only two countries that haven't ratified it are Somalia and the United States). Establishing the standards all civilized countries should attempt to meet in caring for their children, the CRC is comprehensive in scope. Among other things it calls for the protection of children from abuse and abandonment, as well as the provision of basic needs, including prenatal healthcare. The CRC urges governments to abolish prejudicial treatment of children, including treatment before they are born. Although the convention does not directly address the issue of abortion, it can be read to challenge the use of prenatal sex selection, a practice in which parents choose to abort female fetuses and carry male fetuses to full term, which is especially evident in China and India. In China, where traditional preferences and low-tech means have been accelerated by its "one-child" population policy and cheap, accessible ultrasounds, preferential sex selection (before and after pregnancy) have distorted the gender ratio in the country.

The United Nations has also been a pivotal IGO in promoting the rights of women. As one example, in the 1940s women's rights were viewed as something separate from the universal human rights of all people. Largely due to efforts of the UN and related agencies, this status changed in the 1990s to completely incorporate, in theory at least, women's rights within the notion of universally applicable human rights.[35] One of the most important documents attempting to institutionalize these ideas is the 1979 Convention on the Elimination of All Forms of Discrimination Against Women (CEDAW).

CEDAW, which has the force of international law, has been ratified by 165 of the member states of the United Nations and is considered to be the most wide-ranging attempt to eliminate all forms of discrimination against women. Many refer to it as the "International Bill of Rights of Women," in that it establishes minimum standards for combating discrimination based on gender. It is also the only human rights treaty that affirms the reproductive rights of women. The convention recognizes that socially defined gender roles require provisions against discrimination and abuse to go beyond equal treatment of men and women, promoting positive definitions of responsibilities that apply rights standards to all. CEDAW asserts the inhumanity of torture and cruel and degrading treatment, and stresses that intimate violence is no less severe than violence committed by the state. It also focuses on the need to combat military sexual slavery, workplace abuse, and violence in the family. CEDAW condemns the use of rape as a tool to humiliate women and their communities. Of the countries on which we focus, seven have ratified the document: China (1980), Mexico (1981), Peru (1982), Indonesia (1984), Nigeria (1985), Turkey (1985), and Zimbabwe (1991). The United States joins the likes of Afghanistan and Iran in not having yet ratified the treaty, and is the only industrialized country in the world to hold this dubious honor. Domestic political squabbles have prevented the U.S. Senate from ratifying the convention. Saudi Arabia and North Korea are the most recent countries to sign this convention into domestic law.

This document served as the springboard for the commencement of global conferences on women, held in Mexico City (1975), Copenhagen (1980), Nairobi (1985), and Beijing (1995). Each of these events, and meetings held to monitor the implementation of proposals from each conference, sparked a related increase in the number of women-related NGOs and networks of organizations designed to investigate and resolve issues, including marriage and reproductive rights, healthcare and educational inequities, and physical, sexual, and psychological abuse, in times of both peace and conflict, faced by women.[36] In fact, at each UN-sponsored world conference on women, a meeting in conjunction with NGO representatives was held as a way to complement the work of the conference and increase networking opportunities made available to all participants.

Activists in each country have used the force of CEDAW to accomplish varying aims. Many signatory states have altered their constitutions and national laws in order to enter into compliance with the treaty. In Nepal, CEDAW has empowered women to push for stiffer penalties for rape, as well as legislation that, for the first time, codifies women's right to inherit property. In Botswana, CEDAW was used to challenge citizenship laws under which children of a woman married to a foreigner were not considered citizens of the state (even though children of a man married to a foreigner were).

In 1994 a special rapporteur on violence against women was appointed. This enables more direct investigation and advocacy on behalf of the rights enshrined in CEDAW. For example, the rapporteur conducts field visits to investigate claims of breaches of the human rights of women, seeking information about conditions faced by women from all states party to the treaty. The rapporteur is able to act as an advocate in cases of women and girls, assisting in investigation and working to ensure proper punishment. Additionally, since an optional protocol took effect in December 2000, women may bypass their national governments and complain directly to the United Nations.

The UN and justice: Tribunals, truth commissions, and courts. The United Nations and other IGOs have been integral in dealing with violent legacies of states in transition and international crimes against humanity. This work demonstrates the enabling role that international organizations can play in assisting countries during transitional periods. There are two primary types of institutions designed with this type of mandate: war crimes tribunals and TRUTH COMMISSIONS.

Criminal tribunals are established nationally (and sometimes internationally), often following the breakup of a regime, the end of a war, or other act of aggression. Two of the most famous such tribunals were the Nuremberg and Tokyo trials following World War II. Yet these initial tribunals, though international in name, were largely controlled by the victorious Allied powers to prosecute aggressors from the defeated Axis states.[37] War tribunals are based in the Geneva Conventions, and attempt to locate and prosecute "persons responsible for serious violations of international humanitarian law" committed oftentimes during warfare. Ad hoc international criminal tribunals have been established to investigate the war in the former Yugoslavia (operating since 1991), and the genocide in Rwanda. Additionally, there is much consideration of launching tribunals to investigate violence in Cambodia and East Timor.

Tribunals are quite concrete—their goal is to investigate claims of human rights violations and link atrocities to hold trials and punish responsible individuals. A major part of the investigation of such tribunals includes the perusal of murder sites and purported mass graves in which aggressors attempted to conceal the evidence of their crimes. One of the difficulties faced by the Rwandan tribunal, based in Arusha, Tanzania, is the sheer number of accomplices and perpetrators of the crimes, which number in the tens and possibly hundreds of thousands. As Ian Martin states, "The number of direct participants in crimes against humanity is beyond the capacity of any justice system to arraign and judge."[38] Additionally, some of the accused have launched websites, inciting fear that pictures taken illegally in the courtrooms, or even the names of witnesses, could dangerously become public knowledge.[39] The operation of tribunals is often a very slow process, and some of the accused have been released because of time limits. Yet the court has detained forty-four suspects to place on trial, and it has already passed the first genocide convictions under international law, including a conviction against Jean Kambanda, the prime minister at the time of the carnage. Journalists and media employees accused of inciting hatred before and during the genocide also stand accused. In April 2001, four Rwandans (a university professor, a businessman, and two nuns) were indicted for murder during the 1994 genocide. They were not indicted at the international tribunal, but in a Belgian court.[40] All countries that have signed the convention on torture or the Geneva Conventions on war crimes are obliged to change their domestic laws to accommodate the treaties and to empower their courts with jurisdiction to try individuals accused of such crimes. Even with this obligation, such actions remain unusual.

In the International Criminal Tribunal for Yugoslavia, rape and sexual enslavement were prosecuted as formal crimes for the first time, although Yugoslavia was hardly the first place where rape was used as a weapon of war. Inclusion of these crimes was not raised at the Nuremberg trials because the organizers didn't want to hold the defendants accountable for something they themselves could be accused of. The tribunal recognized, after hearing testimony from girls as young as age twelve, that rape constitutes a form of torture and should legitimately be considered a war crime and a crime against humanity. Three soldiers received sentences ranging from twelve to twenty-eight years for their crimes in the eastern Bosnian town of Foca.[41] This is an important precedent for other tribunals. In the Rwandan genocide, for example, rape was systematic.

In 2001 Peru established a truth commission to investigate twenty years of political violence by guerrilla fighters and government troops. The new democracy has created the space so that finally the arduous and emotionally wrenching task of investigating the killings and disappearances of thousands of ordinary people can begin. Peru's truth commission has more power than many similar commissions in the region; it has a mandate to turn over to prosecutors the names of specific wanted individuals to account for their crimes. However, the commission's work is likely to be frustrated by the fact that it is seriously underfunded and because its work must be completed in less than a year, by July 2003, when a report is to be presented to the public. Consequently, many bodies will be left in their shallow graves, and after all this time only a few families will find peace in knowing exactly what happened to their loved ones.[42]

For these tribunals to be established, governments must grant their approval, and oftentimes the logistics of a tribunal need to be approved by the affected national legislatures. While this can provide a lengthy hindrance to the commencement of tribunals, an opening is usually found after a change of regime or the death of an authoritarian leader. For example, a breakthrough was made in 2000 when Senator John Kerry of the United States successfully brokered an agreement between the Cambodian government and the United Nations to begin investigating the 1975–1979 Khmer Rouge massacre of approximately 1.7 million civilians. This agreement, which became possible only after Khmer Rouge leaders voluntarily surrendered to Cambodian authorities in 1998 and 1999, is still awaiting approval by the Cambodian parliament. Regarding a possible tribunal investigating the atrocities in East Timor, Indonesia has repeatedly rejected calls for an international tribunal, insisting that it is an internal matter to be handled within Indonesia alone. Former president Wahid once stated that even if former general Wiranto, who is widely blamed for either ordering or failing to stop the militia violence, were convicted, he would be pardoned in the interest of maintaining national harmony. But a provisional commission of East Timorese and international legal experts, formed by the UN Transition Administration in East Timor (UNTAET), has started, and Indonesia's Ad Hoc Human Rights Tribunal for East Timor passed its first verdicts in August 2002, acquitting six of seven defendants.

Additionally, the Security Council plans a war crimes tribunal for Sierra Leone, which would be the fourth special court established since the end of the Cold War. A key controversy concerning this court surrounds arguments over the youngest age at which a war crimes suspect could be tried. After heated debates between the government, which wanted all persons no matter their age to be tried, and UNICEF, which argued that no one under eighteen should be tried, especially because the youngest were coerced and drugged into fighting, a compromise was reached allowing the court to try persons older than fifteen. However, anyone under eighteen will be tried in a separate juvenile chamber and those found guilty will be sentenced to community service, foster care, or other forms of rehabilitation.

Since 1948 there has been an initiative to establish an International Criminal Court (ICC) to replace ad hoc, conflict-specific tribunals and establish a lasting organization, a permanent war crimes tribunal, in their place. The ICC, which entered into force July 1, 2002, does not replace national courts, but rather will serve as a court of last resort when they are unwilling or unable to handle cases. The idea of such a court was tabled by superpower politics during the Cold War, but was resurrected in the early 1990s. In 1998, 160 states signed an agreement to create this permanent court (with the conspicuous exception of the United States, which has expressed concern that politically motivated cases will be brought against it.) The court, which will only deal with crimes committed after its establishment, is located in the Hague, with the International Court of Justice. (The ICJ is empowered to hear cases waged between governments, while the ICC will allow individuals and groups to prosecute individuals for genocide, war crimes, and crimes against humanity. Additionally, the ICJ is a civil court, while the ICC prosecutes criminal cases.) At the ICC, established under the Rome Convention, a panel of eighteen judges will hear cases—with the maximum allowable penalty of life imprisonment. The court is designed to put on trial not only the most notorious abusers of human rights, but their assistants and orderlies as well. Now that the ICC is a permanent fixture in international law, it is hoped that the Security Council politicking that has taken place in order to establish ad hoc tribunals will be averted.

Somewhat similar to international tribunals, truth commissions are designed to air grievances about past wrongs committed by individuals or groups as a way to prevent future crimes against humanity, to restore a semblance of "normalcy" after periods of unrest, and to promote a human rights culture. Yet truth commissions are different from war crimes tribunals in a few, very important ways. Trials are designed to punish, and may deprive individuals or life, liberty, or property. Truth commissions vary in their aims; they often seek to promote individual and structural healing, to piece together past reality and establish a historical memory so that it can never be denied. Because they are separate from courts of law, truth commissions do not usually have the right of subpoena; they are less bound by concerns of DUE PROCESS and may admit hearsay and other forms of evidence that would be unacceptable in a war crimes tribunal.[43]

The most widely known truth commission is the Truth and Reconciliation Commission of South Africa. However, other truth commissions (some dating back to the 1970s) have been established in Haiti, Guatemala, Uganda, Bolivia, Argentina, Zimbabwe, Uruguay, Chile, Nigeria, and the Philippines. Not all truth commissions are the same, and few follow the model established in South Africa, which granted widespread amnesty to participants in exchange for their role in the investigation. Some of these commissions, such as the ones in Guatemala and El Salvador, are established under UN auspices, while others are domestic initiatives alone. Some, but not most, allow amnesties, which are explained below. A few truth commissions are established for the primary purpose of honoring those hurt by abuse and promoting closure, while others pass on the information they gather to courts for prosecution. Truth commissions are generally established after a civil war, or after an authoritarian government steps aside, as part of a DEMOCRATIC TRANSITION. East Timor fits this description. Its truth commission, established after the 1999 referendum and riots, makes creative use of local customs. Those who are accused of the most serious crimes will be brought before courts, but because there are too many people to handle, the approximately 10,000 East Timorese who participated in lesser crimes with Indonesian-backed militias will come before the truth commission. Many of these people are hiding out in West Timor, afraid they might be lynched if they return home. The truth commission will bring those who want to come home back to appear before local village councils. If they admit their crimes and apologize, they will be sentenced to community service. According to local custom, they will then be safe from acts of revenge.

One of the more controversial aspects of truth commissions is whether they are just "some-of-the-truth commissions," whether they are just "Kleenex commissions," and whether they do more harm than good. Many people grate at the idea of granting amnesties to individuals who admit to committing atrocities, in return for their cooperation with the commission. The trade-off is viewed as necessary in order to allow a more complete airing of misdeeds, including public testimony that often allows victims (or their families) to confront the perpetrators of the crime. Several truth commissions have televised their proceedings. They vary over whether they name the names of those who come forward. Despite their differences, the goal of truth commissions is to make sure that the acts of injustice cannot be ignored, even if, in the end, the commissions breach justice by "letting some people off the hook."[44] For a variety of reasons truth commissions often face powerful resistance and need money, a broad mandate, and high-level backing if they are to succeed. South Africa's Archbishop

Desmond Tutu, in his justification for amnesties in the South African trials of apartheid leaders, argued that criminal justice can be sacrificed if it leads to a greater sense of social justice.

*   *   *

It should be clear that IGOs have played a pivotal role in the world community, sometimes fostering cooperation among governments, and other times taking action against governments that are perceived to be violating universal norms of conduct. As we have discussed, there are limitations with each organization, and generally IGOs are constrained by the fact that they are established by governments to act in the interest of governments. This means that they are beholden to the interests and concerns of powerful elite groups, and that political agendas, as we have seen above, tend to dominate over the humanitarian interests that they profess to promote. And despite the talk of inclusion and equal voting privileges for small states as well as big states, weaker governments of the third world can get caught in big-power agendas that limit their voice and ability to take action, as we have seen. In the end, while states participating in IGOs give up some degree of sovereignty in order to work in concert with others, that power can be snatched back when viewed as necessary. We now turn to another type of collaborative organization, which consists of groups of people who organize outside state authority to promote particular agendas in the global community.

International Nongovernmental Organizations

In Chapter 6 we discussed the influence of some NGOs, namely transnational corporations. International NGOs are private, transnational associations of individuals or groups that organize around a shared interest or understanding, and have strong ties to civil society, which we introduced in Chapter 10. NGOs are extremely diverse, in their size, organizational structure, and range of issues. Their numbers exploded in the 1980s, to the point that many countries have thousands, if not tens of thousands, of NGOs or affiliates. Even though scarce resources for programming and advocacy present formidable obstacles to groups in the third world, NGOs have a strong presence. They include universities, civic organizations, churches, and other religious institutions. You are probably aware of many such organizations, even if you do not identify them as NGOs per se: Habitat for Humanity, the International Red Cross/Red Crescent, the International Planned Parenthood Federation, Greenpeace, Oxfam, WarChild, Amnesty International, Catholic Relief Services, Lutheran World Relief, Bread for the World, Save the Children, and Goodwill Industries International are just some of the most widely recognized. These organizations are powerful in that they help countries incorporate ideas into national (and international) policies and programs. They are also vital in shaping and conveying public opinion to large gatherings of policymakers. They may be national, or international, in scope. NGOs are often able to open previously closed discussions or bring attention to taboo topics, including violence against women, the environmental toll of free trade, and child labor. NGOs rarely work alone.

Rather, they work together with other organizations and with governments, in order to promote their cause, often by hosting international meetings in conjunction with other associational conferences, as of the United Nations, a presence that has increased dramatically since the early 1970s.

What can NGOs accomplish that national governments cannot? NGOs such as Amnesty International have been especially critical in exposing human rights abuses and educating citizens about their rights, with less government interference that mars the work of peacekeeping missions, as we discussed above. NGOs work in dangerous circumstances and under many rules; and they are often subject to retaliation. Often, these organizations voice impatience with the slow action of other government-based organizations. Nongovernmental organizations are less beholden to bureaucratic and electoral interests, and they have power that IGOs such as the UN, which is bound to act only on the expressed interests of its members through the Security Council, do not. Even though they are made up of individuals and interest groups, their target audience is most often the governments of countries or world opinion. Many of the issues that we have discussed throughout this book have an NGO (oftentimes more than one) associated with it. For example, the Global Alliance Against Traffic in Women is a wide-reaching NGO with a presence in each major region of the world. Some of the programs it has sponsored include the networking of Burmese women's groups along the tense Thai-Myanmar border, as well as the coordination of training workshops and the publication of handbooks on human rights in multiple languages. Sometimes it takes a committed group of people organized in an association independent of the government to be able to distribute such materials to groups who need them most. The Lawyers' Committee for Human Rights is another widely recognized NGO that works at both the grassroots and global levels to connect skilled professionals with the people who could most use its skills and resources.

One of the best-known associations of NGOs dedicated to the promotion of human rights is Amnesty International, which works for the advocacy and promotion of human rights. Its success, in part, is due to its wide-reaching network of local (often university-based), national, and international offices. One of the key areas that Amnesty International focuses on is advocacy for individual political prisoners and prisoners of conscience—people who suffer persecution for their beliefs. Amnesty International has been particularly effective in targeting governments, through annual reports and policy papers that reveal violations of universal standards of human rights. Additionally, its members coordinate campaigns for the release of political prisoners throughout the world, and spearhead an international campaign against the use of capital punishment. One of this organization's greatest strengths is its work in raising the awareness of particular issues by publicly turning the spotlight on countries that abuse human rights.

Another NGO that campaigns for issues and also works "on the ground" is the International Committee of the Red Cross/Red Crescent (ICRC). This is a highly acclaimed and almost universally accepted organization that works largely independently of governments so that it can remain impartial in handling humanitarian crises during times of both peace and war. Because the ICRC is not tied to any official government, or even to the United Nations, it can accomplish tasks or change its mandate without needing to muster the will of the international community or the consensus of multiple nation-states. Unlike the campaigning organizations discussed above, ICRC personnel attempt not to change opinion, but rather to take action. The ICRC attempts to promote the most universal perspective of humanity, pursuing the protection and humane treatment of all individuals, even combatants wearing enemy uniforms.

Its record of humanitarian interventions is quite impressive. The complexities facing refugees, particularly related to legally defined "genuine refugees" versus "DISPLACED PERSONS," serves as a case in point. The ICRC has successfully procured legal exemptions to allow its representatives to come to the aid of displaced persons in conflict-rife areas, where other international organizations, notably those affiliated with the UN, lack jurisdiction to respond.[45] It has also been quite active in repatriating prisoners of war, including 10,000 Iraqi prisoners held in Iran.

The ICRC has been absolutely pivotal in promoting global cultural values, especially related to times of war. In fact, as an NGO it was a key player in the drafting and signing of the first Geneva Convention in 1864, also known as the "Red Cross Convention," which when combined with follow-up conventions provides the universally acknowledged rules of warfare. The ICRC stressed that states need to protect the worth and dignity of individuals "even when this is most difficult and costly for states."[46] It has also been instrumental in advocating the need for quality medical care, even during times of strife, and especially for the protection of medical-care providers who identify themselves in war-torn areas with the recognizable symbol of either the red cross or the red crescent.

Yet not all NGOs attempt to maintain the neutrality that the ICRC advocates. Two NGOs that attempt to promote advocacy within particular substantive topics—medicine and journalism—irrespective of geopolitical borders, are the Paris-based associations Doctors Without Borders (Médecins sans Frontièrs, MSF) and Reporters Without Borders (Reporteurs sans Frontièrs, RSF). MSF was founded in Paris in 1971 in order to challenge the neutrality of the ICRC. The organization unites medical professionals around the world in order to provide emergency assistance, especially in areas of conflict. In 1999, MSF won the Nobel Peace Prize for its humanitarian work with victims of wars, famine, and other disasters. MSF has also been very active in refugee issues, particularly in camps and temporary settlements. MSF doctors have served in Vietnam, Lebanon, Afghanistan, Kosovo, East Timor, and elsewhere. Their work includes both prevention and treatment. For example, MSF doctors have been working with local community leaders in Nigeria since the spring of 2000 in an attempt to fight malaria in the Niger Delta, where the disease is endemic. Prior to the genocide in Rwanda in 1994, individuals associated with MSF tried to make the signals of the coming onslaught known. MSF is famous for its fierce independence, but it does not attempt to appear neutral in the face of conflict. One struggle mission participants underscore is that their provision of assistance often supports, if not outright strengthens, the cause of the crisis in the first place. Yet bound by the Hippocratic oath of medicine, MSF doctors feel obliged to treat all human beings, irrespective of their crime or intentions.

The goal of RSF, founded in 1985, is to publicize threats to the free flow of information, especially by highlighting the arrest and torture of journalists who suffer because of their profession. RSF, which consults regularly with the United Nations and other global organizations, tallies arrests, attacks, and murders of journalists caught in the line of duty. Based on RSF data, over 600 journalists were targeted and killed for their work in the 1990s. Not surprisingly, many journalists suffer this fate when they investigate and attempt to report on corruption, abuse of power, or drug trafficking, especially if they highlight the complicity of politicians. More than half the members of the United Nations impose limits on freedom of the press. Turkey is notorious for attacks on journalists, and there are many reports of media employees being tortured while in Turkish custody. Under previous regimes journalists in Nigeria have been harassed, kidnapped, and subjected to other forms of pressure and obstruction for trying to cover up contentious issues. According to the RSF barometer of press freedoms, Iran is considered the biggest jail for journalists in the world.

A new direction in press freedom that RSF and other NGOs are pressing is the freedom of information flow on the Internet. Increasingly, many non-Western countries are imposing restrictions on communication via this channel, either by installing filters that block access to websites, forcing computer users to register, or by sharply limiting access for all citizens. Iranian medical students, for example, do not have access to anatomy slides that are posted on the Internet, which they could use to help pinpoint diagnoses. Myanmar has legislation that calls for a fifteen-year jail sentence if people who simply own a computer fail to declare it to the government.

Other NGOs promote environmental causes. The better-known environmental NGOs include the Nature Conservancy, Greenpeace, and the World Wildlife Fund. These are huge, multinational organizations with very large budgets to accomplish advocacy, education, and mobilization around environmental issues. These NGOs, even more than others, have linked arms with similar-minded organizations in networks to accomplish great feats. Greenpeace, for example, states that one of its primary goals is to stop the "chemicalization" of the planet, especially by ending the threat of nuclear weapons and nuclear power as well as other forms of dirty technology, and to limit ozone depletion through the production and use of greenhouse gases. Yet Greenpeace is also linked with other human rights and environmental organizations promoting responsive government and biodiversity. Greenpeace has offices in forty countries, with an especially strong presence in East Asia, Western Europe, and North America, and some presence in South America.

Churches and religious institutions are other examples of NGOs that have crossed over into multiple issue areas in order to promote human welfare. The Catholic Church and its related institutions, for example, is a widely recognized NGO with a high degree of activism in the third world. Caritas, a Catholic social justice NGO, attempts to promote Christian ideals of social justice and charity by working with and for the most impoverished peoples in the world. Like many NGOs, Caritas has an international-level umbrella organization, but most of its work is increasingly being conducted at the regional, even the state, level. Another religiously affiliated NGO is the International Association for Religious Freedom (IARF), which, having been established in 1900, predates many other

Figure 17.4   The International Olympic Committee and the Role of Sports in International Relations

Another NGO that exerts much influence on countries' behaviors is the International Olympic Committee (IOC), which decides the host country for this premier international event. Landing a spot as the host of the Olympic Games is the envy of many third world countries. Athletic events and their related organizations can also serve as a tool for multilateral international influence. As the film *Forest Gump* humorously memorialized, it was an amateur Ping-Pong tournament between China and the United States that led to the formalized commencement of relations between these two countries in the early 1970s. Recent cultural and athletic exchanges between the United States and Iran, including weightlifting, fencing, and soccer, have attempted to pave the way to improved diplomatic relations. Things soured a bit when the Iranian junior fencing team was required, upon its arrival at Chicago's O'Hare Airport, to be fingerprinted (as required of all Iranians arriving in the United States).[47] They turned around and took the return flight back to Tehran. U.S. basketball coach Gary LeMoine is attempting a possibly more successful approach. LeMoine was asked by the Iranian government to coach the Iranian national basketball team to Olympic victories. His diplomacy on and off the court in Iran could help lead to a thaw in relations between Iran and the West, as has been accomplished in other, less political programs.

China, for example, recently competed for two Olympic Games, the prestigious 2000 millennium games, which were awarded to Sydney, Australia, and the 2008 games, which China successfully landed. Most accounts of the decision to deny Beijing's first bid surround the IOC's concerns with China's record on human rights.[48] In their 1993 application, the Beijing committee famously argued, "Neither now nor in the future, will there emerge in Beijing organizations opposing Beijing's bid and the hosting of the 2000 Olympics."[49] This didn't fly with the IOC, and the statement was changed in China's application for the 2008 games.

Should China, a country notorious for its human rights abuses, have the honor of hosting one of the most visible international sporting events? Some argue that, human rights abuse and political posturing aside,

many long-term benefits may come of Beijing's hosting the games. For one, China would be in the sustained international spotlight for nearly a decade as it prepares to welcome millions of athletes and patrons to the games. Such limelight may nudge the leadership into a more conciliatory space for dealing with perceived challenges to the regime, although this outcome is by no means certain. For example, the Chinese sealed their contested borders during the 1990 Asian Games, and required citizens to possess special documents in order to travel to and from the capital during the event period. Of course, international corporate sponsors have their eyes on the huge Chinese market and the current international cultural appeal of "things Asian" as well.

Yet the sporadic inclusion of non-Western states in global events such as the Olympic Games reveals again how marginalized the third world can be, even in organizations that are ostensibly designed to include all of the world's citizens in nonpolitical affairs. For many non-Western states, the idea of recruiting, training, and completely sponsoring a national Olympic team is an absurdity, given the financial struggles that many of these states face. If a country is in the spotlight, international assistance can pave the way, although this is short-lived and limited. Athletes from East Timor, for example, competed in their first Olympic Games in 2000, in Sydney, after the success of an international effort to purchase basic sports equipment, including shoes. Such apolitical venues have also not been immune to political struggles: South Africa was banned from the games from 1960 until 1992 because of international response to the apartheid regime. Cold War politics also reared its ugly face at the Olympic Games. In 1980, President Jimmy Carter ordered the U.S. Olympic team to boycott the summer games in Moscow to retaliate against the Soviets for their invasion of Afghanistan. (In return, the Soviets boycotted the 1984 Los Angeles games.) North Korea and Cuba both skipped the 1984 and 1988 games as a political statement. China threatened to boycott the 1996 Atlanta games if it was not selected as host for the 2000 games, and over allegations of drug use among Chinese athletes.

NGOs. The goal of the IARF, which is one of many NGOs affiliated with the United Nations, is to promote the universal right of freedom of religion. IARF includes peoples of many faiths, including Buddhists, Hindus, Humanists, Sikhs, Universalists, Christians, and indigenous peoples, in its advocacy and operation. The IARF has linked arms with many other initiatives and NGO networks, participating, for example, in the Jubilee 2000 effort to increase third world debt relief for the most impoverished nations.

NGOs have become increasingly prominent within state networks of global power and influence in recent decades. They serve a particularly prominent role within the United Nations, where they increasingly work in a consultative capacity. Although NGOs are currently confined to ECOSOC committees, without any formal access to the General Assembly and its committees, there is much pressure to change this. Within the United Nations, NGOs cannot vote, because they do not represent a state, but they are often welcome participants in UN debates because of their grassroots experience and data, which states may not be able or may not have the desire to gather. As interest groups, they actively lobby delegates when the General Assembly is in session, and organize parallel meetings when the UN sponsors global conferences on special topics.[50] They also provide a connection between grassroots citizenry and international diplomatic channels that otherwise does not exist.[51] Additionally, NGOs work with UN agencies in the field, taking on massive grassroots tasks that the overburdened and overly bureaucratized UN agencies would be less able to accomplish. For example, over 500 NGOs work with the UN High Commissioner on Refugees to intervene in crisis situations where refugees are involved.[52] An NGO's inclusion under consultative status, however, can be blocked by an appeal of member states. For example, China blocked UN accreditation for the New York–based Human Rights in China (HRC), which is highly critical of the current regime.[53]

While we have emphasized the role of nongovernmental organizations at the international level, it should be noted that much of their work is implemented by regional and national NGOs working in concert. One of the main strengths of NGOs is their ability to foster partnerships and alliances with groups of similar interest, some civic, others government-based, in order to accomplish their goals. For example, the Inter-African Committee on Traditional Practices Affecting the Health of Women and Children, which is a network of affiliates in twenty-six African and three European countries, has worked to raise awareness of female genital cutting by concentrating on public awareness campaigns and educational opportunities in communities.

Global Challenges—
and Responses

As we have discussed throughout this book, state borders have less salience, or meaning, than ever. Either because boundaries are more permeable, or because problems cross borders so readily, many issues take on a cross-national, even global dimension. The question becomes, then, what are the best methods to approach these far-reaching issues? First, we take a brief look at some of the key global issues of our world today. Because of the scope and breadth of these issues, many feel that real solutions to these problems can only be found in a multilateral response, meaning the conduct of activities by three or more states. Since the 1970s, international conferences have been held, based on the recognition that solution of global problems would need the cooperation and input of the international community.

Environment

If there is a single issue that most clearly demonstrates the interconnectivity of this planet's residents, it is the issue of our global environment. Pollution, whether in the form of air, water, land, or otherwise, is not confined to artificially designed political borders. Fish swim in shared waters, wading between the sovereign areas of particular states and the universal seas. Air damaged in one region often worsens as it travels to another, irrespective of human-drawn borders. Often the impact of environmental degradation does not affect the individual or group that engages in it, but rather neighbors near and far. Throughout the late 1990s, for example, smog from Indonesian forest fires blanketed many states in Southeast Asia for weeks. Most scientists agree that modern environmental problems are initiated and worsened by human activity.

Yet the problem of transborder pollution is only one piece of the environmental issue. Additionally, the world is host to increased weather-related natural disasters, including severe storms and sudden weather swings such as tsunamis, or extreme bouts of heat or cold. As Secretary-General Kofi Annan reported, carbon emissions have quadrupled since 1950, water tables are falling, and the livelihood of one-sixth of the inhabitants of this planet is threatened by soil degradation.[1] Deforestation is also a problem, caused in part by increased agriculture and changing food patterns among humans. Increased consumption of meat products taxes agricultural lands and efficiency and constricts resources. As two scholars put it, "Eating animals that eat plants is less efficient than eating plants directly."[2] China has an even more pointed problem in destroying its forests: the production of single-use chopsticks. Each year mainland China produces and discards 45 million pairs of the eating utensils, mass produced from birch or poplar trees, and exports over 10 billion pairs to neighboring countries. If the current rate of timber use is sustained, China could wipe out its remaining forests in ten years, some argue.[3]

Many are familiar with the problem of global warming, also known as the GREENHOUSE EFFECT, brought on by industrial emissions that trap heat close to the earth's atmosphere and contribute to higher average temperatures across the planet. These phenomena are not natural—they are consequences of human consumption patterns. Reports from the UN's Intergovernmental Panel on Climate Change demonstrate the culpability of humans in past global temperature increases, and indicate that this increase could be as much as 10.4 degrees Fahrenheit over the next century.[4] The greatest greenhouse gas–emitting nations include China, India, and Brazil. Himalayan glacier cores drilled in the southern part of the Qinhai-Tibet plateau in southwestern China show that the 1990s was the warmest decade of the last millennium. The samples showed four times the ash and twice the chlorides of the previous 900 years. Additionally, the core samples showed evidence of six severe droughts over the last 1,000 years, caused by the irregularities of the Asian monsoon cycle.[5] Equatorial glaciers in Peru and Africa, including the white ice caps of Mount Kilimanjaro, demonstrate similar reductions. The effects of such warming are far-reaching. For example, a review by the Intergovernmental Panel on Climate Change concluded that warmer temperatures are likely to increase infectious disease epidemics, such as yellow fever and malaria.[6]

Since 1985 there have been a series of international meetings to combat these problems. After meetings in Montreal, Canada, in 1987, governments committed to reducing all substances, but especially human-made materials, that deplete the world's ozone layer. At the Rio de Janeiro meetings in 1992, a greater cooperation was forged between developed and less developed states, promoting "common but differentiated" responsibilities for the environment. The goal is to foster all countries' right to development while chipping away at a growing problem at the same time. The spirit of Rio was widely adopted as a workable solution to environmental issues, and further negotiations led to a comprehensive first set of actions that were approved at the Kyoto, Japan, meetings in 1997. Signatories agreed to reductions in greenhouse gas emissions, differentiated by their economic status: the lion's share of the responsibility is placed on developed countries, from which the largest share of harmful emissions originates. The Kyoto Protocol requires thirty of the most developed countries to cut combined emissions of greenhouse gases an average of 5 percent below their 1990 levels by 2012 (less developed countries will be required to reduce emissions during the second "commitment period," at a later date). The allowance of different emission rates, based on level of development, led to some bizarre bargaining proposals from developed countries, which sought out poorer, low-emissions states to participate in a "trade" of emissions rights for the right price. Amendments were made to the protocols at the Beijing meetings in 1999, yet none of the industrialized countries that signed the treaty have ratified it, claiming that the protocol shifts far too much of the burden onto the developed countries. The irony that it is the developed countries that are responsible for most of the polluting is not lost on many.

Due largely to industrial sprawl and the need to clear forests to make room for agricultural crops, desertification is becoming an increasingly serious issue, which contributes to an overabundance of carbon dioxide in the earth's atmosphere. Land degradation and desertification reduce ability to produce sufficient food, which perpetuates poverty in many areas. "Much of the rural population of Africa relies on semi-arid land for rain-fed farming."[7] The combined effects of these changes in the earth's atmosphere could produce widespread flooding, especially of low-lying areas.

While flooding brought on by increased temperatures is a problem in many low-lying areas of the globe, the availability of drinking water dominates environmental agendas in other areas. The challenge of water scarcity and the larger issue of "water security" also demand global attention. Access to safe, clean water is a political issue in many regions of the world, especially, although not exclusively, in the Middle East. Agriculture of each type (fisheries, forestry, livestock) tends to be the major responsibility of women in the third world, and women shoulder much of the responsibilities for family food security. In response, many organizations have targeted education and training programs toward women to help overcome some environmental problems especially related to agriculture. The UN's Food and Agricultural Organization (FAO) has launched programs in Zambia, Cambodia, and Nepal to educate women in new forms of agricultural production. The pilot programs have trained 400 female farmers in new water management techniques, as well as crop diversification programs, to help increase productivity in rural areas.

The FAO reports that only about 20 percent of agricultural land in developing countries is irrigated; more irrigated land will be needed to sustain an increase in food production. Food requirements in developing countries are expected to double over the next thirty years, at the same time that 20 million hectares of agricultural land will become too drained to produce crops or will be lost to urban sprawl.[8] Eleven of twenty-six water-deficient countries are in Africa. Additionally, water control could be used as a form of ecoterrorism if, for example, one government attempts to block the water supply from a river or other source from traveling to another region. Turkey, for example, controls the waters of the Tigris and Euphrates, on which both Syria and Iraq are dependent.

Environmental issues provide a good example of the theoretical dilemma known as the "free-rider" problem. This image is used to show that individuals (or groups) can benefit from attempts to solve a problem without contributing to this cause. Similarly, they can attempt to skirt limits or constraints designed to decrease the depletion of a particular resource without being caught. This gives individuals and groups little incentive to put forth the effort or the resources to solve problems, which is the main reason why issues such as environmental degradation need larger, global responses in order to successfully combat further decay. Exacerbating this free-rider problem is the long-term perspective on change; we may not see the lasting effects of changes made today for many years to come. This delay in results often limits people's sense of urgency for taking action now, and underscores the need for global organizations and specialized institutions that can reach large audiences to take leadership on this issue. While there are many internationally organized and supported environmental programs, many of them coordinated through the UN Environment Program (UNEP), the UN's support for grassroots activism is more empowering and often more successful than larger-scale events. Two greenbelt programs, in Kenya and India, have received the praise and support of the global environmental community. In Kenya, Wangari Maathai organized women to replant 10 million trees while providing much-needed education on indigenous and women's rights, as well as the importance of sustainable agriculture. The Kenyan government persecuted participants for their involvement. In a similar example of grassroots activism in India, the Chipko movement mobilized thousands of women to embrace trees and advocate conservation as way to prevent erosion, flooding, and famine resulting from widespread logging.

There are also many large-scale efforts to protect biodiversity, in the rainforests and beyond. A key document framing these efforts is the Convention on International Trade in Endangered Species (CITES). Turkey, a recent signatory of CITES, is a growing center of illegal animal trafficking, especially chimpanzees. An increasing number of baby chimps are being smuggled into Turkey with the complicity of Nigerian poachers. Wild chimpanzees, which are an endangered species, are also sold widely in Thailand, Japan, Russia, and Mexico.[9] This trade is all the more disturbing because their mothers are often killed in order to reach the baby chimpanzees, and once the chimps reach age five, they become aggressive, so their owners have them killed or excessively tranquilized. Yet this work is controversial. In an effort to limit the trade in elephants, CITES banned all forms of ivory trading. However, since 1997 Zimbabwe and a number of other southern African countries fought and won the right to sell off their legal stockpiles of ivory and use the money to pay for their elephant conservation programs. The problem is that this limited legal trade has opened up a loophole that poachers are making the most of. Smuggling operations have proliferated, especially in Nigeria, the Congo, and West Africa. Environmentalists are again seeking a total ban on all commercial ivory trading. This is opposed by those dependent on the income created by the ivory trade, who call for an end to Western colonial environmentalism.

The Human Rights of Refugees and Global Migrants

The people of the world are on the move, especially in the third world. Some estimates claim that recently as many as 20 million people have fled their countries in an attempt to escape violence, persecution, or warfare. An additional 25 million more may be considered DISPLACED PERSONS, who have left their homes but remain in their countries, often in makeshift camps that lack even the basic necessities to live.[10] They are overwhelmingly women and children (over 80 percent), with unique vulnerabilities. Refugees are common targets for exploitation and harassment. Their abusers are soldiers, militia members, and even

Many displaced persons travel on foot, like these refugees returning home to East Timor exhausted and dehydrated after spending weeks in squalid camps (UN Photo)

refugee camp officials. The problems that these people face are enormous. Not only do they need assistance in the short term, including food, shelter, clothing, and protection, but their long-term needs are enormous as well. Refugees cannot remain as such forever; they desire either repatriation in their home country, or asylum in a country of choice that would allow them to start their lives relatively anew.

Some of the key sources of human displacement include Kosovo, East Timor, the Congo, Chechnya, Angola, Afghanistan, Sierra Leone, and Colombia. As Mexico is for the United States, Turkey has become a gatekeeper of sorts in recent years for illegal immigrants traveling to Europe. Because of tighter restrictions on immigration within the European Union, Turkey has become a transit route of choice for immigrants from India, Afghanistan, Pakistan, and many African states. Many smugglers charge $3,000 per person.[11] Illegal human smuggling from China has also been on the rise in recent years, and the deaths of migrants in transit—for example, fifty-eight people suffocated in a cargo container crossing into England—reveal the dangerous ends to which some people are prepared to go. These cases also reveal the lucrative underworld business that is thriving as some prey on the aspirations of others for a better life.

Since its establishment in 1951, the UN High Commission for Refugees

(UNHCR), which twice received the Nobel Peace Prize (1954 and 1981), claims to have assisted more than 30 million people in these processes. One of the major responsibilities of the UNHCR is to find "durable solutions" for the world's refugees. This includes searching out possibilities for repatriation, through a voluntary return to their homeland, integration into another country via the granting of asylum, or resettlement in a third country. Unfortunately, the tasks facing this agency, and others related to the handling of refugees, are increasing.

As we discussed in Chapter 12, much conflict in today's world is different; it is often, although not exclusively, targeted at civilians, using displacement and systematic violence, hatred, fear, and other psychological weapons. Sierra Leone, Sudan, Angola, Indonesia, Sri Lanka, Iraq, Afghanistan, Chechnya, and Yugoslavia are just a few areas in our world today where large numbers of people are not safe in their own home communities, and where there have been large-scale movements of people within or outside their countries. For the most part, conflict within each one of these regions is confined to single countries; they are wars within, rather than between, nation-states. The internal nature of these conflicts, over which states can claim SOVEREIGNTY, makes any response by the outside community more difficult, because aggressors (and their supporters) may frame it as an unwelcome invasion of internal matters. World leaders struggle to cope with these changes and with these forms of violence. It is illegal under international law to force "genuine" refugees to return to the country from which they fled, even though the United States and other countries have done so. But how should international organizations respond?

Until the mid-1980s most Mexican migrants made their way to Mexico City. However, a disastrous earthquake and a long economic crisis pushed migrants to go farther in search of work. While many are concerned about the costs to the communities left behind, for example, the separation of families such emigration causes, this outmigration serves as an important source of income for these countries, as wages are sent home. In addition, where there is high unemployment with few prospects, this outmigration functions as a safety valve, releasing pressure on already overburdened governments. Even where unemployment is relatively low (Mexico has the lowest unemployment rates in Latin America), as long as the wage differentials are as high as ten to one (as they are on average between the United States and Mexico), people will continue to leave their countries. The United States and other developed countries have attempted to build the walls higher, to militarize the borders to cut down on illegal migration. However, these zealous actions have only meant that people are forced to find ever more difficult and dangerous routes.

Terminological debates about "types" of refugees capture the emerging problem: while a technical definition exists, based in the 1951 UN Convention Relating to the Status of Refugees, many feel it is far too narrow and that it fails to provide an accurate picture of modern migration. This difficulty is only compounded by the complex reasons people have to flee: some, although they are believed to be a minority, seek better economic opportunities. Of course, it is often difficult to untangle individuals' motivations, and economic rationales can be as much about "pure survival" as political rationales. Others fear political persecution and violence. In fact, many flee violence for a safe but poverty-filled future. The reasons people pack up may be diverse, but their situation as displaced people tends to be uniformly dangerous. Many trade one set of insecurities for another, as they seek asylum in countries experiencing conflict. The Convention Relating to the Status of Refugees confines the status of "refugee" to "a person who, owing to a well-founded fear of being persecuted for reasons of race, religion, nationality, or membership of a particular social group of political opinion is outside the country of his nationality and unable, or, owing to such fear, is unwilling to avail himself of the protection of that country."

Yet the numbers of displaced persons, trapped in their own countries, fleeing from persecution, and often forcibly relocated, may outnumber the official count of refugees. Most estimates of internally displaced people place the totals around 17 million, although there are formidable difficulties in measuring such peoples. This has been the case because people (and governments) have used an overly restrictive definition of who is a refugee. Today, individuals are forced to seek safety because of their gender, their sexual orientation, their beliefs, or their region of origin. Others are economic, political, or wartime refugees. In today's world, there are many issues that are used to segregate people.

High levels of population density can cause simmering tensions to implode. Recently in the Indonesian region of Central Kalimantan, on the island of Borneo, indigenous Dayaks, native to the region, killed more than 300 Madurese who had been resettled from the crowded southeast coast of Java. Government troops fled when they too were attacked by the Dayaks.[12] Once again, the survivors of this attack will probably have to flee this island, which some had adopted as their second or even third home: many have spent more time "on the run," looking for a place to settle, than they have ever spent living in a single place. In other areas of our world, internal refugees are holed up in internment camps, ostensibly for their own safety, but in reality to prevent them from aiding the opposition groups that purportedly threaten the government. Whole families have been murdered while they slept in such camps. Children, who make up large numbers of this population, are forced to educate themselves, or put up with the woefully inadequate makeshift schools. They end up finding other ways to spend their time, including adopting varied survival tactics such as the illicit distribution of drugs, weapons, and sexual favors. Refugee camps are far from the "safe havens" you might expect: there have been, for example, widespread reports of rapes of Somali women in Kenyan camps. Afghan refugees in Iran have been attacked and killed by mobs. Indonesian militias routinely raided refugee camps in West Timor, stoning, beating, and sometimes killing displaced citizens from the east. Burmese refugees in Thailand were attacked when members of the Burmese military crossed over the border and destroyed their camp; killing four refugees, injuring scores, and leaving many without any shelter in an already perilous situation. Of the more than 20 million displaced persons in the world today, it is estimated that half of them can be found in African states, 4 million in Sudan alone.[13] Officially, because of terminological quandaries, they are the responsibility of their home governments, which in many cases are the source of their persecution in the first place.

Contrary to popular belief, it is other third world states that serve as the host countries for refugees. As Figure 18.1 demonstrates, the ratio of refugee population to total population in less developed states, especially Iran, Sudan, and Guinea, is much higher than the ratio in the developed countries, including Germany, the United States, and Canada. Iran, which has its own issues with exiles who will not return home, hosts the largest number of refugees in the world, mostly Afghans and Iraqis who have lived there for decades and whose welcome is beginning to wear thin. Economic struggles and high unemployment rates have motivated Western and non-Western governments to reject new arrivals, confine refugees to camps and prisons, and even to deport them. China hosts refugees from Vietnam and Laos, as well as a sizable population of North Koreans (approximately 50,000) who live in refugee-type situations in China's northern provinces.

Another form of migration can be found in human trafficking, which includes the trade in human beings as a source of cheap labor. One of the fastest-growing criminal enterprises and a multibillion-dollar industry, trafficking in humans is third only to trafficking in guns and drugs. Although males and females are subject to this form of forced labor, it is estimated that nearly 1 million women are sold into servitude each year. Women are trafficked from one poor country to another, or to developed countries, where they are often lured by hopes of finding work as waitresses, models, or entertainers. However, once under the control of the sometimes vast criminal enterprises that run these rackets, women work in bondage as sweatshop laborers, prostitutes, or domestic servants.

Children are a major commodity in this trade. The Central Intelligence Agency (CIA) has reported that as many as 50,000 women and children from Asia, Latin America, and Eastern Europe are brought to the United States each year and forced to work as abused laborers, servants, or prostitutes. Sexual slavery has been documented in 190 countries, including the United States. In Italy alone, for example, it is estimated that there are 15,000 Nigerian sex workers throughout the country. Today, throughout what is still the "Slave Coast" in Africa, children are lured from their homes, often by procurers offering their poverty-stricken parents high sums of money, other times by deceiving the parents that their children will be educated. They are then sent to countries including Gabon, Côte d'Ivoire, and Nigeria, where they are sold into forced labor. Trafficking in children for use in the sex trade is also on the rise, especially in Thailand, Cambodia, and Sierra Leone. A popular myth that children are free of AIDS and that sex with a virgin can cure the disease has greatly contributed to the growth of this form of child labor—in nearly every corner of the world.

Healthcare and Disease

In Chapter 7 we discussed the connection between health and poverty. The deprivation of citizens in the third world, sometimes due to economic malaise, violence, and war, has in many cases led to a complete failure in public health systems. A recent UN report titled "Health and Sustainable Development" argued: "Poverty is an important reason that babies are not vaccinated, clean water and sanitation are not provided, drugs and other treatments are unavailable, and

Figure 18.1 Refugees and Migration

Guinea
1:17
5.88% of total population
(453,000 refugees)

Iran
1:36
2.77% of total population
(1,835,000 refugees)

Sudan
1:80
1.25% of total population
(363,000 refugees)

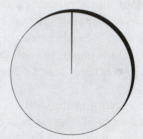

Germany
1:288
0.34% of total population
(285,000 refugees)

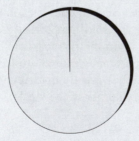

United States
1:530
0.188% of total population
(638,000 refugees)

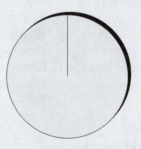

Canada
1:577
0.173% of total population
(53,000 refugees)

Sources: U.S. Committee for Refugees.

mothers die in childbirth."[14] Six major communicable diseases cause 90 percent of deaths from illness in the world today: HIV/AIDS, malaria, tuberculosis, pneumonia, diarrhoeal diseases, and measles.

Health crises demonstrate the world's deepening INTERDEPENDENCE, in that they require the coordinated response of nonstate actors. Many people view the struggle over HIV medicines and vaccines for other diseases to be part of the classic struggle between haves and have-nots. At the global level, though, many efforts have been undertaken—but they are not enough. For example, the United Nations announced a goal to completely eradicate polio through a wide-reaching vaccination plan cosponsored by the World Health Organization (WHO). The UN International Children's Fund (UNICEF) coordinated the vaccination of 450 million children in 1998, and only approximately 6,000 active cases of the disease remain. You may think that the biggest hurdle would be the required financing: over $500 million is still needed to continue vaccination programs. But armed conflict in regions of polio outbreak, with Angola as the starkest example, actually stands as an even larger obstacle.[15]

One of the most prescient examples of the world health crisis that is disproportionately affecting the third world is the HIV/AIDS pandemic. In January 2000 the most powerful arm of the United Nations, the SECURITY COUNCIL, discussed HIV/AIDS as a threat to international peace and security during the "Month of Africa." For the first time ever, a health crisis was placed on the agenda of this body. This move dramatically signified the importance of this global health crisis and its ramifications for all aspects of life and security. One of the Security Council's topics of concern was the higher HIV infection rate among girls, which we discussed in Chapter 7. Additionally, the Security Council considered the role of soldiers as the major carriers of HIV and, alarmingly, discussed the role of international peacekeepers in continuing the spread of this deadly virus.[16] Since 1980, more UN peacekeeping troops have died of AIDS (or will soon die) than have been killed in combat. Infection rates among soldiers in Africa are so high that they have a greater risk of dying from AIDS than from warfare.[17]

In 1996 the UN Economic and Social Council (ECOSOC) launched a special program on HIV/AIDS to bring together existing resources found in the WHO, UNICEF, and other agencies to streamline HIV/AIDS research and programs on a global scale. Many NONGOVERNMENTAL ORGANIZATIONS (NGOs) and NGO networks have mobilized people and resources to combat disease and illness. The NGO Networks for Health, for example, is coordinated by five health-focused NGOs, including CARE and Save the Children, to promote the awareness and availability of family planning materials, reproductive health, child survival, and HIV/AIDS information. Their programs have been especially visible in Armenia, Malawi, and Nicaragua. Much of the controversy in the past has surrounded AIDS medications and their cost. Yet some doctors suggest that we need to worry less about the cost of the drugs and more about the shortage of condoms (for males and females alike). Even the most basic means of prevention is out of reach of the poorest who need it.

Perhaps more governments need to follow the examples of Uganda and Thailand, and break taboos by instituting aggressive public education campaigns. However, we should not underestimate how difficult this will be for many governments, since religious leaders often object to the explicit language that is necessary to inform people how the disease is transmitted, or how widespread it has become. In many countries, conservatives block the distribution of female condoms or vaginal microbicides (which a woman can use with or without her partner's cooperation or knowledge). Adding to the tragedy is the fact that very often a woman is already pregnant before she becomes aware of her HIV status. Many women are only tested when they go to clinics for prenatal care. Screening for HIV is physically and financially inaccessible for many people worldwide. Yet testing is crucial where there are programs that provide pregnant women with a short course of anti-AIDS medicines, such as AZT. Because such programs offer a 50 percent success rate in preventing the transmission of the disease to their unborn children, pregnant women can play a huge role in containing the spread of HIV. However, as important as such programs are, they are limited in their effectiveness. Although a combination or cocktail of anti-AIDS drugs is known to successfully extend the lives and productivity of infected people for years, at a cost of approximately $15,000 per year the cocktail is out of reach for the vast majority. AIDS activists are pushing drug companies to lower their costs. Generic manufacturers could produce a cocktail of AIDS medicines for a cost per patient of about $600 a year. However, even that sum would break the healthcare budgets of most countries, many of which do not have the ability to create and maintain the healthcare delivery systems to administer and monitor use of these drugs. Therefore, health infrastructures must be built where none exist. Expensive laboratory work must be done on a continual basis to monitor this complicated regimen of drugs. Otherwise, it is feared that drug-resistant strains will develop, as they have for malaria and tuberculosis. Still, we need to remember that the anti-AIDS drugs now available offer treatment, not a cure. And they do nothing to prevent transmission of the disease. Prevention and education remain critical in this process, despite their expense. But the failure to treat the disease will lead to even higher costs—which we cannot even begin to tabulate.

Weapons Proliferation

The proliferation or spread of weapons is an issue of increasing concern in the post–Cold War era, in which larger numbers of states are deciding to invest resources to acquire conventional weapons, as well as nuclear and other weapons of mass destruction (WMDs). Without any doubt, conventional weapons are dangerous, but their impact is limited. The advent of the nuclear age in the 1940s changed all this, as the destruction of the entire planet became a possibility. Paul Bracken states that we are in a "second nuclear age."[18] He argues that while Western militaries dominated the world for the past 200 years, we are now entering a different era constituting a distinct shift in the world's balance of power, as non-Western states, particularly throughout Asia, acquire weapons to challenge Western dominance. Especially concerning are the WMDs, an umbrella category including biological and chemical agents that can, as their label suggests, bring harm to large groups of people in one blow. One of the gravest dangers of WMDs is the difficulty of their detection; a sufficiently lethal dose of agents could be loaded into a container and shipped, largely undetectable, anywhere around the world. Unfortunately, multibillion-dollar efforts by the United States ($60 billion at last count) to provide antimissile defensive systems only exacerbate the desire and urgency to build weapons that can evade such error-prone mechanisms. There is much uncertainty about WMDs. Yet what is certain is that the atmosphere is a much different one than of DETERRENCE based on "mutual assured destruction" (MAD) that marked the nuclear race during the Cold War. Now, individuals and groups can wreck havoc on a determined population without threatening themselves and with a much broader blanket of anonymity.

Many believed that the end of the Cold War in the late 1980s would lead to a safer, less militarized world. This has not been the case. Especially within the richer countries of the third world, the acquisition of advanced weaponry, with which comes attention and inclusion in the world's "elite nuclear club," has significantly increased since the mid-1990s. In 1998 alone, India detonated five atomic bombs, followed by Pakistan's own tests; North Korea fired a multistage rocket over Japan; and Iran, India, and Pakistan each tested intermediate-range ballistic missiles. China, which recently officially increased its defense budget by 17.7 percent, deployed short-range missiles aimed at Taiwan and fortified its longer-range missile system. Currently, in Asia and the Middle East, Israel, Syria, Iraq, Iran, Pakistan, India, China, and North Korea are all resituating their military focus "from infantry to disruptive technologies," based on chemical, biological, and nuclear weapons capable of being delivered by ballistic missiles.[19]

Although almost all the governments of Latin America are democracies and there are no major conflicts between them, many analysts fear that this region may be headed for an arms race as well. Setting this off may be Chile's efforts to modernize its aging defense force through the purchase of twelve F-16s. Two decades ago the United States prohibited arms sales to the region, which was dominated by military dictatorships notorious for their abuse of human rights. However, recognizing the political and economic progress the region has made since then, President Bill Clinton ended the ban in 1997. Now Chile wants to spend $600 million buying sophisticated weapons technologies from U.S. MULTINATIONAL CORPORATIONS (MNCs) such as Lockheed Martin. Lockheed and other U.S. corporations are pleased with this turn of events and are eager to diversify their arms sales to South America, which could prove to be a particularly lucrative market. Critics of the policy argue that Chile's rearmament is unnecessary and potentially destabilizing. Although there is no race yet, Brazil and Argentina are considering arms purchases to keep from falling behind. Still-fragile democracies often find it difficult to tell their militaries no. National pride may propel these countries to shift more of their budgets away from education and other needs, to the detriment of their overall human development goals. Yet U.S. proponents of such deals argue that they amount to routine modernization of aging equipment. They contend that these arms sales will provide a needed boost to the U.S. economy, and if the United States doesn't sell them the arms, someone else will. Peru proved that during the U.S. ban when it bought aircraft from Belarus.

Although Africa has joined South America, Antarctica, and the South

Pacific as a nuclear weapons–free zone, there are two regions of Africa that may be headed toward conventional arms races. One is in West Africa, as the Sierra Leonean conflict pulls in more states, including Liberia, Guinea, and Nigeria. The other is in southern Africa. Although there is some disagreement about how it all began, tiny, democratic Botswana recently increased its defense budget by $70 million over a three-year period. The country is involved in a minor land dispute with Namibia; otherwise, its greatest security threat is poachers. Botswana has no known disputes with its largest and most powerful neighbor, South Africa. However, South Africa, along with Namibia, Zimbabwe, and Zambia, reacted so negatively to news of Botswana's massive arms purchases that some called it a "provocation."[20] Similarly, South Africa has been criticized for spending billions of dollars on top-of-the-line equipment to modernize its military when there is so much development work to be done. In addition, massive investments in what already is the largest military in Africa will almost certainly spur its neighbors to follow suit.

The other new development related to arms proliferation is their location. Increasingly, we have the capability to wage an arms race that is unlimited by the globe; it is taking place in space, through the placement of satellites, radar systems, and arms above the earth's atmosphere. The United States was the only delegation within the Conference on Disarmament to oppose the establishment of a committee on the prevention of an arms race in space. Currently, most weapons systems employed in outer space are for defensive purposes. The increasing presence of these weapons, though, threatens to challenge the integrity of past arms control agreements.

In addition to the desire to defend themselves and mount a credible threat in the face of a U.S.-dominated world, many non-Western countries are involved in international arms sales, on both the supply and demand sides of the equation. Although the global economic slowdown in 2001 contributed to sharp declines in international arms sales in the third world, the United States continues to be the largest arms supplier. Israel is among the world's biggest spenders.[21] But it isn't the only one; China knowingly assists the leaders of North Korea, Iran, Iraq, and Pakistan in their weapons programs, providing specialty steels, guidance systems, and technical expertise. Russia has been instrumental in China's military advances in recent years, including its limited forays into space. Russia has also entered into new arms sales agreements with Iran. These weapons transfers reflect the disdain with which many countries of the third world approach the "nuclear club," and their desire to become a part of it.

Another type of weapon that greatly impacts ordinary people, especially the rural poor of the third world, is land mines. They have been used on a large scale since World War I, and the problems surrounding them are many: they have long life-spans, and they are not cleared after war or conflict ceases. They are masterfully hidden during conflict, they remain concealed today by overgrown foliage, and they tend to victimize innocent civilians who are unsuspecting of their presence (most researchers estimate that 80 percent of land-mine casualties are civilians). The people most likely to encounter mines are the economically poor, especially peasant farmers and their children. Complicating matters even more, many of the mines are washed out of the ground and deposited elsewhere, often on previously cleared land. Additionally, a mine can cost as little as $3 to make, and over $1,000 to clear. There are millions of active mines scattered in over seventy countries on every continent, although Africa is the most heavily mined continent on earth. People have been killed or injured by land mines in every country in southern Africa, with the exception of Lesotho and Mauritius. It is believed that Somalia, Ethiopia, Eritrea, and Sudan each have 500,000 land mines, with 250,000 in Rwanda. It is currently estimated that there is one mine for every fifty-two people in the world.[22] Land mines have exacted a huge human toll in many war-scarred countries, especially Angola, Afghanistan, Cambodia, Mozambique, and Vietnam. In addition to the physical toll they take when they explode, their presence also denies people the use of land that could be vital to their subsistence.

If there is one topic that demonstrates the interconnectedness between NGOs, INTERNATIONAL GOVERNMENTAL ORGANIZATIONS (IGOs), and national governments in recent years, it is the International Campaign to Ban Landmines (ICBL), an international effort including over 1,000 organizations based in sixty countries. The coalition was awarded the 1997 Nobel Peace Prize for its efforts. In March 1999 the most quickly promulgated arms treaty in history, known as the Ottawa Treaty, entered into force, banning antipersonnel land mines. This treaty, in the works since 1971, was finally adopted in 1997 in a novel process: it abandoned formal UN channels and explicitly incorporated voices from NGOs. As a result of the "back doors" that were used to move the process along, many refer to the Ottawa Treaty as a "breakaway treaty." The final process took only a little over a year to conclude.[23]

The International Red Cross/Red Crescent (ICRC) movement, in cooperation with countries such as Canada (which spearheaded the effort), South Africa, Belgium, and Norway, as well as multiple IGOs and NGOs, worked on this treaty, which has been ratified by 112 governments around the world. Former mine producers that have signed the Ottawa Treaty include Brazil, Canada, Chile, Nicaragua, Peru, South Africa, Thailand, Uganda, and the United Kingdom. The remaining mine producers that oppose the treaty include China, Cuba, Iran, Iraq, Russia, Serbia, Singapore, the United States, and Vietnam. The treaty prohibits the use, stockpiling, production, and transfer of antipersonnel land mines. In addition to banning further production of these weapons, the campaign establishes an international fund, administered by the United Nations, to promote and finance victim assistance programs. Additionally, it promotes land-mine awareness programs, all in the effort to eradicate the mines worldwide.

As if the problem with major weapons systems weren't enough, the presence of small, portable weapons—such as machine guns, assault rifles, and hand grenades—is on the rise. Indeed, these are the weapons—rather than nuclear bombs—that are responsible for most of the injuries and deaths in today's world. Small-arms proliferation seems to be out of control, and free trade and open borders have only expanded it. It is estimated that over $10 billion worth of automatic rifles, machine guns, mortars, and other light arms are sold each year. It may not sound like a lot in terms of money, but this trade is extremely deadly. Some analysts estimate that the Rwandan genocide was carried out with less than $25 million in imported arms,[24] with much of the killing done with a huge cache of machetes imported from China, whose military is known for exporting small weapons throughout Africa. Technical improvements in the manufacturing of weapons, which make them lighter and easier to conceal, exacerbate the problem. This trade in small arms is illegal, and difficult to track or control. No one, not individual countries, not the UN, keeps good records on the small-arms trade. And there's no movement for this issue like there is for land mines. However, recognizing that the black market in these weapons assists drug cartels, urban gangs, and GUERRILLAS, the Organization of American States (OAS) has attempted to curb the trade. The OAS began a program of registering guns to help track where they ended up, establishing uniform procedures among its members.[25] At the global level, the United Nations hosted a conference on the illicit trade in small arms in July 2001. It was a controversial meeting, as the agenda only included the illegal trade of arms, so that the big dealers, including the United States, Russia, and China, didn't lose a huge export industry.

Some regional attempts to contain the arms trade have been promoted by the OAS, the Organization of African Unity (OAU), and the European Union (EU). A major global initiative targeted to change the behavior of arms-providing states is Oscar Arias's International Code of Conduct on Arms Transfers. Arias, who crafted a Central American peace plan barring outside aid to guerrillas in El Salvador and Nicaragua in the 1980s, brought together sixteen other Nobel laureates with international nongovernmental organizations to present this initiative to the United Nations. The plan calls for developed countries to refuse to sell arms to countries that violate basic human rights or are involved in armed aggression or TERRORISM. If such a plan were to be implemented, it could dramatically change the global weapons landscape. For example, the United States routinely ships weapons to countries whose militaries are known to be abusive, including Colombia, Turkey, Indonesia, Saudi Arabia, and Egypt. Such trade would be barred under the proposed code. It also calls for all countries to report their weapons sales and purchases to the UN, under the current system of voluntary compliance. Arias points out that if 10 percent of the world's military spending, approximately $1 trillion annually, were spent on human development, preventable disease and hunger could be ended, and education and sanitation could be made universal. In addition, former U.S. president Jimmy Carter joined Arias in calling for a two-year moratorium on weapons sales to less-developed, nondemocratic countries. Few countries have heeded these calls. As discussed above, in 1997 President Clinton, lobbied hard by U.S. arms manufacturers and especially Chilean governmental representatives, lifted the twenty-year ban on Latin American arms sales. While this trade brings in a huge profit to the weapons manufacturers, few realize the size of the U.S. subsidy, which stood at $7.6 billion in 1995 alone.[26]

Conclusions: The Future of Global Capacity for Response

What are the advantages of responses by global or regional actors? Multilateral responses can give less powerful countries a stronger voice, because they can find strength in numbers. In the United Nations, for example, two-thirds of all member states are developing countries. Although, as we have seen, there are limits to what individual countries can achieve, the sheer number of third world countries in the UN provides a channel for diplomatic influence that they cannot find elsewhere. Multilateral efforts can also compel action when individual states either will not or cannot comply, due largely to financial constraints. The UN, for example, distributed a survey in preparation for the Millennium Summit in the fall of 2000. Two-thirds of respondents stated that their government had not done enough to protect the environment; people in developing countries were among the most critical.[27] Multilateralism can also promote an internationally acceptable setting in which nations can more freely negotiate in an atmosphere of compromise and diplomacy, which would be more difficult to achieve with individual states.

Yet an "international community" seems to exist in symbol more than reality. Contrary to the exasperated claims of some, we do not have a world government, nor are we close to achieving one. The coordinated response of major powers is about as close as we have come to a singular community in action, and as we have demonstrated, this response has been limited. Much of the world, especially the powerful countries, continues to view matters in a bilateral framework.[28]

What differences exist between regional and global responses? Because of the limited scope and number of actors, it may be easier to build consensus for action within a regional context, although this is not always the case. Global responses take more time to craft consensus (or at least to verify the absence of opposition). Some regions have issues for which it is hard to see what countries would be the intervening force, because of historical or contemporary problems that make no one trustworthy. The larger organizations bring more economies of scale, more people to the table, but they are also more bureaucratically cumbersome, a common criticism of the United Nations, and it is easier in the larger global organizations to leave out voices of the disenfranchised and less powerful. Or, even if the opportunity to speak and participate is present, many of the non-Western countries feel they still have no teeth in these institutions. Regional organizations and specialized NGOs overcome some of these problems of size, but they can also lack influence and might. Yet even international organizations such as the United Nations do not have compelling force; more powerful countries can avoid institutions of the UN if they feel their sovereignty would be impeded. The clearest recent example of such diversion was the action of the North Atlantic Treaty Organization (NATO) in Kosovo taken on behalf of the Albanian Serbs: the U.S.-led coalition bypassed the Security Council because they were assured that China and Russia would have vetoed the measure as an unwanted and unwarranted intrusion of state sovereignty. The UN later took on more of a role, providing a Security Council resolution and a UN-sanctioned peacekeeping force.[29]

Yet an overarching concern for the non-Western world, in the face of much multilateral activity, is the responsiveness of such forces to the needs and concerns of the less powerful. Organizations, large and small, make decisions affecting individuals, who have little or no impact on the process. The need to include disparate, less powerful voices is especially magnified at higher levels. While the problems inherent in this enterprise have been brought to our attention through street demonstrations against the WORLD BANK and the INTERNATIONAL MONETARY FUND (IMF), the same is true with the United Nations and nongovernmental organizations that take actions in the name of the people. How to make such organizations more representative and more accountable will remain a huge task for the future. If these institutions are perceived to be overtly partisan, they will lose their LEGITIMACY and ability to act. Multilateral institutions are favored because they seemingly prevent (or at least limit) the impulse for self-interest or self-delusion. But they are problematic because, in the search for consensus, they can sit idly by while massacres, such as the genocide in Rwanda in 1994, take place. Faced with changing conceptions of sovereignty and global action, many speak of a forthcoming "borderless world." Yet perceptions from the third world contend that some borders, especially economic, social, and power distinctions, remain as sturdy as ever, if not stronger.

Linking Concepts and Cases

We have discussed a wide range of issues and concerns in the last few chapters. To illustrate these ideas further, it may be useful to consider the following questions as you study the cases. What different postures toward the international community do you observe the leaders of these countries taking? What are the perceived trade-offs between isolation and integration? Do you observe any differences between how leaders may want to be seen and how they are actually perceived? What do countries seek from international or regional cooperation? What regional or global issue stands as a priority for each of these countries? In which countries has the international community tried to alter behavior through the threat of punitive action? Why are some attempts more successful than others?

Case Study: Mexico

The Fox government has been hoping that part of the "democracy premium" gained from the relatively recent political transition will allow for significant changes in Mexico's relations with the rest of the world. Some analysts argue that the government has been more innovative and successful in its foreign policy than in any other area. Energized by his surprise win in 2000, President Vicente Fox has adopted an unusually ambitious and activist foreign policy agenda. This marks a break with the past. With a few notable exceptions, for decades the Institutional Revolutionary Party (PRI) took an isolationist approach to the world. Under the "Estrada Doctrine" (named after a foreign minister), the PRI chose a policy of nonintervention in the affairs of other countries. It rarely condemned other governments or spoke up against human rights abuses. PRI governments were careful to uphold the principle of SOVEREIGNTY so as to keep others from discussing Mexico's own record.

Now Mexico's celebrated democratization can be treated as an asset that gives the country the credibility it needs to play a larger role on the world stage. President Fox is promising a more "mature" foreign policy, which he defines as a more engaged approach. He believes that Mexico is ready to take a much more active role in world affairs, especially through activities within the UNITED NATIONS. Past Mexican governments considered the UN to be dominated by developed countries and were distrustful of it. They chose not to compete in UN SECURITY COUNCIL elections for rotating membership. Upon coming into power, however, Fox campaigned for Mexico to take over for Jamaica in a nonpermanent seat within the Security Council and won it. Moreover, Fox has expressed his interest in seeing that a permanent seat in the Security Council be created for Latin America. He claims that Mexico's appointment to such a position would be widely supported throughout the region. In another break with past policy, the Mexican government says it is willing to consider invitations for its troops (or civilians such as engineers, medical personnel, etc.) to take part in international PEACEKEEPING OPERATIONS (PKOs). Until now, the only such participation for Mexicans in peacekeeping was in El Salvador after its war, as highway patrol officers.

As mentioned before, part of Mexico's reluctance to take a more active role in the world was motivated by a desire to deflect outside criticism of its own undemocratic record. According to Fox, that has all changed, although he admits that Mexico still has some work to do to strengthen its judicial system and promote respect for human rights. However, not only has Fox appointed an ombudsman for human rights, but he has established a special prosecutor's office to investigate CORRUPTION and crime at home. Based on the progress his country has made, Fox argues that Mexico is ready to become a "proactive defender of human rights" abroad.[1] One of the first tests of Mexico's readiness will be whether Fox will be able to persuade the Mexican Congress to ratify the convention creating the International Criminal Court (ICC).

Perhaps even a bigger test of the president's determination to depart from the principle of nonintervention will be whether Mexico will criticize others for their human rights abuses. If it does, this proactive stance will amount to one of the biggest foreign policy changes undertaken by the new government. It will not be easy (nonintervention is named as a central principle in the Mexican Constitution), but it appears that the shift is under way. Even before he was inaugurated, Fox met with Alejandro Toledo, who was running for president of Peru. Such a meeting clearly indicated the president-elect's willingness to side with the prodemocracy movement against the AUTHORITARIAN Fujimori government. This new policy is already contributing to some changes in Mexico's relationship with Cuba. For years, Mexico was one of the few Latin American countries that refused to join the U.S. denunciations of Cuba. However, to the Castro government's dismay, it can no longer count on Mexico to always be in its corner. While the Fox government continues to denounce the U.S. embargo against Cuba, it has stated that it will support the prodemocracy movement there and has urged Castro to pursue political reforms.

In a larger sense, Mexico is seeking to broaden its relationship with Latin America and Europe while deepening its relations with its North American neighbors. As discussed in Chapter 3, Mexico's economy has rapidly become more closely tied to that of the United States and Canada since 1994, through the North American Free Trade Agreement (NAFTA). Fox wants to see NAFTA grow into what he calls a "NAFTA-plus," something more like the European common market. A NAFTA based on the European model would mean allowing for the free movement of labor between member states. Mexico also sees itself as a bridge linking the United States and Latin America. The Fox government says it hopes that NAFTA-plus will eventually include extending membership to other countries in the region. It also looks forward to the creation of regional aid projects and resource transfers in Latin America like those that helped the poorer members of the European Union (EU) begin catching up with the richer ones.

While Mexico's international relations are dominated by its relationship with the United States, Fox has maintained that he will not allow this relationship to distract Mexico from its ties to the rest of the region. That may be something the president will have to prove, since Brazil and other Latin American countries view Mexico as a vassal of the United States.[2] While Mexico is now more dependent on the United States than ever before, over the years it pursued a foreign policy quite independent of its neighbor. Mexico played an important role in balancing U.S. policy in Central America, and was at the center of diplomatic efforts to end the wars in El Salvador and Nicaragua.

Most analysts predict that President Fox will build on this tradition, assuming center stage in more arenas and taking a more active role in building ties with other Latin American countries. He looks forward to Mexico serving as a mediator for inter-American disputes and as a leader in expanding trade ties between the countries of the region. Especially concerned about the regional ramifications of the conflict in Colombia, Mexico is joining others who are seeking to create a counterweight to those (namely the United States) who are pursuing with Plan Colombia a nonpolitical, military solution to Colombia's civil war. Similar to the role it played to support peace talks in Central America in the 1990s, Mexico will serve as one of ten mostly European and Latin American "support nations," joining international efforts to promote peace talks between the Colombian government and leftist GUERRILLAS. It will also take part in efforts to help mend growing strains between Venezuela, Brazil, and Ecuador associated with Colombia's spreading civil war. While its interest in being a good international citizen is welcomed by many, such efforts are not entirely selfless. Along with Costa Rica, Mexico is already housing nearly 24,000 refugees, many of them from the Colombian conflict, and even the U.S. government predicts that Plan Colombia will trigger "major flows" of people.[3] Mexico's own interests are at stake in finding a political solution to the Colombian conflict—and soon.

Case Study: Peru

Although Peru has long ties with the United States and other external actors, the country's primary international interest has been its relationship with its neighbors. This relationship has been ambivalent at best. At various times since its independence, Peru has asserted its desire for regional cooperation. The country took an early interest in promoting inter-American solidarity at the 1826 Panama Conference. At the Lima Conference of 1847–1848, Peru joined Bolivia, Chile, Colombia, and Ecuador in calling for a defensive alliance and eventual confederation. A longtime member of the Organization of American States (OAS) and the Andean Community of Nations (CAN), Peru has welcomed the economic cooperation that comes with integration, but has never pursued it fully. It is not part of the free trade zone or the customs union that functions between CAN's other four members (Bolivia, Colombia, Ecuador, and Venezuela). Similarly, Peruvian governments have expressed their interest in strengthening relations with Mercosur, and establishing a common foreign policy among CAN members. Yet at other times Peru has threatened to quit such integration efforts altogether.

Such ambivalence toward its neighbors may be explained by a history of difficult relations in the region. As much as it recognizes the need for cooperation, Peru has just as consistently asserted its desire for independence and determination to pursue what it views as its national interest. As a result, Peru has often found itself in competition with its neighbors—all whom are seeking commercial advantage. The IRREDENTIST conflicts that have divided the region are based in Spain's failure to mark clear boundaries between its administrative units during colonialism. Consequently, Peru has had long-standing border disputes with Chile and Ecuador. Relations with Chile have been tense since the 1879 War of the Pacific, in which Peru lost large tracts of land to Chile. Peru and Ecuador have fought a series of brief wars for the last sixty years, over a sixty-mile stretch of Amazonian territory that was never well demarcated. The dispute over the Cenepa River Basin, known as "the Alsace-Lorraine of the Andes," is over territory, water, and mineral rights. For Ecuador, the Cenepa provides the country with badly needed access through the Amazon to distant markets and the Atlantic. But Peruvian presidents have treated who controls the Cenepa as a matter of national pride. Peru's conflicts with Chile and Ecuador have proven to be highly politicized, emotionally charged issues that have periodically disrupted inter-American relations. In both conflicts, each side blames the other for behaving aggressively. Analysts have accused all the governments involved of making the border disputes into nationalist issues used to divert public attention away from domestic problems.[4]

At least for now, it appears that the border disputes have been put to rest, thanks to the mediation of OAS "guarantor countries" (Brazil, Argentina, Chile, and the United States), which sent peacekeepers to create a demilitarized zone between Peru and Ecuador in the mid-1990s. However, regional rivalries were not helped by the Fujimori government's huge military budgets, or its purchase of fighter jets. Some analysts believe that such actions have set the region perilously close to an arms race—a dangerous and unnecessary waste of precious funds, given the fact that the parties involved are democracies that pose no serious security threat to each other. What Peru and its neighbors do have in common is concern about Plan Colombia, and whether a further militarization of the region will push fleeing drug traffickers, refugees, and rebels into their countries.

Whereas the conflict in Colombia is almost certain to demand Peru's attention in the near future, for the past few years Peru's internal strife has taken priority over its foreign relations. However, international observers, most notably those from the OAS, played a crucial part in the 2000 elections. Their criticism of the elections process through both rounds of voting helped to delegitimize and isolate the Fujimori government. However, the members of the OAS do not like to meddle (or see the United States meddle) in the political affairs of others.

They did characterize the vote as tainted, marred by irregularities, but the OAS never went as far as to condemn the 2000 elections.

The international community's failure to take decisive action greatly disappointed Peru's opposition movement. Even after the opposition candidate, Alejandro Toledo, made it clear that he would boycott what was widely perceived as a fraudulent process, the OAS decided against calling for new elections, arguing that such a demand was beyond its mandate. This stance cost the OAS some credibility with many Peruvians, who saw the organization as allowing Alberto Fujimori to make his own reforms. Although the U.S. Senate threatened sanctions, in the end, international concern had relatively little to do with the resumption of democratic reforms in Peru. Whether it was the Peruvian people or Fujimori himself who brought the president down, domestic forces must be credited with the ouster of this government and the transition to democracy in Peru.

With the tumultuous events of 2000–2001 behind it, Peru's new democratic government as led by Toledo is likely to resume its traditional role in world affairs. As a small to medium-size power, Peru has been impressively active in a variety of capacities. Its diplomatic corps has long enjoyed a reputation of being first rate. Peruvian career diplomat Javier Perez de Cuellar served two terms as UN Secretary-General, from 1982 to 1992. Peru was instrumental in the negotiation of peace accords in Central America. It accepted a leadership role in the negotiation of several multilateral conventions, including the Law of the Sea Conferences. Backed by several NONGOVERNMENTAL ORGANIZATIONS (NGOs), Peru also successfully negotiated with the United States in 2002 a $5 million debt-for-nature swap, to fund conservation work in its Western Amazon rainforests. As long as its DEMOCRATIC TRANSITION goes smoothly, look for similar accomplishments, and for Peru to return as a voice for the non-Western world at the UN, in the NON-ALIGNED MOVEMENT (NAM), and in other international arenas.

Case Study: Nigeria

With its economic resources and the largest population of any country in Africa, Nigeria is a regional power—and some believe it to have the potential to be a superpower. However, during the last years of the Abacha government, Nigeria had become an international pariah of sorts, isolated for its role as a hub in the transshipment of illegal narcotics and slapped with a variety of minor sanctions for its human rights abuses. That status has changed dramatically since Nigeria's latest attempt at democracy in 1999, as the country has resumed its traditional place in international politics. A founding member of the Organization of African Unity (OAU), Nigeria has taken an interest in a variety of issues that do not directly affect the country, such as the Western Sahara. These efforts have won it the title "Africa's leader" and for many years Nigeria was viewed as the voice for the region at international forums. Nigeria has assumed leadership roles in a number of INTERNATIONAL GOVERNMENTAL ORGANIZATIONS (IGOs), including the Organization of Petroleum-Exporting Countries (OPEC) and the Commonwealth. Over the years the country has been a major contributor of troops to UN peacekeeping missions in the Congo, Lebanon, Iran, and Iraq, among others. If Africa ever gets a permanent seat on the Security Council, there is a good chance that two old rivals, South Africa and Nigeria, would campaign hard for it.

The international community has celebrated Nigeria's transition to civilian rule with promises of more foreign aid and debt relief. World leaders say they are determined to do what they can to nurture this new democratic experiment. Motivating this interest is the growing recognition that what happens in this country affects much of the rest of the continent. Experts on Africa maintain that an effective democratic transition in Nigeria will contribute positively to the political liberalization throughout the region. On the other hand, a return to authoritarianism and continued fragmentation in Nigeria will undoubtedly be followed by state decay and disintegration in neighboring countries.

Similarly, Nigerian leaders have taken the position that their country cannot achieve its economic goals if West Africa is unstable. Consequently, Nigeria has imposed what some call a "Pax Nigeriana." It has played the role of regional power broker, and has claimed West Africa, where Nigeria has its greatest security concerns, as its sphere of influence. Willing to violate the OAU's principle of noninterference in the internal affairs of others, Nigeria views itself as an arbiter of both civil and interstate disputes—to the point that some characterize it as being hegemonic.[5] When it went into Liberia it was the first African country ever to intervene in the affairs of a neighbor not threatening war. In addition, Nigeria is a major financial contributor and therefore dominant member of the Economic Community of West African States (ECOWAS). Nigeria has played a central role in that organization's military wing, ECOMOG (the Economic Community of West African States Monitoring Group). After years of sending troops to intervene in the civil war in Liberia, it went on to Sierra Leone, where Nigeria led the ECOMOG intervention in 1998. Although some question its motives, Nigerian leaders argued it went into both countries to prevent the conflicts from spilling over into neighboring states. Ironically, dictator Sani Abacha sent 15,000 Nigerian soldiers to reinstall the democratically elected government of President Tejan Kabbah. By the time the Lomé Accord was signed in 1999, Nigerian troops had suffered heavy casualties and were ready to come home— just as the country was moving toward its own democratic transition. Nigerians were looking forward to the peace dividend of approximately $1 million per day—the estimated expenditure by Nigeria on the Sierra Leone conflict—that would come with their exit from this conflict. It should be noted that Nigeria has spent more on international peacekeeping operations in Africa than the United States, Britain, or France. It has been willing to do what the "world's leaders" have shied away from.[6]

However, both the peace and the UN peacekeeping mission in Sierra Leone fell apart almost immediately. In the future, more than UN peacekeepers, it appears the international community is depending on Nigeria to take the lead in African conflicts. As more of the burden shifts to Nigeria, all parties' commitment to the African Crisis Response Initiative (ACRI) will be sorely tested. Regional peacekeeping operations are hardly a new policy; during the COLD WAR the West relied on Nigeria to intervene throughout Africa on the side of "moderate" pro-Western factions. Under the ACRI this relationship will be formalized, as the United States in particular seeks to prepare Nigerians for this and other regional peacekeeping tasks. President Olusegun Obasanjo appears up to the task; he has promised that Nigeria would commit as many peacekeeping troops as necessary to resolve the crisis in Sierra Leone (which spread to Liberia and Guinea and which some aid workers considered to be one of the worst humanitarian crises in the world). Sending U.S. Army Special Forces to train five battalions at a cost of $10 million is just a start. Disciplining these troops, who were notorious for their human rights abuses and corruption, is crucial. In Sierra Leone it was often said that ECOMOG stood for "Every Car Or Moving Object Gone."[7]

Back at home, the newly democratic Nigerian government contends with a vast range of challenges. First among them is the need to build a human rights culture that will provide a more solid basis for the CONSOLIDATION of democracy. The nation is reconstructing its historical memory, by sorting through the past and recognizing the abuses perpetrated over the years by a series of military governments. To facilitate this process, in 2000 Obasanjo allowed for the creation of Nigeria's first TRUTH COMMISSION, known as the Oputa Panel. Although it is patterned on the South African Truth and Reconciliation Commission, it is different in that the Oputa Panel cannot provide AMNESTY for those who admit their crimes. Of the 10,000 petitions sent to the panel, 200 were to be investigated. Several extremely influential people were called to appear and answer questions about their involvement in a variety of human rights abuses. One of several former generals and dictators called to testify before the panel was President Obasanjo. Obasanjo outraged many of his old friends who refused to appear before the panel when he broke ranks to answer charges of past misdeeds.

For all the attention it is getting from the world media, it is yet unclear as to whether Obasanjo's attempt to lead Africa and the world in a war against AIDS will prove more than ephemeral. In May 2001 the president hosted an AIDS summit, in which African leaders pledged to spend more of their budgets on healthcare as they called on the world to contribute billions of dollars to a global trust fund against AIDS. There is no disputing that such efforts are sorely needed. But unfortunately, suspicions have been raised that this effort, and much of Obasanjo's international activity overall, is a public relations gimmick meant to buy the world's goodwill. The Obasanjo government argues that the president's high profile reinforces international confidence in Nigeria's political stability, and that this will attract badly needed foreign investment. Others worry that too much emphasis on Nigeria's military enhances the LEGITIMACY of that institution, and undermines a still fragile CIVIL SOCIETY. Similarly, a growing number of Nigerians believe that Obasanjo enjoys basking in the glow as leading statesman of one of the world's newest democracies a little too much—to the detriment of some very pressing problems at home.

Case Study: Zimbabwe

Because it is a relatively small, landlocked country, most people might expect Zimbabwe to be relatively uninvolved in foreign affairs and very inward-looking. However, Zimbabwe has long had a special place on the international stage.

The fate of Rhodesia was a recurrent topic at UN meetings for years. Since the country's independence, the Zimbabwean government has been unusually vocal at international fora. A leader of the frontline states bordering South Africa, Zimbabwe was key in the antiapartheid movement (and suffered for it). Similarly, Zimbabwe was punished by the United States when it refused to vote alongside the superpower at the UN. On the other hand, for being willing to stand up to the United States, Zimbabwe's President Robert Mugabe won the admiration of many non-Western people.

However, by the end of its first twenty years in power the Mugabe government's relationship with the rest of the world was deteriorating very rapidly. Many analysts are concerned that Mugabe is taking the country down with him—just when it appears that Zimbabwe may need the world most. One of the few friends the president has left is Libya's Muammar Qaddafi, who is providing Zimbabwe with hundreds of millions of dollars in credit to help with the country's fuel shortages. Meanwhile, the Zimbabwean economy continues to take a nosedive, and Mugabe is trying to save his political position by focusing on land reform and lashing out at all who are critical of him. Although land distribution is certainly necessary and a legitimate issue that resonates with many Zimbabweans, it is the way that Mugabe is conducting the land reform that is causing international consternation. Mugabe's refusal to interfere with farm invasions was viewed by many both within and outside Zimbabwe as contributing to a growing lawlessness in the country. Led by Britain, a growing number of countries have criticized the government's handling of land reform and the growing deterioration in human rights.

Yet Mugabe's response to international concerns has been to strike out in defiance. He has especially singled out Zimbabwe's former colonizer, Britain, for his anger. Mugabe has argued that because it was the British whose policy created the problem, Britain has an obligation to pay for the land redistribution and reform. Britain points out that over the last twenty years, it and the United States have paid millions of dollars for land reform (the Zimbabwean government says it needs billions). The donors argue that they finally suspended the aid because the land being transferred wasn't going to the poor, but to Mugabe's cronies. In the Abuja Agreement of September 2001, Nigeria and South Africa brokered a deal in which Britain agreed to pay Zimbabwe $53 million to help cover the costs of compensation to farmers whose land is expropriated—if the Mugabe government ensured that the redistribution of land occurred in an orderly and legal fashion. The two parties agreed, but nothing changed in Zimbabwe.

As a result, at the start of the twenty-first century, relations between Zimbabwe and Britain were said to be at their lowest point since independence. After years of issuing stern warnings, the EU and the Commonwealth considered a range of punitive measures against the Mugabe government. While many people argue that crude economic sanctions will only hurt the poor, there is some talk of targeted sanctions, such as a travel ban on Mugabe and the political elite, or a freeze on their foreign bank accounts. Most analysts warn against cutting off all development aid to the country, but ask that it be channeled through charities and NGOs. Three weeks before the 2002 presidential elections, the EU did impose targeted "smart sanctions" on President Mugabe, members of his family, and senior administration officials after the Zimbabwe government expelled a group of elections observers sent by the EU. After the elections, the Commonwealth used a stronger penalty (and largely symbolic gesture) and suspended Zimbabwe, the first time an elected government was punished in this way.

Some Commonwealth members, especially African governments, feel that Britain and the United States are going too far to vilify and isolate Zimbabwe. The leaders of the region's two most powerful democracies, Nigeria and South Africa, fear that such a public trouncing might actually worsen the situation. Olusegun Obasanjo and Thabo Mbeki have attempted to intercede between Britain and Zimbabwe and between the Zimbabwe African National Union–Patriotic Front (ZANU-PF) government and the Movement for Democratic Change (MDC). They have encouraged the Zimbabwean president to restore respect for the rule of law and to modify his approach to land redistribution. They have broken with the West to recognize Mugabe's presidential win as flawed but legitimate. However, in the end, despite the African leaders' concern about interference from the West, Obasanjo and Mbeki supported the Commonwealth suspension.

More trouble is likely to follow. UN Secretary-General Kofi Annan has informed Mugabe that Zimbabwe now meets none of the basic requirements necessary to receive UN assistance for land reform. For his part, opposition leader Morgan Tsvangirai welcomes the international pressure that is building on the president. He argues that the government is vulnerable and a tougher international approach could have a dramatic effect. While his party applauds the use of targeted smart sanctions (such as a ban on the sale and supply of arms and equipment used for internal repression), the MDC opposes the use of broader sanctions for fear that they will hurt the poor. In addition, such sanctions might give the government just the excuse it needs to impose a state of emergency and crack down on the opposition.

Given the concerns of Tsvangirai and others, many analysts call instead for "constructive engagement," or a less heavy-handed approach from the international community. They fear that a continuation of vocal condemnations by the rest of the world will only work to back Mugabe into a corner, further isolating the country. Those who know Mugabe best say that he is desperate and will not go down without a fight. South African president Thabo Mbeki has been criticized for taking this position and for being "soft" on Mugabe. However, worried that Mugabe's actions will scare foreign investors away from the region, Mbeki has sometimes taken a harder line. He acknowledges the need for land reform (in Zimbabwe and in South Africa, for that matter), but Mbeki insists that it must occur in the context of the law, without violence. This is a message for the people back home as much as it is for Zimbabweans. The South African president fears events in Zimbabwe may prove contagious, and he should be worried. Already the South African government has begun evicting squatters, and has warned South Africans that land invasions are unacceptable and that it will not put up with the kind of land seizures that have destabilized Zimbabwe. Still, it can't be surprising that Mbeki isn't pushing for international sanctions; given its extremely precarious economic condition, the loss of millions of dollars of foreign aid could actually contribute to Zimbabwe's collapse. This would mean more misery for a people already beset with problems. It certainly is not in South Africa's interests for things to go this far, given the thousands of Zimbabwean refugees who would almost certainly flood over its borders. For these reasons Zimbabwe has become a crucial test for South Africa and the world; it is important that the countries of the region receive the financial support they need from developed countries to take the lead in resolving what could become everyone's problem.

Case Study: Iran

Iran, similar to many countries of the third world, has long been struggling to find its way in the international community. Since the mid–twentieth century, it has vacillated between the U.S.-led post–World War II alliance system, to isolation after the 1979 revolution, to a gradual and conflicted opening of arms to the international community. While some of the Iranian leadership desire closer ties with the international community, others feel this will only weaken Iran. For now, at least, President Mohammed Khatami is pursuing a greater role abroad for Iran. One hallmark of his tenure has been a proactive foreign policy, not only linking with the Muslim nations of the Middle East, but also solidifying bilateral relations with China, Japan, and Russia and enhancing Iran's activism in international organizations as well.

Iran has long been a regional leader in the Middle East. It has also been involved in some of the region's keenest controversies. The collapse of the Soviet Union increased the regional importance of Iran by allowing the restoration of ties between the Caucasus and Central Asia. These newly independent states, concerned about their survival, found an economic and security mentor in Tehran. Yet one of the most important regional issues facing Iran is the long animosity between Iran and Iraq, a tension that erupted again in an eight-year war from 1980 to 1988. Iran accepted UN Security Council Resolution 598, which called for the cessation of hostilities and the exchange of prisoners of war. It was not a solution that Iran agreed to lightly—Ayatollah Ruhollah Khomeini compared signing the resolution to "drinking poison."[8] It was a war that ended out of exhaustion more than solution. The economies, militaries, and societies of both Iran and Iraq had been pushed beyond their limits.

Since the fall of 2000, leaders of both countries have attempted to make amends; such moves are important symbolically, even if no major agreements have been signed. True reconciliation between these two countries will be unlikely in the short term, as each side continues to support the other country's opposition (Iraq funds the opposition People's Mujahidin [MKO], and Iran's Revolutionary Guards assist multiple Iraqi opposition groups). Yet ironically, Iran was one of the few countries that opposed the U.S.-led, UN-sponsored war in Iraq following the invasion of Kuwait in 1990. This demonstrated that many in Iran view the West as a more dangerous enemy than their former archrival Iraq.

Another regional issue that pulls at the Iranian leadership is the changing power relations in Afghanistan. Relations with the country's former rulers, the Taliban, were strained from the onset. For one, over 2 million refugees fled

Taliban rule and have settled in Iran since 1996. Additionally, Islamists in Iran challenged many Taliban interpretations of the Quran. As we discussed in Chapter 10, this group adhered to a very rigid interpretation of Islam that has failed to generate the support of many Islamic countries, including the Islamic Republic of Iran. In fact, Iran actively supported the main opposition movement in Afghanistan, the Northern Military Alliance. Tensions reached a boiling point in August 1998, when Taliban forces killed nine Iranian diplomats and journalists. In response, Iran massed over 100,000 troops along its western border with Afghanistan. Iran not only criticized Taliban and Pakistani leaders, whom they claimed were responsible for training and educating many Taliban forces, but the United Nations as well, which Iranians accused of being impotent in this crisis.

Iran's strides to strengthen its military have raised the eyebrows of many. Particularly disconcerting to some is the solidifying weapon alliance between Iran and Russia, including Russian assistance for an Iranian nuclear complex. Despite their differences, especially involving Iranian support of Chechen rebels, they have collaborated in support of Afghan resistance groups, and have both voiced concern at the eastward expansion of the North Atlantic Treaty Organization (NATO). Some sources argue that Iran has an active nuclear arms program, thanks to Russian know-how and support. Tehran is working to improve its Sahab-3 missile, now in development, which has a range of approximately 1,000 miles.

With gradual political openings since Khatami's presidency, the safety of NGO establishment and involvement has increased as well. This is especially true of Iran's nascent green movement. Various NGOs, including Isfahan Green Message, the Wildlife and Nature Conservancy Foundation, and BoomIran, have worked to encourage public environmental preservation as well as governmentally financed land monitoring (including an antifreeway campaign) and natural resource management, especially around the Caspian Sea.

Iran was a charter member of the United Nations, and it has a rocky history of ties with the organization. Its leaders strongly condemned the UN for failing to find fault with Iraq for the invasion that sparked war in 1980. In 1987, President Ali Khamenei portrayed the UN as "a paper factory for issuing worthless, ineffective orders."[9] This tenor has mellowed somewhat, as Iranian leaders increase their bilateral and multilateral relations and seek rapprochement with their neighbors. Within the United Nations, Iranian diplomats often invoke the importance of territorial integrity and claim to speak for the Muslim world, drafting a proposal that an Islamic country be made a permanent member of the Security Council during future reforms. Yet these same diplomats are often the target of criticism by others, especially with respect to Iran's problematic human rights record. Even though Iran was long a pariah of the international community, and spurned international efforts, it has worked closely with the UN in recent years. Tehran helped negotiate an end to Tajikistan's civil war, which concluded with a peace treaty in June 1997, and has been active in efforts to curb drug trafficking. Iran's standing in the world community was enhanced by its pro-Kuwaiti views during the Gulf War, and it felt "rewarded" when the UN passed a resolution identifying Iraq as the instigator of the Iran-Iraq War, demanding Iraq pay $100 billion in reparations.[10]

The Islamic Republic of Iran has the potential to exert great influence—regionally and internationally. Domestic debates on the pros and cons of greater incorporation into the world community and continued international tensions surrounding Tehran's policies will frame what direction this influence will take.

Case Study: Turkey

Turkey's status as both a metaphorical and a physical "bridge" between Europe, the Middle East, and Central Asia is clearly reflected in the country's regional and international memberships and activities. As a border state to continents (Europe and Asia) and civilizations (Islamic, secular, Western, and non-Western), Turkey is greatly impacted by affairs that surround it. Turbulent regional issues have dominated much of Turkey's multilateral ties. As we discussed above, Turkey was in a precarious position on the question of sanctions on Iraq, for both financial and ethnic reasons. Financially, it was estimated that Turkey lost over $30 billion from these sanctions. With Iraq's hands tied, Turkey also lost its major oil supplier as well. And Turkey's domestic Kurdish crisis, which we discussed in Chapter 12, was complicated by Iraqi attacks against its own Kurdish citizenry, and especially multilateral attempts to ameliorate the situation. Kemal Atatürk's statement "peace at home, peace in the world" continues to evoke a modern sense of priority that captures much of Turkey's views on regional and global issues.

Turkey's human rights problems certainly have the potential to stain its international (and regional) reputation. Turkey has long sought membership in the European Union, and its applications were consistently rejected from 1987 to 1999. It will now be late 2004 before the matter is even taken up once again. As we discussed above, the biggest area of concern from the EU is Turkey's human rights record—the situation seems to have only worsened as the EU membership edges closer. The continuation of capital sentences, as well as widespread stories of torture and abuse, promise to delay Turkey's full-fledged acceptance. And the government has made it clear that it will not tolerate internal criticism of its record. For example, Sema Piskinsut, the head of the parliament's human rights commission, used to display torture implements she collected from police stations in her office. As a result, she was dismissed from her position.[11] Criticism of Turkey's record complicates its EU application, on both sides of the process: EU members lose a sense of urgency to include the Turks, and some Turkish politicians leery of losing sovereignty to the "Christian Club"—as the EU is referred to in some circles—also gain a hand.[12]

Additionally, Turkey still refuses to officially recognize its genocide of over 1 million minority Christian Armenians between 1915 and 1923. Large numbers of Armenians were either methodically massacred or forcibly sent to Syria, where many died of hunger in the desert. Foreign legislatures, including the French National Assembly, the European Parliament, the Belgian Senate, and the Russian Duma, have each called on Turkey to recognize the Armenian massacre as a genocide.

Turkey's relations within the United Nations continue to be challenged by multiple issues, including the Kurdish question, the status of Cyprus, and its own shifting alliances. As we discussed in Chapter 10, one of Turkish leaders' most pressing domestic concerns is the Kurdistan Workers' Party (PKK). Other countries and multilateral institutions have taken on this issue as well, in part because of concerns of overzealous persecution by Turkish authorities of ethnic Kurds, and in part because of the international borders that are affected by this ethnic group. Iran and Syria also have significant Kurdish populations, many of whom lead rival groups to the PKK. For this reason, it was in Turkey's interest to gain favor with the world community by assisting in their protection, at the same time that they were limiting the punch of one of their own "problem groups." As long as competing Kurdish forces were active around Turkey's borders, the PKK's power would be in check. Turkey's ability to maintain such a balance, though, often complicates its own tensions. The dilemma faced by Turkey is huge: an independent Kurdish state would only aggravate their own problems, but continued attacks against Kurds in Iraq would send hordes of refugees across the Turkish border, which doesn't bode well for Ankara either. Any operation to protect Iraqi Kurds required the use of Turkish air bases, and struck a sensitive chord among some Turkish military leaders, who feared that this international protection of Kurdish nationals, with the complicity of the Turkish government, could eventually be replicated in Turkey as well. Many fear the eventual creation of an autonomous Kurdish state could create an even greater security problem for Ankara.[13] When sweetheart deals with rival Kurdish groups across Turkish borders collapsed, the military crossed over into Iraqi territory to destroy PKK bases, prompting outcries from every direction: the Iraqi Kurds, who were caught off guard, the Iraqi government, whose territory was violated, as well as Turkey's global allies. Such incursions were commonplace throughout the late 1990s.

Cyprus, an island in the eastern Mediterranean Sea that has been divided into a Turkish-influenced north and Greek-influenced south since 1974, is another irritant in Turkey's global reputation. In 1974, following an attempted military coup on the island by a group favoring union with Greece, Turkish forces landed on Cyprus under the guise of restoring calm and order and protecting the minority Turkish population on the island. The Turkish incursion was met with immediate UN condemnation from the Security Council, which criticized Turkey's intrusion into the sovereign Republic of Cyprus. A PKO has been supervising the cease-fire and maintaining a buffer zone between ethnic Turkish residents in the north and ethnic Greeks in the south. The goal of the dialogue, which was reinitiated in 1997, is to foster a resolution in this standoff between the Greek Cypriot National Guard and Turkish forces, which number over 20,000.

Each of these dilemmas demonstrates the bind facing Turkish decisionmakers. As they attempt to integrate more with global institutions and with their neighbors to the west, they will face increased pressure in their domestic dealings. For many of the reasons we have discussed throughout this book, though, other options, especially a return to isolation, are out of the question.

Case Study: China

China views itself as a global player, especially since its economic transformation of the mid-1980s. Indeed, many analysts, Chinese and non-Chinese alike, predict that China is the most likely country to become an Asian and potentially world superpower in the twenty-first century. Chinese leaders' deft skills in crafting alliances to avoid an "embarrassing" global debate on its human rights record demonstrate its power in regional and international channels. Beijing has squelched most discussions of its record, by mustering support from Asian, African, and Arab nations that also hope to be immune from such scrutiny—especially Indonesia, Kenya, Malaysia, and Thailand. Much of this global reach derives from its size and influence in Asia, as well as its self-proclaimed but often disputed position as spokesperson for non-Western interests.

Regionally, Chinese leaders played an important role in bringing reclusive North Korea into greater participation in the world community, especially by hosting the North Korean president, Kim Jong Il, in early 2000 and 2001. China's attempts to stabilize the North Korean situation are largely out of self-interest—estimates vary, but it is believed that during particularly difficult times, such as the winter months, approximately 500 North Korean refugees cross the border into northeastern China each week. Beijing has also been a leading advocate of closer ties between North and South Korea, widely referred to as the "Sunshine Policy." Ironically, China has much security to lose if North and South Korea reunify—a united Korean peninsula could reopen major power lunges for influence, and could invite foreign troops even closer to Chinese soil. Even though China officially laments the presence of 37,000 U.S. troops in Korea, their withdrawal could have a potentially destabilizing effect. The People's Republic of China (PRC) has also attempted to play the mediator role in the ongoing dispute (the fires of which it helps fan) between India and Pakistan, especially following their nuclear tests in the spring of 1998. China (allied with Pakistan) and the United States (allied with India) jointly proposed a meeting of the Security Council P-5 in Geneva in response to the crisis. China perceives India to be its greatest threat, which helps explain the assistance the country has provided to Pakistani leaders in the development of long-range missiles that could carry nuclear weapons.

While China is providing weapons capability to Pakistan (as well as Iran), it is receiving assistance from Russia. The deepening alliance between Russia and China (strained after the surprise withdrawal of Soviet support from China in 1959 largely in protest of Mao's policies) causes concern in the region, especially for the Japanese. China often acts in concert with Russia in the United Nations, harshly criticizing U.S.-led efforts to isolate Iraq and the continued U.S. and British air strikes against Saddam Hussein. The two countries' diplomatic relations have blossomed in recent years, sparked primarily by growing resentment of the hegemonic role of the United States and NATO powers, demonstrated in their eyes most convincingly in the 1998 NATO-led war in Yugoslavia.

NGOs have been extremely limited in China, because of their perceived challenge to the monopoly of the Chinese Communist Party's role in policymaking. The leadership's hostility toward NGOs was evident in 1995, when the UN's Fourth World Conference on Women was held in Beijing, when the concurrent NGO gathering was forced to the distant suburban outskirts. Yet NGOs have been permitted to form around some limited issues, including the environment. China's first legal environmental NGO is Friends of Nature. This group attempts to raise public awareness of environmental sustainability and biodiversity in a society known for cooking everything that flies and crawls. So far, Friends of Nature has led the effort to save the last golden monkeys from Yunnan province, rallying support for their cause through promotion in newspapers and television as well as university-based "green clubs." The NGO has also campaigned against the capture and sale of songbirds, a traditional urban pet in areas too cramped for cats or dogs.

In the United Nations, Chinese delegates tend to view themselves as the self-proclaimed leaders of the developing countries, in large part because of the power they hold with their veto option in the Security Council. PRC diplomats use this veto infrequently, but strategically, often to lash out at Taiwan's supporters. For example, in February 2000, China vetoed a resolution to extend the peacekeeping operation in Macedonia, because Macedonia had recently recognized Taiwan as an independent country. It has taken similar action against Guatemala, often voting against any measure the state sponsors, because Guatemala has lobbied other UN members for the admission of Taiwan to the UN. While China often preaches the importance of sovereignty from its soapbox, this claim is never meant to include the territory of Taiwan, for which the principle of Chinese territorial integrity is deemed much more important. China is not likely to budge on the contested issue of Taiwan's relationship with the United Nations any time soon. These acts have impelled others to bend to China's will—South Africa, for example, switched its diplomatic recognition from Taiwan to China in 1997, in part because it recognized it would need China's support in order to lobby for a new permanent seat on the Security Council.

Given China's size, its economic and military might, and its strategic position in many multilateral institutions, its influence in global matters in coming decades is much more likely to increase than to decrease. The big question that remains is the extent to which norms are shifted: Will China do most of the adapting, by gradually moving in line with the UNIVERSAL DECLARATION OF HUMAN RIGHTS (UDHR), for example? Or will China chart an EXCEPTIONALIST, Middle Kingdom–type exemption to global ideals and values?

Case Study: Indonesia

In the past, Indonesia was a pivotal regional actor. It was a catalyst, for example, in efforts to organize non-Western countries during the Cold War. Yet current struggles with domestic stability have forced its leaders to respond to, rather than formulate, many of the global policies affecting it. And although Indonesia has spent much of its postindependence history ostensibly charting an "independent" foreign policy, its reliance on international monetary aid and support has increased, especially since the economic collapse of 1997. The instability of the Indonesian state, rocked by economic, political, and ethnic crises, arouses concern among its neighbors in the region and among the global community alike.

Throughout the Cold War, Indonesia was a proud "holdout" during the superpower-dominated contest, occupying a position that became known as "rowing between two reefs." Indicative of this approach, which is different from neutrality, Indonesia was a founding member of the Non-Aligned Movement, an organization of developing countries that formed in 1961 in opposition to the bipolarity of the Cold War. The NAM grew out of a joint conference of African and Asian leaders in 1955, known as the Bandung Conference, named for the Indonesian city in which it was held. In the face of rising superpower tensions, and the division of many countries into blocs that supported either one side or the other, leaders of many former colonial countries gathered to convey their assessment on world affairs. Since the 1960s the NAM has provided a forum to discuss decolonization, debt relief, total nuclear disarmament, and UN Security Council reform. The organization has also sent fact-finding missions and relief to conflict zones, including Somalia and Bosnia-Herzegovina. All the while, members of the organization claimed independence from the "East-West ideological conflict," concentrating instead on North-South economic cleavages. Yet even though Indonesian leaders publicly proclaimed "an active and independent foreign policy," the 1965 anticommunist coup won it the favor and support of many of the Western powers—especially the United States. Although the NAM is less independent than it claims to be, it remains a valuable forum for many non-Western countries.

Because of Indonesia's internal struggles, it faces an increasingly serious refugee problem. Although, at the current time, most of the refugees are more accurately described as internally DISPLACED PERSONS spread across regions of the Indonesian state, this may not be the case for much longer. West Timor is still home to approximately 100,000 East Timorese refugees fleeing the violence that followed the 1999 referendum. Militias run many of the refugee camps in West Timor, and several UN workers who were sent to ameliorate the situation have been killed. According to Doctors Without Borders, which has had a presence in Indonesia since 1995, religious tension in the Moluccas Islands has sent approximately 100,000 internally displaced people into special camps on the islands in search of safety. People fleeing violence in other regions of the archipelago, including West Kalimantan and Aceh, have also sought refuge in provisional camps.

Ideological and ethnic tension exists between Indonesia and its giant neighbor to the northwest, China. For almost four decades, this animosity was dominantly ideological in nature, as Indonesia was the focal point of anticommunist struggle in the region. As we discussed previously, much of the impetus for forming the Association of Southeast Asian Nations (ASEAN) in the late 1960s was to fortify an anticommunist alliance among states in the region. This focus gradually subsided, though, and China now holds "dialogue status" within the organization. Indonesia's treatment of its sizable ethnic Chinese population is now a focal point of tensions between the two countries. In the riots of 1998 and thereafter, ethnic Chinese communities throughout Indonesia—especially Chinese women—have been targeted in mob attacks, mass rape, and discrimination. Ethnic Chinese business communities in Indonesia have been scapegoated as well, especially as Indonesian families watch their disposable income plummet.

Multilateral institutions, especially the United Nations and the International Monetary Fund (IMF), have played a key although not always positive role in Indonesia since 1997. As we discussed in Chapter 7, IMF demands for the financial bailout package in 1998, after the collapse of the Indonesian currency, led to wide-scale looting and riots that toppled President Suharto. Indonesia's relations with the UN in recent years have mostly surrounded the independence of East Timor in 1999 and the violence that ensued. Regionally, Australia was a main player in urging Indonesian president B. J. Habibie to call for the East Timor referendum, and the Commonwealth also provided a large number of peacekeeping troops in the aftermath of the vote. The smoke has yet to settle. Even though members of the international community demanded that Indonesia establish a war crimes tribunal for the East Timor violence, then-president Abdurraham Wahid feared a surge of NATIONALISM, which he argued could completely unravel the state. Calls for the tribunal lessened after Wahid's argument received the endorsement of UN Secretary-General Kofi Annan.

As the world's fourth most populous state, Indonesia certainly possesses regional and global influence. In recent years, however, and likely for quite some time in the foreseeable future, its focus will likely be on sheer state survival rather than global activism. The international community has the power to help or hinder state leaders and ordinary citizens alike. Indonesia today is more fragile than ever.

Now It's Your Turn

What significant events or issues would you add to this discussion that have become prominent since this book was published? Have any of the concerns we covered in this chapter been significantly resolved—or have any situations dramatically worsened? What role do you believe truth commissions can and do serve in promoting peace and justice? If you were the leader of a country torn apart by conflict, how would you best prescribe picking up the pieces and moving on? In your mind, have any recent events warranted an international tribunal or the commissioning of a peacekeeping operation? Are there any countries that seem to be impacted by regional or global matters more than they are able to influence affairs themselves? How differently would you look at some of the IGOs and NGOs that we studied in this chapter if you were a resident or a leader in one of the third world countries that we are studying? Some people argue that, in general, the richer the country and the more its economy is geared toward trade, the more active and complex its foreign policy. The corollary would then be that the poorer the country, the more focused its leaders tend to be on domestic issues. Do you find this to be the case with the countries that we have studied? Why or why not?

Suggested Readings

Africa

Beyala, Calixthe. *Loukoum: The Little Prince of Belleville*. London: Heinemann, 1995. France and Cameroon: fiction, a seven-year-old boy's view of life in an African immigrant quarter of Paris.

Darko, Amma. *Beyond the Horizon*. London: Heinemann, 1995. Ghana and Germany:

fiction, a disturbing story of how one woman found herself working as a prostitute in Germany after being conned by her husband into coming to the "paradise" of Europe.

Emecheta, Buchi. *Kehinde*. London: Heinemann, 1994. Nigeria and the UK: fiction, a Nigerian woman who enjoyed success in London follows her husband back to Nigeria, only to find that she cannot accept the social mores of her culture.

———. *The New Tribe*. London: Heinemann, 2000. Nigeria and the UK: fiction, a tale of mixed-race adoption and the alienation associated with the loss of one's culture.

Asia

Wang, Shuo. *Please Don't Call Me Human*. Trans. Howard Goldblatt. New York: Hyperion East, 2000. China: black humor mocking China's authoritarian politics and attempts to regain face after China's loss following defeat at an international sports competition.

Women of South Asian Collective, ed. *Our Feet Walk the Sky: Women of the South Asian Diaspora*. San Francisco: Aunt Lute Books, 1993. India and diaspora: multicultural and multidisciplinary collection of essays, short stories, and memoirs by women from South Asia.

Middle East

al-Shaykh, Hanan. *I Sweep the Sun off Rooftops*. St. Leonards: Allen and Unwin, 1994. Varia: short stories presenting concerns shared by a cross-section of Arab women and refugees, including cultural clashes, international power relationships, and regional (in)security.

Daneshvar, Simin. *A Persian Requiem: A Novel*. Trans. Roxanne Zand. New York: G. Braziller, 1992. Iran: historical fiction, set at the beginning of World War II and presenting the international power struggle with a human face.

Mahfouz, Naguib. *Journey of Ibn Fattouma*. Trans. Denys Johnson-Davis. New York: Doubleday, 1992. Varia: epic journey through timeless Middle East, ripe with cultural comparisons.

Marcom, Micheline Ahorian. *Three Apples Fell from Heaven*. New York: Riverhead Books, 2001. Turkey: novel about the Armenian genocide in Turkey after 1915.

Dealing with a Superpower: Third World Views of the United States

Robbers have come; bandits have come. We have been left wounded, bleeding and dying. Is there a Good Samaritan passing by?
—Reverend Israel Akanji, Nigeria[1]

The United States has become too heedless of others' sensitivities and too confident of its own righteousness.
—Statement in *The Nation,* a Pakistani daily newspaper, following Bush's 2002 State of the Union address[2]

At the beginning of the twenty-first century, the United States remains the sole superpower—a "great power" with "great wealth."[3] In responding to and solving global problems, the role of the United States is critical, but certainly not always benign. Many American students are surprised to hear that the United States is viewed with both respect and contempt beyond its borders. Some have a difficult time seeing that actions of the United States are viewed as threatening to many, because Americans tend to believe that their actions are taken in the name of some larger, more noble cause. Yet it is important to remember that others take actions, some of which we deem irresponsible or even reprehensible, with seemingly good motivations as well.

It is clear that in the early years of the twenty-first century, the United States stands as the world's strongest country, the world's lone superpower. What does this mean? How long can it last? Whether or not it is technically accurate by definition, many view the United States as an empire—willing and able to exert influence beyond its borders. Sometimes this happens in the pursuit of a worthy goal. Other times, U.S. actions have been less noble. One particularly controversial example may help illustrate this dilemma. For over twenty years, U.S. presidents have intermittently considered some form of missile defense as a way to protect the United States and some of its allies from attack by unfriendly states. Yet the current pursuit of this initiative, which requires the United States to break hard-won arms accords, is viewed by other states as a unilateral expansion of already dominant U.S. capability, since it would neutralize others' ability to respond defensively to a U.S. attack. Initiatives to extend the military arms race into outer space, including space-based lasers and interceptors, add to this perception. The view from beyond U.S. borders is that technological advances found only in the United States will likely benefit only the United States.[4]

Another example can be found in U.S. trade laws. With domestic legislation sanctioning Cuba, Iran, and Libya, the U.S. government attempts to economically punish not only these states, but also countries (and private corporations) that do business with them. The U.S. perspective is that countries should not do business with known terrorists, a contention voiced more strongly after the events of September 11, 2001. The perspective beyond U.S. borders, though, is that the United States does not have the authority to tell other countries with whom they should be conducting business. As an example of this animosity, the European Union (EU) united behind France after the United States objected to French investment in Iran's South Pars gas field in the late 1990s.[5] These actions increasingly are causing countries to claim that the United States is invoking extraterritoriality, or the attempt to impose one's rules and laws outside of one's own sovereign territory. The treatment of Taliban and Al-Qaida detainees in Guantanomo Bay Naval Base at Camp X-Ray, and the U.S. insistence that they not be treated as prisoners of war, have evoked similar calls. Many argue that the detainees, after they were hooded, shackled, and even drugged in flight, were dropped into legal limbo in Cuba, beyond the jurisdiction of any court system except for U.S.-designed military tribunals.[6]

Some perceive the United States as a country that abides by laws only when it is useful, while attempting to force others to follow U.S. laws and policies, even in foreign countries. In this sense, many countries of the world believe that the United States holds an EXCEPTIONALIST view of its place in the world. The examples are plentiful. The United States condemned the Iraqi invasion of Kuwait in 1990, yet the same U.S. leaders had ordered the invasion of Panama in 1989 in order to capture President Manuel Noriega and try him for criminal drug operations in the United States. The United States produces the most greenhouse emissions of any other country in the world, yet U.S. presidents have sought exceptions from international environmental treaties designed to combat these ills. The lack of U.S. support for the International Criminal Court (ICC), which we discussed in Chapter 17, including the demand that U.S. military personnel be exempt from its jurisdiction, is yet another case in point. U.S. leaders rejected international protocols on germ warfare and demanded amendments to an accord on the illegal sale of small arms. Even if these policies do not convey a growing sense of isolationism, as some claim, there has been a clear increase in U.S. unilateralism, condemned even by U.S. allies. U.S. policies on sanctions, particularly those on Cuba, in force since 1960, and Iraq since 1990, are increasingly counterproductive and, in the opinion of many, violate the same human rights norms that the United States champions in its case against the Cuban and Iraqi leadership.

There are still others examples of U.S. exceptionalism. In 1997, President Bill Clinton, facing Pentagon pressure, refused to sign the 1997 covenant outlawing land mines because an exception of the Korean peninsula was not granted. In 1999 the U.S. Senate rejected the Nuclear Test Ban Treaty because—even though U.S. leaders are clear that they would like the rest of the world to halt weapons development—they don't want to have their own hands tied. On the grounds that outsiders would be able to call for inspections in an imperfect system, President George W. Bush also discarded the biological weapons draft protocol from 1972 (which 143 countries, including the United States, had ratified), and opposed international efforts to limit the trade in small arms. Such policies lead some to view the United States as displaying an "arrogance of power," to borrow from a phrase coined by J. William Fulbright.

Additionally, the United States often withholds support for international organizations that conduct work seen as being in opposition to the policy goals of some interest groups in the country—even if the action is perfectly legal in other societies of the world. One clear example of this is the U.S. condemnation of organizations that provide family planning or abortion services. Recent presidents Ronald Reagan, George H. W. Bush, and George W. Bush each denied funding to any agency that even mentions abortion as an option. These presidents describe themselves as taking a moral stance on such "right to life" issues. Meanwhile, these same presidents have sided with businesses to oppose international efforts to eliminate child labor. The United States is one of the few countries in the world that executes juveniles, and it has refused to sign treaties prohibiting the use of child soldiers. To many, the contradiction is glaring.

Such actions have contributed to much of the animosity, mistrust, and ill will the United States encounters worldwide. Sometimes this hostility is manifested in condemnations of U.S. actions, or the exclusion of the United States from international bodies. In the spring of 2001, for example, the United States for the first time failed to be reelected to a seat on UN Human Rights Commission (which former first lady Eleanor Roosevelt helped create in the late 1940s). Shortly thereafter, the United States lost its seat on the UN's International Narcotics Control Board—the primary drug enforcement commission in the UNITED NATIONS system. Some interpreted the Narcotics Board vote to be an expression of dissension against U.S. drug control policies. After these actions, both of which resulted from secret ballots, some countries' leaders expressed a sense of sweet justice. It is important to emphasize that it was not only countries from the third world that voted the United States off of these seats: negative votes included U.S. allies in the Western, developed world. On the Human Rights Commission, country representatives expressed dissension related to U.S. votes on issues we have discussed throughout this book. This included two times that the United States spoiled a unanimous vote on resolutions: it was the sole abstention on a resolution about the availability of AIDS medications (with fifty-two votes in favor), as well as on a resolution outlining humans' right to food (with fifty-two votes in favor). Former U.S. secretary of state Madeleine K. Albright often stated that the United States is an "indispensable" power. Yet increasingly, because of such actions, many countries, Western and non-Western alike, are finding the United States to be an "untrustworthy partner."[7]

Some countries (friend and foe alike) have taken to referring to the United States as a HEGEMON: a strong, controlling force in the world that attempts to impose its will on others. This used to be a favorite derisory term employed by leaders of the People's Republic of China and other countries to characterize the United States, but now it is catching on with others as well. Many people accuse the United States of behaving as a "hyperpower" consumed with maintaining its political, military, economic, and cultural dominance.[8] This impression is based in the view that strong countries take actions in their interest irrespective of how they will affect others. But no matter how strong a power or country is, it can be humbling to realize what it cannot accomplish. Harsh U.S. rhetoric against undemocratic leaders such as Saddam Hussein, Slobodan Milosevic, and Fidel Castro seems only to have increased their domestic popularity, and has even won them international support as well. Policy intentions often have the opposite outcomes from what their designers have in mind. Attempts to take a strong stance against a regime or policy sometimes winds up strengthening those who are in power or who are taking the undesired action in the first place, and marginalizing those whom reformers want to help. Even the big boys cannot get their way all of the time.

Throughout the book, we have discussed the importance of SOVEREIGNTY, and ways that its meaning may be changing at the turn of the twenty-first century. Many of the actions of U.S. leaders highlighted above are taken in the name of preserving precisely this principle. Yet others have argued that advocates of this principle are looking to a bygone era. As editorial columnist Robert Wright argued, how much sovereignty does a state possess when a dozen people can raze two of the largest buildings in the largest city of that country?[9]

After September 11

Following the events of September 11, 2001, it became common to discuss the ways the world had permanently changed. While it certainly is true that few Americans will view themselves or their personal safety in the same way for a very long time, many voices in the third world argued that it wasn't the world, but rather the United States and its self-image that had been changed by those tragic events. Although both the method and the magnitude of the actions on that day shocked many, much of the world has lived for a long time in fear of violence and TERRORISM.

In this chapter, we have discussed a tendency in the United States to "go it

---

Figure 20.1   Could the Next Superpower Come from the Third World?

The era of the lone superpower can hardly continue forever. And increasingly it looks as though the next major power could come from the third world. As history has shown us, a single country cannot remain the preeminent power forever. If you reflect on the lessons of history for a moment, empires based in Greece, Rome, Turkey, and China once ruled large regions of the world, seemingly unchallenged. Many point to the People's Republic of China as a potential superpower for the twenty-first century. With the world's largest population, a vast amount of territory, and a huge economy, China appears to at least be a candidate for the potential future role. If so, it would be the first nation in history to have gone into decline after a period of greatness, only to recover its former glory.[10]

alone" and to take unilateral action to accomplish its goals. In the weeks following September 11, the Bush administration crafted a wide-reaching coalition of support, uniting many countries of the world, Western and non-Western alike, against terrorism. Indeed, few countries explicitly condemned the U.S.- and British-led strikes on Afghanistan, which began approximately one month after the attacks in New York and Washington—although many in the third world, notably China, Pakistan, and Indonesia, expressed their concern for the war's toll on civilians. Yet after the war was launched, some expressed apprehension over the emergence of the BUSH DOCTRINE, which divided the world neatly in two: linking any country that "supports" terrorists to be on the same playing field as terrorists themselves.[11] While it may be temptingly simple to view the world in such stark terms, the reality of life in the early twenty-first century is rarely that clean cut, as is evident in the case studies presented in this volume. In their efforts to support the U.S. coalition in the war in Afghanistan, many countries, especially Pakistan, Turkey, and Indonesia, have invited intense opposition among their own populations. President Bush later firmly placed Iran, Iraq, and North Korea in this category as terrorist states, labeling these countries part of an "AXIS OF EVIL" in his 2002 State of the Union address. This call provoked angry responses not only from these countries, but from others as well, including U.S. allies in Europe and countries that have supported the U.S. war on terrorism.[12] Yet as we have discussed throughout this chapter, the tendency to take unilateral action, when it is deemed to be in the interests of the United States, is not a development that suddenly emerged after September 11, even if the events of that day accelerated this long-held propensity.

As we discussed in Chapter 12, definitions of terrorism are quite complicated, and are largely dependent upon one's perspective. After the fall of the Taliban's stronghold in Kandahar, Afghanistan, other potential targets for the "new war on terrorism" in the third world were announced, notably Iraq, Iran, Somalia, Yemen, and the Philippines. The domestic support the U.S. administration had for war in Afghanistan may not carry over to these areas for long, even if, in the perspective of the Bush administration, it is all a continuation of a project begun with support in Afghanistan. Even some of its closest allies in Europe have made it clear that the United States is making a mistake if it connects support for the action in Afghanistan to be a carte blanche for backing attacks in Iraq, for example. Others have argued that the broad-sweeping title "war on terrorism" invites widespread misuse of the term, permitting countries to clamp down on pesky minorities or separatist groups who challenge governments. Human Rights Watch has documented many such attempts—especially in Egypt, China, Malaysia, and Zimbabwe. China has argued against "dual standards" in the war on terrorism—because it has assisted in the U.S. fight against Al-Qaida, it also seeks U.S. and Western support in its battle against Uighur separatists in Xinjiang province. They at least partially succeeded in this goal when the United States added the East Turkistan Islamic Movement (ETIM) to its list of terrorist organizations in September 2002. Zimbabwe's Robert Mugabe has extended his definition of terrorism to include journalists who wrote stories about attacks on whites and other political violence—engaging in what he terms "media terrorism."[13] The escalation could become dangerous as disagreeing parties label each other terrorists to justify a fierce response in the eyes of the world.

As was the case during the COLD WAR, in the era of the "war on terrorism," human rights concerns seem to have taken a back seat. It's been an old saying that politics makes for strange bedfellows—perhaps now as long as leaders condemn Al-Qaida they can get away with anything they want in their own territories. And if they can link their own domestic struggles to Al-Qaida, as the Russians are doing with the Chechens and the Chinese with the Xinjiang separatists—who can deny their right to demolish them? Consequently, many human rights activists fear that the post–September 11 world is a time of regression, in which the human rights era of the post–Cold War 1990s is ending with the war on terror.[14] The U.S. government is promoting repression in the name of security and arguing that it should be given tremendous latitude in its use of secrecy and policies that amount to egregious violations of human rights. For example, the United States is holding suspected Taliban and Al-Qaida prisoners in six-by-eight-foot wire cages in Cuba without access to their embassies or attorneys, and is submitting them to closed military tribunals that include capital punishment in their sentencing.

Since September 11, Americans have joined in a resounding chorus of "Why do they hate us?" as they ponder the source of such anger targeted at the United States. It may be difficult to understand why groups of people would want to undertake such damaging acts against not only the United States, but especially U.S. civilians. (Remember our point from Chapter 12, though, that terrorists consider civilians accomplices of larger sources of evil.) Certainly, there is no single answer to this question, but we urge you to consider the importance of competing perceptions in the world. And it is not only an issue of trying to figure out why someone would take such actions against the United States—some Americans were surprised by others' responses to the terrorist attacks. While world opinion generally expressed condolences to the United States, there were pockets of sentiment that were less than supportive. These views, expressed in celebrations—some muted, some not—in Internet chat rooms, in newspaper editorials, and on the streets, included rejoicing that the world's lone superpower had been brought to its knees. It was not uncommon to hear acceptance of the attack, in that it may finally foster a sense of understanding for the way the rest of the world lives. Clearly these views were the minority, and U.S. embassies abroad were almost universally showered with expressions of support and outrage at the attack, but we must acknowledge that the sentiment was there, from the Palestinian territories to Beijing.[15] After the war in Afghanistan began in October 2001, anti-American protests broke out in many cities throughout the world, including Jakarta, Islamabad, and elsewhere.

One does not need to agree with a view in order to try to understand it, and all perceptions are based on a combination of facts and fears. Also, one does not need to argue that the United States in any way deserved the destruction that it experienced in order to question the motivations and anger behind those who perpetrated such acts. It is not un-American to attempt to see the world through others' eyes; in fact, such an exercise is likely to increase commitment to the ideals on which the United States was founded and continues to foster. We must be cautious, though, with broad generalizations that, for example, attribute the anger against the West to some vague notion of "Islamic civilization." Most of the largest Islamic countries in the world show only pockets of anti-American fury, and the rage found in much of the Arab and Islamic world is a relatively recent development since the 1970s.[16] While the roots of these feelings of discord are indeed complex, they stem in large part from the fact that almost every Arab country today is less democratic than it was three decades ago—and that the United States is seen as one of the main forces continuing to prop up corrupt, elitist governments. The contradictions in policy and action are not lost on most people. This has led to feelings of disillusionment for many, anger for some, and raw hatred for others.

Linking Concepts and Cases

In the preceding chapter we discussed how variously situated third world countries have attempted to deal with the United States as a superpower. We focused on non-Western views of the United States and especially its current response to TERRORISM. How would you characterize each country's response to the 2001 terror attacks on the United States as well as the Bush administration's response? What are the important characteristics of the relationship between each of these case studies and the United States beyond the war on terrorism? What is the likely future trajectory for these bilateral ties, and which issues are more or less likely to be important in the next five to ten years?

Case Study: Mexico

"Poor Mexico. Poor United States. So far from God. So near to each other." This is novelist Carlos Fuentes's spin on a saying attributed to a Mexican dictator notorious for opening the country to foreign domination. Yet it expresses the ambivalence many Mexicans have about sharing a border with the United States, which is known throughout Latin America as "the colossus of the north." Mexico's foreign policy is dominated by its relationship with the United States, and Mexico is so often described as having a love-hate relationship with its neighbor that the saying has become trite. Although Mexico is increasingly recognized as influencing U.S. styles and tastes, the influence of U.S. culture in Mexico is almost unavoidable. Many Mexicans fear losing their identity in the shadow of the enormous power of the United States. As one analyst put it, this proximity means that Mexico and the United States are prisoners of each other's problems.[1]

The Mexican-U.S. relationship is one of interdependence, yet it is not and has never been one of equal dependence. Since the North American Free Trade Agreement (NAFTA) was instituted in 1994, cross-border trade between the United States and Mexico has boomed. Mexico depends on its neighbor for nearly 66 percent of its imports and exports, 80 percent of its tourism, and 70 percent of its foreign investment. Whereas Mexico has been forced to consider U.S. interests on a number of issues, the United States has essentially ignored Mexico's interests. For many years, it seemed that the United States was more interested in promoting stability than DEMOCRACY in Mexico. Mexicans are often characterized as sensitive to threats of U.S. imperialism, and perhaps rightfully so. Part of this is due to the fact that for years Mexico has been treated by the United States as a junior partner.[2]

However, President Vicente Fox wants a new partnership with the United States that reflects the profound political and economic change his country has experienced in the last ten years. He wants his northern neighbor to recognize that it is greatly dependent on Mexico's cooperation on a number of difficult issues, which demands the creation of a fuller, more mature, and more equal partnership. Such a partnership would allow Mexico and the United States to be able to talk about their areas of disagreement without worrying about jeopardizing their long-term relationship. Fox set the stage for this new relationship by clearly letting the United States know that the annual ritual of U.S. certification of Mexico's cooperation with drug control efforts is offensive and humiliating. Such assertiveness reflects a new self-confidence evident since the democratic elections in 2000. As Foreign Minister Jorge G. Castañeda put it, "We are not scared of engaging the U.S. anymore."[3]

Engaging the United States means discussing problems that have been festering for years. Too often the United States has treated Mexico as a source of its problems and never considered how it might be contributing to problems in Mexico. From the perspective of many Mexicans, the United States needs to consider not only what it wants from Mexico, but also its own responsibilities in this relationship. For example, a significant number of guns from the United States are used in crimes in Mexico, and the United States needs to do more to stop the flow of illegal weapons across its southern border. Similarly, no one needs to remind Mexicans of the violence associated with the drug cartels that operate there, yet many people resent the approach the United States has taken in its war on drugs, which they consider a violation of SOVEREIGNTY. For example, while Americans are exasperated with Mexico's hesitance to allow U.S. drug enforcement agents to operate on Mexican soil, Mexicans ask Americans to see it the other way around—how would Americans feel about letting Mexican agents travel freely in the United States in search of drug users?[4]

From Mexico's point of view, an even more crucial issue that President Fox hopes to address with the United States is migration. Concerned about the increasing dangers faced by Mexicans seeking work in the United States, Fox hopes some day to deepen NAFTA by negotiating open borders between member countries, much as is the case in the European Union (EU). The Mexican president has also been trying to make it easier for the estimated 4 million Mexicans living illegally in the United States to get temporary legal work and to extend to them protections that they do not currently enjoy. In this effort, Fox has stated that he considers himself the leader not only of Mexico's 100 million residents, but also of the 18–23 million Mexicans and Mexican Americans living in the United States.

Although Fox's forthrightness on this issue may startle some in the United States, until September 11 it appeared that Presidents Fox and Bush had struck up a genuine friendship and that Mexico was going to be at the top of the Bush foreign policy agenda. Prior to the terrorist attacks on the United States,

President Bush appeared receptive to the idea of a limited reform that would reduce illegal immigration without threatening the welfare of U.S. citizens. In part this interest was based in political pragmatism: Bush knew that winning the Latino vote was crucial for Republicans. Although Bush raised expectations by publicly considering the idea of a full amnesty and permanent status for Mexicans living in the United States illegally, talk of such reform has stopped for the time being. Now U.S. anti-immigration sentiment has grown and most politicians' primary concern is national security.

Despite criticism at home for breaking Mexico's constitutional commitment to a noninterventionist foreign policy, President Fox did pledge Mexico's unconditional support for the U.S. war on terror.[5] In the months following September 11 it became clear that migration issues have been moved to the back burner. President Fox initially said that he understood the reasons for this and implied that he was willing to be patient—within limits. However, a year after the attacks, Mexico was feeling abandoned and relations were strained. The most pro-U.S. president in years, Fox paid a political price for being viewed as too cozy with Washington. However, in some important ways the Mexican-U.S. relationship has been fundamentally altered since the 2000 elections. What is perhaps most interesting about this relationship at the turn of the century is that in many ways, President Fox has achieved one of his goals. According to Robert Pastor, there has been a reversal of the two countries' traditional roles. In the past it was the United States that made the proposals and Mexico that said "yes" but not "when." Now it is Mexico making the proposals and it is the United States saying "yes" but not "when."[6]

According to Jorge Castañeda, it is only when democracies work together that a more equitable relationship is possible.[7] Once the United States is ready to resume the discussion with Mexico concerning their common interests, it will be important for Americans to understand that agreement between the two democratic states is likely to be more difficult than it has been in the past. It is very much in the interests of the United States for democracy in Mexico to work. However, a democratic Mexico means that President Fox will be constrained by his own constituency. Now more than ever, Mexico's president cannot appear to be a "yes man" to the United States, and the United States will need to understand this.

Case Study: Peru

In many ways Peru is a pivotal country for the United States. However, the Peruvian-U.S. relationship has had it ups and downs, and at times that relationship has been strained.[8] Since the mid-nineteenth-century guano boom the United States has had significant economic interests in Peru. Over the years these interests expanded into political and strategic areas. Peru has accommodated U.S. interests and supported the United States on a host of regional and international issues. But Peru has been disappointed in its expectations of receiving reciprocal treatment in return. As a result, many Peruvians have becomes distrusting and resentful of the extensive U.S. presence and interference in Peru's internal and external affairs. When Peru has sought to diversify its ties, pursue multilateral diplomacy, or promote ideological pluralism, it has occasionally made for tension between the two countries.

During the COLD WAR, Peru was viewed by the United States as a highly sensitive security zone. Since then, the country has been of particular importance to the United States as the Andes have become a major battlefield in the U.S. war on drugs. Since the 1980s, U.S. forces have worked closely with local police in crop eradication and drug interdiction in Peru, Bolivia, and Ecuador. By the early 1990s, the war on drugs was the centerpiece of U.S. policy in the region and Peru became a major recipient of U.S. military assistance. Some economic aid was set aside for crop substitution and "alternative development," with the view that drug eradication was a development issue. However, the brunt of economic assistance was conditioned on the Peruvian government's cooperation in the use of a military approach to fighting the drug war. U.S. "Andean strategy" has aimed to cut off the cocaine trade at its source of supply. For several years, it appeared that this strategy was working, as coca cultivation in Peru plummeted in the late 1990s. The Clinton administration celebrated the end of Peru's status as the world's biggest producer of coca leaf—well aware that authoritarian measures were behind much of this success.

Yet the United States has competing priorities in Peru, and has often seemed torn over how best to proceed. As Cynthia McClintock has pointed out, on the one hand is the State Department and its advocacy of democratic integrity. On the other hand, these interests must compete against the very influential Central Intelligence Agency (CIA), the Pentagon, and the White House through its adviser on drugs. While U.S. administrations have insisted that there is no trade-off between the insistence on fair elections and the war on drugs, many Peruvians have doubted the sincerity of such claims.[9] For many, U.S. policy toward Peru during the 1990s was best described as ambivalent. Convinced that counternarcotics operations in the region could not continue without Alberto Fujimori's support, the United States overlooked the growing authoritarianism of the Fujimori government. Humanitarian and drug-fighting assistance continued as the democracy eroded because the United States feared that the instability associated with the drug war in Colombia could spread to Peru. Although U.S. military assistance was appropriated only to fight the drug war, some of this money was diverted by Peru for use in its war against the Shining Path GUERRILLAS, under the argument that the terrorists were playing a central part in the drug trade. Consequently, the United States became an important ally for the Peruvian government in its civil war.

By the time Peruvians put a stop to Fujimori's "re-reelection" in 2000, President Bill Clinton was relieved at his old ally's resignation. The United States then called for a rapid restoration of democracy, despite the fact that U.S. reticence had been criticized as compromising it. Whatever the case, it is likely that the inconsistent approach favored by the United States will continue to characterize the Peruvian-U.S. relationship under Bush and Alejandro Toledo. This is due in large part to the fact that the United States still has competing priorities in the Andes. While many of the major players that dominated this relationship in the 1990s are now gone, the drug war remains.

This may be a mixed blessing for the new democratic government of Peru.

Whereas democratization has been relatively successful in several Latin American countries, it is most tenuous not only in Peru, but also in the entire Andean region, where the U.S. war on drugs is concentrated. While Plan Colombia's supporters argue that the drug trade is responsible for the weakness of democracy in the region, others are concerned that U.S. policy will result only in a further militarization of these countries. There is already talk not only of the United States tripling its aid to Peru to fight drug trafficking, but also of a U.S. military operation on Peru's border with Colombia.[10] This is just one of many reasons why the Andes are widely considered the hemisphere's best bet for a major crisis.

However, after September 11 it appeared that Latin America has fallen off the radar screen. U.S. priorities were shifting, budgets were being diverted—would the war on terrorism take precedence over the war on drugs? According to a former U.S. ambassador to Peru, the war on terrorism and the war on drugs are a lot alike. In neither case is the United States likely ever to win a final victory, but the consequences of not dealing with these problems could be even worse than waging a war without end.[11] And in the Andes, there have long been connections between narcotrafficking and terrorism. At this point no one is saying that there is much of a chance of an attack on the United States from the region, but the combination of guerrillas and drug lords makes for plenty of instability. If Shining Path is making a comeback, it poses a very real threat to Peru's fragile democracy. Recent attacks, first in remote areas of Peru followed by a Lima bombing just hours before a visit by President Bush in 2002, suggest that Shining Path is regrouping. Moreover, indications are that Peru may no longer be winning its war on drugs. Since 1999 there has been a spike in drug cultivation, as the price of coca has hit all-time highs while that of likely substitutes such as coffee dropped below the cost of production. Some analysts say that Peru could soon be the heroin capital of Latin America; the only crop substitution program working in Peru is the replacement of coca with the more lucrative opium poppy.[12]

Are there any lessons Peru can teach the United States on how to fight a war on terrorism? Until recently it was thought that with its draconian approach of using summary trials in military courts, the Fujimori government appeared to win a fifteen-year war on terror. Yet it is increasingly recognized today in Peru that the trampling of civil rights in the name of security led to the imprisonment of hundreds of innocents. The no-holds-barred war on terror may have only created martyrs and contributed to long-term problems, as these groups were never destroyed, just forced into dormancy. Still, unlike most other people of the region, because they were so traumatized by Shining Path, Peruvians are uniquely sympathetic to the U.S. war on terror.[13]

Case Study: Nigeria

Despite its enormous significance, U.S. presidents generally have shown little interest in Nigeria, or in Africa, for that matter. Bill Clinton was the first U.S. president to visit Nigeria since President Jimmy Carter's trip in 1977. Yet Nigeria is too big to ignore. Only South Africa rivals it as a regional superpower. Described as Africa's equivalent to Brazil, India, or Indonesia, Nigeria is vital to U.S. interests for several reasons. It is the fifth largest U.S. supplier of oil, exporting more than 2 million barrels a day. In addition, with a population of 120–130 million, it is not only the region's most populous country, but also the largest market in sub-Saharan Africa, offering tremendous trade opportunities. One in six Africans are Nigerian. And present-day Nigeria is part of the region that was home to the ancestors of most African Americans. Still, the United States generally takes a back seat to Europe on African affairs. Although Nigeria has historically been more closely tied to Britain and the EU, that may change as the United States seeks a strategic partner and an alternative to Middle Eastern oil in Africa.

In part, Nigeria cannot be ignored because if Nigeria falls, it will shake the rest of Africa.[14] President Clinton once described Nigeria as a pivot point on which all of Africa's future turns. For the first time in decades, Nigeria is once again attempting to get a fledgling democracy off the ground. If this democracy can become strong, it could become a model for the rest of the continent. Economic prosperity in Nigeria would almost certainly affect others in the region. However, until recently the U.S. approach to Nigeria has been described as paradoxical, alternating between close diplomacy and benign neglect.[15] Interestingly, the last period of reconciliation in Nigerian-U.S. relations was during the Carter era, when Olusegun Obasanjo first tried his hand as head of state (then as a military dictator).

The Nigeria-U.S. relationship hit its lowest point during the Sani Abacha regime, after it became clear that the results of the presidential elections of 1993 would never be respected. However, despite claims by the United States about its concern for the democratic process, in the mid-1990s it was Nigeria's role in the international drug trade that provoked the most serious U.S. response. Not a producer of narcotics, Nigeria has become a leading hub in the transshipment of drugs from Latin America and Asia. Lower prices for oil and a worsening economy in the late 1980s had driven many Nigerians into this risky but highly lucrative line of work. Nigerian "swallowers," or human couriers, are believed to be responsible for nearly 40 percent of the heroin entering the United States. The Nigerian government greatly resented U.S. accusations and interference and basically thumbed its nose at the world.

But as bad as things got, neither side was willing to use oil as a weapon. The United States wanted to buy it from Nigeria, and Nigeria wanted to sell it to the United States. Randall Robinson, head of the African American lobby TransAfrica, tried to change that. In the 1990s, African American celebrities joined an energetic campaign that compared Nigeria under Sani Abacha to apartheid South Africa. Robinson and others called for a boycott of Nigerian oil, noting that nearly half of the oil Nigeria sells goes to the United States. However, despite these efforts, the United States and Western allies never seriously considered an oil boycott, arguing that sanctions on oil from Iran, Libya, and Iraq were already driving up prices. Instead, Nigeria was slapped with a series of relatively mild military and diplomatic sanctions. Meanwhile, U.S. oil companies joined others in dramatically increasing their investments in Nigeria. That hypocrisy, combined with the U.S. decision not to press Abacha on the 1993 elections, disappointed and angered many Nigerians.

Although the United States did not press as hard as some would have liked, U.S. relations with Nigeria during the Abacha years were worse than with any other regional power, except for Iran. However, that all appears to have changed with the DEMOCRATIC TRANSITION in Nigeria. Its return to democracy was celebrated around the world, and Nigeria was brought back into the fold. In 1999 the State Department identified Nigeria as one of four democratic "priorities" for the United States (along with Indonesia, the Ukraine, and Colombia). The United States wants a moderate ally in the region and recognizes that Nigeria is a regional powerhouse essential to any international effort to stabilize the region. Since the debacle in Somalia, the slogan "African solutions for African problems" has become popular. The Clinton administration argued that by helping Nigeria, we are helping ourselves. There are certain problems in Africa that the United States cannot ignore, and one convenient compromise is to promote Nigeria's role as a regional peacekeeper, since it is cheaper to train and equip Nigerian troops than it is to send U.S. forces.

President Obasanjo also wants Nigeria to be recognized as West Africa's unrivaled military leader. But he needs the international community to pay for his country's peacekeeping services in Sierra Leone and Liberia (which cost Nigeria heavy casualties and an estimated $8 billion over the last decade). The United States has pledged more than $50 million toward that effort, dramatically increasing the military assistance it provided Nigeria. Several hundred U.S. troops trained 3,000 Nigerians, to serve under UN command in Sierra Leone. Since its return to democracy Nigeria has recently become a major recipient not only of U.S. military aid, but also of U.S. economic assistance. In terms of trade, Nigerian goods such as cocoa and cotton will have duty-free access to U.S. markets under the Africa Growth and Opportunity Act. This is welcomed in Nigeria, but thus far the United States has not taken the more significant step of canceling the country's bilateral debt, or pushing international financial institutions to do the same. Most Nigerians are eager for debt relief, and they want to be sure that the money saved goes to those who need it most, not to those who are now in power.

As President Obasanjo has admitted, the new democracy is under stress. From a U.S. perspective, the north-south conflict has sometimes taken the guise of a PROXY WAR, as young Muslims who favor posters of Osama bin Laden fight Christians waving tee shirts with U.S. flags. When Obasanjo expressed his support for the U.S. war on terrorism, some Nigerian Muslims organized a protest. For many dispossessed Nigerians and people around the world, bin Laden is a hero—or at least not the monster most Americans see. Many Nigerians, especially Muslims, are horrified by the how the U.S. sanctions on Iraq have hurt the Iraqi people. They resent what they consider to be U.S. favoritism toward Israel. Some Nigerians even go as far as to applaud the attacks on the United States as "the work of God," so that Americans can begin to get a sense of the suffering of others.[16] Such sentiments are disturbing for many Americans to hear, but unless the United States manages to change the way it is viewed in much of Nigeria and elsewhere, the democracies the United States says it cares so much about could be undermined.

Case Study: Zimbabwe

As mentioned in Chapter 13, it could be argued that the United States has been on the wrong side of history in much of southern Africa. During the Cold War the United States at various times directly and indirectly supported white governments in the region, for economic as well as strategic reasons. U.S. paranoia that Africans were procommunist became a self-fulfilling prophecy, as black nationalists had nowhere but the Soviet Union and China to turn. This did not make for an auspicious start to relations between the United States and the new government of Zimbabwe. Although the United States welcomed Zimbabwe's independence in 1980 with a significant aid package, relations between the two countries cooled quickly. This difficult relationship fell to its lowest point in the mid-1980s and again at the turn of the twenty-first century. At times the Zimbabwe-U.S. relationship has been marked by outright hostility.

Yet despite his Marxist rhetoric, in the early years of his rule Robert Mugabe defied skeptics and managed to create in Zimbabwe something of a success story. Mugabe was willing to compromise his socialist principles and followed a pragmatic course, resisting militant demands. Agricultural production was impressive, and the government promoted a policy of racial reconciliation. To the shock and dismay of whites, who had predicted that the country would go down the tubes without their leadership, Zimbabwe continued to be a strategic asset in southern Africa, an anchor or force of stability in the region.

However, Zimbabwe-U.S. relations could be described as a train wreck waiting to happen. At independence, Zimbabwe was eager to assert itself in international forums. As an aspiring leader of the third world in the Non-Aligned Movement (NAM) and as one of the "frontline states" opposed to the racist government in South Africa, Zimbabwe was determined to shape its own policy. The government had taken an outspoken stance in criticizing U.S. policy, especially U.S. policy on apartheid South Africa. From Mugabe's point of view, not only was the United States failing to support the black majority in its efforts to oust the racist government, but it was again collaborating with the racists. In a variety of well-publicized speeches, Mugabe denounced U.S. policy as hypocritical, asking why the United States wasn't sanctioning the apartheid regime when it was willing to use sanctions to promote change in Nicaragua, Poland, and Libya. Over time, the rhetoric became more hostile, as the Mugabe government accused the United States of STATE-SPONSORED TERRORISM, and of "international bullyism," for supporting rebels in Angola, Mozambique, and elsewhere.

Many Westerners were offended by Mugabe's outspokenness. What was viewed as anti-Americanism was too much for the conservative Reagan administration. The last straw, though, came when Zimbabwe indicated that it would vote its own conscience at the UNITED NATIONS on issues important to the United States. In an attempt to force Zimbabwe back into line, in 1983 the United States slashed foreign aid to the country from $75 million a year to $45 million. After a Zimbabwean diplomat vented his anger on former president Jimmy Carter, aid to Zimbabwe was frozen in 1986. In both these cases, Mugabe demonstrated a character trait that defines him today. Ever defiant, he is notoriously resistant to Western pressure. In the 1980s Mugabe described the

U.S. policy as tantamount to blackmail. Swearing that Zimbabwe would be no one's puppet, Mugabe famously proclaimed that Zimbabwe "would rather be poor, eat grass, and be sovereign."

Although relations improved and aid resumed in the years that followed, by 2001 Zimbabwe-U.S. relations were again at a low point. In response to Secretary of State Colin Powell's condemnation of Mugabe's "totalitarian methods" and his calls for free and fair elections, the Mugabe government answered that the United States must not try to impose leaders on Zimbabwe. The United States was told to leave Zimbabwe alone and mind its own business. In response, the U.S. Senate passed the Zimbabwe Democracy and Economic Recovery Act of 2001. Instead of general trade sanctions, which have been criticized as hurting the poor, these are targeted, personal sanctions. Much like the European Union, the United States imposed travel and economic sanctions against Mugabe, his family, and his associates, as well as other government officials. As political conditions worsened in 2002, the United States also considered barring from Zimbabwe aid flows and bilateral trade worth millions. President Mugabe characterizes such policies as racist, coming from a racist government that knows nothing of democracy. The Mugabe government describes its efforts as a continuation of the liberation struggle and reminds the world that Zimbabwe is nobody's colony. In this the president has received the sympathy of several members of the NAM and the South African Development Community (SADC), who worry that the United States has gone too far in interfering in the internal affairs of Zimbabwe. The United States is not the world's policeman, they argue.

Normally, the Bush administration would wholeheartedly agree with such a statement. Since September 11, the attention of the United States has been diverted elsewhere, and this has served to benefit the Mugabe government. Another result of the terrorist attacks on the United States is that the government of Zimbabwe, like the governments of some other countries, has found a way to exploit and manipulate the tragedy to its own political advantage. Since President Bush announced his war on terrorism, the Mugabe government has "jumped on the antiterrorism bandwagon." Mugabe says Zimbabwe is also in a war against terror—it is all the same (except that the ruling party has labeled its opponents as terrorists). The Zimbabwe government says it agrees with President Bush that anyone who in any way finances, harbors, or defends terrorists is a terrorist. Like the United States, Zimbabwe will make no distinction between terrorists and supporters of terrorists. In this "just war," any tactics, no matter how repressive, are warranted by the terrorist menace. All dissent is to be crushed as a righteous cause. The government has pushed through new "security laws" that go further than even those the Rhodesian government dared to undertake. These laws make "acts of insurgency, banditry, sabotage, and terrorism" punishable by death. In addition, it is a crime to speak poorly of or undermine the authority of the president—this is punishable by life imprisonment or even death. In the end, the Mugabe government argues that all it is doing is following the U.S. example. In protecting its citizens from the "scourge" of terrorism, it joins the Bush administration in arguing that in the name of security, some civil rights must be restricted.[17]

Case Study: Iran

With the more recent history of strained ties between Iranian leaders and the United States, it may be tempting to ignore the forty-year ties prior to the Islamic Revolution. Such an omission would be a mistake, though. In fact, the coziness of the Shah with Western leaders after World War II is indeed the source of much of the mistrust that has permeated the relationship since. The Iranians viewed the West, especially the United States, as double-talking supporters of a corrupt and antidemocratic regime. Iran long considered the United States its archenemy, and the animosity on both sides, especially after 1979, when American hostages were taken at the U.S. embassy in Tehran after President Jimmy Carter allowed the Shah to seek refuge in the United States, was fierce. Yet increasingly, neither side can ignore the other. Iran's access to oil in the Persian Gulf solidifies its status as a central player in Gulf affairs. Even though U.S. influence in Middle Eastern affairs may wane in the future, U.S. support of Israel, which Iran and other Muslim states find abhorrent, will continue to color bilateral and multilateral ties throughout the region.

Although chilled for over three decades, Iranian-U.S. relations have in recent years hinted at a thawing, although by no means will they completely normalize. President Muhammad Khatami has welcomed person-to-person exchanges and dialogue, but has been limited by other powerful forces in the Iranian government that continue to view the United States as the "Great Satan." Almost all commercial transactions between the United States and Iran are banned, under a 1995 executive order that was reinforced with the 1996 Iran-Libya Sanctions Act. This U.S. law imposes penalties on foreign firms that invest in either Iran or Libya, which both stand accused by the U.S. government of supporting terrorism. It is not only the clerics in Tehran who detest this action: Germany and other European governments have expressed their displeasure at this perceived U.S. meddling in their financial affairs.

The major concern from the U.S. perspective is Iran's ties to terrorism and weapons proliferation—the ostensible reason why Iran was included in Bush's "AXIS OF EVIL." Iran had been officially placed on the U.S. State Department's list of state supporters of terrorism in 1984. And because of U.S. antiterrorism laws, U.S. representatives to international financial institutions oppose Iranian applications for loans to assist in the country's debt relief.[18]

The United States alleges Iranian complicity in the bombing of U.S. Marine headquarters in Beirut (1983), and in the 1996 Khobar (Saudi Arabia) bombing of U.S. military barracks, which killed nineteen members of the U.S. Air Force. Iran has been implicated through its ties to the Shiite group Hezbollah. U.S. Attorney General John Ashcroft has claimed that "elements of the Iranian government . . . supported and supervised" Hezbollah's actions.[19] Yet Iran denies any involvement. Former president Bill Clinton in 1999 sent a secret letter to Mohammad Khatami, asking for help in solving the Khobar case.[20]

Iran's concerns with the United States are as deep-rooted as the contrary perspective. Iran views the United States as the source of most of its problems—there is much remaining anti-American sentiment tied to the CIA-engineered coup that toppled the popular government of Prime Minister Mohammad Mosaddeq in 1953, as well as U.S. support for the unpopular regime of Shah

Mohammed Reza Pahlavi. After the Islamic Revolution of 1979, hundreds of millions of dollars worth of military equipment, which the former Shah had ordered and paid for, was embargoed, and the financing was impounded. Permitting the ailing Shah to enter the United States was viewed by many ordinary Iranians as part of a larger, Western, anti-Iranian conspiracy to again restore a dynasty (as had been done in 1953). Iranian animosity only increased after President Ronald Reagan's decision to support Iraq during the 1980–1988 Iran-Iraq War, and continued while the United States attempted to maintain its influence in the region, which often necessitated hostile acts toward Iran. For example, in July 1988 a missile fired from a U.S. vessel shot down an Iranian plane flying to Dubai, and 250 Iranians were killed. Iranian leaders were also upset that the international community seemed to be taking little action against its neighbor, Iraq, which had killed tens of thousands of Iranians with chemical weapons. Iran alleged that German chemical firms were assisting Iraq with its production of weapons of mass destruction.[21] Iranian leaders felt they were being snubbed at the conclusion of the Gulf War, when they were excluded from postwar discussions, even though they tacitly assisted the effort to oust Saddam Hussein from Kuwait. Iranians also believe that the United States is unduly and unfairly hindering the development of the Iranian economy, which was already punished a great deal during the eight-year Iran-Iraq War. Even though Iran is the second largest oil producer in the Gulf today, U.S. containment efforts have hurt its energy sector. Iranian leaders feel that they are adrift in a hostile international environment that has been made so largely by efforts of the United States.

What is the outlook for the future? Iranian leaders will continue to be divided over how to accommodate Western power without losing their Islamic identity. Rapprochement with the United States will not be entered into lightly—and its likelihood was significantly hampered after Bush's inclusion of Iran in the "Axis of Evil." The statement has energized hard-liners within Iran and was taken as an affront to many ordinary Iranian citizens, who felt personally attacked—flag burnings and chants of "Death to America" returned in earnest after Bush's 2002 State of the Union address. To some, the inclusion of Iran was ironic because of the Islamic Republic's key role in the 2001 Bonn negotiations that established the Afghani interim government, when the U.S. and Iranian delegations "were practically hugging and kissing each other," according to one observer.[22] Within the United States, the debate between those who want to extend an olive branch to the reforming Iranian regime, and those who seek greater confrontation in order to isolate Iran's Muslim leaders, is likely to continue. Since 1980 the United States has lacked diplomatic ties with Iran; Pakistan represents Iranian interests in Washington, Switzerland represents U.S. interests in Tehran. Other Western powers, however, have normalized their political relations with Iran. In 1999 the United Kingdom (the last EU country without a diplomatic emissary to Iran) exchanged ambassadors with Iran. While it used to be forbidden for the Iranian media to discuss normalizing relations with the United States, this is no longer the case.[23] Under the Clinton administration, the United States lifted its trade ban against carpets and food products (notably pistachios, dried fruit, and caviar) from Iran in March 2000. Iran now purchases grain and medicines from the United States. U.S. companies are still forbidden from investing in Iran, as well as from buying oil or gas, although most use loopholes to do it anyway. Given increases in oil prices, many argue that now is a good time to normalize relations. Whether these limited commercial ties will help break through decades of animosity and distrust is yet to be seen.

Case Study: Turkey

In many ways, Turkey's primary ties (political, economic, security) are with the West. In some of these relations, especially Turkey's relations with the European Union, which continues to bar Turkey from membership even in the midst of expansion, progress is intermittent. Ties between Turkey and the United States, which are dominated by economic assistance and security concerns, are less simple to characterize.

The United States and Turkey have long had linkages, and their formal relationship was established in 1930. Under the spirit of the Truman Doctrine, since 1947 the United States has provided almost $20 billion in economic and military assistance to Turkey. For over fifty years, the U.S.-Turkish relationship has been based on Turkey's desire to foster good relations with the United States in return for Turkey's provision of military bases within reach of the tense regions of the Middle East. (Yet oddly, only three presidents—Dwight Eisenhower, George H. W. Bush, and Bill Clinton, have visited Turkey.) Turkey was a "frontline state" against the Soviet Union in the Cold War, and against Iraq in the Gulf War. It has been a member of the North Atlantic Treaty Organization (NATO) since 1952, in which Turkey serves as the "east anchor"—two NATO headquarters are in Izmir.[24] From Turkish ground, the United States has been able to exert pressure throughout the region. For example, the United States uses Incirlik air base in southern Turkey to patrol the no-fly zone in northern Iraq. Strategically today, the U.S. attempt to counter the resurgence of a "troublemaking Iran" has promoted a closer allied military relationship with Turkey.

Turkish-U.S. relations may be considered a situation of active engagement based on strategic considerations. Turkey's regional importance was on the rise after the end of the Cold War, and especially after the end of the Persian Gulf War of 1991. For this reason, the importance of Turkish-U.S. relations also increased. Turkish support during the Gulf War captured this nicely, even if, after the war, Turkish leaders were less enthusiastic about U.S. and British chastisement of Saddam Hussein. In many ways, Turkey is a pivotal state in the region—in terms of geography, population, and economic power. By stating such, we argue that substantive changes in Turkey can easily affect, possibly dramatically, surrounding states in the region. Turkey has long invited U.S. cooperation, especially militarily, as Turkey attempts to project its power beyond borders. In many ways, U.S. interests in Turkey have rotated around the question of central importance for the United States: How can Turkey, which is seen by many Europeans as a "barrier" to the Islamic world, help in containing its bellicose neighbors Iran and Iraq?[25]

Friction points between the United States and Turkey include human rights, especially the treatment of the Kurdistan Workers' Party (PKK) and the assessment of the Armenian genocide. Additionally, Turkey's attempts to normalize relations with two of its border states, Iraq and Iran, have raised U.S. ire, especially Turkey's support for a pipeline carrying Iranian gas to Turkey. The United States has also expressed concerns over Turkey's role in drug trade and drug trafficking, especially in the eastern and southeastern sections of the country, through which drugs from Iran pass en route to Europe. The United States offered aid (approximately $500 million) for Turkey's anti-drug-trafficking efforts, but it was rejected by Ankara because it had a clause on human rights improvement. Ankara was put in a particularly untenable position during the U.S.-led war in Afghanistan, and in the continuing war against terrorism. As a secular state with an Islamic majority, Turkey is particularly prone to criticism for supporting the United States in its "war against Islam," as some have perceived the war against terrorism to be. Nonetheless, the Turkish government remains guardedly allied with the United States in these efforts. It will not be an easy balancing act to maintain for long, though, and it is important to recognize Turkey's own fragile domestic situation. Two-thirds of Turks opposed the U.S.-led war in Afghanistan and Ankara's support of it. Many were concerned that the actions had the real potential of triggering war between Christians and Muslims.[26] Turkey's complexities were in the spotlight in the lead-up to the war in Iraq, as the Turkish parliament rebuffed the U.S. offer of billions of aid dollars in return for allowing U.S. troops to be stationed in the country. Because of Ankara's increasing commercial ties with Tehran—as well as its long-standing security concerns with this border state—Turkish leaders were particularly enraged by Bush's inclusion of Iran in the "Axis of Evil" designation. Similarly, while the Turks have concerns about the Saddam Hussein regime and its instability, they have made it clear that they do not support another war in the region, which they feel could likely spill over into other conflicts and destabilize much of the Middle East.

As with many of the Turkish issues we have discussed throughout this book, Turkish-Western relations are embedded in the country's ongoing efforts to define itself between the European and Islamic worlds. Turkey's international response—and regional activism—are predicated on competing domestic concerns to promote secularization, guard against Islamic extremism, and develop a larger role for the Turkish Republic in regional and international matters.

Case Study: China

The United States opened a formal diplomatic relationship with the People's Republic of China during the 1970s, under the leadership of staunchly anticommunist president Richard M. Nixon. Previously, the United States had supported the rival of the Chinese Communist Party, the Nationalist Party, which had been exiled to Taiwan after its defeat in 1949. Nixon's rationale for rapprochement with China, for which he faced much criticism, was that one could view the world in terms of a "strategic triangle" encompassing the United States, China, and the Soviet Union. Opening formal ties with China would exploit hostilities between the two communist giants and ultimately, it was hoped, limit the influence of communism throughout the world. After the 1970s, the U.S. relationship with China, like the relationship between most Western powers and China, became centered around its commercial strengths, especially the vast market that it provided for Western goods and services. This commercial focus continues, although its importance may wane as China exerts its growing strength in other arenas.

For the last twenty years, China-U.S. relations have had cycles of highs and lows, from Tiananmen Square (1989), to Bill Clinton's successful China tour (1998), to the bombing of the Chinese embassy in Belgrade (1999), to the collision of a Chinese jet with a U.S. Navy surveillance plane (2001). In this unfortunate encounter, which claimed the life of Chinese pilot Wang Wei, the U.S. crew was held for nineteen days, and three months elapsed before the plane was released. The relationship that began in the 1970s as a Cold War compromise is now facing the tensions of rising power and struggle for influence. More than 20 percent of Americans say they shun any products made in China, an increase of 5 percent since months prior to the spy-plane crisis.[27] Yet these swings in public opinion rarely last long, and after approval of Permanent Normal Trade Relations (PNTR) with China, commerce is only likely to increase.

Each U.S. president struggles with a neat and catchy way to characterize Sino-U.S. relations. For the past twenty years, both countries have been pursuing a policy of engagement, even though, at times for primarily domestic concerns, they both have hesitated to call it such. To some, there was a surprising revelation in the midst of the spring spy-plane crisis that highlighted some of the paradox in current China-U.S. relations. After the U.S. Army decided to outfit all soldiers in black berets, rather than reserving them for the elite Army Rangers, the government's supplier requested exemption from the long-standing Pentagon/Department of Defense rule that uniforms needed to be produced in the United States with U.S. materials. To the dismay of many, the supply company ordered berets from a British firm, which used a factory in China. After the spy-plane incident, this part of the contract was ditched.[28] There is, of course, more to the story than just China-U.S. relations. Bilateral ties collided with army pride (challenging the view that only the elite should wear black berets), as well as the economic interests of Canadian and British firms.

As we discussed above, Beijing had much to say in response to Bush's 2002 State of the Union address, which it perceived as arrogant, self-interested, and at the heart of Washington's HEGEMONIC impulses. Beijing (along with South Korea) argues that the address was particularly irresponsible given ongoing discussions with North Korea, a country that has now been put on the defensive. Similarly, both countries find fault with the Bush administration's insistence on "no negotiation" with North Korea, even after they restarted their nuclear development program. Similarly, Beijing has made it very clear to the United States that it will not support a U.S.-dictated regime in Afghanistan, nor an enlarged role for the United States in Central Asia, China's own backyard.

In the future, it is likely that Sino-U.S. tensions will continue, as the world's strongest power and the most likely country to rival that unchallenged power continue to bump elbows (and spy planes). Chinese suspect that the United States is determined to limit the development of their country and influence; this belief is based in U.S. efforts to arm Taiwan, and other perceived challenges to Chinese sovereignty, including meeting with Tibetan leaders in the halls of the White House. Yet China's status as a tremendous trading partner is the focal point of most of its bilateral ties, and its U.S. relations are not much different. But how long trade can continue to gloss over important differences between the two, and perhaps more important, how a financial/trade showdown may repair itself, remain to be seen. China's leaders (and society) are increasingly assertive in the global front, and how the dominant world power accommodates these changes will have much impact on China's future actions.

Case Study: Indonesia

Indonesia's ties with the Western world have long been strained. Some of this derives from Indonesia's experience with the Dutch and its prolonged fight for acceptance as an independent state. As a founder of the Non-Aligned Movement in the 1960s, Indonesia's leaders positioned the country to be a voice largely independent of the West, and indeed, sometimes in opposition to it. The official policy line espoused Indonesia's "free and active" foreign policy. The latter part of the Sukarno era was very anti-Western and specifically anti-American. After the 1965 anticommunist coup, the United States cultivated a close relationship with Suharto's Indonesia, viewing it as a regional stronghold against communism. Yet Western powers maintained a cozy relationship with Suharto at great cost: ignoring human rights atrocities and propping up a military regime, all in the name of regional stability.

In the post–Cold War period, the inconsistencies of the Indonesian-U.S. relationship have come to the surface, and have been exacerbated by instability throughout the archipelago. Throughout the decades of the Suharto regime, the United States supported a government known to be obliterating human rights. The U.S. and other governments worked to maintain stability, often at any cost. This included pledging financial assistance, although with strings attached.

Since the devastating economic and consequent social and political collapse in 1997–1998, the focus of most Western powers' relations with Indonesia has been to promote stability. The United States and Britain have been major players in this regard, as has Indonesia's regional neighbor, Australia. It has been difficult, however, to craft a coherent policy in the face of the multifaceted crises in Indonesia since this period. From 1998 to 2001, Indonesia had four presidents at the helm, each with a tenuous hold on state power. Indonesia's status as the world's fourth most populous country, stretching geographically across strategic sea-lanes for communication and transport, helps cement its role as a regional dynamo, even in the midst of its struggles.

Political newcomer Megawati Sukarnoputri stepped into office in the summer of 2001 with more than a handful of domestic challenges. Her task became even more difficult after the September 11 attacks and the U.S.-led war in Afghanistan. As the leader of the state with the world's largest Islamic population, her support of Washington (she was one of the first world leaders to meet with Bush after September 11 in a prescheduled visit) rankled many Indonesian citizens. Many viewed her initially unqualified support of U.S. efforts to be blasphemous against the Islamic people. This was seen to be particularly egregious because both her predecessor (Abdurrahman Wahid) and her vice president (Hamzah Haz) are closely allied with a coalition of influential Islamic political parties. U.S. efforts to encourage Indonesian authorities to detain individuals with possible connections to Indonesian cells of Al-Qaida have been met with vigorous resistance, and discussion from Washington that Indonesia could be the next center of Osama bin Laden's organization has been met with defiance. The Bush administration is considering redirecting military aid to Indonesia—truncated by Congress because of Jakarta's human rights abuses—to "counterterrorism" aid, which may not be very welcomed by the Indonesian military. A general in the Indonesian forces made it clear that he will not accept money with strings attached, stating that Indonesia will not be "ordered around."[29]

Many Indonesians express doubt about the direction of world politics and the exclusion, as they see it, of voices from the third world. Indonesian society has often expressed skepticism toward GLOBALIZATION, using instead the term "*gombal*ization" in both public and private discourse. *Gombal* is the term for a piece of old cloth that is viewed as good enough only for dusting shoes or cleaning utensils.[30] There is great consensus within the country that former president Wahid signed the INTERNATIONAL MONETARY FUND's letter of intent in January 2000 because Washington imposed upon him. His successor, Megawati, has delicately tried to balance close relations with the West without provoking anger at home, a task that became all the more difficult after the war on terrorism began. To many Indonesians, George Bush and Tony Blair are waging war on Islam itself, and they are furious that the Indonesian president failed to challenge this action.

Now It's Your Turn

How do recent events complement or challenge the material presented in the case studies? If you were to brief a U.S. government delegation on the perceptions of a particular bilateral relationship between the United States and the third world, what issues and perspectives would you highlight? Do you believe that many Americans understand or can agree with some concerns expressed by people in the third world? Why or why not? How would you explain the animosity expressed in some corners of the world toward the United States? What do you think are the sources of the love/hate relationship between the Western and the non-Western world? If you had to outline a policy plan for future U.S. relations with one of our case studies, what would it look like? How would this proposal be different if you were to chart if from the perspective of a third world country?

Suggested Readings

Asia

Prashad, Vijay. *The Karma of Brown Folk.* Minneapolis: University of Minnesota Press, 2000. India and diaspora: nonfiction, examining the myth of South Asians as the "model minority" in the United States.

Latin America and the Caribbean

Dandicat, Edwidge. *Breath, Eyes, Memory.* New York: Soho, 1994. Haiti and the United States: fiction, a young Haitian immigrant's past haunts her as she tries to acclimate herself to her new home in the United States.

Powell, Patricia. *Me Dying Trial*. London: Heinemann, 1993. Jamaica and North America: fiction, the lives of three generations of Jamaican women as they pursue the American dream.

Middle East

Asayesh, Gelareh. *Saffron Sky: A Life Between Iran and America*. Boston: Beacon Press, 1999. Iran: nonfiction, struggle of a woman attempting to be accepted in her new life in St. Petersburg, Florida, without losing her Iranian cultural connections.

Halo, Thea. *Not Even My Name: From a Death March in Turkey to a New Home in America, a Young Girl's True Story of Genocide and Survival*. New York: Picador, 2000. Turkey: nonfiction, story of a Pontic Greek family who emigrated from Turkey to the West.

Siletz, Ari B. *The Mullah with No Legs*. Yarmouth, UK: Intercultural Press, 1992. Iran: short stories written by an Iranian American.

PART 5

CONCLUSIONS

22

Are We Living in a New Era?

Our world in the early twenty-first century is rife with potential conflicts as well as potential new alignments. Interactions between the governments, societies, cultures, and economies of the Western and non-Western world may very well chart whether this future follows a path of peace and prosperity or stagnation and decline. If there is one lesson that we have highlighted throughout the course of this book, though, it is that it will take an increased recognition of all of the world's peoples in order to craft any meaningful, lasting solutions to the current challenges we face.

Has September 11 changed everything? In UN SECRETARY-GENERAL Kofi Annan's speech to the World Economic Forum, he said that one of the lessons of the terrorist attack that has not received much attention is that we can't ignore inhumane conditions in the rest of the world. The economic and social problems of others have a direct impact on U.S. national security (and world security). Annan is joined by many others who argue that TERRORISM isn't the only scourge threatening world security. According to Oscar Arias, "Terrorism is one of many challenges to humanity, but the basic threats to world peace are poverty, inequality, illiteracy, disease, and environmental degradation."[1]

Fighting terrorism will require a multidimensional strategy, not just a defense strategy.[2] Sickness, for example, is closely related to political stability; countries with high infant mortality rates are more likely to fall into civil wars. The absence of political voice or economic opportunity serves as an "incubator" for terrorists. We should do whatever we can to reduce the number of "failed states," since such places (e.g., Somalia and Afghanistan) become havens for groups like Al-Qaida. As disastrous as U.S. policy in Somalia was, it would be a mistake to stay away from similar situations in the future. As former assistant secretary of state Susan Rice puts it, we must not leave them to rot.[3] Perhaps helping is smarter than running away. Maybe we just need to do a better job at it than we have in the past.[4]

The question can be raised in terms of foreign aid, which could be a much more effective instrument for change than it has been. Used in the proper way, foreign aid can be one of the best weapons against terrorism. The Bush administration says that it understands this argument, but its budget increased defense spending by $46 billion at the same time that foreign aid spending was increased by only $300 million (less than 1% of the defense increase). (Although Bush declared that he will ask Congress to increase it by 50 percent over the next few years, a year after September 11 Bush had only asked for an additional $300 million for foreign aid, and was limiting his attentions mostly to Afghanistan and Pakistan). With the Marshall Plan, the United States once recognized how poverty bred instability and that promoting the development of other countries was a national security issue for the United States. However, during the COLD WAR U.S. foreign aid was used to promote stability by propping up dictators—U.S. assistance to Indonesia's Suharto fits this mold precisely. The United States needs to remember the important role that aid can play in promoting stability, but this time it must not just use it to bribe authoritarians into helping in the war on terror. Already the United States appears headed back to the Cold War mindset, which rationalizes looking the other way when allies commit atrocities against their own people. Look what such a policy has bought the United States; it is still paying for cozying up to the Shah all those years. Now the biggest aid recipients are Pakistan, Uzbekistan, and Azerbaijan—it appears that narrowly defined national security interests are trumping human rights.

Kofi Annan contends that in its war on terror, the United States must also be concerned with the image it projects abroad. The United States claims to be leading the forces of the civilized world against "evil"—but is the United States "civilized"? For many people around the world, including some of its closest allies in the West, the United States has already lost the moral high ground with its self-righteous unilateralism. With President Bush's "AXIS OF EVIL" speech, the United States made clear its intent to broaden the war against terror. This has been done without consulting its allies, yet the United States persists even in the face of mounting criticism, declaring that it will "do what's right" even when it's unpopular. Yet many people who were horrified by the events of September 11 and who were quick to support the United States in its aftermath mistrust how the United States uses its military power. Some of its allies in Europe characterize the U.S. approach to terrorism as simplistic, absolutist, and unhelpful. The United States too quickly reduces all the problems of the world to terrorism (as it may be doing with Colombia: in February 2002 the Bush administration began framing U.S. policy there as being about defeating terrorism, with U.S. activities having crossed the line from counternarcotics to counterterrorism).

Particularly after September 11, Americans are astonished to find so much global anger directed against them. It is not unusual to hear people living in other countries express their sympathy for the victims but wonder if perhaps the United States didn't have it coming. For much of the world the United States is a bully that is full of big talk about human rights but, when it comes down to it, acts only in its own self-interest. Fidel Castro describes the U.S. war on terror as "a war of the old colonizers against the colonized of the past, of the most developed against the least developed, the richest against the poorest."[5] Some believe that the United States has a double standard when it comes to defining terrorism—especially in its embrace of the Ariel Sharon government of Israel.

World leaders such as Oscar Arias hope that the United States will seek justice, not revenge. That does not appear to many to be what is happening. The human rights of others have been pushed to the side in the interests of U.S.

security. However, according to Michael Ignatieff, respect for human rights is the best guarantee of security. Repression will only fuel violence and close off avenues for dialogue and peaceful change. Portraying Islam as a bogeyman that justifies undemocratic measures and the flaunting of international norms only hardens Islamic groups and radicalizes them while confirming all that they ever thought about the United States.[6]

As this book goes to press, the United States continues its war on terrorism. The government is reacting to what may well be the defining public event of our lifetimes. Given that, most U.S. citizens, at least, would probably answer that yes, everything has changed since September 11. Yet a more important question perhaps is one put forward by David Beckman, president of Bread for the World: "Is this a change-the-world moment?" That is one question we leave to you.

Acronyms

ABRI	Angkatan Bersenjata Republik Indonesia
ACRI	African Crisis Response Initiative
AD	Alliance for Democracy (Nigeria)
ANC	African National Congress
APRA	American Popular Revolutionary Alliance (Mexico)
ASEAN	Association of Southeast Asian Nations
ASG	Abu Sayyaf Group (Philippines)
CAN	Andean Community of Nations
CCP	Chinese Communist Party
CEDAW	Convention on the Elimination of All Forms of Discrimination Against Women
CIA	Central Intelligence Agency
CITES	Convention on International Trade in Endangered Species
CRC	Convention on the Rights of the Child
ECOMOG	ECOWAS Monitoring Group
ECOSOC	Economic and Social Council (UN)
ECOWAS	Economic Community of West African States
EPZ	export processing zone
ERPI	Insurgent People's Revolutionary Army (Mexico)
EU	European Union
EZLN	Zapatista National Liberation Army (Mexico)
FAO	Food and Agricultural Organization (UN)
FIS	Islamic Salvation Front (Algeria)
FPI	Islamic Defenders Front
FTAA	Free Trade Area of the Americas
FTZ	free trade zone
GATT	General Agreement on Tariffs and Trade
GDI	Gender Adjusted Development Index
GDP	gross domestic product
GEM	Gender Empowerment Measure
GNI	gross national income
GNP	gross national product
HDI	Human Development Index

HIPC	highly indebted poor country
HRC	Human Rights in China
IARF	International Association for Religious Freedom
IBRD	International Bank for Reconstruction and Development (World Bank)
ICBL	International Campaign to Ban Landmines
ICC	International Criminal Court
ICFTU	International Confederation of Free Trade Unions
ICJ	International Court of Justice (UN)
ICRC	the International Committee of the Red Cross/Red Crescent
IFI	international financial institution
IGO	international governmental organization
ILO	International Labour Organization
IMF	International Monetary Fund
IOC	International Olympic Comømittee
IPCC	Intergovernmental Panel on Climate Change
ISI	import substitution industrialization
KMT	Nationalist Party (China)
LDC	less developed country
LLDC	least less developed country
LRA	Lord's Resistance Army (Uganda)
MAD	mutual assured destruction
MDC	Movement for Democratic Change (Zimbabwe)
MKO	People's Mujahidin (Iran)
MNC	multinational corporation
MNLF	Moro National Liberation Front (Malaysia)
MOSOP	Movement for the Survival of the Ogoni People (Nigeria)
MRTA	Tupac Amaru Revolutionary Movement
MSF	Médecins sans Frontièrs
NAFTA	North American Free Trade Agreement
NAM	Non-Aligned Movement
NEPAD	New Partnership for African Development
NIC	newly industrializing country
NIDL	new international division of labor
NIEO	new international economic order
NIMBY	"not in my backyard"
NYM	Nigerian Youth Movement
OAS	Organization of American States
OAU	Organization of African Unity
OIC	Organization of the Islamic Conference
OPC	Odua People's Congress ö(Nigeria)
OPEC	Organization of Petroleum-Exporting Countries
P-5	permanent five members of the UN
PAN	National Action Party (Mexico)
PAP	People's Armed Police (China)
PAP	poverty alleviation program
PDI-P	Indonesian Democratic Party of Struggle

PDP	People's Democratic Party (Nigeria)
PKI	Communist Party of Indonesia
PKK	Kurdistan Workers' Party
PKO	peacekeeping operation
PLA	People's Liberation Army (China)
PLO	Palestine Liberation Organization
PNTR	Permanent Normal Trade Relations
PPP	purchasing power parity
PQLI	Physical Quality of Life Index
PRC	People's Republic of China
PRD	Party of Democratic Revolution (Mexico)
PRI	Institutional Revolutionary Party (Mexico)
RENETIL	Resistencia Nacional dos Estudantes de Timor-Leste
RPP	Republican People's Party (Turkey)
RSF	Reporteurs sans Frontièrs
RUF	Revolutionary United Front (Sierra Leone)
SADC	South African Development Community
SAP	structural adjustment program
QSEATO	Southeast Asia Treat Organization
SIN	National Intelligence Service (Peru)
SOE	state-owned enterprise
TINA	"there is no alternative"
UDHR	Universal Declaration of Human Rights
UDI	Unilateral Declaration of Independence
UNAMIR	UN Assistance Mission for Rwanda
UNCTAD	UN Conference on Trade and Development
UNDP	United Nations Development Programme
UNEP	UN Environment Program
UNHCR	UN High Commission(er) for Refugees
UNICEF	UN International Children's Fund
UNTAET	UN Transition Administration in East Timor
WHO	World Health Organization
WID	women in development
WMD	weapon of mass destruction
WTO	World Trade Organization
ZANLA	Zimbabwe African National Liberation Army
ZANU	Zimbabwe African National Union
ZANU-PF	Zimbabwe African National Union–Patriotic Front
ZAPU	Zimbabwe African People's Union
ZIPRA	Zimbabwe People's Revolutionary Army

Glossary

abertura   A Portuguese term borrowed from the Brazilian experience, describing a political opening that may or may not lead to democratization. *See* **political liberalization**.

absolute poverty   The term used by the United Nations to describe dire material hardship, a standard of living beneath human dignity. It is a crushing poverty in which people lack access to the basic necessities of life such as food, clean water, shelter, and healthcare.

accountability   A characteristic of democracy existing when government is held responsible for its actions; governments that are promoting accountability seek to control corruption not only by reducing the incentive to steal, but also by raising the costs and risks of official misconduct and demonstrating to the population that no one can violate the law with impunity.

acephalous society   A "headless society" in which there is no full-time executive; rather, groups of people are governed by committee or consensus. *See* **stateless society.**

amnesty   A pardon granted by governments to individual and often groups of offenders as a gesture of reconciliation, often during a transition or change of regime.

aspiration gap   Disparity between what is desired or hoped for and what can be attained. This concept helps us understand the consequences of unmet expectations.

austerity plan   Another name for a structural adjustment policy, denoting the hardship associated with implementing such measures.

authoritarianism   A nondemocratic political system in which the ruler depends on coercion rather than popular legitimacy to remain in power. Such systems are characterized by their abuse of human rights. Power is concentrated in the executive branch of government, and executives act with little if any interference from legislatures or judiciaries.

"Axis of Evil"   Phrase included in President George W. Bush's 2002 State of the Union address, labeling Iran, Iraq, and North Korea as threats to world peace due to their attempts to obtain nuclear, chemical, or biological weapons and their alleged support of terrorism.

bottom-up approach   Describes an approach to change or development when policies or projects are initiated and directed from the grassroots or masses.

bourgeoisie   Originally from the French word *bourg* for "market town," it became a prominent term of analysis in Marxist socialism, separating the working class (known as the proletariat) from the landowning merchant classes and capitalist entrepreneurs, known as the bourgeoisie. In the Marxist framework, it is the bourgeoisie who will be eliminated by class struggle to produce a classless, communist society.

Bush Doctrine   President George W. Bush's foreign policy approach following the terrorist attacks of September 11, 2001. He conceptually divided the world community into two categories—those who support terrorists versus those who fight terrorists. The doctrine may be summed up in his statement that "either you are with us, or you are with the terrorists." In many parts of the world, this simplification was rejected as self-serving and unreflective of the complexities of the twenty-first century.

cadre party   A type of political party dominated by personality-driven cliques and factional groupings that depends on local notables to choose and groom candidates. Cadre parties are recognized for their limited recruitment and are often found in states with limited franchise, or the right to vote. The term *cadre* has also been used to refer to the most dedicated members of a political party.

case study   A detailed examination of a particular phenomenon or institution (in this context, a state). A method that seeks to find and demonstrate causal connections by tracing them through a series of cases, which are then compared.

caudillo   A political strongman, often a member of the military.

Chapter VII   Reference to the section of the UN Charter that permits the Security Council to "order binding action, including economic sanctions and the use of armed force." It sets enforcement mechanisms to prevent or deter threats to international peace. So-called Chapter VII authority has been used often since the end of the Cold War to justify intervention in conflict or unstable circumstances.

civil society   Generally refers to voluntary social interactions between individuals that are independent of the government. Civil society organizations are commonly recognized as intermediaries between the government and the family. As a concept, civil society (also known as "public space") includes nongovernmental organizations, social movements, and professional associations.

class (of society)   A number of people or things grouped together. A group of people who are linked together because of certain things held in common, such as occupation, social status, or economic background.

cleavage   A socially supported division between groups in society who are significant enough to have forms of expression. Cleavages are often based on ethnicity, socioeconomic factors, or gender. Scholars have highlighted two dominant patterns of such divisions: Coinciding cleavages are clear and distinct, in which multiple competing viewpoints or points of division line up in clearly divided categories, presenting a situation that is more ripe for conflict. Crosscutting cleavages are mixed between and among various groups, producing an outcome in which cleavages are dispersed throughout society; therefore those seeking support from the population must appeal to a wider variety of groups.

clientelism Sometimes called a patron-client relationship, clientelism is a form of participation in which influential persons obtain the benefits of personal allegiance, sometimes in the form of votes or payoffs. The patron controls the allocation of resources, and the client is bound to the patron in a relationship of dependent loyalty.

Clinton Doctrine Centerpiece of policy associated with the presidency of William Jefferson Clinton, which holds that, in certain circumstances, human rights, especially the suppression of crimes against humanity, take precedence over a state's rights to sovereignty. Such ideas were articulated more commonly after the crises in Rwanda and Bosnia, but never consistently. Sometimes the concept is also referred to as the Annan Doctrine, in reference to UN Secretary-General Kofi Annan.

Cold War The period of intense U.S.-Soviet rivalry that ran from World War II until the dissolution of the Soviet Union in 1991. Although this antagonism was played out in many different ways across every part of the world, it is known as being "Cold" because, fearing nuclear catastrophe the two parties never engaged in direct military confrontations.

collective security The principle that aggression against one state is taken as an aggression against all. Agreement to collectively resist aggression against another is a founding idea of the United Nations. Collective security arrangements are pursued by states in the hope of deterring threatening action.

common external tariff A shared commercial policy coordinating the tax imposed on imports entering through any state that is part of a trade zone. A protectionist measure aimed at protecting the domestic producers of member states against foreign competition.

common market Allows for the free circulation of goods, services, and capital between member states.

comparative advantage Liberal principle that holds that efficiency is maximized through specialization in production.

comparative studies Seeks to comprehend the complexity of human experience by adopting an eclectic, multidisciplinary approach. Utilizes the comparative method to produce generalizations that describe, identify, and explain trends—and even predict human behavior. This approach identifies relationships and interactions between actors, as well as patterns of behavior, by making comparisons (of two or more countries or of one country over time) to find similarities and differences in experience.

comprador   The indigenous elite who dominate the economies and politics of many non-Western countries. They often enter into sweetheart deals with foreign interests—at great cost to the local majority.

consolidation   Said to exist when democracy has put down deep roots and is durable—when democracy "is the only game in town." Democracies become consolidated by becoming more inclusive, by respecting human rights, and by guaranteeing equal representation to minorities and other marginalized groups. Stability, citizen loyalty, and a widespread belief that the system is good are all signs of consolidation.

convergence   Said to be attained when less developed countries "catch up" with developed countries.

corporatism   Terminology describing relations between groups and political authority; government restricts the development and operation of independent organizations. In corporatist systems, society is divided by functions (such as unions, professional associations, etc.), and government attempts to coordinate society by balancing groups that must negotiate with government for legal or economic benefits.

corruption   Official misconduct or the abuse of power for private gain. A problem in both developed and less developed countries that has contributed to the breakdown of both military and civilian governments, as populations call for accountability and transparency.

cross-national analysis   A study comparing two or more countries in order to make larger generalizations.

cultural relativism   The view that worldwide there is no commonly held morality. Rather, human rights and other ethical issues vary depending on the group, and consequently, the promotion of any set of moral codes as somehow universal is misplaced and imperialistic.

Cultural Revolution   Formally called the Great Proletarian Cultural Revolution, a chaotic period in modern Chinese history, officially from 1966 to 1969, when Chairman Mao Zedong directed the Red Guards to attack officials to prevent the spread of capitalism and materialism. Many individuals (especially businesspeople and intellectuals) were sent to the Chinese countryside to "learn from the peasants" while others were sent to "reeducation" camps to have their problems rectified. Most analysts today argue that the chaos of the Cultural Revolution did not truly end until Mao's death in 1976.

customs union   A form of economic integration in which states agree to promote trade among members by eliminating tariffs and nontariff barriers, and to cooperate to protect their producers by setting a common tariff against nonmember states. *See* **common external tariff.**

delegative democracy   A political system that has an outward appearance of being democratic, and is more democratic than authoritarian. However, such systems are led by elites whose commitment to democracy is said to have limits. In delegative democracies, the executive claims to personify the nation's interests and therefore has the exclusive right to interpret them.

democracy (political) "Government by the people," existing in several variations and operating through different kinds of constitutional systems. A type of government or political system that is based on a decentralization of power and built on the principle of popular sovereignty: in democracies people choose their representatives, who compete for political office through free and fair elections held on a regular basis. Consequently, citizen participation and respect for civil liberties are integral to democracy, as citizens must have the freedom to hold political leaders accountable for their actions.

democracy dividend Popular expectation that after years of abuse, the transition to democracy will bring an economic expansion, an end to corruption, and an improved quality of life. There is usually much goodwill created by a democratic transition; however, this honeymoon is often short-lived and the resulting disillusionment is dangerous for fragile new democracies.

democratic institutionalization The process of crafting, nurturing, and developing democratic institutions to ensure participation, representation, accountability, respect for human rights, and so on. Institutionalization refers to the development of regularized processes; as democratic institutionalization occurs, "the rules of the game" become stabilized and formalized.

democratic transition A phase of political liberalization in which a political system is democratizing (opportunities for political participation and competition are expanded, free and fair elections are scheduled, and so on). Not every political liberalization results in a democratic transition and not all democratic transitions result in democracy—they can turn out many different ways.

deterrence Defense policy in which a country attempts to prevent attack by threatening credible retaliation. The logic of deterrence is that an initiating action will cause mutual suicide. The greatest deterrents are considered to be nuclear weapons—the mere possession of nuclear weapons is believed sufficient to deter an enemy, because unless a country's entire nuclear arsenal could be wiped out by a first strike, the destruction caused by the inevitable retaliation would be too great a price to pay.

development There is little agreement on how best to describe development. The UN defines political development as "the achievement of a stable democracy that promotes the economic well-being of its citizens in an equitable, humane, and environmentally concerned manner." Some identify it as a process associated with increasing humans' choices and opportunities. Development is now widely recognized as promoting material and immaterial forms of well-being; it is associated with improved living standards, although it rests on political participation, human security, and is concerned with the distribution of and access to resources. Often confused with "growth," development should be understood as both a process and an end.

"development with a human face"   Poor economic performance in countries adopting structural adjustment programs and highly visible antiglobalization protests combined to push even its most ardent advocates to undertake a broad reassessment of the neoliberal model. As a result the International Monetary Fund and other international financial institutions pledged to take the hardest edges off of the still-prescribed economic reforms. "Development with a human face" describes the resulting initiatives, such as poverty alleviation programs (PAPs), which are aimed at helping countries construct safety nets to carry them through the period of adjustment.

devotee party   Type of political party that is dominated by a charismatic leader.

disintegration   When political reconfiguration spirals out of control. Divides are aggravated by internal and external demands for change, the military is unwilling or unable to prevent a breakup, and states are incapable of meeting their challenges. Weak states are said to "implode"—to decay and collapse from within.

displaced persons   People who are forced to flee their homes but who have not crossed internationally recognized borders. The numbers of internally displaced people are often higher than the official count of refugees, and considered to be more reflective of the magnitude of human suffering.

divide and conquer   A common means of colonial conquest in which a usurping power sets two parties against each other, aggravates tensions to the point that they bleed each other dry, and then moves into the vacuum. Also known as "divide and rule."

due process   The expectation that certain procedures must always be followed in making policy; guarantees of fair legal procedures designed to protect the rights and liberties of individuals.

economic liberalization   Neoliberal economic reforms that dismantle government controls and promote opening up economies to foreign trade and investment. Also known as "market reforms."

efficacy   An attitude about one's competence to effect change; a perception of ability or the sense that one's participation can make a difference. A sense of efficacy is an important factor in the decision to be engaged in public affairs—people with a strong sense of efficacy are more likely to be active in civic life than those who believe their actions would be worthless. The antonym of *efficacy* in this sense would be *alienation*.

electoral democracy   A political system that allows for elections, but offers little else in the way of political reform.

elite revolution   Special type of revolution that is rapid and swift, with minimal participation by those outside of the initiating core and limited violence. Also known as a "revolution from above."

elites   Those who hold more power than others, whether cultural, political, economic, social, or otherwise. According to elite theory, elites are always outnumbered by those ostensibly holding less power, oftentimes referred to as the masses. Elites possess certain advantages, of wealth, privilege, education, training, status, political power, and the like.

empire   The largest, most complex form of state organization, distinguished from a chiefdom by the size of the territories and the populations it controls. Empires are usually vast and impose a centralized government or single sovereign over a collection of different communities or nations. Empires often dominate regional and international trade; known for their large militaries, they frequently amass great riches through conquest and demands for tribute.

essential functions   The most basic duties expected of elected governments, such as collecting taxes, enforcing laws, designing policies, and being responsive to the majority.

exceptionalist   A belief or behavior that demonstrates the view that one's group is different from the norm, and therefore above the rules by which others are supposed to abide. An exceptionalist view of a group or event emphasizes the singular, unique qualities of whatever is being examined—making it seem that any particular circumstance is difficult to compare to another.

export processing zone (EPZ)   A special trade area established by less developed countries to attract foreign investment. In the hopes of creating jobs, obtaining technology transfers, and other benefits, EPZs offer low or no taxes and guarantee cheap, docile labor and minimal government regulation or interference with regard to health or environmental codes or the repatriation of profits.

extraterritoriality   Imposing one's rules and laws outside of one's own sovereign territory. Extraterritoriality was invoked during the colonial period; now, many developing countries view the United States as attempting to return to this state of affairs by insisting that foreign countries abide by U.S. laws or policies.

fallacy of electoralism   The mistake of focusing on elections as "proof" of democracy and ignoring other political realities.

fatwa   A religious judgment issued by Muslim clerics.

formal sector   The "above-ground" part of the economy, calculated into gross domestic product (as opposed to the "informal sector").

founding elections   The first elections marking a democratic transition, symbolizing a departure from authoritarianism.

Four Tigers   Hong Kong, Taiwan, Singapore, and South Korea—distinguished by their record of strong growth rates and their shared reliance on state capitalism.

General Agreement on Tariffs and Trade (GATT)   International economic organization formed to help liberalize and manage global trade after World War II. Established to promote the rules of conduct for free trade (such as lowering tariff rates and discouraging protectionist policies) and to provide a forum for the resolution of trade disputes. GATT was eventually overwhelmed by the growth in the volume of world trade and was replaced with the World Trade Organization (WTO) in 1995.

General Assembly An organ of the United Nations in which each member state is represented; it is primarily a deliberative organization centered around debate and discussion. Some matters, including those on peace and security and the admission of new members, require a two-thirds majority; others are adopted by a simple majority. Decisions of the General Assembly have no legally binding force on governments, but they represent the weight of world opinion.

globalization Describes the world's increasing interconnectedness, particularly in regard to communications, economies, and cultures, and associated with faster and greater international flows of trade, investment, and finance as well as migration, cultural diffusion, and communication—more specifically, a process describing the spread of capitalism and "modernization" worldwide. Alternatively viewed as a positive force that promotes development and brings the world closer together, or as a negative phenomenon contributing to worsening underdevelopment and the homogenization of the world's cultures.

grassroots-based project An initiative designed, implemented, and controlled by local communities. Often lauded for being not only more democratic in principle but more effective in operation. *See* **bottom-up approach.**

greenhouse effect An increasingly substantiated but not universally accepted theory that the earth is experiencing a gradual rise in temperatures and that this is due to human activity. This global warming is associated with buildup of "greenhouse gases" (most notably carbon dioxide), which are released by the burning of fossil fuels. A layer of these waste gases collects in the upper atmosphere, so that instead of escaping into the outer atmosphere, the sun's heat is trapped, warming the earth (much like the glass traps heat in a greenhouse). Although scientists continue to disagree about the rate of warming, many highly respected climatologists expect that if trends continue, the greenhouse effect will contribute to massive alternations in climate, which will contribute to a variety of consequences, some of them near cataclysmic.

growth A summation of economic performance referring to an increase in the volume of trade or economic output of a country, measured by gross domestic product (GDP), gross national income (GNI), or gross national product (GNP). Growth is usually a key indicator of a healthy economy, measured against the previous performance of each national economy, not a single worldwide standard (e.g., a 10 percent growth rate in a small economy, albeit impressive, actually indicates a smaller amount of absolute economic activity than a single-digit growth rate in a larger economy).

guerrilla From the Spanish, literally "little war." Guerrillas are loosely organized nonuniformed combatants, often small in number. Guerrilla tactics are mobile and swift, incorporating the element of surprise with sabotage, hit and run, and ambush, all in violation of conventional laws of warfare.

hegemon A strong, controlling force that attempts to impose its preferences on others. Used in discussions of international affairs to describe the dominance of a specific country. If the nineteenth century was the period of British hegemony, the post–Cold War era is one of U.S. hegemony, with the United States being the sole remaining superpower.

highly indebted poor country (HIPC)   A country falling into this category is eligible for a program of debt relief if it makes the required neoliberal economic reforms.

human security   Defined as the absence of structural violence, which is understood as widespread poverty and other forms of economic, social, and environmental degradation. Human security is a new but increasingly recognized understanding of security that goes far beyond issues of armaments and territorial security. It addresses individual and collective perceptions of present and potential threats to physical and psychological well-being.

identity   The collective aspect or characteristics by which a person or group is known. Humans have multiple identities that they choose to emphasize, depending on context. Common identities uniting people in action include race, class, gender, and region.

ideology   The belief systems of individuals and groups; a linked set of ideas that describe the world, help people understand their role within society, and arouse them to take action, whether to change or preserve the existing situation.

import substitution industrialization (ISI)   A development strategy especially popular in the mid–twentieth century that seeks to diversify economies and lessen the dependence of less developed countries (LDCs) on foreign imports of manufactured goods. It encourages industrialization headquartered within LDCs by subsidizing and protecting local producers from foreign competition.

informal sector   Also known as the "informal economy," the informal sector is a shadow economy comprising semilegal or illegal activities that are unreported, unregulated, and untaxed—and therefore not included in the calculation of a country's gross domestic product. Because it is so often the case that their opportunities in the formal economy are limited, women compose a large number of informal-sector workers.

integration   A process that increases the quantity and quality of interconnectedness between countries through small or large steps; promotes cooperation between countries based on common security or economic concerns. For example, the European Union began in the 1950s as an agreement on coal and steel and over the years has moved increasingly toward the creation of a single market—the world's largest.

interdependence   A political and economic relationship based on mutual vulnerability between two countries, each of which is sensitive to what happens in the other. The term implies that even developed countries are bound to less developed countries by interdependence, as opposed to those who characterize the relationship as one of dependence—largely the dependence of less developed countries on developed countries.

international economic system   The network of world trade, which is based on the remains of what was known as the Bretton Woods system. Formed in the post–World War II period, this international economic system has been dominated by developed countries under U.S. leadership. Bretton Woods gave lip service to Liberal economic policies such as open economies and free trade. However, even its most ardent advocates routinely practiced protectionist policies that have hamstrung the development of less developed countries. Consequently, critics of this system argue that it is structured to benefit the already rich, to the detriment of the poor.

international financial institution (IFI)   An organization that governs fiscal matters within and between states. Most IFIs (such as the International Monetary Fund and the World Bank) promote the neoliberal agenda and are run by developed countries—with very little input from the less developed countries over which they have tremendous influence.

international governmental organization (IGO)   An organization with two or more member states that may serve as a forum for discussion to promote cooperation on either regional or functional (issue-oriented) matters. The largest IGO is the United Nations; however, IGOs can be very limited in scope and membership as well.

International Monetary Fund (IMF)   Central to the world financial system, this international organization is dedicated to promoting market economics. Established soon after the 1944 Bretton Woods conference, the IMF is a global lending agency originally created to aid in the postwar recovery of Europe and Japan. Rich countries continue to dominate the IMF, which operates under a weighted voting system based on the amount of money members donate to the organization. The IMF is charged with several responsibilities, including the stabilization of exchange rates and promotion of fiscal conservatism. One of its most important roles is to assist with balance of payments problems, and in this capacity it serves as an international credit bureau—for countries. (Just as is the case with individuals, countries are assigned credit ratings. If the IMF blackballs a country, it will have a very difficult time obtaining credit—from the IMF, or from any IFI, for that matter. On the other hand, in order to remain in good stead with the IMF, countries must accept conditionality, or demonstrate their willingness to submit to neoliberal economic reforms such as those promoted by structural adjustment programs.)

international political economy (IPE)   The study of the interrelationship between politics and economics at the international and transnational levels; examines how international politics affects the world's economies and how economics affects international political relationships. Advocates of this approach contend that an understanding of IPE is necessary since economic factors shape most areas of political life. IPE focuses on issues such as world markets, global financial institutions, and multinational corporations.

intifada   From the Arabic, meaning "shivering" or "shaking off." The term was first applied to the Palestinian uprising against Israeli occupation from 1987 to 1993, in protest of killings near a Palestinian settlement. Another intifada began in the fall of 2000.

irredentist war A form of violent interstate conflict stemming from a nation's efforts to redraw political boundaries to include territory considered its homeland or to unite with its people living on the other side of a border.

jihad An Arabic word signifying "struggle." Although it has recently been taken to narrowly mean a "holy war," its more accurate meaning encompasses the internal struggle faithful Muslims undergo in their attempts to contend with the challenges facing them. Jihad also encompasses the requirements for a permissible and legitimate war, similar to other faith traditions' teachings on justifiable combat.

legitimacy The popular perception on the part of large numbers of people that the government, its leaders, and its policies are valid, right, just, and worthy of support. A legitimate regime is not necessarily the same as a legal regime, nor does it mean that a regime is democratic. A political regime is legitimate when it is accepted by the majority of its citizens as right and proper enough to be obeyed in most instances. Legitimacy can be achieved through all sorts of means, including propaganda, clientelism, and coercion.

legitimate trade The trade of raw materials in Africa, which Europeans began to pursue more ardently to serve the needs of industry. For a variety of reasons, by the early nineteenth century the "legitimate trade" had displaced the "illegitimate trade" (the term abolitionists had used for the slave trade) along the African coast.

liberal democracy A political system that has undertaken (and continues to undertake) comprehensive political reform in which democratic institutions are routinized and internalized and civil and political rights are protected—so much so that democracy is said to be "consolidated."

liberation theology A movement that started within the Catholic Church in Latin America and has spread to other Christian churches and regions of the world; an action-oriented ideology that promotes social justice through local activism. Liberation theology teaches that the cause of poverty is capitalism, and that the Church should lead a revolution to establish governing systems that will redistribute wealth, end all forms of imperialism, and promote democracy. It was especially popular throughout the 1980s, but has faced opposition because of its use of Marxist revolutionary ideals.

mandatory system Territories taken from Germany and its allies after World War I were administered under Article 22 of the Charter of the League of Nations. The League appointed states such as Britain, France, and South Africa to help prepare the mandates for their eventual independence, yet in many cases the mandatory system was considered no more than "a fig leaf for colonialism." Later, when the mandates became trust territories administered by the United Nations, the mandatory powers were held somewhat more accountable for their actions.

maquiladora A subsidiary of a multinational corporation that assembles imported parts and exports manufactured goods; originally the assembly plants that have proliferated along the U.S.-Mexican border since the implementation of the North American Free Trade Agreement (NAFTA). However, the term is now sometimes used to describe such enterprises wherever they exist in the non-Western world.

mass party   A type of political party that attempts to be as inclusionary as possible, oftentimes attempting to incorporate less politically engaged individuals and groups into the political process. Mass parties are marked by a formal nationwide structure, and are used to mobilize large groups of voters.

masses   Relative to the elites, the masses are those who lack power and influence and who always outnumber the elites; the vast majority of the population in a country tend to be lumped into the category of the "masses" or the "common people."

mercantilism   A precapitalist stage of development marked by accumulation of capital and accomplished through trade and plunder on a worldwide scale. This aggressive economic policy was the guiding force behind the conquest of many areas; it provided the capital base for Europe's industrialization. In its more contemporary form, mercantilism describes the situation when a power seeks commercial expansion to achieve a surplus in its balance of trade.

military professionalism   Critical to the survival of democracies, this term refers to the military's depoliticization. Where it exists, coup d'états are unthinkable, as the military recognizes the supremacy of civilian rule and views itself as serving civilian government.

mother country   Another name for a colonizing country; its use denotes the exclusive ties that bound the colonies to the mother country much like an umbilical cord. Also refers to the parental role the colonizers portrayed themselves as playing in the non-Western world.

multinational corporation (MNC)   A business enterprise headquartered in one country (usually a developed country) with activities abroad stemming from direct foreign investment located in several countries. As MNCs conglomerate and form near-monopolies, international trade is increasingly dominated by a handful of corporations. Enormously powerful because they are so flexible, they can readily move capital, goods, and technology to fit market conditions.

multinational state   A political unit of organization that includes two or more ethnic or national groups. Largely due to colonialism's arbitrary boundaries, a nation may or may not reside within the political boundary of a state, thereby producing a multinational state.

nation-state   An ideal-type term that combines two concepts—a nation is considered to be a group of people who recognize a similarity among themselves because of common culture, language, or history. Nations often but do not always coincide with political boundaries of states, thereby producing multinational states. A state is considered to be a political entity with legal jurisdiction and physical control—an internationally recognized government.

nationalism   A set of political beliefs that center around the shared sense of characteristics attributable to a group of people known to each other as a nation.

Nationalism has been used to promote the interests and needs of a particular group of people, and has been a particularly strong rallying force, both uniting and dividing groups.

neocolonialism   A term used to describe the condition from which many non-Western states today suffer, as they continue to be indirectly controlled by their former colonizers or other developed countries; said to exist because less developed countries operate under so many of the constraints of colonialism that they are considered independent only in name.

neoliberalism   The contemporary version of procapitalist liberal economic strategy, which holds that all benefit from an open economy and free trade, or the unencumbered movement of goods and services between states. It is the dominant view held by the governments of developed countries and most international financial institutions, such as the World Bank and the International Monetary Fund. Neoliberals fervently believe that globalization is a positive force and that the current international economic system based on free competition can work for all if countries will just embrace it. Most third world countries then must adopt the proper reforms, promote openness, and prepare for a period of austerity so as to get their economic houses in order.

new international division of labor (NIDL)   Whereas the "old" international division of labor described the relationship between developed and less developed countries, with the former as producers of manufactured goods and the latter as producers of raw materials, use of the term *NIDL* points to how the product cycle has shifted, so that more less developed countries are moving into manufacturing, while developed countries go on to economies dominated by the service sector.

new international economic order (NIEO)   A comprehensive attempt by less developed countries to reform the international economic system. Debated in the 1960s and 1970s at the UN Conference on Trade and Development (UNCTAD) and other forums, the Group of 77 called for a series of changes (from increased foreign aid, to a code of conduct for multinational corporations, to elaborate efforts to stabilize the price of exports from less developed countries) aimed at "leveling the playing field" of opportunities for development. Although some of the proposals continue to be discussed today, only marginal changes have come of the NIEO so far.

newly industrializing country (NIC)   Also known as a new industrial economy or an emergent economy. NICs are countries such as China, Mexico, South Korea, and Taiwan that in the last few decades have shifted from agrarian to increasingly industrial economies, due largely to strong state intervention and investment by multinational corporations. The high productivity of the cheap labor force in these countries has enabled the NICs to compete aggressively in the international market with developed countries, effectively driving their textile and other sectors out of business. *See* **Four Tigers.**

Non-Aligned Movement (NAM)   Formed in 1961 in opposition to the polarizing tendencies of the Cold War, the NAM is an alliance of over 100 countries that shunned military alliances and coalitions with other states—especially the dominant powers during the Cold War, during which time the NAM advocated the neutrality of its members. Prime Minister Nehru of India, and Presidents Tito of Yugoslavia, and Nasser of Egypt, founded the movement as a vehicle for non-aligned countries to come together to solve mutual problems without benefit of military alliance. A summit is held every three years.

nongovernmental organization (NGO)   A private association of voluntary membership that works together to accomplish set goals. The numbers of NGOs in the world exploded throughout the 1980s, and continue to swell in numbers. General examples of NGOs include universities, churches, and civic and professional associations. Increasingly at the global level, the "on-the-ground" competency of NGOs is being recognized in policy- and decisionmaking. One of the foremost examples of the partnership between NGOs and international organizations was the Ottawa Treaty, which was born of the efforts of the International Campaign to Ban Landmines.

parliamentary system   A democratic constitutional system in which citizens select members of parliament and executive authority is dependent on parliamentary confidence. Variously characterized as flexible and unstable, gridlock is much less likely in a parliamentary than in a presidential system. Since the majority party in parliament selects the executive, the prime minister can usually be confident that his or her initiatives will be warmly received by the legislature. In a parliamentary system, new elections are called by the prime minister, and can be called at any time (within a certain time frame). As opposed to presidential systems, effective executives can be kept in power indefinitely. However, the system is self-correcting for executive abuse, since the legislative branch can censure and rid itself of an errant executive with much more ease than the painstaking process of impeachment necessary in a presidential system.

party system   Referencing the collection of political parties in a given state or region—analysts often distinguish between single-party systems and multiparty systems, based on the number of active and viable parties in the regime. For example, a one-party-dominant system is one in which there are political alternatives but in which a single party exercises a near monopoly on power, either due to the lack of alternatives or because of the overwhelming support of citizens. A multiparty system is one in which there are two or more major contenders for power.

patrimonialism (or neopatrimonialism)   A form of governance that exists when the ruler treats the state as his or her own personal property. Appointments to government office are assigned on the basis of loyalty to the ruler, who plays the role of a benevolent but stern parent, often through a mixture of co-optation and repression.

patron-client relationship   A method of co-optation based on a relationship of reciprocity, in which the powerful patron (a leader, party, agency, or government) allocates resources to his or her clients (the people) with the expectation that the clients will pledge to the patron their political loyalty. Also known as "clientelism."

peacekeeping operation (PKO) A noncombat military operation mandated by the UN Security Council and sent into conflict areas in an attempt to promote a peaceful transition. PKOs consist of outside forces acting on the consent of all major belligerent parties. Their tasks range from keeping apart hostile parties to helping them peacefully work together. PKOs have monitored cease-fires, created buffer zones, and helped to create and sustain nascent political institutions. PKO forces are often distinguished by their famous "blue berets."

personalist regime Also known as a personally appropriated state—an authoritarian style of government. This regime exists when a single, highly charismatic individual, who represents him- or herself as the personification of the nation, holding unchecked power. It may exist under civilian or military rule, when the leader seeks to guarantee his or her personal control in perpetuity, as "president for life," or through a hereditary republic.

political culture The context out of which political action is taken, recognizing the importance of systems of values and beliefs. While few people would deny that culture impacts people's views on politics and government, it has been difficult to articulate the precise connections between these variables and political outcomes. In 1959, Gabriel Almond and Sidney Verba identified three root (or "civic") cultures in the countries they studied: participant, subject, and parochial.

political liberalization A process of political reform based on the extension of civil and political rights, and the promotion of a more open political system. Signs that a system is liberalizing politically include a variety of changes, such as an increasing tolerance of dissent and the release of political prisoners. Although they are often associated with democratization, not all political liberalizations will result in democracy. Also known as an *abertura*.

political spectrum Conceptual map used to compare and contrast political ideologies. Along a horizontal line, ideologies are listed according to their views on change, the role of government in economic matters, and the relationship between religious institutions and their place in politics. The modern convention of the "left-right" political spectrum derives from legislative arrangements in the National Assembly of France, when those who supported the monarch and the Church sat on the right of the monarch, and those who favored democracy and revolution sat on the left.

populist An agenda, political party, campaign, or image designed to appeal to the "common people" rather than to the minority elite, rallying them around a shared sense of belonging and promising many things to many people. The term was originally used to describe political movements in Europe at the end of the nineteenth century that appealed to the rural poor. The term is now used to describe mass political movements, or a party platform that purports to represent sentiment akin to the collective voice of the ordinary person on social and economic issues.

praetorianism Military supremacy in politics; a type of increased involvement by soldiers in politics when military officers threaten or use force to influence political decisions and outcomes. The term derives from the Praetorian Guards of the Roman Empire, who were established as a unit to protect the emperor but who abused their power to overthrow and select the emperor themselves.

presidential system   A type of democratic constitutional system in which citizens directly select both their legislators and their executive. Because the executive and legislative branches are elected separately, it is not uncommon for one party to hold the presidency and another to dominate the legislature. As a result, gridlock is much more likely in a presidential than in a parliamentary system. Although there are checks and balances between the various branches of government, the executive is relatively independent of the legislature, and power tends to concentrate in the executive. The rigidity of a fixed presidential term means that it is harder to remove an errant executive from power, and effective executives are constitutionally prohibited from serving beyond the prescribed term.

proletariat   The socioeconomic group (or class) identified in Marxist socialism, defined by their relationship to the means of production. The proletarians are the workers who will unite together in revolutionary zeal to overcome the more powerful and entrenched bourgeoisie. Karl Marx argued that most workers own nothing but their labor (unlike artisans, who may own their machinery or tools). The proletariat is commonly called the "working class."

proxy war   During the Cold War, in an attempt to avoid the massive casualties associated with mutual assured destruction, the superpowers took sides in conflicts around the world, choosing intermediaries and supplying and arming them to play out the East-West rivalry with less risk of escalation to nuclear war.

reconfiguration   A form of crisis management in which governments take very small steps or affect the appearance of reform while maintaining significant restrictions on civil liberties, political participation, and competition. Analysts maintain that reconfiguration is not necessarily antidemocratic in nature—even incremental steps may add up to more substantive reforms, which may in turn contribute to democratization.

reform (political)   *See* **political liberalization.**

relative deprivation. A comparative statement that reveals the sense that individuals or groups are not doing as well as other groups.

relative poverty   Denotes a trend in terms of the gap between rich and poor countries. While some countries have made progress in eliminating absolute poverty, rising incomes during the economic boom of the 1990s have actually contributed to widening inequality overall. Consequently, while absolute poverty is said to have declined, for many less developed countries relative poverty has increased .

rescue package   An assortment of loans, credits, and other forms of aid offered by the International Monetary Fund and other international financial institutions to countries suffering from massive economic dislocation (such as much of Asia during the "Asian flu" of the late 1990s). Aimed at stabilizing these economies, however, such packages are only offered to countries willing to accept certain conditions, such as a neoliberal series of economic reforms.

resource mobilization   A conceptual approach to collective behavior and social movements that emphasizes what resources are needed to be successful, taking into account both the material and the nonmaterial needs of participants in collective action.

revolution   Meaning "to turn around," a revolution is the attempt (often sudden) to promote fundamental change in political and social institutions of society, often accompanied by violence and economic and cultural upheaval.

revolution of rising expectations   The recognition that improvement (often in the economy, but also in life choices and options) is often not as great as predicted or promised. Leaders often deliver inflated promises to their people, and rapid change can often increase hopes and desires for the future. The concept of "rising expectations" is used to distinguish from the "revolution of falling expectations," in which people anticipate a bad future and the future turns out to be even worse than expected.

rule of law   A situation in which the power of individuals is limited by a supreme set of rules that prevent arbitrary and unfair actions by governmental officials. A reliance on written rules to govern and operate rather than the vice and virtue of rulers.

secession   The act of withdrawing or breaking away from some organized entity such as a nation, as when Bangladesh seceded from Pakistan in 1971.

Secretary-General   The chief administrative officer of the United Nations. The Secretary-General is nominated by the Security Council and elected by two-thirds of General Assembly members for a five-year renewable term. In addition to presiding over the United Nations, increasingly the Secretary-General has become more visible in mediating and responding to global issues outside UN organizations. Kofi Annan, of Ghana, was reelected to a second five-year term in June 2001.

secularism   The separation of civil or educational institutions from ecclesiastical control; the act of de-emphasizing spiritual or religious perspectives in political, cultural, or social life.

Security Council   The most powerful organ within the UN system. Its representatives include five permanent veto members (P-5) and rotating, nonveto members. The ten nonpermanent members are elected to two-year terms by the General Assembly. Under the UN Charter, the Security Council possesses as its primary responsibility the maintenance of international peace and security. The council works to achieve this through many means: mediation, cease-fire directives, and the use of peacekeeping forces, to name a few.

self-determination   The right of a people who share cultural ties and live in a given territory to choose their own political institutions and government. A central international political concept of the twentieth century associated with nationalism and anticolonial movements.

shariah   Sometimes known as *shariat,* from the Arabic word meaning "way" or "road." *Shariah* is Muslim religious (or canonical) law based on rules for moral conduct developed over the first few centuries after the death of Mohammed. *Shariah* governs both the individual and social lives of believers, and provides followers with a basis for judging actions as good or evil. Despite debates over the degree of observance and the role of authorities for enforcement, most agree that a common understanding of *shariah* unites most Muslims around the world.

social movement   Human beings with a common purpose engaged in discussion and action designed to bring about change. Social movements are responses to a perceived state of affairs and often identify specific groups in society as the source of the problem to be rectified. Oftentimes, collective actions stimulate a countermovement in response.

sovereignty   Freedom from foreign control; a principle widely accepted in international law that speaks to a state's right to do as it wishes in its own territory; a doctrine that holds that states are the principle actors in international relations and the state is subject to no higher political authority. Also refers to widespread international acceptance of a particular country's control of territory.

state   An organized political entity that occupies a specific territory, has a permanent population, is controlled by a government, and is regarded as sovereign. Currently there are approximately 190 recognized states worldwide.

state capitalism   An economic system that mixes capitalism with government planning; private enterprise accounts for most of the country's economic activity, but the government intervenes on the side of business with subsidies and other supports aimed at promoting domestic producers' competitiveness on the world market.

state society   A centralized form of political organization; an outgrowth of the sedentarization of human populations, the intensification of agricultural production, and population booms. State societies are distinguished by increasing social stratification as classes emerge and power is centralized in the hands of full-time political leaders. This broad category includes many different forms of political organization, from simple, small states to immense empires.

stateless nation   A group of people (with a shared identity based on language, ethnicity, religion, or common heritage) who consider themselves to have no country to call their own; people without citizenship in any state.

stateless society   A smaller, decentralized grouping of the type in which the earliest humans lived. It is relatively democratic in that power is shared and there are no full-time political leaders. Also known as an "acephalous society."

state-owned enterprise (SOE)   A business that is owned and operated wholly or partially by the government. In many countries, SOEs have been concentrated in sectors thought vital to the national economy. They were built from nationalized properties, as an attempt to reclaim a country's resources from foreign domination or to promote import substitution industrialization. Throughout much of the world, SOEs have been large employers. However, they have been criticized as notoriously inefficient drains on state budgets. Also known as a "state-owned industry."

state-sponsored terrorism (or state terror)   Violent methods used by government forces or vigilante groups acting with at least the tacit approval of state officials to intimidate and coerce people, often the state's own citizens.

structural adjustment program (SAP)   The neoliberal prescription offered by international financial institutions to indebted countries. As a condition for international assistance (*see* **rescue package**), countries must commit to an SAP, usually a three- to five-year program that includes a variety of reforms associated with economic liberalization (e.g., privatization, devaluation of currency, cutting social spending, raising taxes, welcoming foreign investment, etc.).

structuralism   A school of thought that includes a range of opinion from radical to reformist. Structuralists share the view that the current international economic system works to the benefit of the already rich and globalization is inherently disadvantageous to poor countries. Structuralists are highly critical of neoliberal programs, which they see as dooming much of the world to underdevelopment.

sustainable development   An approach that considers the long-term impact on the environment and resources of current development strategies.

sweatshop   A place of labor, usually a factory. Term used derisively to describe a business establishment profiting from inhumane conditions of work.

terrorism   The use of violence or the threat of violence and intimidation to achieve aims and spread a message. Terrorists aim for symbolic targets to manipulate adversaries and to achieve political, religious, or ideological objectives.

theocracy   From the Greek for "government of God," a system of rule based on religion and dominated by clergy. Rules are often inspired by some form of holy book.

top-down approach   As opposed to a bottom-up approach, top-down policies are ostensibly aimed at benefiting the majority and are initiated by elites.

totalitarianism   A full-blown dictatorship, marked by the severity and magnitude of the state's interference in the lives of its citizens. In totalitarian systems the state, guided by an overarching ideology, attempts to exercise absolute control over virtually every aspect of citizens' lives. Power is concentrated in the hands of the leader or party and dissent is not tolerated. There is no right of political competition or participation, leaders are not accountable for their actions, and the state violates civil and human rights with impunity. Classic examples of totalitarian states include fascist regimes such as Nazi Germany, as well as communist party–dominated states such as Stalin's Russia and Mao's China.

transparency   A policy promoted to reduce corruption; exists when the government is open about its spending and budgetary matters, and people are encouraged to report misconduct.

truth commission   An official mechanism launched usually during periods of political transition to investigate wrongs of the recent past, especially human rights abuses. Truth commissions represent attempts to deal with the past by promoting the public acknowledgment of wrongdoing, sometimes as an alternative to criminal prosecution. There are multiple models of truth commissions, which vary in the scope of crimes examined, mandate and investigation, and the types of justice employed. Most truth commissions are established to achieve an accurate historical description of what took place, to promote reconciliation, and to help promote more durable democracies by creating a culture of human rights. Truth commissions are viewed by many as but one part of the complex healing process after difficult periods, but much disagreement about their long-term impact remains.

United Nations (UN)   Preceded by the League of Nations, the UN was founded in 1945 as an international governmental organization that now includes almost all of the world's states. It provides a forum at which complaints are heard and conflicts are discussed and sometimes resolved. The UN is also involved in promoting human development through the work of its specialized agencies that promote standards for world heath, education, and the environment, in addition to commonly accepted terms for trade and commerce.

Universal Declaration of Human Rights (UDHR)   The most comprehensive international statement on human rights. With over thirty articles pertaining to a wide array of political, civil, economic, social, and cultural rights, the UDHR was put forward in 1948 as a general resolution of the United Nations.

universalism   The view that conceptions of human rights and morality do not depend on whether a group or culture recognize them as such; rather, these principles are universal. Universalists argue that human rights are timeless, global in relevance and scope; there is a common morality that applies across cultures, and human rights are an entitlement all people share—no matter who they are or where they live.

vanguard party   Literally the "leading" party—Vladimir Lenin's term for the Communist Party, supposed to take a front role in the overthrow of capitalism and transition to communism. Lenin prescribed that a single, elite, highly disciplined party would be necessary to lead the revolution of the proletarians, or the workers. Lenin's idea of a vanguard party has been used by Marxist socialist states such as China and North Korea to argue against the creation of competing political parties, producing a monopoly of control with which other socialists disagree.

weapons of the weak   Forms of confrontation that often go unnoticed because they tend to be concealed, disguised, or subtle—employed by the ostensibly powerless, including women, minorities, and peasants. Commonly used tactics include rumor, deception, hoarding, and suicide.

World Bank   Also known as the International Bank for Reconstruction and Development (IBRD), the World Bank was formed as part of the Bretton Woods system in 1944, along with its counterpart organization the International

Monetary Fund (IMF). Like the IMF, the World Bank is controlled by developed countries, as voting power is based on a country's financial contribution to the Bank. Its responsibilities are wide ranging; although it was originally created to fund the reconstruction of postwar Europe and to promote a stable international economic system, it now focuses its efforts on long-term loans and projects in the non-Western world and more recently in Eastern Europe and the former Soviet republics.

World Trade Organization (WTO)   Founded in 1995, the WTO is an institution designed to promote free trade and mediate trade disputes; an updated and expanded product of the General Agreement on Tariffs and Trade (GATT), which focused on manufactured goods. Compared to GATT, the WTO has much more extensive monitoring and enforcement powers, although some less developed countries fear that this international governmental organization will work primarily for the benefit of developed countries.

zero-sum game   A situation in which there can only be one winner and one loser. One actor's gain is another's loss (as opposed to non-zero-sum game, in which all can be winners or all can be losers).

Notes

Chapter 1
Introducing Comparative Studies

1. The former dictators of Haiti, Zaire (now the Democratic Republic of Congo), Indonesia, and Somalia.

2. Naomi Chazan, Peter Lewis, and Robert Mortimer, *Politics and Society in Contemporary Africa* (Boulder: Lynne Rienner, 1999).

3. Frank L. Wilson, *Concepts and Issues in Comparative Politics: An Introduction to Comparative Analysis* (Upper Saddle River, N.J.: Prentice Hall, 1996).

4. David J. Elkins and Richard E. B. Simeon, "A Cause in Search of Its Effect, or What Does Political Culture Explain?" *Comparative Politics* 11, no. 2 (January 1979).

5. Andre Gunder Frank, *Capitalism and Underdevelopment in Latin America* (New York: Monthly Review Press, 1967).

6. Samuel P. Huntington, *The Clash of Civilizations and the Remaking of World Order* (New York: Simon and Schuster, 1996).

7. Monte Palmer, *Comparative Politics: Political Economy, Political Culture, and Political Interdependence* (Itasca, Ill.: F. E. Peacock, 1997).

8. Colin Leys, *Underdevelopment in Kenya: The Political Economy of Neo-Colonialism, 1964–1971* (London: Heinemann, 1975).

9. Thomas Friedman, *The Lexus and the Olive Tree* (New York: Farrar, Straus, and Giroux, 1999).

10. Howard J. Wiarda and Harvey F. Kline, *An Introduction to Latin American Politics and Development* (Boulder: Westview Press, 2001); Austin Sarat and Thomas R. Kearns, "The Unsettled Status of Human Rights: An Introduction," in *Human Rights: Concepts, Contests, Contingencies,* eds. Austin Sarat and Thomas R. Kearns (Ann Arbor: University of Michigan Press, 2001); and Edward W. Said, *Reflections on Exile* (Cambridge: Harvard University Press, 2001).

11. Thomas L. Friedman, "Global Village Idiocy," *New York Times,* May 12, 2002.

12. Joshua S. Goldstein, *International Relations,* 4th ed. (New York: Longman, 2001).

13. Michael E. Porter, "Attitudes, Values, Beliefs, and the Microeconomics of Prosperity," in *Culture Matters: How Values Shape Human Progress,* eds. Lawrence E. Harrison and Samuel P. Huntington (New York: Basic Books, 2000).

14. Friedman, *The Lexus and the Olive Tree.*

15. Ibid.

16. Jack Donnelly, *International Human Rights* (Boulder: Westview Press, 1998).

17. Richard H. Ullman, "Human Rights: Toward International Action," in *Enhancing Global Human Rights,* eds. Jorge I. Domínguez, Nigel S. Rodley, Bryce Wood, and Richard Falk (New York: McGraw Hill, 1979).

18. Michael Ignatieff, *Human Rights as Politics and Idolatry* (Princeton: Princeton University Press, 2001).

19. The UDHR gives equal time to both individual and group rights; it recognizes that protections, privileges, and opportunities are not only for individuals, but also should extend to the family, community, nation, and other groups.

20. Amartya Sen, "Democracy as a Universal Value," *Journal of Democracy* 10, no. 3 (July 1999); and Ignatieff, *Human Rights as Politics and Idolatry.*

21. Vojin Dimitrijevic, "Human Rights and Peace," in *Human Rights: New Dimensions and Challenges,* ed. Janusz Symonides (Brookfield, Vt.: Ashgate, 1998); and Ullman, "Human Rights."

22. Hilary French, "Coping with Ecological Globalization," in *State of the World 2000,* ed. Lester R. Brown (New York: W. W. Norton, 2000).

23. David Stoez, Charles Guzzetta, and Mark Lusk, *International Development* (Boston: Allyn and Bacon, 1999); and French, "Coping with Ecological Globalization."

24. Lester R. Brown, forward to *State of the World 2001,* eds. Lester R. Brown and Linda Starke (New York: W. W. Norton, 2001); and Christopher Flavin, "Rich Planet, Poor Planet," in *State of the World 2001.*

25. "AIDS Statistics Updated Live," *AIDS Javascript Clock of World HIV,* www.poz.ca; Steve Connor, "Million Still Suffer, Caught in Middle of an AIDS Turf War," *The Independent* (London), January 25, 2002; and Chris McGreal, "Orphans of AIDS Face Lonely Struggle for Life," *The Guardian* (London), December 1, 2001.

26. Laurie Garrett, *Betrayal of Trust: The Collapse of Global Public Health* (New York: Hyperion, 2000).

27. Elizabeth Reid, "A Future, If One Is Still Alive: The Challenge of the HIV Epidemic," in *Hard Choices: Moral Dilemmas in Humanitarian Intervention,* ed. Jonathan Moore (Lanham, Md.: Rowman and Littlefield, 1998).

28. Lori Heise, "In Fighting AIDS, We Cannot Delay," *New York Times,* June 27, 2001.

Chapter 2
Precolonial History

1. Octavio Paz, "Critique of the Pyramid," cited in Ana Carrigan, "Chiapas: The First Postmodern Revolution," in *Our Word Is Our Weapon: Selected Writings of Subcomandante Marcos,* ed. Juana Ponce de Leon (New York: Seven Stories Press, 2001), p. 428.

2. Roland Oliver, *The African Experience* (Boulder: Westview Press, 1999); and Robert W. July, *A History of the African People* (Prospect Heights, Ill.: Waveland Press, 1992).

3. Oliver, *The African Experience.*

4. Milton W. Meyer, *Asia: A Concise History* (Lanham, Md.: Rowman and Littlefield, 1997).

5. Benjamin Keen and Keith Haynes, *A History of Latin America* (Boston: Houghton Mifflin, 2000).

6. Ibid.; and Peter Bakewell, *A History of Latin America* (Malden, Mass.: Blackwell, 1997).

7. Meyer, *Asia.*

8. Ibid.; and Rhoads Murphey, "The Historical Context," in *Understanding Contemporary China,* ed. Robert E. Gamer (Boulder: Lynne Rienner, 1999).

9. Keen and Haynes, *A History of Latin America.*

10. Ibid.; Irene Silverblatt, *Moon, Sun, and Witches* (Princeton: Princeton University Press, 1987); and Susan Migden Socolow, *The Women of Colonial Latin America* (Cambridge: Cambridge University Press, 2000).

11. Keen and Haynes, *A History of Latin America.*

12. Meyer, *Asia.*

13. Murphey, "The Historical Context."

14. Ibid.

15. G. Mokhtar, conclusion to *UNESCO General History of Africa: Ancient Civilizations of Africa,* ed. G. Mokhtar (London: Heinemann, 1981).

16. Ironically, the largest states were often the most fragile, disintegrating much more easily than smaller states (and even stateless nations), which proved to be more cohesive and durable. Stateless societies on the frontier, such as the Chichemecas in northern Mexico or the Araucanians in southern Chile, took the longest to conquer. Small, mobile groups able to live off the land were hard to suppress—until in some cases the Europeans decided that it just wasn't worth it.

17. July, *A History of the African People.*

18. Meyer, *Asia;* David Landes, *The Wealth and Poverty of Nations: Why Some Are So Rich and Some Are So Poor* (New York: W. W. Norton, 1998); Murphey, "The Historical Context"; and Edward L. Farmer, Gavin R. G. Hambly, Byron K. Marshall, et al., *Comparative History of Civilizations in Asia* (Reading, Mass.: Addison-Wesley, 1977).

Chapter 3
Colonialism: Gold, God, and Glory

1. Hilaire Belloc, "The Modern Traveller," cited in Margery Perham II, *Lugard: The Years of Authority, 1899–1945* (London: Collins, 1960), p. 45.

2. David Landes, *The Wealth and Poverty of Nations: Why Some Are So Rich and Some Are So Poor* (New York: W. W. Norton, 1998); and Jared Diamond, *Guns, Germs, and Steel: The Fate of Human Societies* (New York: W. W. Norton, 1997).

3. A. Adu Boahen, "Africa and the Colonial Challenge," in *UNESCO General History of Africa: Africa Under Colonial Domination, 1880–1935,* ed. A. Adu Boahen (London: Heinemann, 1985).

4. Peter Bakewell, *A History of Latin America* (Malden, Mass.: Blackwell, 1997); Diamond, *Guns, Germs, and Steel;* and Landes, *The Wealth and Poverty of Nations.*

5. This terminology was used by Ali Mazrui in his video series *The Africans,* no. 4, 1986.

6. Milton W. Meyer, *Asia: A Concise History* (Lanham, Md.: Rowman and Littlefield, 1997).

7. Mark A. Burkholder and Lyman L. Johnson, *Colonial Latin America* (New York: Oxford University Press, 1998).

8. Walter Rodney, "The Colonial Economy," in *UNESCO General History of Africa;* and Emory C. Bogle, *The Modern Middle East: From Imperialism to Freedom, 1800–1958* (Upper Saddle River, N.J.: Prentice Hall, 1996).

9. Bogle, *The Modern Middle East.*

10. Benjamin Keen and Keith Haynes, *A History of Latin America* (Boston: Houghton Mifflin, 2000).

11. Meyer, *Asia.*

12. Edward L. Farmer, Gavin R. G. Hambly, Byron K. Marshall, et al., *Comparative History of Civilizations in Asia* (Reading, Mass.: Addison-Wesley, 1977).

13. Susan Migden Socolow, *The Women of Colonial Latin America* (Cambridge: Cambridge University Press, 2000).

14. Keen and Haynes, *A History of Latin America.*

15. Boahen, "Africa and the Colonial Challenge"; and Farmer, Hambly, Marshall, et al., *Comparative History of Civilizations in Asia.*

16. Farmer, Hambly, Marshall, et al., *Comparative History of Civilizations in Asia.*

17. Whereas the colonizers often argued that they had intervened to end anarchy and bring peace to the inhabitants of the territory, in fact the colonizers encouraged fissures and played different groups off each other, to prevent unity and ensure their continued dominance.

18. Not yet democracies themselves until well into the twentieth century, the Spanish and Portuguese certainly never claimed to be promoting self-rule for their colonies in Latin America.

19. Peter Mansfield, *A History of the Middle East* (New York: Penguin Books, 1991).

20. Keen and Haynes, *A History of Latin America*.

21. Some traditional authorities refused to cooperate with the Europeans. A Peruvian curaca, Jose Gabriel Condorcanqui, opposed Spanish abuses of the Indians and led the largest colonial rebellion in all of Spanish America.

22. Bakewell, *A History of Latin America;* Boahen, "Africa and the Colonial Challenge"; and Keen and Haynes, *A History of Latin America*.

Chapter 4
Independence or In Dependence?

1. Julie Frederikse, *South Africa: A Different Kind of War* (Johannesburg: Ravan Press, 1987), p. 30.

2. Mahmood Mamdani, *Citizen and Subject: Contemporary Africa and the Legacy of Late Colonialism* (Princeton: Princeton University Press, 1996).

3. Jay Kinsbruner, *Independence in Spanish America: Civil Wars, Revolutions, and Underdevelopment* (Albuquerque: University of New Mexico Press, 2000).

4. Benjamin Keen and Keith Haynes, *A History of Latin America* (Boston: Houghton Mifflin, 2000).

5. David Landes, *The Wealth and Poverty of Nations: Why Some Are So Rich and Some Are So Poor* (New York: W. W. Norton, 1998); Adam Hochschild, *King Leopold's Ghost* (Boston: Houghton Mifflin, 1998); and David M. Davidson, "Negro Slave Control and Resistance in Colonial Mexico," in *People and Issues in Latin American History,* eds. Lewis Hanke and Jane M. Rausch (New York: Markus Wiener, 1993).

6. Edward L. Farmer, Gavin R. G. Hambly, Byron K. Marshall, et al., *Comparative History of Civilizations in Asia* (Reading, Mass.: Addison-Wesley, 1977).

7. Susan Migden Socolow, *The Women of Colonial Latin America* (Cambridge: Cambridge University Press, 2000).

8. Ali A. Mazrui, "Seek Ye First the Political Kingdom," in *UNESCO General History of Africa: Africa Since 1935,* ed. Ali A. Mazrui (London: Heinemann, 1993); and Farmer, Hambly, Marshall, et al., *Comparative History of Civilizations in Asia*.

9. Mazrui, "Seek Ye First the Political Kingdom."

10. Peter Bakewell, *A History of Latin America* (Malden, Mass.: Blackwell, 1997).

11. Mark A. Burkholder and Lyman L. Johnson, *Colonial Latin America* (New York: Oxford University Press, 1998); and Emory C. Bogle, *The Modern Middle East: From Imperialism to Freedom, 1800–1958* (Upper Saddle River, N.J.: Prentice Hall, 1996).

12. Laith Kubba, "The Awakening of Civil Society," *Journal of Democracy* 11, no. 3 (July 2000).

13. Bakewell, *A History of Latin America*.

14. Burkholder and Johnson, *Colonial Latin America;* and Keen and Haynes, *A History of Latin America*.

15. Bogle, *The Modern Middle East;* and J. Isawa Elaigwu, "Nation-Building and Changing Political Structures," in *UNESCO General History of Africa*.

16. Burkholder and Johnson, *Colonial Latin America*.

17. Landes, *The Wealth and Poverty of Nations*.

18. Ibid.

19. Farmer, Hambly, Marshall, et al., *Comparative History of Civilizations in Asia*.

20. A. Adu Boahen, "Colonialism in Africa: Its Impact and Significance," in *UNESCO General History of Africa*.

21. Keen and Haynes, *A History of Latin America.*

22. Ibid.; and Boahen, "Colonialism in Africa."

Chapter 5
Linking Concepts and Cases

1. Lynn V. Foster, *A Brief History of Mexico* (New York: Facts on File, 1997).

2. Peter Bakewell, *A History of Latin America* (Malden, Mass.: Blackwell, 1997); and Benjamin Keen and Keith Haynes, *A History of Latin America* (Boston: Houghton Mifflin, 2000).

3. Richard Graham, *Independence in Latin America* (New York: McGraw Hill, 1994).

4. Bakewell, *A History of Latin America;* and Keen and Haynes, *A History of Latin America.*

5. Ibid.

6. Mark A. Burkholder and Lyman L. Johnson, *Colonial Latin America* (New York: Oxford University Press, 1998).

7. Bakewell, *A History of Latin America;* and Keen and Haynes, *A History of Latin America.*

8. Peter Flindell Klaren, *Peru: Society and Nationhood in the Andes* (New York: Oxford University Press, 2000).

9. Ibid., p. 43.

10. The Spanish *mita* built on Inca practice, but there were crucial differences. For the Inca, *mita* was part of a larger social contract in which reciprocal benefits linked the community and state. For the Spanish, however, *mita* was purely exploitative, as the state provided no return to the community.

11. According to Peter Klaren, however, the state did offer some limits on colonial expropriation. For example, indigenous people could appeal to colonial courts for relief, and some became adept at resorting to Spanish legal institutions to defend their interests. But such policies served as safety valves, effectively strengthening the system against radical or revolutionary challenges. Klaren emphasizes that because the system did sometimes rule on behalf of oppressed groups, it in no way vindicates or balances the colonial legacy, which is overwhelmingly negative. Klaren, *Peru.*

12. Klaren, *Peru.*

13. Ibid.; Burkholder and Johnson, *Colonial Latin America;* and Graham, *Independence in Latin America.*

14. Cynthia McClintock, *Revolutionary Movements in Latin America* (Washington, D.C.: U.S. Institute of Peace Press, 1998).

15. Keen and Haynes, *A History of Latin America.*

16. Ibid., p. 43.

17. Klaren, *Peru.*

18. Ibid.; and Washington Office on Latin America, "Deconstructing Democracy: Peru Under Alberto Fujimori," February 2000, www.wola.org.

19. Keen and Haynes, *A History of Latin America;* Klaren, *Peru;* and Thomas E. Skidmore and Peter H. Smith, *Modern Latin America* (New York: Oxford University Press, 1992).

20. Michael Crowder, *The Story of Nigeria* (London: Faber and Faber, 1978).

21. Robin Law, "The Oyo-Dahomey Wars, 1726–1823: A Military Analysis," in *Warfare and Diplomacy in Precolonial Nigeria,* eds. Toyin Falola and Robin Law (Madison: University of Wisconsin–Madison, 1992).

22. Peter M. Lewis, Pearl T. Robinson, and Barnett R. Rubin, *Stabilizing Nigeria* (New York: Century Foundation Press, 1998).

23. Karl Maier, *This House Has Fallen: Midnight in Nigeria* (New York: PublicAffairs, 2000).

24. Ian Phimister, *An Economic and Social History of Zimbabwe, 1890–1948* (London: Longman, 1988).

25. Ibid.

26. Other groups, such as Asians and Coloureds (biracial people today known as "brown Zimbabweans") were also subjected to the color bar, although they generally had more advantages than blacks. Although the black-white struggle dominates most analyses of Zimbabwe, these groups also played a significant though often covert role in the liberation struggle.

27. Phimister, *An Economic and Social History of Zimbabwe.*

28. Ibid.

29. In the 1920s the Watch Tower prophesized the Second Coming and claimed that a whirlwind would blow whites and nonbelievers away.

30. Phimister, *An Economic and Social History of Zimbabwe.*

31. Ibid.

32. Ibid.

33. Ibid.

34. Masipula Sithole, "Zimbabwe: In Search of Stable Democracy," in *Democracy in Developing Countries: Africa,* eds. Larry Diamond, Juan Linz, and Seymour Martin Lipset (Boulder: Lynne Rienner, 1988); D. E. Needham, E. K. Mashingaidze, and Ngwabi Bhebe, *From Iron Age to Independence: A History of Central Africa* (London: Longman, 1985); Victor de Waal, *The Politics of Reconciliation: Zimbabwe's First Decade* (Trenton, N.J.: Africa World Press, 1990); and A. J. Wills, *An Introduction to the History of Central Africa: Zambia, Malawi, and Zimbabwe* (New York: Oxford University Press, 1985).

35. Elton L. Daniel, *The History of Iran* (Westport, Conn.: Greenwood Press, 2001).

36. Mike Edwards, "The Adventures of Marco Polo, Part I," *National Geographic,* May 2001; and Daniel, *The History of Iran.*

37. Daniel, *The History of Iran.*

38. The title "Shah" reappropriates a pre-Islamic Iranian title for "king."

39. Daniel, *The History of Iran.*

40. Ibid.

41. Stephen Kinzer, *Crescent and the Star: Turkey Between Two Worlds* (New York: Farrar, Straus, and Giroux, 2001).

42. Douglas A. Howard, *The History of Turkey* (Westport, Conn.: Greenwood Press, 2001).

43. Kinzer, *Crescent and the Star,* p. 4.

44. Ibid.

45. Ibid.

46. As one person put it, "In this country it is allowed to say bad things about God, but not about Atatürk." Kinzer, *Crescent and the Star,* p. 36. Similar sentiment was also expressed in a recent modern history of Turkey: "If indeed a country can be said to be the creation of a single individual, then Turkey is a new country, the creation of Mustafa Kemal Atatürk." Howard, *The History of Turkey,* p. 1.

47. Lucian W. Pye, *China: An Introduction,* 3rd ed. (Boston: Little, Brown, 1984).

48. Much of the story surrounding the Great Wall is based in legend. While some smaller walls were built prior to the Qin Dynasty, and joined together during the Qin emperor's reign, the bulk of the wall was completed during China's Ming Dynasty (1366–1644), and significantly renovated thereafter. There is evidence to challenge its status as part of China's ancient past. Historian Arthur Waldron has produced extensive research challenging the myth behind the wall, citing, among other points, that even though Marco Polo traveled extensively throughout the region in the thirteenth century, he made no mention of the structure. Similarly, contrary to popular beliefs, the Great Wall cannot be viewed from space, at least not without significant satellite magnification. Yet perceptions of the wall's visibility from space predate space travel by humans—*Ripley's Believe It or Not* made the claim as early as 1930. See David C. Wright, *The History of China* (Westport, Conn.: Greenwood Press, 2001).

49. Pye, *China.*

50. Barney War, "Teaching Indonesia: A World-Systems Perspective," *Education About Asia* 3, no. 3 (Winter 1998).

51. Milton W. Meyer, *Asia: A Concise History* (Lanham, Md.: Rowman and Littlefield, 1997); and Björn Schelander and Kirsten Brown, *Exploring Indonesia: Past and Present* (Honolulu: Center for Southeast Asian Studies, 2000).

52. Schelander and Brown, *Exploring Indonesia.*

53. Meyer, *Asia: A Concise History.*

54. Robert Cribb and Colin Brown, *Modern Indonesia: A History Since 1945* (New York: Longman, 1995).

55. Chris Manning and Peter van Diermen, "Recent Developments and Social Aspects of *Reformasi* and Crisis: An Overview," in *Indonesia in Transition: Social Aspects of Reformasi and Crisis,* eds. Chris Manning and Peter van Diermen (Singapore: Institute of Southeast Asian Studies, 2000).

Chapter 6
Globalization: Cause or Cure for Underdevelopment?

1. United Nations, *2000 Millennium Report* (New York: United Nations, 2000).

2. Lester Brown and Linda Starke, eds., *State of the World 2001* (New York: W. W. Norton, 2001).

3. Nancy Birdsall, "Life Is Unfair: Inequality in the World," in *Annual Editions: Developing World 01–02,* ed. Robert J. Griffiths (Guilford, Conn.: McGraw Hill/Dushkin, 2001).

4. United Nations Development Programme (UNDP), *Human Development Report 2000* (New York: UNDP, 2000).

5. Ibid.

6. "Terrorism Is Not the Only Scourge," *The Economist,* December 22, 2001.

7. Joshua S. Goldstein, *International Relations,* 4th ed. (New York: Longman, 2001).

8. Birdsall, "Life Is Unfair"; and "World Development Indicators 2002," www.worldbank.org.

9. Amartya Sen, cited in Nicholas D. Kristof, "Stark Data on Women," *New York Times,* November 5, 1991.

10. United Nations, Department of Economic and Social Affairs, "The World's Women 2000: Trends and Statistics," www.unstats.un.org.

11. Victoria Brittain and Larry Elliott, "Educating Girls Is Life-Saving for the World," in *Annual Editions: Developing World 01–02.*

12. Douglas Frantz, "As Turkey's Schools Open, a Million Are Left Out," *New York Times,* September 15, 2000.

13. "What Is the World Trade Organization?" www.wto.org.

14. Thomas L. Friedman, *The Lexus and the Olive Tree* (New York: Farrar, Straus, and Giroux, 1999).

15. "Africa's Elusive Dawn," *The Economist,* February 24, 2001.

16. Daniel T. Griswold, "The Blessings and Challenges of Globalization," in *Annual Editions: Developing World 01–02.*

17. Thomas L. Friedman, "Protesting for Whom?" *New York Times,* April 24, 2001.

18. Griswold, "The Blessings and Challenges of Globalization."

19. Jackie Smith and Timothy Patrick Moran, "WTO 101: Myths About the World Trade Organization," in *Annual Editions: Developing World 01–02.*

20. "Africa's Elusive Dawn," *The Economist,* February 24, 2001.

21. Goldstein, *International Relations.*

22. T. J. Pempel, "The Developmental Regime in a Changing World Economy," in

The Developmental State, ed. Meredith Woo-Cumings (Ithaca, N.Y.: Cornell University Press, 1999).

23. Kathleen Schalch, "Study Finds American Firms Doing Business in China Are Not Improving Conditions for Chinese Workers," *National Public Radio: All Things Considered,* May 5, 2000.

24. Ibid.

25. Friedman, "Protesting for Whom?"

26. Goldstein, *International Relations.*

27. Beatrice Newbery, "Labouring Under Illusions," in *Annual Editions: Developing World 01–02.*

28. Goldstein, *International Relations.*

29. Ibid.

30. Lawrence K. Altman, "UN Forecasts Big Increase in AIDS Death Toll," *New York Times,* July 3, 2002.

31. Joseph Kahn, "Losing Faith: Globalization Proves Disappointing," *New York Times,* March 21, 2002.

32. Kofi A. Annan, "Trade and Aid in a Changed World," *New York Times,* March 19, 2002.

33. Goldstein, *International Relations;* and Richard Sokolsky and Joseph McMillan, "Foreign Aid in Our Own Defense," *New York Times,* February 12, 2002.

34. David Ransom, "The Dictatorship of Debt," *New Internationalist,* no. 312 (May 1999), www.oneworld.net; Marie Michael, "Food or Debt? The Jubilee 2000 Movement," in *Annual Editions: Developing World 01–02;* and Elisabeth Bumiller, "Bush, in Monterrey, Speaks of Conditional Global Aid," *New York Times,* March 23, 2002.

35. Michael, "Food or Debt?"

36. Peter Piot, cited in Lawrence K. Altman, "UN Warning AIDS Imperils Africa's Youth," *New York Times,* May 28, 2000; and Lawrence K. Altman, "UN Forecasts Big Increase in AIDS Death Toll."

37. "World Development Indicators 2002," www.worldbank.org.

38. Goldstein, *International Relations;* World Bank, *World Development Indicators 1998* (Washington, D.C.: World Bank, 1998); "Debt: The Facts," *New Internationalist,* no. 312 (May 1999), www.oneworld.net.

39. Tony Hawkins, "Nigeria: Pursuing Forgiveness," *Financial Times* (London), March 30, 2001; Susan George, *The Debt Boomerang: How Third World Debt Harms Us All* (Boulder: Westview Press, 1992); and "Debt: The Facts."

40. Eduardo Galeano, *Open Veins of Latin America* (New York: Monthly Review Press, 1973).

41. Alan Beattie, "Entering a Critical Phase: Development and Debt," *Financial Times* (London), November 30, 2001.

42. Michael, "Food or Debt?"

Chapter 7
Structural Adjustment: Prices and Politics

1. Douglas Farah, "Nigerians' Hopes in Elected Leader Fade," *Washington Post,* March 21, 2001, p. A23.

2. Thomas L. Friedman, *The Lexus and the Olive Tree* (New York: Farrar, Straus, and Giroux, 1999), p. 294.

3. Elisabeth Rosenthal, "Without 'Barefoot Doctors' China's Rural Families Suffer," *New York Times,* March 14, 2001.

4. Tim Weiner, "Roadblocks Right and Left for Mexican President," *New York Times,* January 22, 2001.

5. Nancy Birdsall, "Managing Inequality in the Developing World," in *Annual Editions: Developing World 01–02,* ed. Robert J. Griffiths (Guilford, Conn.: McGraw Hill/Dushkin, 2001).

6. Freedom House, "Freedom in the World, 1999–2000," www.freedomhouse.org; and Ginger Thompson, "Mexican Labor Protest Gets Results," *New York Times,* October 8, 2001.

7. This is quite ironic, since of the least liberalized countries in the region, the People's Republic of China was also the NIC least affected by the Asian crisis. In a remarkable exception to neoliberal rules, China has not been subjected to an SAP and in the meantime it soaks up the largest amount of the world's foreign investment.

8. Edward Goldsmith, "Empires Without Armies," in *Annual Editions: Developing World 01–02.*

9. Julius E. Nyang'oro and Timothy M. Shaw, "The African State in the Global Economic Context," in *The African State at a Critical Juncture: Between Disintegration and Reconfiguration,* eds. Julius E. Nyang'oro and Timothy M. Shaw (Boulder: Lynne Rienner, 1998).

10. United Nations Development Programme (UNDP), *Human Development Report 1999* (New York: UNDP, 1999).

11. Gary Younge, "Penalizing the Poor," *The Guardian,* March 19, 2001.

12. Seth Mydans, "Before Manila's Garbage Hill Collapsed," *New York Times,* July 18, 2000.

13. Barnaby Phillips, "Nigerian Police Having Problems Keeping Oil from Being Stolen," *National Public Radio: Morning Edition,* July 19, 2000.

14. Valentine Moghadam, *Gender and National Identity: Women and Politics in Muslim Societies* (London: Zed Books, 1994).

15. Ibid.

16. Human Rights Watch, "The Damaging Debate on Rapes of Ethnic Chinese Women," September 8, 1998, www.hrw.org.

17. Tim Weiner, "Terrific News in Mexico City: Air Is Sometimes Breathable," *New York Times,* January 5, 2001.

18. Daniel C. Esty, "Environmental Protection During the Transition to a Market Economy," in *Economies in Transition: Comparing Asia and Eastern Europe,* eds. Wing Thye Woo, Stephen Parker, and Jeffrey Sachs (Cambridge: MIT Press, 1997).

19. Susan George, *The Debt Boomerang: How Third World Debt Hurts Us All* (Boulder: Westview Press, 1992).

20. "Nigeria: Environmental Damage," *New York Times,* September 19, 2001.

21. David Stoez, Charles Guzzetta, and Mark Lusk, *International Development* (Boston: Allyn and Bacon, 1999).

22. "Trading in Bushmeat: Africa's Vanishing Apes," *The Economist,* January 12, 2002; and John Nielson, "Hunting of Many Animals for Meat in the Rain Forests Leaves Many Conservationists Worried," *National Public Radio: Sounds Like Science,* November 10, 1999.

23. Andrew C. Revkin, "Hungry People v. Rare Wildlife: A Call for New Farming Methods," *New York Times,* May 9, 2001.

24. Daniel T. Griswold, "The Blessings and Challenges of Globalization," in *Annual Editions: Developing World 01–02.*

25. "Health Aid for Poor Countries," *New York Times,* January 3, 2002.

26. Ibid.; and "Terrorism Is Not the Only Scourge," *The Economist,* December 22, 2001.

27. Ken Silverstein, "Millions for Viagra, Pennies for Diseases of Poor," *The Nation,* July 19, 1999; Laurie Garrett, *Betrayal of Trust: The Collapse of Global Public Health* (New York: Hyperion, 2000); and Elizabeth Olson, "UN Says Millions of Children Die Needlessly," *New York Times,* March 14, 2002.

28. "India's AIDS Crisis," *New York Times,* April 2, 2001.

29. David Brown, "AIDS Spurs a Crisis of Orphanhood Across Africa," *Washington Post,* July 13, 2000; and Lawrence K. Altman, "UN Forecasts Big Increase in AIDS Death Toll," *New York Times,* July 3, 2002.

30. Editorial, "Trafficking in Children," *New York Times,* May 4, 2001.

31. George, *The Debt Boomerang*.

32. Joseph Kahn, "International Lenders' New Image: A Human Face," *New York Times,* September 26, 2000.

Chapter 8
Alternative Approaches to Development

1. "Breaking the Poverty Cycle," *Asiaweek* 26, no. 40 (October 13, 2000).

2. Jorge Nef, *Human Security and Mutual Vulnerability* (Ottawa: International Development and Research Centre, 1999).

3. United Nations Development Programme (UNDP), "A Decade to Eradicate Poverty," in *Annual Editions: Developing World 01–02,* ed. Robert J. Griffiths (Guilford, Conn.: McGraw Hill/Dushkin, 2001); and John Tessitore and Susan Woolfson, eds., *A Global Agenda: Issues Before the Fifty-fourth General Assembly of the United Nations* (Lanham, Md.: Rowman and Littlefield, 1999).

4. Julius E. Nyang'oro and Timothy M. Shaw, "The African State in the Global Economic Context," in *The African State at a Critical Juncture: Between Disintegration and Reconfiguration,* eds. Julius E. Nyang'oro and Timothy M. Shaw (Boulder: Lynne Rienner, 1998); and Theodore H. Cohn, *Global Political Economy: Theory and Practice* (New York: Longman, 2000).

5. Michael Hardt and Antonio Negri, "What the Protesters in Genoa Want," *New York Times,* July 20, 2001; and Thomas L. Friedman, "Evolutionaries," *New York Times,* July 20, 2001.

6. Nyang'oro and Shaw, "The African State in the Global Economic Context"; UNDP, *Human Development Report 1999* (New York: UNDP, 1999); and "Meanwhile, in Another World," *The Economist,* February 9, 2002.

7. Meredith Woo-Cumings, "Introduction: Chalmers Johnson and the Politics of Nationalism and Development," in *The Developmental State,* ed. Meredith Woo-Cumings (Ithaca, N.Y.: Cornell University Press, 1999); and Jorge Castañeda, *Utopia Unarmed* (New York: Knopf, 1993).

8. Adebayo Adedeji, "Popular Participation, Democracy, and Development: Is There a Dialectical Linkage?" in *Nigeria: Renewal from the Roots? The Struggle for Democratic Development,* eds. Adebayo Adedji, Onigu Otite, Kunle Amuwo, et al. (London: Zed Books, 1997).

9. Ibid.

10. David Stoez, Charles Guzzetta, and Mark Lusk, *International Development* (Boston: Allyn and Bacon, 1999); and Ginger Thompson, "Small Loans Help Millions of World's Poorest, Coalition Says," *New York Times,* October 8, 2001.

11. "An Alarm Call for Latin America's Democrats," *The Economist,* July 28, 2001.

12. Cuba was excluded because it is not a democracy. At the Summit of the Americas in 2001, participants signed a declaration that prevents authoritarian governments from participating in the FTAA.

13. David Ransom, "The Dictatorship of Debt," *New Internationalist,* no. 312 (May 1999), www.oneworld.net.

Chapter 9
Linking Concepts and Cases

1. "Rich Is Rich and Poor Is Poor," *The Economist,* October 28, 2000; and "Mexico," *The World Factbook 2002,* www.odci.gov.

2. Robert M. Dunn Jr., "Mexico's Fast Start on Free Trade," *New York Times,* July 5, 2001; "Slowing Economy, Quickening Politics," *The Economist,* May 19, 2001; and Gretchen Peters, "Fox Falls Short on Tall Pledges," *Christian Science Monitor,* December 3, 2001.

3. Cynthia McClintock, *Revolutionary Movements in Latin America* (Washington, D.C.: U.S. Institute of Peace Press, 1998).

4. Susan George, *The Debt Boomerang: How Third World Debt Harms Us All* (Boulder: Westview Press, 1992); and McClintock, *Revolutionary Movements in Latin America*.

5. It now appears that the proceeds from the sale of state-owned industries may have gone into the pockets of Fujimori and his adviser, Vladimiro Montesinos.

6. George, *The Debt Boomerang*.

7. Douglas Farah, "Nigeria's Oil Exploitation Leaves Delta Poisoned," *Washington Post,* March 18, 2001.

8. "Nigeria's Economy: More Pain, Little Gain," *The Economist,* July 28, 2001.

9. "An Ill Wind from the South-West," *The Economist,* September 30, 2000.

10. Tony Hawkins, "End Game Lies in the Economy," *Financial Mail,* October 18, 2002; "Southern Africa's Food Shortage," *The Economist,* June 1, 2002; and "From Breadbasket to Basket Case," *The Economist,* June 29, 2002.

11. "Hunger in Southern Africa: Can Famine Be Averted?" *The Economist,* August 3, 2002.

12. Lawrence K. Altman, "UN Forecasts Big Increase in AIDS Death Toll," *New York Times,* July 3, 2002; and "Zimbabwe," *The World Factbook 2002,* www. odci.gov.

13. Julius E. Nyang'oro and Timothy M. Shaw, "The African State in the Global Economic Context," in *The African State at a Critical Juncture: Between Disintegration and Reconfiguration,* eds. Julius E. Nyang'oro and Timothy M. Shaw (Boulder: Lynne Rienner, 1998); and Robert I. Rotberg, "Africa's Mess, Mugabe's Mayhem," *Foreign Affairs* 79, no. 5 (September–October 2000).

14. Rachel L. Swarns, "Zimbabwe Starts Arresting White Farmers Defying Eviction," *New York Times,* August 17, 2002; and "From Breadbasket to Basket Case," *The Economist,* June 29, 2002.

15. Anoushiravan Ehteshami, *After Khomeini: The Iranian Second Republic* (New York: Routledge, 1995).

16. Ibid.

17. "Islamic Banking: Forced Devotion," *The Economist,* February 17, 2001.

18. Elton L. Daniel, *The History of Iran* (Westport, Conn.: Greenwood Press, 2001).

19. Robert D. Kaplan, "Turkey's Precarious Success," *New York Times,* February 27, 2001.

20. Libby Rittenberg, "Introduction: The Changing Fortunes of Turkey in the Post-Soviet World," in *The Political Economy of Turkey in the Post-Soviet Era: Going West and Looking East,* ed. Libby Rittenberg (Westport, Conn.: Praeger, 1998).

21. Michael R. Gordon, "Threats and Responses: The Allies: U.S. Presses Turkey's Case on Europe and Cyprus," *New York Times*, December 3, 2002, p. 22.

22. Molly Moore, "IMF Grants Turkey $10 Billion to Stem Financial Crisis," *Washington Post,* December 6, 2000.

23. Heinz Kramer, *A Changing Turkey: The Challenge to Europe and the United States* (Washington, D.C.: Brookings Institution, 2000). Faruk Selcuk confirms this pattern of "persistent and slowly increasing inflation" as well. See Faruk Selcuk, "A Brief Account of the Turkish Economy, 1987–1996," in *The Political Economy of Turkey.*

24. "Turkey's New Politician: The Weight of Money," *The Economist*, October 19, 2002, p. 48.

25. Geoffrey Murray, *China: The Next Superpower—Dilemmas in Change and Continuity* (New York: St. Martin's, 1998).

26. Debra E. Soled, ed., *China: A Nation in Transition* (Washington, D.C.: Congressional Quarterly, 1995).

27. Murray, *China.*

28. "China's Stockmarket: Home-Grown High," *The Economist,* December 23, 2000.

29. William E. James, "Lessons from Development of the Indonesian Economy," *Education About Asia* 5, no. 1 (Spring 2000).

Chapter 10
From Ideas to Action: The Power of Civil Society

1 Siamak Namazi, "Three Years Later: Reformist Students Rally at Tehran University," *The Iranian,* May 22, 2000.

2. Sandra Mackey, *The Iranians: Persia, Islam and the Soul of a Nation* (New York: Penguin, 1996).

3. Ibid.

4. Ibid.

5. David Martin, "The People's Church: The Global Evangelical Upsurge and Its Political Consequences," *Christianity Today,* January–February 2000.

6. Ibid.

7. Roger Eatwell, *Fascism: A History* (New York: Penguin, 1997).

8. Orville Schell, "Letter from China," *New Yorker,* July 1994, reprinted in *The China Reader: The Reform Era,* eds. Orville Schell and David Shambaugh (New York: Vintage Books, 1999).

9. A. W. Samii, "The Contemporary Iranian News Media, 1998–1999," *Middle East Review of International Affairs* 3, no. 4 (December 1999).

10. This definition is based on the classic perspective on political culture that was developed in the 1950s and 1960s. Its most common source is Sidney Verba, "Comparative Political Culture," in *Political Culture and Political Development,* eds. Sidney Verba and Lucian Pye (Princeton: Princeton University Press, 1965).

11. Gabriel A. Almond and Sidney Verba, eds., *Civic Culture: Political Attitudes and Democracy in Five Nations* (Princeton: Princeton University Press, 1963).

12. David J. Elkins and E. B. Simeon, "A Cause in Search of Its Effect, or What Does Political Culture Explain?" *Comparative Politics,* January 1979.

13. Roberta Garner, *Contemporary Movements and Ideologies* (New York: McGraw Hill, 1996).

14. Benjamin R. Barber, *Jihad vs. McWorld* (New York: Times Books, 1995).

15. See Benjamin R. Barber, "Beyond *Jihad vs. McWorld*," *The Nation,* January 21, 2002.

16. Donald K. Emmerson, "Will Indonesia Survive?" *Foreign Affairs* 79, no. 3 (May–June 2000).

17. Célestin Monga, *The Anthropology of Anger: Civil Society and Democracy in Africa,* trans. Linda L. Fleck and Célestin Monga (Boulder: Lynne Rienner, 1996).

18. Leslie Bethell, ed., *Ideas and Ideologies in Twentieth-Century Latin America* (Cambridge: Cambridge University Press, 1996).

19. Other key documents and meetings out of which liberation theology was developed: Medellín 1968–1969 (the Second General Conference on Latin American Bishops, which met to discuss the implications of Vatican II for Latin America), the *Letter Addressed to the People of the Third World* (1976), and the Council of Latin American Bishops at Puebla in 1979.

20. While many of these ideas were and continue to be extremely popular at the grassroots levels in many countries, the institutional Catholic Church has responded with harsh criticism. Leonardo Boff, for example, was required to spend a year in "obedient silence" from 1985 to 1986 because of opposition from Rome toward some of his writings. He was eventually forced out of the priesthood for mixing politics and religion too much.

21. In recent years there have been many books and edited collections that focus on non-Western views of feminism. For a sampling, see Kumari Jayawardena, *Feminism and Nationalism in the Third World* (London: Zed Books, 1986); Guida West and Rhoda Lois Blumberg, eds., *Women and Social Protest* (New York: Oxford University Press,

1990); Jane Jaquette, ed., *The Women's Movement in Latin America: Participation and Democracy* (Boulder: Westview Press, 1994); and Bethell, *Ideas and Ideologies in Twentieth-Century Latin America.*

22. Jaquette, *The Women's Movement in Latin America.*

23. Jane Jaquette, "Introduction: From Transition to Participation: Women's Movements and Democratic Politics," in Jaquette, *Women's Movements in Latin America.*

24. Andrew Heywood, *Political Ideas and Concepts: An Introduction* (New York: St. Martin's, 1994).

25. Bager Moin, *Khomeini: Life of the Ayatollah* (New York: St. Martin's, 2000).

26. Heywood, *Political Ideas and Concepts.*

27. This definition is based on the pioneering work on this subject conducted by Sidney Verba, Victor H. Nie, and Jae-on Kim, *Participation and Political Equality: A Seven-Nation Comparison* (New York: Cambridge University Press, 1978).

28. Maurice Duverger, *Political Parties: Their Organization and Activity in the Modern State* (New York: John Wiley, 1963).

29. International Confederation of Free Trade Unions, *Annual Survey of Trade Union Rights, 2000* (Washington, D.C.: International Confederation of Free Trade Unions, 2000).

30. Sarah Bachman, "Underage Unions: Child Laborers Speak Up," *Mother Jones,* November–December 2000.

31. Sidney Tarrow, *Power in Movement: Social Movements and Contentious Politics* (New York: Cambridge University Press, 1998); and William A. Gamson, "The Social Psychology of Collective Action," in *Frontiers in Social Movement Theory,* eds. Aldon D. Morris and Carol McClurg Mueller (New Haven, Conn.: Yale University Press, 1992).

32. Carmen Ramos Escandon, "Women's Movements, Feminism, and Mexican Politics," in Jaquette, *The Women's Movement in Latin America.*

33. Maruja Barrig, "The Difficult Equilibrium Between Bread and Roses: Women's Organizations and Democracy in Peru," in Jaquette, *The Women's Movement in Latin America.*

34. Ibid.

35. Monga, *The Anthropology of Anger.*

36. Mary Beth Sheridan, "Dissident Soaps Put Mirror to Mexico," *Los Angeles Times,* December 18, 1997.

37. Hadani Ditmars, "Let Googoosh Sing," September 18, 2000, www.salon.com.

38. Vivienne Walt, "Persian Pop vs. the Revolution," February 24, 2000, www.salon.com.

39. Elaine Sciolino, "Iran's Well-Covered Women Remodel a Part That Shows," *New York Times,* September 26, 2000.

40. See Albert O. Hirschman, *Exit, Voice, and Loyalty; Responses to Decline in Firms, Organizations, and States* (Cambridge: Harvard University Press, 1970).

41. Douglas Frantz, "Turkish Women Who See Death as a Way Out," *New York Times,* November 3, 2000.

42. Ke'an Wang, *Literature and Information on Preventive Medicine,* January 2000, www.usembassy-china.org.cn/english/sand+/estnews1201.htm.

43. Stephen Ellis, "Tuning In to Pavement Radio," *African Affairs* 88, no. 352 (July 1989).

44. Leigh A. Payne, *Uncivil Movements: The Armed Right Wing and Democracy in Latin America* (Baltimore: Johns Hopkins University Press, 2000).

45. David Rieff, "The False Dawn of Civil Society," *The Nation,* February 22, 1999.

46. Alison Brysk, "Democratizing Civil Society in Latin America," *Journal of Democracy* 11, no. 3 (July 2000).

Chapter 11
Linking Concepts and Cases

1. Octavio Paz, "Latin America and Democracy," in *Democracy and Dictatorship in Latin America: A Special Publication Devoted Entirely to the Voice and Opinions of Writers from Latin America,* eds. Octavio Paz, Jorge Edwards, Carlos Franqui, et al. (New York: Foundation for the Independent Study of Social Ideas, 1982).

2. Ginger Thompson, "Mexican Rebels Set Off on Protest Caravan to the Capital," *New York Times,* February 26, 2001.

3. Tim Weiner, "Weakened Rights Bill for Mexico's Indians Takes Effect," *New York Times,* August 16, 2001.

4. Tim Weiner, "Pummeling the Powerful with Comedy," *New York Times,* June 15, 2001.

5. "Love in the PRI," *The Economist,* August 11, 2001; Ginger Thompson, "A Rare Leader Tries to Save Mexico's Fallen Party," *New York Times,* November 1, 2001; and Gretchen Peters, "Down But Not Out," *Christian Science Monitor,* December 13, 2001.

6. Ginger Thompson and Tim Weiner, "Great Expectations of Mexico's Leader Sapped by Reality," *New York Times,* September 4, 2001.

7. Francisco Durand, "The New Right and Political Change in Peru," in *The Right and Democracy in Latin America,* eds. Douglas A. Chalmers, Maria do Carmo Campello de Souza, and Atilio A. Borón (New York: Praeger, 1992); and Ernesto García Calderon, "Peru's Decade of Living Dangerously," *Journal of Democracy* 12, no. 2 (April 2001).

8. Steven Levitsky and Cynthia Sanborn, "A Hard Choice in Peru," *New York Times,* May 9, 2001.

9. Clifford Krauss, "This Time, 80's Populist Sounds Capitalist Theme in Peru," *New York Times,* May 31, 2001.

10. David Scott Palmer, "Democracy and Its Discontents in Fujimori's Peru," *Current History,* February 2000.

11. Clifford Krauss, "Peru's New Leader, an 'Indian Rebel with a Cause,'" *New York Times,* June 5, 2001.

12. "Toledo Reaches the Palace, at Last," *The Economist,* June 9, 2001; Steven Levitsky and Cynthia Sanborn, "A Hard Choice in Peru," *New York Times,* May 9, 2001; and Clifford Krauss, "Son of the Poor Is Elected in Peru over Ex-President," *New York Times,* June 4, 2001.

13. "Peru's New Government: Teething Troubles," *The Economist,* December 8, 2001.

14. Funso Afolayan, "Nigeria: A Political Entity and a Society," in *Dilemmas of Democracy in Nigeria,* eds. Paul A. Beckett and Crawford Young (Rochester, N.Y.: University of Rochester Press, 1997).

15. Peter M. Lewis and Pearl T. Robinson, *Stabilizing Nigeria* (New York: Century Foundation Press, 1998).

16. Norimitsu Onishi, "Rising Muslim Power in Africa Causes Unrest in Nigeria and Elsewhere," *New York Times,* November 1, 2001.

17. "Zimbabwe's Tighter Belts, and Shorter Tempers," *The Economist,* October 28, 2000.

18. Not all women are MDC supporters. Older, rural women with less formal education are some of ZANU-PF's staunchest supporters, and many of them fear the uncertainty that would come with a new government.

19. Sam Moyo, "The Land Occupation Movement and Democratization in Zimbabwe: Contradictions of Neoliberalism," *Millennium* 30, no. 2 (2001).

20. Ibid.

21. Jane Flanagan, "Women Fight Mugabe with 'Chitter-Chatter,'" *Ottawa Citizen,* February 11, 2002.

22. Rachel Swarns, "Zimbabwe Uses Food as a Political Tool, Aid Groups Say," *New York Times,* December 12, 2002.

23. "Hell No, I Won't Go," *The Economist,* February 23, 2002.

24. Rachel L. Swarns, "Prominent Legislator in Zimbabwe Faults Plan to Limit Media," *New York Times,* January 31, 2002.

25. "Green Danger," *The Economist,* November 11, 2000.

26. "Khatami Faces a Treacherous Second Term," *The Economist,* June 9, 2001.

27. "The Clergy in Defence of Their Own," *The Economist,* May 12, 2001.

28. Elaine Sciolino, "Runaway Youths a Thorn in Iran's Chaste Side," *New York Times,* November 5, 2000.

29. "Is It Wise to Abolish Virtue?" *The Economist,* June 30, 2001.

30. Ergun Özbudun, *Contemporary Turkish Politics: Challenges to Democratic Consolidation* (Boulder: Lynne Rienner, 2000); and "Is It Wise to Abolish Virtue?"

31. Robert Marquand, "China Displays New Tolerance for Abrasive, Urban Art," *Christian Science Monitor,* September 26, 2001; and Jianying Zha, *China Pop: How Soap Operas, Tabloids, and Bestsellers Are Transforming a Culture* (New York: New Press, 1995). In the chapter titled "The Whopper," Zha highlights the phenomenon of "McArt"—artists displaying their work at local McDonald's venues. Those who failed to secure the necessary permits, though, were shut out before the show even began.

32. Robert Cribb and Colin Brown, *Modern Indonesia: A History Since 1945* (New York: Longman, 1995).

33. "Burning Books," *The Economist,* May 26, 2001.

Chapter 12
The Call to Arms: Violent Paths to Change

1. Mao Zedong, "Report on an Investigation of the Peasant Movement in Hunan: March 1927," in *Selected Readings from the Works of Mao Tsetung* (Peking: Foreign Languages Press, 1971), p. 30. Quote from 1927.

2. Juana Ponce de Leone, ed., *Our Word Is Our Weapon: Selected Writings of Subcomandante Marcos* (New York: Seven Stories Press, 2001), p. 17. Quote from 1994.

3. Walter Laqueur, *The New Terrorism: Fanaticism and the Arms of Mass Destruction* (New York: Oxford University Press, 1999).

4. For more on the multiple definitions of terrorism and its components, see Donna M. Schlagheck, *International Terrorism: An Introduction to the Concepts and Actors* (Lexington, Mass.: Lexington Books, 1988).

5. Noam Chomsky, *Pirates and Emperors: International Terrorism in the Real World* (New York: Claremont, 1986).

6. For a concise summary of approaches to violence in the literature, see Jack A. Goldstone, ed., *Revolutions: Theoretical, Comparative, and Historical Studies,* 2nd ed. (New York: Harcourt Brace, 1994).

7. "Guns in China: The Wild West," *The Economist,* November 10, 2001.

8. "Football Hooligans They Aren't," *The Economist,* November 3, 2001.

9. Arend Lijphart, *Democracy in Plural Societies: A Comparative Exploration* (New Haven: Yale University Press, 1977).

10. Charles Euchner, *Extraordinary Politics: How Protest and Dissent Are Changing American Democracy* (Boulder: Westview Press, 1996).

11. Michael Renner, "How to Abolish War," *The Humanist,* July–August 1999.

12. Daniel C. Diller, ed., *The Middle East,* 8th ed. (Washington, D.C.: Congressional Quarterly, 1994).

13. Ibid.

14. Yahya Sadowski, "Ethnic Conflict," *Foreign Policy* 111 (Summer 1998).

15. "Terrorism in the Philippines: The Jolo Conundrum," *The Economist,* November 24, 2001.

16. "Dealing with Iraq: Unfinished Business," *The Economist,* December 8, 2001.

17. "Iran's Kurds: The Lucky Ones?" *The Economist,* December 23, 2000.

18. Barbara Crossette, "Iraq Is Forcing Kurds from Their Homes, the UN Reports," *New York Times,* December 11, 2000.

19. Ibid.

20. Tina Rosenberg, "A Guerrilla War Stoked by a Thirst for Cash," *New York Times,* December 27, 2001.

21. John T. Fishel, "Colombia: Civil-Military Relations in the Midst of War," *Joint Force Quarterly* 25 (Summer 2000).

22. Ibid.

23. Toyin Falola, *The History of Nigeria* (Westport, Conn.: Greenwood Press, 1999).

24. Eleanor O'Gorman, "Writing Women's Wars: Foucaldian Strategies of Engagement," in *Women, Culture, and International Relations,* eds. Vivienne Jabri and Eleanor O'Gorman (Boulder: Lynne Rienner, 1999).

25. Kate Dunn, "Why Zimbabwe Entered the Fray," *Christian Science Monitor,* August 27, 1998; Jon Jeter, "The 'Endgame' in Zimbabwe?" *Washington Post,* March 3, 2001; and Sita Ranchod-Nilsson, "'This, Too, Is a Way of Fighting': Rural Women's Participation in Zimbabwe's Liberation War," in *Women and Revolution in Africa, Asia, and the New World,* ed. Mary Ann Tetreault (Columbia: University of South Carolina Press, 1994). Kabila was assassinated in 2000. Zimbabwe continued to offer its support to the slain president's son and successor, Joseph Kabila.

26. Laqueur, *The New Terrorism.*

27. Amy Caiazza, "Why Gender Matters in Understanding September 11: Women, Militarism, and Violence," *Institute for Women's Policy Research,* no. 1908 (November 2001).

28. David Scott Palmer, "The Revolutionary Terrorism of Peru's Shining Path," in *Terrorism in Context,* ed. Martha Crenshaw (University Park: Pennsylvania State University Press, 1995).

29. Amy Knight, "Female Terrorists in the Russian Socialist Revolutionary Party," *Russian Review,* no. 38 (1979); and Laqueur, *The New Terrorism.*

30. Adel Darwish, "From Boredom to Bombs: Two Female Terrorists," *WIN Magazine,* no. 20 (April 1999).

31. Craig S. Smith, "China's Efforts Against Crime Make No Dent," *New York Times,* December 26, 2001.

32. Clifford Krauss, "Jailed Unjustly, Peruvians Try to Rebuild Shattered Lives," *New York Times,* July 17, 2000.

33. U.S. Department of State, *Country Reports on Human Rights, 2000* (Washington, D.C.: U.S. Government Printing Office, 2000); and Amnesty International, *Annual Report 2001* (New York: Amnesty International, 2001).

34. Ranchod-Nilsson, "'This, Too, Is a Way of Fighting.'"

35. The article that cited this figure noted that the distinction between armed civilian and regular solider is blurred in many contexts, which may inflate the statistic. "The First Casualty: War and Its Victims," *The Economist,* August 25, 2001.

36. Mary Kaldor, *New and Old Wars: Organized Violence in a Global Era* (Stanford, Calif.: Stanford University Press, 1999).

37. Coalition to Stop the Use of Child Soldiers, "Global Report on Child Soldiers 2001," www.child-soldiers.org/news; Juan Forero, "A Child's Vision of War: Boy Guerrillas in Colombia," *New York Times,* December 20, 2000; and "Charity Decries Use of Children in War," *CNN World News,* October 31, 1996.

38. "HIV/AIDS an Extra Danger for LRA Child Soldiers," United Nations Integrated Regional Information Network, July 31, 2001.

39. Kenneth Walker, "UNICEF Works to Deprogram Children Who Have Been Kidnapped in Sierra Leone and Forced to Commit Murder for the Rebels," *National Public Radio: Morning Edition,* July 6, 2000; and Coalition to Stop the Use of Child Soldiers, "Global Report on Child Soldiers 2001."

40. Seth Mydans, "Burmese Rebel Chief More Boy Than Warrior," *New York Times,* April 10, 2000; and "Burmese Rebel Twins and Fourteen Followers Surrender in Thailand," *Associated Press,* January 17, 2001.

41. Rosenberg, "A Guerrilla War Stoked by a Thirst for Cash."

42. J. Isawa Elaigwu, "Nation-Building and Changing Political Structures," in *UNESCO General History of Africa: Africa Since 1935,* ed. Ali A. Mazrui (London: Heinemann, 1993).

43. Ergun Özbudun, *Contemporary Turkish Politics: Challenges to Democratic Consolidation* (Boulder: Lynne Rienner, 2000).

44. Marvine Howe, *Turkey Today: A Nation Divided over Islam's Revival* (Boulder: Westview Press, 2000).

45. Miguel Angel Centeno, *Democracy Within Reason: Technocratic Revolution in Mexico* (University Park: Pennsylvania State University Press, 1997).

46. Sorayya Shahri, "Women in Command: A Successful Experience in the National Liberation Army of Iran," in *Frontline Feminisms: Women, War, and Resistance,* eds. Marguerite R. Waller and Jennifer Rycenga (New York: Garland, 2000).

47. Vesna Kesic, "From Reverence to Rape: An Anthropology of Ethnic and Genderized Violence," in *Frontline Feminisms.*

48. Kaldor, *New and Old Wars.*

49. John McBeth, "Bombs, the Army, and Suharto," *Far Eastern Economic Review* 164, no. 4 (February 1, 2001).

50. Ibid.

51. "In the Hands of the Militia," *The Economist,* September 16, 2000.

52. Frederick J. Hacker, *Crusaders, Criminals, Crazies: Terror and Terrorism in Our Time* (New York: W. W. Norton, 1976).

53. Linda Diebel, "Peru's Rebels Are Down But Not Out," *Toronto Star,* November 9, 1997.

54. Douglas Farah, "Al Qaeda's Road Paved with Gold," *Washington Post,* February 17, 2002.

55. Mike Crawley, "Somali Banking Under Scrutiny," *Christian Science Monitor,* November 28, 2001.

56. Laqueur, *The New Terrorism;* and "Uganda: Stolen Children, Stolen Wives," *Amnesty International,* AFR 59/02/97, September 18, 1997.

57. James Bennet, "Arab Press Glorifies Bomber as Heroine," *New York Times,* February 11, 2002.

58. "Nuclear, Chemical, and Biological Threats: The Terror Next Time?" *The Economist,* October 6, 2001.

59. Laqueur, *The New Terrorism.*

60. Palmer, "The Revolutionary Terrorism of Peru's Shining Path."

61. See Goldstone, *Revolutions;* and Theda Skocpol, *States and Social Revolution: A Comparative Analysis of France, Russia, and China* (New York: Cambridge University Press, 1979).

62. Elton L. Daniel, *The History of Iran* (Westport, Conn.: Greenwood Press, 2001).

63. Ellen Kay Trimberger, "A Theory of Elite Revolutions," *Studies in Comparative International Development* 7 (1972). Trimberger also included the Meiji Restoration of 1868 as an example of this specific type of revolution.

64. Ibid. This point explicitly challenges the theories of Huntington and others who argued against the inclusion of mass mobilization because of its potentially destabilizing outcomes.

65. Margaret Randall, *Sandino's Daughters: Testimonies of Nicaraguan Women in Struggle* (New Brunswick, N.J.: Rutgers University Press, 1995).

66. Jack A. Goldstone, "The Outcomes of Revolutions," in Goldstone, *Revolutions.*

67. Jack A. Goldstone, "Revolutions in World History," in Goldstone, *Revolutions.*

68. Stéphane Courtois, Nicolas Werth, Jean-Louis Panné, et al., *The Black Book of Communism: Crimes, Terror, and Repression,* ed. Mark Kramer, trans. Jonathan Murphy (Cambridge: Harvard University Press, 1999).

69. Schlagheck, *International Terrorism.*

70. Dariush Zahedi, *The Iranian Revolution Then and Now: Indicators of Regime Instability* (Boulder: Westview Press, 2000).

71. Robin Wright, "Iran's New Revolution," *Foreign Affairs* 79, no. 1 (January–February 2000).

72. Ibid.

73. Ibid.

Chapter 13
Linking Concepts and Cases

1. Ginger Thompson and Tim Weiner, "Zapatista Rebels Rally in Mexico City," *New York Times,* March 12, 2001.

2. Several other guerrilla groups have formed elsewhere in Mexico since the Zapatistas came forward. For example, the Insurgent People's Revolutionary Army (ERPI) is a self-proclaimed Marxist revolutionary movement fighting the Mexican government in Guerrero state.

3. Robert Jones Shafer, *A History of Latin America* (Lexington, Mass.: D. C. Heath, 1978); Thomas E. Skidmore and Peter H. Smith, *Modern Latin America* (New York: Oxford University Press, 1992); and Peter Bakewell, *A History of Latin America* (Malden, Mass.: Blackwell, 1997).

4. Juana Ponce de Leon, ed., *Our Word Is Our Weapon: Selected Writings of Subcomandante Marcos* (New York: Seven Stories Press, 2001).

5. "Mexico: Rebels in Search of a Cause," *The Economist,* April 21, 2001.

6. Ginger Thompson, "Mexico Congress Approves Altered Rights Bill," *New York Times,* April 30, 2001.

7. "Mexico: Rebels in Search of a Cause."

8. "Human Rights in Mexico: Untouchable?" *The Economist,* November 3, 2001; Kevin Sullivan and Mary Jordan, "Fox Takes Steps to End Army's Rights Abuses," *Washington Post,* November 11, 2001; and Kevin Sullivan, "Memories of Massacre in Mexico," *Washington Post,* February 14, 2002.

9. Cynthia McClintock, *Revolutionary Movements in Latin America* (Washington, D.C.: U.S. Institute of Peace Press, 1998).

10. Peter Flindell Klaren, *Peru: Society and Nationhood in the Andes* (New York: Oxford University Press, 2000).

11. The name *Shining Path* comes from one of Peru's most prominent authors, Jose Carlos Mariategui, who wrote, "Marxist-Leninism will open the shining path to revolution."

12. M. Elaine Mar, "Violence in Peru: Shining Path Women," *Harvard Magazine,* May–June 1996; and McClintock, *Revolutionary Movements in Latin America.*

13. Guzmán broke with China after Mao's death, considering Deng to be a traitor to the revolution. Shining Path preferred its isolation and sought no external support.

14. Carlos Ivan Degregori, "After the Fall of Abimael Guzmán: The Limits of Sendero Luminoso," in *The Peruvian Labyrinth,* eds. Maxwell A. Cameron and Philip Mauceri (University Park: Pennsylvania State University Press, 1997).

15. Klaren, *Peru.*

16. Ibid.

17. Human Rights Watch, "Peru: Torture and Political Persecution in Peru," December 1997; and U.S. Department of State, *Country Reports on Human Rights, 2000* (Washington, D.C.: U.S. Government Printing Office, 2000).

18. Degregori, "After the Fall of Abimael Guzmán"; and McClintock, *Revolutionary Movements in Latin America.*

19. Although most terrorist leaders have been captured or killed, a revamped Shining Path (the Red Path) is enjoying a revival of sorts. Not only did it carry out an attack on an army barracks in 2001, it is said to be planning an assault on the U.S. embassy and may be behind a "Yankees Out of Afghanistan" graffiti campaign in Lima.

20. Clifford Krauss, "Candidates in Peru's Presidential Race Peck at Fading Military," *New York Times,* May 25, 2001.

21. Abraham Lama, "Military Reforms Key Feature of Transition to Democracy," *Inter Press Service,* December 14, 2001.

22. J. Samuel Fitch, "The Armed Forces and Democracy in Latin America," *Canadian Journal of Latin American and Caribbean Studies* 25, no. 50 (September 2000); and McClintock, *Revolutionary Movements in Latin America.*

23. Peter M. Lewis and Pearl T. Robinson, *Stabilizing Nigeria* (New York: Century Foundation Press, 1998).

24. Toyin Falola, *The History of Nigeria* (Westport, Conn.: Greenwood Press, 1999).

25. Kent Hughes Butts and Steven Metz, *Armies and Democracy in the New Africa: Lessons from Nigeria and South Africa* (Carlisle Barracks, Pa.: Strategic Studies Institute, U.S. Army War College, January 6, 1996); Falola, *The History of Nigeria;* and Christina Lamb, "Life's So Unfair, Says General," *Sunday Telegraph* (London), February 28, 1999.

26. Quoted in Karl Maier, *This House Has Fallen: Midnight in Nigeria* (New York: PublicAffairs, 2000), p. xxi.

27. Falola, *The History of Nigeria;* and Maier, *This House Has Fallen.*

28. Falola, *The History of Nigeria.*

29. Terence Ranger, *Peasant Consciousness and Guerrilla War in Zimbabwe* (London: James Currey, 1985).

30. Ngwabi Bhebe and Terence Ranger, "Volume Introduction: Society in Zimbabwe's Liberation War," in *Society in Zimbabwe's Liberation War,* eds. Ngwabi Bhebe and Terence Ranger (Oxford: James Currey, 1996).

31. From this point on ZANU became known as ZANU-PF—with *PF* indicating "Patriotic Front."

32. Dickson A. Mungazi, *Colonial Policy and Conflict in Zimbabwe* (New York: Crane Russak, 1992).

33. Richard P. Werbner, "In Memory: A Heritage of War in Southwestern Zimbabwe," in *Society in Zimbabwe's Liberation War,* eds. Ngwabi Bhebe and Terence Ranger (Oxford: James Currey, 1996).

34. Ranger, *Peasant Consciousness and Guerrilla War in Zimbabwe.*

35. Andrew Meldrun and Chris McGreal, "Mugabe Takes a Stride into Tyranny," *The Guardian* (London), January 10, 2002.

36. Ibid.; "Africa's Own Mussolini," *The Economist,* February 24, 2001; and Chris McGreal, "Zimbabwe Coup Plot," *The Guardian* (London), May 29, 2001.

37. Houman Sadri, "Iran," in *The Political Role of the Military: An International Handbook,* eds. Constantine P. Danopoulos and Cynthia Watson (Westport, Conn.: Greenwood Press, 1996).

38. Jerrold D. Green, "Countermobilization in the Iranian Revolution," in *Revolutions: Theoretical, Comparative, and Historical Studies,* 2nd ed., ed. Jack A. Goldstone (New York: Harcourt Brace, 1994).

39. Mark J. Roberts, *Khomeini's Incorporation of the Iranian Military* (Washington, D.C.: Institute for National Strategic Studies, National Defense University, 1996).

40. Ibid.

41. Michele Kelemen, "State Department's Annual Report on Global Terrorism," *National Public Radio: Morning Edition,* May 1, 2001. This was part of a larger pattern, even recognizing a general decrease in Iranian sponsorship of terrorism since 1992. In 2000 the U.S. State Department designated Iran the world's "most active state-sponsor of terrorism." See Walter Laqueur, *The New Terrorism: Fanaticism and the Arms of Mass Destruction* (New York: Oxford University Press, 1999).

42. "Lebanon: How Respectable Is Hizbullah?" *The Economist,* December 1, 2001.

43. *U.S.-Iran Relations: A Road Map for Normalization* (Washington, D.C.: Atlantic Council of the United States, 1998).

44. Laqueur, *The New Terrorism*.

45. Robert D. Kaplan, "Turkey's Precarious Success," *New York Times*, February 27, 2001.

46. Douglas Frantz, "Military Bestrides Turkey's Path to the European Union," *New York Times*, January 14, 2001.

47. Ibid.

48. "Blast and Counterblast: Turkey's Generals and Its Civilians," *The Economist*, August 18, 2001.

49. Stephen Kinzer, "Turkey Considers Scaling Back Military Challenge to Greece," *New York Times*, June 8, 2000.

50. Ely Karmon, "The Demise of Radical Islam in Turkey," *Middle East Review of International Affairs* 1, no. 4 (December 1997).

51. Ibid.

52. "Guns in China: The Wild West," *The Economist*, November 10, 2001.

53. Peter Yu Kien-hong, *The Party and the Army in China: Figuring Out Their Relationship Once and for All*, Working Paper no. 7 (Singapore: East Asian Institute, 1998).

54. Ibid.

55. "Java's Angry Young Muslims," *The Economist*, October 20, 2001; and John McBeth, "Bombs, the Army, and Suharto," *Far Eastern Economic Review*, February 1, 2001.

56. Donald K. Emmerson, "Voting and Violence: Indonesia and East Timor in 1999," in *Indonesia Beyond Suharto: Policy, Economy, Society, Transition*, ed. Donald K. Emmerson (Armonk, N.Y.: M. E. Sharpe, 1999).

57. "The Black Bats Strike Back," *The Economist*, August 11, 2001.

58. Rajiv Chandrasekaran, "Witnesses Detail Slaughter of 118 Madurese on Borneo: Police Deployed for Protection Had Earlier Fled," *Washington Post*, Februrary 28, 2001.

59. Ibid.

60. Emmerson, "Voting and Violence."

61. This is the term Donald Emmerson, an election monitor with the Carter Center and a scholar of Indonesian politics, used to describe the situation. See ibid.

62. Emmerson, "Voting and Violence."

63. Jacqueline Siapno, "Gender, Nationalism, and the Ambiguity of Female Agency in Aceh, Indonesia, and East Timor," in *Frontline Feminisms: Women, War, and Resistance*, eds. Marguerite R. Waller and Jennifer Rycenga (New York: Garland, 2000).

64. "Flying the Flag in Irian Jaya," *The Economist*, November 4, 2000.

65. Calvin Sims, "Indonesia Cracks Down on Separatists in Irian Jaya," *New York Times*, December 4, 2000.

66. "A Separatist Murdered," *The Economist*, November 17, 2001.

Chapter 14
Ballots, Not Bullets: Seeking Democratic Change

1. Octavio Paz, "Latin America and Democracy," in *Democracy and Dictatorship in Latin America: A Special Publication Devoted Entirely to the Voice and Opinions of Writers from Latin America*, eds. Octavio Paz, Jorge Edwards, Carlos Franqui, et al. (New York: Foundation for the Independent Study of Social Ideas, 1982), p. 15.

2. Philippe C. Schmitter and Terry Lynn Karl, "What Democracy Is . . . and Is Not," in *The Global Resurgence of Democracy*, eds. Larry Diamond and Marc F. Plattner (Baltimore: Johns Hopkins University Press, 1993).

3. Ibid.

4. Ibid.; Juan J. Linz and Alfred Stepan, *Problems of Democratic Transition and*

Consolidation (Baltimore: Johns Hopkins University Press, 1996); and Larry Diamond, Juan J. Linz, and Seymour Martin Lipset, "Introduction: What Makes for Democracy?" in *Politics in Developing Countries: Comparing Experiences with Democracy,* eds. Larry Diamond, Juan J. Linz, and Seymour Martin Lipset (Boulder: Lynne Rienner, 1995).

5. Schmitter and Karl, "What Democracy Is . . . and Is Not."

6. Adebayo Adedeji, "Popular Participation, Democracy, and Development: Is There a Dialectical Linkage?" in *Nigeria: Renewal from the Roots? The Struggle for Democratic Development,* eds. Adebayo Adedeji, Onigu Otite, Kunle Amuwo, et al. (London: Zed Books, 1997).

7. Rachel L. Swarns and Norimitsu Onishi, "Africa Creeps Along Path to Democracy," *New York Times,* June 2, 2002; Larry Diamond, "Introduction: In Search of Consolidation," in *Consolidating Third Wave Democracies,* eds. Larry Diamond, Marc F. Plattner, Yun-han Chu, and Hung-mao Tien (Baltimore: Johns Hopkins University Press, 1997); Diamond, Linz, and Lipset, "Introduction: What Makes for Democracy?"; Schmitter and Karl, "What Democracy Is . . . and Is Not"; and Freedom House, "Freedom in the World 1999–2000," www.freedomhouse.org.

8. Diamond, Linz, and Lipset, "Introduction: What Makes for Democracy?"

9. Gregory D. Schmidt, "Delegative Democracy in Peru? Fujimori's 1995 Landslide and the Prospects for 2000," *Journal of Inter-American Studies and World Affairs* 42, no. 1 (Spring 2000); Jeffrey Herbst, "Understanding Ambiguity During Democratization in Africa," in *Pathways to Democracy: The Political Economy of Democratic Transitions,* eds. James F. Hollifield and Calvin Jillson (New York: Routledge, 2000).

10. Larry Diamond, "Is the Third Wave Over?" *Journal of Democracy* 7, no. 3 (July 1996); Guillermo O'Donnell, "Delegative Democracy," *Journal of Democracy* 5, no. 1 (January 1994); and Larry Diamond and Marc F. Plattner, introduction to *The Global Resurgence of Democracy.*

11. Kenneth M. Roberts, *Deepening Democracy? The Modern Left and Social Movements in Chile and Peru* (Stanford, Calif.: Stanford University Press, 1998); and Linz and Stepan, *Problems of Democratic Transition and Consolidation.*

12. Diamond and Plattner, introduction to *The Global Resurgence of Democracy;* and Linz and Stepan, *Problems of Democratic Transition and Consolidation.*

13. Freedom House, "Freedom in the World, 1999–2000."

14. O'Donnell, "Delegative Democracy"; and Merilee Grindle, *Challenging the State: Crisis and Innovation in Latin America and Africa* (Cambridge: Cambridge University Press, 1996).

15. Malaysia's Mahathir Mohammad was the strongest spokesperson for this exceptionalist view that continues to be advocated by some third world leaders. Modern Chinese leaders, for example, argue that universal standards for human rights simply do not exist; rather, developed countries use them as a guise for meddling in their internal affairs. They emphasize differing levels of economic development and political conditions that should justify varying approaches toward rights and democracy.

16. Amartya Sen, "Democracy as a Universal Value," *Journal of Democracy* 10, no. 3 (July 1999).

17. Seymour Martin Lipset, *Political Man* (Garden City, N.Y.: Doubleday, 1959); and Linz and Stepan, *Problems of Democratic Transition and Consolidation.*

18. According to this view popular with neoliberals, no democracy with a per capita income approaching that of South Korea or Taiwan has ever broken down, while (with some notable exceptions) new democracies in countries with per capita incomes of less than $1,000 have rarely lasted more than a few years.

19. Emmanuel Sivan, "Illusions of Change," *Journal of Democracy* 11, no. 3 (July 2000); and Laith Kubba, "The Awakening of Civil Society," *Journal of Democracy* 11, no. 3 (July 2000).

20. Although this may currently be the case, no condition is permanent. In a 1993 essay on the global resurgence of democracy, Samuel Huntington contends that the tur-

bulence of the era may give rise to new ideologies with universalist aspirations. An example would be Islamist movements, which reject liberal democracy's association with individualism and materialism. Or an economically advanced or militarily powerful country such as China or Russia may one day offer a successful and attractive alternative nondemocratic model of governance that struggling countries may find appealing.

21. Samuel P. Huntington, "Democracy's Third Wave," in *The Global Resurgence of Democracy.*

22. Linz and Stepan, *Problems of Democratic Transition and Consolidation.*

23. Ibid.; and Diamond, "Introduction: In Search of Consolidation."

24. Linz and Stepan, *Problems of Democratic Transition and Consolidation;* Diamond, "Introduction: In Search of Consolidation"; and Schmitter and Karl, "What Democracy Is . . . and Is Not."

25. Linz and Stepan, *Problems of Democratic Transition and Consolidation;* and Diamond, "Introduction: In Search of Consolidation."

26. Schmitter and Karl, "What Democracy Is . . . and Is Not"; and Larry Diamond, "Three Paradoxes of Democracy," in *The Global Resurgence of Democracy,* p. 104.

27. Diamond and Plattner, introduction, *The Global Resurgence of Democracy;* Diamond, "Introduction: In Search of Consolidation"; and Linz and Stepan, *Problems of Democratic Transition and Consolidation.*

28. Jorge G. Castañeda, *Utopia Unarmed: The Latin American Left After the Cold War* (New York: Knopf, 1993).

29. Diamond, "Introduction: In Search of Consolidation"; and Arturo Valenzuela, "External Actors in the Transitions to Democracy in Latin America," in *Pathways to Democracy.*

30. Larry Diamond, "How People View Democracy: Findings from Public Opinion Surveys in Four Regions," presentation to Stanford Seminar on Democratization, January 11, 2001, www.democracy.stanford.edu; "Yours Discontentedly, Latin America," *The Economist,* May 13, 2000; "An Alarm Call for Latin America's Democrats," *The Economist,* July 28, 2001; Swarns and Onishi, "Africa Creeps Along Path to Democracy"; and Mike Williams, "Democracy Under Fire in Latin America," *Atlanta Journal and Constitution,* November 17, 2002.

31. Catherine Boone, "'Empirical Statehood' and Reconfigurations of Political Order," in *The African State at a Critical Juncture,* eds. Leonardo A. Villalon and Phillip A. Huxtable (Boulder: Lynne Rienner, 1998).

32. Juan J. Linz, "The Perils of Presidentialism," in *The Global Resurgence of Democracy.*

33. O'Donnell, "Delegative Democracy"; Grindle, *Challenging the State;* and Scott Mainwaring, "Latin America's Imperiled Progress: The Surprising Resilience of Elected Governments," *Journal of Democracy* 10, no. 3 (July 2000).

34. O'Donnell, "Delegative Democracy."

35. Linz, "The Perils of Presidentialism."

36. Donald L. Horowitz, "Comparing Democratic Systems," in *The Global Resurgence of Democracy.*

37. Arend Lijphart, *Patterns of Democracy: Government Forms and Performance in Thirty-six Countries* (New Haven, Conn.: Yale University Press, 1999); Linz, "The Perils of Presidentialism"; and Horowitz, "Comparing Democratic Systems."

38. Linz, "The Perils of Presidentialism."

39. Ibid.; and Linz and Stepan, *Problems of Democratic Transition and Consolidation.*

40. Linz and Stepan, *Problems of Democratic Transition and Consolidation;* Diamond and Plattner, introduction, *The Global Resurgence of Democracy;* Diamond, Linz, and Lipset, "Introduction: What Makes for Democracy?"; and Horowitz, "Comparing Democratic Systems."

41. Linz and Stepan, *Problems of Democratic Transition and Consolidation.*

42. Ibid.

43. "Fiasco in Tabasco," *The Economist,* October 21, 2000.

44. John Dearlove, "Village Politics," in *China in the 1990s,* eds. Robert Benewick and Paul Wingrove (Vancouver: UBC Press, 1995), p. 121.

45. Philip Rowan, "Democracy's Memorabilia," *Washington Post,* November 31, 2000.

46. Rafael Ruiz Harrell, "Building Trust with Mexico," *New York Times,* May 22, 2001; Diamond and Plattner, introduction *The Global Resurgence of Democracy;* and Adedeji, "Popular Participation, Democracy, and Development."

47. Harrell, "Building Trust with Mexico"; Diamond and Plattner, introduction, *The Global Resurgence of Democracy;* and Adedeji, "Popular Participation, Democracy, and Development."

48. Linz and Stepan, *Problems of Democratic Transition and Consolidation.*

49. After Abacha's death in 1998, his wife was stopped at the Lagos airport with thirty-eight suitcases full of money.

50. Diamond and Plattner, introduction, *The Global Resurgence of Democracy.*

51. Larry Diamond, "The Uncivic Society and the Descent into Praetorianism," in *Politics in Developing Countries.*

52. Diamond, Linz, and Lipset, "Introduction: What Makes for Democracy?"

53. Robert Dahl, *Democracy and Its Critics* (New Haven, Conn.: Yale University Press, 1989).

54. Howard J. Wiarda and Harvey F. Kline, *An Introduction to Latin American Politics and Development* (Boulder: Westview Press, 2001); Sonia E. Alvarez, *Engendering Democracy in Brazil: Women's Movements in Transition Politics* (Princeton: Princeton University Press, 1990); and Diamond, "Three Paradoxes of Democracy."

55. Diamond, "The Uncivic Society."

56. Diamond, Linz, and Lipset, "Introduction: What Makes for Democracy?"; and Diamond, "The Uncivic Society."

57. Neil MacFarquhar, "In Bahrain, Women Run, Women Vote, Women Lose," *New York Times,* May 22, 2002.

58. Alvarez, *Engendering Democracy in Brazil;* Abraham Lama, "Women Lawmakers Unite Behind Gender Issues," *Inter Press Service,* September 13, 2001; and Cal Clark and Rose J. Lee, *Democracy and the Status of Women in East Asia* (Boulder: Lynne Rienner, 2000).

59. Jane S. Jaquette, "Regional Differences and Contrasting Views," *Journal of Democracy* 12, no. 3 (July 2001).

60. United Nations, *Human Development Report, 1999* (New York: United Nations, 1999), p. 133.

61. Clark and Lee, *Democracy and the Status of Women in East Asia.*

62. Alvarez, *Engendering Democracy in Brazil;* Clark and Lee, *Democracy and the Status of Women in East Asia;* and Allison Brysk, "Democratizing Civil Society in Latin America," *Journal of Democracy* 11, no. 3 (July 2000).

63. O'Donnell, "Delegative Democracy"; and Schmidt, "Delegative Democracy in Peru?"

64. Linz and Stepan, *Problems of Democratic Transition and Consolidation;* Diamond, Linz, and Lipset, "Introduction: What Makes for Democracy?"; and Tim Weiner and Ginger Thompson, "Harsh Spotlight Shines on Mexico's Army," *New York Times,* July 9, 2002.

65. Linz and Stepan, *Problems of Democratic Transition and Consolidation.*

Chapter 15
Political Transitions: Real or Virtual?

1. Jon Miller, "Presidential Candidates in Peru Complain of Harassment from Police," *National Public Radio: Morning Edition,* December 21, 1999.

2. Dilip Hiro, "Rafsanjani: Preparing to Bridge Right-Left Divide," *Dawn* (Internet edition), February 15, 2000, www.dawn.com.

3. Larry Diamond and Marc F. Plattner, introduction, *The Global Resurgence of Democracy,* eds. Larry Diamond and Marc F. Plattner (Baltimore: Johns Hopkins University Press, 1993).

4. Emmanuel Sivan, "Illusions of Change," *Journal of Democracy* 11, no. 3 (July 2000).

5. Paul Keller, "Peru Lags Behind on Road to Democracy," *Financial Times* (London), July 12, 2000.

6. Sivan, "Illusions of Change"; and Laith Kubba, "The Awakening of Civil Society," *Journal of Democracy* 11, no. 3 (July 2000).

7. Merilee Grindle, *Challenging the State: Crisis and Innovation in Latin America and Africa* (Cambridge: Cambridge University Press, 1996); Catherine Boone, "'Empirical Statehood' and Reconfigurations of Political Order," in *The African State at a Critical Juncture,* eds. Leonardo A. Villalon and Phillip A. Huxtable (Boulder: Lynne Rienner, 1998); and Larry Diamond, Juan J. Linz, and Seymour Martin Lipset, "Introduction: What Makes for Democracy?" in *Politics in Developing Countries: Comparing Experiences with Democracy,* eds. Larry Diamond, Juan J. Linz, and Seymour Martin Lipset (Boulder: Lynne Rienner, 1995).

8. Boone, "'Empirical Statehood.'"

9. Grindle, *Challenging the State;* and Leonardo A. Villalon, "The African State at the End of the Twentieth Century: Parameters of the Critical Juncture," in *The African State at a Critical Juncture.*

10. Douglas A. Chalmers, "Corporatism and Comparative Politics," in *New Directions in Comparative Politics,* ed. Howard J. Wiarda (Boulder: Westview Press, 1985); and Roy C. Macridis and Steven R. Burg, *Introduction to Comparative Politics* (New York: HarperCollins, 1991).

11. Phillip A. Huxtable, "The African State Toward the Twenty-First Century: Legacies of the Critical Juncture," in *The African State at a Critical Juncture.*

12. Boone, "'Empirical Statehood.'"

13. Grindle, *Challenging the State.*

14. Roger Cohen, "Yes, Democracy Is Imperfect, Even in Those Places That Never Heard of Chads," *New York Times,* November 30, 2000.

15. Anthony Faiola, "Some in Latin America Fondly Recall the Good Side of Dictatorships," *Washington Post,* May 31, 1998, p. A24.

16. Howard J. Wiarda and Harvey F. Kline, *An Introduction to Latin American Politics and Development* (Boulder: Westview Press, 2001).

17. Although this scenario sounds a lot like Nigeria's, most (but not all) analysts are still optimistic about the authenticity of its transition.

18. I. William Zartman, "Introduction: Posing the Problem of State Collapse," in *Collapsed States: The Disintegration and Restoration of Legitimate Authority,* ed. I. William Zartman (Boulder: Lynne Rienner, 1995).

19. Larry Diamond, "Is the Third Wave Over?" *Journal of Democracy* 7, no. 3 (July 1996); Guillermo O'Donnell, "Delegative Democracy," *Journal of Democracy* 5, no. 1 (January 1994); and Diamond and Plattner, introduction, *The Global Resurgence of Democracy.*

20. Juan J. Linz and Alfred Stepan, *Problems of Democratic Transition and Consolidation: Southern Europe, South America, and Post-Communist Europe* (Baltimore: Johns Hopkins University Press, 1996).

21. Monte Palmer, *Comparative Politics: Political Economy, Political Culture, and Political Independence* (Itasca, Ill.: F. E. Peacock, 1997); and Zartman, "Introduction: Posing the Problem of State Collapse."

22. Andrew J. Nathan, *China's Transition* (New York: Columbia University Press, 1997).

23. Diamond and Plattner, introduction, *The Global Resurgence of Democracy.*

24. Diamond, Linz, and Lipset, "Introduction: What Makes for Democracy?"; Villalon, "The African State at the End of the Twentieth Century"; Julius E. Nyang'oro and Timothy M. Shaw, "The African State in the Global Economic Context," in *The African State at a Critical Juncture.*

Chapter 16
Linking Concepts and Cases

1. Andreas Schedler, "Mexico's Victory: The Democratic Revelation," *Journal of Democracy* 11, no. 4 (October 2000).

2. Daniel C. Levy and Kathleen Bruhn, "Mexico: Sustained Civilian Rule Without Democracy," in *Politics in Developing Countries: Comparing Experiences with Democracy,* eds. Larry Diamond, Juan J. Linz, and Seymour Martin Lipset (Boulder: Lynne Rienner, 1995).

3. "President Fox Celebrates Second Anniversary," *Latin American Regional Reports,* December 17, 2002.

4. "Deconstructing Democracy: Peru Under Alberto Fujimori," Washington Office on Latin America, February 2000, www.wola.org.

5. Cynthia McClintock and Abraham Lowenthal, foreword, *The Peruvian Labyrinth: Polity, Society, Economy,* eds. Maxwell A. Cameron and Philip Mauceri (University Park: Pennsylvania State University Press, 1997).

6. Juan Forero, "Peru Support of Free Trade Draws Praise in Bush Visit," *New York Times,* March 24, 2002.

7. "A Murky Democratic Dawn in Post-Fujimori Peru," *The Economist,* April 7, 2001; David Gonzalez, "New Chance for Peru's Chief to Take Reins," *New York Times,* January 13, 2002; "Peru's New Government: Teething Troubles," *The Economist,* December 8, 2001; Steven Levitsky and Cynthia Sanborn, "A Hard Choice in Peru," *New York Times,* May 9, 2001; and Ernesto García Calderon, "Peru's Decade of Living Dangerously," *Journal of Democracy* 12, no. 2 (April 2001).

8. Larry Diamond, "The Uncivic Society and the Descent into Praetorianism," in *Politics in Developing Countries.*

9. "Three Years of Democracy," *The Economist,* April 6, 2002.

10. Jocelyn Alexander, JoAnn McGregor, and Terence Ranger, *Violence and Memory: One Hundred Years in the "Dark Forests" of Matabeleland* (London: James Currey, 2000).

11. Rachel L. Swarns, "New Laws Make Mark on Zimbabwe," *New York Times,* February 2, 2002.

12. Scott Peterson, "Iran Opens Door—a Little—to U.S.," *Christian Science Monitor,* February 25, 2000.

13. "Reform, but Only as Largesse," *The Economist,* June 23, 2001.

14. Robert Cribb and Colin Brown, *Modern Indonesia: A History Since 1945* (New York: London, 1995).

15. "Indonesia: Fraying at the Edges," *The Economist,* August 21, 1999, p. 33.

16. Donald K. Emmerson, "Will Indonesia Survive?" *Foreign Affairs* 79, no. 3 (May–June 2000).

Chapter 17
Sovereignty and the Role of International Organizations

1. Francis Mading Deng, "State Collapse: The Humanitarian Challenge to the UN," in *Collapsed States: The Disintegration and Restoration of Legitimate Authority,* ed. I. William Zartman (Boulder: Lynne Rienner, 1995).

2. This perspective is based largely on the views on "new regionalism" expressed

by Sheila Page in her book *Regionalism Among Developing Countries* (New York: St. Martin's, 2000), pp. 5–6.

3. Michael Hirsh, "Calling All Regio-Cops: Peacekeeping's Hybrid Future," *Foreign Affairs* 79, no. 6 (November–December 2000).

4. Page, *Regionalism Among Developing Countries.*

5. Carol B. Thompson, "Beyond the Nation-State? Democracy in Regional Economic Context," in *Democracy and Socialism in Africa,* eds. Robin Cohen and Harry Goulbourne (Boulder: Westview Press, 1991).

6. Page, *Regionalism Among Developing Countries.*

7. Lincoln Bizzozero, "Uruguayan Foreign Policies in the 1990s: Continuities and Changes with a View to Recent Regionalisms," in *National Perspectives on the New Regionalism in the South,* vol. 3, eds. Björn Hettne, András Inotai, and Osvaldo Sunkel (New York: St. Martin's, 2000).

8. Rachel L. Swarns, "African Leaders Drop Old Group for One That Has Power," *New York Times,* July 9, 2002.

9. Richard Joseph, *Smart Partnerships for African Development: A New Strategic Framework,* U.S. Institute of Peace Special Report, May 15, 2002; and "Great Expectations," *The Economist,* June 22, 2002.

10. Somalia went without a representative in the plenary for years until Abdikassim Salad Hassan returned in September 2000.

11. Kofi Annan, *Globalization and Governance,* report issued to the 2000 Millennium Summit of the United Nations.

12. Karen A. Mingst and Margaret P. Karns, *The United Nations in the Post–Cold War Era,* 2nd ed. (Boulder: Westview Press, 2000).

13. Because much of the world did not recognize the Communist Party's leadership of the People's Republic of China on the mainland, the "China seat" was occupied by the Nationalist Party, which operated from Taiwan after its loss to the CCP in 1949. The Taiwanese government of the Republic of China occupied this position until 1971, when the People's Republic of China (PRC) first joined the United Nations.

14. Mingst and Karns, *The United Nations in the Post–Cold War Era.* China's figure was updated to include the February 2000 PRC veto of the Macedonian PKO.

15. Hirsh, "Calling All Regio-Cops," p. 5.

16. Howard Schneider, "In Iraq, It's Almost Business as Usual," *Washington Post National Weekly Edition,* March 5–11, 2001.

17. This action in Korea, which required a Security Council mandate, was only made possible because the Soviet Union, one of the P-5 states with veto power, boycotted the Security Council over the UN's refusal to accept the recently established PRC as a member in place of the nationalist representatives from the Republic of China on Taiwan.

18. Mary Kaldor, "Humanitarian Intervention: A Forum," *The Nation,* May 8, 2000. In this piece, Kaldor argues that "a genuine humanitarian intervention is much more like policing than warfighting or traditional peacekeeping." See also Kaldor's book *New and Old Wars: Organized Violence in a Global Era* (Stanford, Calif.: Stanford University Press, 1999).

19. The British government has offered to establish a UN military war college in Britain to train PKO participants, which Secretary-General Annan has endorsed.

20. Michael O'Hanlon, "How to Keep Peace in Africa Without Sending Troops," *New York Times,* January 8, 2001.

21. Irwan Firdaus, "Three E. Timorese Sentenced in Deaths of Aid Workers," *Associated Press,* May 5, 2001.

22. However, the 2000 resolution on the human rights situation in Chechnya was the first time one of the P-5 was a subject of a country resolution.

23. PKOs aren't the only area in which the United States has fallen behind financially. In general budgetary arrears, the United States is in the company of Brazil, Yugoslavia, Argentina, and Iraq as the states that owe the most in overdue bills to the

United Nations. (The U.S. share, approximately $170 million, constitutes 68 percent of all arrears owed to the United Nations.)

24. Anthony Mango, "Finance and Administration," in *A Global Agenda: Issues Before the Fifty-fifth General Assembly of the United Nations,* eds. John Tessitore and Susan Woolfson (New York: Rowman and Littlefield, 2000).

25. Deng, "State Collapse."

26. Holly Burkwalter, "Humanitarian Intervention: A Forum," *The Nation,* May 8, 2000.

27. "Clinton to UN: Learn to Say No," *Miami Herald,* September 28, 1993. These statements, before the Rwandan genocide, were the basis for Presidential Directive no. 25, which was used to rationalize U.S. inaction in Rwanda.

28. The number of Hutu killed during the civil war and genocide is less clear, with estimates varying between 10,000 and 100,000. Yet not all of these Hutu were killed by the Rwandan Patriotic Front: many moderate Hutu were singled out as traitors by the Hutu government and its supporters. Alan J. Kuperman, "Rwanda in Retrospect," *Foreign Affairs* 79, no. 1 (January–February 2000). See also Ian Martin, "Hard Choices After Genocide: Human Rights and Political Failures in Rwanda," in *Hard Choices: Moral Dilemmas in Humanitarian Intervention,* ed. Jonathan Moore (Lanham, Md.: Rowman and Littlefield, 1998).

29. William Shawcross, *Deliver Us from Evil* (New York: Simon and Schuster, 2000), cited in *The Economist,* May 13, 2000.

30. Burkwalter, "Humanitarian Intervention."

31. Tina Rosenberg, "The Unbearable Memories of a UN Peacekeeper," *New York Times,* October 8, 2000.

32. Deng, "State Collapse."

33. These two opposing views are expressed by Mahmood Mamdani in "Humanitarian Intervention: A Forum," *The Nation,* May 8, 2000.

34. Ibrahim A. Gambari, "The Role of Foreign Intervention in African Reconstruction," in *Collapsed States.*

35. Mingst and Karns, *The United Nations in the Post–Cold War Era.*

36. Nitza Berkovitch, "The Emergence and Transformation of the International Women's Movement," in *Constructing World Culture: International Nongovernmental Organizations Since 1875,* eds. John Boli and George M. Thomas (Stanford, Calif.: Stanford University Press, 1999).

37. Richard J. Goldstone, "Bringing War Criminals to Justice During an Ongoing War," in *Hard Choices.*

38. Martin, "Hard Choices After Genocide," p. 159.

39. "Accused Online: The Rwanda Genocide Trial," *The Economist,* February 10, 2001.

40. "Trial in Belgium Against Four Rwandans for War Crimes," *National Public Radio: Morning Edition,* April 30, 2001.

41. "War Crimes Tribunal in the Hague Establishes Sexual Enslavement as a Crime Against Humanity," *National Public Radio: All Things Considered,* February 22, 2001.

42. Juan Forero, "Where the Bodies Are Buried in Peru," *New York Times,* February 18, 2002.

43. Robert I. Rotberg and Dennis Thompson, eds., *Truth v. Justice: The Morality of Truth Commissions* (Princeton: Princeton University Press, 2000).

44. This is a dominant perspective expressed by many, although not all, of the contributors to the Rotberg and Thompson collection on truth commissions. Rotberg and Thompson, *Truth v. Justice;* and Priscilla B. Hayner, *Unspeakable Truths: Confronting State Terror and Atrocity* (New York: Routledge, 2001).

45. "When Is a Refugee Not a Refugee?" *The Economist,* March 3, 2001.

46. Martha Finnemore, "Rules of War and Wars of Rules: The International Red Cross and the Restraint of State Violence," in *Constructing World Culture.*

47. John Ward Anderson, "Slam-Dunk Diplomacy," *Washington Post,* December 6, 2000.

48. The announcement that China would host the 2008 games was made in July 2001. Asia is considered to be underrepresented in its past history of hosting this international event. With 60 percent of world's population, the region has only hosted two summer games, in Tokyo and Seoul.

49. Jonathan Kolatch, "Chinese Games: If Beijing Were Awarded the 2008 Olympics, It Would Be Good for Both China and the West," *The Gazette* (Montreal), July 15, 2000, p. B5.

50. Mingst and Karns, *The United Nations in the Post–Cold War Era.*

51. Ibid.

52. "When Is a Refugee Not a Refugee?"

53. Karin D. Ryan, "Human Rights," in *A Global Agenda.*

Chapter 18
Global Challenges—and Responses

1. Kofi Annan, *Globalization and Governance,* report issued to the 2000 Millennium Summit of the United Nations.

2. David G. Victor and Jesse H. Ausubel, "Restoring the Forests," *Foreign Affairs* 79, no. 6 (November–December 2000): 131.

3. Philip P. Pan, "China's Chopstick Crusade: Environmentalists Dig in Their Heels over Eliminating Disposable Utensils," *Washington Post Weekly Edition,* February 19–25, 2001.

4. "Intergovernmental Panel on Climate Change Concludes That Humans Have Contributed Substantially to Global Warming," *National Public Radio: All Things Considered,* October 26, 2000.

5. *ChinaInfo, China Science News,* September 19, 2000, reprinted in *Beijing Environment, Science, and Technology Update* (U.S. embassy in the People's Republic of China), September 22, 2000.

6. "Study Showing How Shifts in the World's Climates Will Affect Outbreaks of Infectious Diseases," *National Public Radio: Morning Edition,* April 3, 2001.

7. Gail V. Karlsson, "Environment and Sustainable Development," in *A Global Agenda: Issues Before the Fifty-fifth General Assembly of the United Nations,* eds. John Tessitore and Susan Woolfson (New York: Rowman and Littlefield, 2000), p. 139.

8. Kofi Annan, *We the Peoples: The Role of the United Nations in the Twenty-First Century,* report issued to the UN General Assembly, spring 2000.

9. "Chimp Trade in Turkey Targeted by Animal Activists," *Turkey Update,* www.turkeyupdate.com.

10. "When Is a Refugee Not a Refugee?" *The Economist,* March 3, 2001.

11. "Turkey's Role as Gatekeeper for Illegal Immigrants Trying to Get from Asia and Africa into Europe," *National Public Radio: Weekend Edition Sunday,* April 29, 2001.

12. "Wahid Wanders While Borneo Burns," *The Economist,* March 3, 2001.

13. "When Is a Refugee Not a Refugee?"

14. "Health and Sustainable Development: Report of the Secretary-General," Commission on Sustainable Development Acting as the Preparatory Committee for the World Summit on Social Development, April 30–May 2, 2001, p. 5.

15. "Efforts Being Made to Eradicate Polio," *National Public Radio: All Things Considered,* July 29, 1999.

16. Nancy van Itallie, "Health," in *A Global Agenda.* Van Itallie states that this revelation led to the first health-related resolution in the Security Council, sponsored by Richard Holbrooke, for "voluntary and confidential testing and counseling" of UN peacekeepers.

17. Elizabeth Reid, "A Future, If One Is Still Alive: The Challenge of the HIV Epidemic," in *Hard Choices: Moral Dilemmas in Humanitarian Intervention,* ed. Jonathan Moore (Lanham, Md.: Rowman and Littlefield, 1998).

18. Paul Bracken, "The Second Nuclear Age," *Foreign Affairs* 79, no. 1 (January–February 2000). See also Paul Bracken, *Fire in the East: The Rise of Asian Military Power and the Second Nuclear Age* (New York: HarperCollins, 1999).

19. Bracken, "The Second Nuclear Age."

20. Robert I. Rotberg, "Botswana's Race to Arm," *Christian Science Monitor,* August 13, 1996.

21. Thom Shanker, "Global Arms Sales to Developing Nations Are Tumbling, Study Finds," *New York Times,* August 8, 2002.

22. See www.oneworld.org/guides/landmines.info.html.

23. For a detailed account of the ICBL treaty, see Maxwell A. Cameron, Robert J. Lawson, and Brian W. Tomlin, eds., *To Walk Without Fear: The Global Movement to Ban Landmines* (New York: Oxford University Press, 1998).

24. "Controlling Deadly Trade," *Christian Science Monitor,* June 26, 1998.

25. Ibid.

26. Oscar Arias, "Stopping America's Most Lethal Export," *New York Times,* June 23, 1999.

27. Annan, *Globalization and Governance.* Gallup International conducted this survey in 1999 that included 57,000 adults in sixty countries.

28. Michael Hirsh, "Calling All Regio-Cops: Peacekeeping's Hybrid Future," *Foreign Affairs* 79, no. 6 (November–December 2000).

29. Ibid.

Chapter 19
Linking Concepts and Cases

1. "Fox Announces 'More Dynamic' International Role for Mexico," *EFE News Service,* January 6, 2001.

2. "Breaking Foreign Policy Taboos," *The Economist,* August 26, 2000.

3. Nfer Muoz, "Mexico, Costa Rica Host Most Refugees," *Inter Press Service,* February 19, 2001.

4. Gabriel Marcella and Richard Downes, introduction to *Security Cooperation in the Western Hemisphere: Resolving the Ecuador-Peru Conflict,* eds. Gabriel Marcella and Richard Downes (Boulder: Lynne Rienner, 1999); and Ronald Bruce St. John, *The Foreign Policy of Peru* (Boulder: Lynne Rienner, 1992).

5. Okon Akiba, *Nigerian Foreign Policy Towards Africa: Continuity and Change* (New York: Peter Lang, 1998).

6. Leonard H. Robinson Jr., "Clinton Visit Raises Hopes for Nigeria," *Chicago Sun-Times,* August 27, 2000.

7. Ivan Watson, "Green Berets Train Nigerian Troops to Quell Violence in Sierra Leone," *San Francisco Chronicle,* January 26, 2001.

8. "Economic Squeeze Made Iran Accept Peace," *United Press International,* July 19, 1995.

9. Elaine Sciolino, "Iranian President Paints a Picture of Peace and Moderation," *New York Times,* September 22, 1998, p. A12.

10. Hooman Peimani, *Iran and the United States: The Rise of the West Asian Regional Grouping* (Westport, Conn.: Praeger, 1999).

11. "Darker Clouds, a Few Gleams Yet," *The Economist,* November 4, 2000.

12. "That Controversial G-Word," *The Economist,* February 3, 2001.

13. Heinz Kramer, *A Changing Turkey: The Challenge to Europe and the United States* (Washington, D.C.: Brookings Institution, 2000).

Chapter 20
Dealing with a Superpower: Third World Views of the U.S.

1. Marc Lacey, "President Urges Nigeria to Fight Tyranny of AIDS," *New York Times,* August 28, 2000.

2. Jefferson Morley, "'Axis of Evil' Worries Friends and Foes Alike," *Washington Post,* February 1, 2002.

3. Salman Rushdie, "America and Anti-Americans," *New York Times,* February 4, 2002.

4. The only other countries that did not vote for the November 2000 UN resolution, "Prevention of an Arms Race in Outer Space," were the United States, Israel, and Micronesia.

5. Hooman Peimani, *Iran and the United States: The Rise of the West Asian Regional Grouping* (Westport, Conn.: Praeger, 1999).

6. "The Rights of Terrorists," *The Economist,* January 19, 2002. The situation was even more egregious because John Walker Lindh, who is a U.S. citizen, was sent to the United States for trial, bypassing Cuba entirely.

7. William vanden Heuvel, former U.S. deputy representative at the UN, now chairman of the Franklin and Eleanor Roosevelt Institute in Hyde Park, New York, cited in Barbara Crossette, "U.S. Is Voted Off Rights Panel of the UN for the First Time," *New York Times,* May 4, 2001.

8. "Rogue Nation," *The Nation,* May 28, 2001.

9. Robert Wright, "America's Sovereignty in a New World," *New York Times,* September 24, 2001.

10. Geoffrey Murray, *China: The Next Superpower—Dilemmas in Change and Continuity* (New York: St. Martin's, 1998).

11. It has not been unusual for U.S. presidents, and other powerful members of their administrations, to announce paradigms for U.S. foreign policy. In the 1820s, James Monroe argued (in what later became known as the Monroe Doctrine) that the United States should limit European expansion into the Western Hemisphere, straining relations with Europe, and announced the United States as the "protector" of the Americas. The Truman Doctrine was used throughout the Cold War to contain totalitarian, namely communist, regimes. In the 1980s, Ronald Reagan challenged the legitimacy of nondemocratic, especially communist regimes and proclaimed both the right and the responsibility of the United States to provide assistance to movements that challenge them. The Powell Doctrine (named for former chairman of the Joint Chiefs of Staff and current secretary of state Colin Powell) stated that U.S. troops should enter battle only with decisive force and clear objectives (it was actually an idea promoted by Secretary of Defense Casper Weinberger). We discussed the Clinton Doctrine in Chapter 17, namely the justification of the right to intervene in another state's sovereign affairs when there are gross violations of human rights.

12. "China Berates Bush for 'Axis of Evil,'" *Reuters World Report,* January 31, 2002; Jefferson Morley, "'Axis of Evil' Worries Friends and Foes Alike," *Washington Post,* February 1, 2002; Thomas E. Ricks, "European Security Leaders Alarmed by Bush's Stance: U.S. Officials in Munich Stress Urgency of Anti-Terror Initiative," *Washington Post,* February 3, 2002; and Thomas L. Friedman, "Crazier Than Thou," *New York Times,* February 13, 2002.

13. Human Rights Watch, "Opportunism in the Face of Tragedy: Repression in the Name of Anti-Terrorism," www.hrw.org/campaigns/september11/opportunismwatch.htm.

14. Michael Ignatieff, "Is the Human Rights Era Ending?" *New York Times,* February 5, 2002.

15. For expression of these views, see, among others, Nicholas D. Kristof, "The Chip on China's Shoulder," *New York Times,* January 18, 2002; and "Terrorism and America: Five Asia Pacific Perspectives," *East-West Center Observer,* Fall 2001.

16. Fareed Zakaria, "Why Do They Hate Us? The Politics of Rage," *Newsweek,* October 15, 2001.

Chapter 21
Linking Concepts and Cases

1. Roderic Ai Camp, *Politics in Mexico: The Decline of Authoritarianism* (New York: Oxford University Press, 1999).

2. Ibid.; and Daniel C. Levy and Kathleen Bruhn, "Mexico: Sustained Civilian Rule Without Democracy," in *Politics in Developing Countries: Comparing Experiences with Democracy,* eds. Larry Diamond, Juan J. Linz, and Seymour Martin Lipset (Boulder: Lynne Rienner, 1995).

3. Mary Jordan and Kevin Sullivan, "Mexico Steps into the Spotlight," *Washington Post,* January 31, 2001.

4. Camp, *Politics in Mexico.*

5. Ginger Thompson, "Fox Pledges Full Support for U.S.," *New York Times,* September 28, 2001; and "Let Us Be Your Frontier Post," *The Economist,* October 13, 2001.

6. Robert A. Pastor, quoted in "Mexico's President Rewrites the Rules," *New York Times,* September 8, 2001; and Christopher Marquis, "U.S. Hasn't Kept Promise to Latin America, Critics Say," *New York Times,* May 18, 2002.

7. Jorge G. Castañeda, "A Promising Start for a Border Partnership," *Los Angeles Times,* February 14, 2001.

8. For example, throughout the 1980s Peru adopted a military policy relatively independent of the United States, buying weapons from the Soviet Union. This independence, joined with President Garcia's economic NATIONALISM, made for difficult relations with the United States.

9. Cynthia McClintock, quoted in "U.S. Retreats on Peru Vote," *New York Times,* May 31, 2000.

10. Elizabeth Bumiller, "Bush Vows to Keep Andes Region Stable," *New York Times,* March 24, 2002.

11. Dennis Jett, "Remember the Drug War?" *Washington Post,* January 13, 2002.

12. "Spectres Stir in Peru," *The Economist,* February 16, 2002.

13. Scott Wilson, "Peru Fears Reemergence of Violent Rebels," *Washington Post,* December 10, 2001; Jude Webber, "Critics Liken Bush's Tribunals to Peru's 'Faceless' Judges Trials," *Houston Chronicle,* November 18, 2001; and Juan Forero, "Reeling from Blast, Peru Prepares for a Visit from Bush," *New York Times,* March 22, 2002.

14. Karl Maier, *This House Has Fallen: Midnight in Nigeria* (New York: PublicAffairs, 2000).

15. Stephen Wright, *Nigeria: Struggle for Stability and Status* (Boulder: Westview Press, 1998).

16. Norimitsu Onishi, "Rising Muslim Power in Africa Causes Unrest in Nigeria and Elsewhere," *New York Times,* November 1, 2001.

17. "George Bush's Delusion," *The Guardian* (London), January 31, 2002; and Human Rights Watch, "Opportunism in the Face of Tragedy: Zimbabwe," www.hrw.org.

18. Geoffrey Kemp, *Forever Enemies? American Policy and the Islamic Republic of Iran* (Washington, D.C.: Carnegie Endowment, 1994).

19. Afshin Valinejad, "Iran Denies Bombing Involvement," *Associated Press,* June 22, 2001.

20. James Risen and Jane Perlez, "News Analysis: Terror, Iran, and the U.S.," *New York Times,* June 23, 2001.

21. Hooman Peimani, *Iran and the United States: The Rise of the West Asian Regional Grouping* (Westport, Conn.: Praeger, 1999).

22. Scott Peterson, "In Iran, 'Death to America' Is Back," *Christian Science Monitor,* February 12, 2002, p. 1.

23. Peimani, *Iran and the United States.*

24. Heinz Kramer, *A Changing Turkey: The Challenge to Europe and the United States* (Washington, D.C.: Brookings Institution, 2000).

25. Ibid.

26. Steven A. Cook, *U.S.-Turkey Relations and the War on Terrorism* (Washington, D.C.: Brookings Institution, 2001).

27. John Dillon, "More Americans Are Ready to Reduce Trade with China," *Christian Science Monitor,* May 15, 2001.

28. "Badge of Honor: The Great Beret Affair," *The Economist,* June 16, 2001.

29. Raymond Bonner and Jane Perlez, "Finding a Tepid Ally in the War on Terror, U.S. Presses Indonesia to Arrest Two Clerics," *New York Times,* February 18, 2002.

30. Ann Marie Murphy, "Indonesia and Globalization," in *East Asia and Globalization,* ed. Samuel S. Kim (New York: Rowman and Littlefield, 2000).

Chapter 22
Are We Living in a New Era?

1. Mike William, "Slow-Burning Problems Could Singe U.S.," *Montreal Gazette,* February 14, 2002, p. A19.

2. Thomas L. Friedman, "Better Late Than . . ." *New York Times,* March 17, 2002.

3. Jon Sawyer, "U.S. Wrestles with Notion That Massive Aid Can Stop Terrorism," *St. Louis Dispatch,* December 3, 2001.

4. Nicholas D. Kristof, "The Wrong Lessons of the Somalia Debacle," *New York Times,* February 5, 2002.

5. Diego Cevallos, "Latin America: Region Largely Backs U.S.-British Air Strikes," *Inter Press Service,* October 8, 2001.

6. Michael Ignatieff, "Is the Human Rights Era Ending?" *New York Times,* February 5, 2002.

Selected Bibliography

Adedeji, Adebayo. "Popular Participation, Democracy, and Development: Is There a Dialectical Linkage?" In *Nigeria: Renewal From the Roots? The Struggle for Democratic Development,* edited by Adebayo Adedeji, Onigu Otite, Kunle Amuwo, et al., 3–19. London: Zed Books, 1997.

Afolayan, Funso. "Nigeria: A Political Entity and a Society." In *Dilemmas of Democracy in Nigeria,* edited by Paul A. Beckett and Crawford Young, 45–62. Rochester, N.Y.: University of Rochester Press, 1997.

———. "Women and Warfare in Yorubaland During the Nineteenth Century." In *Warfare and Diplomacy in Precolonial Nigeria,* edited by Toyin Falola and Robin Law, 78–86. Madison: University of Wisconsin–Madison Press, 1992.

Aguero, Felipe. "Transition Pathways: Institutional Legacies, the Military, and Democracy in South America." In *Pathways to Democracy: The Political Economy of Democratic Transitions,* edited by James F. Hollifield and Calvin Jillson, 73–92. New York: Routledge, 2000.

Ai Camp, Roderic. *Politics in Mexico: The Decline of Authoritarianism.* New York: Oxford University Press, 1999.

Akiba, Okon. *Nigerian Foreign Policy Towards Africa: Continuity and Change.* New York: Peter Lang, 1998.

Alexander, Jocelyn, JoAnn McGregor, and Terence Ranger. *Violence and Memory: One Hundred Years in the "Dark Forests" of Matabeleland.* London: James Currey, 2000.

Almond, Gabriel A., and Sidney Verba, eds. *Civic Culture: Political Attitudes and Democracy in Five Nations.* Princeton, N.J.: Princeton University Press, 1963.

Alvarez, Sonia E. *Engendering Democracy in Brazil: Women's Movements in Transition Politics.* Princeton: Princeton University Press, 1990.

Annan, Kofi. *Globalization and Governance.* Report issued to the 2000 Millennium Summit of the United Nations.

———. *We the Peoples: The Role of the United Nations in the Twenty-First Century.* Report issued to the UN General Assembly, spring 2000.

Bakewell, Peter. *A History of Latin America.* Malden, Mass.: Blackwell, 1997.

Barber, Benjamin R. *Jihad vs. McWorld.* New York: Times Books, 1995.

Barrig, Maruja. "The Difficult Equilibrium Between Bread and Roses: Women's Organizations and Democracy in Peru." In *The Women's Movement in Latin America: Participation and Democracy,* edited by Jane Jaquette, 151–176. Boulder: Westview Press, 1994.

Benewick, Robert, and Paul Wingrove, eds. *China in the 1990s.* Vancouver: UBC Press, 1995.

Berkovitch, Nitza. "The Emergence and Transformation of the International Women's Movement." In *Constructing World Culture: International Nongovernmental*

Organizations Since 1875, edited by John Boli and George M. Thomas, 116–121. Stanford, Calif.: Stanford University Press, 1999.

Bethell, Leslie, ed. *Ideas and Ideologies in Twentieth-Century Latin America.* Cambridge: Cambridge University Press, 1996.

Bhebe, Ngwabi, and Terence Ranger. "Volume Introduction: Society in Zimbabwe's Liberation War." In *Society in Zimbabwe's Liberation War,* edited by Ngwabi Bhebe and Terence Ranger, 6–34. Oxford: James Currey, 1996.

Birdsall, Nancy. "Life Is Unfair: Inequality in the World." In *Annual Editions: Developing World 01–02,* edited by Robert J. Griffiths, 8–16. Guilford, Conn.: McGraw Hill/Dushkin, 2001.

―――. "Managing Inequality in the Developing World." In *Annual Editions: Developing World 01–02,* edited by Robert J. Griffiths, 42–45. Guilford, Conn.: McGraw Hill-Dushkin, 2001.

Bizzozero, Lincoln. "Uruguayan Foreign Policies in the 1990s: Continuities and Changes with a View to Recent Regionalisms." In *National Perspectives on the New Regionalism in the South.* Vol. 3, edited by Björn Hettne, András Inotai, and Osvaldo Sunkel, 177–197. New York: St. Martin's, 2000.

Boahen, A. Adu. "Africa and the Colonial Challenge." In *UNESCO General History of Africa: Africa Under Colonial Domination, 1800–1935,* edited by A. Adu Boahen, 1–18. London: Heinemann, 1985.

―――. "Colonialism in Africa: Its Impact and Significance." In *UNESCO General History of Africa: Africa Under Colonial Domination, 1800–1935,* edited by A. Adu Boahen, 782–809. London: Heinemann, 1985.

Bogle, Emory C. *The Modern Middle East: From Imperialism to Freedom, 1800–1958.* Upper Saddle River, N.J.: Prentice Hall, 1996.

Boli, John, and George M. Thomas, eds. *Constructing World Culture: International Nongovernmental Organizations Since 1875.* Stanford, Calif.: Stanford University Press, 1999.

Boone, Catherine. "'Empirical Statehood' and Reconfigurations of Political Order." In *The African State at a Critical Juncture,* edited by Leonardo A. Villalon and Phillip A. Huxtable, 129–142. Boulder: Lynne Rienner, 1998.

Bracken, Paul. *Fire in the East: The Rise of Asian Military Power and the Second Nuclear Age.* New York: HarperCollins, 1999.

―――. "The Second Nuclear Age." *Foreign Affairs* 79, no. 1 (January–February 2000): 146–156.

Brittain, Victoria, and Larry Elliott. "Educating Girls Is Life-Saving for the World." In *Annual Editions: Developing World 01–02,* edited by Robert J. Griffiths, 208–209. Guilford, Conn.: McGraw Hill/Dushkin, 2001.

Brown, Lester R. Foreword to *State of the World 2001,* edited by Lester R. Brown and Linda Starke, 17–20. New York: W. W. Norton, 2001.

Brysk, Alison. "Democratizing Civil Society in Latin America." *Journal of Democracy* 11, no. 3 (July 2000): 151–165.

Burkholder, Mark A., and Lyman L. Johnson. *Colonial Latin America.* New York: Oxford University Press, 1998.

Butts, Kent Hughes, and Steven Metz. *Armies and Democracy in the New Africa: Lessons from Nigeria and South Africa.* Carlisle Barracks, Pa.: Strategic Studies Institute, U.S. Army War College, January 6, 1996.

Caiazza, Amy. "Why Gender Matters in Understanding September 11: Women, Militarism, and Violence." *Institute for Women's Policy Research,* no. 1908 (November 2001): 2–3.

Calderon, Ernesto García. "Peru's Decade of Living Dangerously." *Journal of Democracy* 12, no. 2 (April 2001): 46–58.

Castañeda, Jorge G. *Utopia Unarmed: The Latin American Left After the Cold War.* New York: Knopf, 1993.

Centeno, Miguel Angel. *Democracy Within Reason: Technocratic Revolution in Mexico.* University Park: Pennsylvania State University Press, 1997.

Chalmers, Douglas A. "Corporatism and Comparative Politics." In *New Directions in Comparative Politics,* edited by Howard J. Wiarda, 56–79. Boulder: Westview Press, 1985.

Chalmers, Douglas A., Maria do Carmo Campello de Souza, and Atilio A. Borón. *The Right and Democracy in Latin America.* New York: Praeger, 1992.

Chazan, Naomi, Peter Lewis, and Robert Mortimer. *Politics and Society in Contemporary Africa.* Boulder: Lynne Rienner, 1999.

ChinaInfo, China Science News. September 19, 2000. Reprinted in *Beijing Environment, Science, and Technology Update.* U.S. embassy in the People's Republic of China, September 22, 2000.

Chomsky, Noam. *Pirates and Emperors: International Terrorism in the Real World.* New York: Claremont, 1986.

Clark, Cal, and Rose J. Lee. *Democracy and the Status of Women in East Asia.* Boulder: Lynne Rienner, 2000.

Cohn, Theodore H. *Global Political Economy: Theory and Practice.* New York: Longman, 2000.

Cook, Steven A. *U.S.-Turkey Relations and the War on Terrorism.* Washington, D.C.: Brookings Institution, 2001.

Cortright, David, and George Lopez. *The Sanctions Decade: Assessing UN Strategies in the 1990s.* Boulder: Lynne Rienner, 2000.

Courtois, Stéphane, Nicolas Werth, Jean-Louis Panné, et al. *The Black Book of Communism: Crimes, Terror, and Repression,* edited by Mark Kramer. Trans. Jonathan Murphy. Cambridge: Harvard University Press, 1999.

Crenshaw, Martha, ed. *Terrorism in Context.* University Park: Pennsylvania State University Press, 1995.

Cribb, Robert, and Colin Brown. *Modern Indonesia: A History Since 1945.* New York: Longman, 1995.

Crowder, Michael. *The Story of Nigeria.* London: Faber and Faber, 1978.

Dahl, Robert. *Democracy and Its Critics.* New Haven, Conn.: Yale University Press, 1989.

Daniel, Elton L. *The History of Iran.* Westport, Conn.: Greenwood Press, 2001.

Danopoulos, Constantine P., and Cynthia Watson, eds. *The Political Role of the Military: An International Handbook.* Westport, Conn.: Greenwood Press, 1996.

Davidson, David M. "Negro Slave Control and Resistance in Colonial Mexico." In *People and Issues in Latin American History,* edited by Lewis Hanke and Jane M. Rausch, 200–206. New York: Markus Wiener, 1993.

de Waal, Victor. *The Politics of Reconciliation: Zimbabwe's First Decade.* Trenton, N.J.: Africa World Press, 1990.

Dearlove, John. "Village Politics." In *China in the 1990s,* edited by Robert Benewick and Paul Wingrove, 120–131. Vancouver: UBC Press, 1995.

Degregori, Carlos Ivan. "After the Fall of Abimael Guzmán: The Limits of Sendero Luminoso." In *The Peruvian Labyrinth,* edited by Maxwell A. Cameron and Philip Mauceri, 179–191. University Park: Pennsylvania State University Press, 1997.

Deng, Francis Mading. "State Collapse: The Humanitarian Challenge to the UN." In *Collapsed States: The Disintegration and Restoration of Legitimate Authority,* edited by I. William Zartman, 207–219. Boulder: Lynne Rienner, 1995.

Diamond, Jared. *Guns, Germs, and Steel: The Fate of Human Societies.* New York: W. W. Norton, 1997.

Diamond, Larry. "How People View Democracy: Findings from Public Opinion Surveys in Four Regions." Presentation to Stanford Seminar on Democratization, January 11, 2001.

———. Introduction to *The Global Resurgence of Democracy,* edited by Larry Diamond and Marc F. Plattner, 9–26. Baltimore: Johns Hopkins University Press, 1993.

———. "Introduction: In Search of Consolidation." In *Consolidating Third Wave Democracies,* edited by Larry Diamond, Marc F. Plattner, Yun-han Chu, and Hung-mao Tien, xv–xlix. Baltimore: Johns Hopkins University Press, 1997.

————. "Introduction: What Makes for Democracy?" In *Politics in Developing Countries: Comparing Experiences with Democracy,* edited by Larry Diamond, Juan J. Linz, and Seymour Martin Lipset, 1–66. Boulder: Lynne Rienner, 1995.

————. "Is the Third Wave Over?" *Journal of Democracy* 7, no. 3 (July 1996): 20–37.

————. "Three Paradoxes of Democracy." In *The Global Resurgence of Democracy,* edited by Larry Diamond and Marc F. Plattner, 95–107. Baltimore: Johns Hopkins University Press, 1993.

————. "The Uncivic Society and the Descent into Praetorianism." In *Politics in Developing Countries: Comparing Experiences with Democracy,* edited by Larry Diamond, Juan J. Linz, and Seymour Martin Lipset, 417–492. Boulder: Lynne Rienner, 1995.

Diller, Daniel C., ed. *The Middle East.* 8th ed. Washington, D.C.: Congressional Quarterly, 1994.

Dimitrijevic, Vojin. "Human Rights and Peace." In *Human Rights: New Dimensions and Challenges,* edited by Janusz Symonides. Brookfield, Vt.: Ashgate, 1998.

Donnelly, Jack. *International Human Rights.* Boulder: Westview Press, 1998.

Durand, Francisco. "The New Right and Political Change in Peru." In *The Right and Democracy in Latin America,* edited by Douglas A. Chalmers, Maria do Carmo Campello de Souza, and Atilio A. Borón, 239–258. New York: Praeger, 1992.

Duverger, Maurice. *Political Parties: Their Organization and Activity in the Modern State.* New York: John Wiley, 1963.

Eatwell, Roger. *Fascism: A History.* New York: Penguin, 1997.

Ehteshami, Anoushiravan. *After Khomeini: The Iranian Second Republic.* New York: Routledge, 1995.

Elaigwu, J. Isawa. "Nation-Building and Changing Political Structures." In *UNESCO General History of Africa: Africa Since 1935,* edited by Ali A. Mazrui, 435–467. London: Heinemann, 1993.

Elkins, David J., and E. B. Simeon. "A Cause in Search of Its Effect, or What Does Political Culture Explain?" *Comparative Politics,* January 1979, pp. 127–145.

Ellis, Stephen. "Tuning In to Pavement Radio." *African Affairs* 88, no. 352 (1989): 321–330.

Emmerson, Donald K. *Indonesia Beyond Suharto: Policy, Economy, Society, Transition.* Armonk, N.Y.: M. E. Sharpe, 1999.

————. "Voting and Violence: Indonesia and East Timor in 1999." In *Indonesia Beyond Suharto,* edited by Donald K. Emmerson, 354–357. Armonk, N.Y.: M. E. Sharpe, 1999.

————. "Will Indonesia Survive?" *Foreign Affairs* 79, no. 3 (May–June 2000): 98–101.

Escandon, Carmen Ramos. "Women's Movements, Feminism, and Mexican Politics." In *The Women's Movement in Latin America: Participation and Democracy,* edited by Jane Jaquette, 199–222. Boulder: Westview Press, 1994.

Esty, Daniel C. "Environmental Protection During the Transition to a Market Economy." In *Economies in Transition: Comparing Asia and Eastern Europe,* edited by Wing Thye Woo, Stephen Parker, and Jeffrey Sachs, 357–385. Cambridge: MIT Press, 1997.

Euchner, Charles. *Extraordinary Politics: How Protest and Dissent Are Changing American Democracy.* Boulder: Westview Press, 1996.

Falola, Toyin. *The History of Nigeria.* Westport, Conn.: Greenwood Press, 1999.

Falola, Toyin, and Robin Law, eds. *Warfare and Diplomacy in Precolonial Nigeria.* Madison: University of Wisconsin–Madison Press, 1992.

Farmer, Edward L., Gavin R. G. Hambly, Byron K. Marshall, et al. *Comparative History of Civilizations in Asia.* Reading, Mass.: Addison-Wesley, 1977.

Finnemore, Martha. "Rules of War and Wars of Rules: The International Red Cross and the Restraint of State Violence." In *Constructing World Culture: International Nongovernmental Organizations Since 1875,* edited by John Boli and George M. Thomas, 149–168. Stanford, Calif.: Stanford University Press, 1999.

Fitch, J. Samuel. "The Armed Forces and Democracy in Latin America." *Canadian Journal of Latin American and Caribbean Studies* 25, no. 50 (September 2000): 275–277.

Flavin, Christopher. "Rich Planet, Poor Planet." In *State of the World 2001,* edited by Lester R. Brown and Linda Starke, 3–20. New York: W. W. Norton, 2001.

Foster, Lynn V. *A Brief History of Mexico.* New York: Facts on File, 1997.

Frank, Andre Gunder. *Capitalism and Underdevelopment in Latin America.* New York: Monthly Review Press, 1967.

Frederikse, Julie. *South Africa: A Different Kind of War.* Johannesburg: Ravan Press, 1987.

French, Hilary. "Coping with Ecological Globalization." In *State of the World 2000,* edited by Lester R. Brown, 184–202. New York: W. W. Norton, 2000.

Friedman, Thomas L. *The Lexus and the Olive Tree.* New York: Farrar, Straus, and Giroux, 1999.

Galeano, Eduardo. *Open Veins of Latin America.* New York: Monthly Review Press, 1973.

Gambari, Ibrahim A. "The Role of Foreign Intervention in African Reconstruction." In *Collapsed States: The Disintegration and Restoration of Legitimate Authority,* edited by I. William Zartman, 221–233. Boulder: Lynne Rienner, 1995.

Gamer, Robert E. *Understanding Contemporary China.* Boulder: Lynne Rienner, 1999.

Gamson, William A. "The Social Psychology of Collective Action." In *Frontiers in Social Movement Theory,* edited by Aldon D. Morris and Carol McClurg Mueller, 53–76. New Haven, Conn.: Yale University Press, 1992.

Garner, Roberta. *Contemporary Movements and Ideologies.* New York: McGraw Hill, 1996.

Garrett, Laurie. *Betrayal of Trust: The Collapse of Global Public Health.* New York: Hyperion, 2000.

George, Susan. *The Debt Boomerang: How Third World Debt Harms Us All.* Boulder: Westview Press, 1992.

Goldsmith, Edward. "Empires Without Armies." In *Annual Editions: Developing World 01–02,* edited by Robert J. Griffiths, 24–27. Guilford, Conn.: McGraw Hill/Dushkin, 2001.

Goldstein, Joshua S. *International Relations.* 4th ed. New York: Longman, 2001.

Goldstone, Jack A. "The Outcome of Revolutions." In *Revolutions: Theoretical, Comparative, and Historical Studies,* 2nd ed., edited by Jack A. Goldstone, 194–195. New York: Harcourt Brace, 1994.

———. "Revolutions in World History." In *Revolutions: Theoretical, Comparative, and Historical Studies,* 2nd ed., edited by Jack A. Goldstone, 315–318. New York: Harcourt Brace, 1994.

Goldstone, Richard. "Bringing War Criminals to Justice During an Ongoing War." In *Hard Choices: Moral Dilemmas in Humanitarian Intervention,* edited by Jonathan Moore, 195–210. Lanham, Md.: Rowman and Littlefield, 1998.

Gould, Benina Berger. "Ritual as Resistance: Tibetan Women and Nonviolence." In *Frontline Feminisms: Women, War, and Resistance,* edited by Marguerite R. Waller and Jennifer Rycenga, 213–234. New York: Garland, 2000.

Graham, Richard. *Independence in Latin America.* New York: McGraw Hill, 1994.

Green, Jerrold D. "Countermobilization in the Iranian Revolution." In *Revolutions: Theoretical, Comparative, and Historical Studies,* 2nd ed., edited by Jack A. Goldstone, 136–146. New York: Harcourt Brace, 1994.

Grindle, Merilee. *Challenging the State: Crisis and Innovation in Latin America and Africa.* Cambridge: Cambridge University Press, 1996.

Griswold, Daniel T. "The Blessings and Challenges of Globalization." In *Annual Editions: Developing World 01–02,* edited by Robert J. Griffiths, 47–55. Guilford, Conn.: McGraw Hill/Dushkin, 2001.

Hacker, Frederick J. *Crusaders, Criminals, Crazies: Terror and Terrorism in Our Time.* New York: W. W. Norton, 1976.

Hanke, Lewis, and Jane M. Rausch, eds. *People and Issues in Latin American History.* New York: Markus Wiener, 1993.

Hayner, Priscilla B. *Unspeakable Truths: Confronting State Terror and Atrocity.* New York: Routledge, 2001.

"Health and Sustainable Development: Report of the Secretary-General." Commission on Sustainable Development Acting as the Preparatory Committee for the World Summit on Social Development, April 30–May 2, 2001.

Heiner, Robert, ed. *Social Problems and Social Solutions: A Cross-Cultural Perspective.* Boston: Allyn and Bacon, 1999.

Herbst, Jeffrey. "Understanding Ambiguity During Democratization in Africa." In *Pathways to Democracy: The Political Economy of Democratic Transitions,* edited by James F. Hollifield and Calvin Jillson, 245–258. New York: Routledge, 2000.

Hettne, Björn, András Inotai, and Osvaldo Sunkel, eds. *National Perspectives on the New Regionalism in the South.* Vol. 3. New York: St. Martin's, 2000.

Heywood, Andrew. *Political Ideas and Concepts: An Introduction.* New York: St. Martin's, 1994.

Hirschman, Albert O. *Exit, Voice, and Loyalty: Responses to Decline in Firms, Organizations, and States.* Cambridge: Harvard University Press, 1970.

Hirsh, Michael. "Calling All Regio-Cops: Peacekeeping's Hybrid Future." *Foreign Affairs* 79, no. 6 (November–December 2000): 6–8.

Hochschild, Adam. *King Leopold's Ghost.* Boston: Houghton Mifflin, 1998.

Hollifield, James F., and Calvin Jillson, eds. *Pathways to Democracy: The Political Economy of Democratic Transitions.* New York: Routledge, 2000.

Hoon, Shim Jae. "North Korea: A Crack in the Wall." *Far Eastern Economic Review,* April 29, 1999, pp. 10–14.

Horowitz, Donald L. "Comparing Democratic Systems." In *The Global Resurgence of Democracy,* edited by Larry Diamond and Marc F. Plattner, 127–133. Baltimore: Johns Hopkins University Press, 1993.

Howard, Douglas A. *The History of Turkey.* Westport, Conn.: Greenwood Press, 2001.

Howe, Marvine. *Turkey Today: A Nation Divided over Islam's Revival.* Boulder: Westview Press, 2000.

Huntington, Samuel P. "Democracy's Third Wave." In *The Global Resurgence of Democracy,* edited by Larry Diamond and Marc F. Plattner, 3–25. Baltimore: Johns Hopkins University Press, 1993.

———. Introduction to *The Global Resurgence of Democracy,* edited by Larry Diamond and Marc F. Plattner, 3–25. Baltimore: Johns Hopkins University Press, 1993.

Huxtable, Phillip A. "The African State Toward the Twenty-First Century: Legacies of the Critical Juncture." In *The African State at a Critical Juncture,* edited by Leonardo A. Villalon and Phillip A. Huxtable, 279–294. Boulder: Lynne Rienner, 1998.

Ignatieff, Michael. *Human Rights as Politics and Idolatry.* Princeton: Princeton University Press, 2001.

James, William E. "Lessons from Development of the Indonesian Economy." *Education About Asia* 5, no. 1 (Spring 2000): 31–36.

Jaquette, Jane. "Regional Differences and Contrasting Views." *Journal of Democracy* 12, no. 3 (July 2001): 111–125.

———, ed. *The Women's Movement in Latin America: Participation and Democracy.* Boulder: Westview Press, 1994.

Jayawardena, Kumari. *Feminism and Nationalism in the Third World.* London: Zed Books, 1986.

Joseph, Richard. *Smart Partnerships for African Development: A New Strategic Framework.* U.S. Institute of Peace Special Report, May 15, 2002.

July, Robert W. *A History of the African People.* Prospect Heights, Ill.: Waveland Press, 1992.

Kaldor, Mary. *New and Old Wars: Organized Violence in a Global Era.* Stanford, Calif.: Stanford University Press, 1999.

Karlsson, Gail V. "Environment and Sustainable Development." In *Global Agenda: Issues Before the Fifty-fifth General Assembly of the United Nations,* edited by John Tessitore and Susan Woolfson, 133–145. New York: Rowman and Littlefield, 2000.

Karmon, Ely. "Radical Islamic Political Groups in Turkey." *Middle East Review of International Affairs* 1, no. 4 (December 1997).

Keen, Benjamin, and Keith Haynes. *A History of Latin America.* Boston: Houghton Mifflin, 2000.

Kemp, Geoffrey. *Forever Enemies? American Policy and the Islamic Republic of Iran.* Washington, D.C.: Carnegie Endowment, 1994.

Kesselman, Mark, Joel Krieger, and William A. Joseph. *Introduction to Comparative Politics: Political Challenges and Changing Agendas.* Boston: Houghton Mifflin, 2000.

Kim, Samuel S., ed. *East Asia and Globalization.* New York: Rowman and Littlefield, 2000.

Kinsbruner, Jay. *Independence in Spanish America: Civil Wars, Revolutions, and Underdevelopment.* Albuquerque: University of New Mexico Press, 2000.

Klaren, Peter Flindell. *Peru: Society and Nationhood in the Andes.* New York: Oxford University Press, 2000.

Knight, Amy. "Female Terrorists in the Russian Socialist Revolutionary Party." *Russian Review* 38, no. 2 (1979): 139–159.

Kramer, Heinz. *A Changing Turkey: The Challenge to Europe and the United States.* Washington, D.C.: Brookings Institution, 2000.

Kubba, Laith. "The Awakening of Civil Society." *Journal of Democracy* 11, no. 3 (July 2000): 84–90.

Kuperman, Alan J. "Rwanda in Retrospect." *Foreign Affairs* 79, no. 1 (January–February 2000): 98–101.

Laqueur, Walter. *The New Terrorism: Fanaticism and the Arms of Mass Destruction.* New York: Oxford University Press, 1999.

Law, Robin. "The Oyo-Dahomey Wars, 1726–1823: A Military Analysis." In *Warfare and Diplomacy in Precolonial Nigeria,* edited by Toyin Falola and Robin Law, 9–25. Madison: University of Wisconsin–Madison Press, 1992.

Levitsky, Stephen. "Latin America's Imperiled Progress: Fujimori and Post-Party Politics in Peru." *Journal of Democracy* 10, no. 3 (July 1999): 78–92.

Levy, Daniel C., and Kathleen Bruhn. "Mexico: Sustained Civilian Rule Without Democracy." In *Politics in Developing Countries: Comparing Experiences with Democracy,* edited by Larry Diamond, Juan J. Linz, and Seymour Martin Lipset, 171–217. Boulder: Lynne Rienner, 1995.

Lewis, Peter M., and Pearl T. Robinson. *Stabilizing Nigeria.* New York: Century Foundation Press, 1998.

Leys, Colin. *Underdevelopment in Kenya: The Political Economy of Neocolonialism, 1964–1971.* London: Heinemann, 1975.

Lijphart, Arend. *Democracy in Plural Societies: A Comparative Exploration.* New Haven, Conn.: Yale University Press, 1977.

———. *Patterns of Democracy: Government Forms and Performance in Thirty-six Countries.* New Haven, Conn.: Yale University Press, 1999.

Linz, Juan J., and Alfred Stepan. "The Perils of Presidentialism." In *The Global Resurgence of Democracy,* edited by Larry Diamond and Marc F. Plattner, 108–126. Baltimore: Johns Hopkins University Press, 1993.

———. *Problems of Democratic Transition and Consolidation.* Baltimore: Johns Hopkins University Press, 1996.

Lipset, Seymour Martin. *Political Man.* Garden City, N.Y.: Doubleday, 1959.

Mackey, Sandra. *The Iranians: Persia, Islam, and the Soul of a Nation.* New York: Penguin, 1996.

———. *The Middle East.* 8th ed. Washington, D.C.: Congressional Quarterly, 1994.

Macridis, Roy C., and Steven R. Burg. *Introduction to Comparative Politics*. New York: HarperCollins, 1991.

Maier, Karl. *This House Has Fallen: Midnight in Nigeria*. New York: PublicAffairs, 2000.

Mainwaring, Scott. "Latin America's Imperiled Progress: The Surprising Resilience of Elected Governments." *Journal of Democracy* 10, no. 3 (July 2000): 101–114.

Mamdani, Mahmood. *Citizen and Subject: Contemporary Africa and the Legacy of Late Colonialism*. Princeton: Princeton University Press, 1996.

Mango, Anthony. "Finance and Administration." In *A Global Agenda: Issues Before the Fifty-fifth General Assembly of the United Nations*, edited by John Tessitore and Susan Woolfson, 271–301. New York: Rowman and Littlefield, 2000.

Manning, Chris, and Peter van Diermen. "Recent Developments and Social Aspects of *Reformasi* and Crisis: An Overview." In *Indonesia in Transition: Social Aspects of Reformasi and Crisis*, edited by Chris Manning and Peter van Diermen, 1–11. Singapore: Institute of Southeast Asian Studies, 2000.

Marcella, Gabriel, and Richard Downes. "Introduction." In *Security Cooperation in the Western Hemisphere: Resolving the Ecuador-Peru Conflict*, edited by Gabriel Marcella and Richard Downes, 211–230. Boulder: Lynne Rienner, 1999.

Martin, David. "The People's Church: The Global Evangelical Upsurge and Its Political Consequences," *Christianity Today*, January–February 2000, p. 12.

Martin, Ian. "Hard Choices After Genocide: Human Rights and Political Failures in Rwanda." In *Hard Choices: Moral Dilemmas in Humanitarian Intervention*, edited by Jonathan Moore, 157–176. Lanham, Md.: Rowman and Littlefield, 1998.

Mazrui, Ali A., ed. "Seek Ye First the Political Kingdom." In *UNESCO General History of Africa: Africa Since 1935*, edited by Ali A. Mazrui, 105–126. London: Heinemann, 1993.

———. *UNESCO General History of Africa: Africa Since 1935*. London: Heinemann, 1993.

McBeth, John. "Bombs, the Army, and Suharto." *Far Eastern Economic Review*, February 1, 2001, pp. 24–28.

McClintock, Cynthia. *Revolutionary Movements in Latin America*. Washington, D.C.: U.S. Institute of Peace Press, 1998.

McClintock, Cynthia, and Abraham Lowenthal. Foreword to *The Peruvian Labyrinth: Polity, Society, Economy*, edited by Maxwell A. Cameron and Philip Mauceri, vii–xiv. University Park: Pennsylvania State University Press, 1997.

Meyer, Milton W. *Asia: A Concise History*. Lanham, Md.: Rowman and Littlefield, 1997.

Michael, Marie. "Food or Debt: The Jubilee 2000 Movement." In *Annual Editions: Developing World 01–02*, edited by Robert J. Griffiths, 78–83. Guilford, Conn.: McGraw Hill/Dushkin, 2001.

Mingst, Karen A., and Margaret P. Karns. *The United Nations in the Post–Cold War Era*. 2nd ed. Boulder: Westview Press, 2000.

Moghadam, Valentine. *Gender and National Identity: Women and Politics in Muslim Societies*. London: Zed Books, 1994.

Moin, Bager. *Khomeini: Life of the Ayatollah*. New York: St. Martin's, 2000.

Mokhtar, G. Conclusion to *UNESCO General History of Africa: Ancient Civilizations of Africa*, edited by G. Mokhtar, 732–737. London: Heinemann, 1981.

Monga, Célestin. *The Anthropology of Anger: Civil Society and Democracy in Africa*. Translated by Linda L. Fleck and Célestin Monga. Boulder: Lynne Rienner, 1996.

Moyo, Sam. "The Land Occupation Movement and Democratization in Zimbabwe: Contradictions of Neoliberalism." *Millennium* 30, no. 2 (2001): 311–330.

Mungazi, Dickson A. *Colonial Policy and Conflict in Zimbabwe*. New York: Crane Russak, 1992.

Murphey, Rhoads. "The Historical Context." In *Understanding Contemporary China*, edited by Robert E. Gamer, 29–62. Boulder: Lynne Rienner, 1999.

Murphy, Ann Marie. "Indonesia and Globalization." In *East Asia and Globalization,* edited by Samuel S. Kim, 209–232. New York: Rowman and Littlefield, 2000.

Murray, Geoffrey. *China: The Next Superpower—Dilemmas in Change and Continuity.* New York: St. Martin's, 1998.

Namazi, Siamak. "Three Years Later: Reformist Students Rally at Tehran University." *The Iranian,* May 22, 2000.

Nathan, Andrew J. *China's Transition.* New York: Columbia University Press, 1997.

Needham, D. E., Elleck K. Mashingaidze, and Ngwabi Bhebe. *From Iron Age to Independence: A History of Central Africa.* London: Longman, 1985.

Newbery, Beatrice. "Labouring Under Illusions." In *Annual Editions: Developing World 01–02,* edited by Robert J. Griffiths, 86–89. Guilford, Conn.: McGraw Hill/Dushkin, 2001.

Norris, Pippa, and Ronald Inglehart. "Women and Democracy: Cultural Obstacles to Equal Representation." *Journal of Democracy* 12, no. 3 (July 2001):126–140.

Nyang'oro, Julius E., and Timothy M. Shaw. "The African State in the Global Economic Context. In *The African State at a Critical Juncture: Between Disintegration and Reconfiguration,* edited by Julius E. Nyang'oro and Timothy M. Shaw, 27–44. Boulder: Lynne Rienner, 1998.

O'Donnell, Guillermo. "Delegative Democracy." *Journal of Democracy* 5, no. 1 (January 1994): 55–69.

O'Gorman, Eleanor. "Writing Women's Wars: Foucaldian Strategies of Engagement." In *Women, Culture, and International Relations,* edited by Vivienne Jabri and Eleanor O'Gorman, 91–116. Boulder: Lynne Rienner, 1999.

Oliver, Roland. *The African Experience.* Boulder: Westview Press, 1999.

Özbudun, Ergun. *Contemporary Turkish Politics: Challenges to Democratic Consolidation.* Boulder: Lynne Rienner, 2000.

Page, Sheila. *Regionalism Among Developing Countries.* New York: St. Martin's, 2000.

Palmer, David Scott. "Democracy and Its Discontents in Fujimori's Peru." *Current History* 99 (February 2000): 60–65.

———. "The Revolutionary Terrorism of Peru's Shining Path." In *Terrorism in Context,* edited by Martha Crenshaw, 249–308. University Park: Pennsylvania State University Press, 1995.

Palmer, Monte. *Comparative Politics: Political Economy, Political Culture, and Political Independence.* Itasca, Ill.: F. E. Peacock, 1997.

Payne, Leigh A. *Uncivil Movements: The Armed Right Wing and Democracy in Latin America.* Baltimore: Johns Hopkins University Press, 2000.

Paz, Octavio. "Latin America and Democracy." In *Democracy and Dictatorship in Latin America: A Special Publication Devoted Entirely to the Voice and Opinions of Writers from Latin America,* edited by Octavio Paz, Jorge Edwards, Carlos Franqui, et al., 5–17. New York: Foundation for the Independent Study of Social Ideas, 1982.

Peimani, Hooman. *Iran and the United States: The Rise of the West Asian Regional Grouping.* Westport, Conn.: Praeger, 1999.

Pempel, T. J. "The Developmental Regime in a Changing World Economy." In *The Developmental State,* edited by Meredith Woo-Cumings, 137–181. Ithaca, N.Y.: Cornell University Press, 2001.

Perham, Margery, II. *Lugard: The Years of Authority, 1899–1945.* London: Collins, 1960.

Phimister, Ian. *An Economic and Social History of Zimbabwe, 1890–1948.* London: Longman, 1988.

Ponce de Leon, Juana, ed. *Our Word Is Our Weapon: Selected Writings of Subcomandante Marcos.* New York: Seven Stories Press, 2001.

Pye, Lucian W. *China: An Introduction.* 3rd ed. Boston: Little, Brown, 1984.

Ranchod-Nilsson, Sita. "'This, Too, Is a Way of Fighting': Rural Women's Participation in Zimbabwe's Liberation War." In *Women and Revolution in Africa, Asia, and the*

New World, edited by Mary Ann Tetreault, 62–88. Columbia: University of South Carolina Press, 1994.

Randall, Margaret. *Sandino's Daughters: Testimonies of Nicaraguan Women in Struggle.* New Brunswick, N.J.: Rutgers University Press, 1995.

Ranger, Terence. *Peasant Consciousness and Guerrilla War in Zimbabwe.* London: James Currey, 1985.

Reid, Elizabeth. "A Future, If One Is Still Alive: The Challenge of the HIV Epidemic." In *Hard Choices: Moral Dilemmas in Humanitarian Intervention,* edited by Jonathan Moore, 269–286. Lanham, Md.: Rowman and Littlefield, 1998.

Renner, Michael. "How to Abolish War." *The Humanist,* July–August 1999, pp. 15–21. Reprinted in *Global Issues 00–01,* edited by Robert M. Jackson. Guilford, Conn.: McGraw Hill/Dushkin, 2000, pp. 181–187.

Rittenberg, Libby. "Introduction: The Changing Fortunes of Turkey in the Post-Soviet World." In *The Political Economy of Turkey in the Post-Soviet Era: Going West and Looking East,* edited by Libby Rittenberg, 3–16. Westport, Conn.: Praeger, 1998.

Roberts, Kenneth M. *Deepening Democracy? The Modern Left and Social Movements in Chile and Peru.* Stanford, Calif.: Stanford University Press, 1998.

Roberts, Mark J. *Khomeini's Incorporation of the Iranian Military.* Washington, D.C.: Institute for National Strategic Studies, National Defense University, 1996.

Rodney, Walter. "The Colonial Economy." In *UNESCO General History of Africa: Africa Under Colonial Domination, 1800–1935,* edited by A. Adu Boahen, 332–350. London: Heinemann, 1985.

Rotberg, Robert I., and Dennis Thompson, eds. "Africa's Mess, Mugabe's Mayhem." *Foreign Affairs* 79, no. 5 (September–October 2000): 47–61.

———. *Truth v. Justice: The Morality of Truth Commissions.* Princeton: Princeton University Press, 2000.

Rothstein, Richard. "Immigration Dilemmas." In *Arguing Immigration,* edited by Nicolaus Mills, 48–66. New York: Simon and Schuster, 1994.

Ryan, Karin D. "Human Rights." In *Issues Before the Fifty-fifth General Assembly of the United Nations,* edited by John Tessitore and Susan Woolfson, 157–172. New York: Rowman and Littlefield, 2000.

Sadowski, Yahya. "Ethnic Conflict." *Foreign Policy* 111 (Summer 1998): 12–23.

Sadri, Houman. "Iran." In *The Political Role of the Military: An International Handbook,* edited by Constantine P. Danopoulos and Cynthia Watson, 207–222. Westport, Conn.: Greenwood Press, 1996.

Said, Edward W. *Reflections on Exile.* Cambridge: Harvard University Press, 2001.

Samii, A. W. "The Contemporary Iranian News Media, 1998–1999." *Middle East Review of International Affairs* 3, no. 4 (December 1999).

Schedler, Andreas. "Mexico's Victory: The Democratic Revelation." *Journal of Democracy* 11, no. 4 (October 2000): 5–19.

Schelander, Björn, and Kirsten Brown. *Exploring Indonesia: Past and Present.* Honolulu: Center for Southeast Asian Studies, 2000.

Schell, Orville. "Letter from China." *New Yorker,* July 1994. Reprinted in *The China Reader: The Reform Era,* edited by Orville Schell and David Shambaugh, 246–256. New York: Vintage Books, 1999.

Schlagheck, Donna M. *International Terrorism: An Introduction to the Concepts and Actors.* Lexington, Mass.: Lexington Books, 1988.

Schmidt, Gregory D. "Delegative Democracy in Peru? Fujimori's 1995 Landslide and the Prospects for 2000." *Journal of Inter-American Studies and World Affairs* 42, no. 1 (Spring 2000): 99–132.

Schmitter, Philippe C., and Terry Lynn Karl. "What Democracy Is . . . and Is Not." In *The Global Resurgence of Democracy,* edited by Larry Diamond and Marc F. Plattner, 39–52. Baltimore: Johns Hopkins University Press, 1993.

Selcuk, Faruk. "A Brief Account of the Turkish Economy, 1987–1996." In *The Political Economy of Turkey in the Post-Soviet Era: Going West and Looking East,* edited by Libby Rittenberg, 17–36. Westport, Conn.: Praeger, 1998.

Sen, Amartya. "Democracy as a Universal Value." *Journal of Democracy* 10, no. 3 (July 1999): 3–18.

Shafer, Robert Jones. *A History of Latin America.* Lexington, Mass.: D. C. Heath, 1978.

Shahri, Sorayya. "Women in Command: A Successful Experience in the National Liberation Army of Iran." In *Frontline Feminisms: Women, War, and Resistance,* edited by Marguerite R. Waller and Jennifer Rycenga, 185–192. New York: Garland, 2000.

Shawcross, William. *Deliver Us from Evil.* New York: Simon and Schuster, 2000.

Siapno, Jacqueline. "Gender, Nationalism, and the Ambiguity of Female Agency in Aceh, Indonesia, and East Timor." In *Frontline Feminisms: Women, War, and Resistance,* edited by Marguerite R. Waller and Jennifer Rycenga, 275–296. New York: Garland, 2000.

Silverblatt, Irene. *Moon, Sun, and Witches.* Princeton: Princeton University Press, 1987.

Sithole, Masipula. "Zimbabwe: In Search of Stable Democracy." In *Democracy in Developing Countries: Africa,* edited by Larry Diamond, Juan J. Linz, and Seymour Martin Lipset, 217–257. Boulder: Lynne Rienner, 1988.

Sivan, Emmanuel. "Illusions of Change." *Journal of Democracy* 11, no. 3 (July 2000): 69–83.

Skidmore, Thomas E., and Peter H. Smith. *Modern Latin America.* New York: Oxford University Press, 1992.

Skocpol, Theda. *States and Social Revolution: A Comparative Analysis of France, Russia, and China.* New York: Cambridge University Press, 1979.

Smith, Jackie, and Timothy Patrick Moran, "WTO 101: Myths About the World Trade Organization." In *Annual Editions: Developing World 01–02,* edited by Robert J. Griffiths, 68–71. Guilford, Conn.: McGraw Hill/Dushkin, 2001.

Socolow, Susan Migden. *The Women of Colonial Latin America.* Cambridge: Cambridge University Press, 2000.

Soled, Debra E., ed. *China: A Nation in Transition.* Washington, D.C.: Congressional Quarterly, 1995.

St. John, Ronald Bruce. *The Foreign Policy of Peru.* Boulder: Lynne Rienner, 1992.

Stoez, David, Charles Guzzetta, and Mark Lusk. *International Development.* Boston: Allyn and Bacon, 1999.

Tarrow, Sidney. *Power in Movement: Social Movements and Contentious Politics.* New York: Cambridge University Press, 1998.

Thompson, Carol B. "Beyond the Nation-State? Democracy in Regional Economic Context." In *Democracy and Socialism in Africa,* edited by Robin Cohen and Harry Goulbourne, 216–227. Boulder: Westview Press, 1991.

Tilly, Charles. "Reflections on the History of European Statemaking." In *The Formation of National States in Western Europe,* edited by Charles Tilly, 3–83. Princeton: Princeton University Press, 1975.

Trimberger, Ellen Kay. "A Theory of Elite Revolutions." *Studies in Comparative International Development* 7, no. 3 (1972): 191–207.

Tripp, Aili Mari. "The New Political Activism in Africa." *Journal of Democracy* 12, no. 3 (July 2001): 141–155.

Ullman, Richard H. "Human Rights: Toward International Action." In *Enhancing Global Human Rights,* edited by Jorge I. Domínguez, Nigel S. Rodley, Bryce Wood, and Richard Falk, 1–20. New York: McGraw Hill, 1979.

United Nations. *United Nations Human Development Report, 1999.* New York: Oxford University Press, 1999.

United Nations Development Programme. "A Decade to Eradicate Poverty." In *Annual Editions: Developing World 01–02,* edited by Robert J. Griffiths, 17–23. Guilford, Conn.: McGraw Hill/Dushkin, 2001.

U.S. Department of State. *Country Reports on Human Rights, 2000.* Washington, D.C.: U.S. Government Printing Office, 2000.

———. *Country Reports on Human Rights, 2001.* Washington, D.C.: U.S. Government Printing Office, 2001.

Valenzuela, Arturo. "External Actors in the Transitions to Democracy in Latin America." In *Pathways to Democracy: The Political Economy of Democratic Transitions,* edited by James F. Hollifield and Calvin Jillson, 116–129. New York: Routledge, 2000.

van Itallie, Nancy. "Health." In *A Global Agenda: Issues Before the Fifty-fifth General Assembly of the United Nations,* edited by John Tessitore and Susan Woolfson, 202–208. New York: Rowman and Littlefield, 2000.

Verba, Sidney. "Comparative Political Culture." In *Political Culture and Political Development,* edited by Sidney Verba and Lucian Pye, 512–560. Princeton: Princeton University Press, 1965.

Verba Sidney, Victor H. Nie, and Jae-on Kim. *Participation and Political Equality: A Seven-Nation Comparison.* New York: Cambridge University Press, 1978.

Victor, David G., and Jesse H. Ausubel. "Restoring the Forests." *Foreign Affairs* 79, no. 6 (November–December 2000): 131.

Villalon, Leonardo A. "The African State at the End of the Twentieth Century: Parameters of the Critical Juncture." *The African State at a Critical Juncture,* edited by Leonardo A. Villalon and Phillip A. Huxtable, 3–26. Boulder: Lynne Rienner, 1998.

Vogler, John. "Environment." In *Issues in World Politics,* edited by Brian White, Richard Little, and Michael Smith, 222–245. New York: Palgrave, 2001.

Wang, Ke'an. *Literature and Information on Preventive Medicine.* January 2000.

War, Barney. "Teaching Indonesia: A World-Systems Perspective." *Education About Asia* 3, no. 3 (Winter 1998): 17–23.

Werbner, Richard P. "In Memory: A Heritage of War in Southwestern Zimbabwe." In *Society in Zimbabwe's Liberation War,* edited by Ngwabi Bhebe and Terence Ranger, 192–205. Oxford: James Currey, 1996.

West, Guida, and Rhoda Lois Blumberg, eds. *Women and Social Protest.* New York: Oxford University Press, 1990.

Wiarda, Howard J., and Harvey F. Kline. *An Introduction to Latin American Politics and Development.* Boulder: Westview Press, 2001.

Wills, A. J. *An Introduction to the History of Central Africa: Zambia, Malawi, and Zimbabwe.* New York: Oxford University Press, 1985.

Wilson, Frank L. *Concepts and Issues in Comparative Politics: An Introduction to Comparative Analysis.* Upper Saddle River, N.J.: Prentice Hall, 1996.

Woo, Wing Thye, Stephen Parker, and Jeffrey Sachs, eds. *Economies in Transition: Comparing Asia and Eastern Europe.* Cambridge: MIT Press, 1997.

Woo-Cumings, Meredith. "Introduction: Chalmers Johnson and the Politics of Nationalism and Development." In *The Developmental State,* edited by Meredith Woo-Cumings, 1–31. Ithaca, N.Y.: Cornell University Press, 1999.

Wright, David C. *The History of China.* Westport, Conn.: Greenwood Press, 2001.

Wright, Robin. "Iran's New Revolution." *Foreign Affairs* 79, no. 1 (January–February 2000): 133–145.

Wright, Stephen. *Nigeria: Struggle for Stability and Status.* Boulder: Westview Press, 1998.

Yu Kien-hong, Peter. *The Party and the Army in China: Figuring Out Their Relationship Once and for All.* Working Paper no. 7. Singapore: East Asian Institute, 1998.

Zahedi, Dariush. *The Iranian Revolution Then and Now: Indicators of Regime Instability.* Boulder: Westview Press, 2000.

Zartman, I. William. "Introduction: Posing the Problem of State Collapse." In *Collapsed States: The Disintegration and Restoration of Legitimate Authority,* edited by I. William Zartman, 1–14. Boulder: Lynne Rienner, 1995.

Zedong, Mao. "Report on an Investigation of the Peasant Movement in Hunan: March 1927." In *Selected Readings from the Works of Mao Tsetung.* Peking: Foreign Languages Press, 1971.

Zha, Jianying. *China Pop: How Soap Operas, Tabloids, and Bestsellers Are Transforming a Culture.* New York: New Press, 1995.

Index

About the Book

Comparative Politics of the Third World offers just the right blend of theory and substance to introduce students in a meaningful way to the developing—or not developing—world. Avoiding overgeneralization on the one hand and the problems of a strictly country-by-country approach on the other, authors Green and Luehrmann consistently link concepts pertaining to history, politics, economics, and international relations to a set of eight case studies: the "classic" cases of Mexico, Nigeria, Iran, and China, and the "alternative" cases of Peru, Zimbabwe, Turkey, and Indonesia. Their approach, an accessible and even compelling narrative, is directed specifically at today's undergraduate students.

December Green is associate professor of political science and director of the International Studies Program at Wright State University. Among her publications are *Gender Violence in Africa: African Women's Responses* and *Namibia: The Nation at Independence*. **Laura Luehrmann** is assistant professor of political science at Wright State University.